'The historical assumption that green investment c͜... economy needs to be challenged. Destroying the natural resource base upon which economies thrive, and life depends, has never made for good economics. As the world struggles to recover from one of the worst economic crises in living memory we have an opportunity to promote inclusive and sustainable development based upon green growth, energy efficiency and the sustainable use of natural resources. *Cents and Sustainability* offers a coherent argument and a collection of evidence to show how prudent policies, market innovation and sheer common sense can lead to green development solutions that cost less, destroy less and benefit all. This message of this book is clear. It's time to act!'
Dr Noeleen Hezyer, Under-Secretary-General of the United Nations, and UN Executive Secretary of the Economic and Social Commission for Asia and the Pacific

'The combination of the recent economic crisis and the growing public aware-ness of the potential future climate crisis has led to demand worldwide for a new green growth paradigm. It is clear that economic growth can no longer be built on the basis of environmental degradation and over-use of natural resources. The costs of inaction on climate change, biodiversity loss, over-use of water and the build-up of toxic chemicals in the environment are simply too high – not just for the environment, but also for human health and the economy. A new growth model, achieving both economic development and environmental sustainability, is needed. *Cents and Sustainability* is a very timely contribution to the development of this new growth model, providing the evidence base of those policies that have already succeeded in decoupling environmental degradation from continued economic growth.'
Dr Helen Mountford, Head of Climate Change, Natural Resources and Environmental Outlooks Division, OECD Environment Directorate, and co-author of the 2008 OECD Environmental Outlook to 2030

'Since the *Limits to Growth* publication in the early 1970s, some authors have advocated slowing economic growth in wealthy countries to achieve environ-mental sustainability. Yet this will also slow economic growth in developing countries, making it impossible to lift 2 billion people out of poverty, locking in rapid population growth in many developing countries which itself would be environmentally unsustainable, not to mention inhumane and unjust. Is it possible then to reconcile the need for strong economic growth to break the poverty trap whilst also achieving an environmentally sustainable future? Over twenty years ago *Our Common Future* argued that it was and suggested decoupling GDP growth from environmental pressures as a way forward. Twenty years on no nation has really tried to achieve what could be accom-plished through a genuine commitment to decoupling. How do I know this? The recent publication *Factor Five*, that I developed with the authors here of *Cents and Sustainability*, shows that 80 per cent resource productivity oppor-tunities still exist throughout the global economy. Hence I urge all leaders and

decision makers to read this book, along with *Factor Five*, and to commit to achieving the scale of decoupling needed to ensure we stay within the ecological limits of the planet. If decoupling is implemented rapidly, with a focus on resource productivity, as this book shows, it will lead to higher economic and jobs growth, not less.'
Dr Ernst Von Weizsäcker, Co-Chair, UNEP International Panel for Sustainable Resource Management, lead author of *Factor Five: Transforming the Global Economic Through 80% Resource Productivity Improvements*

'Since the publication of the Brundtland Report [*Our Common Future*], problems of unsustainable economic growth have become even more severe. Unless standards of living can be increased while sharply reducing environmental pressures, the world is headed for disaster. Fortunately, such decoupling is not only possible, as this book shows; it is almost always the most economic approach. Bad environmental policies are usually bad economic policies as well.'
Professor Robert Repetto, United Nations Foundation Fellow, Professor for the Economics of Sustainable Development, Yale School of Forestry and Environmental Studies

'*Cents and Sustainability* presents the latest, even more compelling evidence that national solutions for sustainability are ready and waiting, tried and true. The book presents development patterns that are far more attractive for both human welfare and the environment. It explains how the development model of the previous centuries is dangerously misguided and how the political controversies of economy versus environment put us on a pathway to an insecure future. Now, almost 20 years on from Agenda 21, and in the lead up to the next Earth Summit in 2012, this book takes a fresh look at our sustainable future.'
Andrew Higham, United Nations Framework Convention on Climate Change (UNFCCC) Technology Sub-Programme, and co-editor of *Climate Change and Energy Insecurity: The Challenge for Peace, Security and Development*

'*Our Common Future* was a wake-up. The publication showed the real possibilities for economic growth and development, outlining the advantages of basing such development on policies that upkeep the environmental resource base and showing how much could be gained by not depleting them, as has largely been the case in the past. The book *Cents and Sustainability* is a welcome reminder of what can and should be done to integrate economic growth and environmental sustainability. It also is serving notice, reminding us of what needs to be done to achieve the necessary scale of decoupling of economic growth from environmental pressures to secure the resources to sustain coming generations.'
Professor Walter Leal, Distinguished Professor of Sustainable Development and Chairman, International Climate Change Information Programme (ICCIP), HAW Hamburg, Germany

'In 1987, *Our Common Future* offered the prospect of decoupling as the resolution between environment and development. Since then the debate has been dismal and confused. Is significant, profitable decoupling somehow impossible, as traditional economists might think, or not permissible to speak of as an incomplete answer, as some on the further green edge seem to believe? Neither. *Cents and Sustainability* offers abundant evidence that, supported by appropriate policies and institutions, the technical ability exists for us to do much, much more to decouple human development from environmental degradation. The only negative is that this empowering work was not with us in the 1990s.'
Professor Stephen Dovers, Director, Fenner School of Environment and Society, Australian National University, Canberra, Australia

'*Cents and Sustainability* shows how economic growth can be decoupled from environmental pressures, with government simultaneously addressing negative environmental externalities and investing in R&D and education. The opposition to such government leadership has historically come from affected industry sectors who have threatened that policy changes and added regulation would significantly harm their bottom line, lead to job losses, and even force their business offshore. *Cents and Sustainability* presents historical experience and data to show that such fears are unfounded. Drawing on my own work, this new book shows that in all cases industry's estimates of the costs of compliance with environmental regulation have been at least twice and sometimes as much as 100 times more than the actual costs turned out to be. This is partly because it is hard to foresee the role innovation will play in bringing down the costs of action. When governments have phased in effective policies to reduce environmental pressures, new incentives and markets emerge – resulting in lower than predicted compliance costs. Cents and Sustainability provides an overview of these historical lessons to embolden greater leadership and co-operation today between government and industry to achieve significant decoupling of economic growth from environmental pressures.'
Professor Hart Hodges, Director of Centre for Economic and Business Research, Department of Economics, Western Washington University and author of *Falling Prices: Cost of Complying With Environmental Regulations: Almost Always Less than Advertised*

'*Cents and Sustainability* helps move the debate beyond "growth versus the environment", focusing on the potential for dramatic increases in resource productivity. Now more than ever, realizing the vision of sustainable development is imperative to achieve a prosperous, just and ecologically viable common future.'
Professor Eban Goodstein, Director of the Bard Centre for Environmental Policy, Bard College, Annandale-on-Hudson New York, and author of *The Trade-off Myth: Fact and Fiction about Jobs and the Environment*

'In these dangerous times of hype and spin about environment "versus" the economy, it is refreshing to get an update on what has proved to be one of the most important books of the modern era: *Our Common Future*, and its message of sustainable development. Quite simply, we cannot flourish without both economic growth to help the poor to have a more equitable share of the amenities of living, and environmental sustainability, to ensure the ecological underpinnings of our economy – and lives! – are secure over the generations. Of course there are always trade-offs, but it is false to assert it is an either/or situation – species or jobs, wealth or forests, etc. We can do well by doing good, and in fact must if the world is to be both sustainable and just. *Cents and Sustainability* is an important road map to achieve these complementary goals.'

Professor Stephen H. Schneider, Stanford University, USA, contributor to IPCC Assessments, and author of *Science as a Contact Sport*

'*Cents and Sustainability* explains how economic development can be made to support environmental protection and not detract from it. Drawing together 20 years of theory and research, this volume highlights the path forward toward environmental sustainability.'

Professor Daniel Esty, Director of the Yale Center for Environmental Law and Policy and the Center for Business & Environment at Yale, and lead author of *Green to Gold: How Smart Companies Use Environmental Strategy to Innovate, Create Value, and Build Competitive Advantage*

'The most recent science on climate change and other global environmental changes is compelling. The Earth's environment is changing faster than we earlier thought, lending a sense of urgency to move from identification of the problem to implementation of solutions. The book *Cents and Sustainability* does just that. Central to any solution to the global change challenge is the decoupling of the continued economic growth required to enhance human well-being from the environmental impacts that such growth has traditionally caused. Practical examples of such decoupling abound in this wonderful book, giving us hope and inspiration that humanity can indeed move quickly onto a much more sustainable pathway.'

Professor Will Steffen, Executive Director, Climate Change Institute, Australian National University. and Science Advisor to the Commonwealth Department of Climate Change and Energy Efficiency, Australia

'The biggest problem facing the environmental movement is to present a convincing picture of a global economy that can generate improved living standards for all, and particularly for the billions of people now living in poverty, while drastically reducing the adverse impacts of economic activity on the environment. A sustainably growing economy could provide more and better health, education and other services, increased leisure as well as extending material prosperity across the planet, with a combination of more environmentally efficient technology and active efforts to undo the consequences of past environmental mistakes. *Cents and Sustainability* is an important contribution to the formulation of a realistic vision of sustainable "economic" growth through its focus on decoupling economic growth from environmental pressures and how to combine this with efforts to reduce poverty.'

Professor John Quiggan, ARC Federation Fellow in Economics and Political Science, University of Queensland, Brisbane, Australia

'Since The Brundtland Commission report was published, we have long awaited a book that tackles the formidable analytic task of developing a framework and realistic strategy to simultaneously achieve environmental sustainability, economic and jobs growth, and poverty reduction. With *Cents and Sustainability* the wait is over. I hope *Cents and Sustainability* enjoys exceptional circulation success: it surely deserves to be on the desk – nay, in the head – of political leaders, policy analysts, environmental economists, systems ecologists, and all who play a prominent part in the management of our Only One Planet.'

Professor Norman Myers, Green College, and External Fellow of the James Martin Institute, Oxford University, and adjunct or visiting professor at over 7 Universities including the United Nations University

'Historically, society has treated the environment as a cost to business and an impediment to progress. The challenge facing humanity is to merge the paradigms of sustainable development, progress and economic growth. *Cents and Sustainability* shows that there does not have to be a trade-off between the economy and the environment, but this requires new thinking, new practice and effective policy to address market failures. Transitioning to a sustainable economy, if done wisely, may not harm economic growth significantly, in fact it could even help it. The transition, if focussed on improving resource productivity, will lead to higher economic growth than business as usual, while at the same time reducing pressures on the environment and enhancing employment. I commend the authors for their valuable contributions.'

Dr Andrew Johnson, Commonwealth Scientific and Industrial Research Organisation (CSIRO) Group Executive, Environment, Brisbane, Australia

'As *Cents and Sustainability* shows the book *Limits to Growth*, published almost 40 years ago, created some unintended confusion because it did not distinguish between economic growth and the physical growth of the economy (and its associated pollution). Hence, when the *Limits to Growth* publication called for "growth" to be limited, people assumed they meant "economic" as well as "physical" growth. This inadvertently has inspired some to argue for zero economic growth. I have been to extremely poor countries experiencing zero (and even negative) economic growth. It is not something any human should wish on another. Zero economic growth gives no hope of reducing

extreme poverty. *Cents and Sustainability* confirms what I have long felt, that there is another way – decoupling business profits and economic growth from physical growth and pollution by as much as 75–90 per cent. Decoupling of this order, combined with restoration of natural capital, offers a way to achieve environmental sustainability and enable economic growth to continue to help us reduce poverty. Much of my work compliments the message in Cents and Sustainability and provides further evidence that we can achieve such levels of decoupling and restoration of natural capital. As *Natural Capitalism* showed, doing this is also the best strategy to improve business profitability and competitiveness. If this is done, it would unleash the biggest economic and employment boom ever, and create a just and sustainable future for all.'
Hunter Lovins, President and Founder of the Natural Capitalism Solutions, Boulder, USA and co-author of *Natural Capitalism: The Next Industrial Revolution, Factor 4: Doubling Wealth, Halving Resource Usage*, and *The Climate Protection Manual for Cities*

'*Cents and Sustainability* empowers readers by challenging widespread assumptions about the relationship between economic growth and environmental impacts. It gives us hope that, if we pursue intelligent policies with commitment, we can redefine this relationship. When people believe it will be expensive and painful to address issues such as climate change, we fall into a self-fulfilling cycle of denial and impotence. When we accept the fundamental environmental constraints, we naturally apply human creativity to provide myriad ways of having better lives while living within the Earth's capacity. It's really about adjusting priorities: if we focus on environmental improvement we will find many opportunities to both reduce costs and environmental pressures. As *Cents and Sustainability* shows, energy and water costs make up usually between only 2–3 per cent of total business and household costs in OECD countries. Hence opportunities to improve the efficiency of their use have often been neglected. As a result of this, I have found in my work with business and government, that it is possible to cost effectively achieve in the order of 50–80 per cent improvements in resource efficiency. As *Cents and Sustainability* shows, if governments lead with effective policy, incentives and rolling loans to drive such large improvements in resource productivity, it will boost the economy and jobs, whilst reducing environmental pressures.'
Adjunct Prof Alan Pears AM, RMIT University, Melbourne, Australia

'*Cents and Sustainability* illustrates what a significant proportion of the global investor capital community now recognise, namely that the stock of our natural and social capital affects the level of long term investor returns. Business is reliant upon the environment for inputs and waste outputs in production, along with ecosystem services for the maintenance and growth of its assets. This reliance on the environment by business exemplifies the need to significantly decouple business profits and economic growth from environment pressures to sustain long term profits and economic growth. *Cents and*

Sustainability shows that some companies have already reduced greenhouse emissions by over 60 per cent whilst improving their bottom line. Investors now know that considering environmental and social issues does not limit financial returns; it clarifies the investment proposition and drives opportunity and innovation.'
Nick Edgerton, Manager ESG (environmental, social, governance) Research and Engagement Sustainable Funds, Colonial First State, Sydney, Australia

'Globally, buildings are responsible for around 40 per cent of greenhouse gas emissions. Many studies now show that green building design and retrofits are one of the most cost effective ways to reduce greenhouse gas emissions. Not only does this help the environment and reduce operating costs, but greening buildings can lead to measurable improvements in labour productivity, staff retention and reduced absenteeism. As far back as 1995, Bill Browning and Joseph Romm showed that this was because green buildings provide a work space that people enjoy being in through improvements in natural lighting, comfort, air quality, and amenity. This is just one of the many practical "win–win" strategies outlined in this book, that debunks the myth that there has to be major trade-offs between the environment and the economy. This book is full of practical examples, such as this, which show how action on climate change can improve productivity, the bottom line and thus economic growth. As such, this book is an important contribution to the debate on how to mitigate climate change in a way that also simultaneously boosts jobs and economic growth.'
Archie Kasnet, Partner, Aedi Group, Social Entrepreneur, Boston, USA

'There is now a growing consensus among the nations of the world that climate change should not exceed the 2 degree guardrail. *Cents and Sustainability* provides timely and valuable assistance to leaders and decision makers in achieving this goal. *Cents and Sustainability* shows that there are significant greenhouse gas reductions to be made from simultaneously taking concerted action on recycling and waste reduction, water efficiency and recycling and, most importantly, biodiversity conservation and ecosystem-based management and restoration. This book makes the case, as did *Our Common Future*, for nations to adopt a more systemic approach to addressing the climate change problem. In 2010, the International year of Biodiversity, *Cents and Sustainability* explains clearly why all nations should be taking such an integrated approach to the climate change problem and the broader challenges of environment and development. With the UN 2012 Earth Summit only two years away, this book is a timely resource that can help inspire all nations to develop purposeful and effective national strategies for sustainable development.'
Professor Brendan Mackey, Fenner School of Environment and Society, The Australian National University, Chair, International Union for Conservation of Nature's (IUCN) Climate Change Task Force

'Population growth and climate change, combined with our current approaches to doing business and managing water, are placing our livelihoods, our communities, and the environment at risk. *Cents and Sustainability* suggests concrete alternatives for managing both water and business in ways that will help sustain our communities long-term. The book shows that, across many sectors, leading companies are achieving 50–90 per cent freshwater savings. It also provides new evidence of the economic, jobs and business cost-benefits of implementing water efficiency and water demand management strategies.'

Cheryl Davis, Project Manager for the Global Platform, International Water Association and Manager, Workforce Development Initiative, San Francisco Public Utilities Commission, USA

'In the 21st century, we need an economy that grows and increases its value, but at the same time uses fewer resources. Our work, referenced in *Cents and Sustainability*, shows such "decoupling" can be achieved through a transition from a linear (cradle to grave) to a closed loop (cradle to cradle) economy. Manufacturers are the key economic actors here as they can re-design their products to enable easier and higher levels of recycling and remanufacturing. Finally, incentives can be provided to encourage companies to move from simply selling products to also leasing products and selling a service instead. Such an approach rewards companies for making durable products. It provides a business model which creates sustainable profits by internalizing the costs of waste whilst creating new jobs through increasing levels of remanufacturing.'

Walter Stahel, Founder of the Product-Life Institute, Geneva, and author of *The Performance Economy*

'In the years since *Our Common Future* was published, we have learned much more about how to achieve sustainable development while decoupling economic growth from environmental pressure. In Massachusetts, USA, companies have utilized forward-thinking approaches to production that reduce the use of toxic chemicals before costly safety measures or, worse, pollution control or remediation measures are required. Between 1990 and 2005, Massachusetts companies reduced their use of toxic chemicals by 40 per cent and onsite releases of toxic chemicals by 91 per cent. This was achieved without harming profits — rather economic and worker health and safety benefits have exceeded costs. This book, *Cents and Sustainability*, is a wonderful compilation of similar examples of how addressing environmental pressures can be achieved in ways that represent a win-win for businesses, the global economy and society.'

Pam Eliason, Senior Associate Director and Industry Research Program Manager of the Massachusetts Toxics Use Reduction Institute, Lowell, Massachusetts, USA

'There have been three times that significant global momentum for action on the environment has been built: the 1972 UN Stockholm Conference on the Human Environment, the 1992 World Summit on Environment and Development in Rio, and in the last few years thanks to Al Gore's *An Inconvenient Truth*, The Stern Review and IPCC's 4th Assessment. In 1972 and 1992, momentum for action was rapidly lost as the world economy went into recession and the mistaken assumption that action on the environment harms jobs and the economy came to dominate. Post-Copenhagen, it is vital that we do not let history repeat itself. This new publication *Cents and Sustainability* shows that, far from harming economic growth, rapid action on climate change and the environment is the key to unlocking new sources of "green" jobs and productivity growth to underpin lasting global prosperity.'
Molly Harris Olsen, Director of Eco Futures Pty Ltd and Convenor of the National Business Leaders Forum for Sustainable Development; Philip Toyne, Director of Eco Futures Pty Ltd and Co-Founder of Landcare

'We now know that we can only create a sustainable future if we take an integrated approach to our pressing problems of environmental degradation, resource limitations and poverty alleviation. *Cents and Sustainability* is a guide to that approach. Every decision-maker who wants to make a difference should be drawing on this wonderful resource.'
Emeritus Professor Ian Lowe, Griffith University, President, Australian Conservation Foundation and Patron of The Natural Edge Project

'In the pursuit of prosperity and raising billions out of poverty we have inadvertently hard-coupled our ever upward development pathway with a voracious and wasteful use of natural resources. To avoid overshoot and collapse in our socio-economic and bio-physical systems we must decouple! We must kick start a sustainability revolution – one which sees an endless drive towards the limits of resource efficiency and at the same time one which sees prosperity grow and poverty diminish. To do this we need to bring Cents into the Sustainability debate in a much more powerful way. There is no trade off between the economy and the environment. The long-term health of the former is hard-coupled to the health of the latter!'
Greg Bourne, CEO World Wildlife Fund, Australia. Chair of the Sustainable Energy Authority of Victoria and a Member of the CSIRO Sector Advisory Council to the Natural Resource Management and Environment Sector

'The future is about environmental protection which is affordable, practical, implementable, transferable and most importantly socially acceptable. This can only be achieved through decoupling economic growth from environmental pressures which means not only addressing the often forgotten environmental externalities and negative feedbacks in our current rear guard management approach, but being practical and getting ahead of the game. This requires engaging in proactive and invigorating policy integrated with practical

on-ground options for action that redefine the way we do business. This means going from local sustainability demonstrations to transformative action which involves a "whole of community" approach and addresses the way we fundamentally communicate with each other in a positive way. This book addresses the need for a new era of engagement which gets us out in front of the bus and lays the path for the bus to follow. I commend *Cents and Sustainability* to all local community leaders, sustainability officers and change agents.'
Greg Bruce, Executive Manager, Integrated Sustainability Services Townsville City Council

'*Cents and Sustainability* shows that today's environmental challenges are really a series of great opportunities disguised as insolvable problems. One of the barriers to people seeing the opportunities is the belief that action on the environment will cost too much and hence the more we do for the environment the worse of the economy will be. Such win/lose belief systems offer no hope to reconciling our need to grow the economy with our need to conserve the ecosystems upon which our economy depends. *Cents and Sustainability* shows that economic growth (monetary growth) and the physical growth of the economy (with its associated pollution) are two different things and thus can be decoupled. With its decoupling framework, this book is significant for providing a sound and politically viable way to transform our economies so that their growth restores rather than harms the environment.'
Candia Bruce, Director, Working On Sustainability, Associate Fellow of the Australian Institute of Management

Cents and Sustainability

Cents and Sustainability

Securing Our Common Future by Decoupling Economic Growth from Environmental Pressures

Michael H. Smith, Karlson 'Charlie' Hargroves and Cheryl Desha

London • Washington, DC

First published in 2010 by Earthscan

Earthscan Ltd, Dunstan House, 14a St Cross Street, London EC1N 8XA, UK
Earthscan LLC, 1616 P Street, NW, Washington, DC 20036, US

Earthscan publishes in association with the International Institute for Environment and
Development

For more information on Earthscan publications, see www.earthscan.co.uk or write to
earthinfo@earthscan.co.uk

ISBN 978-1-84407-529-4

Typeset by MapSet Ltd, Gateshead, UK
Cover design by Andrew Corbett

A catalogue record for this book is available from the British Library

Library of Congress Cataloging-in-Publication Data

Smith, Michael H., 1969-
  Cents and sustainability : making sense of how to grow economies, strengthen communities and
revive the environment in our lifetime / Michael H. Smith, Karlson "Charlie" Hargroves and Cheryl
Desha.
       p. cm.
  Includes bibliographical references and index.
  ISBN 978-1-84407-529-4 (hardback : alk. paper)
  1. Economic development—Environmental aspects. 2. Climatic changes—Economic aspects. 3.
Climatic changes—Environmental aspects. 4. Greenhouse gas mitigation. 5. Environmental policy.
6. Economic policy. I. Hargroves, Karlson, 1974- II. Desha, Cheryl. III. Title.
  HD75.6.S616 2010
  338.9'27—dc22
                                                                              2010022793

For further publications by The Natural Edge Project
see www.naturaledgeproject.net

At Earthscan we strive to minimize our environmental impacts and carbon footprint through reducing waste, recycling and offsetting our CO_2 emissions, including those created through publication of this book. For more details of our environmental policy, see www.earthscan.co.uk.

This book was printed and bound
in the UK by CPI Antony Rowe.
The paper used is FSC certified.

Contents

Forewords

I

Dr Gro Brundtland
Former Prime Minister of Norway, Chair of the World Commission on Environment and Development, Director General of the World Health Organization, Special Envoy on Climate Change for the United Nations Secretary-General Ban Ki-moon

When we published *Our Common Future* in 1987 it was intended as an urgent message to the world. We warned that if action were not taken rapidly then the current unsustainable form of development would lead to significant environmental degradation and greatly exacerbate current levels of poverty. Now, some 20 years on it is clear that this warning has not been heeded to the extent to which it was intended and as a result we have some significant challenges to face in the coming decade. *Our Common Future* sought to bring about recognition that the many crises facing the planet are interlocking elements of a single problem relating to the lack of sustainability in our development. As the world today faces rapidly rising food and oil prices, climate change, lack of water and sanitation, the importance of what we discussed 20 years ago is finally being understood.

I think there is more of an understanding today about sustainability issues, especially because of increased awareness and understanding on the climate issue. Climate change is the most dramatic part of the broader sustainable development picture. The climate issue itself has led to an increased understanding of the main messages we were seeking to communicate in *Our Common Future*, namely that:

- the problems we face are in fact shared by all;
- there is no way to avoid them or for someone else to solve the problem;
- it is going to hit all of us in our lifetimes (not in our grandchildren's);
- there is a need for greater global cooperation to successfully address these issues in time.

You can see the changes already. Global warming is accelerating. Leading climate scientists are warning that humanity may already have passed the thresholds for dangerous climate change. Sir John Holmes, the UN relief coordinator, warned that 12 of the 13 major relief operations in 2007 were climate related, and that this combination of disasters effectively amounted to a climate change 'mega disaster'.

This issue of climate change has entered the minds of many more people. It has helped to widen the perspectives we tried our best to communicate some 20 years ago. When you consider climate change and how to mitigate and adapt to it you get into many aspects of sustainable development. For instance, investments in avoided deforestation have significant biodiversity benefits, investing in hybrid cars and higher car fuel efficiency standards reduces urban pollution, and greater investment in public transport and cycling infrastructure provides significant public health benefits and reduced obesity. The climate change issue is also motivating countries, businesses and people everywhere to find ways to reduce the burning of non-renewable fossil fuels in their homes and in transport. Climate change has helped us widen our perspective and understand more about the seriousness of the lack of sustainability as well as inspiring a new momentum for change globally.

This new book, which rigorously seeks to build on from *Our Common Future*, will greatly help to ensure that this new momentum for change is well informed and supported to achieve the changes needed for genuine sustainable development. Twenty years ago, *Our Common Future* was widely endorsed by the World Bank, the Organisation for Economic Co-operation and Development (OECD), and many governments around the world. But despite this overwhelming endorsement, by the early 1990s, with many countries in economic recession, some government leaders and vested interests reduced momentum for change by playing on citizens' fears that sustainable development would significantly harm economic growth and cause job losses. Hence the central message of this new book – 'that economic growth, profitability, social justice and environmental protection can all be achieved simultaneously and are reinforcing' – is of vital importance.

In this new book the team from The Natural Edge Project has summed up the key message from *Our Common Future* simply and elegantly, and I quote:

> *If business, governments and citizens continue with development that is not sustainable, we will indeed become economically richer for a time but significantly poorer environmentally and socially long term. However, if we choose to truly embrace and commit to achieving sustainable development, it is not too late to help all people and future generations become better off and improve their quality of life in every way – economically, socially, and environmentally. It is not too late if business, government and the citizens of the world make the commitment to leave a positive legacy of sustainable prosperity, environmental sustainability and opportunity for future generations.*

This new book and its online companion is a key resource for decision-makers and those wanting to find ways to constructively address long-standing challenges to achieving sustainable development. Over my career, in many positions of responsibility, an unspoken rule has often applied, that is if you wish to achieve change, help people to understand that the economic costs of action are far less than those of inaction. In other words, demonstrate, where possible, that cost-effective practical solutions exist based on a rigorous economic cost–benefit analysis. This book brings together such studies, which do just this across the major aspects of sustainable development. This new book, in showing how effective and proven strategies of achieving social and environmental sustainability are already helping economic growth, has the potential to be truly world changing.

This new publication is informed by a range of significant studies that have appeared since *Our Common Future* was published, including the Intergovernmental Panel on Climate Change (IPCC) assessment reports, the UK *Stern Review* and the UN Environment Programme (UNEP) *GEO-4* report. It includes projects with which I have been involved, like the Commission on Macroeconomics and Health: Investing in Health for Economic Development, chaired by Professor Jeffrey Sachs, which I initiated while Director General of the World Health Organization (WHO). The Commission's report showed that the economic benefits of scaling up investment in health in Africa from US$6 billion per year to US$27 billion would lead to: 'eight million lives saved from infectious diseases and nutritional deficiencies [which] would translate into a far larger number of years of life saved for those affected, as well as a higher quality of life'. The economic benefits of this were shown to be significant, leading to at least US$66 billion in direct benefits, as the report outlines:

> the actual benefits could be much larger than this if the benefits of improved health help to spur economic growth (and help nations to escape the poverty trap), as we would expect. The improvements in life expectancy and reduced disease burden would tend to stimulate growth through: faster demographic transition (to lower fertility rates), higher investments in human capital, increased household saving, increased foreign investment, and greater social and macroeconomic stability.

Such investments would significantly help poor countries break out of the poverty trap and be able to shift from negative to positive economic growth. At the same time, the cost of such an investment to the wealthy countries is minimal, estimated at one thousandth of their annual wealth. In other words, the cost of such an investment to the relatively wealthy countries would barely be noticed in a nation's annual GDP figures. Throughout this book you will find the latest economic studies, such as this study on health, that are building momentum to embolden efforts globally for action to rapidly achieve sustainable development. This work addresses the central concerns of those hesitant about making a commitment to sustainable development and communicates clearly that we already know how to achieve sustainable development cost effectively.

This book also shows that we do not have much more time to wait. Drawing on evidence from the latest IPCC and Millennium Ecosystem Assessment reports, this publication shows that such commitment and actions to achieve sustainable development are needed now. I commend the team from The Natural Edge Project and their partners for undertaking to develop a response to *Our Common Future* to mark its 20th anniversary. This book, *Cents and Sustainability*, brings together significant evidence from the last 20 years to demonstrate that environmental and social sustainability and economic growth need not be incompatible but rather can reinforce each other.

II

Dr Rajendra Pachauri
Director General of the Energy and Research Institute, Delhi, Chief of the Intergovernmental Panel on Climate Change, Co-recipient of the Nobel Peace Prize

It gives me great pleasure to contribute this foreword to *Cents and Sustainability* and to support a response by our next generation to the seminal publication *Our Common Future*, following its recent 20th anniversary. The book, *Our Common Future* (also known as the Brundtland report), will forever be remembered for its early enunciation and popularization of the concept of 'sustainable development'. This leading work has paved the way for numerous efforts, such as the 1992 Earth Summit in Rio de Janeiro where the UN Framework Convention on Climate Change (UNFCCC) was first launched. However, the importance of considering sustainability in development policies and practice has not been widely realized till recently. As is often the case it is only the occurrence or the threat of a crisis that spurs human society to unusual actions and changes in pathways.

In the case of sustainable development, I think the wake-up call has really come from the sudden growth in awareness and understanding of the scientific concerns regarding human-induced climate change. Along with a comprehensive assessment of a range of issues set to challenge mankind, *Our Common Future* took an overview of a range of findings related to climate change in 1987 and clearly outlined the growing scientific consensus at the time that:

> *After reviewing the latest evidence of the greenhouse effect in October 1985, the World Meteorological Organisation (WMO), the UN Environment Programme (UNEP) and the International Council of Scientific Unions (ICSU), (which three years later formed the IPCC) scientists from 19 industrialised and develop-*

ing countries concluded that climate change must be considered a 'plausible and serious probability'. They estimated that if present trends continue, the combined concentration of CO_2 and other greenhouse gases in the atmosphere would be equivalent to a doubling of CO_2 from pre-industrial levels, possibly as early as the 2030s, and could lead to a rise in global mean temperatures greater than any in mankind's history. Current modelling studies and experiments show a rise in globally averaged surface temperature, for such a doubling, of somewhere between 1.5 and 4.5 degrees Celsius.

This remarkable work outlined in detail the risks and potential responses to mitigate and adapt to climate change, covering areas such as energy efficiency opportunities, renewable energy, biomass and policies to price carbon dioxide emissions in detail. *Our Common Future* was one of the first works to demonstrate that through implementing such climate change mitigation solutions economic growth could cost effectively be decoupled from greenhouse gas emissions. As *Our Common Future* stated:

During the past 13 years, many industrial countries saw the energy content of growth fall significantly as a result of increases in energy efficiency averaging 1.7 per cent annually between 1973 and 1983. And this energy efficiency solution costs less, by savings made on the extra primary supplies required to run traditional equipment ... The costs of improving the end-use equipment is frequently much less than the cost of building more primary supply capacity. In Brazil, for example, it has been shown that for a discounted, total investment of $4 Billion in more efficient end-use technologies (such as more efficient refrigerators, street lighting, or motors) it would be feasible to defer construction of 21 gigawatts of new electrical supply capacity, corresponding to a discounted capital savings for new supplies of $19 Billion in the period 1986 to 2000.

Our Common Future concluded that with the right mix of policy and a carbon price signal to further encourage 'the design and adoption of more energy efficient homes, industrial processes and transportation vehicles ... [and] investments in renewables ... within the next 50 years, nations have the opportunity to produce the same levels of energy services with as little as half the primary supply currently consumed'.

During the time the UN Brundtland Commission was drafting *Our Common Future*, tragedies such as the African famines, the leak at the pesticides factory at Bhopal, India, and the nuclear disaster at Chernobyl, USSR helped to focus world attention on *Our Common Future*'s main messages. Also from 1987 through to 1999, scientists investigating ice core samples from

Antarctica discovered that atmospheric carbon dioxide and methane levels had already exceeded the 'natural' peak atmospheric levels for the last 400,000 years. The 1987 Vostok ice core results also showed that humanity is actually adding human-made greenhouse gases to a peaking of the natural cycle of carbon dioxide (CO_2) and methane (CH_4). Carbon dioxide levels in the atmosphere are now over 380 parts per million (ppm). The growing awareness of the seriousness of this situation led to the formation of the Intergovernmental Panel on Climate Change (IPCC) in 1988 by the UN Environment Programme (UNEP) and the World Meteorological Organization (WMO) to provide objective information about climate change to the public and to policy-makers. The IPCC was established in 1988 through a resolution of the UN General Assembly. One of its clauses was significant in having stated:

> *Noting with concern that the emerging evidence indicates that continued growth in atmospheric concentrations of 'greenhouse' gases could produce global warming with an eventual rise in sea levels, the effects of which could be disastrous for mankind if timely steps are not taken at all levels.*

The IPCC's first report was published in 1990 and it broadly agreed with the conclusions about climate change outlined three years earlier in *Our Common Future*. It warned of the risks of inaction, called for a 60 per cent reduction in greenhouse gas emissions and outlined ways to mitigate climate change. In many ways Our Common Future in 1987 laid a foundation which helped world leaders to embrace the first IPCC report in 1990. In 1990 Margaret Thatcher, then UK Prime Minister, stated the following about the IPCC's first report:

> *Today with the publication of the report of the Intergovernmental Panel on Climate Change, we have an authoritative early-warning system: an agreed assessment from some three hundred of the world's leading scientists of what is happening to the world's climate. They confirm that greenhouse gases are increasing substantially as a result of man's activities, that this will warm the Earth's surface with serious consequences for us all ... There would surely be a great migration of population away from areas of the world liable to flooding, and from areas of declining rainfall and therefore of spreading desert. Those people will be crying out not for oil wells but for water.*

Since 1990, the IPCC has published three more assessments. By 2007, when the IPCC published its Fourth Assessment, the scientific work had advanced to the point where we, the IPCC, could say that there is absolutely no doubt that we, the human race, have substantially altered and are continuing to alter the Earth's atmosphere.[1] As stated in the Fourth Assessment Report, 'warming of the climate system is unequivocal', and 'most of the global average warming over the past 50 years is very likely due to anthropogenic greenhouse gases increases'. Eleven of the warmest years since instrumental records have been kept occurred during the last twelve years. In the 20th century the increase in average temperature was 0.74°C, sea level rose by 17cm and a large proportion of the northern hemisphere snow cover receded.[2]

Many aspects of the climate science are far better understood today, such as the science of abrupt climate change, which has found that anthropogenic factors can lead to some impacts that are abrupt or irreversible, depending on the rate and magnitude of climate change. For instance, the rapid melting of the Arctic sea ice, which is another amplifying effect as it allows more solar energy to be absorbed, could imply metres of sea-level rise. Other such positive feedbacks that are also of great concern to the IPCC and need to be better understood by decision-makers are discussed in Chapter 1 of this book. The increased evidence of abrupt changes in the climate system, the fact that CO_2 equivalent levels are already at 455ppm, plus the current high rate of annual increases in global greenhouse gas emissions reinforces the IPCC's Fourth Assessment finding that humanity has a short window of time to bring about a reduction in global emissions if we wish to limit temperature increase to around 2°C at equilibrium. The IPCC's Fourth Assessment calls for global greenhouse gases to peak no later than 2014–2015 and to rapidly decrease after that to 80 per cent below 1990 levels by 2050 to achieve this.

This is a significant and historic challenge but the team from The Natural Edge Project shows in this book that a wide range of research, investigations and practice now exist demonstrating that it is achievable. In this book the authors will update the climate-change related material in *Our Common Future* and show that there is now a wealth of studies and empirical evidence to demonstrate the substantial potential to significantly and rapidly decouple economic growth from greenhouse gas emissions cost effectively. For example, *The Stern Review* found that the costs of inaction on climate change would range from 5 to 20 per cent of GDP leading to a global recession. Conversely, the IPCC found in the Fourth Assessment Report that achieving equilibrium (using best estimate climate sensitivity) of around 2.0–2.4°C would lead to a reduction in average annual GDP growth rate of less than 0.12 per cent up to 2030 and beyond up to 2050.

In this publication, The Natural Edge Project builds on *The Stern Review* and the IPCC Fourth Assessment to explain succinctly why the costs of mitigation have been misunderstood and exaggerated in the past. It shows that economic modelling has made clear for almost 20 years that the costs of action are relatively small compared to the costs of inaction. This book shows that one of the reasons why the costs of action are relatively small is that there are multiple co-benefits for actions that reduce emissions of greenhouse gases at the local level in terms of economic development, poverty alleviation, employment, energy security, reduced air pollution, better biodiversity outcomes and local environmental protection. The book provides a detailed overview of how best to reduce the costs of mitigation and for the first time brings together an overview of those countries leading in implementing strong climate change policy globally from which other countries can learn.

Still, some decision-makers fear that if their government or business commits to ambitious short-term targets by 2020 this may harm their economies or profits or reduce their business competitiveness. This book, and others like it, shows that this does not need to be the case. The authors demonstrate that energy efficiency, smarter building codes and regulations, retrofitting buildings, better demand management and avoided deforestation (plus reforestation and soil sequestration), and smarter approaches to sustainable transport, can provide significant reductions rapidly within the next 5–12 years while maintaining strong economic and job growth.

Complementing this book, The Natural Edge Project has developed a comprehensive 600-page online capacity-building programme entitled 'Energy Transformed: Sustainable Energy Solutions for Climate Change Mitigation', which provides technical detail to complement the IPCC's Third Working Group's publications on climate change mitigation. The Natural Edge Project's online resource is a comprehensive resource to assist and empower people globally to play their part to reduce greenhouse gas emissions. I also highly recommend it for the university sector and for professional groups such as engineers and architects who have a key role to play in helping business and government to reduce their emissions.

Finally, I am also very pleased that the authors discuss how poverty reduction and climate change mitigation strategies can be combined to help countries escape the poverty trap. Perhaps the greatest challenge of the 21st century is how to end extreme poverty while also achieving environmental sustainability. There are 1.6 billion people who do not have access to electricity, and there are similar numbers who have no access to clean water and live in a state of environmental insecurity. The Natural Edge Project is to be commended for tackling this vitally important issue and highlighting where in the world communities, regions and nations are already creating solutions to this great challenge of our time.

Notes

1 IPCC (2007) *Climate Change 2007: The Physical Sciences Basis*, Contribution of Working Group I to the Fourth Assessment Report of the Intergovernmental Panel on Climate Change, Cambridge University Press, Cambridge, see 'Global climate projections'.
2 Pauchari, R. (2007) 'Coping with Climate Change: Is Development in India and the World Sustainable?', 2007 K. R. Narayanan Oration, Australian National University (ANU).

III

Dr Kenneth G. Ruffing

Coordinator of the OECD African Economic Outlook, former Deputy Director and Chief Economist of the OECD Environment Directorate, and Deputy Director of the UN Division for Sustainable Development

The leitmotif of this book is how to decouple environmental pressures from economic growth while simultaneously making progress towards attaining the Millennium Development Goals. It thus addresses a number of economic, social and environmental dimensions of sustainable development.

Ultimately, environmental pressures can be reduced only be reducing the level of output (negative economic growth) or by transforming the economic processes that underpin growth in such a way as to reduce the pressures (emissions of pollutants, greenhouse gases and destructive use of natural resources) per unit of output. Since buoyant economic growth is a necessary, but by no means sufficient condition, for achieving most of the goals, the former is not an option. That leaves us with decoupling. Because environmental pressures are multiple, there is no single overarching solution – no magic bullet. There is, instead, a need for a 'decoupling agenda'. In fact, governments with well-established environmental programmes are all pursuing such agendas without necessarily labelling them as such.

The literature on environmental indicators distinguishes between 'relative' and 'absolute' decoupling. In the former situation, the environmental pressures continue to increase, but at a slower rate than the relevant driving variable (usually GDP). In the latter situation the environmental pressures actually fall in absolute terms, while the relevant driver continues to grow.

The book restates the case for reducing environmental pressures. Failure to do so will entail very high costs to ourselves and future generations; and the technological means and the policy tools needed already exist and, in most cases, have been deployed in one country or another. Finally, the costs of implementing a decoupling agenda are eminently affordable, amounting to only a few percentage points of future increases in GDP. These costs have been extensively assessed by the OECD and others.

Goals of environmental policy

The policy challenge is to achieve absolute decoupling in a cost-effective way to the point that the requirements of environmental sustainability are met. These can be summarized by four criteria: regeneration, substitutability, assimilation and avoiding irreversibility. A few words describing each are provided below using language that was agreed by OECD Environmental Ministers in May 2001.

Regeneration means that renewable resources shall be used efficiently and their use shall not be permitted to exceed their long-term rates of natural regeneration. Substitutability means that non-renewable resources shall be used efficiently and their use limited to levels that can be offset by substitution by renewable resources or other forms of capital. Assimilation means that releases of hazardous or polluting substances to the environment shall not exceed its assimilative capacity; concentrations shall be kept below established critical levels necessary for the protection of human health and the environment. When assimilative capacity is effectively zero (e.g. for hazardous substances that are persistent and/or bio-accumulative), a zero release of such substances is effectively required to avoid their accumulation in the environment. Avoiding irreversibility means that irreversible adverse effects of human activities on ecosystems and on biogeochemical and hydrological cycles shall be avoided; the natural processes capable of maintaining or restoring the integrity of ecosystems should be safeguarded from adverse impacts of human activities; and the differing levels of resilience and carrying capacity of ecosystems must be considered in order to conserve their populations of threatened, endangered and critical species.

In the recent report, the *OECD Environmental Outlook to 2030*, the costs of policy inaction were found to be particularly high for water pollution, especially in developing countries; for air pollution the costs were as much as a few percentages of GDP in the US, the European Union (EU) and China; and for climate change, the costs of inaction were in the range of 1–10 per cent of global output.

The roles of the main actors

Governments, business and households can all contribute to the common task of decoupling. The voluntary actions of business and households can directly reduce the intensity of some environmental pressures; they can also reveal the relatively low costs entailed by many measures which reduce environmental pressures; and they can help raise environmental consciousness which can lead to heightened expectations (and demand) for government action.

Business can benefit from voluntary action to reduce environmental pressures, especially when the measures reduce costs (eco-efficiency) or help the firm to secure a competitive edge in certain markets. Households can also benefit directly by reducing costs (for example, water and energy) through more efficient behaviour.

However, voluntary actions are no substitute for action by governments, especially since the costs of pollution are often borne only to a small degree by the polluters themselves, but mostly by others. Government policy measures are thus required to 'internalize' these costs, and thus make the 'polluter pay', a principle politically binding on OECD member countries. With regard to natural resource use, the problem is often that of open access to common resources such as fisheries. Without restrictions on access to ensure that resource use is kept within the limits of sustainable use, resources will be overused. This is because it is not in the interest of any single producer to reduce effort since this will only serve to increase the profits of other producers if they do not follow suit. Once access is controlled by a suitable regulatory framework, charges can be levied equal to the value of the resource rents. Application of this second OECD principle, that of 'user pays', is a necessary but not always sufficient condition for ensuring sustainable use of natural resources.

Environmental policy measures

Government has an array of measures at its disposal for implementing environmental policy, including: direct regulation of the command and control variety; economic instruments such as environmental taxes and tradable emission permits; and information tools, such as pollutant release and transfer registries and environmental labelling. These instruments can be used singly, or in combination, and the judicious selection of a suitable policy instrument (or mix) can substantially reduce the cost of achieving environmental goals.

Information for decision-making is crucial for making sound policy and for monitoring progress. Indicators to measure decoupling have been developed and are regularly published by the OECD as part of its key indicators, as well as by the European Commission, and many national governments. These are based on a small subset of environmental data that are now regularly collected by members of the European Commission and by other OECD countries. The more extensive pollutant release and transfer registry systems often track dozens of particular pollutants known to have negative impacts on human health and the environment. These inventories are also increasingly being made available online. An OECD-coordinated programme to assess the potential impacts of chemicals produced in high volumes also generates information useful to governments and the general public in deciding on the stringency of environmental regulations.

Estimates of the cost of more ambitious environmental policies

Efficient environmental policies are important since direct expenditures for pollution prevention and control in OECD countries already range from 0.5 to 2.1 per cent of GDP. It is important to recognize that increasing environmental expenditure in itself does not reduce GDP; instead it redirects economic activity toward the purchases of goods and services required for environmental management. The size of the environmental goods and services industry was estimated at more than US$650 billion worldwide in 2005, about 1 per cent of world GDP. Jobs are created in the waste management industry in the supply of engineering goods (pipes, pumps, filters, etc.) for wastewater management, consultancy services for undertaking environmental impact assessments, and specialized energy products, such as wind turbines, solar panels, etc.

However, there is an indirect effect on GDP. It has been estimated, for example, that the additional costs of implementing measures to reduce a number of environmental pressures could lower GDP in OECD countries by about 1.2 per cent in 2030, and more ambitious measures to reduce CO_2 to a safe level by 2050 could cost even more, slowing the rate of GDP growth by about 0.1 per cent per year over 25 years. This indirect impact on GDP arises from increasing the capital and/or operating costs of production in areas affected by regulation as calculated by mathematical economic models that assume full employment and an economy-wide savings rate that does not change in response to the increase in capital-output ratios which some types of environmental policies would impose on business.

So securing environmental stability does come at a cost. The displacement effect mentioned above means lower final consumption of goods and services purchased by households as some labour and capital are transferred to the sectors producing environmental goods and services; and slightly lower productivity (by raising the cost of production) which would mean slightly lower GDP in the future than would otherwise be the case. However, the environmental benefits that would accrue to ourselves and future generations are widely estimated to exceed these costs when both are properly calculated.

Introductions

I

Jim MacNeill, OC

Secretary-General of the World Commission on Environment and Development, and chief architect and lead author of its report, Our Common Future *(1987)*

When we launched *Our Common Future* at a major event in London on 27 April 1987, I never expected that within a year our recommendations would be endorsed by the UN system, regional bodies like the Association of Southeast Asian Nations (ASEAN), OECD and the Commonwealth, as well as the World Bank and all of the regional banks. Nor did I expect that within two years, our recommendations would begin to reshape curricula in universities and graduate schools and would become a preoccupation of a growing number of leading companies worldwide. Nor that within five years, our recommendation that an international conference be held to review progress and develop plans for a global transition to more sustainable forms of development would be realized through the 1992 Earth Summit in Rio.[1] I also never expected that within a few years the words 'sustainable development' would become part of the common everyday lexicon of humankind. I must add in that respect that I also never thought that the concept of sustainable development could and would be interpreted in so many different ways. I sometimes think that a new way to define 'infinity' is the ever-expanding number of interpretations of sustainable development. Many of these, of course, are totally self-serving. In fact, the concept raises profound questions about values and about our relationship with nature, on whose integrity and stability all life depends, as well as implying a revolution in the way we now do business.

In 1987, we thought the concept was plain enough. We defined sustainable development in several ways including ethical, social and ecological. A number of the definitions appeal to me: for example, development based on 'consumption standards that are within the bounds of the ecological possible and to which all can reasonably aspire'. Or development that, 'at a minimum ... must not endanger the natural systems that support life on Earth: the atmosphere, the waters, the soils and the living beings'.[2] Only one definition grabbed the headlines, however, and stuck, unfortunately to the exclusion of all the others. It's the one that features the need for intergenerational equity:[3]

> *Development which meets the needs and aspirations of the present generation without compromising the ability of future generations to meet their own needs.*

In addition to defining the concept from various perspectives, the Commission put forward a number of broad directions that development must take if it is to be sustainable. We called these directions and the policy changes needed to achieve them 'strategic imperatives'.[4] They range from ensuring a sustainable level of population, to increasing equity within and between nations, to reducing poverty, reducing the energy and resource content of growth, reorienting technology, and merging environment and economics in decision-making. We also discussed other imperatives like opening information systems, supporting human rights and empowering indigenous peoples.

These imperatives are fundamental to any transition to sustainability. Some of them have received considerable attention since 1987 and we've seen some progress. In no case, however, has it been at the pace and scale needed to keep up with the unsustainable trends we charted in *Our Common Future*. Our failure to address these imperatives more effectively and rapidly is, I think, linked directly to our failure to make any real progress on the most critical of the imperatives: the urgent need to 'merge environment with economics in our processes of decision-making', not only in the cabinet chambers of government but also in the board rooms of industry and the kitchens of our own homes.

I call this the 'forgotten imperative of sustainable development'. Yet, it is the most important imperative of all. If we change the way we make decisions, we will change the decisions we make – if we don't, we won't. One of the key assumptions underlying *Our Common Future* was that we could and would change the way we make decisions. This new book by The Natural Edge Project, *Cents and Sustainability*, will help us move significantly in that direction.

We have in fact made some progress on this imperative but, in my experience, mainly in the corporate sector in Europe and Asia.[5] In the governmental sector, with perhaps a few small exceptions, there has been very little movement. We devoted an entire chapter of *Our Common Future* to the institutional and legal changes needed for sustainable development and, in my view, we could hardly have been more clear. Some of us who were there will recall that during the late 1960s and 1970s, governments in over 100 countries established special environmental protection and resource management agencies. But, without exception, they failed to make their powerful central economic, trade and sectoral agencies in any way responsible for the environmental implications of the policies they pursued, or the revenues they raised, or the expenditures they made. Moreover, almost without exception, the new environmental agencies were given extremely limited mandates. They were told to focus on the downstream end of the development cycle. In fact, they were told to take development as a given and to worry about ways and means to deal with the negative effects of development on health, property and ecosystems. Moreover, they were told to do so almost exclusively with add-on technologies, add-on policies and add-on politics.

Our economic, trade, energy and other sectoral agencies, on the other hand, retained their historic mandates intact, along with their unfettered control over the tax system and over a critical menu of incentives, such as grants and subsidies to industry, fossil fuel and nuclear energy, agriculture, fisheries, forestry, etc. These are, of course, the policies that command the biggest budgets. These are the policies that encourage farmers to spend their ecological capital or build it up. These are the policies that encourage the forest industry to draw down its forest capital or build it up; that encourage industry to build environment into product design or not; and manufacturing processes and marketing that encourage consumers to use more or less energy, or to purchase or not purchase environmentally friendly products.

What is the most significant statement of environmental policy that any government makes in any given year? Clearly, it's not the report of the minister of environment. As I have observed and stated repeatedly since my days in the OECD, it is the budget of the minister of finance. The government's annual budget sets out the framework of incentives and disincentives within which businessmen, farmers and households make their decisions. It determines, more than any other single statement of government policy, whether development will move in directions that are sustainable or unsustainable. In terms of power and resources, with few exceptions, the environment agency is the low man on every totem pole. In my years with the OECD, the Commission and the World Bank, visiting governments around the world, I often noted that if there were 25 ministers in the government, the last on the protocol list, and the weakest, is the environment minister. Unless, of course, they had a sports minister, or an urban affairs minister – in which case, environment may rise a few ranks. Yet, as you all know, whenever there's an environmental problem – whether it's a polluted well or soil erosion or climate change – everyone expects the environment minister to solve it. I remember a meeting in Oslo in the mid-1980s sitting around a table discussing this with Mrs Brundtland. She was then Prime Minister and had been Norway's Environment Minister for years. She said, and I paraphrase, 'Yes, Jim, you know, it's true. Environment ministers do spend most of their time trying to repair the damage caused by the policies of their colleagues.' The Earth can no longer bear the consequences of these institutional arrangements. It is past time to make the strongest ministers in government responsible for the ecological consequences of their policies. In 1960, global population stood at 3 billion and global GDP came in around US$6 trillion. Today, with population at 6.5 billion and GDP around US$60 trillion, our economic and ecological systems are now totally interlocked: till death do them part. It is time for governments to end the institutional divorce between the environment and the economy. It is time for every public agency to become an environmental agency, a green agency, a sustainable development agency.

This book by The Natural Edge Project will help to build momentum for such a change. The single most significant barrier for institutions wishing to embrace sustainable development has been the dominant belief that the more one does to help the economy the worse off the environmental and social outcomes will be, and the more one does for the environment or society the worse off the economy will be. *Cents and Sustainability* brings a wealth of evidence together to challenge this conventional wisdom. By demonstrating how best economic growth can be decoupled from environmental pressures, it provides an invaluable resource to decision-makers seeking to embed the environment into their economic decision-making. The most compelling reasons for protecting the environment are often economic. Environmental problems become incredibly expensive and even sometimes impossible to solve if you wait to a later stage to attempt to solve them. The earlier environmental problems are identified, the cheaper they are to solve. *Cents and Sustainability* builds on this 'delay dilemma' – most effectively noted in *The Stern Review* in regards to the issues of climate change – and shows that the same is true for other environmental and social challenges. It shows that the costs of inaction significantly outweigh the costs of action for decoupling economic growth from other major environmental pressures. It also shows that proactively addressing many social problems, such as extreme poverty, corruption, illiteracy, unemployment, poor education and health standards, significantly helps economic growth rather than harming it, and underpins environmental actions. In *Our Common Future* we called for a new form of economic growth that is forceful and also environmentally and socially sustainable. *Cents and Sustainability* shows how this goal can be achieved.

In doing so, it also demonstrates the sea-change occurring in the field of economics. When I began my career 50 years ago, environmental externalities were seen as largely irrelevant by most economists and not worthy of study. Economic textbooks in the 1950s and 1960s made statements like 'the weather is clearly an exogenous or non-economic variable, affecting individual choices but unaffected by them'[6] and 'rainfall affects the economy but is not affected by the economy'.[7] Many decision-makers and economists today went through university at a time when environmental economics was not taught to them and such attitudes were common. Even today environmental economics tends to be taught to economists as a sub-discipline of economics rather than as central to economics, which is shocking given the interdependence of the world economy and ecology.[8]

At a time when, globally, there is better access to education than ever before, too few receive any formal education in economics, even though many of the most critical societal decisions are made on the basis of economics. It is not wise simply to hope that our decision-makers will make the right choices, especially given the fact that there are still powerful vested interests who do not want to see a transition to sustainable development.

In the end, it is up to each and every one of us to leave as positive a legacy as possible to future generations. *Cents and Sustainability*, with its inspiring world class success stories, our earlier 1987 report to the United Nations entitled *Our Common Future*, and free online education and training packages by The Natural Edge Project will help empower you to play your part in helping achieve a sustainable future.

Jim MacNeill is a former Chairman of the World Bank's Independent Inspection Panel in Washington, DC, and Chairman Emeritus of the International Institute for Sustainable Development (IISD) in Winnipeg. Earlier in his career MacNeill was the Secretary-General of the World Commission on Environment and Development, Director of Environment for the Organisation for Economic Co-operation and Development, the Canadian Ambassador and Commissioner General responsible for the 1976 UN Conference on Human Settlements in Vancouver, and Deputy Minister for Urban Affairs in Pierre Elliot Trudeau's administration. MacNeill has over five decades of experience as a policy adviser to leaders of governments, industry and international organizations in the fields of energy, natural resources, management, environment and sustainable development. He is an author, speaker, and recipient of many honours and distinctions, national and international.

Notes

1 World Commission on Environment and Development (WCED) (1987) *Our Common Future*, Oxford University Press, Oxford, Chapter 12, p343.

2 WCED (1987) *Our Common Future*, Oxford University Press, Oxford, Chapter 2, p44.

3 WCED (1987) *Our Common Future*, Oxford University Press, Oxford, Chapter 2, p43.

4 WCED (1987) *Our Common Future*, Oxford University Press, Oxford, Chapter 2, pp49–65.

5 Cogan, D. (2006) *Corporate Governance and Climate Change: Making the Connection*, Ceres Publications, Boston, MA.

6 de Graaf, J. V. (1957) *Theoretical Welfare Economics*, Cambridge University Press, Cambridge, p6.

7 Klein, L. R. (1962) *An Introduction to Econometrics*, Prentice Hall, Englewood Cliff, NJ, p16.

8 MacNeill, J. (1991) *Beyond Interdependence: The Meshing of the World's Economy and the Earth's Ecology*, Oxford University Press, Oxford.

II

Robert Purves, AM

Chair of the Purves Environment Fund, founding member of the Wentworth Group of
Concerned Scientists, Chair of Australia's peak environmental business association
Environment Business Australia and board member of WWF International

Welcome to *Cents and Sustainability*. As a major sponsor for this work, we, the Purves Environment Fund, are proud to welcome you to this new book by The Natural Edge Project, the culmination of over three years of dedicated effort by the team and its partners. The focus of this book is the critical issue of how we can continue to develop our global economy and societies without exceeding the limits of the natural world we inhabit. The team has delivered a strong response from the next generation to the seminal book *Our Common Future*, and presents a wealth of understanding to inform our efforts into the coming decades. In my opinion the members of The Natural Edge Project are representatives of Australia's, and the world's, next generation of decision-makers and thought leaders.

As with The Natural Edge Project's previous publications, *The Natural Advantage of Nations: Business Opportunities, Innovation and Governance in the 21st Century* and *Factor Five: Transforming the Global Economy through 80% Improvements in Resource Productivity*, this new book is a tremendous achievement and a timely and important contribution. I commend it as essential reading for anyone who is concerned with long-term sustainability and prosperity. Ours is the first generation which has the potential to drive the world's climate and many of its ecosystems past irreversible tipping points through our pollution and environmental pressures. Hence, the choices we all make over coming decades will determine the quality of our lives in the future and the legacy we leave our children, and our children's children.

Thanks to significant global efforts such as Al Gore's film, *An Inconvenient Truth*, the IPCC's Fourth Assessment Report, the UK *Stern Review* and books such as Tim Flannery's *The Weathermakers*, there is now significant momentum for change. However, having the global spotlight turned onto the issue of sustainable development, does not mean that it will lead to meaningful change. This book reminds us that over the last 100 years there have been a number of times where similar momentum has grown and, unfortunately, swiftly eroded. This book shows how Rachel Carson's seminal work *Silent Spring*, published in 1962, helped build momentum for action leading to the 1972 UN Stockholm Conference on the Human Environment; unfortunately, the impact of the OPEC oil crisis quickly changed the world's focus in 1973. Similarly the book shows that there was significant momentum for change following the development and publication of *Our Common Future* and leading up to the 1992 World Summit on Environment and Development in Rio. However, the impact of a worldwide economic recession again led to a change in global focus and valuable momentum was lost. Now that the momentum is again growing, the coming decade may in fact be the last time we have a global opportunity to act in time before the environment is pushed beyond its capacity. Even after the impacts of the recent global credit crunch many are seeing sustainable development-related strategies as robust approaches to spur economic growth. A clear message throughout this book is that we all need to play our part if we are to successfully address the range of challenges in time to make a real difference. This book explains why not just business, or government, or individuals, but the whole of society needs to act together.

As *Cents and Sustainability* explains, one of the main reasons for hesitancy on action to reduce environmental pressure is the prevalence of the belief that such action will harm economic growth and lead to job losses, and hence become an election issue. This book shows, based on a number of significant studies, reports and modelling, that the opposite is in fact true, and that, if wisely implemented, action on the environment can help business competitiveness and long-term economic and job growth, in fact influencing elections. The authors point out that this may be the most important 'convenient truth' of our generation. Furthermore, the book suggests that, based on the growing consensus on the seriousness of the current global environmental crisis, and the potential direct impacts on the economy of nations, the only sensible and economically sound approach is rapid and urgent action.

It is clear from the material presented in this book that the costs of inaction on reducing environmental pressures cost effectively will mount up if we do not act, and act soon. This book brings together an array of studies which support this realization, including the *OECD Environmental Outlook to 2030*, published in January 2008, which the authors quote, highlighting the fact that, 'Without more ambitious policies, increasing pressures on the environment could cause irreversible damage within the next few decades.' The authors also quote the statements of the Chair of UNEP's fourth *Global Environment Outlook*, published in November 2007, stating that, 'The systematic destruction of the Earth's natural and nature-based resources has reached a point where the economic viability of economies is being challenged – and where the bill we hand on to our children may prove impossible to pay.' Conversely, as *Cents and Sustainability* shows, the costs of action are usually an order of magnitude less than the costs of inaction, as highlighted by the UK *Stern Review* for climate change. *Cents and Sustainability* brings together studies which, for the first time, assess the economics of acting on multiple environmental issues. It shows that the costs of acting on climate change, biodiversity, air and water pollution, and sanitation simultaneously are miniscule compared to the costs of inaction that we stand to face in the near future.

This book's central message – that if done wisely there is in fact no trade-off between ongoing strong economic growth, jobs and environmental sustainability – is important, particularly as the global economy currently suffers jitters from high oil prices, inflation and the sub-prime mortgage crisis. It is an important message leading into the 2009 post-Kyoto UN Climate Change Conference in Copenhagen (COP15). Here is a truly historic moment for the nations of the world to come together to chart a course for sustainable development this century. This meeting is the key meeting which will decide whether or not we have a global commitment to serious 2020 and 2050 greenhouse gas reduction targets. Again debates about the economic costs of environmental measures, in this case mitigating climate change, are front and centre. As this book shows, there are no excuses, only risks for governments not acting on an ambitious new global framework for action.

Furthermore, we have witnessed a rapid succession of unprecedented natural events, the devastation of Katrina, the massive reduction in sea ice this summer in the Arctic, the devastating droughts in Australia and floods in Europe, and the serious bleaching events on many of the world's coral reefs. As Robert May said in 2005 in his final address as President of the Royal Society in London, '... make no mistake, climate change is undeniably real, caused by human activities, and has serious consequences'. This book's detailed economic argument could make the difference in finally convincing decision-makers of the affordability of action on a strong sustainable development agenda. Hence, the Purves Environment Fund is proud of its role in supporting the development of this sort of outstanding, independent thought leadership.

Preface

In the immortal words of George Santayana, 'Those who cannot remember the past are condemned to repeat it.'[1] Our early 21st-century civilization is not the first to face the prospect of what has become known as an 'environmentally induced economic decline'. Like many before it – including the first civilizations in Mesopotamia, the Roman Empire, the city of Angkor Wat and the Maya in the Yucatán – the impact of today's civilization on its environment is growing to a scale that threatens to degrade it past the point at which it can continue to support life as we know it. However, what makes our present civilization unique is that this scale of impact is threatening the entire planet, and the resulting changes will affect all life on Earth. Jared Diamond[2] and other writers[3] argue that our current civilization ignores the lessons of the history of civilizations at our peril. Diamond wrote in his bestseller *Collapse* that: 'One of the disturbing facts of history is that so many civilizations collapse. Few people, however, least of all our politicians, realize that a primary cause of the collapse of those societies has been the destruction of the environmental resources upon which they depend. Fewer still appreciate that many of those civilizations share a sharp curve of decline. Indeed, a society's demise may begin only a decade or two after it reaches its peak population, wealth, and power.'[4] In this book Diamond describes how one of his students reflected to him after a lecture that 'he wondered whether those people of the next century will be as astonished about our blindness today as we are about the blindness of past civilizations'.

Drawing a compelling parallel Diamond points out that past civilizations have collapsed due to a range of behaviours that we are again seeing evidence of, such as: large-scale damage to natural systems, such as through deforestation and soil erosion; the dependence on long-distance trade for resources; and increasing levels of internal and external violence and conflict. There is also some evidence that sudden climate change and changes in rainfall patterns were additional factors in the decline of some past civilizations. Experts have warned for a long time that our civilization could suffer a similar decline, if we do not take heed of the signs and work to transition to a new environmentally sustainable form of development. These early warnings included extinctions (1681),[5] overfishing (1712),[6] deforestation, desiccation and degradation of soils, and dryland salinity (1864),[7] acid rain (1872),[8] asbestos (1898),[9] PCBs (1899),[10] benzene (1897),[11] radiation (1896),[12] greenhouse gas emissions (1896)[13] and damming rivers (1900s). However, despite the fact that, by 1900, the first warning signs of the 'unsustainable' nature of the industrial revolution had been issued by respected scientists and experts of the day, little action was taken by leaders at the time.[14] A similar pattern, of a lack of action on early warnings, can be seen on the issue of climate change. By the 1930s, scientists realized that the US and North Atlantic region had warmed significantly during the previous half-century. Scientists supposed this was just a phase of a mild natural cycle, with unknown causes. However, a scientist and coal engineer named Guy Stewart Callendar postulated that the increase in temperature was associated with an increase of atmospheric CO_2 concentrations to the order of 10 per cent over the past 100 years. Callendar published a number of academic papers[15] and estimated that a doubling of CO_2 could gradually bring a 2°C rise in future centuries and even that this might result in a self-sustaining warming.[16] By 1972, much more was known about climate science. Drawing on such understanding, Barbara Ward and Rene Dubois issued the following warning in the book *Only One Earth*, the official book of the UN Conference on the Human Environment, in Stockholm: 'The sum of all likely fossil fuel demands in the early decades of the next century [could] greatly increase the emission of CO_2 into the atmosphere and by doing so bring up average surface temperature uncomfortably close to that rise of 2 degrees Celsius, which might set in motion the long-term warming-up of the planet.'[17]

The UN and member countries have initiated a number of major international conferences and events over the last 40 years in response to such warnings in order to build international cooperation and inform action. Of these events the most influential have been the UN Conference on the Human Environment, held in Stockholm in 1972, and the UN Conference on Environment and Development, held in Rio de Janeiro in 1992. Whilst these events were attended by a significant number of the world's leaders, on the whole their influence has been weak, with many commentators reporting that much more could have been achieved, and that the momentum generated by each event was soon lost.

One of the main reasons for the loss in momentum was the fact that soon after each of the two events the global economy experienced a period of recession. The economic recessions shifted attention away from issues perceived to be medium- to long-term issues, such as those related to environmental pressures, and firmly onto short-term issues such as increased unemployment and reduced economic activity, issues that demand the attention of politicians, business leaders and citizens alike. Furthermore, as it has long been perceived that action to reduce environmental pressures will result in job losses and reduced profits, any momentum that has been gained in this area was quickly lost in the face of each of the 1972 and 1992 recessions. However, as this book will show, the response to the 2008 global financial crisis by many world leaders was in fact a shift towards action on the environment and climate change as a way to stimulate economic growth and create jobs. This shift was greatly helped by the leadership of Sir Nicholas Stern and his team, through *The Stern Review*, and then in subsequent articles,[18] with Stern stating: 'The credit crunch provide[s] an opportunity to invest in measures such as energy efficiency to tackle global warming as a way of stimulating economic growth. Spending on renewable and other low-carbon industries could help stimulate the economy ... We're going to have to grow out of this ... and [action on climate change] is an area which looks as though it could well grow strongly and with the right support could be one of the major engines of growth.'[19]

Such leadership and clarity on these issues is important because, as Jim MacNeill, former Secretary-General of the World Commission on Environment and Development, responsible for the report *Our Common Future*, has explained to us, certain interests in society have long played on the prevalence of the mistaken assumption that action on the environment harms the economy and jobs. He explained that certain interests have in fact formed 'blocking coalitions' to mount significant media and political lobbying campaigns, based on this false assumption, to reduce political will in order to delay and even block efforts to reduce environmental pressures. Such campaigns portray addressing environmental concerns as a luxury, and suggest that only after achieving strong economic growth can a nation or company afford to act.

Unfortunately, some in the environment movement and in the field of ecological economics have unwittingly helped these vested interests convince politicians and the public that we have to choose between the economy and the environment. For many years writers have developed academic works that challenge the structure of the global economy and question its suitability for our global society. Such works tend to have argued that there is strong coupling between economic growth and the physical growth of the economy, and further that decoupling is all but impossible. Assuming this, these works then pursue the question of whether it is possible to have prosperity without economic growth because, discounting decoupling, they can see no alternative. Hence, this argument plays perfectly into the hands of those that seek to hinder action on the environment in order to protect short-term profits through promoting the idea that we have to choose between economic growth and the environment. This book is focused on demonstrating that significant decoupling can be achieved and, even if some take the view that this cannot be done, there is no sign of any government committing to 'slow' economic growth and, as such, efforts to decouple are the only realistic option and need to be better informed and accelerated.

Ironically, much of this belief that economic and the physical growth are strongly coupled stems from a misunderstanding of the 1972 book *Limits to Growth*. The publication, which sold 9 million copies, created much unintended controversy and confusion partly because it did not consistently distinguish between 'economic growth' and the 'physical growth of the economy'. The original *Limits to Growth* publication did not explain why economic growth and the physical growth of the economy are not the same and that they can be significantly decoupled. Therefore, when the authors called for 'growth' to be limited, many people assumed they meant 'economic growth' rather than 'physical growth' as they intended. As Jim MacNeill explains, '*Limits to Growth* gave birth to a widespread movement advocating zero or even negative growth.'[20] However, as economist Dr Steve Dodds explains, 'Discouraging economic growth would do little to encourage a more sustainable society. Indeed, engineering a recession is likely to have perverse consequences, increasing unemployment, reducing the willingness of consumers and firms to adopt improved social and environmental practices, and encouraging farmers and resource based industries to eat into our natural capital to maintain cash flows and living standards.'[21]

In a globalized economy, halting economic growth in wealthier countries will also slow economic growth in poor countries and thus make it very difficult to reduce global poverty[22] and address rapid population growth, which both have major impacts on the environment, as shown in Chapter 4. As Diamond points out, it is no coincidence that the 12 countries that face the worst levels of poverty and overpopulation are the same countries that have the worst levels of environmental degradation – namely, in alphabetical order, Afghanistan, Bangladesh, Burundi, Haiti, Iraq, Madagascar, Mongolia, Nepal, Pakistan, Rwanda, the Solomon Islands and Somalia.[23]

Furthermore as Dr Kenneth Ruffing, former Deputy Director and Chief Economist of the OECD Environment Directorate, points out in his foreword to this volume, 'Ultimately, environmental pressures can be reduced only by reducing the level of output (negative economic growth) or by transforming the economic processes that underpin growth in such a way as to reduce the pressures (emissions of pollutants, greenhouse gases and destructive use of natural resources) per unit of output. Since buoyant economic growth is a necessary, but by no means sufficient condition, for achieving most of the [Millennium Development Goals], the former is not an option. That leaves us with decoupling.'

Hence, rather than asking if a society can be prosperous without economic growth, this book asks the question: is it possible to significantly decouple economic growth from environmental pressures, and so allow the basis for breaking the poverty trap? Over 20 years ago the report to the World Commission on Environment and Development, published as *Our Common Future*, showed that it is possible to decouple GDP growth from environmental pressures through price signals and effective policy reform. For instance, *Our Common Future* showed that GDP growth had increased whilst energy use and greenhouse gas emissions had reduced during the 1970s. *Our Common Future* stated that 'Sustainable development ... requires a change in the content of (economic) growth, to make it less material and energy intensive and more equitable.' Changing the 'quality of economic growth' was one of the main stated themes and recommendations from *Our Common Future*. Dr Gro Brundtland gave powerful expression to this in her foreword, where she called for 'a new form of economic growth that is forceful and environmentally and socially sustainable'.

At the time, the work was heavily criticized as many still held the mistaken assumption that large trade-offs between economic growth and environmental sustainability were inevitable, as described above. The reason for writing this book, *Cents and Sustainability*, is that now, 20 years on, there is a wealth of research and practice that provides compelling evidence to support the claims made in *Our Common Future*, which needs to be communicated. For instance investigations by the OECD have found that for every major environmental pressure at least one OECD country has absolutely decoupled it from its economic growth.[24] Hence, the imperative to communicate such advances. Leaders of this agenda such as Ernst von Weizsäcker, Amory Lovins and Hunter Lovins have argued for many years that factor 4–10 reductions in environmental pressures are possible through improvements in resource productivity through whole system design and biomimicry. Their publications,[25] and many others, show that it is now possible to achieve in the order of 60–80 per cent resource productivity improvements across major sectors of the economy, thus for instance making it possible to meet higher percentages of energy demand through renewable energy more rapidly.[26] They show that combining this factor 4–10 scale decoupling through resource productivity, with investments in renewable energy and restoration of natural ecosystems, provides a strategy to achieve environmental sustainability.

Even those often traditionally seen as critics of 'decoupling' do in fact support decoupling as long as the scale of the decoupling is significant enough to achieve environmental sustainability. In a World Bank debate Herman Daly observed that, 'Some folks, like Amory Lovins, think that GDP could grow 10 fold or more with a constant throughput. I tend to doubt it. I believe the coupling is stronger than that, but if Amory is right that's fine with me. Let GDP grow forever as long as throughput is constrained and held constant.'[27] Tim Jackson recently wrote that 'The message here is not that decoupling is unnecessary. On the contrary, absolute (large scale) reductions in physical throughput (and associated waste and pollution) are essential.'[28]

The challenge of how to cost effectively and rapidly decouple economic growth from environmental pressure by a factor 5–10 whilst restoring the environment and reducing poverty has been the focus of our research team since our formation in 2002.[29] Since 2002, we have focused on researching innovations in sustainable technology, design, policy and education, and communicating this research in a series of books that present evidence for decoupling, culminating in this publication, *Cents and Sustainability*. In our first, 2005, publication, *The Natural Advantage of Nations: Business Opportunities, Innovation and Governance in the 21st Century*, we worked with a number of leading experts to create one of the first books to look at how national systems of innovation can be harnessed to address the scale of the decoupling needed. A key feature of this work was a chapter by Dr Paul Weaver based on the Sustainable Technology Development programme from the Netherlands, which was the first nation to embrace the goal of researching how to achieve factor 10–20 levels of decoupling (with an updated summary in Chapter 2).

A more recent example of our research in this area has been our team's work with Ernst von Weizsäcker, to develop an update to the groundbreaking 1997 book *Factor Four: Doubling Wealth and Halving Resource Usage*. The resulting 2009 book, *Factor Five: Transforming the Global Economy through 80% Improvements in Resource Productivity*, shows in detail how as much as 80 per cent reductions in greenhouse gas emissions can be achieved across each of the major sectors of the economy, including the buildings, steel,[30] cement,[31] transportation and agricultural sectors.

One of the significant barriers to realizing such achievements, however, has been the lack of training of engineers, designers, planners and managers, in undertaking developing an integrated approach that captures synergies across and between entire technical systems. It was this understanding, inspired by the mentoring of Amory Lovins, that motivated our team to develop the book, *Whole System Design: An Integrated Approach to Sustainable Engineering*, led by our teams technical specialist, Peter Stasinopoulos. The book first sets out the basis of an integrated approach to whole system design drawing on the leading work in the field and compares it to the traditional design approach. The book then presents a series of worked examples to demonstrate the effectiveness of a whole system approach to sustainable design realizing large resource productivity improvements, namely in the design of industrial pumping systems, server farms, passenger vehicles and residential building design. In each case the book shows that this approach can yield factor 2–10 improvements over traditional design methods.[32]

To further complement *Cents and Sustainability*, our team has also published several free online textbooks, which provide additional detail on how to achieve decoupling. For instance, *Energy Transformed: Sustainable Energy Solutions for Climate Change Mitigation*, developed with CSIRO (the Commonwealth Scientific and Industrial Research Organization), provides a set of 30 comprehensive free-access online units showing how to achieve significant levels of decoupling of economic growth from greenhouse gas emissions through energy efficiency, demand management, renewable energy and sustainable transport.[33] *Water Transformed: Sustainable Water Solutions for Climate Change Adaptation*, being developed with the Australian Government Department of Climate Change, will provide 24 free-access online units showing how to decouple economic growth from potable freshwater usage through water efficiency, demand management and water recycling.[34]

Building on this work, and using the framework of decoupling, here we show in *Cents and Sustainability* that many cost-effective opportunities to reduce environmental pressures still exist across the economy, mainly due to the fact that in the past resources (such as energy, water and materials) and pollution have been relatively inexpensive.[35] However with the recent moves in a number of countries to introduce carbon trading and/or carbon taxation and enact stricter pollution controls, and considering the likely imminent peaking of world oil production, this situation is set to change, and it is now evident that an emphasis on reducing environmental pressures, particularly associated with climate change, will be a key part of national and corporate strategy.

Cents and Sustainability shows that when governments have made the necessary policy and regulatory changes, economic growth has been significantly decoupled from many environmental pressures such as ozone-depleting chemicals, air pollutants including sulphur and nitrogen oxide emissions, asbestos, benzene, DDT and leaded petrol to name a few.[36] Furthermore, many aspects of a decoupling strategy have strong economic multipliers that will significantly boost economic growth and create new jobs. For instance, a respected 2008 study showed that US green stimulus spending – retrofitting buildings, mass transit, shifting to rail freight, smart grid, wind power, solar power and next generation biofuels – could create 2 million new jobs in the US within two years.[37] This book will thus assist governments focused on multi-factor productivity[38] gains that drive economic growth – resource and labour productivity, technical innovation, investment in 'green' infrastructure, and improving skills and training to create 'green jobs'. As Sir Nicholas Stern has observed:

> The next few years present a great opportunity to lay the foundations of a new form of growth that can transform our economies and societies. Let us grow out of this recession in a way that both reduces risks for our planet and sparks off a wave of new investment which will create a more secure and cleaner economy. And in so doing, we shall demonstrate for all, that low-carbon growth is not only possible, but that it can also be a productive and efficient route to overcome world poverty.[39]

A Call for Leadership, Action and Results

This book is dedicated to help inspire and inform efforts and leadership at the local, regional, national and global scales to translate good intentions into action and results. There is no more time for inaction. As a response to *Our Common Future*, this book also marks a number of significant anniversaries, such as it being 20 years since former UK Prime Minister Margaret Thatcher warned in a speech to the UN that 'We are seeing a vast increase in the amount of carbon dioxide reaching the atmosphere ... The result is that change in future is likely to be more fundamental and more widespread than anything we have known hitherto',[40] and called for a meaningful global treaty on climate change. It is 50 years since the World Council of Churches called for wealthy nations (0.7 per cent) and corporations (0.3 per cent) to commit a total of 1 per cent of GDP per annum to reduce extreme poverty. It is 100 years since former Republican President Theodore Roosevelt called on world leaders to meet at The Hague to work together on the conservation of natural resources.[41]

The reality is that the 21st century provides the last real chance to achieve the necessary bipartisan leadership and action to avoid large-scale dangerous climate change, lift billions of people out of poverty, prevent significant species extinction and allow our global civilization to thrive long term on this planet. We are in effect the last generation with the opportunity to make the changes needed to ensure we do not 'compromise the ability of future generations to meet their own needs'. This book is intended to provide a valuable enabler to achieve this future and is in honour of Dr Gro Brundtland, Dr Jim MacNeill and the many contributors and reviewers of *Our Common Future*.

Michael H. Smith, Karlson 'Charlie' Hargroves and Cheryl Desha
July 2010

Notes

1   Santayana, G. (1905) *Life of Reason, Reason in Common Sense*, Scribner's, p284.
2   Diamond, J. (2006) *Collapse: How Societies Choose to Fail or Succeed*, Random House.
3   Marsh, G. P. (1864) *Man and Nature: Or, Physical Geography as Modified by Human Action,* University of Washington Press, reprint 2003; Ponting, C. (1991) *A Green History of the World: The Environment and the Collapse of Great Civilisations*, Penguin; Redman, C. (1999) *Human Impact on Ancient Environment*, University of Arizona Press; Fagan, B. (1999) *Floods, Famines, and Emperors: El Nino and the Fate of Civilisations*, Basic Books; St Barbe Baker, R. (1944) *I Planted Trees*, Lutterworth Press, London.
4   Diamond, J. (2006) *Collapse: How Societies Choose to Fail or Succeed*, Random House.
5   Strickland, H. E. and Melville, A. G. (1848) *The Dodo and its Kindred*, vol 1, London, p26.
6   Taylor, J. (1999) *Making Salmon: An Environmental History of the Northwest Fisheries Crisis*, Washington University Press, Seattle.
7   Marsh, G. P. (1864) *Man and Nature: Or, Physical Geography as Modified by Human Action*, University of Washington Press, reprint 2003.
8   Smith, R. A. (1872) *Air and Rain*, Longmans Green & Co., London.
9   Deane, L. (1898) '*Report on the Health of Workers in Asbestos and Other Dusty Trades*', in HM Chief Inspector of Factories and Workshops, Annual Report for 1898, pp171–172, HMSO, London (see also the Annual Reports for 1899 and 1900, p502).
10 Harremo, P., Gee, P., MacGarvin, M., Stirling, A., Keys, J., Wynne, B. and Vaz, S. G., (2002) *Late Lessons from Early Warnings: The Precautionary Principle 1896–2000*, Environmental issue report no 22, European Environment Agency.
11 LeNoir, C. (1897) 'On a case of purpura attributed to benzene intoxication', *Bul. Mem. Soc. Med. Hop.*, vol 3, pp1251–1261.
12 Edison, T. A. (1896) 'Effect of X-rays upon the eye', *Nature*, vol 53, p421.
13 Arrhenius, S. (1896) 'On the influence of carbonic acid in the air upon the temperature of the ground', *Philosophical Magazine,* vol 41, pp237–276.
14 Harremo, P., Gee, P., MacGarvin, M., Stirling, A., Keys, J., Wynne, B. and Vaz, S. G. (2002) *Late Lessons from Early Warnings: The Precautionary Principle 1896–2000*, Environmental issue report no 22, European Environment Agency.

15 Callendar, G. S. (1938) 'The artificial production of carbon dioxide and its influence on climate', *Quarterly Journal Royal Meteorological Society*, vol 64, pp223–240; Callendar, G. S. (1939) 'The composition of the atmosphere through the ages', *Meteorological Magazine*, vol 74, pp33–39; Callendar, G. S. (1940) 'Variations in the amount of carbon dioxide in different air currents', *Quarterly Journal Royal Meteorological Society*, vol 66, pp395–400; Callendar, G. S. (1941) 'Infra-red absorption by carbon dioxide, with special reference to atmospheric radiation', *Quarterly Journal Royal Meteorological Society*, vol 67, pp263–275; Callendar, G. S. (1949) 'Can carbon dioxide influence climate?', *Weather*, vol 4, pp310–314; Callendar, G. S. (1958) 'On the amount of carbon dioxide in the atmosphere', *Tellus*, vol 10, pp243–248; Callendar, G. S. (1961) 'Temperature fluctuations and trends over the Earth', *Quarterly Journal Royal Meteorological Society*, vol 87, pp1–12.
16 Weart, S. (2008) *The Discovery of Global Warming*, American Institute of Physics, see 'Money for Keeling: Monitoring CO_2 levels'.
17 Ward, B. and Dubois, R. (1972) *Only One Earth. The Care and Maintenance of a Small Planet*, Pelican Publishing, England.
18 Stern, N. (2009) 'Time for a Green Industrial Revolution', *New Scientist*, 21 January.
19 Jowit, J. (2008) 'Now is the time to tackle global warming – Stern', *Guardian*, UK, 7 October.
20 MacNeill, J., Winsemius, P. and Yakushiji, T. (1991) *Beyond Interdependence: The Meshing of the World's Economy and the Earth's Ecology*, Oxford University Press, Oxford.
21 Dodds, S. (1997) 'Economic growth and human well-being', in Hamilton, C. and Diesendorf, M. (eds) *Human Ecology, Human Economy: Ideas for an Ecologically Sustainable Future*, Allen & Unwin, Sydney, pp99–124.
22 Also, when industrialized nations have had periods of slow or negative economic growth, this has lowered levels of tax revenue to government thus reducing government's capacity to fund overseas development aid and environmental sustainability initiatives.
23 Diamond, J. (2006) *Collapse: How Societies Choose to Fail or Succeed*, Random House, pp515–516.
24 OECD Secretariat (2002) *Indicators to Measure Decoupling of Environmental Pressure and Economic Growth*, OECD, Paris.
25 Hawken, P., Lovins, A. and Lovins, L. H. (1999) *Natural Capitalism: Creating the Next Industrial Revolution*, Earthscan, London, Chapter 9, pp176–177; von Weizsäcker, E., Lovins, A. B. and Lovins, L. H. (1997) *Factor Four: Doubling Wealth, Halving Resource Use*, Earthscan, London.
26 von Weizsäcker, E., Hargroves, K., Smith, M., Desha, C. and Stasinopoulos, P. (2009) *Factor Five: Transforming the Global Economy through 80% Improvements in Resource Productivity*, Earthscan, London.
27 Daly, H. (2004) 'Can economic growth solve our environmental problems?' A debate with Herman Daly and Paul Portney, The World Bank Group.
28 Jackson, T. (2009) *Prosperity Without Growth*, Earthscan, London.
29 Smith, M. and Elliot, F. (2002) *Factor 10: A Future Worth Having*, Australian National University.
30 von Weizsäcker, E., Hargroves, K., Smith, M., Desha, C. and Stasinopoulos, P. (2009) *Factor Five: Transforming the Global Economy through 80% Improvements in Resource Productivity*, Earthscan, London.

31 Smith, M., Hargroves, K., Desha, C. and Stasinopoulos, P. (2009) 'Factor 5 in eco-cements', *CSIRO ECOS Magazine*, no 149.
32 Stasinopoulos, P., Smith, M., Hargroves, K. and Desha, C. (2008) *Whole System Design: An Integrated Approach to Sustainable Engineering,* Earthscan, London, and The Natural Edge Project, Australia.
33 Smith, M., Hargroves, K., Stasinopoulos, P., Stephens, R., Desha, C. and Hargroves, S. (2007) *Energy Transformed: Sustainable Energy Solutions for Climate Change Mitigation*, The Natural Edge Project, Australia.
34 Smith, M., Hargroves, K., Stasinopoulos, P. and Desha, C. (2010) *Water Transformed: Sustainable Water Solutions for Climate Change Adaptation*, The Natural Edge Project, Australia.
35 Lovins, A. and Lovins, H. (1997) *Climate: Making Money, Making Sense,* Rocky Mountain Institute.
36 Smith, M., Hargroves, K. and Desha, C. (2010) *Cents and Sustainability: Securing Our Common Future By Decoupling Economic Growth from Environmental Pressures*, Earthscan, London, www.naturaledgeproject.net/centsandsustainability.aspx.
37 Pollin, R., Garrett-Peltier, H., Heintz, J. and Scharber, H. (2008) *Green Recovery – A Program to Create Good Jobs and Start Building a Low-Carbon Economy*, Political Economy Research Institute.
38 Gittens, R. (2010) 'The truth about productivity', *Sydney Morning Herald*, 30 January.
39 Stern, N. (2008) 'Green routes to growth: Recession is the time to build a low-carbon future with the investment vital for economy and planet', *Guardian*, 23 October.
40 BBC (2009) *A Brief History of Climate Change*, BBC.
41 Barney, G. (1982) *The Global 2000 Report to the President: Entering the Twenty-first Century*, Appendix A 'Lessons from the past', Volume Two, Technical Report, Penguin Books, pp685—687.

Acknowledgements

The authors would like to thank the following individuals and groups for making the development of this publication possible. First, a special thank you must go to the authors' families. Mike would like to thank his wife, Sarah Chapman, for her love, support and for sharing a life-long passion for environmental sustainability. Charlie would like to thank his wife, Stacey, for her patient and loving support and along with his family for bringing joy into his life. Cheryl would like to thank her family for their love and support of her commitment to sustainable engineering. The authors would like to thank Dhruv Sanghavi (author of Chapter 12), Peter Stasinopoulos (co-author of Chapter 10), and Connor Kretch (contributions to Chapter 8) for their contributions to the book. The authors would also like to thank Angie Reeve, Nathan Keilar and David Sparks for research support, Fatima Pinto for her tireless efforts in managing The Natural Edge Project (TNEP) office, and Candia Bruce from Working On It for her amazing support for our team.

The work was copy-edited by Stacey Hargroves, based at Griffith University, whom the authors thank for her patience and invaluable attention to detail. Work on original graphics and enhancements to existing graphics has been carried out by the gifted graphic designer Roger Dennis.

We would like to thank Dr Gro Harlem Brundtland, Dr R. Pachauri, Dr Kenneth Ruffing, Jim MacNeill and Robert Purves for their significant contributions to sustainable development over many years. The pioneering work of these leaders has inspired and informed the development of this book, and we are most grateful for the contribution of the forewords and introductions.

The authors would also like to thank the sponsors of the book:

- The Purves Environmental Foundation, for providing a grant towards the development of the book, in particular Robert Purves and his team members Alison Atherton and Zoe Hamilton.
- Griffith University, for both providing a grant towards the development of the book, in particular Deputy Vice Chancellor (Research) Professor Ned Pankhurst, and providing TNEP members based at Griffith University with in-kind administrative hosting, in particular the director of the Urban Research Program (URP), Professor Brendan Gleeson, and the URP centre manager, Dr Stephen Horton.

- Australian National University, for providing in-kind hosting for members of TNEP, in particular the director of the Fenner School of Environment and Society, Professor Stephen Dovers, the executive director of the ANU Climate Change Institute, Professor Will Steffen, and the associate dean (undergraduate) for the ANU Faculty of Engineering and Information Technology, Dr Paul Compston.
- Curtin University, for the ongoing mentoring by Professor Peter Newman, Professor of Sustainability, Curtin University Sustainability Policy Institute.

We wish to acknowledge the following, for their significant contributions to the field of the economics of sustainable development, whose work has inspired this publication: Arthur Pigou, Christian Azar, Daniel Esty, David Pearce, Duncan Austin, Eban Goodstein, Edward B. Barbier, Elinor Ostrom, Ernst von Weizsäcker, Francis Cairncross, Gro Harlem Brundtland, Hart Hodges, Heather Cooley, James K. Boyce, Jeff Kenworthy, Jeffrey Sachs, Jim MacNeill, Joseph Stiglitz, Kenneth Arrow, Kenneth Ruffing, Leo Jansen, Lester Brown, Matthew Riddle, Michael Porter, Mike Young, Nicholas Stern, Noeleen Hezyer, Norman Myers, Patrick ten Brink, Paul Ekins, Paul Weaver, Pavan Sukhdev, Peter Gleick, Peter Newman, Philip Sutton, Robert Pollin, Robert Repetto, Stephen Dovers, Steve Hatfield-Dodds, Stephen Schneider and Walter Stahel. We would also like to acknowledge the pioneering work on decoupling economic growth from environmental pressures by the OECD Environment Directorate. In particular, we would like to acknowledge the work by the team behind the *OECD Environmental Outlook to 2030*, led by Lorents Lorentsen, and including Rob Visser, Helen Mountford and Jan Bakkes. This work is a significant contribution to understanding decoupling economic growth from environmental pressures and has greatly informed this book. We would also like to thank Earthscan for their dedicated efforts, and in particular Jonathan Sinclair Wilson, Rob West, Michael Fell, Anna Rice, Claire Lamont and Hamish Ironside.

List of Abbreviations

ACIA	Arctic Climate Impact Assessment
ANU	Australian National University
ASEAN	Association of Southeast Asian Nations
BAT	best available technology
BAU	business as usual
CBD	Convention on Biological Diversity
CCA	Climate Change Agreement
CDM	Clean Development Mechanism
CEO	chief executive officer
CFC	chlorofluorocarbon
CH_4	methane
CITES	UN Convention on International Trade in Endangered Species of Wild Fauna and Flora
CNG	compressed natural gas
CO	carbon monoxide
CO_2	carbon dioxide
CO_2e	non-CO_2 greenhouse gases
CPR	collective producer responsibility
CSIRO	Commonwealth Scientific and Industrial Research Organization
DDT	dichlorodiphenyltrichloroethane
DHA	docosa-hexaenoic acid
EAF	electric arc furnace
EEQ	enhanced environmental quality
EG	economic growth
EPs	Equator Principles
EPA	eicosa-pentaenoic acid
EPA	Environment (Protection) Act
EPR	extended producer responsibility
EU	European Union
FAO	Food and Agriculture Organization of the UN
FIT	feed-in tariff
GAVI	Global Alliance for Vaccines and Immunization

GDI	gross domestic income
GHG	greenhouse gas
GPI	genuine progress indicator
$GtCO_2$	billion tonnes of carbon dioxide
GW	gigawatt
GWP	global warming potential
HC	hydrocarbons
HEI	higher education institution
ICPD	International Conference on Population and Development
IEA	International Energy Agency
IISD	International Institute for Sustainable Development
IPCC	Intergovernmental Panel on Climate Change
IPR	individual producer responsibility
IUCN	International Union for the Conservation of Nature (now World Conservation Union)
MtC	million tonnes of carbon
NEP	negative environmental pressure
NF_3	nitrogen trifluoride
NFEE	National Framework for Energy Efficiency
NGO	non-governmental organization
NNI	net national income
NO	nitrous oxide
NO_x	nitrogen oxides
NPF	novel protein foods
O_3	tropospheric ozone
OBF	oxygen blast furnace
ODA	official development assistance
OECD	Organisation for Economic Co-operation and Development
Pb	lead
PBL	problem-based learning
PCB	polychlorinated biphenyl
PM	particulate matter
$PM_{2.5}$	particulate matter under 2.5 micrometres, or microns
PM_{10}	particulate matter under 10 micrometres, or microns
POP	persistent organic pollutant
ppm	parts per million
RCR	rapid curriculum renewal
R&D	research and development
REACH	Registration, Evaluation and Authorization of Chemicals
REN21	Renewable Energy Policy Network for the 21st Century
SCR	standard curriculum renewal
SO_2	sulphur dioxide
SO_x	sulphur oxides
STD	Sustainable Technology Development
TNEP	The Natural Edge Project

UNDESA	UN Department of Economic and Social Affairs
UNECE	UN Economic Commission for Europe
UNEP	UN Environment Programme
UNESCAP	UN Economic and Social Commission for Asia and the Pacific
UNFCCC	UN Framework Convention on Climate Change
USCAP	US Climate Action Partnership,
US EPA	US Environmental Protection Agency
WCED	World Commission on Environment and Development
WEF	World Economic Forum
WFEO	World Federation of Engineering Organizations
WHO	World Health Organization
WIC	women, infants and children
WRI	World Resources Institute
WSSD	World Summit on Sustainable Development

1

Securing 'Our Common Future'

Are We Destroying the World We Are Creating?

If you don't know how to fix it, please stop breaking it.
Severn Cullis-Suzuki, daughter of David Suzuki,
speaking at the 1992 Rio Earth Summit at 12 years of age

Even a cursory overview of human history will conclude that the last few centuries have witnessed remarkable change, with now the majority of the world shifting from local agrarian communities to densely populated, highly urbanized, industrial cities. For much of this transition, nature was considered to be plentiful and innovation was focused on increasing labour productivity. A lack of financial capital was addressed by the formation of banking systems and stock exchanges, and access to cheap energy was achieved by generating energy from oil, natural gas and coal. Governments and business, working together have created remarkable material prosperity and economic growth for many living today. Much has improved; for instance, poverty has been reduced, life expectancy has risen, access to education and health services has increased (for instance, with polio now largely eradicated), democratic governance has spread, and there have been huge leaps forward in technology and communication. Agricultural production now helps to support a global population of over 6 billion people and an increase in global trade has helped to build a foundation for greater peace and security. In many ways these are the best of times; however, with these advances, new issues have emerged, particularly related to the scale of environmental pressures, that if not addressed, will have real impacts on future prosperity and economic growth.

A wide range of significant recent reports[1] by the likes of the World Bank, United Nations Environment Programme, the Intergovernmental Panel on Climate Change, and the United Nations Millennium Ecosystem Assessment have identified a set of key issues that now need to be addressed as we move into the next century, including:

- Cheap energy from fossil fuels, which fuelled the first industrial revolution, now threatens future prosperity through the generation of significant quantities of greenhouse gas emissions, and the resulting impacts on our climate system. Already we are seeing the intensity of cyclones, hailstorms, flooding, heatwaves and bushfires increase. If climate change is not mitigated, such changes risk being complemented by sea-level rises, shifting rainfall patterns, reduced water availability and agricultural production, the further spread of vector-borne diseases, and loss of species, to name a few of the negative changes forecast this century.
- Advances in agriculture, which have increased food production and under-pinned exponential population growth, have often relied on over-extraction of groundwater and fresh water that cannot be sustained.
- The scale of deforestation, loss of habitat and species loss is reducing the earth's ecosystems' resilience and capacity to assimilate pollution and other environmental pressures, a service that we depend on.
- The forecast rising demand this century for finite non-renewable resources such as oil, natural gas, coal and minerals is resulting in many nations and companies already competing to sure up access to the remaining reserves, which some warn could lead to ongoing 'resource wars'.

By 2050 it is predicted that there will be 9 billion people on earth. Already, it is no longer physically possible, using the previous industrial revolution model of development, to sustain for everyone long term the standards of living enjoyed in the West. This is because the scale of the resources required would exceed the earth's capacity to regenerate them.

As George Monbiot, in his 2006 publication *Heat*, laments, 'Ours are the most fortunate generations that have ever lived. Ours might also be the most fortunate that ever will'.[2]

As we showed in the Preface, early 21st-century civilization is not the first to face the risk of '*environmentally induced economic decline*'. The challenge of how to achieve economic prosperity, whilst not undermining the environ-mental base upon which the economy depends, is a long-standing challenge faced by many civilizations. What is different today is the sheer scale of devel-opment and its impact that is affecting the entire planet's biosphere. Perhaps if the planet were twice or three times as big we would not be writing this book, and it would be another group of young engineers and scientists long off in the future that would be concerned about the environmental sustainability of their future on this earth. However, as the growing number of significant reports in this area are now showing, current forms of development are environmentally unsustainable, and if we do not take action in the next two decades irreversible thresholds are likely to be breached leading to dangerous and unpredictable impacts on the biosphere.

> *Two decades after* Our Common Future *emphasized the urgency of sustainable development, environmental degradation continues to threaten human well-being ... While progress towards sustainable development has been made through meetings, agreements and changes in environmental governance, real change has been slow.*
>
> UNEP, *GEO-4*, 2007[3]

On the positive side, we are now at a point in the development of humankind where there is the economic means, technological know-how, and a sophisticated global communication network that can be harnessed to tackle these large-scale global problems. The goal is to achieve a transition to a global society that can continue to grow economically whilst sustaining the environment. To achieve such a future we need to absolutely disconnect or 'decouple' economic growth from a wide range of environmental pressures. This is because the combined impact of different environmental pressures – such as air, water and land pollution; overconsumption of water, fish, wood and other natural resources; and inappropriate land management leading to loss of topsoil, erosion of coastal environments and desertification – interact with each other resulting in an amplification of their negative effects. Hence, seeking to decouple economic growth from one environmental pressure is insufficient to create a basis for environmental sustainability. Impacts from global warming by itself can be mitigated, however, since they are compounded by impacts from deforestation, excessive freshwater extraction and growing volumes of waste and chemical pollution. Hence, economic growth needs to be significantly decoupled from a range of environmental pressures to ensure that ongoing economic growth does not push some ecosystems past ecological thresholds to collapse. Many studies are showing that such decoupling needs to occur rapidly as environmental pressures are compounding each other currently to such an extent that this risks leading to a significant number of negative amplification effects[4] occurring, faster than previously predicted.[5]

There is now concern that due to complexity and uncertainties involved in understanding ecosystems, their resilience may have been overestimated, and this means that as pressures on these ecosystems continue to grow there is growing risk that they can be overstressed, leading to significant disruption and even collapse. This growing concern has been supported by a number of key investigations including an analysis of the world's ecosystems prepared by the UN, the World Bank and the World Resources Institute (WRI) in 2000, finding that 'There are considerable signs that the capacity of ecosystems, the biological engines of the planet, to produce many of the goods and services we depend on is rapidly declining.'[6] Then further in 2005, the UN's Millennium Ecosystem Assessment Report, conducted by 1360 experts in 95 nations, issued a stark warning: 'Human activity is putting such strain on the natural functions of Earth that the ability of the planet's ecosystems to sustain future generations can no longer be taken for granted.'[7] The report detailed how over

60 per cent of the ecosystem services that support life on earth are being seriously degraded or used unsustainably. Imagine how fast people would act if roughly 60 per cent of their bodily systems were sick and in serious decline.[8]

In addition, there has been a misconception that humankind can pull back once the environmental pressures look to be causing too much damage. However, often by the time the ecosystem shows signs of not being able to assimilate the pressures, it has already been stressed beyond its capacity, and its decline is either irreversible, or the environmental pressure would need to be dramatically and rapidly reduced to allow the ecosystem to recover. For example, the wider impacts of using chemical pesticides in agriculture may not be noticeable until it is too late to reverse them as they bio-accumulate up through the food chain to form concentrations that are lethal to top-level predators, like the bald eagle in the US, or the fox in the UK. Rachel Carson pointed this out in her critically acclaimed 1962 book *Silent Spring*. In such a case even after the use of chemical pesticides, such as DDT, was largely stopped there was a long delay before reductions in concentration in top chain predators were recorded, as the remaining chemicals made their way through the system.[9]

> We are crossing natural thresholds that we cannot see and violating deadlines that we do not recognize. Nature is the time keeper, but we cannot see the clock.
>
> Lester Brown, *Plan B 3.0*, 2008[10]

This is similar to the situation with greenhouse gas emissions, with UNEP pointing out that, 'even if atmospheric concentrations of greenhouse gases were to be stabilized today, increases in land and ocean temperatures due to these emissions would continue for decades, and sea levels would continue to rise for centuries, due to the time-lags associated with climate processes and feedbacks'.[11] The feedbacks mentioned by UNEP refer to the situation where a trend already under way (such as global temperature rise) begins to reinforce itself regardless of whether the original stimulus or cause is removed (for example greenhouse gas may continue to be released from melting permafrost, or increased warming may continue to occur due to the melting of the highly reflective polar ice caps even if greenhouse gas emissions are reduced).

Environmental pressures not only exact a burden on the planet's ecosystems, they also come at a cost to the economy. According to UNEP, 'The systematic destruction of the Earth's natural and nature-based resources has reached a point where the economic viability of economies is being challenged – and where the bill we hand on to our children may prove impossible to pay.'[12] In most cases, the cost of declining ecosystem services, such as the regulation of climate, cleaning air and water, pollination, prevention of soil erosion and assimilating waste, becomes apparent only when the services start to break down. Ecological economists are increasingly identifying and quantifying the costs to the mainstream economy from the impact of environmental pressures. When Costanza et al calculated the value of nature's ecosystem services in 1997 they found it was worth a combined value of at least US$36 trillion annually,[13] compared to the annual gross world product at the time of approximately US$39 trillion. This provides a striking measure of the value of ecosystems to the economy, but also gives a sense of the scale of the economic risks to economies from not acting to reduce environmental pressures. According to a 2006 review of the economics of climate change, led by Sir Nicholas Stern, 'We estimate the total cost of business-as-usual climate change to equate to an average reduction in global per capita consumption of 5 per cent at a minimum now and for ever.'[14] *The Stern Review* also describes that this cost would increase to as much as 20 per cent per year if the modelling was to take into account the impacts related to human health, various amplifying effects, and the disproportionate burden of climate change on the poor and vulnerable globally. A particular area of concern also comes from the possible effects from global warming on the intensity of 'natural disasters', particularly when they are compounded by other environmental pressures. For instance, clearing land for farming can result in life-threatening mudslides, either under torrential rain and flooding, or during earthquakes. There was a good example in northern Pakistan in 2005 where locals claimed that intact forest cover prevented landslides which caused extensive damage elsewhere.

Understanding the Threat of Rising Greenhouse Gas Emissions

The threat of rising greenhouse gas emissions may be the greatest threat humanity has ever faced. Why is this so? In short, before the industrial revolution the change in average global temperature has been estimated to have oscillated between −9°C and +2°C for over 400,000 years, relative to 1950. (an average of temperatures change across the entire globe).[15] These oscillations in temperature coincided with oscillations in atmospheric carbon dioxide levels between approximately 180 and 280 parts per million (ppm). Within this band of temperature and carbon dioxide levels a delicate balance has evolved involving a certain amount of water remaining frozen at the poles, in glaciers and in vast areas of permafrost (where the land itself remains constantly frozen close to the poles); it involves the oceans finding a delicate balance of salinity, pH levels (just the right balance of acidity and alkalinity) and temperature that allows vibrant and diverse aquatic ecosystems to grow (such as coral reefs); and this balance has enabled an abundant ocean ecosystem to evolve with many species unique to particularly parts of the world depending on the level of this balance. Today, the global temperatures and carbon dioxide levels are at a peak of the natural oscillation and, hence, humanity is currently adding greenhouse gas emissions to an already developed natural peak. This is why today, carbon dioxide levels are already at 391ppm, approximately 100ppm higher than previous 'natural peaks' over the last 650,000 years, not to mention the additional 25 per cent global warming caused by non-CO_2 gases, many new to the environment. Calculations by NASA estimate that since 1950 the average global temperature in 2005 increased by 0.64°C,[16] and when combined with the increase in temperature expected due to time lags and from committed energy-intensive infrastructure and plants of 0.6°C, NASA estimates that we have already locked in a 1.24°C increase. This means that we are fast approaching +2°C of global warming at which many scientists warn will lead to dangerous climate change. As with many environmental challenges of the past, there have been early warnings about the risks of emitting greenhouse gases. In 1896 Svante Arrhenius published a study showing that the burning of fossil fuels, which added carbon dioxide gas to the earth's atmosphere, would raise the planet's average temperature.[17] However, this 'greenhouse effect' was only one of many speculations about global climate changes and was not regarded as being a credible threat at the time. Even if it were true, Arrhenius's calculations suggested that global warming would occur over thousands of years. Al Gore in his acceptance speech for the 2007 Nobel Peace Prize said: 'Even in Nobel's time, there were a few warnings of the likely consequences. One of the very first winners of the Prize in chemistry worried that "We are evaporating our coal mines into the air." After performing 10,000 equations by hand, Svante Arrhenius calculated that the Earth's average temperature would increase by several degrees if we doubled the amount of CO_2 in the atmosphere.'[18] According to the Intergovernmental Panel on Climate Change (IPCC), since 1950 the concentration of greenhouse gas emissions (expressed as a CO_2 equivalent) has increased by just over 50 per cent from 320ppm[19] to 455ppm in 2007[20] – an increase of around 1.4 times, fast approaching Arrhenius's warning of a doubling.

More recently such concerns were outlined in the official supporting publication to the 1972 UN Conference on the Human Environment, in Stockholm, *Only One Earth*, by Barbara Ward and Rene Dubois, who wrote, 'We do not have to postulate the fantasy of three and a half billion cars on the planet to begin to wonder whether the sum of all likely fossil fuel demands in the early decades of the next century might not greatly increase the emission of CO_2 into the atmosphere and by doing so bring up average surface temperature uncomfortably close to that rise of 2 degrees Celsius which might set in motion the long-term warming-up of the planet'.[21] Since 1988 the IPCC has released a series of comprehensive assessment reports that have informed global debate and shaped understandings around the seriousness of the climate change situation, and as Dr Rajendra Pachauri, the IPCC Chairperson, explains in his foreword to this book, 'The increased evidence of abrupt changes in the climate system, the fact that CO_2 equivalent levels are already at 455ppm, plus the current high rate of annual increases in global greenhouse gas emissions reinforces the IPCC's Fourth Assessment finding that humanity has a short window of time to bring about a reduction in global emissions if we wish to limit temperature increase to around 2°C at equilibrium.' Further, NASA,[22] the European Union (EU)[23] and participants of the 2009 Copenhagen Meeting[24] all support a call for emissions to be reduced in a serious effort to prevent average global temperature rises from exceeding 2°C. However, the reality may be that even if we stop emissions levels growing as soon as 2015 and then gradually reduce them each year by as much as 3 per cent – as is considered feasible – findings released in 2009 suggest that 'there is still a 55 per cent chance of exceeding a 2°C rise in global average temperatures, and a 1 in 3 chance that the world will still be more than 2°C warmer in 100 years' time'.[25] Hence urgent action is needed if we are to ensure global warming does not result in global temperatures reaching or exceeding 2°C.

In order to achieve such a goal, the IPCC, and many other bodies, are calling for reductions in greenhouse gas emissions in the order of 25 to 40 per cent by 2020 and 80 per cent of 2005 levels by the year 2050. Specifically, the emissions being referred to include both the actual emissions of carbon dioxide (CO_2) gas, as well as the emissions of a range of other greenhouse gases which are represented as an equivalent volume of CO_2 gas based on their relative ability to contribute to global warming (known as their global warming potential or GWP). Carbon dioxide is released primarily from fossil-fuel related emissions, peat and permafrost releases, and deforestation. In 2005 an estimated 34 billion tonnes of CO_2 (or $34GtCO_2$) was emitted globally. Other identified greenhouse gases, referred to as non-CO_2 greenhouse gases (CO_2e), include methane, carbon dioxide, nitrous oxide, hydrofluorocarbons, perfluorocarbons and sulphur hexafluoride. When converted to an equivalent volume of CO_2 these gases contribute an estimated further 12 billion tonnes of CO_2e (or $12GtCO_2$e). Hence the total level of greenhouse gas emissions in 2005 was in the order of 46 billion tonnes. Considering that the potential for the earth's biosphere to assimilate CO_2 has been estimated at around 11.4 billion tonnes (give or take 4 billion tonnes),[26] from land and ocean absorption, we are currently emitting in the order of four times as much as the planet can assimilate.

However, the IPCC has also clearly explained that targets as high as 80 per cent may prove to be insufficient given the unpredictable potential for feedbacks to increase emissions even further – such as rising temperatures triggering the release of additional greenhouse emissions from the vast stores of carbon in nature, stating that 'It appears that, as climate warms, these feedbacks will lead to an overall increase in natural greenhouse gas abundances. For this reason, climate change is likely to be greater than the estimates we have given.'[27] The occurrence of feedbacks and amplification effects means that efforts to minimize the increase in average global temperature need to be accelerated before the feedbacks strengthen and begin to contribute to global concentrations, with or without reductions in emissions levels. Many now consider an increase of 2°C as being the point at which such feedbacks become irreversible, and caution that it would then take centuries to allow the global average temperature to come back down.[28]

The following three examples outline some of the examples of feedbacks of most concern. However, for a detailed account of these and coverage of related issues, please refer to the UNEP *GEO-4*,[29] *The Stern Review*[30] and Lester Brown's *Plan B*,[31] all of which are critical reading.

The melting of sea ice

The thawing of Arctic sea ice to water results in a drastic increase in heat absorption at the poles, from around 10 to 80 per cent. This is known as the 'albedo' effect, where the replacement of highly reflective sea ice with darker open water greatly increases the heat absorbed from sunlight.[32] As the average global temperature increases, this increases the amount of ice melt, which then allows for greater heat absorption by the oceans, which then contributes to the average global temperature increase ... hence a feedback loop. This is of particular concern given that, due to the nature of the global climate system, heat is unevenly distributed towards the poles resulting in an increase in average temperature in the Arctic region around 2.5 times higher than the global average.[33] Furthermore, scientists now estimate that the Arctic sea ice will completely melt during summer as soon as 2030, rather than 2070 or 2100 as was previously estimated.[34]

The thawing of permafrosts

The rate of global temperature rise may also be increased by the release of methane (with a GWP 21 times that of CO_2) from peat deposits, wetlands and thawing permafrost,[35] which has the potential to release billions of tonnes of carbon into the atmosphere.[36] Models suggest that up to 90 per cent of the upper layer of permafrost will thaw by 2100,[37] with some scientists even estimating that 'the Arctic permafrost contains twice as much carbon as the entire global atmosphere'.[38] Arctic permafrost has warmed by up to 2°C in recent decades and methane emissions from thawing permafrost in northern Siberia increased an estimated 58 per cent between 1974 and 2000.[39] In total, it has been estimated that methane emissions each year from thawing permafrost and wetlands could increase by more than 50 per cent of current methane emissions – equivalent to 10–25 per cent of current human-induced emissions.[40]

The weakening of the capacity of the ocean to absorb carbon dioxide

Scientists are warning that levels of carbon dioxide in the atmosphere have grown more quickly than expected since 2000, partly due to a 'weakening' of the earth's natural carbon sinks.[41] According to the scientists from the University of East Anglia, the British Antarctic Survey and the Global Carbon Project, the decline of the effectiveness of the oceans to act as carbon sinks is the result of intensifying winds in Antarctica's Southern Ocean disrupting the sea's ability to store carbon. There are also signs that there has been an additional relative weakening of oceanic sinks as a result of changes in other atmospheric factors, including surface air temperatures and water temperature fluxes.[42] Over the last 200 years, the planet's oceans have absorbed nearly half the carbon dioxide produced by human activities.[43] However, as greenhouse gas emissions and ocean temperatures have gradually increased, the buffering capacity of the oceans have decreased, due to ocean acidification, changes to biological processes and increased temperatures, leading to a reduced ability to absorb more carbon dioxide.[44]

Coupled with such feedbacks a number of direct impacts from increasing average global temperature will be experienced, and will have impacts across the world's economies. These include:

- Impacts on agricultural production. Lester Brown points out that 'since crops in many countries are grown at or near their thermal optimum, even a relatively minor increase during the growing season of 1 or 2 degrees Celsius can shrink the grain harvest in major food-producing regions, such as the North China Plain, the Gangetic Plain of India, and the US Corn Belt'.[45] Brown outlines numerous reasons for this, including reduced photosynthesis, impacts on pollination and crop dehydration, and goes on to outline the particular implications for corn (maize), one of the three world grain staples, stating that, 'corn is particularly vulnerable. In order for corn to reproduce, pollen must fall from the tassel to the strands of silk that emerge from the end of each ear of corn. Each of these silk strands is attached to a kernel site on the cob. If the kernel is to develop, a grain of pollen must fall on the silk strand and then journey to the kernel site. When temperatures are uncommonly high, the silk strands quickly dry out and turn brown, unable to play their role in the fertilization process.' Furthermore, two studies cited by Brown found that in the Philippines pollination of rice fell from 100 per cent at 34°C to near zero at 40°C, and in India a 2°C rise led to a decline in irrigated wheat yields ranging from 37 to 58 per cent.[46]

- Access to fresh water. Climate change threatens to significantly reduce water availability and lead to greater frequency of droughts in many countries. This will threaten agricultural production and subsistence farming upon which a significant percentage of the world's population and local economies depend. Already one-third of the world's population lives in countries that are experiencing moderate to high levels of water shortage. According to the Organisation for Economic Co-operation and Development (OECD) that number could rise to two-thirds within 30 years unless serious efforts are made to conserve and use water more efficiently.[47] As the IPCC stated in their Fourth Assessment Report:

> *Climate change is expected to exacerbate current stresses on water resources from population growth and economic and land-use change, including urbanisation. On a regional scale, mountain snow pack, glaciers and small ice caps play a crucial*

role in freshwater availability. Widespread mass losses from glaciers and reductions in snow cover over recent decades are projected to accelerate throughout the 21st century, reducing water availability, hydropower potential, and changing seasonality of flows in regions supplied by meltwater from major mountain ranges (e.g. Hindu-Kush, Himalaya, Andes), where more than one-sixth of the world population currently lives.[48]

Entering a Period of Consequences

Given the threat of rising global temperatures, and the fact that this can cause feedbacks that further increase the temperature, governments, business and civil society around the world need to work together to achieve significant reductions in greenhouse gas emissions in the coming decades. But climate change is not the only major threat to long-term national and regional prosperity and economic growth. In addition there is a range of emerging environmental pressures that will affect national and regional economic prosperity, including:

- land degradation, loss of topsoil and desertification affecting global crop yields and amplifying natural disasters;
- overharvesting of the world's fisheries leading already to the collapse of certain fish stocks;
- environmental and human health costs from air and water pollution;
- declines in freshwater supplies for environmental flows from the cumulative effect of unsustainable rates of extraction and usage;
- increased levels of toxins and hazardous substances affecting both environmental and human health;
- the potential for increasing economic hardship and growing conflict due to reduced access to resources such as metals, water and oil.[49]

For example, the latest studies suggest that within the next 30 years the world's production of oil will begin to decline, leading to significantly higher oil prices, and the risk of continued conflict over securing remaining reserves. Hence not only is the use of oil as a fuel a significant contributor to global warming, its long-term availability is questionable, with oil production already peaking in over 60 countries around the world.[50]

The entire global economy is remarkably dependent on oil for transport, fertilizers, plastics, chemicals and pharmaceuticals. Sprawling cities have been planned and designed all over the world based on the assumption that cheap oil would continue. This makes family budgets and national economies highly vulnerable to increases in oil prices because these prices can flow into the costs of basic everyday items, like the cost of food. Also, high oil prices threaten a country's balance of payments, as many OECD countries are now importing a significant percentage of their oil usage. For instance, Australia is already importing 50 per cent of its oil, a figure set to reach 100 per cent by 2020. According to an Australian senate enquiry, by 2015, '... imported oil would subtract about $30 billion a year from the Australian national export bill'.[51] Furthermore, the price of oil can have a strong inflationary effect, which can lead to reserve banks lifting interest rates, making it harder for businesses to borrow, and reducing levels of consumer confidence and disposable income.[52] Hence, the price of oil has and will continue to have a significant effect on the short- and long-term prosperity of nations. It will thus present a significant challenge for continued economic growth, especially as the International Energy Agency (IEA) cautions that 'The rapidly growing appetite for fossil fuels in China and India is likely to help keep oil prices high for the foreseeable future – threatening a global economic slowdown [in coming decades]'.[53] Since 1965 there have been five periods of high world oil prices, all of which were followed by economic recessions of varying degree.[54]

The several main reasons why many experts are now concerned that world oil production may peak sometime in the next three decades and then start to decline are as follows:

- There are few, if any, large or medium-sized oil fields left to be discovered; the last year that more oil was discovered was in the 1980s.
- As storage of oil is costly there is limited oil storage relative to demand and modern economies work on a just-in-time delivery strategy.
- Two-thirds of the remaining oil reserves are located in the Middle East, a region that for many decades has seen conflict and instability.
- Oil reserves are finite and a number of oil-rich countries are holding back on developing their full reserves.

A peaking and then decline of world oil production could affect efforts to reduce greenhouse gas emissions from transportation positively or negatively. The negative risk is that since economies are so dependent on oil, many nations may feel that they have to rapidly turn to 'proven technologies', such as coal conversion to oil and oil shales production, before geo-sequestration technologies are commercial, leading to higher greenhouse gas emissions per gallon of oil used. The positive effect of peaking of world oil production is that ongoing and rising higher oil prices could lead to increased investment in urban design and planning, public transport and cycling, rail, shipping, and broadband infrastructure to simultaneously reduce dependency on oil and greenhouse gas emissions.

It is vital that the second option is chosen because according to the findings of *The Stern Review*, inaction to respond to climate change over the coming decades 'could create risks of major disruption to economic and social activity, on a scale similar to those associated with the great wars and the economic depression of the first half of the 20th century. And it will be difficult or impossible to reverse these changes'.[55]

One of the reasons why we find ourselves in this situation is that, in the past, there has not been a systematic effort to ensure that new energy sources, technologies or chemicals were environmentally sustainable and safe for human health. This is partly because, historically, our knowledge and understanding of such complex systems as the earth's atmosphere and biosphere was still evolving. For instance, it was not until the 1950s that the early science of climate change became solid enough for scientists to issue warnings of the dangers of rising greenhouse gas emissions.

The lack of knowledge in these areas led for instance to Thomas Midgley Jr (1889–1944), an American mechanical engineer turned chemist, developing both lead for petrol and chlorofluorocarbons.[56] Midgley died believing that both were of great benefit to the world, and while lauded at the time for his discoveries, today he bears a terrible legacy of being responsible for two of the most hazardous and destructive inventions in human history.[57]

Much like the unintended consequences of Midgely's innovations, Rachel Carson's *Silent Spring* sounded the alarm over the bio-accumulation of a number of pesticides, including DDT, in the food chain in 1962, and this single work may have done more than any other to awaken the world to the environmental and health risks from the use of new technologies and substances without proper assessment, testing and safeguards. Today we have no such excuses: since the 1950s, our knowledge of the earth's biosphere and human health has increased exponentially. We can now ensure that new technologies and energy sources undergo rigorous environmental sustainability assessment. We have the means to implement *Our Common Future*'s recommendation that 'National and international institutional mechanisms are needed to assess potential impacts of new technologies before they are widely used, in order to ensure that their production, use and disposal do not overstress environmental resources.'[58] Given such an imperative, significant effort has gone into developing methodologies for sustainable technology assessment to help foresee and prevent problems before they are allowed to occur.[59] Also, concerned consumer groups and organizations are increasingly performing assessments on new and existing products in the market. However, even today new technologies are entering the market without effective consideration of the wider environmental impacts. For instance, it was only in June 2008 that scientists for the first time warned that there is a significant risk of increased global warming from the use of the gas nitrogen trifluoride (NF_3) in flat screen televisions.[60] Nitrogen trifluoride is estimated to have a global warming potential 17,000 times as powerful as carbon dioxide, but as it was only produced in small quantities in 1997 it was not included in the Kyoto protocol. However, more recently the market for flat screens has dramatically increased, and thus the increased levels of NF_3 in the atmosphere are causing concern, although they are yet to be monitored.

Warnings against not acting to reduce environmental pressures have been raised for many years, and at the turn of the 21st century the calls for action came from many concerned voices, including:

- 1997, *The Engineer's Response to Sustainable Development*, The World Federation of Engineering Organizations (WFEO): 'Engineers around the world understand that they have a tremendous responsibility in the implementation of sustainable development. Many forecasts indicate there will be an additional five billion people in the world by the middle of the 21st century. This future "built environment" must be developed while sustaining the natural resources of the world and enhancing the quality of life for all people'.[61]

- 1997, Economists' letter on global warming to American Economics Association with over 2000 signatories: 'The balance of evidence suggests a discernible human influence on global climate. As economists, we believe that global climate change carries with it significant environmental, economic, social, and geopolitical risks and that preventive steps are justified. Economic studies have found that there are many potential policies to reduce greenhouse gas emissions for which the total benefits outweigh the total costs.'[62]

- 1998, UNESCO 'World Declaration on Higher Education for the Twenty-First Century': considering the urgency of sustainable development, 'Higher education itself is confronted therefore with formidable challenges and must proceed to the most radical change and renewal it has ever been required to undertake.'[63]

- 2000, United Nations, the World Bank and the WRI: 'There are considerable signs that the capacity of ecosystems, the biological engines of the planet, to produce many of the goods and services we depend on is rapidly declining.'[64]

- 2001, Professor S. C. Rockefeller: 'We cannot care for people in a world with collapsing ecosystems, and we cannot care for the Earth in a world where widespread poverty, injustice, economic inequity, and violent conflict exists.'[65]

- 2001, Robert T. Watson, Chair, 2001 Intergovernmental Panel on Climate Change: 'The question is not whether climate will change further in the future in response to human activities, but rather by how much (magnitude), where (regional patterns), and when (the rate of change). It is also clear that climate change will, in many parts of the world, adversely effect socio-economic sectors, including water resources, agriculture, forestry, fisheries, and human settlements, ecological systems (particularly coral reefs) and human health (particularly vector-borne diseases). Indeed, the IPCC Third Assessment Report concluded that most people will be adversely affected by climate change.'[66]

- 2005, World Economic Forum, *Global Governance Initiative 2005*: 'The world's leaders have made solemn promises to humanity. They are breaking those promises. In multiple declarations spanning decades, the world's governments have agreed on a comprehensive agenda to turn the world away from environmental overload, unnecessary pandemics, pervasive malnutrition and poverty, and war. Some promises, such as the Millennium Development Goals, are specific commitments to achieve such targets as halving global poverty and hunger by 2015. Others, dealing with such topics as peace and security, are broader. But all are essential. They are the building blocks of global stability in what has become a tightly interconnected world. It is thus inexcusable that they are being honoured far more in the breach than in the observance.'[67]

- 2005, UN Economic and Social Commission for Asia and the Pacific (UNESCAP) Ministerial Conference on Environment and Development: 'It is now an urgent challenge to find ways to ensure that the old paradigm "grow first, clean up later" is replaced by an integrated approach that enables economic growth to support and reinforce sustainability rather than undermine it.'[68]

- 2005, UN Millennium Ecosystem Assessment: 'Although evidence remains incomplete, there is enough for the experts to warn that the ongoing degradation of 15 of the 24 ecosystem services examined is increasing the likelihood of potentially abrupt changes that will seriously affect human well-being.'[69]

- 2006, UK *Stern Review*: 'Our actions now and over the coming decades could create risks of major disruption to economic and social activity, on a scale similar to those associated with the great wars and the economic depression of the first half of the 20th century. And it will be difficult or impossible to reverse these changes.'[69A]

- 2007, Achim Steiner, UN Under Secretary-General and UNEP Executive Director: 'The systematic destruction of the Earth's natural and nature-based resources has reached a point where the economic viability of economies is being challenged – and where the bill we hand on to our children may prove impossible to pay.'[70]

- 2007, Fatih Birol, the Chief Economist of the IEA: 'I can tell you that we, in the next seven to eight years, need to bring about 37.5 million barrels per day of oil into the markets … What we expect is 25 million barrels per day, and this is in the case of no slippages, no delays in the projects, and everything goes on time, which is very rare. So, there is a gap of 13.5 million barrels per day.'[71]

- 2007, Dr Rajendra Pachauri, IPCC Chair: '2015 was the last year in which the world could afford a net rise in greenhouse gas emissions, after which "very sharp reductions" are required.'[72]

- 2007, Robert Corell, Chairman of the Arctic Climate Impact Assessment (ACIA): warning that Arctic ice is 'moving at 2 metres an hour on a front 5 kilometres (3 miles) long and 1,500 metres deep'.[73]

- 2007, the Intergovernmental Panel on Climate Change Fourth Assessment Report: 'to ensure that warming does not exceed 2–2.4°C [widely regarded as the temperature at which there is a high risk of dangerous climate change], global emissions must peak by 2015, and we must be on track to reduce global emissions by 50–85% by 2050'.[74]

- 2008, *UNEP Year Book 2008*: 'There is a critical need to substantially increase research investments for understanding the processes of climate change, assessing the likely impacts on people and places, and expanding

the adaptive capabilities of human and natural systems ...'[75]
- 2008, *OECD Environmental Outlook to 2030*: 'The challenge for all countries is to put in motion a transition to a more secure, lower-carbon energy system, without undermining economic and social development. Vigorous, immediate and collective policy action by all governments is essential to move the world onto a more sustainable energy path.'[76]
- 2009, US President Barack Obama, address to the UN General Assembly: 'It is hard to change something as fundamental as how we use energy. It's even harder to do so in the midst of a global recession. Certainly, it will be tempting to sit back and wait for others to move first. But we cannot make this journey unless we all move forward together. As we head into Copenhagen, let us resolve to focus on what each of us can do for the sake of our common future.'[77]

When considering the evidence of the negative impacts on the environment it is difficult to understand how a 'business-as-usual' assumption could still be held even by the most ardent sceptic, leading to the question, is it denial of the truth, or the fear of the ramifications of admitting the truth, that now holds us back? With the growing evidence that in fact the scientists were right, if we take a rational evidence-based approach we can no longer hold to the assumption that our activities are not threatening the climatic and ecosystems upon which we depend. As these warnings are not new, why, then, has there been insufficient action to date to address these issues?

As Jim MacNeill, the former secretary-general of the World Commission on Environment and Development, and chief architect and lead author of its report *Our Common Future*, explained to us at a meeting in Canada, in the early stages of developing this book, certain interests in society have organized media and political lobbying campaigns against action on the environment and sustainable development. In these campaigns they have long played on the prevalence of the mistaken assumption that action on the environment significantly harms the economy and jobs. Such campaigns were very successful in reducing political will for action around major international conferences seeking to achieve cooperation on the much-needed action, such as at the United Nations Conference on the Human Environment, held in Stockholm in 1972, and the United Nations Conference on Environment and Development, held in Rio de Janeiro in 1992. Such campaigns have been so successful because concerns about action on the environment harming business competitiveness, jobs and economic growth have resonated in the past with many politicians, business leaders and citizens who have a strong commitment to maximizing business, jobs and economic growth. Economic growth is closely associated with political success, greater business opportunities, a better investment climate, less unemployment, and greater job security. Economic growth is also essential to enable global poverty reduction. Is it possible, then, to reconcile the need for strong economic growth to break the poverty trap and help create more jobs whilst also achieving an environmentally sustainable future?

Over 20 years ago *Our Common Future* argued that this was achievable through delinking economic growth from environmental pressures, combined with strategies to restore the environment and reduce poverty. Because *Our Common Future* was one of the first books to argue that economic growth and environmental sustainability could be reconciled, it was criticized by some for making this claim partly because of the prevalence at the time of the belief that large trade-offs between economic growth and environmental sustainability were inevitable. Much of the reason for the development of this book is to respond to such critiques and show that there is a wealth of research and practice now indicating that economic growth can be significantly decoupled from environmental pressures. This, combined with a renewed effort to reduce global poverty, provides a plausible strategy to achieve sustainable development over coming decades, one that can achieve wide support across society as it can meet multiple needs.

Using a decoupling framework as a basis for action in reducing environmental pressures can provide the basis for a clear set of strategies to navigate the inherent complexity involved in steering society to reduce environmental pressures while allowing it to prosper. Natural systems are complex, social systems are complex, institutional systems are complex ... our 21st-century world is increasingly complex. We can easily get overwhelmed by the complexity and scale of these global problems. Al Gore described this reaction in his award-winning and world-changing film, *An Inconvenient Truth*, where he discussed the tendency for people making this realization to jump from 'denial' to 'despair'. Our motivation for writing this book is to help provide a realistic way forward whereby all can play their part to embrace the imperative to reduce our environmental pressures in a positive and innovative way.

Dealing with Unprecedented Complexity

Few would disagree with the observation that traditionally the significant amounts of economic growth and prosperity that the world has achieved to date have correlated with increasing levels of negative environmental pressure. Furthermore, this pressure is now causing the degradation of natural systems on a global scale, and if continued may threaten the viability of our economies.

> *We have in the past been concerned about the impacts of economic growth upon the environment. We are now forced to concern ourselves with the impacts of ecological stress ... upon our economic prospects.*
>
> *Our Common Future*, 1987, p5.

Hence, in order to truly secure our common future, the societies of the world need to work towards the unified goal of decoupling economic growth from environmental pressures, beginning with the areas at most risk, while under-pinning current and future economic growth, employment and prosperity.

> *Economic growth always brings risk of environmental damage, as it puts increased pressure on environmental resources. But policy-makers guided by the concept of sustainable development will necessarily work to assure that growing economies remain firmly attached to their ecological roots and that these roots are protected and nurtured so that they may support growth over the long term. Environmental protection is thus inherent in the concept of sustainable development, as is a focus on the sources of environmental problems rather than the symptoms.*
>
> *Our Common Future*, 1987, p40

As explained in this book, increasingly our political leaders understand that action on the environment can assist, not harm, economic growth. Even with the recent global financial crisis, created by the sub-prime mortgage crisis in the US, many forward-thinking leaders across the world swiftly looked to strategies that both spurred economic growth and reduced the environmental and resource-related costs. There is a range of evidence to support such a focus, including the performance of the Finnish economy in the early 1990s when GDP dropped till around 1994 and then recovered without a noticeable spike in environmental pressures, followed by a relative slowing of CO_2 emissions and energy consumption, as seen in Figure 1.1.

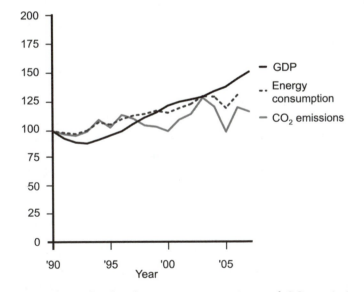

Figure 1.1 *Relative levels of energy consumption and CO_2 emissions compared to GDP in Finland 1990–2007*

Source: Based on data from the IMF (2009)[78] and Statistics Finland (2008)[79]

Many nations now understand that continuing to avoid such a focus leads to serious economic risks, as highlighted in *The Stern Review*: 'The world does not need to choose between averting climate change and promoting growth and development. Changes in energy technologies and in the structure of economies have created opportunities to decouple growth from greenhouse gas emissions. Indeed, ignoring climate change will eventually damage economic growth.'[80] Sir Nicolas Stern, speaking to the *Guardian* ahead of a speech to launch a new climate change economics centre at the London School of Economics said, when considering the global financial crisis, that, 'We're going to have to grow out of this ... and this is an area which looks as though it could well grow strongly and with the right support could be one of the major engines of growth.'[81] This sentiment is being widely supported with, for example, the UN Secretary-General Ban Ki-moon stating in his 2007 UN Bali Climate Change Conference address, 'I am convinced that climate change, and what we do about it, will define us, our era and, ultimately, the global legacy we leave for future generations. Action is possible now and it makes economic sense. The cost of inaction will far outweigh the cost of action'.[82]

Agreeing with this position, the British government made a landmark decision (passed by 463 votes to 3) in October 2008 to commit to increase its greenhouse gas reduction target from 60 per cent to around 80 per cent by 2050, despite strong pressure to cut such targets in light of the financial crisis, thus becoming the first country to have such a legally binding framework on climate change.[83] Ed Miliband, Secretary for Energy and Climate Change, said at the time, 'If you accept that what is required is an economic transition to deal with climate change then the problems in the financial system actually make a stronger case for pushing ahead with that transition ... In our view it would be quite wrong to row back and those who say we should, misunderstand the relationship between the economic and environmental tasks we face.' Miliband went on to say, 'It's the first legislation of its kind in the world. It will tie this and future governments into legally binding emission targets – an 80 per cent cut by 2050, with five-year carbon budgets along the way.'[84] Across the Atlantic Ocean, the then President-elect Barack Obama, at the time boldly signalled a sea-change in the US administration's attitude, stating in November 2008 that, 'Now is the time to confront this challenge once and for all ... Delay is no longer an option. Denial is no longer an acceptable response.' He went on to say:

> *My presidency will mark a new chapter in America's leadership on climate change that will strengthen our security and create millions of new jobs in the process ... When I am president, any governor who's willing to promote clean energy will have a partner in the White House. Any company that's willing to invest in clean energy will have an ally in Washington. And any nation that's willing to join the cause of combating climate change will have an ally in the United States of America.*[85]

The Chinese government also clearly understands the imperative to reduce environmental pressures, with the 11th five-year plan for China, launched in 2005, placing for the first time 'scientific' (sustainable) development as its primary goal rather than economic growth. As the *People's Daily* newspaper reported:

> *The recognition that economic growth is not equal to economic development and that growth is not the final goal of development, will be included in the 11th Five-Year Plan for the first time ... Top leaders have criticized old concepts of economic growth many times, saying that 'economic development at the center' does not mean 'with speed at the center'. Blind pursuit of economic growth has led to blind investment, damage to the environment and false statistics. The country's helmsmen are worried that without changing China's concept of growth, the economy might develop an unbalanced structure with a lack of driving power.*[86]

Chinese Deputy Minister of Environment Pan Yue stated in 2005:

> *This [Chinese economic] miracle will end soon because the environment can no longer keep pace. Acid rain is falling on one third of the Chinese territory, half of the water in our seven largest rivers is completely useless, while one fourth of our citizens do not have access to clean drinking water. One third of the urban population is breathing polluted air, and less than 20% of the trash in cities is treated and processed in an environmentally sustainable manner. Finally, five of the ten most polluted cities worldwide are in China.*[87]

Such realizations have led to a range of strategic responses by the Chinese government (many highlighted in Chapter 6) including a programme involving the 1000 largest heavy industry companies in China (estimated to represent 33 per cent of the national energy consumption) to work towards contributing up to 25 per cent of the savings required to achieve the overall Chinese government target of a 20 per cent reduction in energy use per unit of GDP by 2010.[88]

Hence the success of such government commitment will determine the future economic impacts that climate change will have on nations of the world. The longer action is delayed on a meaningful scale the higher the resulting costs from the environmental damage will be to future generations, adding to the already high cost of environment-related costs to the economy. Thus, to pay for such costs, governments in the future will need to raise taxes, privatize public assets, or borrow money. Some argue that future generations will be wealthier and more able to pay, but this assumes that the costs of inaction will not rise, and if they do it will be a predictable and manageable increase. However, *The*

Stern Review is clear that due to the complexity of natural systems and the potential for feedbacks and amplification effects the costs of inaction will continue to rise unless action is taken. The IPCC is also clear that there are real risks of abrupt and irreversible changes to ecosystems in the coming decades, and that these will have significant impacts on economies around the world.

Even though the challenges we face are great, the good news is that at the time this book hits the shelves in 2010 our global community is in a very strong position to enable change on a meaningful scale. Those moving early to respond to this challenge are learning that there are in fact a number of ways that reducing pressure on natural systems can underpin continued economic growth.[89] However, the timeframe for action is short and the consequences of inaction will be long lasting. In order to ensure that the most cost-effective, efficient and successful strategies for action are adopted it is crucial that effective investigations of key elements are undertaken (see Chapter 5) and that efforts from societies around the world are monitored and quickly learned from to inform further efforts. The number of countries now developing national strategies for sustainable development is an encouraging sign, including Cameroon, Canada, Denmark, Finland, France, Germany, Greece, Ireland, Latvia, Mauritius, Mexico, Moldova, the Netherlands, Norway, Philippines, the Republic of Korea, Sweden, Switzerland, the Czech Republic, the UK and the EU. This publication is designed to assist and inform such efforts.

To conclude, the question at the heart of this book is: is it possible to maintain levels of economic growth while achieving significant reductions in the negative environmental pressures that have been associated with it? We hope that by the end of the book you will not only agree that it is indeed possible, but that it is the most pressing imperative of global development this century. To paraphrase Will Durant, a famous historian who died in 1981, 'Civilization exists by consent, subject to change without notice.' As the coming decades unfold, if we do not act now to achieve significant decoupling, the consent we will require will be that of the environment.

Moreover, we hope by the end of this book you will see a way forward within your own area of influence; see a way out of both denial and despair. We hope that you will see that we can reduce our negative impacts on this planet while continuing to increase our prosperity, learning from our mistakes and becoming a better species for it. Life as we know it around the world is going to change, but we have a real opportunity to create a civilization that knowingly and consistently rises to the challenge set out in *Our Common Future* to 'meet the needs and aspirations of the present generation without compromising the ability of future generations to meet their own needs'.

Notes

1   Based on a range of works including: UN Millennium Ecosystem Assessment (2005) *Ecosystems and Human Well-being: Biodiversity Synthesis*, World Resources Institute, Washington, DC; UNEP (2007) *Global Environment*

Outlook: Environment for Development (GEO-4) Report, UNEP; OECD (2008) *OECD Environmental Outlook to 2030*, OECD, Paris; World Bank (2003) *World Bank Development Report 2003: Sustainable Development in a Dynamic World*, Oxford University Press, Oxford; Brown, L. (2008) *Plan B 3.0: Mobilizing to Save Civilization*, W. W. Norton & Company, New York.

2   Monbiot, G. (2006) *Heat*, Penguin Books, UK.

3   UNEP (2007) *Global Environment Outlook: Environment for Development (GEO-4) Report*, UNEP, p34.

4   Brown, L. (2008) *Plan B 3.0: Mobilizing to Save Civilization*, W. W. Norton & Company, New York, p59.

5   Pearman, G. et al (2007) *Evidence of Accelerated Climate Change*, Prepared by the Climate Adaptation Science and Policy Initiative, the University of Melbourne for the Climate Institute; Pittock, B. (2006) 'Are scientists underestimating climate change?', *Earth and Ocean Sciences (EOS), Transactions American Geophysical Union*, vol 87, no 34, pp340–341.

6   World Resources Institute (2000) *World Resources: People and Ecosystems: The Fraying Web of Life*, World Resources Institute, Washington, DC.

7   UN Millennium Assessment Board (2005) *Statement of the Board – Living Beyond our Means: Natural Assets and Human Well Being*, UN Millennium Ecosystem Assessment.

8   UN Millennium Ecosystem Assessment (2005) *Ecosystems and Human Well-being: Synthesis*, Island Press, Washington, DC.

9   Carson, R. (1962) *Silent Spring*, 40th anniversary edition published in 2002 by Houghton Mifflin, Boston, MA.

10   Brown, L. (2008) *Plan B 3.0: Mobilizing to Save Civilization*, W. W. Norton & Company, New York.

11   UNEP (2007) *Global Environment Outlook: Environment for Development (GEO-4) Report*, UNEP, p363.

12   UNEP (2007) 'Media brief: Planet's tougher problems persist, UN report warns', UN Environment Programme.

13   Costanza, R. et al (1997) 'The value of the world's ecosystem services and natural capital', *Nature*, vol 387, pp253–260.

14   Stern, N. (2006) *The Stern Review: The Economics of Climate Change*, Cambridge University Press, Cambridge.

15   Petit, J. et al (1999) 'Climate and atmospheric history of the past 420,000 years from the Vostok Ice Core, Antarctica', *Nature*, vol 399, pp429–436.

16   NASA (2009) 'Global Temperature Anomalies in .01°C', Goddard Institute for Space Studies, Earth Sciences Directorate.

17   Arrhenius, S. (1896) 'On the influence of carbonic acid in the air upon the temperature of the ground', *Philosophical Magazine*, vol 41, pp237–276.

18   Gore, A. (2007) 'Nobel lecture', Nobel Peace Prize Award Ceremony, the Nobel Foundation, Oslo.

19   Petit, J. et al (1999) 'Climate and atmospheric history of the past 420,000 years from the Vostok Ice Core, Antarctica', *Nature*, vol 399, pp429–436.

20   IPCC (2007) *Climate Change 2007: Mitigation of Climate Change*, Contribution of Working Group III to the Fourth Assessment Report of the Intergovernmental Panel on Climate Change, Cambridge University Press, Cambridge.

21   Ward, B. and Dubois, R. (1972) *Only One Earth – The Care and Maintenance of A Small Planet*, Pelican Publishing, Middlesex, UK.

22   Hansen, J. (2005) 'A slippery slope: How much global warming constitutes dangerous anthropogenic interference?', *Climate Change*, vol 68, pp269–279.

23   European Council (2007) *Limiting Global Climate Change to 2°C – The Way Ahead for 2020 and Beyond: Communication from the Commissions to the Council*, the European Parliament, the European Economic and Social Committee and the Committee of the Regions.

24   International Alliance of Universities (2009) *Copenhagen Synthesis: Climate Change: Global Risks, Challenges and Decisions*, International Alliance of Universities, Denmark.

25   Lowe, J. A., Huntingford, C., Raper, S., Jones, C., Liddicoat, S. and Gohar, L. (2009) 'How difficult is it to recover from dangerous levels of global warming?', *Environmental Research Letters*, vol 4, no 014012.

26   IPCC (2007) *Climate Change 2007: The Physical Science Basis*, Contribution of Working Group I to the Fourth Assessment Report of the Intergovernmental Panel on Climate Change, Cambridge University Press, Cambridge: see 'Couplings between changes in the climate system and biogeochemistry'.

27   IPCC (1990) *Climate Change 1990: Scientific Assessment of Climate Change*, Contribution of Working Group I to the First Assessment Report of the Intergovernmental Panel on Climate Change, Cambridge University Press, Cambridge.

28   Lowe J. A., Huntingford, C., Raper, S., Jones, C., Liddicoat, S. and Gohar, L. (2009) 'How difficult is it to recover from dangerous levels of global warming?', *Environmental Research Letters*, vol 4, no 014012.

29   UNEP (2007) *Global Environment Outlook: Environment for Development (GEO-4) Report*, UNEP.

30   Stern, N. (2007) *The Stern Review: The Economics of Climate Change*, Cambridge University Press, Cambridge.

31   Brown, L. (2008) *Plan B 3.0: Mobilizing to Save Civilization*, W. W. Norton & Company, New York, p59.

32   Brown, L. (2008) *Plan B 3.0: Mobilizing to Save Civilization*, W. W. Norton & Company, New York, p64.

33   ACIA (Arctic Climate Impact Assessment) (2004) *Impacts of a Warming Arctic*, Arctic Monitoring and Assessment Programme, Cambridge University Press, Cambridge.

34   Adam, D. (2007) 'Ice-free Arctic could be here in 23 years' *Guardian* (UK), 5 September.

35   ACIA (2004) *Impacts of a Warming Arctic*, Arctic Monitoring and Assessment Programme, Cambridge University Press, Cambridge.

36   IPCC (2007) *Climate Change 2007: The Physical Science Basis*, Contribution of Working Group I to the Fourth Assessment Report of the Intergovernmental Panel on Climate Change, Cambridge University Press, Cambridge, p33; Zimov, S. A. et al (2006) 'Permafrost and the global carbon budget', *Science*, vol 312, no 3780, pp1612–1613.

37   Lawrence, D. M. and Slater, A. G. (2005) 'A projection of severe near-surface permafrost degradation during the 21st century', *Geophysical Research Letters*, vol 32, pL24401. Based on the IPCC's A2 Scenario, cited in Stern, N. (2007) *The Stern Review: The Economics of Climate Change*, Cambridge University Press, Cambridge.

38   Schuur, E. et al (2008) 'Vulnerability of permafrost carbon to climate change: Implications for the global carbon cycle', *BioScience*, vol 58, no 8, pp701–714.

39   Earth Watch Institute (2008) *Selected Examples of Ice-melt around the World*, compiled by Earth Policy Institute, from sources including WWF, Arctic Climate Impact Assessment, UNEP, IPCC, NASA, National Snow and Ice Data Center,

and other scientific literature.

40 Davidson, E. A. and Janssens, I. A. (2006); Gedney, N. et al (2004) and Archer, D. (2005) cited in Stern, N. (2007) *The Stern Review: The Economics of Climate Change*, Cambridge University Press, Cambridge, p14.

41 Raupach, M. et al (2007) 'Global and regional drivers of accelerating CO_2 emissions', *Proceedings of the National Academy of Sciences of the United States of America*, vol 104, no 24, pp10288–10293; British Antarctic Survey (2007) 'Unexpected Increase in Atmospheric CO_2', BAS Press Release, 23 October.

42 Le Quere, C. et al (2007) 'Saturation of the Southern Ocean CO_2 sink due to recent climate change', *Science,* no 316.

43 Kuylenstierna, J. and Panwar, T. (eds) (2007) 'Atmosphere' in UNEP (2007) *Global Environment Outlook: Environment for Development (GEO-4) Report,* UNEP, p65.

44 Royal Society (2005) *Ocean Acidification due to Increasing Atmospheric Carbon Dioxide,* Policy Document 12/05, the Royal Society, London, cited in UNEP (2007) *Global Environment Outlook: Environment for Development (GEO-4) Report,* UNEP, p128; Homer-Dixon, T. (2007) 'Op-ed contributor: A swiftly melting planet', *New York Times,* 4 October; Cox, P., Betts, R., Jones, C., Spall, S. and Totterdell, I. (2000) 'Acceleration of global warming due to carbon-cycle feedbacks in a coupled climate model', *Nature*, vol 408, pp184–187; Jones, C. D. and Cox, P. M. et al (2003) 'Strong carbon cycle feedbacks in a climate model with interactive CO_2 and sulphate aerosols', *Geophysical Research Letters*, vol 30, no 9, p1479.

45 Sanchez, P. (2002) 'The climate change-soil fertility–food security nexus', Speech, Sustainable Food Security for All by 2020, Bonn, Germany, 4–6 September; United States Department of Agriculture (USDA), cited in Brown, L. (2008) *Plan B 3.0: Mobilizing to Save Civilization*, W. W. Norton & Company, New York.

46 Brown, L. (2008) *Plan B 3.0: Mobilizing to Save Civilization*, W. W. Norton & Company, New York.

47 OECD (2002) *Sustainable Development Strategies: A Resource Book*, OECD, Paris.

48 IPCC (2010) 'IPCC statement on the melting of the Himalayan glaciers', Intergovernmental Panel on Climate Change, 20 January, 2010.

49 For a comprehensive overview of these and other related challenges see Brown, L. (2008) *Plan B 3.0: Mobilizing to Save Civilization*, W. W. Norton & Company, New York.

50 Hirsch, R. L. (2005) 'The inevitable peaking of world oil production', *The Atlantic Council of the US Bulletin*, vol XVI, no 3.

51 Senate Economics Committee (2005) *Incentives for Petroleum Exploration in Frontier Areas*, Parliament of Australia, Chapter 3, Schedule 5, pE12.

52 IEA (2004) *Analysis of the Impact of High Oil Prices on the Global Economy*, International Energy Agency, Paris.

53 Kanter, J. (2007) 'IEA says oil prices will stay "very high", threatening global growth', *New York Times*, 31 October.

54 Porritt, J. (2005) *Capitalism as if the World Matters*, Earthscan, London.

55 Stern, N. (2006) *The Stern Review: The Economics of Climate Change*, Cambridge University Press, Cambridge, p10.

56 Lewis, J. (1985) 'Lead poisoning: A historical perspective', US EPA, www.epa.gov/history/topics/perspect/lead.htm, accessed 27 January 2008.

57 Bryson, B. (2000) *A Short History of Nearly Everything*, Black Swan Publishing, London.

58 World Commission on Environment and Development (WCED) (1987) *Our Common Future*, Oxford University Press, Oxford, p61.

59 Cetron, M. J. and Connor, L. W. (1972) 'A method for planning and assessing technology against relevant national goals in developing countries', in Cetron, M. J. and Bartocha, B. (eds) *The Methodology of Technology Assessment*, Gordon & Breach, New York.

60 Prather, M. and Hsu, J. (2008) 'NF_3, the greenhouse gas missing from Kyoto', *Geophysical Research Letters*, vol 35, no l12810.

61 WFEO (1997) *The Engineer's Response to Sustainable Development*, World Federation of Engineering Organizations, Paris.

62 UNESCO (undated) 'Global warming: Economists' letter on global warming: Endorsed by over 2000 economists including six Nobel laureates', http://uneco.org/Global_Warming.html#Economists'%20Letter%20on%20Global%20Wa, accessed 12 July 2009.

63 UNESCO (1998) 'World Declaration on Higher Education for the Twenty-First Century: Vision and Action' and 'Framework for Priority Action for Change and Development in Higher Education', World Conference on Higher Education, Paris, UNESCO.

64 WRI (2000) *World Resources: People and Ecosystems: The Fraying Web of Life*, World Resources Institute, Washington, DC.

65 Rockefeller, S. C. (2001) *The Earth Charter: An Ethical Foundation*, The Earth Charter, printed in *Resurgence*, May/June, pp32–34.

66 Watson, R. (2001) 'Climate Change 2001: Summary', From an address for the Intergovernmental Panel on Climate Change Sixth Conference of Parties to the United Nations Framework Convention on Climate Change, Cambridge University Press, Cambridge.

67 WEF (2005) *Global Governance Initiative 2005: Executive Summary*, World Economic Forum, London.

68 Kwon Chung, R. (2005) *Achieving Environmentally Sustainable Economic Growth in Asia and the Pacific*, UNESCAP, Bangkok.

69 Millennium Ecosystem Assessment (2005) *Ecosystems and Human Well-being: Synthesis*, Island Press, Washington, DC.

69A Stern, N. (2006) The Stern Review: The Economics of Climate Change, Cambridge University Press, Cambridge, pii.

70 UNEP (2007) Global Environment Outlook: Environment for Development (GEO-4) Report, UNEP.

71 Parliament of Australia, Senate (2007) *Australia's Future Oil Supply and Alternative Transport Fuels: Executive Summary*, Commonwealth of Australia.

72 Milmo, C. (2007) 'Too late to avoid global warming', *Independent* (UK), 19 September 2007.

73 Brown, P. (2007) 'Melting ice cap triggering earthquakes' *Guardian* (UK), 8 September, cited in Brown, L. (2008) *Plan B 3.0: Mobilizing to Save Civilization*, W. W. Norton & Company, New York, p4.

74 IPCC (2007) *Climate Change 2007: The Physical Science Basis*, Contribution of Working Group I to the Fourth Assessment Report of the Intergovernmental Panel on Climate Change, Cambridge University Press, Cambridge, Table SPM.6, p20.

75 Harrison, P., McMullen, C., Walker, P., Corell, R., Hassol, S. J. and Melillo, J. (2008) *UNEP Year Book 2008: An Overview of Our Changing Environment*, United Nations Environment Programme, p47.

76 OECD (2008) *OECD Environmental Outlook to 2030*, OECD, Paris, p3.

77   Obama, B. (2009) 'Responsibility for our common future: Address to the United Nations General Assembly', *Real Clear Politics*, 23 September.

78   International Monetary Fund (2009) 'World economic outlook database', www.imf.org/external/pubs/ft/weo/2009/01/weodata/index.aspx, accessed 18 August 2009.

79   Statistics Finland (2008) 'Total energy consumption by energy source and carbon dioxide emission', www.stat.fi/til/ekul/tau_en.html, accessed 18 August 2009.

80   Stern, N. (2007) *The Stern Review: The Economics of Climate Change*, Cambridge University Press, Cambridge, pxvii.

81   Jowit, J. (2008) 'Now is the time to tackle global warming – Stern', *Guardian* (UK), 7 October.

82   UN General Assembly (2007) 'Actions on climate change will define global legacy left for future generations', UN Media Release.

83   Moresco, J. (2008) 'UK adopts stiff emissions law', *Red Herring*, 1 December.

84   *The Age* (2008) 'British MPs pass climate change bill', *The Age*, 19 November.

85   Broder, J. M. (2008) 'Obama affirms climate change goals', *New York Times*, 18 November.

86   *People's Daily Online* (2005) 'New Five-Year Plan to see revolutionary changes', *People's Daily Online*, 12 October.

87   *Spiegel Online* (2005) 'The Chinese miracle will end soon', interview with China's Deputy Minister of the Environment, *Spiegel Online*, 7 March.

88   Lawrence Berkeley National Laboratory (2009) *China Energy Group: Sustainable Development through Energy Efficiency*, Lawrence Berkeley National Laboratory, Berkeley, CA.

89   von Weizsäcker, E., Hargroves, K., Smith, M., Desha, C. and Stasinopoulos, P. (2009) *Factor Five: Transforming the Global Economy through 80% Improvements in Resource Productivity*, Earthscan, London.

2

Achieving Economic Growth and Reducing Environmental Pressures

What is 'Decoupling'?

It used to be taken for granted that economic growth entailed parallel growth in resource consumption, and to a certain extent, environmental degradation. However, the experience of the last decades indicates that economic growth and resource consumption and environmental degradation can be decoupled to a considerable extent. The path towards sustainable development entails accelerating this decoupling process.

Yukiko Fukasaku, OECD, 1999[1]

In 1987, *Our Common Future* was one of the first books to argue that it was possible to reconcile environmental sustainability and economic growth, although at the time and since many questioned this position.[2] This was despite the fact that, by the time *Our Common Future* was published, there were a number of significant examples of such decoupling. One of the first examples came as a result of the 1970s oil shocks, where, for seven years after 1979, the US economy grew by 27 per cent, with oil consumption falling by 17 per cent, and net oil imports from the Persian Gulf falling by 87 per cent. This led to the US oil intensity (barrels per dollar of real GDP) dropping by 35 per cent during 1977–1985.[3] Since then, there have been many further decoupling successes at both global and national levels, including efforts to reduce air and water pollution, largely phasing out the use of ozone-depleting chemicals, as well as lead and asbestos, and significantly reducing sulphur dioxide (SO_2) emissions. These success stories show that where there has been the political will, and the vested interests have been appropriately managed, effective and purposeful

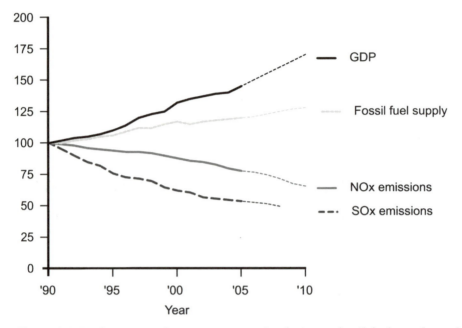

Figure 2.1 *Performance of economic growth relative to fossil fuel supply, and NO$_x$ and SO$_x$ emissions 1990–2005 (with projections to 2010)*

Source: Based on data from the OECD Key Environmental Indicators Report (2008)[4]

policy responses and technical innovation have achieved significant reductions in pollution while maintaining strong economic growth.

A leading example of this has been global and regional efforts to decouple economic growth from SO$_2$ pollution through first the 1983 'Helsinki Protocol' and the United Nations Economic Commission for Europe (UNECE) Second Sulphur Protocol in 1994. The Second Sulphur Protocol committed nations to targets of reductions of 50 per cent by the year 2000, 70 per cent by 2005 and 80 per cent by 2010.[5] Initial perceptions were that it would be incredibly costly, but the arrival of cost-effective low-sulphur fuel and a range of supporting technologies altered the cost situation such that the use of sulphur could be reduced for significantly less cost than anticipated – US$90 per tonne rather than the anticipated US$1000–1500 per tonne.[6] When the costs of sulphur to health and the environment are taken into account, this phase-out has had negligible net impact on economic growth, as seen in Figure 2.1. In this case economic growth and the reduction of environmental pressures, namely the emissions of sulphur dioxide, have been quite compatible,[7] along with reductions in nitrogen oxides (NO$_x$) and fossil fuel consumption.

What Level of Decoupling is Required?

The reality is that if economic growth is not absolutely decoupled from environmental pressure then at some point in the near future the systems that support life on this planet are going to collapse. David Suzuki often says to his audiences that we couldn't kill the planet if we tried but we can make it a place that we don't enjoy living on. So we have two choices, wait and see what the world looks like once we have further increased the global temperature and degraded the ecosystems beyond their ecological limits, or act with unprecedented urgency to decouple as fast as we can before irreversible thresholds are past for both the climate and the world's ecosystems. If the growing consensus about environmental trends is correct then this decision will either be made by the world's decision-makers in the near future, or it will be dictated by the state of the environment, forcing our and future generations to deal with the negative impacts and costs associated with climate change and ecosystem degradation.

If we as a global community do decide to act fast to secure our common future, we will need a number of organizing principles. As Kenneth Ruffing outlines in the foreword to this book, according to the OECD, the goal for the level of decoupling to work towards will be set by four main criteria:[8]

1   Regeneration: Renewable resources shall be used efficiently and their use shall not be permitted to exceed their long-term rates of natural regeneration. (*Meaning that we need to enhance production capacity of renewable resources, while controlling the growth in demand by improving demand management and increasing efficiency of use.*)

2   Substitutability: Non-renewable resources shall be used efficiently and their use limited to levels that can be offset by substitution by renewable resources or other forms of capital. It is interpreted by the authors that substitutability then means that non-renewable resources can be used (assuming the other three criteria are met), but must be used efficiently and when they run out, or are uneconomical, they need to be able to be fully replaced by substitution by renewable resources, hence the ability to source substitutes is the limiting factor on the use of non-renewable resources if the activity using the resource is to be sustained. (*For example if we are to use coal for power generation we can only use it if the other three criteria are met and to the level that it is possible to source alternatives – that also satisfy the other three criteria – to take over once the supply is diminished or uneconomical.*)

3   Assimilation: Releases of substances to the environment shall not exceed its assimilative capacity; concentrations shall be kept below established critical levels necessary for the protection of both human and environmental health. When assimilative capacity is effectively zero (e.g. for hazardous substances that are persistent and/or bio-accumulative), a zero release of such substances is required to avoid their accumulation in the environ-

ment. (*Thus the use of coal in the above example would need to satisfy, for instance, emissions requirements for toxins in waterways and greenhouse gas emissions in the atmosphere to be able to operate.*)

4   Avoiding irreversibility: Irreversible adverse effects of human activities on ecosystems and on biogeochemical and hydrological cycles shall be avoided; the natural processes capable of maintaining or restoring the integrity of ecosystems should be safeguarded from adverse impacts of human activities; and the differing levels of resilience and carrying capacity of ecosystems must be considered in order to conserve their populations of threatened, endangered and critical species.

It is for each nation to undertake specific studies to investigate appropriate levels and pace for decoupling efforts to contribute to achieving these system conditions (see Chapter 5). To provide further clarity on the magnitude of decoupling efforts required, the well-known IPAT formula is commonly used, such that: $I = A \times P \times T$, with I representing the total negative environmental impact, P representing population, A representing affluence, and T representing environmental impact per unit of product/service consumed. The formula shows that there are a range of levers for reducing impact, such as stabilizing population, reducing wasteful consumption patterns and reducing the environmental impact of various products/services. Given that these are the main options, it seems that due to the forecast ongoing increase of global population and affluence levels, the main opportunity for reducing impact is through a focus on 'T', namely to reduce the environmental impact per unit of product or service consumed. A range of studies now show that as much as 60–80 per cent reductions in environmental impact can be achieved across a range of sectors

Such a target may seem unachievable. However, historically, where governments and business have had the courage to try to achieve such targets, such as through the Sulphur Protocols outlined previously, industry has found significantly cheaper ways than forecast to reduce the costs of meeting such environmental regulation, as further explained in Chapter 5, and shown in Table 5.5. This book will show that there are many examples of where purposeful policy, combined with effective R&D, has lowered costs of complying with stringent and progressive environmental regulation to achieve remarkable levels of decoupling.

An effective way to achieve significant improvements in 'T' is to re-optimize the design process to harness opportunities to improve resource productivity and reduce environmental pressures early in the process. A range of leading examples of sustainable design now demonstrate that by taking what is known as a 'whole system design' approach, a range of cost-effective improvements can be made to achieve enhanced resource productivity outcomes while significantly reducing environmental pressures. Such a design process involves looking at the system in which the design is to become part, and then how the subsystems within the design will interact with the overall design. However, traditional design processes encourage what is referred to as an 'incremental' approach where designers focus on a subsystem of a design in relative isolation from the other subsystems and the interaction is not optimized. Over the last 20 years engineers and designers using whole system design techniques have found that across all sectors the potential exists to achieve between 60 and 90 per cent improvements in energy, water and materials productivity cost effectively. Such achievements are leading to a strong basis for informing the design process, as summarized in *Whole System Design: An Integrated Approach to Sustainable Engineering*.[8A] This body of work is important because it shows how, using existing technologies, we can cost effectively achieve environmental sustainability.

Such approaches are being increasingly understood around the world and many nations and regional governments now are embracing and achieving strong decoupling targets to achieve as much as 90 per cent decoupling. Leading the way are countries such as Costa Rica, which has committed to become net climate neutral by 2021, Sweden, which has committed to be independent of oil imports by 2020, and Japan, which has committed to becoming a closed-loop society dramatically reducing waste, and regions such as Massachusetts, where since 1989, the private sector has worked with the government and university researchers to achieve a 90 per cent reduction in toxic chemical emissions by 2005 without harming businesses profits.[9] Hence, it is possible for nations working with the private sector, through a focus on improving efficiencies and resource productivity as well as changing processes and products, to both contribute to the imperative for decoupling globally, and to also unlock new ways to improve their own bottom line.

This may prove to be the most important 'convenient truth' of our generation as if efforts to achieve decoupling did not prove to be cost effective, and even in some cases provide opportunities to increase economic growth, then a decoupling agenda would have little chance of success. For these reasons the publication *The Natural Advantage of Nations*[10] proposed that we are seeing the beginning of a new wave of innovation that is being driven by businesses needing to reduce resource and energy costs, differentiate their products, and innovate for new rapidly growing markets in environmental solutions.

How Can We Represent and Interpret Decoupling Trends?

Before exploring further examples of decoupling it is important to define further what is specifically meant by the term. According to the OECD, the term decoupling 'has often been used to refer to breaking the link between the growth in environmental pressure associated with creating economic goods and services'. Figure 2.2 provides a stylized impression by the authors of a decoupling graph developed to demonstrate the various relevant trends. It is assumed that at the start of the time period the relative growth rates of both

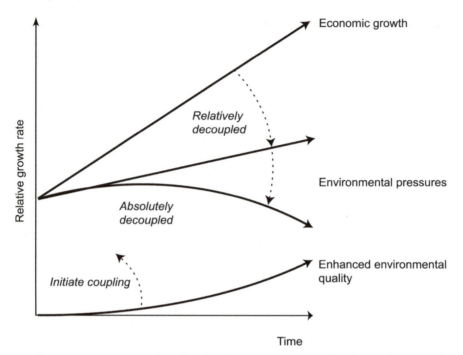

Figure 2.2 *Conceptual and stylized representation of a decoupling graph*

Source: Developed by Karlson Hargroves, Peter Stasinopoulos, Cheryl Desha and Michael Smith

economic growth and environmental pressures are the same so that the trend can be established. As can be seen, the assumption is that economic growth continues to increase, although the resultant environmental pressures no longer grow at comparable rates. In the case where the growth rate of environmental pressures is less but is still rising, it is said to be 'relatively decoupled', and in the case where the growth rate of environmental pressures is decreasing, it is said to be 'absolutely decoupled'. The goal is to first relatively decouple the trends and then absolutely decouple them; however, it is unreasonable to expect that the environmental pressures will reduce to zero, realistically they will instead hit a lower bound signifying the minimum amount of pressure to deliver the economic growth. If this lower bound is still higher than the environment's carrying capacity then options to offset, remediate or substitute for the damage will need to be developed and represented in the figure as 'enhanced environmental quality'. It is intended that these enhanced outcomes are coupled with and enhanced by economic growth.

As economic growth and various environmental pressures are not measured in the same units, dollars verses tonnes of emissions for instance, they cannot be plotted directly on the same set of axes. However, as the purpose of a decoupling graph is to visually represent the behaviour of trends, the relative growth of each can be plotted and compared if they are given the same point of origin. In standard decoupling curves the first year of the data set is used as the origin on the x axis and runs as long as data are available. On the y axis both trends are set to 100 per cent, or an index of 100, to allow the different trends to be compared following the first year of record. Figure 2.1 uses the year 1990 as the beginning of the data set and presents the relative growth rate of GDP (typically 2–3 per cent per year) and the relative growth rates of three trends that had resulted in environmental pressure. Note that with reference to Figure 2.2 the curve for 'fossil fuel supply' is relatively decoupled from the curve for GDP, and both the remaining environmental pressure curves are absolutely decoupled from GDP.

In order to reduce the graph to a figure at the time of consideration the relative growth rate of the negative environmental pressure (NEP) can be calculated as a percentage of the relative growth rate of the economic growth (EG), such that the percentage is equal to $[1-(NEP/EG)] \times 100$ per cent. For example from Figure 2.1, the relative growth rate of SO_x emissions in 2000 was approximately 52 per cent of the relative growth rate of the economic growth. However, this figure does not indicate whether the trend is relatively or absolutely decoupled. Therefore in order to calculate this using the data set, the relative growth of the NEP is either:

a   Coupled, such that $EG_{(n-1)} = NEP_{(n-1)}$ and $EG_{(n)} - NEP_{(n)}$
b   Relatively decoupled, such that $EG_{(n)} > NEP_{(n)}$ and $NEP_{(n)} > NEP_{(n-1)}$
c   Absolutely decoupled, such that $EG_{(n)} > NEP_{(n)}$ and $NEP_{(n)} < NEP_{(n-1)}$

As mentioned above, it is unreasonable to assume that the negative environmental pressures will be reduced to zero, and there will always be a need for a range of initiatives to enhance the environmental quality and restore ecosystem resilience to offset the ongoing presence of environmental pressures. The level of such enhanced environmental quality (EEQ) can be calculated as,

d   %EEQ of EG = $[(EEQ(n) - 100)/(EG(n) - 100)]$.

What Potential Is There for Relative and Absolute Decoupling?

It is important to note that the concept of decoupling is a very recent one, as until the 1970s there was little evidence that economic growth and environmental pressures could be decoupled. In 1987, the Brundtland report, *Our Common Future*, reported statistics that showed that over the period 1972–1986 the relationship between energy use and economic growth in industrial countries had undergone a significant change from the broadly proportional relationship that had prevailed before.[11] In the US, energy intensity had decreased by 25 per cent from 1973 to 1986. Over the OECD nations, it decreased 20 per cent from 1973 to 1985. For the same period, in countries belonging to the IEA, GDP grew by nearly 32 per cent while energy use grew by only 5 per cent. The UK has achieved absolute decoupling of CO_2 emissions

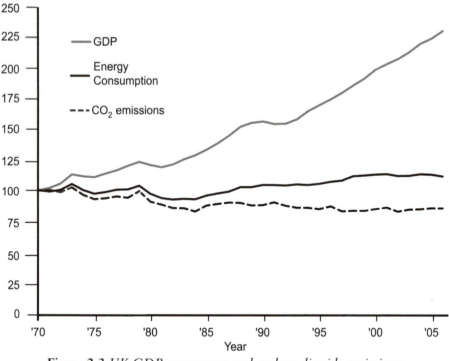

Figure 2.3 *UK GDP, energy use and carbon dioxide emissions trends since 1970*

Source: Data from the UK Department for Environment, Food and Rural Affairs[12] and the WRI[13]

from GDP since 1970,[14] and while over the last 30 years the UK's GDP has doubled, its energy use has only increased marginally, as shown in Figure 2.3.

In the 21st century the challenge of decoupling economic growth from greenhouse gas emissions is inspiring a whole new wave of innovation in more energy-efficient products that provide further opportunities to achieve greater levels of decoupling. For instance, Japanese engineers have designed a vacuum-sealed refrigerator that uses only one-eighth as much electricity as those marketed a decade ago. Gas electric hybrid automobiles, getting nearly 50 miles per gallon, are twice as efficient as the average car on the road. Furthermore, the Climate Group's 2005 report *Carbon Down, Profits Up*[15] showed that 43 companies have increased their bottom line by a total of US$15 billion while developing ways to reduce their greenhouse gas emissions by as much as 60 per cent. Multinationals like IBM and Dupont have succeeded through such measures on reducing greenhouse gas emissions by over 60 per cent since 1990 while saving over US$2 billion each. Such savings can help keep businesses profitable and prevent job losses during tough times. The cost savings from energy and fuel efficiency can also help business pay for the costs of investing in shifting energy production from fossil fuels to low-carbon renewable technologies.

As many companies have already learned, acting on this issue [climate change] is simply good business. Reducing our use of energy reduces costs ... The debate is shifting from whether climate change is really happening to how to solve it. And when so many of the solutions make sense for us as a business, it is clear that we should take action not only as a matter of public responsibility, but because we stand to benefit.

Rupert Murdoch, Founder of News Corporation, 2007[16]

Across most sectors of the economy, examples exist of companies that have cost effectively achieved significant reductions in environmental pressures and resource consumption, and even up to 80 per cent. In the 2009 publication *Factor Five*,[17] an update of the internationally renowned book *Factor Four*, such efforts leading to an 80 per cent improvement in resource productivity were compiled by taking a whole systems approach, as seen in Table 2.1. *Factor Five* gives detailed sector studies which provide a step-by-step approach to achieving large energy and water productivity improvements of 80 per cent or better for the buildings, industry, agriculture, food and hospitality, and transport sectors – the sectors responsible for most of the world's energy demand.

Using such innovations, a number of countries and states, such as the Netherlands, Denmark, Sweden and the UK, have achieved encouraging levels of decoupling of economic growth from greenhouse gas emissions. For instance, for the past 25 years Denmark has experienced an economic growth of 75 per cent without increasing its CO_2 emissions (see Figure 2.4).

States like California, which have strong energy efficiency and demand management regulations and policies, have managed to decouple GDP from

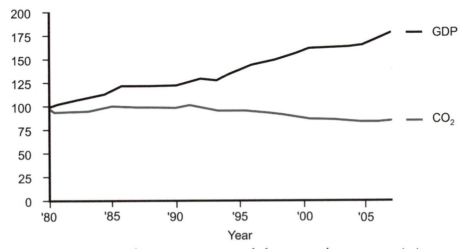

Figure 2.4 *Decoupling economic growth from greenhouse gas emissions in Denmark, 1980–2005*

Source: Based on data from the WRI (2008)[18]

Table 2.1 *Sample of best practice case studies demonstrating large decoupling potential*

Sector	Best practice case studies
Residential buildings	Passive house designs have achieved significant reductions in heating requirements in Germany with an 80% improvement over contemporary German standards, and a 90% improvement over the average German building stock.[19] There are now examples of Passivhaus design in many OECD countries.
Energy in developing countries	Grameen Bank's subsidiary Grameen Shakti uses the bank's original micro-credit financing model to enable the people of Bangladesh to purchase energy-efficient lighting and cooking systems that are powered by solar energy. Since 1997 the company has serviced over 135,000 homes, and in 2008 its service rate was 5000 additional homes per month; 3 million trees have also been planted by customers.[20]
Commercial buildings	There are now many examples of outstanding green buildings, such as the Saunders Hotel Group, a third-generation family business that owns and operates three properties in Boston, MA. It is the first such group to retrofit its hotels to become climate neutral, through a combination of energy efficiency initiatives and purchasing renewable energy. The company is certified by the Climate Neutral Network as the first hotel group in the world to offer climate neutral rooms.[21]
Steel industry	Leading US steel company, Nucor Steel, is around 70% more energy efficient than many steel companies around the world,[22] using state-of-the-art electric arc furnace systems, adopting leading practices such as net shape casting, and implementing options such as energy monitoring systems for energy recovery and distribution between processes.[23]
Cement industry	Ordinary Portland cement manufacture is responsible for 6–8% of global greenhouse emissions and this is rising with demand. The good news is that an Australian company Zeobond Pty Ltd, based in Melbourne, is now making geo-polymer cement which reduces energy usage and greenhouse gas emissions by over 80%.[24] Geo-polymers can be used for most major purposes for which Portland cement is currently used.[25]
Paper and pulp industry	Catalyst Paper International has improved its energy efficiency by 20% across all operations since 1990, saving the company close to US$26 million between 1994 and 2004. At the same time, it has reduced its greenhouse gas emissions by 69% through greater use of biomass and sourcing electricity from hydro power.[26] The pulp and paper sector has the potential in both existing and new mills to become renewable electricity power generators through the use of black liquor gasification combined cycle technologies.[27]
Data centres	Google has achieved 80% energy efficiency improvements in its data centres through efficient data centre design, efficient power supplies and efficient voltage regulator modules on motherboards.[28] Unnecessary components, such as graphics chips, are omitted. Fan energy is minimized by running fans only as fast as required. Finally, Google seeks to use components that operate efficiently across its whole operating range, a strategy that the company estimates could reduce data centre energy consumption by half.[29]

Table 2.1 *continued*

Sector	Best practice case studies
Supermarkets	Supermarket chains Tesco (UK) and Whole Foods (US) are showing that there are numerous ways to significantly reduce electricity usage through, for instance, reducing cooling and heating loads and utilizing more efficient lighting.[30] They are also experimenting with solar energy and wind micro-turbines.[31] Whole Foods Market are set to power an entire store using solar panels and combined cycle co-generation using fuel cells and heat recovery.[32]
Restaurants	Four profitable restaurants – Bordeaux Quay (Bristol, UK),[33] Foodorama (Berlin, Germany),[34] The Acorn House (London, UK)[35] and The Water House (UK) – demonstrate that restaurants can significantly reduce their energy consumption through building design, energy-efficient lighting and cooking equipment, purchasing their electricity from accredited renewable sources, buying organic fresh local food in season, composting and recycling all waste, and investing in carbon offsets.
Transport – vehicle efficiency	Integrating technical advances in light-weighting, hybrid electric engines, batteries, regenerative braking and aerodynamics is enabling numerous automotive and transport vehicle companies to redesign cars, motorbikes, trucks, trains, ships and aeroplanes to be significantly (50–80%) more fuel efficient than standard internal combustion vehicles. Plug-in vehicle technologies are opening up the potential for all transportation vehicles to be run on batteries charged by renewable energy.[36]
Transport efficiency from modal shifts (passenger)	Shifting transport modes can also lead to significant energy efficiency gains. One bus with 25 passengers reduces energy and greenhouse gas emissions per capita by approximately 86% per kilometre compared to 25 single occupant vehicles.[37] Trains are even more efficient. Typically, rail systems in European cities are 7 times more energy efficient than car travel in US cities.[38]
Transport efficiency from modal shifts (freight)	Shifting freight transport from trucks to rail can also lead to large efficiency gains of between 75 and 85%.[39] Several countries are moving to improve the efficiency of their transport sectors by making large investments in rail freight infrastructure, including improving the modal interfaces. For instance, China has invested US$292 billion to improve and extend its rail network from 78,000km in 2007, to over 120,000km by 2020, much of which will be dedicated to freight.

Source: von Weizsäcker et al (2009)[40]

the typical rising electricity demand profile. Figure 2.5 shows that California, through its strong policies, has managed to achieve a significant reduction in electricity demand compared to the rest of the US.

The cost savings from energy and fuel efficiency can help individuals, business and government pay for the costs of investing in shifting energy production from fossil fuels to low-carbon renewable technologies. Denmark, for example, today gets 20 per cent of its electricity from wind and has plans to push this to 50 per cent. Some 60 million Europeans now get their residential electricity from wind farms. By the end of 2007, some 40 million Chinese

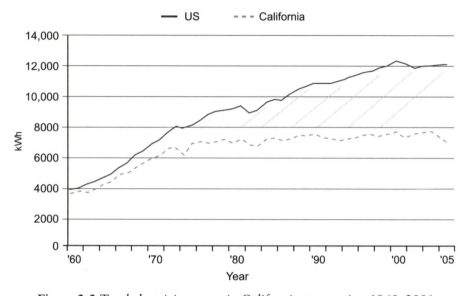

Figure 2.5 *Total electricity usage in California, per capita, 1960–2001*

Source: Based on data from Shirley (2006)[41] and the California Energy Commission[42]

homes will be getting their hot water from rooftop solar water heaters. Iceland now heats close to 90 per cent of its homes with geothermal energy, and in so doing, has virtually eliminated the use of coal for home heating. Iceland, New Zealand, Norway and Costa Rica have committed to becoming net climate neutral – 100 per cent decoupling of economic growth from greenhouse gas emissions – over the next 30 years through energy efficiency, demand management, renewable energy, sustainable transport options and carbon offsets (see Chapter 6 and in particular Table 6.1 for further evidence of leading national programmes and policies). Respected economists such as Nicholas Stern and Paul Ekins, have argued that it is theoretically and practically possible to decouple economic growth from environmental pressures sufficiently to enable economic growth to continue to grow strongly.

> *Changes in energy technologies and in the structure of economies have created opportunities to decouple growth from greenhouse gas emissions ... Tackling climate change is the pro-growth strategy for the longer term, and it can be done in a way that does not cap the aspirations for growth of rich or poor countries.*
> Sir Nicholas Stern, Executive Summary
> of *The Stern Review*, 2006[43]

> *It is clear from past experience that the relationship between the economy's value and its physical scale is variable, and that it is*

possible to reduce the material intensity of GDP. This establishes the theoretical possibility of GDP growing indefinitely in a finite material world.

Paul Ekins, *Economic Growth and Environmental Sustainability*, 2000[44]

Since *Our Common Future* was published in 1987, a wealth of evidence has been developed to show that along with greenhouse gas emissions significant decoupling of other environmental pressures from economic growth can also be achieved. Given the size and scope of this publication, it is not feasible to cover each environmental pressure in detail, instead we have selected five main areas, aligned with the focus areas of the OECD, as this would allow the work in this book to complement and extend such leading efforts. The categories and their corresponding chapters are as follows:

1 greenhouse gas emissions – Chapters 6 and 7;
2 biodiversity loss and deterioration of natural systems – Chapter 8;
3 freshwater extraction – Chapter 9;
4 waste production – Chapter 10;
5 air pollution – Chapter 11 (with a detailed case study from Delhi in Chapter 12).

Greenhouse gas emissions is expanded to cover two chapters because we see it as the overarching issue that affects each of the other areas, as well as being the issue that is posing the largest-scale immediate threat. Then each of the remaining four areas are investigated for particular aspects that can be decoupled from economic growth such as those outlined as a priority or as urgent by the OECD in Table 2.2.

The first area of focus, decoupling economic growth from greenhouse gas emissions, shows that urgent decoupling is needed to avoid dangerous climate change; furthermore, that achieving such decoupling is both technically possible and economically affordable if we act in the coming decade, particularly as the costs of inaction are set to be significant. The remaining chapters then make the case that this is also true for actions to reduce environmental pressures on biodiversity, water resources, waste management, and air quality, such as:

• Biodiversity loss and deterioration of natural systems: South Korea has already shown how biodiversity and natural systems can be restored as a part of their economic development goals. Having lost the majority of its forests by the end of the Korean War, the South Korean government invested in a major national reforestation effort, utilizing village cooperatives involving hundreds of thousands of people to dig trenches and to create terraces for supporting trees on barren mountains. As Se-Kyung Chong, researcher at the Korea Forest Research Institute, writes, 'the result

Table 2.2 *Environmental protection priority areas*

Priority area	Well managed	Priority	Urgent
Climate change		• Declining greenhouse gas emissions per unit of GDP	• Global greenhouse gas emissions • Increasing evidence of an already changing climate
Biodiversity and renewable natural resources	• Forested area in OECD countries	• Forest management • Protected areas	• Ecosystem quality • Species loss • Invasive alien species • Tropical forests • Illegal logging • Ecosystem fragmentation
Water	• Point-source water pollution in OECD countries (industry, municipalities)	• Surface water quality and wastewater treatment	• Water scarcity • Groundwater quality • Agricultural water use and pollution
Air quality	• OECD country SO_2 and NO_x emissions	• Partculate matter (PM) and ground-level ozone • Road transport emissions	• Urban air quality
Waste and hazardous chemicals	• Waste management in OECD countries • OECD country emissions of CFCs	• Municipal waste generation • Developing country emissions of CFCs	• Hazardous waste management and transportation • Waste management in developing countries • Chemicals in the environment and in products

Source: OECD (2008)[45]

was a seemingly miraculous rebirth of forests from barren land. Today forests cover 65% of the country, an area of roughly 6 million hectares. While driving across South Korea in November 2000, it was gratifying for me to see the luxuriant stands of trees on mountains that a generation ago were bare. We can reforest the Earth!'[46] Further to reforestation efforts, South Korea is also taking steps to reduce timber demand, shifting to metal and plastic chopsticks (with China discarding an estimated 25 million trees worth of chopsticks a year), and having one of the highest paper recycling rates in the world of 77 per cent.

• Air pollution: Significant advances have been achieved over the last few decades both in the scientific understanding of air pollution and in the technological innovations to reduce it. Through these advances, air quality has been improved dramatically in many cities, especially in the OECD, at much less cost than first anticipated. The US Environmental Protection Agency (US EPA), for instance, conducted an extensive study which found that the total benefits of the Clean Air Act programmes 1970–1990 saved the US economy US$22 trillion.[47] In other words, if US air pollution trends in 1970 had continued to 1990, then the measurable economic, social, health and environmental costs to the US economy would have been an extra US$22 trillion. By comparison, the actual cost of achieving the pollution reductions observed over the 20-year period was US$523 billion, a small expense compared to the estimated costs of the impacts avoided.

- Freshwater extraction: There are also significant success stories from which we can learn in decoupling economic growth from freshwater extraction. In the US between 1980 and 1995 the amount of fresh water withdrawn per American fell by 21 per cent and water withdrawn per dollar of real GDP fell by 38 per cent.[48] This trend is being seen worldwide in OECD countries, although greater efforts are needed if freshwater supply is to meet demand in the long term. Most industry sectors, homes and commercial buildings can cost effectively reduce water usage by over 50 per cent through using water-efficient appliances, and utilizing and recycling rain and greywater onto gardens. Further, farmers in India, Israel, Jordan, Spain and the US have shown that drip irrigation systems that deliver water directly to crop roots can reduce water use by 30–70 per cent and raise crop yields by 20–90 per cent. Rice farmers in Malaysia saw a 45 per cent increase in their water productivity through a combination of better scheduling of their irrigations, shoring up canals, and sowing seeds directly into the field rather than transplanting seedlings.

- Waste production: Most OECD nations have achieved significant levels of decoupling of economic growth from waste production, although further improvement is both needed and will be cost effective. For instance, in OECD countries in the mid-1990s, approximately 64 per cent of municipal waste was sent to landfill, 18 per cent for incineration and 18 per cent for recycling.[49] In 2005, only 49 per cent of municipal waste was being disposed of in landfill, 30 per cent was being recycled and 21 per cent was being incinerated or otherwise treated.[50] While waste production has only been relatively decoupled from economic growth, the OECD has not advised slowing economic growth to achieve further decoupling. Rather, the OECD has advocated stronger waste reduction policies and better whole system approaches to sustainable design to achieve more significant decoupling in this area. According to the OECD, 'New integrated approaches – with stronger emphasis on material efficiency, redesign and reuse of products, waste prevention, recycling of end-of-life materials and products and environmentally sound management of residues – could be used to counterbalance the environmental impacts of waste throughout the entire life-cycle of materials.'[51]

It is possible for nations to achieve decoupling simultaneously across a range of environmental pressures. A leading overall example of national decoupling comes from the Netherlands where significant progress has been made on decoupling economic growth from a range of environmental pressures, as shown in Figure 2.6. The Netherlands is also one of the first countries to undertake research to investigate the relative levels of decoupling of environmental pressure needed to meet the OECD's sustainability criteria. This has

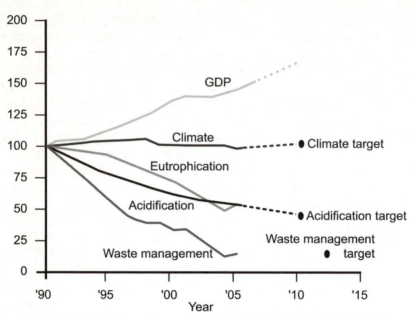

Figure 2.6 *Achieving decoupling in the Netherlands, 1985–2010*

Source: Netherlands Environmental Assessment Agency (2007)[52]

been done through the Netherlands' government Sustainable Technology Development (STD) project, which is one of the first national government programmes to suggest that it is possible to decouple economic growth and environmental damage by as much as 75–95 per cent (a factor of 4–20) over a 50-year period in many critical sectors of the economy.

The STD project has been documented in detail in the 2000 publication *Sustainable Technology Development* by Paul Weaver et al.[53] One of the most remarkable works to enter the sustainability debate, *Sustainable Technology Development* provides a very powerful methodology for generating innovations that are driven by the need to achieve ecological sustainability. The book starts with a 'no-flinching' analysis of just how big a change would be needed to achieve ecological sustainability. This was assessed for a range of issues and the result in all cases is that the changes need to be very big (factor 20–50 improvements). This would not shock most people, but it is very rare for government-sponsored projects to face this level of reality.

Rather than giving up at the point where they discovered that nothing less than wholesale technology innovation and reinvention was required, the project went on to figure out how the necessary efficiency gains and redesigns could be accomplished. The project looked at case studies covering the issues of nutrition (food supply), water management, chemicals supply and alternative engine/fuel systems for cars. The methodology also dealt with how to create the commitment and momentum to ensure that innovation programmes were followed through to their results. The STD project was also a key influence, leading to the development of the Fourth Dutch National Environment Plan that looks specifically at system change to achieve ecological sustainability.

> *Certainly many use growth [of global material and energy flows, population, environmental damage] to forecast disaster. But there is an alternative vision: one of a sustainable future where [economic] growth is not seen as a threat but as a driving force behind innovation.*
>
> Paul Weaver et al, *Sustainable Technology Development*, 2000[54]

Table 2.3 provides a summary from *Sustainable Technology Development* of the Netherlands government's targets for factor 10–50 (depending on the issue) in 50 years from 1990 levels (that is, by 2040). For example, fossil carbon emissions were targeted at factor 25 (p42), oil was factor 40, copper factor 30 and acid deposition factor 50 (p43). Table 2.3 was originally adapted by Phillip Sutton for the 2005 publication *The Natural Advantage of Nations*,[55] to show the specific factor improvements needed (without adjustment for population growth and poverty reduction), ranging from 20 to 99 per cent improvements, including page numbers from the source document. However, the table has now been updated for this publication and includes direct comments from the Chairman of the STD programme (1993–1998) Professor Leo Jansen. Jansen has stated that since the STD project, the Netherlands' GDP grew by 220 per cent between 1990 and 2006, and by 2006, greenhouse gas emissions reduced by 3 per cent relative to the 1990 baseline,[56] although final consumption of petroleum products also grew by nearly 18 per cent from 1995 until 2006.[57]

> *Since the STD programme has been closed, the STD approach has been further developed, spread and applied ... as a stepping stone for transition policies in the Netherlands. Furthermore, the STD approach is embedded and applied in (higher) education for sustainable development.*
>
> Leo Jansen, Chairman of the STD programme and Professor of Environmental Technology at the University of Delft[58]

While it is relatively simple to describe the STD programme with its rationale, underlying philosophy and methodology, or to expand upon case studies, evaluating the programme is somewhat more complex. Measurable results will only be evident in the long term and may be inextricably linked with outcomes from other influences. Hence the updates added to the table above focus on the short-term and indirect indicators of influence, with some more recent trends and achievements. The five-year programme was completed in 1997, and since then many of the case studies have been embedded in continuation activities in the Netherlands.

Table 2.3 *Results of the Netherlands Sustainable Technology Development (STD) project (with recent progress and reflections from the Chairperson of the STD programme)*

Case study area	Programme target	Predicted potential and indicators of progress
Nutrition		
Sustainable multifunctional land use		Factor 20 (95%) over several eco-capacity criteria (p100). **Update:** *Greenhouse gas emissions in the agricultural sector decreased by 19% from 1994 to 2004, while the amount of nitrogen and phosphates used both decreased by 25%. Ammonia emissions decreased by 32%, and mineral losses from soils have more than halved in the preceding 20 years. Manure is being traded between intensive livestock and stockless arable farms to decrease fertilizer use and eutrophication of surface water.*[59]
High-technology closed-cycle horticulture		Wastage of CO_2 can be cut by factor 8 (87%) and water by factor 18 (94%) (p116). **Update:** *The energy per product used in glasshouse horticulture was 54% less (factor 2) in 2005 than it was in 1980. The industry is now investigating the prospect of being a net energy provider, treating glasshouses like solar collectors.*[60]
Novel protein foods	Average factor 20 improvement by 2035 (p145).	In general in many cases: factor 20–30 (95–97%) with half to one-fifth of the cost (p104). Specific examples: Lupin cheese factor 9–21 (89–95%) improvement on dairy cheese production (p112); potato-derived pasta factor 8 (87%) improvement over wheat pasta (p112); by 2035 novel food protein could be produced more efficiently than pork today by factor 80 (99%) or factor 60 (98%) better than meat in 2035 (p143). **Update:** *Several research projects are under way to explore the economic, environmental and social aspects of novel protein foods (NPF) and consumer choices.*[61, 62] *One such project found land use efficiencies of factor 3–4 when meat production was replaced with novel proteins production, while water efficiency increased by factor 30–40.*[63] *Another study, which found that consumer expenditure on NPF has been increasing in the Netherlands, predicted that in the next 30 years NPF will replace 40% of current meat consumption.*[64]
Protein Foods, Environment, Technology and Society (Profetas) (added by Professor Leo Jansen)	As a follow-up to NPF an inter-university programme was constituted to explore and deepen further developments.[65]	The Profetas results show that the environmental benefits of a transition from animal to plant protein may be factor 3–4 for land and energy requirements, but 30–40 or more for water requirements and acidification. The geographical distribution of potential environmental and economic benefits strongly depends on the actual protein crop selected.

Case study area	Programme target	Predicted potential and indicators of progress
Water		
The water-handling system (does not deal with water use efficiency measures)	Factor 20 improvement (p158) by 2040 (p159).	Some of the most important actions need to be taken on the demand side by system users in households, businesses and industry (p152). Abiotic depletion can be reduced by factor 3 (67%) and aquatic eco-toxicity by factor 4 (75%), fossil energy use by around factor 1.25 (15–20%), solid waste production by factor 1.3 (25%). **Update:** *Over a ten-year period to 2006, overall water efficiency improved by 23%.*[66]
The 'Waterpact Twente'[67] (added by Professor Leo Jansen)	An integral sustainable water system in the Twente region.	In a follow-up of STD all relevant stakeholders, municipalities, industries, water authorities, drinking water industry, farmers and the province of Overijssel joined in the Waterpact. In seven years the goals were achieved. The pact is seen as an example for other regions and cities.
Cleaning domestic textiles	Factor 10–20 (p176) by 2040 (p186).	Household by 2025: factor 2.5 (60%) for energy, factor 4 (75%) for water, factor 5 (80%) for detergent (p194). Neighbourhood by 2025: factor 2 (50%) for energy, factor 10 (90%) for water, factor 10 (90%) for detergent (p195). Centralized by 2025: no conclusions reported. More efficient technologies expected to be cheaper: less than half the cost possible by 2005 (p197).
Chemicals		
Chemical and industrial materials	By 2040 no fossil fuels used to source industrial organic chemicals/materials and factor 20 improvements in efficiency of eco-capacity use (p215).	Many promising technology changes identified but no quantitative results reported.
Sourcing organic chemical feed stocks	To supply sufficient biomass to source organic chemicals and materials (plastics, liquid fuels, etc.), and to find effective chemical pathways from biomass to needed organic chemical materials.	The quantity of biomass that can be produced is adequate for chemicals and materials, but there is a shortfall for liquid fuel (p221). Feasible synthesis routes were available for practically all major commodity products. The quantity of phenolic compounds sourced from biomass may not be adequate (p245). **Update:** *The National School in Process Technology is currently undertaking an extensive list of research projects into sourcing organic chemical feed stocks.*[68] *DSM, a Netherlands-based chemical manufacturing company, reported its strongest quarter in 2008, largely resulting from the 17% growth in sales of organically based chemicals.*[69]

Table 2.3 *continued*

Case study area	Programme target	Predicted potential and indicators of progress
Biomass production on saline soils	To find halophytic plants that produces useful biomass as feedstock for the production of chemical products so that biomass production can be expanded by utilizing otherwise unavailable salinized land.	Several appropriate halophytic plants are available. **Update:** *A three-year project which commenced in 2006 is developing bio-saline agro-forestry systems for the Netherlands to both remediate saline wastelands and to produce biomass.*[70]

Motor vehicle propulsion

Hydrogen fuel/ fuel cell cars	To find alternative renewable energy 'carrier' fuel(s) – with high end-use conversion efficiency to offset any inefficiency of the initial production (p249) – that can provide the basis for a significant Dutch industry to replace fossil fuel oil in the refinery sector (p248).	Hydrogen fuel (or hydrogen-rich liquid carriers, such as cyclohexane and methanol) identified as possible alternatives (p248). A hydrogen-fuelled fuel cell car could have an increased energy efficiency of factor 1.75 (43%) compared to conventional internal combustion engine cars (p263). Renewable energy use with carbon removal from the fuel and carbon sequestration could enable CO_2 to be removed from the atmosphere (p265). **Update:** *The Netherlands has developed a fuel cell system and the first Dutch hydrogen vehicles are entering operational service.*[71] *Amsterdam ran a successful three-year trial of hydrogen buses and is currently developing the world's largest hydrogen public transport project in Rotterdam with 20 hydrogen buses and associated refuelling infrastructure.*[72]

Update
Further developments (added by Professor Leo Jansen)

Adaptive Integration of Research and Policy for Sustainable Development[73]	Evaluation of ten research and technology development programmes.	This evaluation confirmed and proved the applicability of the STD approach for sustainable development. The report contains annexes on pitfalls and recommendations for setting up and evaluating research and technology programmes for sustainable development.
Strategic sustainable development	Comparison of sustainable-development-oriented approaches.[74]	Among the investigated approaches the STD approach is 'backcasting', and focused on societal needs.[75]
Climate OptiOns for the Long term (COOL)	The STD approach was applied in a programme to reduce use of energy and CO_2 emissions by factor 4.	The programme was a participatory process based on the STD approach with dialogues on three levels: National, EU and Global.[76]

Case study area	Programme target	Predicted potential and indicators of progress
Transition policies	The STD programme was a stepping stone to the Dutch transition policies.	Transition theory has been developed as a follow-up to STD.[77] In Dutch policies, transitions are to be achieved in the fields of energy, mobility, agriculture and biodiversity.
Plant of the future, Austria	A governmental programme, 2002–2009, with 142 projects to date.	In a number of projects the STD and transition approach was applied.
Education (added by Professor Leo Jansen)		
Delft University of Technology	STD-derived backcasting applied to education of engineers.	The university is investigating the competences of the engineer in ten years working in a developing world as the basis of a programme to embed sustainable development into courses at the university.[78]

Source: Weaver et al (2000);[79] summarized by Philip Sutton in Hargroves and Smith (2005);[80] and updated by Professor Leo Jensen and The Natural Edge Project for this publication.

How Does Decoupling Directly Contribute to GDP?

Historically, political parties tend to rise or fall based on the performance of the GDP. Tony Blair once stated that growth in GDP would be the 'judge and jury' of British Labour's success. Hence to the majority of the governments of the world, increasing GDP is an imperative, as it is directly linked to a range of important 'voter' issues, such as employment, interest rates, health care, education and infrastructure development, and is therefore a strong determinant of political success. This is ironic as many commentators in this area now point out that the measure was never intended by those who invented it to be such an influential indicator. John Maynard Keynes, John Hicks and Simon Kuznets who first developed the system of national accounting (to specifically assist nations manage their economies out of the great depression), warned against using the GDP as a measure of well-being and prosperity. As Simon Kuznets told the US Congress in 1934, 'The welfare of a nation can scarcely be inferred from a measurement of national income ... Goals for more growth should specify of what and for what.'[81] As US Senator Robert Kennedy famously stated in 1968:

> The Gross National Product includes air pollution and advertising for cigarettes, and ambulances to clear our highways of carnage. It counts special locks for our doors, and jails for the people who break them. GNP includes the destruction of the redwoods and the death of Lake Superior. It grows with the production of napalm and missiles and nuclear warheads. And if GNP includes all this, there is much that it does not comprehend. It does not allow for the health of our families, the quality of their education, or the joy of their play. It is indifferent to the decency of our factories and the safety of our streets alike. It does

not include the beauty of our poetry or the strength of our marriages, or the intelligence of our public debate or the integrity of our public officials ... GNP measures neither our wit nor our courage, neither our wisdom nor our learning, neither our compassion nor our devotion to our country. It measures every-thing, in short, except that which makes life worthwhile; and it can tell us everything about America – except whether we are proud to be Americans.[82]

Even though not traditionally reflected in the calculations of GDP, some econo-mists have long made the distinction between economic activity that is created from activities that impact on society and the environment, such as cleaning up oil spills and fighting wars, and economic activity which services the optimal social good and builds sustainable wealth. For instance, in 1848 French econo-mist Frederic Bastiat outlined what he called the 'broken window fallacy', and explained that if someone throws a stone and breaks a shop window, the owner needs to repair it ... this puts people to work ... and hence it would easy to assume that if more windows were broken it would be a positive thing for the overall economy. However, Bastiat pointed out that what is seen is the broken window being repaired, the activity of the workers, and the money they in turn spend. What is not seen is that these workers and resources may have been better employed on something else if not for the broken window. Bastiat believed that when assessing the economic situation one must not only consider the foreseeable and immediate consequences, both good and bad, but one must also look to the longer term, across the whole of society. Bastiat stated that, 'In the economic sphere an act, a habit, an institution, a law produces not only one effect, but a series of effects. Of these effects, the first alone is immediate; it appears simultaneously with its cause; it is seen. The other effects emerge only subsequently; they are not seen; we are fortunate if we foresee them.'[83] What ultimately benefits society is not fixing more broken windows, or repairing damage from wars,[84] or dealing with the impacts of pollution, but instead directing material and human resources to develop goods and services, infra-structure, policies and practices that improve conditions and increase wealth and well-being.

There have been a number of calls for alternative indicators to the GDP, such as the 1972 work of William Nordhaus and James Tobin to propose a 'measure of economic welfare'.[85] This work was later further developed by Herman Daly and John Cobb in 1989 when they proposed substituting GDP with an 'index of sustainable economic welfare',[86] aligned with the much earlier work of John Hicks in 1939, when he suggested that 'the purpose of income calculations in practical affairs is to give people an indication of the amount which they can consume without impoverishing themselves'.[87] Further calls have been made to replace GDP with measures including the 'genuine progress indicator' (GPI), and a measure of 'net national income' (NNI), but GDP remains entrenched in systems of national accounts. A 2009 report by the

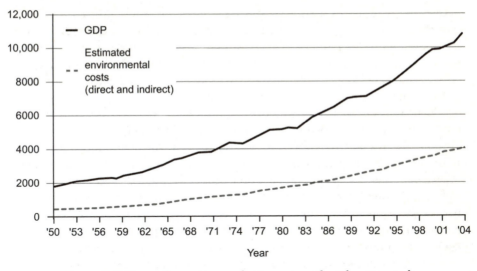

Figure 2.7 *Gross domestic product compared with estimated environmental costs (billions) for the US, 1950–2004*

Source: Data reinterpreted by K. Hargroves from Talberth, J. et al (2006)[88]

'Commission on the Measurement of Economic Performance and Social Progress', initiated by French President Nicholas Sarkozy, and led by notable economists Joseph Stiglitz and Amartya Sen, argued for the adoption of measures of well-being to be used in conjunction with the GDP.[89] Further to the understanding that additional measures need to be compared to GDP, such as 'decoupling indicators' as explained in Chapter 5, it must also be understood that environmental pressures are leading to real and measurable costs that reduce a nation's GDP.

A reinterpretation by the authors of the results of a leading study undertaken by the US public policy think tank, Redefining Progress, demonstrates such costs, with the results shown in Figure 2.7.

As part of a process to calculate an alternative measure to the GDP, the genuine progress indicator (GPI), the group Redefining Progress researched and quantified a number of environmental costs during the period 1970–2004 in the US. These costs included: household pollution abatement; water pollution; air pollution; loss of wetlands; loss of farmland; loss of primary forests; resource depletion; carbon dioxide emissions damage; and ozone depletion.[90] When such costs are aggregated and plotted against GDP it can easily be seen that as GDP increases so do the estimated environmental costs, and increasingly so, with the costs rising from 22 per cent of GDP in 1950 to 37 per cent in 2004. This simplified example is complicated by a number of factors related to measurement and assumptions regarding the distribution of costs, but it provides a clear picture of the trends associated with economic growth and costs related to environmental pressures. Hence, in order to monitor the overall economic progress of a society, the GDP must be held against the level of environmental damage it creates, and in particular the direct and indirect costs associated with this damage. This will then provide an indication of both the economic progress and the level of reliance on damaging the environment that is required to deliver it, potentially providing a strong indicator of a nation's risk of maintaining future economic growth.

Hence a focus on decoupling provides nations with a strategy to reduce the costs related to environmental pressures while undertaking activities that allow an increase in GDP. As GDP is an aggregation of the economic activity of a nation, both 'good' and 'bad' economic activity will contribute to its growth. Hence activities that promote the 'good' and discourage the 'bad' can still lead to overall growth. Furthermore, the 'good' actions that reduce environmental pressures can lead to a range of additional benefits that support economic growth. In particular, investments to reduce the consumption of resources – such as to improve the efficiency and/or productivity of energy, water and other resources – are now being recognized as having a compounding effect on GDP. This is due to the fact that such investments lead to reduced input costs, reduced running and maintenance costs, and reduced waste-related costs, and hence can be recovered over a reasonable timeframe to then deliver ongoing cost savings that can then be invested to achieve even greater improvements, and so on. Furthermore, as such investments can lead to reduced levels of consumption of resources, such as water and electricity, this can lead to delays in or even the avoidance of costly investments in increasing the capacity of energy and water supply infrastructure, as well as plant and infrastructure in extractive industries. Typically such investments are at a local level and can spur job growth and economic development, attracting companies and operations keen to be part of such initiatives.

However, in order to understand how efforts to reduce environmental pressures can enhance economic growth it is important to understand the two main approaches used to calculate GDP.

The most common approach is called the 'expenditure' method, where:

GDP = Consumption + Investment + Government spending
      + Gross (Exports – Imports)

Represented as GDP = C + I + G + (X–M)

The following explains the formula above with reference to how the efforts to reduce environmental pressures can contribute positively to GDP:

- Consumption (C) represents the private consumption in the economy. This includes most personal expenditures of households such as food, rent, medical expenses and so on, but does not include new housing. Thus if a household purchases energy-efficient light bulbs and appliances, organic food, new bicycles, accredited green electricity from renewable energy sources, this all adds positively to GDP.

- Investment (I) is defined as business investments in capital,[91] such as spending on new houses, including those with sustainable aspects. Such investments include a range of activities such as: onsite energy recovery and generation; onsite water recovery, capture and treatment; green retrofitting of buildings; and improvements to operating plant and equipment – all counting positively to a nation's GDP.

- Government spending (G) is the sum of government expenditures on final goods and services. It includes salaries of public servants, military expenditure and any investment expenditure by a government, along with:

  - spending to support and encourage the development of decentralized, low-carbon, renewable energy supply infrastructure (including upgrades to national electricity grids to accommodate such new supply – referred to as a 'smart grid');

  - spending to undertake green retrofitting of the publicly owned built environment infrastructure (such as defence and military bases, schools, housing commission homes, hospitals, university campuses and general government buildings, and public and street lighting), along with increasing environmental performance requirements for new buildings;

  - spending on sustainable transport infrastructure and vehicles (such as in expanding coverage of rail and light-rail infrastructure, increasing the use of low-carbon alternatives for buses and rail services, the construction of bicycle paths and preferential lanes for high-occupancy vehicles);

  - spending on the restoration and enhancement of natural systems and biodiversity, along with improvements to agricultural techniques and practices;

  - spending on national broadband infrastructure that can enable video conferencing to dramatically reduce dependency on air transportation;

  - spending on structural adjustment packages and retraining of workers and business managers to reduce their burden of environmental pressure, to completely transition those unsustainable industries that need to be made redundant, or to create entirely new industries such as recycling of materials and products;

  - spending on overseas development aid to assist developing countries to cost effectively reduce environmental pressures.

- Gross exports (X) is the amount of goods and services produced for overseas consumption, and gross imports (M) are subtracted from the gross exports since imported goods will be included in the accounts for government spending, investment or consumption, and must be deducted to avoid counting foreign supply as domestic. A range of decoupling-related activities can help improve this balance of trade results, including:

  - A transition to sustainable transport systems reduces the amount of oil and gas imports needed. Oil imports over the coming decades will add significantly to import bills for most nations unless they find alternative sustainable transport approaches.

– Efforts to reduce waste and encourage greater recycling will also reduce the amount of new appliances, cars and equipment plus raw materials, metals, chemicals and plastics, and fertilizers, needing to be imported. This can also lead to a surplus of materials being created, thus enabling more exports. For instance, Australia recycles more paper and cardboard products and PET bottles than it can reuse, creating export opportunities.

– Nations which shift their subsidies and incentives to reward businesses that are innovating lower consumption and/or pollution technologies will help the economy to position itself to capture the growing markets for these products.

Hence sustainable consumption, green investments, reducing unnecessary imports and increasing environmentally friendly exports all positively adds to a nation's GDP.

The second most used method for measuring GDP is to measure the total income payable in national income accounts. In this situation, one will sometimes hear of gross domestic income (GDI), rather than gross domestic product. This should provide the same figure as the expenditure method described above. (By definition, GDI = GDP; however, in practice measurement errors will make the two figures slightly off when reported by national statistical agencies.)

Calculating GDP using the 'income' approach involves:

GDP = Compensation of employees + Gross operating surplus + Gross mixed income + Taxes less subsidies on production and imports

Represented as GDP = COE + GOS + GMI + Taxes – Subsidies, where:

• Compensation of employees (COE) measures the total remuneration to employees for work done. It includes wages and salaries, as well as employer contributions to social security and other such programmes. During an economy-wide transition to lower environmental pressures, which would be a period of several decades at least, the economy would have a strong structural tendency to higher levels of employment. The structural tendency to favour higher employment is caused by three things:

– the recycling of revenues from eco-taxes to reduce payroll taxes or other costs of employing labour;

– the greater labour intensity of new ways of doing things where the technology and the manufacturing and operational techniques are not yet highly refined;

– the pump-priming effect of investments brought forward to replace scrapped capital.

- Gross operating surplus (GOS) is the surplus due to owners of incorporated businesses, also called profits, although only a subset of total costs is subtracted from gross output to calculate GOS. There is now significant empirical evidence that, wisely applied, pursuing practices that reduce environmental pressures can help improve a business's bottom line both through eco-efficiency savings in the short term but also by positioning itself for new emerging markets longer term.
- Gross mixed income (GMI) is the same measure as GOS, but for unincorporated businesses. This often includes most small businesses.

Hence once it is clear how GDP is calculated, and the range of decoupling actions that can contribute to its growth, an important consideration in understanding the economic implications of particular investments is the concept of an economic multiplier, which is effectively the direct increase in GDP for each dollar of spending. This measure can then be used to compare how much economic activity can be generated by different combinations of purchasing and investment. A higher economic multiplier will lead to greater economic vitality because business activity is encouraged, creating jobs and encouraging investment. Investments made locally in reducing energy and water demand, and in generating electricity through small-scale renewable options (e.g. solar, wind, hydroelectric and co-generation) can create significant economic multipliers. For instance, as mentioned above, investments to increase energy, water and resource productivity have a high economic multiplier as they not only reduce pollution-related costs but they also reduce the levels of inputs needed, thus reducing energy and water bills and input resource costs, along with delaying and even permanently preventing the need to spend money on expanding resource intensive infrastructure, which is particularly valuable as such investments have low economic multipliers.

Several local and state governments have now analysed the actual and projected economic development effects of energy efficiency or alternative energy projects, including:

- In Osage, Ohio, they found that a US$1.00 purchase of ordinary consumer goods in a local store generates US$1.90 of economic activity in the local economy. In comparison, petroleum products generate a multiplier of about US$1.51; utility services US$1.66; and energy efficiency US$2.23.[92] The reduced demand has delayed investment in energy infrastructure, reducing electricity rates by 19 per cent over an eight-year period, and natural gas rates by 5 per cent over a five-year period.[93] In addition, the programme reduced unemployment to half that of the national average as the lower electricity rates attracted more factories and companies to town, while reducing the emissions and costs of the utility itself.[94]
- The Massachusetts Division of Energy Resources reports that the state has realized a 257 per cent job growth in energy efficiency firms, such as

energy service companies, between 1988 and 1992, indicating vigorous business growth.

- The Wisconsin Energy Bureau found that the use of renewable energy generates about three times more jobs, earnings and sales output in Wisconsin than the same level of imported fossil fuel use and investment. Given a 75 per cent increase in the state's renewable energy use, now representing 6 per cent, the Bureau found that the state would realize more than 62,000 new jobs, US$1.2 billion in new wages and US$4.6 billion in new sales for Wisconsin businesses.

Hence investments to reduce environmental pressures – such as eco-efficiency improvements; building new industries such as recycling and processing; and building low-carbon energy infrastructure – can have a positive effect on local economies. Often these initiatives can lead to lower costs of living in the form of lower utility bills, taxes and rates, or lower costs of local goods and services.

Understanding and Reducing the Risk of Negative Rebound Effects from Decoupling Activities

Eco-efficiency investments, in particular, can yield such cost savings to business and households, that, without appropriate mechanisms and government policies, can result in direct or indirect negative rebound effects which can undermine the intended environmental benefits. Direct negative rebound effects include where the demand and consumption of a good increases due to a price reduction caused by the more efficient production methods and lower operational costs. Thus when a more eco-efficient technology, process or product is introduced into the market, it does not automatically imply that, due to the greater eco-efficiency, there will be a significant reduction in environmental pressures. As the product is cheaper to produce, it will be cheaper to purchase, leading to the potential for more people being able to afford to use the product leading to greater demand for such products. The direct negative rebound effect was first noticed in 1865 in the book *The Coal Question*[95] by William Jevons which showed that improving the efficiency with which coal was used to produce steel by over two-thirds in Scotland, was followed by a tenfold increase in total consumption, between the years 1830 and 1863. This was of course due to the fact that the lower coal consumption required to make steel meant that steel could be produced more cheaply. With steel available at cheaper prices, the demand for steel rose significantly. This occurrence is now referred to as a 'rebound effect', or as the 'Jevons paradox', after the author of *The Coal Question*, William Jevons. So, without effective government policies or market mechanisms in place, simply making production methods more efficient will not necessarily lead to an overall reduction in environmental pressures as consumption levels may grow due to the lower price in the market. However, improving the operational end-use efficiency of products, appliances and transport vehicles does lead to significant reductions

Table 2.4 *Summary of estimates of rebound effects in the US residential sector*

Device	Potential size of rebound	Number of studies
Space heating	10–30%	26
Space cooling	0–50%	9
Water heating	<10–40%	5
Residential lighting	5–12%	4
Appliances	0%	2
Automotive transport	10–30%	22

Source: Greening et al (2000)[96]

in environmental pressures per item and effectively managed can lead to significant reductions overall. For instance, there is no evidence that owners of hybrid vehicles have driven twice as much just because their cars were more fuel efficient as some predicted, with similar results found in green buildings. Furthermore investing in end-use energy and water efficiency can have further positive rebound effects such as delaying the need to build new unsustainable energy (coal- and gas-fired power stations) and water supply infrastructure (more dams, desalination plants run from carbon-intensive electricity) if governments institute effective policies.

However, even here the positive effect can be reduced by negative rebound effects:

- Once homes are effectively insulated and people get used to the extra comfort of having a warm or air-conditioned house, this can lead to them running their heating or air-conditioning systems more often.
- Installing much more energy-efficient lighting can lead to people not being so conscientious in turning them off when they are not needed. Since people know that the light bulbs they have installed are ultra-efficient, and thus cost so little to run, they can neglect the need to turn them off regularly.
- Ultra-efficient transportation vehicles can use so much less petrol per 100 kilometres, this can make it easier for people to financially afford regularly to drive long distances. These sorts of factors have been shown to lead to negative rebound effects as shown in Table 2.4.

Furthermore, indirect negative rebound effects can also occur where the money saved on the particular good or service, due to a reduction in price, is spent on other goods and services that have a negative environmental impact. Such examples include people increasingly taking advantage of cheap airflights and travelling more by air, which uses far more resources than train or bus travel.

And even though there is growing social concern and understanding around the issues related to environmental pressures, particularly in relation to greenhouse gas emissions, surveys have identified a disconnect between the level of environmental concern and the consumption patterns of households.[97] This can be due to a range of factors, including the impact of social pressure to conform to a particular pattern of work and consumption outweighing the individual desire to reduce environmental impact. Also, when people have little spare personal time to research up-coming purchases, it is often easier simply to purchase something that is 'conveniently available' even though it may not be environmentally the best available product in that market. This is often the case as there is a lack of information available to the public to inform them of the sustainability performance of products in the marketplace. The reality is that much of the current global economy, and the goods and services it produces, are intrinsically unsustainable, and will be for some time to come, and hence anything that saves people and businesses money and enables them to purchase more, will often lead to purchasing new products and services that are on the whole unsustainable. Furthermore, as this phenomenon involves the nexus between technical performance and social behaviour, it is a very complex issue to manage, as it can negate many well-intentioned technical and policy innovations designed to reduce environmental pressures and advance societal progress, particularly as the effect can actually see increases in GDP.[98]

To further complicate the issue, it has been found that the rebound effect can result in a range of economy-wide effects (also referred to as 'the inter-sectoral rebound effect' to signify the macroeconomic scale[99]), namely:

- Producers may use cost savings from improvements in efficiency to increase output which results in increasing consumption of capital, labour and materials.
- Efficiency improvements will also increase the labour, capital and materials productivity, which may stimulate further economic growth and subsequently increase resource use.
- Efficiency improvements in the use of a particular resource will decrease the price of goods that contain that resource relative to other goods, thus causing a substitution towards those goods.[100]

These impacts can be significant, as according to long run analyses of the US economy from an industrial ecology perspective by Robert Ayers and colleagues, 'physical rebound' (efficiency improvements in energy and materials) was the main motor of GDP growth (and thus use of energy and materials) over the last 100 years.[101] Another study of clean development mechanisms in India found that implementing aggressive end-use efficiencies caused a rebound of 25 per cent, largely negating the greenhouse rationale for the clean development approach.[102] Hence efforts to reduce overall environmental pressures and levels of resource consumption cannot rely solely on technological or process improvements to productivity, and must be complemented with a range of underpinning mechanisms, government policies, education and initiatives

Whilst clearly negative rebound effects can be significant, it is important to note that they need not be because it is also likely that the businesses and households will use their financial savings from eco-efficiency improvements to further invest in actions that reduce environmental pressures. According to Adjunct Professor Alan Pears, much can be done to encourage these positive amplification effects.[103] Pears argues that it is just as likely that positive environmental change from investments in eco-efficiency initiatives, like energy efficiency, will lead to people in their homes and workplaces undertaking more ecologically sustainable initiatives, not less (leading to a positive amplification effect rather than a negative rebound effect), including:[104]

- the purchase of accredited 'green' power, or third-party-certified carbon offsets;
- reducing the amount of water needing to be heated in the home through installing water-efficient shower heads and tap fixtures, and then investing in options to reduce energy consumption in hot water systems, such as upgrades to solar PV, solar thermal or heat pump systems;
- options to reduce internal heating and cooling loads, such as increased insulation, painting roofs white, double glazing or applying films to windows, installing appropriate window furnishings and pelmets, and planting appropriate vegetation to shade homes;
- reducing the ecological footprint of travel, such as substituting with low-emission transportation options like public transport, bicycles or walking;
- purchasing locally grown goods, preferably organic (meaning that chemical pesticides and fertilizers are not used, considering that it takes more energy to create a tonne of fertilizer than a tonne of steel).

Similarly, business can be encouraged to utilize financial cost savings from eco-efficiency investments to invest in further eco-efficiency opportunities with longer payback periods. For instance, this can be done through governments increasing mandatory energy efficiency standards of new appliances and industrial equipment with longer payback periods to divert money towards reinvestment in energy efficiency and away from other economic activity, reducing the negative rebound effect. Governments can also require companies above a certain size to invest in eco-efficiency opportunities with a designated payback period, (say, initially one- to two-year payback periods, then ramped up over time to three- to four- and then four- to eight-year payback periods), to ensure that savings from short-term eco-efficiency gains are invested in further eco-efficiency opportunities. To ensure that this does not just delay and make the negative rebound even larger, a portfolio policy approach is needed. Government policies and incentives are needed to require companies to go further than simply eco-efficiency and also invest in, for instance, onsite co-generation, renewable energy and other sustainability initiatives such as onsite rainwater harvesting. Government policies, incentives, rebates, education and information can powerfully influence how people and businesses choose to reinvest their financial savings from eco-efficiency initiatives and thus significantly reduce the negative rebound effect and instead encourage positive amplification effects. Governments can do much to help businesses and households move on from just simplistic focus on 'efficiency alone' to encourage them to invest in other initiatives that reduce environmental pressures. Governments can do this by using a range of policies, such as:

- mandatory renewable energy targets supported by feed-in tariffs to encourage the direct substitution for renewable energy from fossil fuel-based energy;
- product stewardship, recycling and waste reduction policies and targets;
- limitations to carbon based energy use and excessive use of natural resources (by physical caps, rationing or higher prices) – using financial instruments to ensure that the price of energy, water and other materials remains relatively constant while the efficiency of their use increases can reduce direct and indirect rebound effects;
- capturing a percentage of the financial benefit from efficiency gains to invest in greening activities, such as national infrastructure improvements and natural resource/habitat restoration, through the use of carbon/ecological taxation.

Notes

1   Fukasaku, Y. (1999) 'Stimulating environmental innovation', *The STI Review*, no 25, issue 2, OECD, Paris.
2   Dunchin, F. and Lange, G. M. (1994) *The Future of the Environment: Ecological Economics and Technological Change*, Oxford University Press, Oxford.
3   Lovins, A. and Datta, E. K. et al (2004) *Winning the Oil Endgame: Innovation for Profits, Jobs, and Security*, Rocky Mountain Institute, Earthscan, London.
4   OECD (2008) *Key Environmental Indicators*, OECD, Paris.
5   UNECE (1994) *The 1994 Oslo Protocol on Further Reduction of Sulphur Emissions*, United Nations Economic Commission for Europe, Geneva, Switzerland.
6   Hodges, H. (1997) *Cost of Complying with Environmental Regulations Almost Always Less than Advertised*, Economic Policy Institute, Washington, DC.
7   Ekins, P. (2000) *Economic Growth and Environmental Sustainability*, Routledge Publishing, New York, Chapter 10: 'Sustainability and sulphur emissions: The case of the UK, 1970–2010'.
8   OECD (2004) *OECD Environmental Strategy: Review of Progress*, OECD, Paris, p16.
8A   Stasinopoulos, P., Smith, M., Hargroves, K. and Desha, C. (2008) Whole System Design: An Integrated Approach to Sustainable Engineering, Earthscan, London, and The Natural Edge Project, Australia.
9   Roelofs, C. R., Moure-Eraso, R. and Ellenbecker, M. (2007) 'Pollution prevention and the work environment: The Massachusetts experience', *Applied Occupational and Environmental Hygiene*, vol 15, no 11, pp834–850.
10   Hargroves, K. and Smith, M. (eds) (2005) *The Natural Advantage of Nations: Business Opportunities, Innovation and Governance in the 21st Century*, The Natural Edge Project, Earthscan, London.
11   World Commission on Environment and Development (WCED) (1987) *Our Common Future*, Oxford University Press, Oxford.

12   Department of Environment, Transport and the Regions (2000) 'General Guidelines on Environmental Reporting – Consultation Draft', Department for Environment, Food and Rural Affairs, UK.

13   WRI (2009) 'Earth Trends – Environmental Information Portal', World Resources Institute, Washington, DC.

14   UK Cabinet Office (2001) *Resource Productivity: Making More with Less*, the Strategy Unit, Cabinet Office, London.

15   The Climate Group (2005) *Carbon Down, Profits Up*, the Climate Group, UK.

16   Murdoch, R. (2007) 'Rupert Murdoch's speech on climate neutrality', *The Australian*, 10 May.

17   von Weizsäcker, E., Hargroves, K., Smith, M., Desha, C. and Stasinopoulos, P. (2009) *Factor Five: Transforming the Global Economy through 80% Improvements in Resource Productivity*, Earthscan, London.

18   Earthtrends (2009) 'Economics, Business and the Environment Searchable Database', World Resources Institute, using data from: Development Data Group (2008) *2008 World Development Indicators Online*, the World Bank, Washington, DC.

19   Clinton Climate Initiative (2008) 'C40 Cities: Buildings, Freiburg, Germany', Clinton Climate Initiative, New York, US.

20   Grameen Shakti (undated) Homepage, www.gshakti.org/, accessed 30 June 2009.

21   US EPA (2004) 'Boston's Saunders Hotel Group awarded for energy efficiency and good environmental practices', Press Release, 18 November, US EPA.

22   Boyd, B. K. and Gove, S. (2000) 'Nucor Corporation and the US steel industry', in Hitt, M. A., Ireland, R. D. and Hoskisson, R. E. (eds) *Strategic Management: Competitiveness and Globalization,* fourth edition, Southwestern Publishing, Oklahoma, US.

23   Worrell, E., Price, L. and Galitsky, C. (2004) *Emerging Energy-Efficient Technologies in Industry: Case Studies of Selected Technologies*, Ernest Orlando Lawrence Berkeley National Laboratory, Environmental Energy Technologies Division, Berkeley, CA.

24   Smith, M., Hargroves, K. Desha, C. and Stasinopoulos, P. (2009) 'Factor 5 in eco-cements', *CSIRO ECOS Magazine*, no 149.

25   CSIRO (undated) 'Geopolymers: Building blocks of the future', www.csiro.au/science/ps19e.html, accessed 4 September 2008.

26   Catalyst Paper Corporation (undated) 'Environmental manufacturing principles', Catalyst Paper Corporation, British Columbia, Canada.

27   Worrell, E., Price, L. and Galitsky, C. (2004) *Emerging Energy-Efficient Technologies in Industry: Case Studies of Selected Technologies*, Ernest Orlando Lawrence Berkeley National Laboratory, Environmental Energy Technologies Division, Berkeley, CA.

28   Google (undated) 'Efficient computing – Step 1: Efficient servers', Google, www.google.com/corporate/green/datacenters/step1.html, accessed 4 April 2010.

29   Google (undated) 'Efficient computing – Introduction', Google, www.google.com/corporate/green/datacenters/step1.html, accessed 4 April 2010.

30   Faramarzi, R., Coburn, B. and Sarhadian, R. (2002) *Performance and Energy Impact of Installing Glass Doors on an Open Vertical Deli/Dairy Display Case*, American Society of Heating, Refrigerating, and Air-Conditioning Engineers (ASHRAE), Winter meetings, Atlanta, US.

31   Tesco (2008) *Sustainability Report: More than the Weekly Shop: Corporate Responsibility Review*, Tesco Inc., Dallas, TX.

32   Whole Foods Market (2008) *Whole Foods Market 2008 Annual Report,* Whole Foods Market, Austin, TX.

33   Bordeaux Quay (undated) 'Eco pages: Saving energy', Bordeaux Quay, www.bordeaux-quay.co.uk/ecopages/eco_saving_energy.php, accessed 4 April 2010.

34   Sonnenberg, B. (2009) 'Berlin's carbon-neutral eatery', *The Associated Press,* 21 January.

35   Carvalho, M. D. (2007) 'The Acorn House bears fruit', *Community Energy,* July.

36   Light Rail Now (2008) 'CTrain light rail growth continues with north east extension', News Release, January, Light Rail Now, TX.

37   Northern Territory government (2007) 'NT greenhouse gas emissions – Transport', www.nt.gov.au/nreta/environment/greenhouse/emissions/transport.html, accessed 4 April 2010.

38   Newman, P. and Kenworthy, J. (2007) 'Transportation energy in global cities: Sustainability comes in from the cold', *Natural Resources Forum,* vol 25, no 2, pp91–107.

39   Freight on Rail (2009) 'Useful facts and figures', Freight on Rail, www.freightonrail.org.uk/FactsFigures.htm, accessed 9 April 2009; Frey, C. and Kuo, P. (2007) 'Assessment of potential reduction in greenhouse gas (GHG) emissions in freight transportation', *Proceedings, International Emission Inventory Conference,* US Environmental Protection Agency, Raleigh, NC, 15–17 May.

40   von Weizsäcker, E., Hargroves, K., Smith, M., Desha, C. and Stasinopoulos, P. (2009) *Factor Five: Transforming the Global Economy through 80% Improvements in Resource Productivity,* Earthscan, London.

41   Shirley, W. (2006) *Decoupling Utility Profits From Sales,* Prepared for Arizona Decoupling Stakeholder Meeting, Regulatory Assistance Project (RAP), Vermont.

42   California Energy Commission (2009) *US Per Capita Electricity Use by State in 2005,* California Energy Commission, Sacramento, CA.

43   Stern, N. (2006) *The Stern Review: The Economics of Climate Change,* Executive Summary, Cambridge University Press, Cambridge, p10.

44   Ekins, P. (2000) *Economic Growth and Environmental Sustainability,* Routledge Publishing, London and New York.

45   OECD (2008) *OECD Environmental Outlook to 2030,* OECD, Paris.

46   Chong, S. K. (2005) 'Anmyeon-do recreation forest: A millennium of management', in Durst, P. et al *In Search of Excellence: Exemplary Forest Management in Asia and the Pacific,* Asia-Pacific Forestry Commission, FAO Regional Office for Asia and the Pacific, Bangkok, pp251–259.

47   US EPA (1999) *The Benefits and Costs of the Clean Air Act 1990 to 2010,* US Environmental Protection Agency, Washington, DC.

48   Hawken, P., Lovins, A. and Lovins, L. H. (1999) *Natural Capitalism: Creating the Next Industrial Revolution,* Earthscan, London.

49   OECD (2001) *OECD Environmental Outlook,* OECD, Paris.

50   OECD (2008) *OECD Environmental Data Compendium,* OECD, Paris.

51   OECD (2008) *OECD Environmental Data Compendium,* OECD, Paris.

52   Netherlands Environmental Assessment Agency (2007) *Environmental Balance 2007,* Netherlands Environmental Assessment Agency (MNP), Bilthoven, the Netherlands.

53   Weaver, P., Jansen, L., Van Grootveld, G., Van Spiegel, E. and Vergragt, P. (2000) *Sustainable Technology Development,* Greenleaf Publishing, Sheffield, UK.

54   Weaver, P., Jansen, L., Van Grootveld, G., Van Spiegel, E., and Vergragt, P. (2000) *Sustainable Technology Development,* Greenleaf Publishing, Sheffield, UK, see the

back cover.

55   Hargroves, K. and Smith, M. (2005) *The Natural Advantage of Nations: Business Opportunities, Innovation and Governance in the 21st Century*, The Natural Edge Project, Earthscan, London.

56   Econstats (2008) 'Netherlands, GDP, current prices', www.econstats.com/weo/C114V019.htm, accessed 27 August 2008; NFIA (2007) *Greenhouse Gas Emissions Down in the Netherlands*, Netherlands Foreign Investment Agency.

57   Eurostat (2008) *Final Energy Consumption of Petroleum Products*, European Commission.

58   Refer to the following for further information: Jansen, L., Weaver, P. and van Dam, R. (2008) 'Education to meet new challenges in a networked society', in Larkley, J. E. and Maynhard, V. B. (2008) *Innovation in Education*, Nova Science Publishers Inc., Hauppage, NY; Jansen, L. (2008) 'Higher education's contribution for sustainable development: The road to take', Special contribution to the Fourth International Barcelona Conference on Higher Education, Higher Education in the World 2008: New Challenges, Changing roles, Steering a Course for Human and Social Development, 31 March, Palgrave Macmillan, Hampshire, UK, www.dhovlaanderen.be/files/Higher%20Education%20contribution%20for%20SD%20-%20Prof.%20Jansen.pdf.

59   UN (2007) *Agriculture and Sustainable Development in the Netherlands*, Agenda 21, United Nations, p13.

60   Rabobank (2007) *Greenhouse Horticulture, from Bulk Energy User to Energy Supplier!* Rabobank Group A, Netherlands.

61   Profetas (undated) 'Protein foods, environment technology and society', www.profetas.nl, Profetas.

62   STW (2008) *Novel Protein Foods: Consumer Oriented Technology Development*, Technologiestitchting STW, Netherlands.

63   Profetas (2008) 'Societal transitions', www.profetas.nl, Profetas.

64   Zhu, X. and van Ierland, E. C. (2005) 'A model for consumers' preferences for novel protein foods and environmental quality', *Economic Modelling*, vol 22, no 4, pp720–744.

65   Aiking, H., de Boer, J. and Vereijken, J. (eds) (2006) 'Sustainable protein production and consumption: Pigs or peas?', *Environment and Policy*, vol 45.

66   VROM (2007) *International Water Association*, Netherlands government.

67   For further information on this programme refer to: Brink, P. (2002) *Voluntary Environmental Agreements: Process, Practice and Future Use*, Greenleaf Publishing, Sheffield, UK.

68   KNAW (2008) *National School in Process Technology (OSPT) – Organic Chemical Technology*, Royal Academy of Netherlands Arts and Science, Netherlands.

69   Market Wire (2008) 'DSM reports best quarter ever and raises full-year outlook', *Market Wire*, July.

70   Biomat.net (2007) 'BIOSAFOR: Biosaline agroforestry: Remediation of saline wastelands through the production of biosaline biomass (for bioenergy, fodder and biomaterials)', CPL Press, Berks, UK.

71   ENC (2006) *First Dutch Hydrogen Car: Made by ECN*, Energieonderzoek Centrum Nederland, Petten, Netherlands.

72   The Engineer Online (2006) *Shell Hydrogen Signs Dutch Bus MoU*, Centaur Media PLC, UK.

73   Hinterberger, F. (2001) *Adaptive Integration of Research and Policy for Sustainable Development – Prospects for the European Research Area*, Project No STPA – 2001-00007.

74 Robèrt, K. H., Schmidt-Bleek, F., Aloisi de Larderel, J., Basile, G., Jansen, J. L., Kuehr, R., Price Thomas, P., Suzuki, M., Hawken, P. and Wackernagel, M. (2002) 'Strategic sustainable development – selection, design and synergies of applied tools', *Journal of Cleaner Production*, vol 10, no 3, pp197–214.

75 Holmberg, J. and Robèrt, K. H. (2000) 'Backcasting from non-overlapping sustainability principles – a framework for strategic planning', *International Journal of Sustainable Development and World Ecology*, vol 7, pp291–308.

76 van de Kerkhof, M. and Wieczorek, A. (2004) 'Learning and stakeholder partici-pation in transition processes towards sustainability: Methodological considerations', *Technological Forecasting & Social Change*, vol 72, pp733–747; van de Kerkhof, M. (2004) *Debating Climate Change: A study of Stakeholder Participation in an Integrated Assessment of Long Term Climate Policy*, Lemma Publishers Utrecht; Hisschemoller et al (2002) *Climate Options for the Long term*, Final Report, RIVM, Bilthoven.

77 Kemp, R. and Rotmans, J. (2005) '*The management of co-evolution of technical, environmental and social systems*', in Weber, M. and Hemmelskamp, J., *Towards Environmental Innovation Systems*, Springer, Berlin, Heidelberg, pp33–55; Martens, P. and Rotmans, J. (2002) *Transitions in a globalising world*, Swets&Zeitlinger B.V., Lisse.

78 Fokkema, J., Jansen, L. and Mulder, K. (2005) 'Sustainability: Necessity for a prosperous society', *International Journal of Sustainability in Higher Education*, vol 6, no 3; Jansen, L., Mulder, K. and Pessers, G. (2006) 'Building capacity for SD: An evaluation of experiences at Delft University of Technology', in Mulder, K., *Sustainability Made in Delft*, Eburon Academic Publishers, Delft, the Netherlands.

79 Weaver, P. et al (2000) *Sustainable Technology Development*, Greenleaf Publishing, Sheffield, UK.

80 Hargroves, K. and Smith, M. (eds) (2005) *The Natural Advantage of Nations: Business Opportunities, Innovation and Governance in the 21st Century*, The Natural Edge Project, Earthscan, London.

81 Kuznets, S. (1962) *The New Republic*, October 20, 1962, cited in Cobb, C., Halstead, T. and Rowe, J. (1995) 'If the GDP is Up, Why is America Down?', *The Atlantic Monthly*, October, p67.

82 Robert Kennedy (Attorney General of the US 1961–1964, US Senator 1964–1968). Most first year economics textbooks now discuss the limitations of the GDP measure by quoting Robert Kennedy, textbooks like Smith, B. (2003) *Principles of MacoEconomic Analysis*, Australian National University, Australia.

83 Bastiat, F. (1848) 'What is seen and what is not seen', in Cain, C. and de Huszar, G. (eds) (1995) *Selected Essays of Political Economy*, the Foundation for Economic Education, Inc., Irvington-on-Hudson, New York.

84 The debts governments incurred from the First World War sowed the seeds for economic recession in the 1930s which sowed the seeds for the Second World War.

85 Nordhaus, W. and Tobin, J. (1972) *Is Growth Obsolete?*, Columbia University Press, New York.

86 Daly, H. and Cobb, J. (1989) *For the Common Good*, Beacon Press, Boston, MA.

87 Hicks, J. R. (1962) *Value and Capital: An Inquiry into Some Fundamental Principles of Economic Theory*, Oxford University Press, Oxford.

88 Talberth, J., Cobb, C. and Slattery, N. (2006) *The Genuine Progress Indicator 2006: A Tool for Sustainable Development*, Redefining Progress, Oakland, CA.

89   Stiglitz, J. and Sen, A. et al (2009) *Report by the Commission on the Measurement of Economic Performance and Social Progress*, Commission on the Measurement of Economic Performance and Social Progress, http://media.ft.com/cms/f3b4c24a-a141-11de-a88d-00144feabdc0.pdf, accessed 4 April 2010.

90   For an overview of the methodology for calculation of environmental costs refer to Talberth, J., Cobb, C. and Slattery, N. (2006) *The Genuine Progress Indicator 2006: A Tool for Sustainable Development, Redefining Progress*, Oakland, CA.

91   Unlike its general meaning, 'investment' in GDP is meant very specifically as non-financial product purchases. Buying financial products is classed as 'saving', as opposed to investment. The distinction is (in theory) clear: if money is converted into goods or services, it is investment; but, if you buy a bond or a share of stock, this transfer payment is excluded from the GDP sum. Although such purchases would be called investments in normal speech, from the total economy point of view, this is simply swapping of deeds, and not part of the real economy or the GDP formula.

92   National Renewable Energy Laboratory (1996) *The Jobs Connection: Energy Use and Local Economic Development*, produced for the US Department of Energy (DOE), Washington, DC.

93   Smart Communities Network (undated) 'Green buildings success stories', www.smartcommunities.ncat.org/success/osage_muni.shtml, accessed 2 June 2008.

94   National Renewable Energy Laboratory (1996) *The Jobs Connection: Energy Use and Local Economic Development*, produced for the US Department of Energy. The document was produced by the Technical Information Program, under the DOE Office of Energy Efficiency and Renewable Energy.

95   Jevons, W. S. (1865) *The Coal Question: An Inquiry Concerning the Progress of the Nation, and the Probable Exhaustion of our Coal-mines*, third edition (1905) Flux, A. W. and Kelley, A. M. (eds), MacMillan and Co, New York.

96   Greening, L. A., Greene, D. L. and Difiglio, C. (2000) 'Energy efficiency and consumption – the rebound effect – a survey', *Energy Policy*, vol 28, pp389–401.

97   Vringer, K., Aalbers, T. and Blok, K. (2007) 'Household energy requirement and value patterns', *Energy Policy*, vol 35, pp553–566.

98   Ayres, R. U., Ayres, L. W. and Warr, B. (2003) 'Energy, power and work in the US economy, 1900–1998', *Energy*, vol 28, pp219–273.

99   Alcott, B. (2005) 'Jevons' paradox', *Ecological Economics*, vol 54, pp9–21; Schipper, L. (2000) 'Editorial: On the rebound: The interaction of energy efficiency, energy use and economic activity', *Energy Policy*, vol 28, pp351–353.

100   Informed by the unpublished paper, Murray, C. (2007) 'The fallacy of win-win outcomes in the economy-environment debate: Why environmental protection and restoration must come at cost – the higher the cost, the better'.

101   Ayers, R. U., Ayers, L. W. and Warr, B. (2003) 'Energy, power and work in the US economy', *Energy*, vol 28, pp219–273.

102   Shrestha, R. M. and Shrestha, R. (2004) 'Economics of clean development power projects under alternative approaches for setting baseline emissions', *Energy Policy*, vol 32, pp1363–1374.

103   Pears, A. (2004) *Energy Efficiency – Its Potential: Some Perspectives and Experiences*, Background paper for International Energy Agency Energy Efficiency Workshop, Paris.

104 Refer to the Townsville City Council CitySolar Community Capacity Building Program for further details, www.townsville.qld.gov.au/services/departments/ integ_sustainability/citisolar/index, accessed 4 April 2010.

3

Factors that can Undermine or Even Block Efforts to Achieve Decoupling

The Key Role of Government to Underpin and Accelerate Efforts to Achieve Decoupling

History shows that successful efforts to decouple economic growth from environmental pressures have been underpinned by effective government policies and strategies which address a range of market, institutional and information failures, as outlined in our first book, *The Natural Advantage of Nations: Business Opportunities, Innovation and Governance in the 21st Century*. Such efforts are usually initiated through a response to some form of disaster, or to respond to growing costs or political pressure related to an environmental issue. For instance, after the famous December 1952 smog in London, which killed thousands of people as a result of the high level of pollution, new regulations were put in place restricting the use of fuels in industry and households to ensure that cleaner forms of energy were used to reduce air pollution. These included the Clean Air Acts of 1956 and 1968, and the City of London (Various Powers) Act of 1954.[1] Reflecting on this situation, Grossman and Krueger state:

> *Even for those dimensions of environmental quality where economic growth seems to have been associated with improving conditions, there is no reason to believe that the process has been an automatic one. In principle, environmental quality might improve automatically when countries develop if they substitute cleaner technologies for dirtier ones, or if there is a very*

pronounced effect on pollution of the typical patterns of structural transformation ... However, a review of the available evidence on instances of pollution abatement suggests that the strongest link between income and pollution in fact is via an induced policy response ...[2]

Governments have a key role to play in guiding, preparing and, in some cases, policing societies to effectively reduce environmental pressures while continuing to grow economies. From reducing perverse subsidies that exacerbate environmental pressures, to providing incentives for low-impact alternatives, there is much that governments can do to underpin efforts by business and industry to prepare for and capture the opportunity of the 'next wave of innovation', that of sustainable development.

For instance governments can:

- Provide rigorous information on the risks and opportunities related to various environmental pressures (*through government scientific research organizations, such as the Commonwealth Scientific and Industrial Research Organization (CSIRO) in Australia, or through funding academic research*).
- Provide funding for related research and development to identify and commercialize innovative solutions to cost effectively reduce environmental pressures (*through national research bodies and grant-providing government departments*).
- Initiate and commit to a research programme, like the Netherlands Sustainable Technology Development programme (as discussed in Chapter 2) that undertakes research on the questions of 'What scale and speed of decoupling of economic growth from environmental pressures is needed to ensure the achievement of environmentally sustainable development' and 'How to achieve large-scale decoupling quickly and cost effectively across all the major environmental pressures for each nation?'
- Reform national systems of innovation to effectively embed and operationalize sustainable development research goals. How to do this is outlined, in detail, in Chapter 13 of our first publication *The Natural Advantage of Nations: Business Opportunities, Innovation and Governance in the 21st Century*.
- Ensure that there is a level playing field for all businesses (*as businesses will be willing to adapt and change to environmental policy as long as all businesses in their sector and market are also required to do so*).
- Provide business and industry with a clear regulatory environment to be able to plan and make investments with confidence (*such as the use of ecological taxes which provides certainty about the level of taxation over long periods of time*).
- Identify energy- and resource-intensive sectors that make a significant contribution to environmental pressures and provide incentives and low-

interest loans for retrofitting of existing plants and the building of new low-carbon plants (*which may, for instance, involve the investment of ecological taxation revenues*).

- Identify where extractive industries are operating at above sustainable yields and assist a transition and structural adjustment to bring back extraction levels to within ecologically sustainable limits (*such as in the management of fisheries and native forests*).
- Review current government policy to identify policies that are blocking efforts to reduce environmental pressures (*such as subsidies for fossil fuel energy*).
- Develop appropriate programmes to target specific areas of action, for instance through encouraging and even requiring a level of improvement in resource productivity for business, government departments and the education sector (*such as the Chinese Top-1000 Enterprises Energy Efficiency Programme*).
- Provide a well-planned and transparent phasing-in of policy changes or new ecological controls or taxes to allow adequate time for industry and business responses (*much like the long lead times on the EU's electronic waste directives*).
- Assist particular industries to develop specific action plans for reducing their environmental pressures, particularly through working with peak industry sector representative groups (*such as the Australian Plantation, Timber Products and Paper Council's Sustainability Action Plan*).
- Control fraudulent claims of companies or products reducing environmental pressures, referred to as 'green-washing', and further add credibility to legitimate actions to do so (*such as through supporting third party independently certified eco-labelling programmes, setting requirements for performance, and applying strong penalties for illegitimate claims*).
- Invest in the ecological infrastructure of the nation to preserve biodiversity and restore habitat and ecosystems upon which the whole economy depends.
- Work with international efforts to harmonize and ratchet up environmental regulations (*as differences in regulatory requirements to reduce environmental pressures in different countries can lead to industry groups running campaigns against such legislation. Such campaigns can undermine and reduce political will for the implementation of much-needed environmental policies, programmes and R&D to underpin decoupling*).
- Work with international efforts to reduce poverty and corruption and reduce the occurrence of preventable disease, (*for instance Denmark, Norway, Sweden and Luxembourg have committed 0.7 per cent of national GDP to assisting other countries' efforts in poverty reduction*).

Options such as these have long been advocated by sustainability experts to assist nations achieve their full potential in respect to decoupling whilst also giving the best chance of such efforts being embraced globally. However, apart from in a few outstanding countries, such as the Germany, Norway, Sweden, Finland, the Netherlands and Costa Rica, such options are generally not employed to their full potential. There are many reasons for this, such as the short-term cycle of political office, given the three- to four-year time horizon, which makes it difficult to plan, let alone create, binding legislation for a nation's future much beyond this period. If two to three administrations come and go, some 12 years can pass without meaningful future planning by the government. Such efforts are further undermined by poverty, corruption, inequality and conflict, with the negative impacts of each on decoupling efforts discussed in Chapter 4. Another major factor in their having been insufficient efforts made by most nations arises from the lack of integration of sustainable development in the central agencies of government such as the treasury, finance, industry/commerce and defence departments. *Our Common Future* emphasized the need here for institutional reform, writing that:

> *Governments, pressured by their citizens, saw the need to clean up the mess ... and established agencies to do this in the 1970s ... but much of their work has been after-the-fact and repair of the damage once it is done. The mandates of the central economic and sectoral ministries are also often too narrow, too concerned with quantities of production or [economic] growth. The present challenge is to give the central economic and sectoral ministries the responsibility for the quality of those parts of the environment affected by their decisions, and to give the environmental agencies more power to cope with the effects of unsustainable development.*

Just over two decades since, the central agencies of most governments are just as concerned with achieving higher economic growth and higher levels of production as they were in 1987. Nevertheless, today a few treasury departments have embraced new ways of ensuring that their decisions take into account potential future environmental negative externalities. Hence, one of the goals of this book is to encourage the use of a *decoupling framework* by the central (treasury, finance, etc.) and environmental agencies, giving them a clear framework to which they can both commit and work together on. A decoupling framework, which includes the twin goals of economic development and the reduction of environmental pressures, provides governments with a clear measure and indicator on which central agencies and environment departments can work together to improve every nation's performance.

Such a new approach is urgently needed because most nations currently have insufficient cooperation across government departments/agencies to enable a truly whole of government approach to develop and successfully implement the purposeful policy and structural adjustment programmes needed to achieve the level of decoupling required. This state of affairs not only increases the risk of damage to the environment affecting the economy as a whole, it also creates significant risk for individual companies. First, this is due to the fact that, as outlined in Chapter 1, the race is on by nations and companies to lead the next wave of innovation in sustainable development. As the Deutsche Bank showed, in their 2010 report entitled *The Green Economy: The Race is On*,[2A] there have been over 154 significant climate change policy changes in a six-month period from October 2009 to March 2010 to help nations position themselves and their domestic companies at the head of this new wave of innovation. Second, nations and companies that do not manage their natural resources sustainably risk exhausting such resources and whole industries collapsing, as happened during the 1990s for the Atlantic cod-fishing industry. Finally, whether considering companies or nations, those that currently have a low, or compliance-level, commitment to achieving relatively easy levels of decoupling will inevitably be faced with an imperative to significantly improve performance over a short period of time, as shown in Figure 3.1. Many are likely to realize too late that they are unprepared. On the other hand, those companies and nations that have achieved leading practices, or even best practice, are likely to be much better placed to make significant improvements when required as they will have a base of experience upon which to confidently build to quickly achieve large-scale decoupling across a range of environmental pressures.

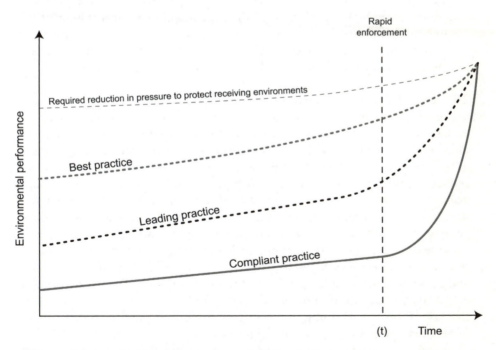

Figure 3.1 *A stylized representation of the level of commitment to reducing environmental pressure over time, for three performance scenarios*

Source: Desha, C. and Hargroves, K. (2009)[3]

Essentially there may be considered to be three commitment scenarios facing any organization across business, government, industry and civil society, namely:

1   Compliant practice: This is the level of commitment to reducing environmental pressure that is required by government legislation and regulatory controls. For instance, it might represent the volumes of various toxic substances that can be released into waterways, a specific level of energy performance rating for a commercial building or appliance, or a price instrument placed on a particular pollution such as greenhouse gas emissions. The term 'beyond compliance' is also gaining increasing popularity as a way to describe practices that aim for more than compliance, but are not leading practice.
2   Leading practice: These are the businesses, organizations or communities who see the need to reduce environmental pressures beyond the mandated levels and who have found cost-effective and even profitable ways to deliver higher levels of performance. This may be motivated by brand development, preparation for future increases in requirements, attracting and retaining top staff concerned about environmental pressures, and to strategically position themselves for future work.
3   Best practice: This is the outstanding, flagship practice that demonstrates significantly higher performance than the mandated levels. These efforts are also motivated by the same aspects that motivate leading practice, but they distinguish themselves by going further than any other in their sector (refer to *Factor Five*[4] for a detailed presentation of such efforts).

The very top line, the 'required reduction', represents the level of environmental pressure the receiving environment can handle or assimilate without damage to the system – thus as environmental pressures persist this requirement will increase as the health and resilience of the receiving systems is adversely affected. As each of the three scenarios are less than the required reduction, the level of environmental pressure will continue increasing to a point (t) where the negative impacts can no longer be further discussed, debated or largely ignored, and at this point there will be a steep increase in compliant practice requirements to protect economic growth. For example, in the case of overfishing and the southern bluefin tuna, mandatory requirements to reduce catch sizes were too low to protect the viability of the overall catch and thus led to a dramatic decrease in fish catch volumes. The period of rapid enforcement that followed involved sudden and strict controls on catches. In the case of global warming, the result of compliant practice (which varies between countries) was estimated to result in the release of around 46 billion tonnes of greenhouse gas emissions ($GtCO_2e$) in 2005, with only a small number of leading and best practice examples. Considering that the planet's ability to accommodate greenhouse gases is close to just 10 billion tonnes per year, we are beginning to see a range of environmental impacts approaching time (t) where the damage reaches a critical point that triggers rapid enforcement. This may be a certain level of sea rise, a certain level of Arctic ice melting, a certain amount of loss of productivity in agriculture, a certain level of coral reef bleaching or a combination of such events. Hence reductions in the order of 80 per cent are required, and are now being shown to be both achievable and cost effective in works such as *Factor Five*.

In looking at Figure 3.1, it is clear that even terms such as 'compliant practice' or 'best practice' are somewhat misleading in inferring good stewardship, given that actual compliance is often so far below what is needed to protect the environment. Furthermore, even the leading and best practice scenarios still require improvement at time (t), leaving organizations and governments currently operating at 'compliance' with significant risks with regard to future capacity and economic implications. There are many reasons why, on the whole, the level of compliant practice is well below the requirements of the receiving environmental system, such as uncertainty around the level of requirement of receiving systems, uncertainty around the impact that reducing environmental pressures will have on businesses and the economy, and pressure from powerful interests to keep compliance levels low. These uncertainties and pressures coupled with the short-term nature of many national governments means that little long-term planning is done. Hence this leads to limited levels of support from governments to improve performance higher than compliance levels. Forward-thinking businesses, organizations and citizens are put in a difficult position, as they can see the impending imperative to reduce pressure, but they are not required to do so, and in many cases would be penalized or blocked from acting.

When considering the pressures being applied to governments to maintain low levels of compliance there are four main contenders that need to be addressed:

1 fear of loss of profitability;
2 fear of losing international competitiveness;
3 fear of job losses;
4 fear of skills shortages and gaps.

Responding to the Fear of Loss of Profitability

Business and industry groups have historically been wary of, and often opposed to, the introduction of environmental policies because they have feared the costs of compliance would adversely affect their bottom line. For example, a number of OECD governments have decided not to introduce energy or carbon taxes due to strong and concerted opposition from energy-intensive industries like steel, aluminium and cement. This is especially true of companies who rely on exports for overall profitability ('trade exposed'), due to competing companies operating under less stringent regulatory conditions in other countries, particularly in developing countries. Some corporations have even threatened to relocate if such strengthening of environmental regulations takes place; the reality of which will be investigated in the next part of this chapter.

Governments today have a range of policy options to effectively respond to concerns about potential loss of profitability. The EU regulatory framework on the Registration, Evaluation and Authorization of Chemicals (REACH) is a good example of how effective policy processes, balanced cost–benefit analysis, and consultation, has helped to overcome fears of increased environmental regulation.[5] Before its introduction in 2007, the REACH framework faced significant resistance from the chemical industry because of the expected impact of higher compliance costs on sectoral competitiveness. Such close consultations with the industry and other stakeholders, extensive cost–benefit impact assessments, and a staged approach to policy implementation (now a standard feature in the EU), were crucial in allaying businesses' fears and enabling the eventual adoption of REACH. Such consultative efforts to address competitiveness concerns about environmental policies will be vitally important to enable the achievement of decoupling more broadly over the coming decades.

The OECD's research in this area, based on many years of experience, has found that a portfolio policy approach, utilizing a variety of government mechanisms and policies (see Table 3.1), is the most effective strategy to underpin the decoupling of economic growth and environmental pressures which ensures minimal negative effects to business competitiveness. The OECD writes that:

> *Significant environmental improvement can be achieved at relatively low cost to the economy and with little negative social impact if the right mix of policies is used. The necessary policies and technological solutions to tackle the key environmental challenges are both available and affordable. Even for a single environmental problem, an instrument mix may be needed given the often complex and inter-connected nature of many environmental challenges, the often large number and variety of sources exerting pressure on the environment, and the many market and information failures. Instrument mixes need to be carefully constructed to ensure that they achieve a given environmental goal in an effective and economically efficient manner, while providing consumers and producers with flexibility in how they meet the targets, so as to enable innovation. Social or equity impacts should be addressed. Instrument mixes should provide clear, short- and long-term policy signals to support appropriate investment decisions. The policy instruments used in a mix should be complementary and reinforcing, rather than duplicative or conflicting.[6]*

Strong examples of effectively combining policy instruments, that have now been extensively documented, include the German best available technology (BAT) legislation,[7] and the use of 'feebates'.[8] The BAT legislation does not involve mandating specific technologies. But rather the German government upwardly adjusts standards that industry has to meet based on the standards met by the best and most cost-effective available technologies. In theory then, whenever a new and improved technology is created globally, German industry is expected to meet the environmental standard achieved by that technology. Of course, regulatory practice is more flexible, ambiguous and much less instantaneous, and is also subject to industry pressure. However, it has provided a significant incentive for German firms to develop new technologies that make it cheaper for them to meet the competition from the best available technologies globally.

Feebates provide a fee on the most environmentally harmful brands of a certain product, and a rebate on the most environmentally benign products. The fee on harmful products provides the income to governments which allows them to then offer the rebate to encourage consumers to purchase more benign products. The feebate scheme is thus geared to be as close to revenue neutral as possible. Operationally, feebates are also quite simple. For example, if you were to buy a new car, or were extending the registration of a car, you would pay an extra fee if the car is deemed an inefficient user of fuel, or alternatively get a rebate if it is fuel efficient. The neutral point would be set so that fees and rebates balanced, so that it does not become an inflationary measure or a disguised tax. To reduce administrative costs, feebates can also be targeted at those consumer products that have the largest ongoing environmental impacts, such as cars and, within the home, refrigerators, washing machines and air-conditioners. A key benefit of feebates is that they can ensure industry knows there will be clear market signals to the consumer to purchase more efficient products, thereby stimulating innovation in this direction. However, government still needs to work with industry to phase in feebates, to ensure industry has time to respond.

When such policy options are used to encourage lower impact operations and products, this helps drive innovation. As Professor Michael Porter from the Harvard Business School, wrote as far back as 1991:

> As other nations have pushed ahead, US trade has suffered. Germany has had perhaps the world's tightest regulations in stationary air-pollution control, and German companies appear to hold a wide lead in patenting and exporting air-pollution and other environmental technologies. As much as 70 per cent of the air pollution-control equipment sold in the US today is produced by foreign companies. Britain is another case in point. As its environmental standards have lagged, Britain's ratio of exports to imports in environmental technology has fallen from 8:1 to 1:1 over the past decade. In contrast, the US leads in those areas

in which its regulations have been the strictest, such as pesticides and the remediation of environmental damage. Such leads should be treasured and extended. Environmental protection is a universal need, an area of growing expenditure in all the major national economies and a major export industry. The strongest proof that environmental protection does not hamper competitiveness is the economic performance of nations with the strictest laws.[9]

Table 3.1, provides an overview of the range of options and approaches available to governments to allow them to take a lead with industry and the community, to underpin decoupling efforts in a way that does not harm competitiveness of industry, but rather potentially improves it.

There is a great deal of experience in Europe of using combinations of different policy options to respond to competitiveness concerns from business and industry. This experience is well captured in the 2008 *OECD Environmental Outlook to 2030* publication[10] and related publications by the OECD:[11]

[Designed well,] in some cases, environmental policies may actually enhance the economic competitiveness of targeted sectors or industries. Firms that are forced to 'clean up' can gain market advantages, either by being the first to exploit 'green' markets or by moving into new technologies that can in turn be marketed or lead to efficiency savings.

OECD Environmental Outlook to 2030, 2008

This sentiment is supported by a mounting body of evidence. Innovest's extensive 2004 report, *Corporate Environmental Governance: A Study into the Influence of Environmental Governance and Financial Performance*, found 'strong evidence for the existence of a positive relationship between environmental governance and financial performance. In 51 of the 60 studies reviewed, a positive correlation was found between environmental governance and financial performance ... results from fund, sector and company analysts are all generally positive.'[12] Innovest's extensive study clearly showed that, sector by sector, companies that are environmental leaders are financially outperforming the laggards.[13] Furthermore, an extensive range of research literature shows clear links between improved environmental performance and a company's financial results.[14]

In 2007 at the United Nations Summit on Corporate Responsibility, Goldman Sachs released a report which found that environmental sustainability leaders outperformed the general stock market by 25 per cent over the previous two years and outperformed their same-sector peers by almost 75 per cent over the same period.[15] Markets in environmentally sustainable solutions are also booming, as shown in Table 3.2.

Table 3.1 *Policy instruments to address loss of profitability and underpin decoupling efforts*

Policy option	Policy overview
Regulatory instruments	Regulatory instruments include, for example, bans on certain products or practices, emission standards, ambient quality standards, technology standards, requirements for the application of certain ('best available') technologies, obligations for operational permits, land use planning and zoning. While these can make environmental outcomes more certain, such regulations tend to be far more effective if they focus on an environmental outcome rather than, for example, specifying the technologies to be used. This provides business with more incentive to find the lowest-cost approaches to achieve the required environmental outcome.
Ecologically inspired taxes ('ecological taxes')	Ecological taxes are a method to ensure that prices of goods and services are influenced by their negative environmental impacts.[16] The strength of a taxation-based approach is that it can provide a clear and predictable level of additional costs for goods and services that carry high environmental pressure burdens, such as greenhouse gas emissions, toxic and hazardous waste production, and destruction of biodiversity. This then allows for a level of certainty for business of the current and future expected costs of such taxes to balance with the costs of acting to reduce these pressures.
Tradable allowance systems	Tradable allowance systems set limits, either as a *maximum* ceiling for 'cap and trade' schemes, or as a *minimum* performance commitment for 'baseline and credit' schemes. The limits can be either in absolute terms or in relative terms, and the permits can be denominated either in terms of rights to emit pollutants (e.g. greenhouse gas emissions), or rights to access natural resources (e.g. water, fish stocks). Cap and trade systems, however, unlike ecological taxation, deliver an uncertain price for tradable allowances that provides significant risk to business when forecasting such costs or encumbrances to consider them against the investment to reduce environmental pressures. However, in the absence of political strength a trading-based system can at least offer a real price for environmental pressures – the risk can be reduced through the purchase of futures, although this brings its own level of risk.
Subsidies for environmental improvement	Currently the majority of government subsidies go to industry practices which carry high environmental pressures, referred to as 'perverse subsidies'. Instead, these subsidies could be used to encourage environmental improvement by encouraging the diffusion of lower-impact products, processes and behaviours. Further incentives can be used to develop lower impact infrastructure such as energy generation plant, along with environmental regeneration projects that can lead to offsets to reduce the burden of ecological taxes or emissions trading schemes.
Voluntary approaches	Governments can enter into voluntary agreements with industry whereby industry agrees to meet certain targets and in return government will hold back on bringing in new policy and regulation. Voluntary agreements are a useful way to get buy-in from business and industry on the need for action, but their effectiveness has to be carefully assessed, and they need careful monitoring and reporting. History shows that voluntary approaches are most useful when used in combination with other policy instruments, or during a phase-in period for the use of another policy instrument.

Source: Based on OECD (2008)[17]

Table 3.2 *Fast-growing markets associated with decoupling environmental pressures*

Market growth	Overview
Investment with environmental and social sustainability criteria	Over 360 investment firms, totalling more than US$14 trillion worth of investments, have now signed the UN Principles of Responsible Investment and 60 banks have endorsed the Equator Principles (EPs), an international standard of sustainability investment for large investments.[18] The EPs are fast becoming the global standard for project finance and have transformed the funding of major projects globally. In 2007, of the US$74.6 billion total debt tracked in emerging markets, US$52.9 billion was subject to the EPs, representing about 71% of total project finance debt in emerging market economies.[19]
Renewable energy	Since 2003, clean energy technologies including solar, biofuels, geothermal, tidal and hydropower have produced more electricity globally than the total energy created by nuclear power plants. Global investment in renewable energies jumped to a record US$100 billion in 2006 according to the UN Environment Programme (UNEP).[20] US bank Morgan Stanley has estimated that global sales from clean energy sources like wind, solar and geothermal power and biofuels could grow to as much as US$1 trillion a year by 2030 and a Cambridge Energy Research Associates 2008 report predicts that alternative energy investments will top US$7 trillion by 2030.[21]
Eco-tourism	Emerging in the 1990s, eco-tourism has been growing 20–34% per year.[22] In 2004, eco/nature tourism was growing globally three times faster than the tourism industry as a whole.[23] According to the International Ecotourism Society, sustainable tourism could grow to 25% of the world's travel market by 2012, taking the value of the sector to approximately US$473 billion a year.[24]
Organic agriculture	With global revenue surpassing US$25 billion annually, organic agriculture is a highly visible and rapidly growing market.[25]
Recycling and remanufacturing	In the US the remanufacturing market is now worth almost US$53 billion. The US recycling sector is worth over US$250 billion a year. A report for the National Recycling Coalition[26] found that the industry in the US created more than 56,000 public and private sector recycling facilities, with 1.1 million jobs, US$236 billion in gross annual sales, and US$37 billion in annual payroll.

Source: Compiled by Smith, M., Hargroves, K., with sources as cited

Given such growing opportunities, many industry representative groups are now shifting from a focus on blocking efforts to reduce environmental pressures, to supporting members to capitalize on the opportunities presented, particularly ahead of inevitable government regulation, given the state of the environment as outlined previously. For example, in Australia there are a number of industry bodies that are seeking to actively inform members of the strategic considerations of reducing environmental pressure, including a number of strategies and frameworks that have been directly informed by The Natural Edge Project, including the Australian Council for Infrastructure and Development's Sustainability Framework,[27] Australian Plantation Products and Paper Industry Council (A3P) Sustainability Action Plan[28] and the Plastics and Chemicals Industry Association Sustainability Framework.[29] Industry groups are well positioned to rapidly support business and industry throughout entire sectors of any national economy, through their ability to identify and assess environmental performance goals and targets across their respective sectors, to provide capacity-building opportunities and training for members, and to rapidly communicate the latest advances. Such respected networks provide a valuable vehicle to allow industry consultation on intended policy initiatives to identify opportunities, risks and barriers to change.

Addressing Fears about Losing International Competitiveness

The debate around the likelihood that strengthening of national environmental policy and decoupling targets will significantly harm a business's international competitiveness, and lead companies to shift location from OECD to developing countries, has occupied a great deal of media and academic review over the last 20 years.[30] To begin to address such concerns it is worth investigating the results of previous efforts to improve environmental regulations with regards to whether or not it has led to the relocation of businesses to so-called 'pollution havens'. Despite what many would assume, on the whole the empirical evidence for shifts to such areas where there are limited or no controls on pollution (and so referred to as a pollution haven), particularly in developing countries, is very weak,[31] and it is more likely to be cheap labour that draws operations offshore to such countries. Furthermore, there is evidence to suggest that overall companies are more likely to remain in or shift to developed countries to enable access to a highly skilled workforce and research and development (R&D) support, rather than locate to developing countries that allow higher levels of pollution but do not provide such support.[32]

> *Factor endowments such as capital intensity, availability of technology and skilled labour, and access to markets and technologies are the key determinants of environmentally sensitive firms' location decisions. Other explanations for why companies if anything tend to move to richer countries are the lack of mobility of these industries and the fact that there is often corruption in countries which have lax environmental regulations.[33] Such factors outweigh rich countries' tendency to apply tighter environmental restrictions in determining firms' location decisions.*
>
> Sir Nicholas Stern, *The Stern Review*, 2006[34]

Many other studies have come to the same conclusions and have shown that there is very little evidence from the last 30 years that firms have decided to move operations based on the avoidance of strengthening environmental policy.[35]

However, environmental policy and pollution regulation will affect the international competitiveness of a very small percentage of genuinely trade-exposed industry sectors. A company's competitiveness can, for instance, be disadvantaged internationally by the imposition of a carbon tax or an emissions trading scheme if the following conditions exist:

1 The industry is particularly emissions intensive and has done little to reduce its intensity, has done little to cost effectively provide low-impact energy, or to reduce the environmental pressures that result.
2 The industry is trade exposed, meaning that it relies on exports for overall profitability and needs to compete with international competitors that may not be under such constraints, such as commitments to meet the Kyoto Protocol.

As *The Stern Review* explains:

> *Sectors open to competition from countries not enforcing climate change abatement policies will not be able to pass on costs to consumers without risking market share. The short-run response to such elastic demand is likely to be lower profits. In the long run, with capital being mobile, firms are likely to make location decisions on the basis of changing comparative advantages. Analysis helps identify which industries are likely to suffer trade diversion and consider relocation: in general the list is short. With the exception of refined petrol and coal, fuel costs are not particularly exposed to foreign trade. Under carbon pricing, the price of electricity and gas distribution is set to rise by more than 15%, but output is destined almost exclusively for domestic markets. In all other cases, price increases are limited to below – mostly well below – 10% ... apart from refined petrol, coal, paper and pulp, iron and steel, fertilizers, air and water transport, chemicals, plastics, fibres and non-ferrous metals, of which aluminium accounts for approximately half of value added ... few industries are negatively affected.*[36]

In such cases, experts have demonstrated that the most effective policy option is to compensate trade-exposed energy-intensive industries through a border tax adjustment. This means that the government would pay the exporter of say aluminium exports, for example, a rebate to offset the increased costs in production caused by the carbon tax or emissions trading scheme to allow a level playing field internationally. But the rebate would only be paid at the point of export, thus ensuring that all companies producing and selling within a country would be subject to the carbon price signal. Border tax adjustments are not a radical idea and are used in a number of countries, including in nations which have goods and services taxes, such as the Australian GST and the European VAT. OECD studies of the effects of border tax adjustments on the cement[37] and steel industries[38] show that they can result in carbon taxes having a negligible effect on the international competitiveness of the steel and cement industries. The benefit is that the industries affected can then innovate their processes in preparation for increasing international requirements this century, without having their international competitiveness harmed in the meantime.

Responding to the Fear of Job Losses

Another major social factor that has held back efforts to achieve decoupling has been the fear that environmental policy and regulation would lead to avoidable job losses. Many believe that at the macroeconomic level, higher environmental standards and more purposeful environmental regulation have contributed to long-term unemployment. It is a common perception that environmental protection has been responsible for plant shutdowns and lay-offs in certain industry sectors such as coal mining, forestry, fishing, and chemical and manufacturing industries. It is a common belief among workers that they may lose their jobs in the future as a result of environmental protection. A 1990 nationwide poll, conducted in the US, found that 33 per cent of those polled felt themselves 'likely' or 'somewhat likely' to lose their job as a consequence of environmental regulation.[39] Economist Eban Goodstein has studied the jobs–environment debates in detail[40] and concluded that at the economy-wide level, these fears are not substantiated, and that there has been no significant trade-off between jobs and the environment.

> ... *at the local level, in sharp contrast to the conventional wisdom, layoffs from environmental protection have been very, very small. Even in the most extreme cases, such as protection of forests or closing down fisheries or steps to address acid rain, job losses from environmental protection have been minute compared to more garden-variety layoff events.*
> Eban Goodstein, *The Trade Off Myth*, 1999[41]

Implemented effectively the likely economy-wide effect of environmental regulation is to shift jobs without increasing the overall level of unemployment. But if decoupling policies are implemented well, as this book will show, there is potential for such policies to create new jobs. Globally there are now significant numbers of people who work in the 'environmental industry sector' as a result of environmental policy and regulatory changes. In fact, regulation-induced plant closings and lay-offs are very rare. Goodstein showed that in the US in the late 1990s, about a million workers were laid off each year because of factors such as import competition, shifts in demand or corporate downsizing. In sharp contrast, annual lay-offs in manufacturing because of environmental regulation were in the order of 100 to 3000 per year. There is significant evidence to suggest that efforts to underpin decoupling can also help create significantly higher employment. Chapters 5 to 10 provide such evidence that decoupling policies to encourage, for instance, energy efficiency and renewable energy, water efficiency and water recycling, remanufacturing and recycling and investment in the ecological infrastructure of nations leads to net job growth. For instance, David Roland-Holst's 2008 study on *Energy Efficiency, Innovation and Job Creation in California*[41A] showed that energy efficiency policies in California have created nearly 1.5 million jobs from 1977 to 2007. He showed that, whilst this has meant reduced jobs growth in the fossil fuel sector, for every 1 job lost in this sector, 50 have been created in the energy efficiency sector.

In addition to this, ecological tax reform, done well, can lead to net job creation because, as von Weizsäcker and Jesinghaus point out,[42] employment (a social good) is currently taxed in a variety of ways, such as payroll taxes, while environmental pollution (a social bad) receives relatively little taxation, and shifting such taxes can result in employment incentives. Supporting this position, in 1994, consultants DRI and other consultancies commissioned by the European Commission modelled a scenario where all the revenues from pollution taxes were used to reduce employers' non-wage labour costs, such as social security payments, superfund payments and payroll tax. The study showed that employment in the UK would be increased by 2.2 million through such tax shifting.[43]

There are a number of other reasons why a strategic approach to underpinning decoupling efforts can lead to higher jobs growth than business-as-usual, including:[44]

- the greater labour intensity in retrofitting the built environment, identifying and implementing efficiencies, and investment in distributed sustainable forms of energy and water supply;
- the greater labour intensity of new industrial processes where the technology and the manufacturing and operational techniques are not yet highly refined;
- the economically stimulating effect of bringing forward investments to achieve a more rapid transition to sustainability, which would also create new jobs.[45]

Furthermore there is strong evidence to support the case that as long as carbon tax revenue is recycled effectively, a carbon tax would have a strong employment dividend. Part of the benefit of this derives from the relative labour intensity of the low carbon-intensive sectors (services, retail, finance, education and health), with these sectors standing to benefit from such a relative price shift.[46]

Why then does this myth, that environmental regulation to achieve decoupling leads to job losses, continue and lead to such opposition from business and industry? This myth persists primarily because there are some industries that are currently extracting resources and creating pollution at unsustainable levels, which will need to be reduced in order to decouple economic growth from environmental pressures to the levels required to sustain prosperity. Some industries are currently operating at such unsustainable levels that they will need to be scaled down and their operations significantly redesigned. Workers currently working within those industries – such as some fisheries, some native forest logging, destruction of rainforests for agriculture and biofuels, and certain types of mining – fear any reduction in production rates will lead to them losing their jobs and livelihoods. So while the real economy-wide effect of environmental regulation is to shift jobs without increasing the overall level of unemployment, this is little comfort to those in the fishing industry, and timber or mine workers who do not have skills to do anything else. It is little comfort to regional communities whose incomes and property values depend on the existence of such industries and the local timber mill or mining plant. Often their trade or specialization has been in the family for three or four generations and a large part of their identity is understandably attached to that tradition. This aspect is often not recognized or acknowledged by the environmental movement nor incorporated into the design of policy responses.

Dealing with this issue, and others related to structural adjustment, may be one of the most important roles for government in the 21st century. Government needs to work with industry, communities and a range of institutions, to design ways to provide support, compensation and retraining for those workers and businesses in the sectors and regions of the economy that will be significantly negatively affected. Also, governments have a role to play in looking at alternative sustainable futures for regional communities that currently have intrinsically environmentally unsustainable industries. Hence a great effort is needed by governments to help these workers and communities revise the basis of their ongoing prosperity by investigating and acting early to find and support new, more environmentally sustainable industries. This includes working with such communities to investigate alternative sustainable business opportunities, such as sustainably managed mixed species plantations, organic agriculture, fish farming and aquaculture, eco-tourism, recycling plants, wind farms, solar arrays, biomass and geothermal plants for electricity. As Table 3.2 shows, the markets for such environmentally sustainable industries are rapidly growing. Hence it is in the collective interests of towns, cities, regions and nations to help support and foster these sustainable industries.

To conclude, there is great experience and understanding globally of how to better achieve decoupling while ensuring business competitiveness is not harmed and jobs are created overall. There is also a great deal of experience in how to manage effectively structural adjustment processes for communities and regions that are negatively affected by structural reform. It is therefore important that this knowledge is better understood to assist business, governments and civil society to work together more effectively, with structural adjustment processes that are not rushed and that are systematically and strategically implemented.

Responding to Fears of Skills Shortages and Gaps

The development of this section was led by Cheryl Desha and Charlie Hargroves drawing on a number of the engagements with higher education institutions related to curriculum renewal. The section provides a summary of the main messages of the book Engineering Education and Sustainable Development: A Guide for Rapid Curriculum Renewal in Higher Education, *by Desha and Hargroves.*

Society is increasingly calling for professionals across government, industry, business and civil society to problem-solve issues related to climate change and reducing environmental pressures. A key factor in determining the extent to which economic growth can be decoupled from environmental pressures, is how well decoupling strategies are researched and implemented. Such research and implementation depends on the level of knowledge and skills of decision-makers, policy-makers, professionals and workers. Unfortunately, studies suggest that our current level of education is not sufficient to enable the required levels of decoupling to be achieved in the timeframes required. For example, modelling by the Australian CSIRO has shown that 3 million Australians (of a population of just over 20 million), will need training or re-training in energy efficiency, green building technologies, sustainable energy and more sustainable agricultural systems to enable Australia to achieve the IPCC's recommended targets for greenhouse gas reductions.[47] This scenario reflects the reality that the effectiveness of a price signal on carbon, either through an emissions trading scheme or a carbon tax, depends largely on society's ability to respond to it. In the absence of the private sector or the community knowing how they can cost effectively respond to a carbon price signal to reduce their greenhouse gas emissions, such measures are unlikely to be successful.

Currently, the state of knowledge, understanding and implementation of even basic environmental and energy management systems in the business sector is poor, and education systems the world over are currently poorly prepared to develop such skills and capacity. For example, a 2008 survey of 300 Australian business chief executive officers regarding operating in a carbon-constrained economy found that two-thirds (67 per cent) of businesses were concerned or unsure about compliance obligations, and only a handful of businesses (less than 3 per cent) had implemented a strategic response to climate change.[48] A 2007 survey of the Australian mining and metals sector also highlighted an alarmingly slow adoption of energy demand management practices, with nearly half (43 per cent) of companies still not having implemented an official energy policy.[49] In the same context, only 10 per cent of companies responding to a 2007 national Australian Industry Group survey on climate change practices felt informed enough to manage the risks associated with climate-related impacts.[50] Furthermore, despite concerted efforts in research on the key role of the higher education institution (HEI) sector, and findings of a range of surveys, reports, papers and declarations by professional, business, academic and governmental agencies,[51] there is yet little precedent to demonstrate how such skills and capacity can be rapidly and systematically included in education programmes, apart from a handful of leading efforts;[52] and relatively few opportunities for professionals to access formal training in sustainable development knowledge and skills. This situation presents significant risk to companies that are now, or will soon be, required to deliver on national commitments to reduce environmental pressures such as greenhouse gas reduction targets, and energy, water and materials intensity targets. Further, there is growing fear within business and industry that if government requirements move too quickly with policies and regulations to underpin decoupling, employers will not have enough people with the necessary knowledge and skills to respond in an informed way and implement the changes in time. As the world moves towards a green economy, a comprehensive approach is therefore clearly needed for a rapid transfer of knowledge, to facilitate the successful design and implementation of effective decoupling measures.

Along with understanding that current education systems are poorly prepared to develop knowledge and skills related to reducing environmental pressures, it is also important to understand that it is logistically impossible for the education system to change 'overnight'. Rather, a strategic approach is needed that melds organizational changes with curriculum renewal over time, and on many levels. The core of the issue is that the typical timeframe required to make systemic changes to national education systems (in the order of 15–20 years) is now converging with the timeframe for the professional community to successfully act to avoid irreversible damage to the planet's ecosystems as discussed in Chapter 1. We refer to this as a 'time lag dilemma' facing the HEI sector, whereby the usual or 'standard' timeframe to significantly update the curriculum for professional disciplines (that is, three to four programme accreditation cycles, or 15–20 years) will be too long to meet changing market and regulatory requirements for knowledge and skills capacity.[53] In hindsight, this may not have been the situation had HEIs acted on the previous major calls for capacity building related to sustainable development, such as in *Our Common Future* in 1987:[54]

> *The changes in attitudes, in social values, and in aspirations that the report urges will depend on vast campaigns of education, debate and public participation. To this end, we appeal to citizens' groups, to non governmental organizations, to educational institutions, and to the scientific community. They have all played indispensable roles in the creation of public awareness and political change in the past. They will play a crucial part in putting the world onto sustainable development paths, in laying the groundwork for Our Common Future.*

Yet even in core fields such as engineering and technology, only a relatively small number of HEIs (concentrated in Europe) subsequently undertook a process of curriculum renewal.[55] Some 20 years later, most HEIs are only just beginning to include such content within existing programmes, as renewed calls are being taken up for capacity building. These include the UN 2005–2014 Decade of Education for Sustainable Development,[56] international calls for university action such as the Talloires Declaration,[57] and national HEI commitments to action such as the American College and University Presidents' Climate Commitment.[58]

The extent of the 'time lag' in delivering graduates with new attributes to employers is now dependent on the level of commitment from HEIs, and their approaches to embedding new content into existing programmes. For example, the average pathway to achieve professional status of a undergraduate bachelor built environment programme (for example in design, engineering or planning) is approximately 3–5 years, from enrolment to graduation, followed by 3–5 years of on-the-job graduate development. Hence, if HEIs take the typical approach over a 15–20 year period to fully renew such bachelor programmes, this will result in a time lag of around 21–29 years: two to three decades before a student completes a fully updated programme and then reaches a decision-making position. However, through adopting a higher level of commitment to undertake a shorter process, this time lag can be reduced to 15–22 years, and it is this difference that will determine the level of risk and benefit for individual institutions. For postgraduate and masters students the time lag will be shorter as students may already be practising in their field and studies may be over 1–2 years, although the time lag may still be in the order of 5–10 years depending on the curriculum renewal process.

Effectively there are two options: a 'standard curriculum renewal' process, or a 'rapid curriculum renewal' process, each of which has direct implications for exposure to future risks and rewards that are also set to increase over the next 20 years, as shown in Figure 3.2. Such implications include:

- Standard curriculum renewal (SCR): In this option there is low to moderate commitment to embedding new knowledge and skills within programmes, driven by compliance requirements (see Figure 3.1), meeting current accreditation requirements, and reacting to student recruitment and retention figures, advisory board contributions and immediate internal institutional pressures. Institutions choosing to continue along the 15–20 year SCR path and wait before acting faster, face a future risk that market and institutional changes might overtake their curriculum renewal progress, causing their product (education) to fall behind employer demand. In short, if commitment is low then the exposure to future risk is high (for example with respect to falling student numbers with diminishing reputation, increasing accreditation difficulties and poaching of key staff by other institutions that are progressing faster) and the future potential

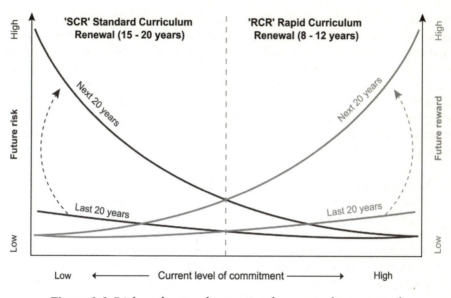

'SCR' Standard Curriculum Renewal (15 - 20 years)

'RCR' Rapid Curriculum Renewal (8 - 12 years)

High

Future risk

Low

Next 20 years

Last 20 years

Next 20 years

Last 20 years

High

Future reward

Low

Low ← Current level of commitment → High

Figure 3.2 *Risk and reward scenarios for curriculum renewal in the higher education institution sector*

Source: Desha, C. and Hargroves, K. (2009)[59]

for rewards is low (for example with respect to recruiting top educators and researchers in the field).

- Rapid curriculum renewal (RCR): In this option there is a high commitment to embedding new knowledge and skills within programmes and the pace of such efforts is being driven by a strategic approach, considering the level of current and predicted demand, rather than reacting to staff, market or institutional drivers. This approach positions institutions well to respond to future changes to industry, regulatory and accreditation requirements. Hence, as the level of commitment increases, future risk exposure to changing market and institutional requirements reduces and the future rewards increase. Such rewards include more students and better staff, keeping programmes ahead of accreditation requirements, strengthening graduate reputation, attracting associated research funding, and securing key academic appointments and industry partnership and funding.

Clearly then, if HEIs have a high level of commitment to capacity building in areas related to reducing environmental pressures early, they can not only reduce fears of future associated skills shortages, but also be well placed to attract increased international students and researchers, increase research leading to opportunities for commercialization, and be in a strong position to provide expertise to other nations, particularly in assisting developing countries. On the other hand, a low commitment will result in: an increasing reliance on finding skills offshore (with capacity in, for example, energy efficiency auditing, product design and manufacture, green buildings or emissions reduction technologies); diminished research and commercialization in the area; and an increasing reliance on foreign imports for both goods and services (and expertise) that comply with increasing requirements.

Hence, to address the fear of future skills shortages, and to position HEIs to capture future benefits, governments around the world can use a range of mechanisms to increase the level of commitment to updating programmes, such as:

- Legislation: Creating the legislative framework for companies to accelerate efforts such as energy efficiency assessments. This in turn provides a signal to professional associations, accreditation bodies and the higher education sector regarding the need for such graduate attributes.
- Accreditation: Influencing professional accreditation requirements, working with accreditation bodies and professional organizations to provide the necessary 'calls for action' in priority knowledge and skills areas, to review and revise the coverage and extent of accreditation requirements.
- Employer and employee needs: Assisting professional organizations to identify current and future industry demands for graduates with specific knowledge and skill capabilities.
- Research: Changing the criteria and selection for research funding to include a sustainability-oriented research priority, given that early integration of emerging content appears to be driven largely by individual interests and research pursuits of the lecturers involved rather than formal strategic integration.
- Teaching: Linking a portion of federal funding of higher education institutions to institutional learning and teaching performance with regard to integrating sustainability knowledge and skills into curricula (in a similar manner to the way in which institutions currently track integration of other priority areas such as indigenous knowledge and research-led teaching).

In Australia, for example, in July 2006 the federal government launched the Energy Efficiency Opportunities Programme, which required more than 220 businesses (representing around 45 per cent of national energy demand) that use more than 0.5PJ (138,890MWh) of energy per year, to undertake an energy efficiency assessment and report publically on opportunities with a payback period of up to four years.[60] Further to this, Victoria was the first state to require all Environmental Protection Agency licence holders using more than 0.1PJ (27,780MWh) to implement opportunities with a payback period of up to three years, through its Industry Greenhouse programme.[61] As a result of implementing these programmes, both state and federal governments have identified a significant skills shortage in the area of undertaking energy efficiency assessments. Subsequently in 2009 the federal government initiated a long-term training strategy for the development of energy efficiency assessment skills, beginning with an extensive survey process across the energy-intensive industries, energy service providers and universities.[62] In 2007, the CSIRO through its 'Energy Transformed Flagship' engaged in providing capacity-building notes for professionals and students looking to up-skill in this area, funding a 30-lecture series (freely available online) aimed at both undergraduate education and professional development, on energy efficiency opportunities.[63] Australia's top engineering professional body, the Institution of Engineers Australia, has also acknowledged that 'The need to make changes in the way energy is used and supplied throughout the world represents the greatest challenge to engineers in moving toward sustainability.'[64]

Once the HEI sector is shown a clear imperative through such programmes, or through the other mechanisms listed above, much can be done to strategically accelerate efforts, even though on the whole there is little precedent. In the following we provide an overview of two national surveys undertaken to address the issue of capacity building, specifically regarding improving the extent of energy efficiency knowledge and skills in engineering education. Although this research was focused on one content area in one discipline, it also provides possible parallels for strategically planning curriculum renewal for a range of sustainable development topics across built-environment-related education in the HEI sector.[65]

In 2007, the National Framework for Energy Efficiency (NFEE) funded a national survey on the state of energy efficiency education in Australia, undertaken by Cheryl Desha and Charlie Hargroves from The Natural Edge Project. With excellent participation by 27 of the 32 universities offering engineering higher education (comprising 62 lecturers and 261 students), the survey identified that even though energy efficiency education was highly variable and ad hoc, there was a range of preferred options for improvement.[66] For example, for more than half of the surveyed courses (55 per cent), lecturers reported that their course could include more (in-depth) energy efficiency content, while most respondents (74 per cent) thought that the increase in content should be in the specific area of *applying* energy efficiency theory and knowledge. More than half (52 per cent) thought their course could include more on information about energy efficiency opportunities. The survey also showed a clear preference for resources to be available through open access, online learning modules (90 per cent) as opposed to restricted access sources (6 per cent) or intensive short courses undertaken in person (13 per cent) or remotely (10 per cent).

However, while there was clearly a desire to integrate energy efficiency content, the Australian survey indicated a substantial shortfall in the inclusion of energy efficiency theory, knowledge, application and assessment in engineering education. Even mainstream contextual topics, such as carbon dioxide and other greenhouse gas emissions from energy generation or the link between greenhouse gas emissions and global temperature change, were only covered in detail by up to a third of surveyed courses, and mentioned by less than half.

Moreover, student survey results indicated only a low to moderate appreciation of how energy efficiency might be directly related to their future careers. Lecturers and students agreed that there was little if any coverage of topics such as product stewardship and responsibility, decoupling energy utility profits from kilowatt-hours sold or incremental efficiency versus whole system design. The survey results indicated that this disconnect – between lecturers recognizing an absence of content, and a lack of action in integrating the content – was likely to be due to the presence of a variety of barriers to implementation. For example, nearly two-thirds (58 per cent) considered the potential for course content overload to be an issue, while more than half (52 per cent) considered having insufficient time to prepare new materials as a challenge to such curriculum renewal.

Hence, in 2009 a follow-up survey was funded by the NFEE, to identify and investigate a shortlist of options that HEIs could consider for timely curriculum renewal in energy efficiency education at the level of the lecturer.[67] In the following we present and briefly discuss these ten shortlisted options along with the identified common barriers to and benefits from their uptake. We then present a range of components to organizational strategies, which could be included to support the uptake of these options. We conclude with a number of observed elements of curriculum renewal identified in the literature that are already helping to structure the process of rapid curriculum renewal.

Through a comprehensive literature review followed by a national survey of engineering educators, the researchers shortlisted ten favoured options amongst HEIs to integrate emerging energy efficiency content within current engineering programmes, as shown below (in order of priority):[68]

1   including a case study on energy efficiency;
2   including a guest lecturer to teach a sub-topic;
3   offering supervised research topics on energy efficiency themes;
4   offering energy efficiency as a topic in a problem-based learning course;
5   including assessment that aligns with the energy efficiency theme within the course (e.g. exam questions and assignments);
6   including tutorials that align with the energy efficiency theme in the course (e.g. presentations/discussions/problem solving);
7   overhauling the course to embed energy efficiency;
8   including one workshop on energy efficiency in the course (experiments);
9   including a field trip related to energy efficiency;
10 developing a new course on energy efficiency.

The research then investigated barriers to and benefits of these options as a critical step[69] in understanding the potential for rapid capacity building at the actual level of implementation. Table 3.3 provides a summary of the identified common barriers to one or more of the shortlisted options, highlighting that putting in place mechanisms to address any of the barriers can have multiple flow-on benefits for addressing other barriers. For example, for key staff who

Table 3.3 *Identified key barriers to and benefits of timely curriculum renewal (energy efficiency content and engineering education)*

Key issues for implementation	Shortlisted options for curriculum renewal									
	1. Case Study	2. Guest Lecturer	3. Supervised Research	4. PBL Topic	5. Include Assessment	6. Tutorials	7. Course Overhaul	8. Workshop	9. Field Trip	10. New Course
Common barriers										
Lack of available data/information	•			•	•	•	•		•	•
Lack of time for preparation	•	•		•	•	•				•
An overcrowded curriculum	•	•	•	•		•		•		•
Prohibitive cost	•	•	•	•	•	•			•	•
Lack of knowledge	•		•	•	•	•	•		•	•
Lack of value attached	•	•	•				•	•	•	
Lack of industry contacts			•				•			
Resistance to top-down directive		•	•					•		
Students' prior learning habits					•		•			
Lecturer apathy									•	•
Administrative coordination								•		
Common benefits										
Improved marketability	•	•					•			•
Cross-functionality of content	•						•			•
Additional research opportunities		•								•
Networking opportunities for students		•	•				•	•		
Networking opportunities for lecturers		•	•				•	•		
Experience in incorporating emerging concepts into curriculum			•							
Addressing the time lag for graduates										
Improved pedagogy – problem-based learning (PBL)				•	•					
Improved pedagogy – generic skills				•	•	•	•		•	
Lecturer professional development (content)			•			•			•	

Source: Desha, C., Hargroves, K. and Reeve, A. (2009)[70]

are tasked with integrating new content, setting up an annual allocation of teaching buy-out funds, or having an avenue for temporarily altering staff teaching–research–service workload allocation to engage in rapid curriculum renewal, would help to address the barrier of insufficient time for preparation, which affects seven of the ten options. Similarly, an annual small-grants programme available for educators to pilot rapid curriculum renewal initiatives would help to address the barrier of prohibitive cost.

With such considerations in mind, HEIs can strategically allocate budget and human resourcing to enable the integration of new content – in this case energy efficiency knowledge and skills – into existing education and training programmes. This could be for example through a 'tiered' approach, where the first three options, including the use of case studies, guest lecturers and supervised research, may be targeted immediately, with other options then implemented among various programmes in the following budget cycles.

For the tools to be successful, an overarching strategic plan is needed, which maps out the timeframe, responsibilities and resource requirements. In the NFEE investigation, despite the scarcity of literature on timely curriculum renewal, a number of key components were identified that might be considered in a HEI's strategic plan to rapidly develop graduates who can fill critical knowledge and skills gaps, such as:

- tracking emerging 'hot topic' areas and emerging knowledge and skills gaps;
- including knowledge and skills in the new topic area in graduate attribute (competency) lists for programmes;
- publicly committing senior management support;
- recruiting staff with expertise in the new knowledge and skills area;
- providing training for staff in the new knowledge and skills area;
- hosting topical events;
- fostering formal and informal interdisciplinary networks;
- collaborating with other HEIs to offer programmes in emerging topic areas;
- directly involving potential employers;
- developing and monitoring curriculum integration targets;
- creating a clear timeline for action;
- permitting workload discussions between faculty involved in rapid curriculum renewal and senior management;
- providing seed funds for new research in the identified knowledge and skills gap area;
- providing seed funds for teaching research on piloting rapid curriculum renewal strategies;
- harnessing other institutional overhauls (such as restructuring) to incorporate curriculum renewal strategies;
- engaging external support (e.g. consultants) for market advice on graduate employment options and potential student expectations.

Table 3.4 *Emerging elements of rapid curriculum renewal*

Element	Summary
Awareness raising and developing a common understanding	• Bringing faculty (academic staff) to a common understanding of challenges, opportunities and implications for curriculum renewal at the department level through activities such as keynote lectures, public addresses, lunchtime seminars, media articles and profiling existing sustainability initiatives. • Senior management in the department identifying what capacity is available to deliver sustainability content within the programme offerings.
Graduate attribute mapping	• Facilitating scoping workshops with faculty and other collaborators within the university hierarchy, to focus on the 'graduate attribute' requirements for graduating students and how sustainability knowledge and skills relate to these requirements. • Rather than starting from scratch, rethinking the relevance of the theory, knowledge and applications to deliver graduate attributes and skills.
Curriculum auditing	• Providing a strategic (risk management) opportunity to review the extent of sustainability content within courses, which then assists in identifying areas of focus for the introduction and consolidation of sustainable development content across a given programme. • Applying a risk management approach to the timing and prioritization of the curriculum renewal process, while acknowledging efforts already undertaken in curriculum renewal for sustainable development.
Course development and renewal	• Planning the curriculum development and renewal over the desired timeframe for full integration. • Considering the merits of possible strategies such as 'niche programmes', 'flagship courses', and institutional considerations like the availability of existing content and management support.
Bridging and outreach	• Extending the utility of course development and renewal to improve recruitment from industry and government, high schools and the community. • Considering opportunities for existing courses to be offered in an intensive format to industry and government as professional development (bridging) or to high-school students and the local community (outreach).
Integration with Campus Operations	• Enhancing the course development and renewal process by linking theory about education for sustainable development curriculum with on-campus application opportunities. • Providing staff with practical experience in their subject matter, and providing students with real project experience.

Source: Desha, C. and Hargroves, K. (2007)[71]

Such strategies are already evident in leading institutions around the world that are setting their own timely agendas, with a number of elements of rapid curriculum renewal already emerging in the higher education sector, as summarized in Table 3.4. Given an imperative for rapid curriculum renewal, a combination of these elements (depending on the existing circumstances of the HEI) may be strategically implemented to achieve such change, in a non-confrontational, proactive and outcomes-based approach that preserves institutional diversity and innovation.

Hence, given the need for rapid up-skilling of the existing and future workforce to address national and international commitments on issues such as greenhouse gas emissions, energy, materials and water productivity, there is simply no more time – and there are no more excuses – for the higher education sector to continue to teach outdated content related to business-as-usual practices. While fears about skills shortages and gaps are currently real and threatening, timely capacity building across all major infrastructure and service professions to address such concerns is possible. In engaging in strategic planning that takes on board the above considerations, the HEI sector certainly has the capacity to respond to current and emerging knowledge and skills shortages. However, government needs to play an active role in driving the timeframe for knowledge and skills development, providing clear signals on impending requirements that can be quickly incorporated into immediate operations and strategic planning by professional associations, industry (employers) and accreditation agencies for professional programmes.

Given such signals and support, HEIs have a limited window in which to address the current skills shortages and gaps. Indeed, a variety of competitors in the form of specialized institutions are quickly emerging in the market where education and training gaps are not being readily filled by the traditional education and training providers, with a range of short courses and programmes on offer.

Notes

1   Wise, W. (2001) *Killer Smog: The World's Worst Air Pollution Disaster*, iUniverse.com Inc.
2   Grossman, G. and Krueger, A. (1994) 'Economic growth and the environment', NBER Working Paper no 4634, National Bureau of Economic Research, Cambridge, cited in Ekins, P. (2000) *Economic Growth and Environmental Sustainability*, Routledge Publishing, New York, p190.
2A Deutsche Bank Climate Change Advisors (2010) *Global Climate Change Policy Tracker – The Green Economy: The Race is On*, Deutsche Bank Group, www.dbcca.com/dbcca/EN/investment-research/investment_research_2296.jsp
3   Developed by The Natural Edge Project in considering opportunities for companies and the HEI sector; see also Desha, C. and Hargroves, K. (2010) *Engineering Education & Sustainable Development: A Guide for Rapid Curriculum Renewal*, The Natural Edge Project and Earthscan Press, London.
4   von Weizsäcker, E., Hargroves, K., Smith, M., Desha, C. and Stasinopoulos, P. (2009) *Factor Five: Transforming the Global Economy through 80% Improvements in Resource Productivity*, Earthscan, London.
5   OECD (2008) *OECD Environmental Outlook to 2030*, OECD, Paris.
6   OECD (2008) *OECD Environmental Outlook to 2030*, OECD, Paris, p432.
7   Braithwaite, J. and Drahos, P. (2000) *Global Business Regulation*, Cambridge University Press, Cambridge.
8   von Weizsäcker, E., Lovins, A. and Lovins, H. (1997) *Factor Four: Doubling Wealth, Halving Resource Use*, Earthscan, London.
9   Porter, M. (1991) 'Green competitiveness', *Scientific American*, 5 April.
10 OECD (2008) *OECD Environmental Outlook to 2030*, OECD, Paris.
11 OECD (2007) *Business and the Environment: Policy Incentives and Corporate Responses*, OECD, Paris; OECD (2007) *Environmental Innovation and Global*

Markets, OECD, Paris; OECD (2007) *Pollution Abatement and Control Expenditures in OECD Countries*, OECD, Paris; OECD (2007) *Instrument Mixes for Environmental Policy*, OECD, Paris.

12   Innovest Strategic Value Advisors (2004) *Corporate Environmental Governance: A Study into the Influence of Environmental Governance and Financial Performance*, Innovest, Denver, CO, p10.

13   Innovest Strategic Value Advisors (2004) *Corporate Environmental Governance: A Study into the Influence of Environmental Governance and Financial Performance*, Innovest, p10.

14   Hart, S. and Ahuja, G. (1996) 'Does it pay to be green? An empirical examination of the relationship between emission reduction and firm performance', *Business Strategy and the Environment*, vol 5, pp30–37; Schaltegger, S. and Figge, F. (1997) 'Environmental shareholder value', *WWZ/Sarasin Basic Research Study*, no 54, WWZ, Basel; Schaltegger, S. and Synnestvedt, T. (2002) 'The link between "green" and economic success: Environmental management as the crucial trigger between environmental and economic performance', *Journal of Environmental Management*, vol 65, pp339–346; Waddock, S. and Graves, S. B. (1997) 'The corporate social performance–financial performance link', *Strategic Management Journal*, vol 18, no 4, pp303–319; Wagner, M. (2001) *A Review of Empirical Studies Concerning the Relationship between Environmental and Economic Performance: What Does the Evidence Tell Us?*, University of Lüneburg, Centre for Sustainability Management, Lüneburg, Germany; Schmidheiny, S. (1992) *Changing Course: A Global Business Perspective on Development and the Environment*, MIT Press, Boston; Halliday, C., Schmidheiny, S. and Watts, P. (2002) '*Walking the Talk: The Business Case for Sustainable Development*', World Business Council for Sustainable Development, Greenleaf Publishing, Sheffield, UK; Verschoor, C. (1999) 'Corporate performance is closely linked to a strong ethical commitment', *Business and Society Review*, vol 104, no 4, p407; Repetto, R. and Austin, D. (2000) *Pure Profit: The Financial Implications of Environmental Performance*, World Resources Institute, Washington, DC; Pfeffer, J. (1998) *The Human Equation: Building Profits by Putting People First*, Harvard Business School Press, Boston, MA.

15   Baue, B. (2008) 'Chapter 13: Investing for sustainability', *State of the World 2008*, Worldwatch Institute, Earthscan, London.

16   von Weizsäcker, E. and Jesinghaus, J. (1992) *Ecological Tax Reform: Policy Proposal for Sustainable Development*, Zed Books, London.

17   OECD (2008) *OECD Environmental Outlook to 2030*, OECD, Paris.

18   UNEP (2008) *Principles of Responsible Investment*, UNEP Finance Initiative.

19   Reuters (2008) 'Equator principles celebrate five years of positive environmental impact and improved business', 8 May.

20   UNEP (2007) Global Trends in Sustainable Energy Investment 2007, UNEP, www.unep.org/Documents.Multilingual/Default.asp?DocumentID=512& ArticleID=5616&l=en, accessed 17 June 2010.

21   Cambridge Energy Research Associates (CERA) (2007) *Crossing the Divide: The Future of Clean Energy*, CERA.

22   Mastny, L. (2001) *Treading Lightly: New Paths for International Tourism*, Worldwatch Paper 159, Worldwatch Institute, Washington, DC, p15.

23   World Tourism Organization (2004) 'Eco-tourism factsheet', International Eco-Tourism Society, Washington, DC.

24   Shum, K. (2007) 'Lifestyles of health and sustainability – Green travel: Trends in eco-tourism', International Ecotourism Society, Washington, DC.

25   Kristiansen, P., Taji, A. and Reganold, J. (2006) *Organic Agriculture: A Global Perspective*, CSIRO Publishing, Australia.
26   R. W. Beck Inc. (2002) *Report to the National Recycling Coalition*, Washington, DC.
27   Toyne, P., Tate, A., Hargroves, K. and Smith, M. (2003) *Sustainability Framework for the Future of Australia's Infrastructure Handbook*, Australian Council for Infrastructure and Development, Australia.
28   Prosser, M., Smith, M., Hargroves, K. and Toyne, P. (2006) *Australian Plantation, Products and Paper Industry Council's (A3P) Sustainability Action Plan – Performance, People and Prosperity*, A3P, Australia.
29   PACIA (2007) *Sustainable Leadership Framework*, Plastics and Chemicals Industry Association, Australia.
30   Copeland, B. and Taylor, M. (2003) *Trade and the Environment*, Princeton University Press, Princeton, NJ.
31   Wilson, J. (1996) 'Capital mobility and environmental standards: Is there a theoretical basis for a race to the bottom?', in Bhagwati, J. and Hudec, R. (eds) 'Vol I, Economic Analysis', *Fair Trade and Harmonization*, MIT Press, Cambridge, MA, p393; Copeland, B. and Taylor, M. (2003) *Trade and the Environment*, Princeton University Press, Princeton, NJ; Jänicke, M., Binder, M. and Mönch, H. (1997) 'Dirty industries: Patterns of change in industrial countries', *Environmental and Resource Economics*, vol 9, no 4, pp467–491; Javorcik, B. and Wei, S. (2004) 'Pollution havens and foreign direct investment: Dirty secret or popular myth?', *Policy Research Working Paper Series 2673*, World Bank, Washington, DC.
32   Antweiler, W., Copeland, B. and Taylor, M. (2001) 'Is free trade good for the environment?' *American Economic Review*, vol 91, no 4, pp877–908.
33   Taylor, M. (2004) 'Unbundling the pollution haven hypothesis', *Advances in Economic Analysis & Policy*, vol 4, no 2, Article 8; Das, M. and Das, S. (2007) 'Can stricter environmental regulations increase export of the polluting good?', *The B. E. Journal of Economic Analysis & Policy*, vol 7, no 1, Article 26; Jänicke, M., Binder, M. and Mönch, H. (1997) 'Dirty industries: Patterns of change in industrial countries', *Environmental and Resource Economics*, vol 9, no 4, pp467–491.
34   Stern, N. (2006) *The Stern Review: The Economics of Climate Change*, Cambridge University Press, Cambridge, 'Executive Summary', p10.
35   Copeland, B. and Taylor, M. (2004) 'Trade, growth, and the environment', *Journal of Economic Literature*, vol 42, pp7–71; Trefler, D. (1993) 'Trade liberalization and the theory of endogenous protection: An econometric study of US import policy', *Journal of Political Economy*, vol 101, no 1, pp138–160; Mani, M. and Wheeler, D. (1997) 'In search of pollution havens? Dirty industry migration in the world economy', World Bank Working Paper 16, World Bank Washington, DC.
36   Stern, N. (2006) *The Stern Review: The Economics of Climate Change*, Cambridge University Press, Cambridge, 'Executive summary'.
37   OECD (2005) *The Competitiveness Impact of CO_2 Emissions Reduction in the Cement Sector*, OECD, Paris.
38   OECD (2003) *Environmental Policy in the Steel Industry: Using Economic Instruments*, OECD, Paris.
39   Goldstein, E. (1999) *The Trade Off Myth: Fact & Fiction About Jobs and the Environment*, Island Press, Washington, DC.
40   Goodstein, E. (1999) *The Trade Off Myth: Fact & Fiction About Jobs and the Environment*, Island Press, Washington, DC.

41 Goodstein, E. (1999) *The Trade Off Myth: Fact & Fiction About Jobs and the Environment*, Island Press, Washington, DC, p15.

41A Roland-Holst, D. (2008) *Energy Efficiency, Innovation and Job Creation in California*, Center for Energy, Resources, and Economic Sustainability, University of California, Berkeley, CA.

42 von Weizsäcker, E. and Jesinghaus, J. (1992) *Ecological Tax Reform: Policy Proposal for Sustainable Development*, Zed Books, London.

43 DRI (1994) *Potential Benefits of Integration of Environmental and Economic Policies: An Incentive-Based Approach to Policy Integration*, Graham and Trotman and the Office for Publications of the European Communities, Brussels.

44 Supported by the findings of INFRAS and ECOPLAN (1996) '*Economic Impact Analysis of Eco-tax Proposals: Comparative Analysis of Modeling Results*', European Commission, Directorate-General XII, Brussels.

45 Sutton, P. (2000) *Is it Possible for a Green Economy to have High Economic Performance?* Green Innovations, Melbourne.

46 Proops, J., Faber, M. and Wagenhals, G. (1993) *Reducing CO_2 Emissions: A Comparative Input–Output Study for Germany and the UK*, Springer Verlag, Berlin.

47 Hatfield-Dodds, S., Turner, G., Schandl, H. and Doss, T. (2008) 'Growing the green collar economy: Skills and labour challenges in reducing our greenhouse emissions and national environmental footprint', report to the Dusseldorp Skills Forum, June, CSIRO Sustainable Ecosystems, Canberra.

48 PriceWaterhouseCoopers (PWC) (2008) 'Carbon countdown: A survey of executive opinion on climate change in the countdown to a carbon economy', PWC, Australia.

49 Proudfoot Consulting (2007) 'Meeting the corporate energy challenge: Are companies walking the talk on energy efficiency?', Proudfoot Consulting, Australia.

50 Australian Industry Group (AIG) (2007) 'Environmental sustainability and industry: road to a sustainable future', AIG, Australia.

51 For example, Leal Filho, W. (ed) (2002) *Teaching Sustainability at Universities: Towards Curriculum Greening*, Peter Lang, Publishing Group, New York; Cortese, A. (2003) 'The critical role of higher education in creating a sustainable future', *Planning for Higher Education*, March-May; Blewitt, J. and Cullingford, C. (2004) *The Sustainability Curriculum: The Challenge for Higher Education*, Earthscan, London; Corcoran, P. and Wals, A. (eds) (2004) *Higher Education and the Challenge of Sustainability: Problematics, Promise, and Practice*, CERC Studies in Comparative Education, Kluwer Academic Publishers, Netherlands; Timpson, W., Dunbar, B., Kimmel, G., Bruyere, B., Newman, P. and Mizia, H. (2009) *147 Practical Tips for Teaching Sustainability: Connecting the Environment, the Economy, and Society*, Atwood Publishing, Madison, WI; Stephens, J. and Graham, A. (2009) 'Toward an empirical research agenda for sustainability in higher education: Exploring the transition management framework', *Journal of Cleaner Production*, vol 18, issue 7, pp611–618; Steinfeld, J. and Takashi, M. (2009) 'Special feature editorial: Education for sustainable development – the challenge of trans-disciplinarity', *Journal of Sustainability Science*, Springer, vol 4, no 1, pp1–2.

52 For example, see Rowe, D. (2007) 'Policy forum sustainability: Education for a sustainable future', *Science*, vol 317, no 5836, pp323–324; Newman, J. and Fernandez, L. (2007) *Strategies for Institutionalizing Sustainability in Higher Education: Report on the Northeast Campus Sustainability Consortium 3rd*

Annual Conference and International Symposium, Yale School of Forestry and Environmental Studies, April; Holmberg, J., Svanström, M., Peet, D., Mulder, K., Ferrer-Balas, D. and Segalàs, J. (2008) 'Embedding sustainability in higher education through interaction with lecturers: Case studies from three European technical universities', *European Journal of Engineering Education*, vol 33, no 3, pp271–282.

53 Desha, C., Hargroves, K. and Smith, M. (2009) 'Addressing the time lag dilemma in curriculum renewal towards engineering education for sustainable development', *International Journal of Sustainability in Higher Education*, vol 10, no 2, pp184–199.

54 Brundtland, G. (1987) 'Our common future, chairman's foreword', in WCED, *Our Common Future*, Oxford University Press, Oxford.

55 Alliance for Global Sustainability (2006) *The Observatory: Status of Engineering Education for Sustainable Development in European Higher Education, 2006*, EESD-Observatory, Technical University of Catalonia, Spain; Alliance for Global Sustainability (2008) *The Observatory: Status of Engineering Education for Sustainable Development in European Higher Education, 2008*, EESD-Observatory, Technical University of Catalonia, Spain.

56 UN General Assembly (2002) 'Proclamation of the Decade of Education of Sustainable Development (2005–2014)', 57th Session, UN General Assembly.

57 University Leaders for a Sustainable Future (undated) 'The Talloires Declaration', www.ulsf.org/programs_talloires.html, accessed 4 April 2010; or University Leaders for a Sustainable Future (ULSF), US.

58 Presidents' Climate Commitment (undated) 'American College and University's Presidents' Climate Commitment', www.presidentsclimatecommitment.org/signatories, accessed 4 April 2010.

59 Desha, C. and Hargroves, K. (2009) 'Re-engineering higher education for energy efficiency solutions', *ECOS*, CSIRO, vol 151, October–November.

60 Australian Federal Department of Resources, Energy and Tourism 'Energy efficiency opportunities', DRET, Australia.

61 Victorian Environmental Protection Agency (undated) 'Environment and Resource Efficiency Plans – EREP', Victorian EPA, Australia.

62 Council of Australian Governments (2009) *National Strategy on Energy Efficiency,* July, Commonwealth of Australia.

63 Smith, M., Hargroves, K., Stasinopoulos, P., Stephens, R., Desha, C. and Hargroves S. (2007) *Energy Transformed: Sustainable Energy Solutions for Climate Change Mitigation*, Griffith University, ANU, and The Natural Edge Project. Australia., www.naturaledgeproject.net/Sustainable_Energy_Solutions_Portfolio.aspx, accessed 4 April 2010.

64 The Institution of Engineers Australia (undated) 'Energy efficiency: The importance of energy efficiency in moving toward sustainability', the Institution of Engineers Australia website, www.engineersaustralia.org.au/.

65 Desha, C. and Hargroves, K. (2009) 'Re-engineering higher education for energy efficiency solutions', *ECOS*, CSIRO, vol 151, October–November.

66 Desha, C., Hargroves, K., Smith, M., Stasinopoulos, P., Stephens, R. and Hargroves S. (2007) *Energy Transformed: Australian University Survey Summary of Questionnaire Results*, The Natural Edge Project, Australia; Desha, C. and Hargroves, K. (2009) 'Surveying the state of higher education in energy efficiency in Australian engineering curriculum', *Journal of Cleaner Production*, vol 18, issue 7, pp652–658.

67 Desha, C., Hargroves, K. and Reeve, A. (2009) *An Investigation into the Options for Increasing the Extent of Energy Efficiency Knowledge and Skills in Engineering Education*, Report to the National Framework for Energy Efficiency, The Natural Edge Project, Australia; Desha, C. and Hargroves, K. (2009) 'Surveying the state of higher education in energy efficiency in Australian engineering curriculum', *Journal of Cleaner Production*, vol 18, issue 7, pp652–658.

68 Desha, C., Hargroves, K. and Reeve, A. (2009) *An Investigation into the Options for Increasing the Extent of Energy Efficiency Knowledge and Skills in Engineering Education*, Report to the National Framework for Energy Efficiency, The Natural Edge Project, Australia.

69 McKenzie-Mohr, D. (2007) *Fostering Sustainable Behaviour: An Introduction to Community-Based Social Marketing*, third edition, New Society Press, Gabriola Island, BC.

70 Desha, C., Hargroves, K. and Reeve, A. (2009) *An Investigation into the Options for Increasing the Extent of Energy Efficiency Knowledge and Skills in Engineering Education*, Report to the National Framework for Energy Efficiency, The Natural Edge Project, Australia.

71 Desha, C. and Hargroves, K. (2007) 'Education for Sustainable Development Curriculum Audit (E4SD Audit): A curriculum diagnostic tool for quantifying requirements to embed sustainable development into higher education – demonstrated through a focus on engineering education', *World Transactions on Engineering and Technology Education*, UNESCO International Centre for Engineering Education (UICEE), vol 6, no 2.

4

Factors that Affect Poorer Nations' Ability to Achieve Decoupling

Escaping the 'Poverty Trap'

As the previous chapters have shown, future generations' economic prosperity will be undermined if the degradation of ecosystems continues, so efforts to reduce a range of environmental pressures are not only good for the environment, but good for the world's economies. Reducing environmental pressures will be particularly challenging for developing countries for a number of reasons outlined in this chapter. Poverty is both a major cause and effect of global environmental problems.

As Professor S. C. Rockefeller has stated:

> We cannot care for people in a world with collapsing ecosystems, and we cannot care for the Earth in a world where widespread poverty, injustice, economic inequity, and violent conflict exists.[1]

Our Common Future is among a number of significant publications to recognize that the call for sustainable development comes from the realization that economic development and issues of poverty reduction and human well-being cannot be separated from environmental pressures.[2] For example the need for fuel in developing countries is the largest single demand on trees, and accounts for just over half of all wood removed from forests.[3] If our global community is to effectively reduce environmental harms it will need to be underpinned by a strong approach to addressing factors that cause and exacerbate poverty.

In the year 2000, 189 nations of the world committed to the United Nations Millennium Development Goals which, among others, set a target of halving the number of people living in poverty by 2015. As 'ensuring environ-

Table 4.1 *UN Millennium Development Goals and environmental sustainability*

Goals	Why ensuring environmental sustainability is so important for achieving the other Millennium Development Goals
1 Eradicate extreme poverty and hunger	Poor people's livelihoods and food security depend on ecosystem goods and services. The poor often have insecure rights to environmental resources, inadequate access to markets, decision-making and environmental information, which limits their ability to protect the environment and improve their livelihoods and well-being.
2 Achieve universal primary education	Time spent by children collecting water and fuel wood reduces time available for schooling. In addition, the lack of energy, water and sanitation services in rural areas discourages qualified teachers from working in poor villages.
3 Promote gender equality	Women and girls are especially burdened by water and fuel collection, reducing their time and opportunities for education, literacy and income-generating activities.
4 Reduce child mortality	Diseases (such as diarrhoea) tied to unclean water and inadequate sanitation, and respiratory infections related to pollution are among the leading killers of children under five.
5 Improve maternal health	Inhaling polluted indoor air and carrying heavy loads of water and fuel wood impacts significantly on women's health. This can make them less fit to bear children and place them at greater risk of complications during pregnancy.
6 Combat major diseases	Up to 20% of the disease burden in developing countries may be due to environmental risk factors (as with malaria and parasitic infections). Further, lack of fuel for boiling water contributes to preventable water-borne diseases.
7 Ensure environmental sustainability	Countries need to integrate the principles of sustainable development into their policies and programmes to focus on reducing biodiversity loss, reducing the proportion of people without sustainable access to safe drinking water and basic sanitation, and achieving significant improvement in the lives of slum dwellers.
8 Develop a global partnership	Many global environmental problems, such as climate change, loss of species diversity and depletion of global fisheries require partnerships and cooperation between rich and poor countries.

Source: Adapted from the UN Millennium Development Goals

mental sustainability' is one of the eight goals it is clear that ensuring a stable environment is just as important as the other challenges facing the world today. In fact, as Table 4.1 illustrates, the other seven Millennium Goals actually rely upon, and are underpinned by, a stable environment in order for their targets to be achieved.

Environmental damage in the long run harms human well-being and contributes to poverty. In turn people living in poverty contribute to pressures on remaining biomass, forests, water resources, fish stocks, farmland and wildlife. As *Our Common Future* stated:

> *The links between environmental stress and developmental disaster are most evident in sub-Saharan Africa. Per capita food production, declining since the 1960s, plummeted during the*

drought of the 1980s, and at the height of the food emergency some 35 million people were exposed to risk. Human overuse of land and prolonged drought threaten to turn the grasslands of Africa's Sahel region into desert. No other region more tragically suffers the vicious cycle of poverty leading to environmental degradation, which leads in turn to even greater poverty.[4]

To reduce poverty and environmental degradation simultaneously it is vital first to understand what factors cause it. This chapter seeks to build on and complement the work of Professor Jeffrey Sachs, Director of the Earth Institute at Columbia University, who has published books such as *The End of Poverty*,[5] which outlines a range of factors and interrelationships within the 'poverty trap'. Professor Sachs shows in this book that domestic resources, which are needed to finance physical and human capital investment and productivity growth, are low, owing to the following factors:

- generalized poverty: where widespread poverty engenders rapid population growth and environmental degradation, as well as increasing the probability of political instability and conflict;
- weak state capacities: where all activities, including administration, and law and order are under-funded;
- weak corporate capacities: where corporate capacities are weak in business, finance and support services, even though there may be a thriving informal sector.[6]

Low productivity, rapid population growth, environmental degradation, political instability, conflict and weak state capacities all serve to reinforce generalized poverty directly and indirectly, and undermine efforts to reduce environmental pressures through impacts such as pollution, emissions and unsustainable consumption. Generalized poverty in turn results in low savings and investment, and low productivity. In addition, external trade and finance relationships interact with these domestic cycles of stagnation and together cause generalized poverty to persist.

Jeffrey Sachs has also identified four international factors which affect whether or not nations can escape the poverty trap, each of which is interrelated and has various cause-and-effect relationships within the nexus of generalized poverty and low savings, investment and productivity:

1   the form of primary commodity dependence;
2   build-up of unsustainable external debt;
3   emergence of an aid/debt service system;
4   degree of access to markets.

The underlying cause of the poverty trap among these complex external and domestic relationships is low productivity, low physical and human capital investment, and low savings. In countries with negative economic growth, savings, capital, low productivity and high indebtedness there is insufficient means for the people to break out of the poverty trap without foreign assistance. In *The End of Poverty*, Professor Sachs shows that the extreme poor find themselves trapped in poverty as the ratio of capital per person (GDP per capita) actually falls from generation to generation because of depreciation of what little capital they have, along with the further loss of natural capital and ecosystem health. Whether capital is accumulated and the poverty trap is broken fundamentally depends on whether households and businesses are able to save some of their current income or contribute some taxes to government at a higher rate than that which capital depreciates. Diminished or depreciated capital can result from a number of factors, such as the passage of time, or the wear and tear of equipment, disease, or the death of skilled workers.

Also, the amount of capital per person declines when the population is growing faster than capital is being accumulated. So even if there is net positive capital accumulation, whether this translates into rising income/economic growth per capita depends on whether the net capital accumulation is large enough to keep up with population growth. Much faster population growth in most developing countries is offsetting comparatively faster GDP growth, causing GDP per capita growth rates in these countries to be low or even negative. Sachs uses a simple economic model to illustrate the point:[7]

> *Suppose that an economy requires $3 of capital for every $1 of annual production. Suppose also that the capital stock depreciates at a rate of 2 per cent per annum. For each $1 million of capital this year, about $835,000 will remain at the end of a decade. Suppose that the economy has one million poor people, each with capital of $900. This results in an annual income of $300 per person ($900 divided by three). The total GNP is therefore $300 million ($300 per person multiplied by 1 million people). The population is growing at two per cent per year, so at the end of the decade there will be about 1.2 million poor people.*
>
> *Assume now that this society is too poor to save ... At the end of the decade, the capital stock that they do own or lease will have depreciated. So instead of $900 million in capital, there will only be $750 million in capital. But also the population has grown from one million to 1.2 million so instead of $900 in capital per person each person now only owns ~$628 per capita. Hence over a decade per capita wealth has dropped from $900 per person to $628 per capita amongst the poor in this country. This leads to households sinking into extreme poverty.*
>
> *Now suppose that due to overseas development assistance the economy begins with the same population but with capital stock that is twice as much equal to $2.4 billion. Assume that per capita income is twice as large at $600 per capita. Assume that as*

before households do not save anything out of incomes up to $300 and of income above $300 they now can save 20 per cent of $300 or $60 per annum.

The capital stock is $2.4 billion so over a decade it will depreciate to $2.2 billion. In other words $200 million will be lost. Also population growth will mean over that decade that in fact per capita wealth (not including saved income) is reduced from $1628 per capita to $900 per capita. But over that same decade per capita saved income is $600 or $600 million. Thus savings are just ahead overall from depreciation costs and this country no longer is experiencing negative economic growth but positive economic growth (albeit at a slow rate).

At this point the poverty trap is broken; a nation now achieving positive economic growth has the potential to break this trap once and for all. Economic growth can become self-sustaining through household savings and public investments supported by the taxation of households and business. Hence overseas foreign aid should not be considered as a handout but rather an essential investment that gives countries, a chance to break the poverty trap. When countries get their foot on the first rung of the ladder of development they are then able to continue an upward climb. The problem is that currently most poverty occurs, globally, because nations are not even on the first rung of development. Once countries and the extremely poor can be assisted onto the first rung, then virtuous cycles can be created. If people and nations are trapped below the first rung on the ladder of development, as Sachs' simple economic model above shows, they will continue to slide into deeper and more extreme poverty due to depreciation, population growth, greater vulnerability to disease, outside shocks (such as climate change) and the pressures this puts on increasingly scarce natural resources and ecosystems. As Sachs states, 'Even if well-governed countries stuck in a poverty trap mobilize domestic resources to pay for the interventions, they will not be able to afford the entire cost, and the difference must be borne by the developed world.'

The results of the failure of the developed world to more effectively help poorer countries break the poverty trap is evident in the number of failed states in the world. A failed state is a state whose government is so ineffective that it can no longer guarantee law and order or control over the country. The US Central Intelligence Agency estimates that there are at least 20 failed states currently and the World Bank estimates that there are an additional 35 fragile low-income countries under stress.[8] The most systematic ongoing effort to analyse failed states is done by the Fund for Peace and the Carnegie Endowment for International Peace, with the 2007 report stating that 'few encouraging signs emerged to suggest the world is on a path to greater peace and stability'.[9]

In his recent update of the seminal book, *Plan B*, Lester Brown points out that:

Ranking on the Failed States Index is closely linked with key demographic and environmental indicators. Of the top 20 failing states, 17 have rapid rates of population growth, many of them expanding at close to 3 per cent a year or 20-fold per century. In 5 of these 17 countries, women have an average of nearly seven children each ... In all but 6 of the top 20 failing states, at least 40 per cent of the population is under 15. Such a large share of young people often signals future political instability. Young men, lacking employment opportunities, often become disaffected, making them ready recruits for insurgency movements. Not surprisingly, there is also often a link between the degree of state failure and the destruction of environmental support systems. In a number of countries on the list – including Sudan, Somalia, and Haiti – deforestation, grassland deterioration, and soil erosion are widespread. The countries with fast-growing populations are also facing a steady shrinkage of both cropland and water per person, hence the rapid population growth, deteriorating environmental support systems, and poverty are reinforcing each other.[10]

To help fragile states break out of the poverty trap and ensure they do not become failed states, an integrated and multi-faceted approach is needed to address endemic poverty, rapid population growth, environmental pressures, and lack of effective governance and institutional capability. In addition to moral, humanitarian and environmental reasons, there are sound security reasons for the OECD to do much more to help break the poverty trap. The dangerous exports of failed states pose significant concerns, whether they be terrorism, drugs, weapons or nuclear proliferation. State failure often spreads to neighbouring countries, much as the conflict in Rwanda spilled over into the Democratic Republic of the Congo, eventually involving several other countries and resulting in the loss of 3.9 million lives over several years. More recently, the conflict in Darfur spread into Chad. With recent acts of terrorism around the world, it is clear that distance and relative military strength are no longer a measure of the potential for acts of conflict. OECD countries are now threatened less by states that are economically and militarily strong than by failing ones. This was the conclusion of the 2002 US National Security Strategy. Former UN Secretary-General Kofi Annan in 2005 summed up the issue in a speech to launch a report reviewing progress on the UN Millennium Goals, stating that:

We live in an interconnected world, in a world where we face many challenges, many threats – threats that no one country, however powerful, can face alone – and that we need to work together to contain these threats, whether it is terrorism, non-proliferation, or environmental degradation and poverty that

> *leads to failed States. And we also know that ignoring failed States creates problems that sometimes come back to bite us.*[11]

Steps needed to eradicate poverty include: filling several funding gaps, like those needed to reach universal primary education; fighting infectious diseases, such as AIDS, tuberculosis, and malaria; providing reproductive health care to contain the HIV epidemic; and ensuring clean drinking water and a healthy environment. According to the studies assembled in this chapter, the approximate annual cost of enabling poorer nations to escape the poverty trap and embark on growing their economies while decoupling negative environmental pressures includes:

- water and sanitation – US$9–30 billion (World Bank);[12]
- universal basic health care – US$33 billion (Jeffery Sachs);[13]
- reproductive health and family planning – US$17 billion (University of California);[14]
- closing the condom gap – US$3 billion (UNFPA and Population Action International);[15]
- universal primary education – US$10 billion (UK Treasury);[16]
- eradication of adult illiteracy – US$4 billion (Lester Brown);[17]
- assistance to preschool children and pregnant women in the 44 poorest countries – US$4 billion (Lester Brown);[18]
- school lunch programmes for the 44 poorest countries – US$6 billion (George McGovern);[19]
- natural disaster prevention – US$4–6 billion (World Bank);[20]
- emergency food aid – US$3.8 billion (UN World Food Programme).[21]

This amounts to US$77–100 billion per annum. This estimate is very close to estimates of the cost to achieve the UN Millennium Development Goals. For instance, using two different approaches, the World Bank estimate that if countries improve their policies and institutions, the additional foreign aid required to reach the Millennium Development Goals by 2015 is US$75–136 billion a year.[22] Additional funding will be needed to restore natural capital and ecosystem services globally, along with additional aid needed for capacity building and improving developing countries' institutional capability to provide these additional services.

However, in a global economy of over US$60 trillion this is a price the OECD nations can readily afford. Professor Sachs explains in detail how our generation is the first in history to have the technologies, knowledge and financial resources to actually eradicate extreme poverty. The achievements in poverty reduction and economic prosperity in Asia have been significant and can now underpin efforts by the OECD to invest in the activities necessary to eradicate extreme poverty. Lester Brown explains:

> *China's annual economic growth of nearly 10 per cent over the last two decades, along with India's more recent acceleration to 7 per cent a year, have together lifted millions out of poverty. The number of people living in poverty in China dropped from 648 million in 1981 to 218 million in 2001, the greatest reduction in poverty in history. India is also making impressive economic progress. Several countries in Southeast Asia are making impressive gains as well, including Thailand, Viet Nam, and Indonesia.[23]*

As of 2007, these countries in particular were making significant progress, but overall much still needs to be done. Sachs writes:

> *The truth is that the cost now [of ending extreme poverty] is likely to be small compared to any relevant measure – income, taxes, the costs of further delay, and the benefits from acting. Most importantly, the task can be achieved within the limits that the rich world has already committed: 0.7 per cent of the gross national product of the high-income world, a mere 7 cents out of every $10 in income. All the incessant debate about development assistance, and whether the rich are doing enough to help the poor, actually concerns less than 1 per cent of rich-world income. The effort required of the rich is so slight that to do less is to announce brazenly to a large part of the world, 'You count for nothing'. We should not be surprised, then, if in later years the rich reap the whirlwind of that heartless response.[24]*

Sachs asks the question, 'Can the US afford 0.7 per cent of GDP?'. The US's current donor assistance is 0.15 per cent of GDP, so to go from that to 0.7 per cent would be an extra 0.55 per cent tax on GDP. Sachs finds that the US economy, growing at 1.9 per cent per annum from 2005, would have reached the same level of increased prosperity on 1 May 2010 paying 0.7 per cent of GDP rather than on 1 January 2010 if it had continued paying 0.15 per cent. Sachs writes:

> *So, for a four month delay in achieving higher levels of prosperity, a billion people could be given an economic future of hope, health and improvement, rather than a downward spiral of despair, disease and decline. To put this further in perspective, the US spent 30 times as much on its military as it does on overseas aid in 2004: US$450 billion on the military compared to $15 billion on overseas aid. By comparison some European countries only spend 2–4 times as much on their military as foreign aid. The lopsided ratio of the US in this area reflects several myths. Most Americans when surveyed assume that the US is already giving far more overseas aid than is in fact the case. Surveys by*

the 'Program on International Policy Attitudes' show that Americans on average believe that foreign aid accounts for 20 per cent of the federal budget, approximately 24 times the actual figure. In 2002 the USA gave $3 per sub Saharan African. Taking out the parts for US consultants, food and other emergency aid, administrative costs and debt relief then the aid per sub Saharan African from the USA comes to 6 cents each in 2002.[25]

Sachs' calculations here assume 0.7 per cent of GDP is invested by governments on overseas aid, as many have promised to do in the past. This is based on a target for government of 0.7 per cent of GDP and for the private sector of 0.3 per cent GDP, being the long-held general consensus of what is needed to significantly reduce global poverty.[26] It is important to point out that this net target of 1 per cent GDP of wealthy nations has its origins as far back as 50 years ago in a statement from the World Council of Churches. Since 1970 the world's nations, on several occasions, have agreed in principle to work towards the 0.7 per cent target, but overall little and insufficient progress has been made. In 1992 the US, Australia and most of the nations of the world were signatories of Agenda 21, which contained the following statement in Chapter 33:13:

Developed countries reaffirm their commitments to reach the accepted United Nations target of 0.7 per cent GNP for ODA and, to the extent that they have not yet achieved that target, agree to augment their aid programmes in order to reach that target as soon as possible and to ensure prompt and effective implementation of Agenda 21.[27]

A decade later, at Monterrey, the Monterrey Consensus, adopted by many countries, stated:

We urge developed countries that have not done so to make concrete efforts towards the target of 0.7 per cent of GNP as ODA to developing countries.[28]

Later in 2002, at the World Summit on Sustainable Development in Johannesburg, South Africa, the conference delegates agreed on the Plan of Implementation, which aimed to:

Make available the increased commitments in official development assistance announced by several developed countries at the International Conference on Financing for Development. Urge the developed countries that have not done so to make concrete efforts towards the target of 0.7 per cent of GNP as ODA to developing countries.[29]

Table 4.2 *Business and the Millennium Development Goals: A framework for action*

Core business activities

Building financial capital – generating income and investment: Through paying local wages, taxes, dividends and royalties, making timely payment to local suppliers and earning foreign exchange.

Creating jobs: Recruiting locally, both within the company and along the supply chain, and facilitating positive organized labour relations.

Developing human resources: Investing in training, skills development, health and safety in the workplace and along the supply chain.

Building local businesses: Through supplier and distribution networks, especially with medium, small and micro-enterprises.

Spreading responsible international business standards and practices: In areas such as environment, health and safety management, human rights, ethics, and quality.

Establishing physical and institutional infrastructure: For example, investing in plant and machinery, telecommunications and transport systems, and legal and financial frameworks and institutions.

Social investment and philanthropy

Building social capital: By supporting education, training, youth development, environmental, and health and nutrition projects in local communities.

Creating and supporting businesses: Building capacity of community leaders and social entrepreneurs.

Micro-credit schemes: Establishing and supporting micro-credit programmes and small business support.

Building institutional and governance capacity: Building the governance capacity and voice of local civil society groups and media organizations.

Supporting and encouraging democratic processes: Assisting with voter education initiatives, community advocacy and participatory decision-making.

Capacity building: Training local technical specialists in environmental management.

Policy dialogue and advocacy activities

Working with governments to improve social infrastructure: By supporting health care and education reform and quality improvement.

Advocating: For increased levels of government aid to developing countries.

Addressing environmental issues: By advocating regulatory and fiscal policies within governments and civil society.

Engaging in global dialogue: On issues such as HIV/AIDS, climate change and biodiversity..

Supporting local and national governments: To achieve the elimination of bribery and corruption, fair and transparent regulations and human rights.

Helping to increase ability to attract and retain foreign and domestic investment: Advocating for improved access for developing country exports to OECD markets.

Source: Nelson and Prescott (2003)[30]

Since the first call 50 years ago by the World Council of Churches, only a handful of the world's nations have achieved this level of official development assistance (ODA) of 0.7 per cent of GDP: Denmark, Norway, Sweden and Luxembourg. Six others have pledged to do so by 2015, namely Finland,

France, Ireland, Belgium, the UK and Spain.[31] It is vital today that all OECD nations raise levels of ODA to relieve the suffering and misery of billions, and enable the building of capacity in developing nations to address multiple crises – from food shortages to disease to drought and climate change.

Much more could also be done by the private sector. The business case for action to eliminate poverty is clear and has been outlined by Jane Nelson and Dave Prescott's report *Business and the Millennium Development Goals: A Framework for Action*, summarized in Table 4.2.[32] In this report Nelson and Prescott cover the myriad of ways the private sector can, and is already starting to, contribute to alleviating poverty and supporting development goals such as the UN Millennium Goals.

As this table highlights, the private sector has a key role to play but it is important to note that it cannot replace the role of governments to coordinate efforts to reduce poverty and environmental pressure simultaneously. Both the scale of the challenge and the importance of coordination of efforts to avoid duplication, make the role of governments crucial. Thus to help achieve the UN Millennium Goals and lift people out of poverty, an integrated and multi-faceted approach is going to be needed to address endemic poverty, rapid population growth and environmental degradation.

We now consider how efforts to reduce poverty and environmental pressures simultaneously are greatly enhanced by improving the effectiveness of foreign development aid, reduce debt corruption and extreme inequality. In addition to these, this chapter then shows how stabilizing population, ensuring universal access to education and health, investing in natural capital and appropriate technologies, are also needed as part of a comprehensive strategy to ensure lasting progress is made to reduce extreme poverty and environmental pressures. We then feature the UN Millennium Villages project to show how bringing all these elements together can achieve rapid reductions in poverty and environmental degradation.

Improving the Effectiveness of Foreign Development Aid to Reduce Poverty

Effective overseas development aid certainly has the potential to help countries escape the poverty trap, but it is important to consider under which conditions overseas such aid is most effective. For instance, a 2008 study on *Foreign Aid and Economic Growth in the Developing Countries* found that 'One per cent of GDP in assistance normally translates to a sustained increase in growth of 0.5 per cent per capita. Some countries with sound policies received only a small amount of aid yet still achieved 2.2 per cent per capita growth. The good-management, high-aid groups grew much faster, at 3.7 per cent per capita GDP'.[33] In poor-policy countries, relatively low private sector investment may explain why the net effect of such aid is small. In 2003, the OECD provided evidence supporting this suggestion:

One factor contributing to low growth rates in developing countries, especially the poorest ones, is insufficient, inappropriate and poorly maintained physical infrastructure. Improving the investment climate will encourage more infrastructure investors to invest. This in turn will make infrastructure services more widely available and encourage other types of investment. Recent research supports the view that using ODA to promote infrastructure development merits greater attention; studies have found a large, positive, causal relationship over a four-year period between 'immediate-impact aid' – i.e. budget and balance-of-payments support, infrastructure and aid for productive sectors – and economic growth. A diversified and competitive financial sector is also important for promoting growth in developing countries as it helps maintain economic stability, makes financial transactions secure, mobilizes external and domestic savings and facilitates the efficient allocation of capital to productive investments.[34]

By contrast, others investigating the issue have found that foreign aid can have a negative impact on growth as it can erode institutional quality and increase rent-seeking and corruption.[35] By and large, the relation between aid and economic growth remains neither definitely positive nor negative because there are many other variables affecting whether or not aid stimulates economic growth. For example, geography has been found to be influential on economic growth but so far this factor has been neglected in many of the aid and economic growth analyses.[36] As the World Bank states:

Foreign aid has at times been a spectacular success. Botswana and the Republic of Korea in the 1960s, Indonesia in the 1970s, Bolivia and Ghana in the late 1980s, and Uganda and Vietnam in the 1990s are all examples of countries that have gone from crisis to rapid development. Foreign aid played a significant role in each transformation, contributing ideas about development policy, training for public policymakers, and finance to support reform and an expansion of public services ... Internationally funded and coordinated programs have dramatically reduced such diseases as river blindness and vastly expanded immunization against key childhood diseases. Hundreds of millions of people have had their lives touched, if not transformed, by access to schools, clean water, sanitation, electric power, health clinics, roads, and irrigation – all financed by foreign aid. On the flip side, foreign aid has also been, at times, an unmitigated failure. While Zaire's former dictator, Sese Seko Mobuto, was reportedly amassing one of the world's largest personal fortunes (invested, naturally, outside his own country), decades of large-scale foreign assistance left not a trace of progress. Zaire (now the Democratic

Republic of Congo) is just one of several examples where a steady flow of aid ignored, if not encouraged, incompetence, corruption, and misguided polices [sic]. *Foreign aid in different times and different places has thus been highly effective, totally ineffective, and everything in between.*[37]

Clearly, then, simply increasing overseas development aid will not be sufficient to ensure poverty is eliminated and a platform for progressive action on environmental goals developed. Overseas development aid will most likely only succeed within good policy and governance environments relatively free of corruption. In addition, if unsustainable debt levels and trade barriers, which particularly harm the poorest countries, are not effectively addressed, this will continue to block the potential for poor countries to trade agricultural and other products with OECD countries and climb the ladder of sustainable development.

For many developing countries caught in the poverty trap, debt relief is an essential first step to enable them to use the majority of overseas development aid for poverty reduction rather than debt repayments. For example, with sub-Saharan Africa spending four times as much on debt servicing as it spends on health care, debt forgiveness can help boost living standards. In 2005, through leadership from the UK government and NGO pressure, heads of the G-8 group of industrial countries meeting in Gleneagles, Scotland, agreed to cancel US$100 billion worth of the multilateral debt that some of the poorest countries owed to the World Bank, the International Monetary Fund and the African Development Bank. This step forward provided relief to 18 of the poorest debt-ridden countries (14 in Africa and 4 in Latin America).

The year after the Gleneagles meeting, the International Monetary Fund had eliminated the debts owed by 18 countries, the first major step toward the debt relief goal set at the G-8 meeting. For Zambia, the US$6 billion of debt taken off the books enabled President Levy Mwanawasa to announce that basic health care would now be free. Burundi has used the debt relief to cancel school fees, enabling 300,000 children to attend school. If the international community continues to forgive debt, it will be a strong step toward eradicating poverty. Yet there is still room for progress. The Gleneagles' commitment eliminates only a minor share of poor-country debt to international lending institutions; many more poor countries, which are currently significantly indebted, would benefit from this.

OECD nations can readily afford to do this, considering that OECD governments currently subsidize environmentally damaging industries totalling over US$650 billion per annum[38] – more than six times the level of debt relief promised and roughly ten times what is spent on overseas development aid. A barrier to the OECD lifting levels of aid has been the concern that increases in aid will be squandered due to corruption, resulting in little overall progress. Hence a key focus this century must be on reducing and eliminating corruption in public and private institutions.

The World Bank has identified corruption as the single greatest obstacle to economic and social development; an obstacle that can cause the growth rate of a country to be 0.5–1.0 per cent lower than that of a similar country with little corruption.[39] Transparency International, the leading NGO working on this issue, highlights how damaging corruption is to achieving the full breadth of social development goals:

> *On the political front, corruption constitutes a major obstacle to democracy and the rule of law. In a democratic system, offices and institutions lose their legitimacy when they are misused for private advantage. Though this is harmful in the established democracies, it is even more so in newly emerging ones. Accountable political leadership cannot develop in a corrupt climate. Economically, corruption leads to the depletion of national wealth. It is often responsible for the funnelling of scarce public resources to uneconomic high-profile projects, such as dams, power plants, pipelines and refineries, at the expense of less spectacular but more necessary infrastructure projects, such as schools, hospitals and roads, or the supply of power and water to rural areas.[40]*

Susan Rose-Ackerman has written widely on corruption and lists the following ways through which poor people are hurt by corruption:

- The poor will receive a lower level of social services.
- Infrastructure investment will be biased against projects that aid the poor.
- The poor may face higher tax or fewer services.
- The poor are disadvantaged in selling their agricultural produce.[41]

The problem of corruption highlights more clearly than any other issue that social, environmental and economic challenges are intertwined. Corruption is widely regarded as one of the biggest impediments to economic growth, social development and environmental sustainability. In 1995, Paolo Mauro presented an article entitled 'Corruption and growth', which helped to demonstrate the negative relationship between corruption and long-term economic growth.[42] The paper showed, using extensive cross-country data, that corruption has the effect of reducing confidence and investment in nations and thus reduces economic growth. Mauro's 1995 study has been verified by a number of empirical studies which have generally concluded that the economic costs of corruption and weak governance are substantial.[43] Given that there is increasing recognition that corruption has significant adverse effects on social, environmental and economic outcomes, the question needs to be asked: why don't countries strive to improve their institutions and eliminate corruption? Why do many countries appear to be stuck in a vicious circle of widespread corruption and low economic growth, often accompanied by ever-changing governments through revolutions and coups? Mauro argues in his 2004 paper that a possible explanation is that when corruption is widespread, individuals do not have incentives to fight it even if everybody would be better off without it.[44] Another is that they simply do not know how to effectively address and eliminate corruption.

Countries like Botswana have shown that it is possible to eliminate corruption and maintain this through a proactive approach. Botswana, since independence in 1966, has been politically stable with a multi-party democracy and has enjoyed four decades of economic growth underpinned by its diamond industry. Botswana is the largest producer of diamonds, by value, in the world and yet has still been able to successfully keep corruption in check; according to Transparency International, Botswana is the least corrupt country in Africa. The poster on the wall in the arrivals hall at Gaborone Airport is a clear sign; 'Botswana has zero tolerance for corruption. It is illegal to offer or ask for a bribe'. Lebang Mpotokwane, chairman of Transparency International in Botswana, says that in a fast-growing economy, there are temptations, but the government has led by example; 'the government is forever preaching to the nation about corruption, and I can't think of any corruption involving government ministers'.[45]

The success of Botswana demonstrates that it is worthwhile to investigate the way in which a country can maintain a very low level of corruption. Some of the reasons for Botswana's success are owed to unique historical developments, such as a peaceful struggle for independence, the discovery of diamonds after independence, and political leaders who refrained from seizing the nation's wealth. Although this course of events cannot be replicated, others can, such as the way Botswana negotiated rents on access to mine diamonds with the major multinational diamond company De Beers. The deals with diamond multinational De Beers were negotiated very carefully and evolved into a real partnership which is often absent in the relations between multinationals from the North and governments in the South. Botswana's overall success would also have been impossible without a national integrity system. This includes high levels of democratic accountability, an independent and efficient judicial system, an Ombudsman to report irregularities in the public service, and free media.[46]

Botswana is not the only success story. When government officials, politicians, judges or the police are earning very low wages they are vulnerable to corruption. Singapore showed that corruption of this type can be quickly eliminated by strong penalties and by raising salaries. However, not all countries and governments have the capacity to do this. In Uganda, to fight corruption, the government publicizes all cheques sent to the local level, so that villagers know what they should be receiving and can make sure those between the national government and the villages are not taking a cut. In Nigeria, the government publishes how much money it is getting in oil royalties so that citizens can see where the money is going. In Thailand, the new constitution includes the notion that citizens have a basic right to know what their government is doing with taxes and money.

However, in a search for opportunities to significantly reduce environmental pressures, corruption remains one of the most difficult challenges to address. Researchers and reformers at all levels – national and international, official and non-governmental, public and private – see their efforts to tackle corruption frustrated by lack of political will and lack of information, as well as lack of common methodologies, appropriate tools of analysis and concerted action.

Addressing Economic Disparity: The Inequality Predicament

Efforts to reduce poverty and environmental pressures simultaneously are threatened by growing global economic disparity. As *Our Common Future* stated in 1987:

> *Such inequalities represent great differences not merely in the quality of life today, but also in the capacity of societies to improve their quality of life in the future ... Within countries, poverty has been exacerbated by the unequal distribution of land and other assets. The rapid rise in population has compromised the ability to raise living standards. These factors, combined with growing demands on the commercial use of good land ... [have] pushed many subsistence farmers onto poor land and robbed them of any hope of participating in their nations economic lives. The same forces have meant that traditional shifting cultivators, who once cut forests, grew crops and then gave the forest time to recover, now have neither land enough nor time to let forests re-establish. So forests are being destroyed, often only to create poor farmland that cannot support for long those that till it.*[47]

Hence, 20 years ago *Our Common Future* argued that broad-based economic growth is critical to accelerating poverty reduction but that this economic growth needed to be pro-poor, and based on greater equity of distribution of wealth to achieve rapid poverty reduction.[48] Twenty years on from the publication of *Our Common Future* global inequality continues to rise.[49] In 2005 two major reports were published on the issue – the UNDP *2005 Human Development Report*[50] and the UN's *The Inequality Predicament*[51] – both agreed that global income inequality continues to increase. According to the UNDP report only nine countries (4 per cent of the world's population) have reduced the wealth gap between rich and poor, while 80 per cent of the world's population have recorded an increase in wealth inequality. The report states that, 'the richest 50 individuals in the world have a combined income greater than that of the poorest 416 million'. According to the UN report, the 2.5 billion people living on less than US$2 a day – 40 per cent of the world's population – receive only 5 per cent of global income, while 54 per cent of global income goes to the richest 10 per cent of the world's population. The UN report also identifies non-economic aspects of global inequality (such as inequalities in health, education, employment, gender and opportunities for social and political participation) as causing and exacerbating poverty. These institutionalized inequalities result in greater marginalization within society. The report emphasizes the inevitable social disintegration, violence and national and international terrorism that this inequality fosters.

The most successful East Asian countries in the 1970s and 1980s showed that rapid growth, combined with low initial inequality and pro-poor distributional change, can help to reduce poverty relatively quickly.[52] Analysis of changes in poverty levels across a sample of developing countries in the 1980s and 1990s also highlights the importance of fast growth for poverty reduction.[53] But income inequality also affects the pace at which growth is translated into poverty reduction. Growth has been found to be less efficient in lowering poverty levels in countries with high initial inequality or in which the distributional pattern of growth favours the rich.[54] In the late 1990s the term 'pro-poor growth' became popular as economists recognized that accelerating poverty reduction required both more rapid growth and lower inequality. Thus these two key social development goals – to eliminate poverty and to reduce global inequality – featured in some form in almost every call for sustainable development, and both of these goals appear to be mutually reinforcing.

Addressing inequality helps to reduce the risks of violence, conflict and war. The most well-established determinant of levels of violence in a country is the scale of income differences between rich and poor, meaning that more unequal societies tend to be more violent. Reducing inequality also correlates with improved levels of public health,[55] which in turn has been shown by the Harvard School of Public Health to correlate with a productive workforce and economic growth.[56]

Stabilizing Population Growth

While progress is being made on the goal of cutting poverty in half by 2015, few of the other Millennium Development Goals – including achieving universal primary school education, reversing the spread of infectious diseases, especially HIV and malaria, and halving the number of people without access to safe drinking water – look like being achieved by 2015. Particularly as the 2008 global economic crisis has plunged hundreds of millions more people below the poverty line. Many experts now argue that a halving of poverty by 2015 will be all but impossible without efforts to address unsustainable population growth. Ensuring access to family planning or reproductive health services was not one of the original Millennium Goals. To address this omission, in 2007 the UK All Party Parliamentary Group on Population Development and Reproductive Health was created. After extensive investigations the group concluded that 'the MDGs are difficult or impossible to achieve with current levels of population growth in the least developed countries and

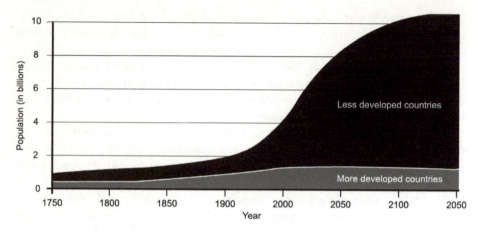

Figure 4.1 *World population growth – medium level projection*

Source: UN (1998)[57]

regions'.[58] Since then the UN has created and approved a new target, that of universal access to family planning and reproductive health services by 2015.[59]

If current trends continue, the global population will exceed 9 billion people by 2050, and according to the UN Department of Economic and Social Affairs (UNDESA) Population Division, 95–99 per cent of this growth will take place in the developing countries – with more than 90 per cent of this growth concentrated in the poorest of these developing countries, as shown in Figure 4.1.[60]

Slowing population growth helps reduce poverty, and, conversely, reducing poverty helps slow population growth. As *Our Common Future* stated:

> *Population growth and development are linked in complex ways. Economic development generates resources that can be used to improve education and health. These improvements, along with associated social changes, reduce both fertility and mortality rates. On the other hand, high rates of population growth that eats into surpluses available for economic and social development can hinder improvements in education and health.*[61]

So, if we are serious about reducing environmental pressures to sustainable levels it will be necessary to address the factors that drive high population growth. Over 40 countries no longer have population growth – with Japan, Russia, Germany and Italy having the lowest fertility rates in the world – and are likely to see a decline in population growth over the coming decades unless immigration levels are increased. The majority of countries have relatively stable population numbers due to the fact that their fertility rates are at replacement level or just below. This group includes China and the US. A third group of countries, with the lowest levels of GDP per capita, is projected to more than double their populations by 2050. And even if these nations quickly reduce population growth to below replacement level, the UN forecasts that global population will not stabilize until 2041, at around 8 billion people.[62]

A first step to slowing world population growth is investing to ensure that all women who want to plan their families have access to the family planning and basic reproductive health services they need. Unfortunately, at present over 200 million couples cannot obtain these services.[63] For instance, around 500,000 women die each year during childbirth with over 90 per cent of cases being in developing countries. This has a devastating effect on the family unit and is a significant contributor to such families remaining in poverty.[64] The benefits of addressing this issue of maternal mortality rates are enormous and the costs have been shown to be minimal.[65] This is well illustrated in Peru where the mortality rate in childbirth was reduced by 50 per cent between 1999 to 2005. Traditionally, most rural Peruvian women give birth at home, supported by family members or midwives. However, when complications arise, the long distance from health care facilities increases the risk of maternal mortality. The Peruvian government, working with aid organizations such as Care International, has built and resourced 450 'birthing centres' where pregnant women in remote regions can stay in the lead-up to their due date. Each birthing centre has a staff 24 hours a day to ensure that health professionals can help with emergencies. If there are serious risks with a pregnancy or birth, the birthing centres have two-way radios to alert hospitals to send ambulances to quickly transport patients to the closest fully equipped hospitals. Such centres can also provide citizens with face-to-face access to trained health professionals who can advise on family planning options and provide basic reproductive health services.

Many couples want to have access to basic family planning and reproductive health services to be able to plan when and how many children they have. This is well illustrated in Iran, which 'in just one decade dropped its near-record population growth rate to one of the lowest in the developing world'.[66] Janet Larson from the Earth Policy Institute explains that in 1979, when Ayatollah Khomeini assumed leadership in Iran, he stopped all family planning programmes. Khomeini sought large families to bolster Iran's army for the 1980s Iran-Iraq war. This led to population growth levels rising to a peak of 3.2 per cent in the early 1980s. The explosive population growth rate strained both the environment and economy. Iran's leaders soon realized that such rapid population growth was stretching social services infrastructure, while also causing unemployment and environmental degradation to increase. So, in 1989 the government restored its family planning programme and, in May 1993, passed a national family planning law. The government ministries of education, culture and health worked together to encourage smaller families. Iran Broadcasting raised awareness, and numerous 'health houses' were created to provide these family planning services. Birth control became free of charge, and to be eligible for a marriage licence, new couples were required to take a class on modern contraception. Janet Larsen writes that:

> *In addition to the direct health care interventions, a broad based effort was launched to raise literacy ... The literacy rate for adult males increased from 48 per cent in 1970 to 84 per cent in 2000, nearly doubling in 30 years. Female literacy climbed even faster, rising from less than 25 per cent in 1970 to more than 70 per cent. Meanwhile, school enrolment grew from 60 to 90 per cent. And by 1996, 70 per cent of rural and 93 per cent of urban households had televisions, allowing family planning information to be spread widely through the media. As a result of these initiatives, family size in Iran dropped from seven children to fewer than three. From 1987 to 1994, Iran cut its population growth rate by half. Its overall population growth rate of 1.3 per cent in 2006 is only slightly higher than the U.S. growth rate. The costs of providing reproductive health and family planning services are small compared with their benefits. Joseph Speidel estimates that expanding these services to reach all women in the developing countries would take close to $17 billion in additional funding from both industrial and developing countries.*[67]

The UN estimates that meeting the needs of the 200 million women who do not have access to effective contraception could each year prevent 52 million unwanted pregnancies, 22 million induced abortions and 1.4 million infant deaths.[68] Put simply, the costs to society of not filling the family planning gap are significant. For Bangladesh, analysts found that, if the government spent US$62 to prevent an unwanted birth, it saved US$615 in reduced social services costs.[69] Furthermore, investing in reproductive health and family planning services leaves more financial resources per child for education and health care, thus accelerating the escape from the poverty trap.

Economists talk of the per capita economic benefits of lower fertility rates which raise the capital stock per person. At the household level, higher fertility rates mean less investment in each child's development (that is, nutrition, schooling and health care). At the national level higher population growth means more capital investment must be provided simply to expand the number of services and infrastructure to keep pace with population growth rather than improving the quality of such services and infrastructure. This has been empirically tested with cross-country studies of economic growth and fertility rates, with researchers finding a statistically significant negative correlation of high fertility rates with economic growth.[70]

Ensuring Universal Access to Education and Health Care

The overwhelming majority of those living in poverty today are the children of people who have lived in poverty. A powerful way to break out of the vicious cycle of poverty is through education, especially the education of girls. Economist Gene Sperling concluded in a 2001 study of 72 countries that 'the expansion of female secondary education may be the single best lever for achieving substantial (voluntary) reductions in fertility rates'.[71] At a time when the HIV epidemic is spreading, schools provide the institutional means to educate young people about the risks of infection, as they provide the means to reach children at the right age. One great need in developing countries, particularly those where the ranks of teachers are being decimated by HIV, is more teacher training.

For example, scholarships could be provided to motivated students from poor families to attend training institutes in exchange for a commitment to teach for an agreed period as a form of return of service. Such an initiative would help create teaching capacity to address the massive problem of lack of primary education and child and adult illiteracy. Globally, there are currently nearly 800 million illiterate adults, and award-winning adult literacy programmes in countries such as Bangladesh and Iran can serve as models.[72]

According to studies by the UK Treasury, an estimated £10 billion (US$16 billion) in external funding, in addition to what is being spent today, is needed for the world to achieve universal primary education.[73] This seems a small price to pay to ensure that in the 21st century all children have a chance to go to school. However, in very poor countries, there are barriers to this. If children do not assist with the farming, there often will be little food for them at night, as Lester Brown explains:

> *Few incentives to get children in school are as effective as a school lunch program, especially in the poorest countries. Since 1946, every American child in public school has had access to a school lunch program … There is no denying the benefits of this national program. Children who are ill or hungry miss many days of school. And even when they can attend, they do not learn as well.*[74]

When school lunch programmes are launched in low-income countries, school enrolment jumps, the children's academic performance improves, and children spend more years in school. The impact on the lives of girls is especially significant. Attracted to school by the lunch, statistics show that they stay longer in school, which can lead to delaying marriage, and having smaller families. It would cost an estimated US$6 billion per annum to run school lunch programmes in the 44 lowest-income countries in addition to what the UN now spends to reduce hunger.[75]

The issue of children's nutrition in the years before they get to school is also critical for their health and development. Former US Senator George McGovern notes that 'a women, infants and children (WIC) program, which offers nutritious food supplements to needy pregnant and nursing mothers should also be available in the poor countries'.[76] After running for 33 years, the US WIC programme has made a significant difference in improving nutrition, health and the development of preschool children from poor families. These extensive years of experience could be used as a basis to create new aid programmes to reach pregnant women, nursing mothers and small children in the 44 poorest countries. Such a programme would help eradicate hunger among millions of small children at a critical time in their early childhood development, and is estimated to cost annually US$6 billion.[77]

While heart disease, cancer, obesity and smoking dominate health concerns in industrial countries, in developing countries infectious diseases are the overriding health concern. Besides HIV/AIDS, the principal diseases of concern are diarrhoea, respiratory illnesses, tuberculosis, malaria and measles. Child mortality is high. These infectious diseases not only take a devastating human toll but they also have a significant negative effect on economic growth. The poorest countries in GDP per capita also correlate with those countries with the worst malaria outbreaks globally. Mosquito bed nets, indoor spraying and the best malaria medicines are all very cost effective in preventing the spread of malaria and vital investments to help most of the countries with negative economic growth break the poverty trap. Yet currently the world only spends tens of millions in aid per annum on fighting malaria when US$2–3 billion is needed.[78]

Currently most people in Africa, where malaria is the most virulent, do not have access to even a 50-cent mosquito net. In a damning analysis of current aid expenditure on AIDS, Sachs and Attaran found several years ago that until the early 21st century the world was only giving Africa an average of US$69 million per annum to fight HIV/AIDS.[79] To put this into context, citizens of the EU have been estimated to spend at least US$11 billion per year on ice cream alone.[80] In recognition of this serious failure, the WHO formed the 'Commission of Macroeconomics and Health', chaired by Professor Sachs, to study and outline the cost benefits to the world of investing to improve health outcomes globally, and in 2001 published *Investing in Health for Economic Development*. This report found that:

> *Evidence presented by the Commission suggests that each 10 per cent improvement in life expectancy is associated with an increase in economic growth of about 0.3 per cent to 0.4 per cent per year, other growth factors being equal. Economic losses from ill health have been underestimated. Countries with the weakest conditions of health and education have more difficulty in achieving sustained growth. In sub-Saharan Africa losses due to HIV/AIDS are estimated to be at least 12 per cent of annual GDP. Economic development in malaria-free zones is at least 1 per cent per year higher than in areas where malaria is endemic.*
>
> *A few health conditions account for a high proportion of avoidable deaths. In 1998, 16 million deaths were caused by communicable diseases, maternal and perinatal conditions, childhood infections, tobacco-related illness and nutritional*

deficiencies. Of the 30 million children not receiving basic immunizations, 27 million live in countries with GDP per capita lower than US$1200. Of the half million women who die annually in pregnancy and childbirth, 99 per cent live in developing countries. The level of spending on health in low-income countries is insufficient to address the health challenges they face.

The recommended increase in spending is large, but so is the potential return. The aggregate additional cost of scaling up interventions in low-income countries is in the order of US$66 billion per year, with around half of this amount coming from donors. The predicted result is to save around eight million lives a year and generate economic benefits of US$360 billion: a sixfold return on investment.[81]

Another significant report exploring the economic benefits of investments in public health is *Millions Saved: Proven Successes in Global Health* by the Center for Global Development. This 2004 report showed that:

The costs of successful public health initiatives are dwarfed by the social and economic benefits of eliminating, treating, or controlling the disease. For example, a tuberculosis program in China treated more than 1.5 million patients over 10 years at a total cost of $130 million, preventing 30,000 TB-related deaths annually and averaging just $15–20 for each healthy life-year saved. The economic returns were enormous: Each dollar invested in the program generated $60 in the form of savings on treatment costs and the increased earning power of healthy people. Similarly, efforts to control river blindness in sub-Saharan Africa between 1974 and 2002 cost less than $1 per protected person and prevented 60,000 cases of blindness. As a result of the program's positive impact on health, an estimated $3.7 billion will accrue from improved worker and agricultural productivity.[82]

Infectious diseases that cause relatively few problems in developed countries continue to spread sickness and death in poorer regions of the world. One of the reasons for this is that poorer countries cannot afford the immunizations that those in the OECD countries take for granted. The largest private–public partnership to address this is the Global Alliance for Vaccines and Immunization (GAVI) whose goal is to make a major contribution to the 'two-thirds reduction in under-five mortality' targeted by the international community in the Millennium Development Goals. GAVI seeks to do this by making advanced vaccine products available in the world's poorest countries and strengthening delivery systems to ensure their children derive full benefit.[83]

Governments, philanthropists and benefactors are donating to such initiatives, for example the Bill and Melinda Gates Foundation had invested more than US$1.5 billion until the end of 2006 to protect children from infectious diseases like measles.[84] Vaccinations are one of the most cost-effective investments that can be made with significant health improvements from an investment of a few cents per child. Immunization programmes, led by the WHO have successfully eradicated a number of diseases, like smallpox, through global immunization programmes, saving billions of dollars in health are expenditures.[85] Lester Brown writes that:

> Similarly, a WHO-led international coalition, including Rotary International, UNICEF, the US Centers for Disease Control and Prevention (CDC), and Ted Turner's UN Foundation, has waged a worldwide campaign to wipe out polio, a disease that has crippled millions of children. Since 1988, Rotary International has contributed $600 million to this effort. Under this coalition-sponsored Global Polio Eradication Initiative, the number of polio cases worldwide dropped from some 350,000 per year in 1988 to fewer than 700 in 2003.[86]

One of the most important plans to help countries break the poverty trap is to implement strategies to curb the HIV epidemic. In 2007 one of the four new targets adopted by the UN and added to the Millennium Development Goals was 'Achieve, by 2010, universal access to HIV treatment for all those who need it.' An important starting point to curb the HIV/AIDS epidemic is through prevention and education. To rapidly reduce the spread of the infection it is vital to target the groups in society which are most likely to spread the disease, such as truck drivers and sex workers, with education programmes and free condoms. In India, for example, studies show that educating the country's 2 million female sex workers about HIV/AIDS risks and the value of using a condom pays huge dividends.[87] As Lester Brown states:

> At the most fundamental level, dealing with the HIV threat requires roughly 13.1 billion condoms a year in the developing world and Eastern Europe. Including those needed for contraception adds another 4.4 billion. But of the 17.5 billion condoms needed, only 1.8 billion are being distributed, leaving a shortfall of 15.7 billion. At only 3.5¢ each, or $550 million, the cost of saved lives by supplying condoms is minuscule.[88]

Also, significant breakthroughs have occurred to reduce the costs of HIV/AIDS medicine. For instance, the cost of anti-retroviral medicine is now under US$300 per year per person, down from nearly US$12,000 per year when first released.[89]

Spurring Economic Growth by Reducing Environmental Pressures

It is physically impossible for all developing nations to achieve Western material living standards with previous modes of development, as meeting such demand would require more capacity than our planet has to offer. To ensure that efforts to reduce poverty lead to reductions in environmental pressures, the world must implement a range of sustainable-development-related innovations, particularly in energy, water and materials consumption, as presented in *Factor Five*.[90] However, past applications of aid have given insufficient attention to these important areas. This is because the investment needs of the extreme poor are diverse, and decision-makers must weigh the need for investment in, for example, improving resource productivity of industry or replanting areas of forest, against investment in education, health, vaccinations and family planning. Development finance has often subsequently not been allocated towards 'sustainable-development'-related investments that lead to reducing environmental pressures because the belief has been that they secure a lower rate of return than other investments.

However, economists can now measure rates of return on investments to both restore environmental systems and reduce the pressure on them, and are therefore able to test these assumptions. The exploration of this area has resulted in a number of reports, including *Investing in Environmental Wealth for Poverty Reduction* by the late UK environmental economist David Pearce. This report finds that rates of return on investments in environmental assets have been significantly underestimated. Taking the example of valuing the worth of forestry assets globally, Pearce argues that properly valuing a forest's ability to store carbon ranges between US$360 and US$2200 per hectare, which makes forests worth far more than if they are converted to grazing or cropland. Indeed, Pearce's study claims that once the price of carbon reaches over US$30 a tonne it becomes more cost effective to conserve forests than to clear them.[91] *The Stern Review* is even more optimistic than Pearce, and estimates that the marginal cost per greenhouse gas abated from avoiding deforestation is the cheapest form of abatement after energy efficiency and demand management.[92] As deforestation is currently responsible for roughly 18 per cent of global greenhouse gas emissions, compensating developing countries for stopping deforestation and funding reforestation schemes, is both a sound investment in reducing poverty (considering the jobs it will create and the direct benefit from carbon sequestration) and one of the most cost-effective and rapid ways the world could make progress on reducing greenhouse gas emissions in the short term.

Stopping deforestation and restoring ecosystem services is also vital to helping developing countries restore soils and clean waterways in order to provide a sustainable base for their agriculture and fisheries, upon which billions of people depend for their livelihoods. Protecting and enhancing nature's resilience will also help developing countries cope and adapt to the future anticipated impacts on temperature, rainfall and sea-level rises from climate change. Conversely, further loss of forests and other natural ecosystems makes developing countries more vulnerable to storms, landslides, flooding, droughts and natural disasters, as previously explained, and this realization has strengthened efforts that have led to China, the Philippines, Sri Lanka, Thailand and Viet Nam initiating total or partial bans on deforestation.[93]

The story of the last 40 years in Niger demonstrates perhaps better than any other the significant benefits of investing in reforestation.[94] Forty years ago Niger was on track to become a failed state, propelled by drought, desertification, unsustainable farming practices and rapid population growth. It was becoming harder and taking longer for firewood and timber to be found and the farming soil's fertility was declining. This, along with a rapidly increasing population (the national average birth rate was seven children per family), was sending Niger into a dangerous poverty spiral. However, from the mid-1980s this began to change. At that time, farmers in several villages were taught to plough carefully around tree saplings when sowing crops of millet, sorghum, peanuts and beans. With careful nurturing, along with other soil and water conservation practices, saplings became trees, putting down roots and a buffer against topsoil erosion and crop loss. The quick-growing trees provided families with wood for charcoal, foliage for animal fodder and fruit for food, and soon became assets that families used to supplement incomes and provide insurance against crop failure. Word of mouth spread the good news until an area of 7 million hectares was being replanted with trees.

While this transformation occurred largely due to the efforts of Niger's farming families it was also assisted by the government. The government gave the farmers secure property rights over the trees in recognition of the farmers' investment in time and labour to plant them. The result of their efforts is today a more sophisticated mix of agro-forestry and a more diverse economy. The effects of this change have been profound: the average distance a woman must walk for firewood in the Zinder region of Niger has declined from two and a half hours to half an hour; poverty is lower; nutrition improved; and communities are less vulnerable to natural disasters. When a regional drought followed by locusts hit in 2005, many of the villages in the green belt of Niger reported no child deaths from malnutrition because they were able to sell wood in local markets to purchase expensive cereals. This success story from Niger demonstrates that the greatest untapped resource in solving the problem of global poverty and environmental decline are those who are currently trapped in poverty and enduring hardship because of environmental degradation – they have more motivation than anyone to change their conditions if just supported to have a chance to do so.

Another area where investment can both reduce levels of poverty and reduce environmental pressures is in improving the quality of drinking water and levels of sanitation. Increasing access to the supply of clean water and sanitation for example, can yield very high rates of return, with benefit-to-cost ratios in the range of 4:1 to 14:1, making such investments extremely attractive from a social investment standpoint.[95] Improved water supplies and sanitation create time savings (that is, time not spent travelling long distances to fetch water) that translate into higher economic output and productivity as well as greater school attendance.

Preserving or rebuilding ecosystem services can not only increase the system's resilience to natural disasters, it can also help to improve water quality, with the services provided by watersheds globally being worth tens of billions of dollars. Currently, 40 per cent of humanity, or 2.6 billion people, do not have regular access to clean water, due in part to the removal or degradation of water catchment areas. About 90 per cent of the sewage and 70 per cent of the industrial waste in developing countries is being discharged untreated into watercourses, and without the natural wetlands and natural aquatic systems this waste is not even treated to primary levels.[96]

In this brief discussion we have shown several examples of why investing in a range of initiatives that both improve conditions and reduce environmental pressures need to be part of any serious strategy to help countries break out of the poverty trap. As Klaus Töpfer, UNEP Executive Director, stated:

> It is clear ... that the environment is something like the red ribbon running through the Millennium Development Goals. It is not a luxury good, only affordable when all other problems have been solved. It is the oxygen that breathes life into all our aspirations for a healthier, fairer and more stable world. We also need to pursue more imaginative and clever methods for paying the poor for the regional and global assets they hold. But these ecosystem services, which largely remove the pollution of the rich countries from the atmosphere, are provided gratis and the people paid nothing for these assets.[97]

Since overseas development aid funding is currently scarce it is necessary to explore the question of the most cost-effective ways to invest in developing countries. Given that there is now significant political will in OECD countries to invest in developing countries for projects that reduce greenhouse gas emissions, aid agencies and governments in developing countries are rethinking ways they can meet their people's urgent needs with solutions that also reduce greenhouse gas emissions. It is very likely that the Clean Development Mechanism of the Kyoto Protocol will be a key part of any post-Kyoto Framework currently being negotiated. Already there are many ways for poverty reduction initiatives to count for Clean Development Mechanism and carbon credits. The book *Factor Five* outlines a number of options for low-carbon approaches to meeting energy demands in developing countries, including low-carbon approaches to heating and cooking, and options to invest in low-carbon approaches to lighting and energy generation, all of which can count for carbon credits. *Factor Five* discusses in detail the example of NGO

Grameen Shakti (a subsidiary of the Grameen Bank), which expands on the Grameen Bank's original micro-credit financing model to enable people to break the poverty cycle through purchasing electricity and cooking systems that are powered by renewable energy (solar panels and biogas plants). This opportunity has already been recognized by the World Bank in the form of a carbon-offsetting deal for the company's solar panel systems. Grameen Shakti was created in 1997, when it serviced 228 homes. As of 2008, the company had serviced over 135,000 homes, its current rate was 5000 additional homes per month. Grameen Shakti's target is to have 1 million solar-powered lighting systems and 1 million biogas plants by 2015. Also in both *Factor Five* and Chapter 11 of this book on air pollution we discuss the benefits of investing in low-carbon transport options and their potential to help reduce poverty as well as greenhouse gas emissions. Further information, case studies and reports on how to reduce poverty whilst also enabling a transition to a low-carbon future will be available from this book's online companion website.

With this in mind, we strongly believe that in the 21st century, it is possible to combine poverty reduction and climate change mitigation goals simultaneously to harness a range of opportunities to not only improve the lives of billions of people but to reduce environmental pressures significantly.

Bringing It Together – Millennium Villages

At the moment one of the best examples in the world of bringing these elements together is the Millennium Project and in particular the Millennium Villages programme. This economic development project is led by Africans, for Africans, and its aim is to achieve the Millennium Development Goals at a local level throughout rural Africa. The project works with village communities to identify and implement practical measures which will rapidly make a real difference to their lives. In each part of the village the project identifies opportunities to make a difference through investing in clean water, vaccines, mosquito nets, along with appropriate technologies, food, food supplements, and health and education services. As economist, Professor Sachs, says, 'It is a kind of aid that can work fast, providing a reliable investment that is easy to monitor and protect against corruption.'[98]

The first Millennium Village began in Sauri, Kenya in August 2004 and achieved remarkable results, rapidly leading to: yields of maize (corn) tripling; malaria rates more than halving; agriculturalists teaching villagers new farming methods; free health care being available; and a school food programme being established.[99] Since the introduction of school lunches, the pupils' school test results have improved dramatically. Improved nutrition has also led to better health, and the mosquito nets treated with insecticide have reduced the malaria rates. Such projects are showing that aid money can make a difference by taking an integrated community-based approach to create real ownership of the process. The programme is also involving government in the process, because without government support it will be impossible to ensure the lessons are passed on to other villages to scale up the process. Another key to the success of the programme has been the collaborative funding model, with the project providing US$50 per person each year, US$20 coming from other donors, US$30 coming from government and US$10 being contributed by the local community, to cover the costs of US$110 for each person every year.

Each Millennium Village requires a donor investment of US$300,000 per year for five years. This includes a cost of US$250,000 per village per year (5000 villagers per village multiplied by $50 per villager) and an additional US$50,000 per village per year to cover logistical and operational costs associated with implementation, community training, and monitoring and evaluation. Considering that there are roughly 500 million Africans living in rural villages and that each villager would receive US$50 per annum from the programme, the annual cost would be in the area of US$25 billion. This seems viable, particularly given that at the 2005 G-8 Summit in Gleneagles, Scotland the G-8 countries promised to reach US$90 billion per annum in aid for Africa, effectively doubling the current level. As Professor Sachs states, 'The point of this is not about transferring money. It is about investing in very practical things.'[100] As of 2007, there are 13 accredited Millennium Villages, with growing interest in the programme. The goal of the programme is for household incomes to grow with diversification into higher-value crops and expanded off-farm jobs, raising household savings, accelerating economic progress and investment.

To conclude, this chapter, and the work that has informed it, have shown that a significant difference can be made to the lives of hundreds of millions of people currently living in extreme poverty while decoupling economic growth from environmental pressures. Furthermore the required levels of investment can easily be afforded by OECD nations. However, many poverty reduction decision-makers are still not persuaded that investing in reducing such pressures can make much of a contribution to poverty reduction. This chapter has emphasized how preventing further environmental degradation, improving environmental quality, and investing in efficient use of resources is actually central to reducing poverty, as the poor are extremely dependent on their local environment. Moreover there is a compelling economic case for investing in both the enhancement of the environment, and the reduction of pressures on the environment, to underpin efforts to secure poverty reduction.[101] Once nations have used such approaches to escape from the poverty trap, it is vital, as they seek to rise up the steps of the ladder of development, that their efforts to raise living standards and build competitive industries do not lead to greater pressure on the environment but, rather, deliver low-impact, low-carbon solutions for their citizens. As explained in Chapter 1, such a transition is needed to avoid dangerous climate change and other ecological thresholds from being passed. But developing countries cannot be expected to make such a transition unless the wealthy countries of the world lead by example. Hence, the rest of this publication focuses on how to achieve a new 'low-impact, low-carbon' form of development through decoupling economic growth from a wide range of environmental pressures. The rest of the book is designed to assist all nations in their efforts to make a rapid transition to sustainable development.

Notes

1   Rockefeller, S. C. (2001) *The Earth Charter: An Ethical Foundation*, The Earth Charter, www.earthcharterinaction.org/resources/files/resurgence.htm, accessed 15 February 2008. A slightly shorter version of this essay appeared in *Resurgence* magazine.
2   World Commission on Environment and Development (WCED) (1987) *Our Common Future*, Oxford University Press, Oxford.
3   Brown, L. (2008) *Plan B 3.0: Mobilizing to Save Civilization*, W. W. Norton & Company, New York.
4   World Commission on Environment and Development (WCED) (1987) *Our Common Future*, Oxford University Press, Oxford.
5   Sachs, J. (2005) *The End of Poverty: How Can We Make it Happen in Our Lifetime*, Penguin Group, New York.
6   Hausmann, R. and Rodrik, D. (2003) 'Economic development as self-discovery', *Journal of Development Economics*, vol 72, p603.
7   Sachs, J. (2005) *The End of Poverty: How Can We Make it Happen in Our Lifetime*, Penguin Group, New York, pp246–250.
8   World Bank (2007) *Global Monitoring Report 2007: Millennium Development Goals*, World Bank, Washington, DC, p5.
9   The Fund for Peace (2007) 'The Failed States Index 2007', *Foreign Policy Magazine*.
10 Brown, L. (2008) *Plan B 3.0: Mobilizing to Save Civilization*, W. W. Norton & Company, New York.
11 Annan, K. (2005) UN Press Release, Transcript of Press Conference by Secretary-General Kofi Annan at the UN Headquarters, 21 March.
12 World Bank (2007) *The Costs of Attaining the Millennium Development Goals*, World Bank, Washington, DC.
13 Commission on Macroeconomics and Health (2002) *Macroeconomics and Health: Investing in Health for Economic Development*, Report of the Commission on Macroeconomics and Health, Chaired by Jeffery D. Sachs, Presented to the World Health Organization, Geneva.
14 Speidel, J., Weiss, D., Ethelston, S. and Gilbert, S. (2007) *Family Planning and Reproductive Health: The Link to Environmental Preservation*, Bixby Center for Reproductive Health and Research Policy, University of California, San Francisco, CA, p10.
15 UNFPA (2005) *Donor Support for Contraceptives and Condoms for STI/HIV Prevention 2005*, UNFPA, New York; UNFPA (2005) *Achieving the ICPD Goals: Reproductive Health Commodity Requirements 2000–2015*, UNFPA, New York; Chaya, N., Amen, K. A. and Fox, M. (2004) 'Condoms count: Meeting the need in the era of HIV/AIDS', Population Action International, Washington, DC.
16 UK Treasury (2005) *From Commitment to Action: Education Department for International Development*, UK Treasury, London.

17   Brown, L. (2008) *Plan B 3.0: Mobilizing to Save Civilization*, W. W. Norton & Company, New York.
18   Brown, L. (2008) *Plan B 3.0: Mobilizing to Save Civilization*, W. W. Norton & Company, New York.
19   McGovern, G. (2001) *The Third Freedom: Ending Hunger in Our Time*, Simon & Schuster, New York, Chapter 1.
20   World Bank (2004) *Natural Disasters: Counting the Cost*, World Bank, Washington, DC.
21   UN WFP (2008) *WFP's Operational Requirements, Shortfalls and Priorities for 2008*, World Food Programme, Rome.
22   World Bank (2007) *The Costs of Attaining the Millennium Development Goals*, World Bank, Washington, DC.
23   Brown (2008) *Plan B 3.0: Mobilizing to Save Civilization*, W. W. Norton & Company, New York.
24   Sachs, J. (2005) *The End of Poverty: How Can We Make it Happen in Our Lifetime*, Penguin Group, New York, p288.
25   Sachs, J. (2005) *The End of Poverty: How Can We Make it Happen in Our Lifetime*, Penguin Group, New York, p310.
26   Sachs, J. (2005) *The End of Poverty: How Can We Make it Happen in Our Lifetime*, Penguin Group, New York, pp337–339.
27   UN Division of Sustainable Development (1992) *Agenda 21: Programme of Action for Sustainable Development*, United Nations, New York.
28   UN (2002) *Monterrey Consensus on Financing for Development*, UN International Conference on Financing for Development, Monterrey, Mexico.
29   UN (2002) *World Summit on Sustainable Development: Plan of Implementation*, United Nations, New York.
30   Nelson, J. and Prescott, D. (2003) *Business and the Millennium Development Goals: A Framework for Action*, The International Business Leaders Forum.
31   Goar, C. (2005) 'Pearson's '69 target still unmet', *The Toronto Star*, 26 January.
32   Nelson, J. and Prescott, D. (2003) *Business and the Millennium Development Goals: A Framework for Action*, The International Business Leaders Forum, UK.
33   Duc, V. M. (2008) *Foreign Aid and Economic Growth in the Developing Countries – A Cross-Country Empirical Analysis*, The Connexions Project, Houston, TX.
34   OECD (2003) *Promoting Private Investment for Development*, OECD, Paris.
35   Knack, S. (2000) *Aid Dependence and the Quality of Governance: A Cross-Country Empirical Analysis*, World Bank Policy Research Paper, World Bank, Washington, DC.
36   Gallup, J. L., Sachs, J. and Mellinger, A. D. (1999) 'Geography and economic development', *International Regional Science Review,* vol 22, no 2, pp179–232.
37   World Bank (1998) *Assessing Aid: What Works, What Doesn't and Why*, Oxford University Press, New York.
38   Roodman, D. (1999) *The Natural Wealth of Nations: Harnessing the Market and the Environment*, Earthscan, London.
39   Mauro, P. (1997) 'The effects of corruption on growth, investment, and government expenditure: A cross country analysis', in Elliot, K. A. (ed) *Corruption and the Global Economy*, Institute for International Economics, Washington, DC, pp 83–107.
40   Transparency International (undated) 'FAQs on corruption', www.transparency.org/news_room/faq/corruption_faq, accessed 12 December 2008.

41   Rose-Akerman, S. (1999) *Corruption and Government: Causes, Consequences, and Reform*, Cambridge University Press, Cambridge.

42   Mauro, P. (1995) 'Corruption and growth', *Quarterly Journal of Economics*, vol 110, pp681–712.

43   Knack, S. and Keefer, P. (1995) 'Institutions and economic performance: Cross-country tests using alternative institutional measures,' *Economics and Politics*, vol 7, no 3, pp207–227; Kaufmann, D., Kraay, A. and Zoido-Lobatón, P. (1999) *Governance Matters*, World Bank Policy Research Working Paper no 2196, World Bank, Washington, DC.

44   Mauro, P. (2004) 'The persistence of corruption and slow economic growth', *IMF Staff Papers, International Monetary Fund*, vol 51, no 1, p1.

45   Biles, P. (2005) 'Botswana: Africa's success story?', *BBC News,* 7 March.

46   Frimpong, K. (2001) *National Integrity Systems Country Study Report: Botswana*, Transparency International, Berlin.

47   WCED (1987) *Our Common Future*, Oxford University Press, Oxford.

48   WCED (1987) *Our Common Future*, Oxford University Press, Oxford.

49   UN (2005) *The Inequality Predicament: 2005 Report on the World Social Situation*, United Nations Department of Economic and Social Affairs, New York.

50   UNDP (2005) *Human Development Report*, UNDP, Paris.

51   UN (2005) *The Report of the World Social Situation 2005: The Inequality Predicament*, UN, New York.

52   World Bank (1993) *The East Asian Miracle: Economic Growth and Public Policy*, Oxford University Press, New York.

53   Dollar, D. and Kraay, A. (2002) 'Growth is good for the poor', *Journal of Economic Growth*, vol 7, pp195–225; Foster, J. and Székely, M. (2001) *Is Economic Growth Good for the Poor? Tracking Low Incomes Using General Means*, Research Department Working Paper 453, Inter-American Development Bank, Washington, DC; Kraay, A. (2006) 'When is growth pro-poor? Evidence from a panel of countries', *Journal of Development Economics*, vol 80, no 1, pp198–227; Ravallion, M. and Chen, S. (1997) 'What can new survey data tell us about recent changes in distribution and poverty?', *World Bank Economic Review*, vol 11, no 2, pp357–382.

54   Bourguignon, F. (2004) 'The poverty-growth-inequality triangle', Paper presented at the Indian Council for Research on International Economic Relations, New Delhi, 4 February; Ravallion, M. and Chen, S. (1997) 'What can new survey data tell us about recent changes in distribution and poverty?', *World Bank Economic Review*, vol 11, no 2, pp357–382; Ravallion, M. and Chen, S. (2003) 'Measuring pro-poor growth', *Economics Letters*, vol 78, no 1, pp93–99.

55   Marmot, M. (2004) *Status Syndrome: How Your Social Spending Directly Affects Your Health and Life Expectancy*, Bloomsbury Publishing, London; Wilkinson, R. (2005) *The Impact of Inequality: How to Make Sick Societies Healthier*, The New Press, New York.

56   Bloom, D. E. and Canning, D. (2005) *Schooling, Health and Economic Growth: Reconciling the Micro and Macro Evidence*, Harvard School of Public Health, Cambridge, MA.

57   UN (1998) *World Population Prospects (The 1998 Revision)*, UN Department of Economic and Social Affairs, Population Division, New York.

58   All Party Parliamentary Group on Population Development and Reproductive Health (2007) *Return of the Population Growth Factor: Its Impact on the Millennium Development Goals,* Her Majesty's Stationery Office (HMSO), London.

59 UN (2007) *Report of the Secretary-General on the Work of the Organization,* United Nations General Assembly, Official Records Sixty-Second Session Supplement no 1 (A/62/1).

60 UNDESA (2004) *World Population Prospects Revision, Analytical Report,* vol 3, UN Department of Economic and Social Affairs, Population Division, New York.

61 WCED (1987) *Our Common Future,* Oxford University Press, Oxford.

62 UNDESA (2004) *World Population Prospects Revision, Analytical Report,* vol 3, UNDESA, Population Division, New York.

63 All Party Parliamentary Group on Population Development and Reproductive Health (2007) *Return of the Population Growth Factor: Its Impact on the Millennium Development Goals,* HMSO, London.

64 Speidel, J. (2006) 'Oral evidence', the All Party Parliamentary Group on Population Development and Reproductive Health, 3 July, cited in All Party Parliamentary Group on Population Development and Reproductive Health (2007) *Return of the Population Growth Factor: Its Impact on the Millennium Development Goals,* HMSO, London.

65 Program for Appropriate Technology in Health (PATH) and UN Population Fund (UNFPA) (2006) *Meeting the Need: Strengthening Family Planning Programs,* PATH and UNFPA, Seattle, pp5–11.

66 Larsen, J. (2001) *Iran's Birth Rate Plummeting at Record Pace: Success Provides a Model for Other Developing Countries,* Earth Policy Institute, Washington, DC.

67 Larsen, J. (2001) *Iran's Birth Rate Plummeting at Record Pace: Success Provides a Model for Other Developing Countries,* Earth Policy Institute, Washington, DC citing Speidel, J., Weiss, D., Ethelston, S. and Gilbert, S. (2007) *Family Planning and Reproductive Health: The Link to Environmental Preservation,* Bixby Center for Reproductive Health and Research Policy, University of California, San Francisco, CA, p10.

68 All Party Parliamentary Group (2007) *Return of the Population Growth Factor: Its Impact on the Millennium Development Goals,* HMSO, London, p22.

69 Family Planning Programs (1994) *Bangladesh: National Family Planning Program,* Diverse Solutions for a Global Challenge, Washington, DC.

70 Barro, R. J. and Martin, S. (2004) *Economic Growth* (second edition), MIT Press, Cambridge, MA, cited in Sachs, J. (2008) *Common Wealth: Economics For A Crowded Planet,* Penguin Group, New York.

71 Sperling, G. (2001) 'Toward universal education', *Foreign Affairs,* September/October, pp7–13; Sperling, G. (2002) 'Educate them all', *Washington Post,* 20 April.

72 UNESCO (2003) 'Winners of UNESCO Literacy Prizes 2003,' UNESCO Press Release, 27 May.

73 UK Treasury (2005) *From Commitment to Action: Education,* Department for International Development, London.

74 Brown, L. (2008) *Plan B 3.0: Mobilizing to Save Civilization,* W. W. Norton & Company, New York.

75 Sachs, J. (2000) 'A new map of the world', *The Economist,* 22 June; McGovern, G. (2001) 'Yes we CAN feed the world's hungry', *Parade,* 16 December.

76 McGovern, G. (2001) 'Yes we CAN feed the world's hungry', *Parade,* 16 December.

77 Sachs, J. (2001) 'A new map of the world', *The Economist,* 22 June.

78   Sachs, J. (2005) *The End of Poverty: How Can We Make it Happen in Our Lifetime*, Penguin Group, New York.

79   Attaran, A. and Sachs, J. (2001) 'Defining and refining international donor support for combating the AIDS pandemic', *The Lancet*, vol 357, no 9249, pp57–61.

80   UN (2002) 'Providing safe drinking water, sanitation to 1 billion in next decade critical challenge for humanity, sustainable development summit told', United Nations Press Release ENV/DEV/674, UN, Vienna, Austria.

81   WHO (2001) *Macroeconomics and Health: Investing in Health for Economic Development*, World Health Organization, Geneva.

82   Levine, R. and the What Works Working Group (2004) *Millions Saved: Proven Successes in Global Health*, Center for Global Development, Washington, DC.

83   The Global Alliance for Vaccines and Immunization (GAVI) (undated) Homepage', www.gavialliance.org, accessed 17 February 2008.

84   Bill and Melinda Gates Foundation (undated) 'Vaccine-preventable diseases', www.gatesfoundation.org, accessed 13 September 2007.

85   WHO (2001) *Macroeconomics and Health: Investing in Health for Economic Development*, World Health Organization, Geneva.

86   Brown, L. (2008) *Plan B 3.0: Mobilizing to Save Civilization*, W. W. Norton & Company, New York.

87   Venkataramana, C. B. S. and Sarada, P. V. (2001) 'Extent and speed of spread of HIV infection in India through the commercial sex networks: A perspective,' *Tropical Medicine and International Health*, vol 6, no 12, pp1040–1061.

88   Brown, L. (2008) *Plan B 3.0: Mobilizing to Save Civilization*, W. W. Norton & Company, New York.

89   Sachs, J. (2005) *The End of Poverty: How Can We Make it Happen in Our Lifetime*, Penguin Group, New York.

90   von Weizsäcker, E., Hargroves, K., Smith, M., Desha, C. and Stasinopoulos, P. (2009) *Factor Five: Transforming the Global Economy through 80% Improvements in Resource Productivity*, Earthscan, London.

91   Pearce, D. (2005) *Investing in Environmental Wealth for Poverty Reduction*, prepared on behalf of the Poverty-Environment Partnership: UNDP, UNEP, IUCN, IIES, World Resources Institute, New York.

92   Stern, N. (2006) *The Stern Review: The Economics of Climate Change*, Executive Summary, Cambridge University Press, Cambridge, Chapter 9.

93   Durst, P. et al (2001) *Forests Out of Bounds: Impacts and Effectiveness of Logging Bans in Natural Forests in Asia-Pacific*, FAO, Asia-Pacific Forestry Commission, Bangkok.

94   Starke, L. (ed) (2008) *State of the World: Ideas and Opportunities for Sustainable Economies*, Worldwatch Institute, Earthscan, London.

95   Pearce, D. (2005) *Investing in Environmental Wealth for Poverty Reduction*, prepared on behalf of the Poverty-Environment Partnership: UNDP, UNEP, IUCN, IIES, World Resources Institute.

96   OECD (2008) *Environmental Outlook to 2030*, OECD, Paris.

97   UNEP (2005) 'Investing in the environment gives big bang for your buck. Poverty and Environment Partnership says natural capital central to development goals', UNEP Media Release.

98   Sachs, J. (2008) *Common Wealth: Economics for a Crowded Planet*, Penguin Press, New York.

99   Millennium Project (2006) *Millennium Villages: A New Approach to Fighting Poverty*, Millennium Villages, www.unmillenniumproject.org, accessed 1 May 2008.

100 Sachs, J. (2008) *Common Wealth: Economics for a Crowded Planet*, Penguin Press, New York.

101 Pearce, D. (2005) *Investing in Environmental Wealth for Poverty Reduction*, prepared on behalf of the Poverty-Environment Partnership: UNDP, UNEP, IUCN, IIES, World Resources Institute, New York.

5

Informing and Developing National Strategies for Decoupling

What Is Needed to Underpin a National Decoupling Agenda?

The rate of change is outstripping the ability of scientific disciplines and our current capabilities to assess and advise. It is frustrating the attempts of political and economic institutions, which evolved in a different, more fragmented world, to adapt and cope. It deeply worries many people who are seeking ways to place those concerns on the political agendas. The next few decades are crucial. The time has come to break out of past patterns.

Our Common Future, 1987[1]

Unfortunately, many nations have been slow to act on this call from the World Commission on Environment and Development in 1987, meaning that the challenge to develop national policy that allows for both strong economic growth and jobs performance, along with lower environmental pressures, will be the defining feature of the 21st century. Encouragingly, over the last 40 years a number of countries around the world have achieved absolute decoupling for at least one environmental pressure, and this wealth of knowledge and experience will prove crucial in the coming years. In fact, investigations by the OECD have found that for every major environmental pressure at least one OECD country has achieved absolute decoupling.[2] These successes have created the momentum for many OECD countries to now include some form of decoupling commitments in national development strategies,[3] leading to the identification and tracking of an initial list of 'decoupling indicators', in the areas of climate change, air pollution, water quality and use, waste management and natural resources management.[4] Such programmes are also finding that if a whole of government approach is taken there can be clear overlaps and co-benefits between efforts related to climate change and most of the other main environmental pressures.

For instance, a major part of a global strategy to reduce greenhouse gas emissions will be a focus on encouraging and assisting developing countries to rapidly reduce deforestation, and the associated losses of biodiversity and impacts on the health of natural systems (discussed further in Chapter 8). Another major part will be the reduction in water consumption through water efficiency and demand management, as not only will many nations of the world face severe water shortages this century, but this will also reduce the associated energy demand related to extraction, storage, treatment and distribution of potable water (discussed further in Chapter 9). For example, a significant study, *Waste Not, Want Not: The Potential for Urban Water Conservation in California*, found that despite the progress already made in improving water efficiency, one-third of California's current urban water use can be saved through conservation and efficiency in the residential, commercial, institutional and industrial sectors.[5] Furthermore, strategies to reduce minerals extraction and waste production through recycling will result in significant reductions in energy demand in a range of industries (discussed further in Chapter 10), along with the associated greenhouse gas emissions. These include: recycling aluminium requires 95 per cent less energy overall, copper (70–85 per cent), lead (60–80 per cent), zinc (60–75 per cent), magnesium (95 per cent), paper (64 per cent), plastics (up to 80 per cent) and glass (60–70 per cent).[6] Finally, acting to reduce air pollution can also directly reduce greenhouse gas emissions (discussed further in Chapter 11), with the OECD highlighting that, 'to comply with agreed or future policies to reduce regional air pollution in Europe, mitigation costs are implied, but these are reduced by 50–70 per cent for SO_2 and around 50 per cent for NO_x when combined with Greenhouse gas policies'.[7] Given such complexity and interconnectivity, it is imperative that governments create robust decoupling strategies in the short term that build momentum to achieve larger levels of decoupling in the medium and longer term. We must learn from what has been achieved and been shown to be possible as there is not the time to undertake lengthy experiments and trials. The stakes are high and growing higher, which means that there is not room for making hasty assumptions about critical variables and unknowns.

While developing decoupling strategies is not the focus of this book, this chapter highlights nine key areas where careful consideration is needed before setting to the task of developing decoupling-related strategies. The purpose of this chapter is to present an overview of each area in an attempt to demonstrate its value and prompt deeper investigations by decision-makers. In the following chapters we will then demonstrate the level of support and current understanding across these critical areas for decoupling five environmental pressures, to further inform efforts.

The following text overviews the nine key areas to consider when planning a decoupling strategy, before entering into a discussion of each area in the rest of the chapter. This chapter is complemented by section 3 of our first publication, *The Natural Advantage of Nations*, which has detailed chapters on how to embed sustainability/decoupling into the institutions of government and national systems of innovation. Implementing such recommendations in combination with the following list items offers nations a strong foundation upon which to rapidly achieve significant levels of decoupling.

1   *Past appreciation – an historical perspective*
    An historical perspective can help to build political momentum for change. All nations have decoupling success stories of which most citizens are unaware. These need to be brought together and communicated to remind citizens and business leaders of what is possible. All nations also have examples of what can happen when insufficient efforts have been made to achieve decoupling. Most people are also unaware that our early 21st-century civilization is not the first civilization to face the prospect of environmentally induced economic decline. Either we continue as we have done in the past and the health of the environment will dictate our future, or we pay attention to the lessons from the last 5000 years and ask:
    - What can be learned from previous civilizations facing similar challenges?
    - More recently, what locally relevant cautionary tales exist to help communicate the costs of inaction on decoupling?
    - More recently, what success stories already exist to highlight the benefits of decoupling?
    - More recently, what solutions have been put forward in the past that have been largely ignored?
    - Today, what action in other countries can inform efforts to face similar challenges?

2   *Ecosystem resilience – assessing and monitoring the resilience of natural systems*
    The assessment, quantification and ongoing monitoring of the state of the environment to provide indications as to the health and levels of resilience of ecosystems is vital to determining the level and speed of decoupling required to avoid passing ecological thresholds and avoiding irreversible ecosystem collapse. Such knowledge is critical to providing a scientific basis for prioritizing efforts to achieve decoupling. This includes understanding where to place priorities, and at what scale and pace actions will be required, asking:
    - What is the likelihood that particular ecosystems are being overstressed to the point that they will pass ecological thresholds and go into decline?
    - Which ecosystems are close to critical levels of resilience and need urgent action?

- How can ecosystem resilience be restored and enhanced?
- How will issues related to the environment be translated and communicated to other parts of government to allow a whole of government approach?

3   *Performance evaluation – appropriate decoupling indicators*
It is necessary to find ways to quantify the achievement of decoupling initiatives in order to inform further efforts. The timeframe for action is tight and large-scale action is yet to begin. Thus, the better the process is monitored and interpreted the greater the probability that society will achieve decoupling to a meaningful extent in the coming decades, underpinning our common future. We may ask:

- What are the priority environmental pressures that need to be decoupled, and what are the sources and drivers of the pressures?
- What specific decoupling indicators and metrics can be used to effectively monitor progress?
- What factors are increasing the pressure on ecosystems, and are they reinforcing each other?
- How will each of the sectoral departments process and internalize information related to environmental pressure to inform their efforts?

4   *Decoupling requirements – determining the required scale and speed of decoupling*
Although difficult to estimate and quantify, the level of decoupling needed to allow the appropriate reduction of environmental pressures will have a crucial influence on decoupling-related strategies. This level of decoupling needs to then be balanced by the capacity to deliver decoupling. There is now a great deal of evidence to show that five to tenfold improvements in efficiency and productivity are technically possible without reducing economic growth and in some cases even increasing it:

- What level of decoupling is needed for the main environmental pressures?
- How fast must each environmental pressure be decoupled?
- What priority is given to each environmental pressure?
- What options have been proven to assist decoupling each environmental pressure?
- How will accountability and responsibility for achieving targets be assigned within government?

5   *The costs of inaction – investigating the costs of inaction on decoupling efforts*
Costs of inaction include both current and anticipated future costs from the loss of ecosystem services, the intensification of natural disasters and direct damages to human health and physical infrastructure. OECD studies show that costs related to future impacts from water and air pollution, biodiversity loss, climate change and natural disasters are already significant, and are all set to rise sharply by 2030. A range of studies have reported economic losses of 2–4 per cent of the GDP of cities and countries

because of air pollution alone, mostly related to public health costs. Where air pollution has been reduced, the economic benefits associated with reduced impacts have far outweighed the costs of action. Hence we may ask:

- What are the various potential costs both direct and indirect from environmental pressures, now and in the future?
- How will these costs be borne by the economy?

6 *The costs of action – estimating the costs of action on decoupling efforts*
The level of real cost in the short to medium term of investing in decoupling activities needs to be investigated, with the goal to both stimulate economic growth and avoid greater costs of inaction in the long term. However, before seeking to investigate such costs it is wise to consider the accuracy of past estimates of the cost of large-scale environmental actions in response to unacceptable levels of environmental pressure or impacts on human health. Hence we may ask:

- What technologies and process improvements have been proven to contribute to reducing environmental pressures cost effectively in the short, medium and longer term?
- What previous estimates of the costs of action have been made for each environmental pressure and how accurate have they proved to be?
- What are the key assumptions that are made in each estimate and are they reasonable?
- What level of innovation is to be expected by business and industry?
- What multiplier effects and co-benefits can be expected through decoupling actions?
- What options are there for restorative projects that not only reduce the pressure but also assist in restoring natural systems?
- What policies and incentives have been used to effectively encourage action to decouple each environmental pressure? (Also understanding policies and incentives which can undermine efforts to achieve decoupling)

7 *Economic resilience – investigating and understanding the resilience of the economy*
The strength and resilience of an economy is a crucial determinant of its ability to decouple environmental pressures. Governments considering large-scale changes to allow reduction in environmental pressures need to first analyse the range of options and opportunities, and how they could affect the economy and in particular the levels of employment. Such investigations are now showing that the decoupling agenda provides numerous opportunities to stimulate the economy and create employment, both leading to a strengthening of the resilience of an economy, especially when the reduction of future costs from inaction are factored into the modelling. With this in mind we may ask:

- How can job losses be minimized and jobs growth in affected sectors be maximized?

- What increases in public environmental awareness and education will be needed to support strategies and policies?
- What education and (re)training requirements will there be to ensure enough people have the skills to implement decoupling in each sector of the economy?
- What new mechanisms will be needed to improve access to information both by the public and within the various sectors?
- How can broad participation and ownership of the strategies be achieved?
- What legislative changes have been made to make decoupling a legal requirement of the key stakeholders?
- What industry sectors will require assistance with the transition and in developing strategic plans; which industry groups will need to be assisted to develop sustainability action plans to help their sector see the opportunities from decoupling?
- What factors will influence cross-sectoral and trans-boundary policy implementation?
- How can decoupling of environmental pressures be linked to strengthen efforts in other policy agendas, such as reducing poverty, improving public health, national security and broader economic development?
- What levels of enforcement will be required, and will this be monetary or legal?

8 *International cooperation – identifying the potential for synergy with global efforts*
A key aspect that will inform the development of decoupling-related strategies will be the level of global commitment and cooperation by both governments and business on reducing a particular environmental pressure. Despite various barriers, progress has been made to develop a range of multilateral agreements, which are forming the basis of a global framework. It is clear, however, that efforts to achieve the goals of such agreements will be continually undermined if efforts to build social capital and reduce inequality and poverty are not also undertaken. We may therefore ask:

- What are the existing national commitments to global environmental agreements and targets?
- What global environmental agreements and targets have not yet been committed to and why?
- Of those not committed to which could be complementary to decoupling efforts, and what would be the ramifications of committing to them?
- How effectively are aid and development contributions being used? What is working and why? What is not working and why?
- What component of a nation's overseas developmental aid budget is also helping to achieve decoupling of poverty reduction and environ-

mental pressures? How can it be made more effective? Should it be increased?

- What mechanisms are needed to ensure that successes are communicated and replicated to assist broader action, nationally and internationally?

9 *Assessing and accounting for the national security benefits of decoupling*
One of the core responsibilities of national governments is to ensure national security, often involving the commitment of significant amounts of resources and funding. A number of strategists and commentators are now identifying that global cooperation to achieve decoupling of economic growth from environmental pressures will be a key component of national security strategy. Security expert Michael Klare argues that the main geographical hotspots for wars and conflict this century could be for oil in the Persian Gulf, the Caspian Sea Basin and the South China Sea, while for water they are the Nile valley, the Middle East, Jordan, the Tigris-Euphrates and the Indus river basins. Hence multilateral efforts to address climate change, and other environmental pressures, will be critical for national security as well as being a moral, humanitarian and economic development imperative. With this in mind we may ask:

- What are the short- and long-term national security risks and threats from climate change, and in particular those related to energy and water?
- How can such risks and threats be reduced as part of decoupling strategies?
- What will be the required balance between securing reserves, or the access to reserves, compared to reducing demand for energy and water?
- How can decoupling strategies to reduce demand strengthen national security?

Many of these elements highlight the synergistic benefits of decoupling in helping long-term economic prosperity, job creation and national security; the core goals of the central agencies of government. Yet relatively few national governments are developing national strategies that focus on achieving decoupling across their economies, and involving all parts of government despite the clarity provided by *Our Common Future*, which stated, 'The present challenge is to give the central economic and sectoral ministries the responsibility for the quality of those parts of the environment affected by their decisions, and to give the environmental agencies more power to cope with the effects of unsustainable development.'[8] The development of decoupling strategies will certainly require a government's treasury and finance departments to be working with at least the environmental agencies, and at most with all other portfolios. The above nine elements are now discussed in further detail with the intention of informing efforts to develop decoupling strategies.

Element 1: Past Appreciation – An Historical Perspective

Committing to the decoupling agenda outlined in this book is not a walk into the unknown, as seeking to find a way to achieve both economic development and environmental sustainability is not a new goal. There are many such examples as our early 21st-century civilization is not the first to face the prospect of environmentally induced economic decline. A range of authors have shown that overstressing the environment has been a significant factor in the demise of many of the most advanced past civilizations.[9] Jared Diamond for instance, argues that our civilization ignores the lessons from our history at our own peril, particularly those related to deforestation, soil management and reliance on resources from outside nations.[10] Diamond shows that many past civilizations have failed to make the required correction to development paths and subsequently collapsed. This was because the environmental factors which caused the collapse crept up on these ancient civilizations, who did not see the problem coming, and once the problem was identified either did not know how to solve it or it was too late. Diamond was not the first to notice this pattern. Famous early 20th-century environmentalist Richard St Barbe Baker wrote:

> *The great Empires of Assyria, Babylon, Carthage and Persia were destroyed by floods and deserts let loose in the wake of forest destruction. Erosion following forest destruction and soil deple-tion has been one of the most powerfully destructive forces in bringing about the downfall of civilizations and wiping out human existence from large tracts of the Earth's surface. Erosion does not march with a blast of trumpets or the beating of drums, but its tactics are more subtle, more sinister.*
> Richard St Barbe Baker, *I Planted Trees*, 1944[11]

For instance, Diamond shows that the Mayan civilization flourished from AD 250 until its collapse around AD 900. Like the Sumerians, some 2000 years before, the Mayans had developed a sophisticated system of agriculture, and as with Sumer, the Mayan demise was partly due to a failing food supply. But in this case, it was deforestation and soil erosion that undermined agriculture. Changes in climate which resulted in a prolonged drought are also thought to have played a role. Food shortages apparently triggered civil conflict among the various Mayan cities as they competed for food. Arthur Demarest argues in *Ancient Maya: The Rise and Fall of a Rainforest Civilization*,[12] using a holistic perspective on the most recent evidence from archaeology, palaeoecology and epigraphy, that no one explanation is sufficient, but that a vicious cycle devel-oped. He argues that a series of erratic, complex events, including loss of soil fertility and drought from deforestation and climate change led to rising levels of internal and external violence. This, he argues, led to the disintegration of the courts of Mayan kingdoms which began a spiral of decline and decay. Today this region is covered by jungle, reclaimed by nature.

A well-documented more recent example comes from Rapa Nui, better known as Easter Island. In AD 900 Polynesian explorers discovered a small island in the South Pacific covered in subtropical rainforest. Life was good to the new settlers and they grew to around 20,000 people, achieving a thriving community expressing its spiritualism through the mystical statues the island is famous for. Eleven clans prospered on the small isolated paradise and soon competition for prestige, power and resources dominated the minds of the leaders. They found that moving the statues required large amounts of logs and rope, a limited resource on the island. And, now that the population was so big they began to feel the limits to the natural resources, including animals, plants and trees. Limits were being reached in many of the activities of the clans – room for farming, available firewood, wood for canoes, construction, bark clothes, nuts and palm sap. As the limits began to press on quality of life they began to fight over them, in the process destroying the statues. By 1600 the deforestation and degradation of the island was complete. The population and the environment collapsed leading to mass starvation and cannibalism, and by 1700 it is estimated that 80 per cent of the population was lost. (In 1995, Rapa Nui National Park was declared a World Heritage park by UNESCO because of its unique cultural expression within the Polynesian region.)

One of the most respected recent academic publications in this field is Joseph Tainter's book *The Collapse of Complex Societies*. Referred to by Diamond, Tainter's book shows that civilizations collapse due to a range of factors feeding back on each other. Tainter argued that societies that collapse usually adhere to a mixture of the following three models in the face of that collapse:[13]

1   The Dinosaur: The best example is a large-scale society in which resources are being depleted at an exponential rate and yet nothing is done to rectify the problem because the ruling elite are unwilling or unable to adapt to said changes. In such examples rulers tend to oppose any solutions that diverge from their present course of action. They will favour intensification and commit an increasing number of resources to their present plans, projects and social institutions.

2   A Runaway Train: An example would be a society that only functions when new sources of resources and goods can be acquired, even if it is with force. Societies based almost exclusively on acquisition, including pillage or exploitation, cannot be sustained indefinitely. The society of the Assyrians and Genghis Khan and the Mongols, for example, both fractured and collapsed when no new conquests were forthcoming.

3   A House of Cards: In this model, societies grow to be so large and include so many complex social institutions that they are inherently unstable and prone to collapse.

Tainter argued that often these three models coexist and reinforce each other, leading to civilizations' collapse. The lesson from Diamond's, Tainter's and Marsh's publications is that advanced and complex civilizations, like ours today, stand the best chance of thriving long term if we identify and address unsustainable aspects of their development as early as possible. Jared Diamond argues that these are vitally important lessons for civilization today:

> *One of the disturbing facts of history is that so many civilizations collapse. Few people, however, least of all our politicians, realize that a primary cause of the collapse of those societies has been the destruction of the environmental resources on which they depended. Fewer still appreciate that many of those civilizations share a sharp curve of decline. Indeed, a society's demise may begin only a decade or two after it reaches its peak population, wealth, and power.*[14]

It is vital that we do not repeat mistakes of the past but rather inform our future with past wisdom. Dr Pachauri, Chair of the IPCC, in his Nobel laureate acceptance speech made this point strongly:

> *Neglect in protecting our heritage of natural resources could prove extremely harmful for the human race and for all species that share common space on planet earth. Indeed, there are many lessons in human history which provide adequate warning about the chaos and destruction that could take place if we remain guilty of myopic indifference to the progressive erosion and decline of nature's resources.*[15]

As unfortunate as it may be, our global civilization is set to see a significant course correction in the 21st century. Either we continue as we have done in the past, and the health of the environment will dictate our future, or we pay attention to the lessons from the last 5000 years and correct our own course. Many are aware that scientists have been warning humanity about the consequences of unsustainable forms of development since the 1960s. Rachel Carson's *Silent Spring*, published in 1962, is probably the most famous of such warnings. However, few are aware that concerns about the lack of sustainability of development go back much further. For instance, one of the first modern political leaders to recognize the need to change was US President Theodore Roosevelt who, between 1907 and 1909, initiated a wide range of environmental conservation initiatives within the US and the region, and called for global cooperation on resource conservation.[16] Roosevelt understood that until the turn of the 20th century the US had built its economic and political strength by exploiting the nation's natural resources. But Roosevelt, like other leading conservationists of the time, no longer believed that these natural resources were infinite in their abundance. In 1909, President Roosevelt asked the leaders of the world to meet at The Hague to consider the conservation of the natural resources of the world – unfortunately this was an invitation the world did not accept.[17]

In Roosevelt's speeches of the time[18] he outlined many of the themes which were subsequently covered in the publications *Limits to Growth* and *Our Common Future* and the Rio Summit on Environment and Development many years later. Environmental history shows that by 1909 many of the key understandings that inform the call for sustainable development and many of the necessary sustainable design solutions and early forms of innovations were available and being actively promoted and discussed, including:

- *Soil rehabilitation*: George Washington Carver argued for the need to focus on soil rehabilitation in the 1905 book How to Build Up Worn Out Soil.[19] Following a fact-finding stay in China in 1907–1909, F. H. King, a US Department of Agriculture official, published a study called *Farmers of Forty Centuries*, based on Chinese methods of farming that had been practised on the same piece of land for thousands of years.[20]
- *Energy generation*: wind-driven mills were operating in Persia from the 7th Century AD for irrigation and milling grain. Wind powered all seafaring ships and transport for thousands of years. Clarence Kemp patented the first solar water heater in 1891,[21] and by 1897, solar water heaters serviced 30 per cent of houses in Pasadena, California.[22] The great Italian engineer Tesla had invented alternating current (AC) electricity by 1895 and was focused on using renewable energy sources such as hydropower to power society.
- *Green buildings and cities*: the Ancient Greeks pioneered passive solar design of their cities so all homes had access to sunlight during winter. Many green buildings today are actually modelled on 19th century building design that needed to keep buildings cool in summer and warm in winter without air-conditioners and heaters to assist. As early as 1892, Ebenezer Howard published *Garden Cities of To-Morrow* which launched the Garden City movement.[23]
- *Transportation*: in 1895 Rudolf Diesel (1858–1913) developed the first 'diesel' engine to run on peanut oil, as he demonstrated at the World Exhibition in Paris in 1900. In 1912 Diesel stated that 'The use of vegetable oils for engine fuels may seem insignificant today. But such oils may become in the course of time as important as the petroleum and coal tar products of the present time.'[24] Unfortunately, Diesel died in 1913 before his vision of a vegetable oil-powered engine was fully realized. France and Great Britain were the first nations to support the widespread development of electric vehicles in the late 19th century. In the US, in 1899 and 1900 electric cars outsold all other types of cars. At the turn of the 20th century, they were produced by Anthony Electric, Baker Motor Vehicle, Detroit Electric, Woods Motor Vehicle and others. Later in 1916, Woods invented a hybrid car that had both an internal combustion engine

and an electric motor.[25] All major cities at this time (1909) had train and light rail systems connecting the suburbs to places of work, with cars seen as a novelty.

Hence, in 1909 the world was poised to consider the realities of the environment and what it meant to development, but within six years the world was at war. In many ways this history parallels the choices we face today, some 100 years later, in 2009, when again we are at a point where serious decisions about our future global development need to be made, with impacts that may rival or even exceed the great depression. What we choose to do about HIV/AIDS and infectious diseases will affect the lives of tens of millions; what we decide to do about providing access to clean water, responding to climate change and halting deforestation will affect the lives of hundreds of millions; what we decide to about energy, water and sanitation will affect the lives billions; and what nations choose to do to about oil dependency will effect international relations, economies, the peace of the world and every person on the planet. Hence, it is critical that we don't repeat the mistakes of our ancestors, and rather learn from their success and failures, locally, regionally and globally.

Element 2: Ecosystem Resilience – Assessing and Monitoring the Resilience of Natural Systems

Despite the importance of ecosystems, they are being modified in extent and composition by people at an unprecedented rate, with little understanding of the implications this will have in terms of their ability to function and provide services in the future.
Millennium Ecosystem Assessment, 2005[26]

The assessment, quantification and ongoing monitoring of the state of the environment is vital to determining meaningful cost-effective strategies to achieve decoupling, including understanding where to place priorities, and at what scale and pace actions will be required. Even though it may seem obvious that all ecosystems are worth restoring and hence all environmental pressures need to be reduced, it is unreasonable to expect that enormous investments in resources can be committed to reduce pressures on all ecosystems at the same time. Hence prioritization is needed – it may actually turn out to be closer to a process of triage, to identify the most critical damages. A wealth of data has been gathered on the state of ecosystems, and many investigations are now providing valuable insight into the resilience of such systems, although this work needs to be brought together and extended in light of each nation's particular situation. The main purpose of such investigations is to provide as much guidance as possible on the likelihood of ecosystems being pressured to the point that they begin to decline, and then when further pressured, lead to failure. The fear is that once ecosystems are pressured to a particular level, this will lead to irreversible decline and collapse, with the subsequent costs of action to restore the services (if at all possible) becoming prohibitively high.

> *Resilience is a measure of a system's ability to survive and persist within a variable environment ... Resilience is something that may be very hard to see, unless you exceed its limits ... Loss of resilience can come as a surprise, because the system is usually paying much more attention to its play than to its playing space. One day it does something it has done a hundred times before it crashes.*
>
> Donella H. Meadows, *Thinking in Systems*, 2009
> (edited by Diana Wright)[27]

Unfortunately, a weakness of the measurement approach is that it tends to measure symptoms of environmental decline. Furthermore, ecological thresholds and tipping points are notoriously hard to measure with certainty. UNEP highlights a range of complicating issues, including 'the intricate nature of ecosystems, the differing spatial reach and temporal implications of biophysical processes, thresholds and feedback loops, and the human dimensions shaping ecosystem dynamics'. UNEP further reflects that 'Science is incomplete on aspects of environmental change, some understanding of biophysical processes and ecosystem dynamics are likely to be wrong, some changes are not predicted and provided for, and existing knowledge is not fully integrated.'[28] Such investigations are further complicated by the range of impacts from environmental pressures acting unpredictably on ecosystems, such as average temperature increases, shifting rainfall patterns, reduced availability of water, and loss of biodiversity and habitat.

Hence many sustainability advocates have recommended a precautionary approach which seeks to build a strategy based on a set of precautionary systems conditions such as regeneration, substitutability, assimilation and avoiding irreversibility, adopted by OECD ministers in 2001 (See Chapter 2). Such a strategy is founded on an understanding that ecosystems are delicate and unpredictable systems, and is informed by a clear understanding of the current conditions within affected ecosystems.

In short, natural ecosystems are complex, and helpful information may be difficult to obtain. Examples include establishing the safe levels of environmental pressures, and establishing the causal links between pollutants and negative environmental effects; especially as there are often lengthy lag times between applying the pressure and recognizing the impact on the ecosystem. For instance, take what seems to be the simple issue of sustainable management of fisheries. Government estimates of the state of fish stocks rely on the catch that fishers report. It is too expensive and difficult for governments themselves to go out into the oceans and take enough samples to know what the state of fish stocks is. Hence often by the time scientific consensus is built on an issue, it is

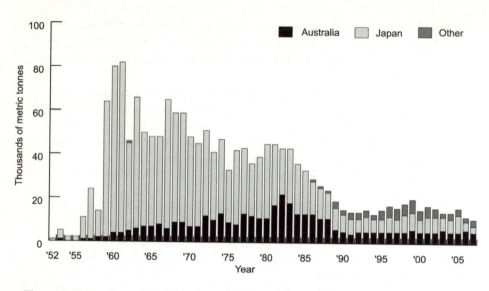

Figure 5.1 *Southern bluefin tuna catch in thousands of tonnes, 1950–2007*

Source: Based on data from Australian government (2004)[29] and OECD (2006)[30]

decades after the concerns were raised by the original scientist. By this time it is often too late and the ecological system is in irreversible decline, or at best solving the problem will require a dramatic reduction of environmental pressures for the ecosystem in question to have a chance to recover. The catch history shown in Figure 5.1 for bluefin tuna illustrates that this fishery has been significantly overfished with stocks crashing through the 1980s.

Element 3: Performance Evaluation – Appropriate Decoupling Indicators

It is helpful to find ways to quantify the achievement of various decoupling agendas and evaluate the success of initiatives, to inform further efforts. As the timeframe for action is tight and large-scale action is yet to have begun, the better the process is monitored and interpreted the greater the probability that our global society will achieve decoupling to a meaningful extent in the coming decades. As outlined previously, the current leading indicator of an economy's success is the GDP, with this measure considered alongside a range of other performance indicators such as balance of trade, level of education and employment, provision of health services, strength of currency, and national interest rates. However, often the GDP is considered over and above other performance indicators and is not directly amended to include the economics of social or environmental performance of a nation. Hence as well as promoting those activities that align with sustainable development and contribute to GDP, additional measures will need to be developed and compared to GDP to inform a strategic decoupling agenda.

Table 5.1 *OECD environmental indicator selection criteria*

Indicator categories	Criteria for the selection of environmental indicators
Policy relevance and utility for users*	An environmental indicator should: • provide a representative picture of environmental conditions, pressures on the environment or society's responses • be simple, easy to interpret and able to show trends over time • be responsive to changes in the environment and related human activities • provide a basis for international comparisons • be either national in scope or applicable to regional environmental issues of national significance • have a threshold or reference value against which to compare, so that users can assess the significance of the values associated with it
Analytical soundness*	An environmental indicator should: • be theoretically well founded in technical and scientific terms • be based on international standards and international consensus about its validity • lend itself to being linked to economic models, forecasting and information systems
Measurability*	The data required to support the indicator should be: • readily available or made available at a reasonable cost:benefit ratio • adequately documented and of known quality • updated at regular intervals in accordance with reliable procedures

Note: * These criteria describe the 'ideal' indicator; not all of them will be met in practice.
Source: OECD (2002)[31]

However, in practice, developing the metrics related to environmental pressures to compare to GDP is very challenging. Furthermore, monitoring such metrics will require a sophisticated approach. In order to quantify the impacts of environmental pressures, the pressures must be broken down into specifics and tangible measurements must be obtained as to the trend of the impacts. As part of the *OECD Environmental Strategy for the First Decade of the 21st Century*, a 2002 study was undertaken of the suitability of a range of indicators to measure decoupling of economic growth from environmental pressures. In this study the OECD suggested a set of criteria for the selection of environmental indicators across the categories of policy relevance and utility for users, analytical soundness and measurability, as outlined in Table 5.1.[32]

The study used these criteria to develop a range of environmental indicators, as shown in Table 5.2. These indicators provide a basis for nations to consider what performance metrics will be used to inform the progress of decoupling efforts. OECD investigations show that at least one nation has now achieved absolute decoupling for all but two of the decoupling indicators shown in Table 5.2.[33]

Table 5.2 *Decoupling indicators proposed by the OECD*

Economy-wide decoupling indicators

Climate change
- Total greenhouse gas emissions per unit of GDP and per capita
- Total CO_2 emissions per unit of GDP and per capita

Air pollution
- Total NO_x emissions per unit of GDP
- Total SO_x emissions per unit of GDP
- Total emissions of fine particulate matter per unit of GDP
- Total volatile organic chemicals (VOCs) emissions per unit of GDP

Water quality and management
- Population not connected to sewage treatment plants versus total population
- Discharges of nitrogen and phosphorus from households into the environment versus total population
- Total freshwater abstraction per unit of GDP

Waste management
- Municipal waste going to final disposal versus private final consumption
- Amount of glass not collected for recycling versus private final consumption
- Amount of paper/cardboard not recycled versus GDP

Decoupling indicators for specific sectors

Energy
- Energy-related emissions per unit of GDP of CO_2, NO_x and SO_x
- Energy-related CO_2 emission per m³ of floor area from the residential and commercial sectors
- CO_2 emissions from electricity generation

Transport
- Road transport-related emissions per unit of GDP of CO_2, NO_x and VOCs
- Passenger car-related emissions per unit of GDP of NO_x and VOCs
- Freight road transport-related emissions per unit of GDP of NO_x and VOCs

Agriculture
- Soil surface nitrogen surplus versus agricultural output
- Emissions from agriculture of methane and nitrous oxide versus agricultural output
- Total agricultural water use versus agricultural output
- Apparent consumption of commercial fertilizers versus final crop output

Manufacturing
- NO_x emissions from manufacturing industry versus manufacturing value adding
- Waste generated by manufacturing industry versus manufacturing value adding
- CO_2 emissions from manufacturing industry versus manufacturing value adding
- Freshwater abstraction by manufacturing industry versus manufacturing value adding

Source: OECD (2002)[34]

Element 4: Decoupling Requirements – Determining the Required Scale and Speed of Decoupling

Although difficult to estimate and quantify, the level of decoupling needed to allow the appropriate reduction of environmental pressures will have a crucial influence on decoupling-related strategies. Governments need to understand the reality of the size of the problem, and the foreseeable and anticipated risks from not acting in the short term, and in particular, over the term of their appointment. At first glance, the scale and speed of decoupling required seems so large as to make it impossible to achieve without at least slowing economic growth. In the EU's 2003 review, *Europe's Environmental Progress at Risk from Unsustainable Economic Activities*, it was said, 'The state of the environment across Europe has improved in several respects over the past decade, but much of the progress is likely to be wiped out by economic growth because governments have yet to make significant strides towards decoupling environmental pressures from economic activity.'[35] In a World Bank debate on this topic in 2004, Herman Daly summed up this debate when he asked:

> *Just how tight is this coupling between GDP [economic growth] and [physical] throughput? That is a debateable question. Ecological economists tend to think that the ... coupling is relatively tight. Some folks, like Amory Lovins, think that GDP could grow 10 fold or more with a constant throughput. I tend to doubt it. I believe the coupling is stronger than that, but if Amory is right that's fine with me. Let GDP grow forever as long as throughput is constrained and held constant.*[36]

There is a surprising amount of evidence to suggest that Amory Lovins and other leaders in the field such as Ernst von Weizsäcker, Joechem Eberhard, Ernst Worrell, Alan Pears, Paul Anastas and Paul Ekins are onto something. There is now a great deal of evidence to show that five to tenfold improvements (i.e. factor 5–10) in efficiency and productivity are technically possible without reducing economic growth and in some cases even increasing it. From a technical and an economic perspective, the World Bank as early as 1992 argued that, 'If the environmental policies required are put in place, it is possible to reduce pollution by factors of 10 or more in the most serious cases, even if energy consumption levels rise fivefold. Furthermore, developing countries would find themselves better-off both economically and environmentally.'[37] This position is supported by a range of investigations including those presented in a background paper for the World Bank's *World Development Report* in 1992 that brought together a range of impressive evidence to show that it is possible to reduce environmental pressures in three major fields of concern on the scale required by a factor of 5–10.

The scale and speed of decoupling efforts will vary across the range of environmental pressures for each nation, however, through the investigations considered in Element 2, and the monitoring of environmental pressures considered in Element 3, nations will be well placed to understand which areas will need to be prioritized. The Netherlands government, as part of its Sustainable Technology Development project as summarized in Table 2.3 on page 44, was one of the first national governments to estimate the scale and speed of change required to achieve nationwide reductions in environmental pressures.

Table 5.3 *Relative pollution (or damage) intensities of polluting or low-polluting practices*

Source and type of emissions or environmental pressures	Index per unit of output		Examples of low-polluting practices
	Polluting	Low polluting	
Electricity production			
Particulate matter	100	< 0.1	Natural gas; clean coal technologies
Carbon monoxide (CO)	100	< 0.1	Scrubbers; low-sulphur fuels
Sulphur dioxide (SO_2)	100	0 to < 5	Low NO_x combustion methods
Nitrogen oxides (NO_x)	100	5 to 10	Emission control catalysts
Motor vehicles: diesel engines			
Particulate matter	100	< 10	Clean fuels and particulate traps
Sulphur dioxide (SO_2)	100	5	Low-sulphur fuels
Motor vehicles: gasoline engines			
Lead	100	0	Unleaded and reformulated fuels; catalytic converters
Carbon monoxide (CO)	100	5	Unleaded and reformulated fuels; catalytic converters
Nitrogen oxides (NO_x)	100	20	Unleaded and reformulated fuels; catalytic converters
Volatile organic compounds	100	5	Unleaded and reformulated fuels; catalytic converters
All fossil fuels for electricity			
Carbon dioxide (CO_2)	100	~ 0	Renewable energy sources
Other areas of concern			
Marine pollution	100	< 10	
Surface water pollution	100	negligible	Sewerage works, effluent control technologies
Soil erosion	100	negligible	Agro-forestry, soil erosion prevention practices
Forestry	100	negligible	Sustainable practices
Industrial effluents and wastes	100	small	Effluent control technologies: waste reduction or prevention

Source: Anderson (1996)[38]

> *In setting a time-horizon of 50 years – two generations into the future – it was found that ten to twenty-fold eco-efficiency improvements will be needed to achieve meaningful reductions in environmental stress. It was also found that the benefits of incremental technological development could not provide such improvements.*
>
> Leo Jansen, Chairman, Netherlands Inter-ministerial
> Sustainable Technology Development Programme, 2000[39]

There are a range of existing bodies of work which can inform the efforts of nations to better understand the scale and speed with which decoupling is needed, such as the work of the IPCC to inform greenhouse gas-related targets. For instance, the IPCC recommends that globally greenhouse gas levels need to be reduced by 80 per cent by 2050, below 1990 levels, and more still by 2100, and this will have specific ramifications for each nation depending on its levels of emissions. There also exist a number of resources and studies such as the OECD work to create international databases on material flows,[40] and at a national level, the work of the CSIRO in undertaking a detailed account of the physical/material flows, and social and economic criteria for Australia.[41] Furthermore, a range of publications have assembled case studies which show that there is significant potential for decoupling in the short to medium term. These publications include *Factor Four: Doubling Wealth, Halving Resource Use*,[42] *Natural Capitalism: Creating the Next Industrial Revolution*,[43] *The Natural Advantage of Nations: Business Opportunities, Innovation and Governance in the 21st Century*,[44] and *Factor Five: Transforming the Global Economy through 80% Improvements in Resource Productivity*.[45] Table 5.3 outlines a number of examples of low-polluting practices for a range of areas that currently carry significant environmental pressures.

Element 5: Cost of Inaction – Investigate the Costs of Inaction on Decoupling Efforts

Costs of inaction include both the current and anticipated future costs from the loss of ecosystem services, the intensification of natural disasters, and direct damages to human health and physical infrastructure. OECD studies show that costs of inaction on water and air pollution, biodiversity loss, climate change and natural disasters are already significant,[46] and are all set to rise sharply by 2030.[47]

A range of studies have reported economic losses of 2–4 per cent of the GDP of cities and countries because of air pollution alone,[48] and mostly related to public health costs. For instance the World Bank in 2007[49] estimated Chinese air pollution health costs at about 3.8 per cent of GDP. Where air pollution has been reduced, the economic benefits associated with reduced impacts have far outweighed the costs of action.[50] In another example, the US EPA conducted an extensive study which found that the total benefits of Clean Air Act programmes saved the US economy US$22 trillion in 1970–1990.[51] In other words, if US air pollution trends in 1970 had continued to 1990, then the measurable economic, social, health and environmental costs to the US economy would have been an extra US$22 trillion. By comparison, the actual cost of achieving the pollution reductions observed over the 20-year period was US$523 billion, a small fraction of the estimated economic costs from inaction. In 1995, the UK government calculated total costs of damage from sulphur to be over £18 billion (US$28 billion) while the costs of action were no more than £1–3 billion (US$1.5–4.5 billion).[52] When the US converted to unleaded gasoline, it saved more than US$10 for every US$1 it invested thanks to reduced health costs, savings on engine maintenance and improved fuel efficiency.[53] The studies reviewed by the OECD[54] show that national measures to reduce agricultural run-off and stormwater management – including introducing targeted measures to reduce a variety of different pollutants such as arsenic and nitrates – result in health benefits costed to be in excess of US$100 million for large OECD economies. Recreational water quality improvements through sewage treatment in France, Portugal, the US and the UK, and drinking water quality improvements in the US, all show that health benefits of drinking water quality and sewage treatment often outweigh the costs of policy implementation.[55]

In non-OECD countries, the costs of inaction with respect to unsafe water supply and sanitation are particularly acute. At the global level, water stress is a major issue, with 1.1 billion people without access to a safe water supply, and 2.6 billion people without access to adequate sanitation facilities.[56] The associated health impacts are alarming – 1.7 million deaths per year, of which 90 per cent are children under five years of age. Achieving the Millennium Development Goal of halving the population without access to water and sanitation by 2015 is expected to cost about US$10 billion per year. But this figure could be far outweighed by the costs of inaction if the goal is not achieved, in terms of impacts on human health and economic productivity. The cost of not meeting this goal (i.e. the cost of inaction) has been estimated at some US$130 billion a year.[57] Hence, investments in water supply and sanitation have a return of as much as 13:1. Globally, the WHO has estimated that the economic benefits of investments in meeting this target would outweigh costs by a ratio of about 8:1.[58] Furthermore, a recent extensive WHO study[59] found that 24 per cent of the global burden of disease, and 23 per cent of all deaths, are attributable to environmental factors. Children are more susceptible to the impacts of environmental pollution than adults. This WHO study[60] estimates that 33 per cent of diseases among 0–14-year-old children can be attributed to environmental factors, and this figure increases to 37 per cent for the 0–4 age group.

In 2008 the Secretary-General of the OECD, Angel Gurría, stated that 'If we want to avoid irreversible damage to our environment and the very high costs of policy inaction, we'd better start working right away.'[61] However, there are a number of key considerations that need to be taken into account when estimating the costs of inaction. It is important to consider a range of potential costs, both direct and indirect, as the OECD outlines, 'these include public finance expenditures (e.g. health service costs, restoring contaminated sites, restoring degraded habitat); direct financial costs borne by households and firms (e.g. increased insurance costs, reduced productivity in resource-based sectors); indirect costs, such as those which arise through markets affected by environmental factors (e.g. employment markets, real estate markets); and social welfare costs, which are not reflected in market prices or national accounts at all – including some non-use values of environmental damage (e.g. ecosystem degradation)'.[62]

It is also important to understand that such direct and indirect costs may not currently be reflected in the existing market prices for goods and services. For instance the costs of inaction on air, water and chemical pollution and waste

Table 5.4 *Potential areas related to costs of inaction on reducing pollution*

Air pollution	Water pollution
• Adverse health impacts	• Adverse health impacts
• Material damages (inducing cultural heritage)	• Increased drinking water treatment requirements
• Reduced agricultural yields	
• Polluted freshwater sources	• Reduced commercial fish stocks
• Reduced visibility	• Reduced recreational opportunities
• Loss of biodiversity	• Loss of biodiversity

Source: OECD (2008)[63]

generation include a wide variety of impacts that affect market prices (e.g. the effects of air pollution on human health,[64] or of water pollution on agricultural productivity), along with impacts that are more difficult to reflect in market terms (e.g. the existence value of affected species habitats). Table 5.4 illustrates the diversity of impacts that are involved from air and water pollution.

A further complication arises from the fact that not only are the costs related to the direct and indirect impacts from water, air and chemical pollution difficult to value, there are also costs relating to ecosystems (e.g. air sheds, watercourses) which are not directly related to some downstream economic activity, and are even more difficult to estimate.

Element 6: Costs of Action – Estimating the Costs of Action on Decoupling Efforts

In order to inform national and international targets and strategies, short- to medium-term costs of decoupling activities need to be investigated, with the long-term goal to both stimulate economic growth and to reduce the potential for costs of inaction. In investigating such costs it is helpful to consider the accuracy of past estimates of the cost of large-scale environmental actions in response to unacceptable levels of environmental pressure or impacts on human health. The fact is that an investigation of historical concerns around costs to industry of environmental responses clearly shows that purposeful action and innovation, effectively implemented, can result in significantly lower costs of action on a range of environmental issues.

Over the last 100 years industry has repeatedly argued that the costs of acting to address early warnings of environmental problems would be prohibitive; a key factor in many early warnings being ignored by decision-makers, governments and politicians. As explained by the European Environment Agency study *Late Lessons from Early Warnings: The Precautionary Principle 1896–2000*[65] in 2002:

> *In many of the case studies, adequate information about poten-*
> *tial hazards was available well before decisive regulatory advice*
> *was taken, but the information was either not brought to the*

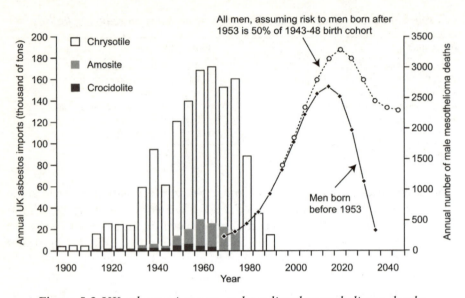

Figure 5.2 *UK asbestos imports and predicted mesothelioma deaths*

Source: Peto (1999)[66]

> *attention of the appropriate decision-makers early enough, or was discounted for one reason or another. It is also true that in some of the case studies, early warnings – and even 'loud and late' warnings – were effectively ignored by decision makers because of short-term economic and political interactions.*[67]

Take the case of asbestos.[68] In the last 20 years the use of asbestos has been nearly completely phased out through the use of a range of replacements. However, despite this significant progress, the first warnings were raised by British factory workers as early as 1898 of the 'harmful and "evil" effects of asbestos dust', but later in 1911 the UK Factory Department, pressured by industry groups, found insufficient evidence to justify action. It was not until the 1980s that pressure from the UK media, trade union and other interests, provoked tightening of asbestos controls on users and producers.[69] This late action is considered to have led to an estimated 150,000 asbestos-related deaths globally,[70] with continuing costs incurred within public health systems. For example, it is estimated that 250,000 cases of mesothelioma, which is normally fatal within one year, will occur in the EU by 2035 based on asbestos exposure. Figure 5.2 shows the peak of asbestos imports into the UK being followed some 50–60 years later by the estimated peak of mesotheliomas.

Such studies show how estimates about the cost of actions to reduce impacts to human health, or indeed to relieve environmental pressures, are a strong determinant in the probability of action being taken. For instance, such estimates affect the development of public policy, business strategy and research agendas, influencing public opinion and subsequently political support, which in turn again influences political and strategic decisions – effectively forming a reinforcing feedback loop. If estimates overstate the costs, the public may conclude that the regulations are too expensive when, in fact, the actual cost might be acceptable. Alternatively, policy analysts may decide that the benefits do not justify the costs, when the benefits may actually exceed the costs ultimately paid. It is therefore critical to balance current projections of the future costs of environmentally related activities with an understanding of how effective past efforts have actually been in forecasting regulatory costs.

Hart Hodges, an economist with the city of Portland, has undertaken a detailed economic analysis of past projections of environmental regulatory costs as they relate to a variety of industries, as shown in Table 5.5.[71] His

Table 5.5 *Industry original estimates of the cost of particular forms of environmental protection compared with the actual costs*

Pollutant	Initial cost estimate	Actual cost estimate	Overestimation as a percentage of actual cost
Asbestos (for the manufacturing and insulation sectors)	US$150 million	US$75 million	100%
Benzene	US$350,000 per plant	Approx. US$0 per plant	Infinite
CFCs	Early 1980s: Predicted financial catastrophe as no 'cheap' alternatives existed	Total cost globally of implementing the Montreal Protocol – US$235 billion in 1997[72]	Less than catastrophe
CFCs in auto air-conditioners	US$650–1200 per new car	US$40–400 per new car	63–2900%
Coke oven emissions 1970s	US$200 million –1 billion	US$160 million	29–1500%
Coke oven emissions US EPA 1980s	US$4 billion	US$250–400 million	900–1500%
Cotton dust	US$700 million per year	US$205 million per year	241%
Halons	1989: phase out not considered possible	1993: phase out considered technologically and economically feasible	n/a
Landfill leachate	Mid-1980s: US$14.8 billion	1990: US$5.7 billion	159%
Sulphur dioxide	1980s: US$1000–1500 per tonne of sulphur dioxide	1996: US$90 per tonne of sulphur dioxide	~750%
Surface mining	US$6–12 per tonne of coal	US$0.50–41 per tonne	500%–2300%
Vinyl chloride	US$109 million per year	US$20 million per year	445%

Source: Hodges (1999)[73]

examples range from asbestos to vinyl, and in all but one instance the estimated cost flowing from regulatory change was at least double the actual cost paid, while in some cases the estimates were found to be massively exaggerated.

The most interesting aspect of this trend is that the inflation of estimated costs holds, regardless of whether industry itself or an independent assessor did the work, which suggests a systematic source of the error rather than a political or agenda-driven influence. The reason for this discrepancy, Hodges argues, is that business groups and economists find it nearly impossible to predict the innovative ways in which industry goes about complying with new regulations. Hart found that the projections were generally based on the 'business-as-usual' assumption that environmental actions would only lead to costs and that the company must directly absorb the burden of these costs. *The Stern Review* explains Hodges result as follows:[74]

> *When such numbers come to light, companies are often accused of inflating initial cost estimates to support their lobbying efforts. But there is a more positive side to the story. The dramatic reduction in costs is often a result of the process of innovation, particularly when a regulatory change results in a significant increase in the scale of production. And the process of complying with new policies may reveal hidden inefficiencies which firms can root out, saving money in the process.*

Further to unforeseen levels of innovation, economists have often overestimated the costs of action in the short term because they do not appreciate the potential for strong multiplier effects, such as from investments in efficiency and local decoupling initiatives such as recycling and distributive approaches to energy and water. Also, economists have tended to underestimate the co-benefits of taking action to reduce environmental pressure on reducing other environmental pressures. Research shows that for the Kyoto Protocol, about half the costs of climate policy might be recovered from reduced air pollution control costs alone.[75] Similarly, further research has found that to comply with agreed or future policies to reduce regional air pollution in Europe, mitigation costs are reduced by 50–70 per cent for SO_2 and around 50 per cent for NO_x when combined with greenhouse gas policies.[76] Indirect co-benefits include reduced dependence on non-renewable resources, such as action to reduce greenhouse gas emissions from transport that will insulate economies from the likely sustained high oil prices into the future.

Other studies are also finding that the costs of action are usually an order of magnitude less than the costs of inaction. For instance, in 2008 the OECD published results of economic modelling that estimated the economic costs of action on the following policy package:[77]

- Assuming a goal of achieving stabilization at 450ppm of CO_2 equivalent by 2030, through implementing a carbon price of US$25 per tonne of carbon.[78]
- Bring forward the introduction and uptake of second generation biofuels, i.e. those using agricultural waste material or woody inputs developed on abandoned or marginal soils, rather than competing with agricultural land use.
- Ensuring clean water and sanitation to 50 per cent of people who currently do not have it. Connecting all urban dwellers with improved sanitation by 2030. For existing sewage treatment, treatment to be upgraded to the next best level in terms of removal of nitrogen compounds.
- Achieving 'maximum feasible reductions' in air pollutant emissions, including reducing SO_x and NO_x air pollution levels to 31 and 37 per cent less, respectively, in 2030, achieving a business-as-usual baseline (and about one-third less than 2005 levels).

The OECD modelling showed that these key environmental challenges can be addressed at a cost of just 0.5 and 2.5 per cent GDP by 2030 and 2050 respectively, equivalent to a reduction in annual GDP growth of just 0.1 per cent of world GDP in 2030. However, this does not consider a range of significant co-benefits available. For instance, according to *The Stern Review*, co-benefits related to reducing deforestation as a greenhouse mitigation scheme might include:[79]

- *Protection/preservation of biodiversity: Tropical forests house 70 per cent of the Earth's plants and animals. Without forest conservation, many of the world's plant and animal species face extinction this century. Essential natural resources are found in frontier forests that cannot be recreated.*
- *Research and development: Frontier forests in Brazil, Colombia and Indonesia are home to the greatest plant biodiversity in the world. Destroying these forests destroys the source of essential pharmaceutical ingredients. Some 40–50 per cent of drugs in the market have an origin in natural products, with 42 per cent of the sales of the top 25 selling drugs worldwide either biologicals, natural products or derived from natural products.*
- *Indigenous peoples and sustainability: About 50 million people are believed to be living in tropical forests, with the Amazonian forests home to around 1 million people of 400 different indigenous groups. Forest conservation affects people beyond those who inhabit them. Over 90 per cent of the 1.2 billion people living in extreme poverty depend on forests for some part of their livelihoods.*

- *Tourism: Forests provide opportunities for recreation for an increasingly wealthy and urbanized population. Brazil had a fivefold increase in tourists between 1991 and 1999, with 3.5 million people visiting Brazil's 150 Conservation Areas.*
- *Consequences for vulnerability to extreme weather events: Forests systems can play an important role in watersheds, and their loss can lead to an increase in flooding. In November 2005 a flash flood occurred in Langkat, Indonesia that killed 103 people with hundreds more missing. The Mount Leuser National Park had lost up to 22 per cent of its forest cover due to logging and, combined with high rainfall, this had caused a landslide to occur.*
- *In 2004, 3000 people died in Haiti after a tropical storm, while only 18 people across the border in the Dominican Republic died. The difference has been linked to extensive deforestation in Haiti where political turmoil and poverty have lead [sic] to the destruction of 98 per cent of original forest cover.*
- *Mangrove forests, depleted by 35 per cent play an important role in coastal defence, as well as providing important nursery grounds for fish stocks. Areas with healthy mangrove or tree cover were significantly less likely to have experienced major damage in the 2004 tsunami.*

Other publications go further than to simply highlight the potential co-benefits, arguing that it is possible to design buildings,[80] developments, industrial processes,[81] agriculture[82] and waste management processes to not only reduce their environmental pressures but to also then achieve enhanced environmental quality, referred to as 'restorative development'. Furthermore examples in books like *Factor Four*,[83] *Natural Capitalism*[84] and *Design for Sustainability*[85] show that humanity now possesses enough knowledge, understanding and skills to significantly decouple economic growth from these pressures, often contributing positively to the economy at the same time.

Element 7: Economic Resilience – Investigating and Understanding the Resilience of the Economy

The strength and resilience of an economy is an important determinant of its ability to decouple environmental pressures. Governments considering large-scale changes to allow reduction in environmental pressures need first to analyse the range of options and opportunities, and how they could affect the economy, in particular levels of employment, as explained in Chapters 3 and 7 in relation to greenhouse gas reductions. Such investigations are now showing that the decoupling agenda provides numerous opportunities to stimulate the economy and create employment,[86] both leading to a strengthening of economic resilience, especially when the reduction of future costs from inaction are factored into the modelling. This is mainly due to the potential for economic multipliers, where investments lead to the generation of economic activity, such as:

- investments to reduce the consumption of energy, water and other resources having a high economic multiplier because of reduced costs associated with sourcing and disposing of such resources;
- such reductions in consumption delaying (and even in some cases preventing) the need to invest large sums in the development of new energy and water supply infrastructure, along with new extractive industries;
- such initiatives saving governments and citizens money, while stimulating multiplier effects, and allowing greater local spending and job creation, and attracting people and businesses.

For example, California's energy efficiency policies created nearly 1.5 million jobs from 1977 to 2007.[87] Such opportunities are particularly attractive during periods of economic recession, when politicians often worry that investments to decouple economic growth from environmental pressures could further harm the economy. However, these opportunities have not historically been captured, such as in 1973 when a global recession rapidly took the world's focus away from the environment onto the economy, despite the momentum for action on the environment being developed as part of the 1972 UN Conference on the Human Environment in Stockholm. Similarly, significant momentum was again created leading up to the 1992 World Summit on Environment and Development in Rio, Brazil. However, the 1992 global economic recession again contributed to a significant amount of that momentum being lost. Since 2006, significant momentum has again been built up, due to leading efforts such as the film *An Inconvenient Truth*, the UK *Stern Review*,[88] and the IPCC Fourth Assessment Report.[89] But, since the global financial crisis hit in 2008–2009, there have again been calls by several national leaders and media commentators for caution on acting 'too fast' to reduce environmental pressures. However, it appears this time the message that decoupling economic growth from environmental pressures is possible and can lead to both economic benefits and reduced future risk, is beginning to take a foothold. Decoupling efforts can not only help national economies grow out of financial crises, they can also strengthen economies against such failures. This is mainly due to the fact that policies and incentives to encourage investment in decoupling (such as energy productivity, renewable energy, energy-efficient appliances, cars and green infrastructure) act to direct investments toward such areas that have positive effects across the economy, rather than just focusing on one or two main areas, such as the real estate market, which led to the 2008 US sub-prime mortgage crisis.

Hence, unlike in 1972 and 1992, there is strong evidence that many of the world's leaders are realizing that 'green' economic growth can underpin economies into the future. For instance, as discussed in Chapter 7, in the face of the 2008 financial and economic crisis, the EU nations, in November 2008, renewed their commitments to 20 per cent greenhouse gas reduction targets by 2020,[90] and British Prime Minister Gordon Brown led an increase of the UK target from 60 per cent to 80 per cent by 2050, passing this into law. In Australia, the much anticipated Federal Treasury modelling, launched in November 2008, found that Australia could tackle climate change while maintaining strong economic growth. As Treasurer Wayne Swan stated, 'The Australian economy will continue strong growth while reducing emissions. Average annual GDP growth will be a whisker less as a result of action. Just one tenth of one per cent less than otherwise would be the case.'[91] US President Barack Obama reinforced this message, saying in an interview with *Time Magazine* that, 'There is no better potential driver that pervades all aspects of our economy than a new energy economy. For us to say we are just going to completely revamp how we use energy in a way that deals with climate change, deals with national security and drives our economy, that's going to be my number one priority ...'[92] There is also strong evidence that rapidly emerging economies can also benefit from a focus on decoupling economic growth from environmental pressures. For instance, as Chapter 7 explains, the Chinese government decided in the early 1980s that a focus on decoupling economic growth from greenhouse gas emissions was essential to boost productivity and reduce dependency on foreign energy sources. From 1980 to 2000, Chinese industry's energy intensity decreased between 3 and 5 per cent per annum, helping to achieve a sixfold increase in national GDP from 1980 to 2000 while keeping increases in energy use relatively low.

When considering the ability of a nation's economy to underpin decoupling efforts, a range of areas need to be investigated. In particular the requirements of structural adjustment and industry transition need to be considered, along with the associated impacts on employment of such efforts and investments in new areas. During a transition to lower environmental pressures a number of inherently unsustainable industries will need to be completely transitioned to new forms, or if this is not possible, significantly downsized and eventually phased out. Workers in regional economies that are dependent on one main industry are understandably very concerned about anything that would affect that industry. There will need to be structural adjustment and compensation packages and retraining for those workers and businesses in the sectors and regions of an economy that will be significantly negatively affected – such as fisheries, forests, farming and some areas of coal mining. Such transitions need to be studied and understood so effective government policy and structural adjustment can be implemented. In addition it is important to undertake specific regional or national research on the potential for decoupling policy, in order to create new 'green' jobs in the local areas that would be negatively affected. Nations should undertake studies of the potential positive and

Table 5.6 *Potential to increase clean energy job growth and investment in the US – Sample of US states with large coal, oil, heavy industry or manufacturing sectors*

American State	Pew Charitable Trusts (2009)				Political Economy Research Institute (2009)		
	Total clean, green businesses (2007)	Clean energy jobs (2007)	Clean energy jobs growth (1998–2007)	Overall job growth (1998–2007)	Clean energy venture capital investment (US$ million) (2006–2008)	Potential clean energy jobs growth	Potential net increase clean energy investment ($US billion per annum)
Ohio	2513	35,267	7.3%	−2.2%	74	67,300	5.6
Kentucky	778	9308	10.0%	3.6%	–	25,700	2
Indiana	1268	17,298	17.9%	−1.0%	26	43,353	3.1
Illinois	2176	28,300	−2.5%	−2.5%	108	69,600	2
Michigan	1932	22,674	10.7%	−3.6%	55	53,800	4.8
Minnesota	1206	19,994	11.9%	1.9%	49	30,000	2.7
Pennsylvania	2934	38,763	−6.0%	−3.0%	233	86,385	6.1
Texas	4802	55,646	15.5%	6.7%	716	153,000	12.7
Wyoming	225	1419	56.4%	14.0%	7	4000	0.3
US	68,203	770,000	9.1%	3.7%	12.6 billion	1.7 million	150 billion

Source: Pew Charitable Trusts (2009)[93] and Political Economy Research Institute (2009)[94]

negative impacts on jobs of any major policy changes at the local and regional level to better understand and design effective structural adjustment and education and retraining programmes.

University research groups and non-governmental organizations (NGOs) can also assist by undertaking state-by-state or regional analysis of how any national environmental policy will affect clean energy and green jobs. For example, in 2009 studies by both the Pew Charitable Trusts, and the Political Economy Research Institute at the University of Massachusetts, investigated the impacts of the American Clean Energy and Security Act, coupled with the clean energy provisions of the Obama/Biden stimulus package passed by the Senate and Congress in February 2009. The Political Economy Research Institute's study found that these two measures have the potential to drive US$150 billion of investment in clean energy per annum, and the creation of up to 1.7 million jobs nationwide.[95] According to the study, 'clean-energy investments create 16.7 jobs for every US$1 million in spending whilst spending on fossil fuels generates 5.3 jobs'. Such results are important as they show that effective policy to decouple economic growth from greenhouse gas emissions can create jobs, even in states of the US with large coal, oil, heavy industry or manufacturing industries, as shown in Table 5.6.

These studies are also significant as they show that the rapid growth in clean energy jobs is fast approaching levels of employment in the industries that will need significant structural adjustment, such as coal, oil and gas. The Pew study found that, 'Between 1998 and 2007, clean energy jobs grew by 9.1

per cent per annum to 770,000 ... the traditional energy sector including utilities, coal, oil and gas companies employs 1.27 million workers in 2007.' Furthermore, both studies found that employees in such industries have valuable skills that will be needed to expand the clean energy sector, with the Political Economy Research Institute study pointing out that:

> *Constructing wind farms, for example, will create jobs for sheet metal workers, machinists, and truck drivers, among many others. Increasing the energy efficiency of buildings through retrofitting requires roofers, insulators, and building inspectors. Expanding mass transit systems employs civil engineers, electricians, and dispatchers. More generally, economic stimulus and green jobs programs will provide a major boost to the construction and manufacturing sectors through much-needed spending on green infrastructure.*[96]

Hence although it may seem at first that transitioning away from carbon-intensive energy generation to clean and renewable options will place a heavy burden on the economy, and cause job losses, research is demonstrating that the resilience of many economies is actually stronger than this and if it is done wisely can support an effective transition.

Element 8: International Cooperation – Identifying the Potential for Synergy with Global Efforts

In developing decoupling-related strategies an important element to consider is the level of international commitment and cooperation across both governments and business to reduce a particular environmental pressure, for the following key reasons:

- Many environmental challenges are inherently global because pollutants created in one country can travel around the world through the atmosphere and oceans.
- It is impossible to address global environmental issues without addressing poverty, as explained in Chapter 4.
- Rapidly developing countries such as in China and India need to be integrally involved if efforts to address global environmental pressures are to be effective.
- Domestic industries across the world's economies must be able to operate on a level playing field to reduce the potential for industries to be exposed to unfair international competitiveness issues.
- Global cooperation will assist in creating global markets for more environmentally friendly technologies and products, providing corporations and nations with greater certainty about the scale of such emerging markets, and reducing risks involved with research and development.

- Global cooperation is needed to facilitate technological transfer to increase rates of global diffusion of sustainable technologies and practices.

While for these and many other reasons it is wise to develop international cooperation to effectively address environmental pressures, there are significant barriers working against it, such as mistrust between nations, concerns over issues of national sovereignty, concerns about the distribution of the costs and benefits, and the fact that domestic political imperatives often require the majority of a government's focus and time. However, despite such barriers, over the last few decades a number of multilateral agreements have been forged related to a range of environmental pressures, inspired by works such as *Our Common Future* which more than 20 years ago outlined the need for global cooperation to address global environmental degradation and extreme poverty.[97] According to UNEP in 2006 there were more than 500 environment-related international treaties and other agreements, of which 323 were regional.[98] Such agreements can form the basis of a global framework that can support increased action to decouple environmental pressures in the coming decades. As Jeffrey Sachs reflected in *Common Wealth: Economics for a Crowded Planet*, 'One of the reasons why we should be confident that our generation can be the one to end extreme poverty, mitigate climate change, and avoid another mass extinction of species, is that a framework for shared global commitment already exists and has been at least adopted in principle by most nations.'[99] Such agreements include the UN Framework Convention on Climate Change, the Convention on Biological Diversity and the UN Convention to Combat Desertification, with most UN member nations being signatories, and inspiring the development of a number of regional institutions and organizations concerned with the environment.

Further to a significant number of agreements related to the marine environment, some 40 per cent of current agreements, a range of specific agreements related to chemicals and hazardous waste, have emerged since 1972. These include the Basel Convention on Transboundary Movements of Hazardous Wastes, the Montreal Protocol on Substances that Deplete the Ozone Layer, the Rotterdam Convention on the Prior Informed Consent Procedure for Certain Hazardous Chemicals and Pesticides in International Trade and the Stockholm Convention on Persistent Organic Pollutants, along with EU directives including the Restriction of Hazardous Substances and the Registration, Evaluation, Authorization and Restriction of Chemical Substances. Each of these agreements will affect industry in some way and need to be carefully considered as part of decoupling strategies, particularly in relation to their impact on imports and exports.

It is clear, however, that efforts to achieve the goals of such agreements will be continually undermined if efforts to build social capital and reduce inequality and poverty are not also undertaken. Low productivity, rapid population growth, political instability, conflict and weakening state capacities, all serve to reinforce generalized poverty, and undermine efforts to reduce environmental pressures. Over 2 billion people have no access to electricity and thus the need for fuel in developing countries is the largest single demand on trees and accounts for just over half of all wood removed from the world's forests.[100] Many developing countries are struggling currently under the combined pressures of a heavy external debt burden, violent conflict, serious health issues such as HIV/AIDS and malaria epidemics, and a lack of investment. Some experts also argue that these problems are exacerbated by trade protectionism from the North.[101] Many of the citizens of these countries suffer from a lack of access to social services, education, energy and basic water sanitation. At best, some become refugees or economic migrants. As a result of these processes, poor countries and poor people are marginalized from the opportunities presented by global economic growth and development.

The publication *Our Common Future* and the 1992 Rio Earth Summit addressed, in detail, the linked issues of poverty and environmental degradation, leading to the 1994 International Conference on Population and Development (ICPD) in Cairo. The ICPD Action Plan was agreed by 179 governments, and emphasized the links between family planning options, access to basic health services, education and gender equity, and with sustainable development as discussed in Chapter 4. The plan of action, a precursor to the Millennium Development Goals, in addition to calling for universal primary education and steep reductions in infant and child mortality, put emphasis on 'ensuring by 2015 access to universal sexual health and reproductive health care, including family planning, assisted childbirth and prevention of sexually transmitted diseases including HIVAIDS'.[102]

Hence there are now a number of multilateral agreements covering the major development challenges to be faced in the coming century, from climate change to poverty reduction, that provide a firm foundation for cooperative action.

Element 9: Assessing and Accounting for the National Security Benefits of Decoupling

One of the core responsibilities of government is to ensure security, often involving the commitment of significant amounts of resources and funding. A number of strategists and commentators are now identifying that global cooperation to achieve decoupling of economic growth from environmental pressures will be a core component of national security strategies. In recent years, a quarter of the world's armed conflicts have involved a struggle for natural resources, with more than 5 million people dying as a result of these conflicts in the 1990s.[103] Security expert Michael Klare argues that wars this century will be fought over increasingly scarce resources, rather than the traditional causes such as trade barriers or land disputes, mostly due to:[104]

- Increasing competition for remaining global oil and gas reserves, with many areas importing significant percentages of their consumption, such as the US (50 per cent) and Europe (70 per cent). By 2020 China will import 50 per cent, with Japan and South Korea almost entirely dependent on oil from overseas.

- Reductions in water availability from the combination of unsustainable water usage and climate change. According to the International Management Institute, nearly a third of the world's expected population will live in regions facing severe water scarcity by 2025.[105]

Klare argues that geographical hotspots for wars and conflict this century will be related to access to oil in the Persian Gulf, the Caspian Sea Basin and the South China Sea, while for access to water the hotspots are the Nile Valley, the Middle East, Jordan, the Tigris-Euphrates and the Indus river basins. The potential for conflict in these regions is heightened because at least two countries border on and share these precious resources, and have never agreed on procedures for dividing up the available supply.

The South China Sea, for example, is bordered by many nations: China and Taiwan, the Philippines, Indonesia, Malaysia and on the west by Viet Nam. All of these nations have expanding oil and natural gas needs. If current projections continue, Asia will rely on these two fuels for over 50 per cent of its energy needs by 2020. The South China Sea is like the Persian Gulf and the Caspian Sea in that its underwater oil resources are within many disputed borders, and the states involved have already shown that they are willing to use military force to protect 'their interests' in the region. Normally borders and hence ownership can be easily determined: when nations that border a sea both claim an Economic Exclusion Zone, one simply works out the halfway point between the two nations. However, in the South China Sea this is very difficult due to the great number of islands. Added to this is China's claim for the Spartly archipelago, a set of over 400 islands, most only visible at low tide, at the south of the South China Sea. In doing this China is seeking a zone of almost the entire South China Sea.[106]

There have already been low-level military disputes, mainly between China and Viet Nam. But these will only be exacerbated by the rapidly growing demand for oil and natural gas by Asian nations, and Asia's relative lack of reserves in such resources. Although several countries including China and Indonesia possess modest supplies of petroleum and natural gas, none possesses truly significant quantities, such as those found in the Persian Gulf and the Caspian Sea areas. By 2000, Asian nations produced approximately 7 million barrels of oil per day but consumed 19 million barrels a day; by 2020 with business-as-usual projections the gap between production and consumption will have doubled, and net imports will approach 25 million barrels per day. This will impact on the South China Sea in subtle ways. Not only will there be increased concern among Asian nations for who controls the oil reserves, but there will be increased shipping of oil through the South China Sea to countries like Japan who will be keen to ensure there is no threat to their shipping routes.

Klare also argues that reduced water availability will be a source of future conflict. Around the world, groundwater extracted from deep wells is the main source of drinking water for over 3 billion people.[107] The failure of governments to limit pumping to the sustainable yield of aquifers means that water tables are now rapidly falling in countries that contain more than half the world's people, including the big three grain producers – China, India and the US.[108] As Chapter 9 shows, there are already a number of regions which are facing shortages of fresh water and many more will suffer the same fate within the next few decades if sustainable water management practices are not rapidly introduced. There have already been wars over water, such as between Israel and Jordon in the mid-1960s.[109] Climate change will exacerbate freshwater shortages significantly, and is already changing the water cycle and affecting water availability. For example, the IPCC in 2008 released a new technical report on *Climate Change and Water*, finding that:[110]

- *By the middle of the 21st century, many semi-arid and arid areas (e.g., the Mediterranean Basin, western USA, southern Africa and North-Eastern Brazil, Murray Darling Basin, Australia) are particularly exposed to the impacts of climate change and are projected to suffer a decrease of water resources due to climate change.*
- *Water supplies stored in glaciers and snow cover are projected to decline in the course of the century, thus reducing water availability during warm and dry periods (through a seasonal shift in streamflow, an increase in the ratio of winter to annual flows, and reductions in low flows) in regions supplied by melt water from major mountain ranges, where more than one-sixth of the world's population currently live.*

Considering again the potential for conflict from countries sharing borders with resources, Turkey, Syria and Iraq have had several conflicts over water extraction from the Tigris and Euphrates rivers. The Nile River flows past ten African countries, and is another case of water conflict, particularly following construction of the Aswan Dam.[111] Klare writes in his publication *Resource Wars: The New Landscape of Global Conflict*, that, 'Unless ways are found to reduce these states' per capita use of the available supply, any increase in utilization by one country in the system will result in less water being available to the others – a situation that could lead to the outbreak of war.'[112]

The region of Asia Pacific will be particularly negatively affected by climate change, with island states already being seriously threatened by sea-level rises. Furthermore, most of the megacities in Asia are on low-lying river deltas which are very vulnerable to the slightest sea-level rises. Professors Dupont and Pearman suggest that climate change will threaten the security of many countries in the following ways:[113]

- Weather extremes and greater fluctuations in rainfall and temperatures will exacerbate food, water and energy scarcities over relatively short timeframes as discussed above.
- Climate change will contribute to destabilizing unregulated population movements in Asia and the Pacific. Experts predict that with current climate models, climate change will increase the number of environmental refugees sixfold over the next 50 years to 150 million, largely from low-lying areas such as Bangladesh.[114]
- Extreme weather events and climate-related disasters will not only trigger short-term disease spikes but also lead to breakdowns of society, lawlessness and loss of security, as witnessed after Hurricane Katrina, in the US in 2006.

Hence multilateral efforts to address climate change and other environmental pressures will be critical for national security, as well as being a moral, humanitarian and economic development imperative. Reducing the potential for resource-based conflict is an urgent consideration given the devastating effects of war, with the repercussions of the First World War being felt for the rest of the 20th century. Professor Sachs writes that 'Another great consequence of World War I was the prolonged financial instability it created in Europe after the war. The war created a morass of interlocking financial and economic problems, including the mountain of debt incurred by combatant countries, the destruction and dismembering of the Ottoman and Hapsburg empires and their displacement by small, unstable and feuding successor states, and the Allied claims for reparation payments from Germany, which embittered the next generation of Germans and was one of the rallying points for Hitler's rise to power ... The economic instability that followed World War I led to the Great Depression of the 1930s and then to World War II.'[115] Furthermore as a result the financial debt incurred, the loss of life, the emotional impact on those involved and their families, and finally the damage to civilians was immense. *Our Common Future* devoted an entire chapter to peace and security and summed up the situation clearly, stating that:

> *Arms competition and armed conflict creates major obstacles to sustainable development. They make huge claims on scarce material resources. They pre-empt human resources and wealth that could be used to combat the collapse of environmental support systems, the poverty, and the underdevelopment that in combination contribute so much to contemporary political insecurity. They may stimulate an ethos that is antagonistic towards co-operation amongst nations whose ecological and economic interdependence requires them to overcome national and ideological antipathies.*[116]

Humanity faces the choice to either proactively build global cooperation to address environmental pressures, or to let current trends continue to the detriment of future national security.

Notes

1   WCED (1987) *Our Common Future*, Oxford University Press, Oxford, p22.
2   OECD Secretariat (2002) *Indicators to Measure Decoupling of Environmental Pressure and Economic Growth*, OECD, Paris.
3   OECD (2002) *Environmental Strategy for the First Decade of the 21st Century*, adopted by OECD Environment Ministers on 16 May, OECD, Paris.
4   OECD Secretariat (2002) *Indicators to Measure Decoupling of Environmental Pressure and Economic Growth*, OECD, Paris.
5   Gleick, P. et al (2003) *Waste Not, Want Not: The Potential for Urban Water Conservation in California*, Pacific Institute, Oakland, CA.
6   von Weizsäcker, E., Hargroves, K., Smith, M., Desha, C. and Stasinopoulos, P. (2009) *Factor Five: Transforming the Global Economy through 80% Improvements in Resource Productivity*, Earthscan, London.
7   Van Minnen, J. G., Onigkeit, J. and Alcamo, J. (2002) 'Long-term reductions in costs of controlling regional air pollution in Europe due to climate policy', *Environmental Science & Policy*, vol 5, no 4, pp349–365, cited in OECD (2008) *OECD Environmental Outlook to 2030*, OECD, Paris.
8   WCED (1987) *Our Common Future*, Oxford University Press, Oxford.
9   Diamond, J. (2006) *Collapse: How Societies Choose to Fail or Succeed*, Random House; Tainter, J. (1993) *The Collapse of Complex Societies*, Cambridge University Press, Cambridge; Marsh, G. P. (1864) *Man and Nature: Or, Physical Geography as Modified by Human Action*, University of Washington Press, Washington, DC; Ponting, C. (1991) *A Green History of the World: The Environment and the Collapse of Great Civilisations*, Penguin, New York; Redman, C. (1999) *Human Impact on Ancient Environment*, University of Arizona Press, Tuscon, AZ; Fagan, B. (1999) *Floods, Famines, and Emperors: El Nino and the Fate of Civilisations*, Basic Books, New York; Fagan, B. (2001) *The Little Ice Age*, Basic Books, New York; Fagan, B. (2004) *The Long Summer: How Climate Changed Civilisation*, Basic Books, New York; St Barbe Baker, R. (1944) *I Planted Trees*, Lutterworth Press, London and Redhill.
10 Diamond, J. (2006) *Collapse: How Societies Choose to Fail or Succeed*, Random House.
11 St Barbe Baker, R. (1944) *I Planted Trees*, Lutterworth Press, London and Redhill.
12 Demarest, A. (2004) *Ancient Maya: The Rise and Fall of a Rainforest Civilization*, Cambridge University Press, Cambridge.
13 Tainter, J. (1993) *The Collapse of Complex Societies,* Cambridge University Press, Cambridge.
14 Diamond, J. (2006) *Collapse: How Societies Choose to Fail or Succeed*, Random House, New York.
15 Pachauri, R. K. (2007) *Nobel Laureate Acceptance Speech*, Nobel Institute, Sweden.
16 Barney, G. (1982) *The Global 2000 Report to the President: Entering the Twenty-First Century, Volume Two: The Technical Report*, Penguin Books, Harmondsworth, UK, pp685–687, see Appendix A 'Lessons from the past'.

17 Barney, G. (1982) *The Global 2000 Report to the President: Entering the Twenty-First Century, Volume Two: The Technical Report*, Penguin Books, Harmondsworth, UK, pp685–687, see Appendix A 'Lessons from the past'.
18 American Memory (undated) 'Proceedings of a 1908 Conference of Governors: Opening Address by the President', http://memory.loc.gov/cgi-bin/query/r?ammem/consrv:@field(DOCID+@lit(amrvgvg16div19)), accessed 1 July 2008.
19 Carver, G. W. (1905) *How to Build Up Worn Out Soils*, Tuskegee Experiment Station, Bulletin Six, Tuskegee, p4.
20 King, F. H. (1911) *Farmers of Forty Centuries*, Dover Publications, New York.
21 Ecssolar (undated) 'A Brief History of the American Solar Water Heating Industry', www.ecs-solar.com/Solar_Articles/briefHistory.pdf, accessed 30 January 2008.
22 Perlin, P. (1999) *From Space to Earth – The Story of Solar Electricity*, Aatec Publications, MI.
23 Howard, E. (1965) *Garden Cities of To-Morrow*, MIT Press, MA. Originally published in 1898 as *To-Morrow: A Peaceful Path to Real Reform* and reissued in 1902 under its present title, *Garden Cities of To-Morrow* holds a unique place in town planning literature. The book was responsible for the introduction of the term Garden City, and set into motion ideas that helped transform town planning.
24 Moon, J. (1974) *Rudolf Diesel and the Diesel Engine*, Priory Press, London.
25 Kirsch, D. (1996) 'The electric car and the burden of history: Studies in Automotive Systems Rivalry in the United States, 1890–1996', PhD dissertation, Stanford University, CA.
26 Millennium Ecosystem Assessment (2005) *Ecosystems and Human Well-Being: Synthesis Report*, World Resources Institute, Island Press, Washington, DC.
27 Meadows, D. (2009) *Thinking in Systems*, Earthscan, London.
28 UNEP (2007) *Global Environment Outlook: Environment for Development Report*, UNEP.
29 Caton, A. and McLoughlin, K. (2004) *Fishery Status Report: Status of Fish Stocks Managed by the Australian Government*, Bureau of Rural Sciences, Canberra.
30 OECD (2006) *OECD Environmental Data – Inland Waters*, OECD Statistics, Paris.
31 OECD (2002) *Indicators to Measure Decoupling of Environmental Pressure and Economic Growth*, OECD, Paris.
32 OECD (2002) *Indicators to Measure Decoupling of Environmental Pressure and Economic Growth*, OECD, Paris.
33 OECD (2002) *Indicators to Measure Decoupling of Environmental Pressure and Economic Growth*, OECD, Paris.
34 OECD (2002) *Indicators to Measure Decoupling of Environmental Pressure and Economic Growth*, OECD, Paris.
35 European Environment Agency (EEA) (2003) *Europe's Environment: The Third Assessment*, EEA, Luxembourg.
36 Daly, H. (2004) 'Can economic growth solve our environmental problems?', A debate with Herman Daly and Paul Portney, World Bank Group, Washington, DC.
37 Anderson, D. (1992) 'Economic growth and the environment', Background Paper for the World Bank (1992) *World Development Report 1992*, World Bank, Washington, DC.
38 Anderson, D. (1996) 'Energy and the environment: Technical and economic possibilities', *Finance and Development*, vol 33, no 2, pp10–13; OECD (2008) *The Costs of Inaction on Key Environmental Challenges*, OECD, Paris.

39 Weaver, P., Jansen, L., van Grootveld, G., van Spiegel, E. and Vergragt, P. (2000) *Sustainable Technology Development*, Greenleaf Publishing, Sheffield, UK, p7.

40 OECD (2007) *Measuring Material Flows and Resource Productivity: The OECD Guide*, OECD, Paris.

41 Foran, B. et al (2005) *Balancing Act: A Triple Bottom Line Analysis of the Australian Economy*, CSIRO, Australia.

42 von Weizsäcker, E., Lovins, A. and Lovins, L. H. (1997) *Factor Four: Doubling Wealth, Halving Resource Use*, Earthscan, London.

43 Hawken, P., Lovins, A. and Lovins, L. H. (1999) *Natural Capitalism: Creating the Next Industrial Revolution*, Earthscan, London.

44 Hargroves, K. and Smith, M. (eds) (2005) *The Natural Advantage of Nations: Business Opportunities, Innovation and Governance in the 21st Century*, Earthscan, London.

45 von Weizsäcker, E., Hargroves, K., Smith, M., Desha, C. and Stasinopoulos, P. (2009) *Factor Five: Transforming the Global Economy through 80% Improvements in Resource Productivity*, Earthscan, London.

46 OECD (2008) *The Costs of Inaction on Key Environmental Challenges*, OECD, Paris.

47 OECD (2008) *OECD Environmental Outlook to 2030*, OECD, Paris.

48 OECD (2008) *OECD Environmental Outlook to 2030*, OECD, Paris.

49 World Bank (2007) *Cost of Pollution in China: Economic Estimates of Physical Damages*, World Bank, Washington DC.

50 UNEP (2007) *Global Environment Outlook: Environment for Development Report*, UNEP.

51 US EPA (1999) *The Benefits and Costs of the Clean Air Act 1990 to 2010*, US Environmental Protection Agency, Washington, DC.

52 Farmer, A. (1997) *Managing Environmental Pollution*, Routledge, New York.

53 Farmer, A. (1997) *Managing Environmental Pollution*, Routledge, New York.

54 OECD (2008) *Cost of Inaction: Technical Report*, OECD, Paris; OECD (2008) *Costs of Environmental Policy Inaction: Summary for Policy-Makers*, OECD, Paris.

55 OECD (2008) *Cost of Inaction: Technical Report*, OECD, Paris; OECD (2008) *Costs of Environmental Policy Inaction: Summary for Policy-makers*, OECD, Paris.

56 WHO/UNICEF (2006) *Joint Monitoring Programme for Water Supply and Sanitation*, WHO/UNICEF, Geneva and New York.

57 Hutton, G. and Haller, L. (2004) *Evaluation of the Costs and Benefits of Water and Sanitation Improvements at the Global Level*, Water, Sanitation and Health, Protection of the Human Environment, WHO, Geneva, Washington, DC.

58 WHO and UNICEF (2005) *Water for Life: Making it Happen*, WHO, Geneva.

59 Prüss-Ustün, A. and Corvalán, C. (2006) *Preventing Disease through Healthy Environments – Towards an Estimate of the Environmental Burden of Disease*, WHO, Geneva.

60 Prüss-Ustün, A. and Corvalán, C. (2006) *Preventing Disease through Healthy Environments – Towards an Estimate of the Environmental Burden of Disease*, WHO, Geneva.

61 OECD (2008) *OECD Environmental Outlook to 2030*, OECD, Paris.

62 OECD (2008) *OECD Environmental Outlook to 2030*, OECD, Paris.

63 OECD (2008) *OECD Environmental Outlook to 2030*, OECD, Paris.

64 Pearce, D. et al (2006) *Cost-Benefit Analysis and the Environment*, OECD, Paris.

65 Harremo, P., Gee, P., MacGarvin, M., Stirling, A., Keys, J., Wynne, B. and Vaz, S. G. (2001) *Late Lessons from Early Warnings: The Precautionary Principle 1896–2000,* Environmental issue report no 22, European Environment Agency.

66 Peto, J. (1999) 'The European mesothelioma epidemic', *British Journal of Cancer,* vol 79, February, pp666–672.

67 Harremo, P., Gee, P., MacGarvin, M., Stirling, A., Keys, J., Wynne, B. and Vaz, S. G. (2001) *Late Lessons from Early Warnings: The Precautionary Principle 1896–2000,* Environmental issue report no 22, European Environment Agency, p168.

68 For a detailed account of this case study refer to: Gee, D. and Greenberg, M. (2001) 'Asbestos: From "magic" to malevolent mineral', in Harremo, P., Gee, P., MacGarvin, M., Stirling, A., Keys, J., Wynne, B. and Vaz, S. G. (2001) *Late Lessons from Early Warnings: The Precautionary Principle 1896–2000,* Environmental issue report no 22, European Environment Agency, Chapter 5.

69 Harremo, P., Gee, P., MacGarvin, M., Stirling, A., Keys, J., Wynne, B. and Vaz, S. G. (2001) *Late Lessons from Early Warnings: The Precautionary Principle 1896–2000,* Environmental issue report no 22, European Environment Agency.

70 Slattery, L. (2004) 'Asbestos industry – corporate murder on a global scale, you will know them by their trail of death', an investigation into the asbestos industry, Review of a Real Life documentary produced in the UK for ITN television, International Committee of the Fourth International, 14 September.

71 Hodges, H. (1997) *Cost of Complying with Environmental Regulations Almost Always Less than Advertised,* Economic Policy Institute, Washington, DC.

72 Bornman, J. F. and van der Leun, J. C. (1998) 'Frequently asked questions', *Journal of Photochemistry and Photobiology,* vol 46.

73 Hodges, H. (1997) *Cost of Complying With Environmental Regulations Almost Always Less Than Advertised,* Economic Policy Institute, Washington, DC.

74 Stern, N. (2006) *The Stern Review: The Economics of Climate Change,* 'Executive summary', Cambridge University Press, Cambridge.

75 Van Vuuren, D. P. and den Elzen, M. J. E. et al (2006) 'Exploring the ancillary benefits of the Kyoto Protocol for air pollution in Europe', *Energy Policy,* vol 34, pp444–460.

76 Van Minnen, J. G., Onigkeit, J. and Alcamo, J. (2002) 'Long-term reductions in costs of controlling regional air pollution in Europe due to climate policy', *Environmental Science & Policy,* vol 5, no 4, pp349–365.

77 OECD (2008) *OECD Environmental Outlook to 2030,* OECD, Paris.

78 Application of a price on carbon across all sectors, via a carbon tax starting at US$25 per tonne of CO_2eq, which increases in real terms by 2.4 per cent per year. The carbon price was phased in by region, starting in OECD countries in 2012, Brazil, India, Russia and China in 2020 and the rest of the world in 2030.

79 Stern, N. (2006) *The Stern Review: The Economics of Climate Change,* Cambridge University Press, Cambridge, Box 12.6.

80 Birkeland, J. (2002) *Design for Sustainability: A Sourcebook of Integrated Eco-Logical Solutions,* Earthscan, London.

81 McDonough, W. and Braungart, M. (2002) *Cradle to Cradle: Remaking the Way We Make Things,* North Point Press, San Francisco, CA.

82 Benyus, J. (1997) *Biomimicry: Innovation Inspired by Nature,* HarperCollins, New York.

83 von Weizsäcker, E., Lovins, A. B. and Lovins, L. H. (1997) *Factor Four: Doubling Wealth, Halving Resource Use,* Earthscan, London.

84   Hawken, P., Lovins, A. B. and Lovins, L. H. (1999) *Natural Capitalism: Creating the Next Industrial Revolution*, Earthscan, London.

85   Birkeland, J. (2002) *Design for Sustainability: A Sourcebook of Integrated Eco-Logical Solutions*, Earthscan, London.

86   Jowit, J. (2008) 'Now is the time to tackle global warming: Lord Stern', *Guardian* (UK), 7 October.

87   Roland-Holst, D. (2008) *Energy Efficiency, Innovation, and Job Creation in California*, Research Papers on Energy, Resources, and Economic Sustainability, UC Berkeley, CA.

88   Stern, N. (2006) *The Stern Review: The Economics of Climate Change*, Cambridge University Press, Cambridge, p104.

89   IPCC (2007) *Climate Change 2007: Mitigation of Climate Change*, Contribution of Working Group III to the Fourth Assessment Report of the Intergovernmental Panel on Climate Change, Cambridge University Press, Cambridge.

90   Italy has agreed to sign the EU's climate plan in December but only on condition the deal is revisited at the end of 2009 once real costs have been analysed.

91   Lane, S. (2008) 'Emissions trading scheme to cost families an extra $1 a day', *ABC PM*, 30 October.

92   Klein, J. (2008) 'The full Obama interview', *Time Magazine*, 23 October.

93   Pollin, R. Heintz, J. and Garrett-Peltier, H. (2009) *The Economic Benefits of Investing in Clean Energy: How the Economic Stimulus Program and New Legislation Can Boost U.S. Economic Growth and Employment*, Political Economy Research Institute in partnership with the Center for American Progress.

94   Pew Charitable Trusts (2009) *The Clean Energy Economy: Repowering Jobs, Businesses and Investments Across America*, Pew Charitable Trust.

95   Pollin, R. Heintz, J. and Garrett-Peltier, H. (2009) *The Economic Benefits of Investing in Clean Energy: How the Economic Stimulus Program and New Legislation Can Boost U.S. Economic Growth and Employment*, Political Economy Research Institute in partnership with the Center for American Progress.

96   Pollin, R. Heintz, J. and Garrett-Peltier, H. (2009) *The Economic Benefits of Investing in Clean Energy: How the Economic Stimulus Program and New Legislation Can Boost U.S. Economic Growth and Employment*, Political Economy Research Institute in partnership with the Center for American Progress.

97   WCED (1987) *Our Common Future*, Oxford University Press, Oxford, p10.

98   UNEP (2006) *UN Reform – Implications for the Environment Pillar*, Issue paper by the Deputy Executive Director, UNEP/DED/040506, UNEP, Nairobi.

99   Sachs, J. (2008) *Common Wealth: Economics for a Crowded Planet*, Penguin, New York.

100   Brown, L. (2008) *Plan B 3.0: Mobilizing to Save Civilization*, W. W. Norton & Company, New York.

101   Stiglitz, J. and Charlton, A. (2005) *Fair Trade for All: How Trade Can Promote Development*, Oxford University Press, Oxford.

102   Sachs, J. (2008) *Common Wealth: Economics for a Crowded Planet*, Penguin, New York.

103   WorldWatch Institute (2003) *Vital Signs*, Worldwatch Institute, Washington, DC.

104   Klare, M. (2001) *Resource Wars: The New Landscape of Global Conflict*, Henry Holt Books, New York.

105 Seckler, D., Amarasinghe, U., Molden, D., de Silva, R. and Barker, R. (1998) *World Water Demand and Supply, 1990 to 2025: Scenarios and issues,* Research Report 19, International Water Management Institute, Colombo, Sri Lanka; Seckler, D., Baker, R. and Amarasinghe, U. A. (1999) 'Water scarcity in the twenty-first century', *International Journal of Water Resources Development,* Special Double Issue: Research from the International Water Management Institute, vol 15, issue 1 and 2, pp29–42.

106 Klare, M. (2001) *Resource Wars: The New Landscape of Global Conflict,* Henry Holt Books, New York.

107 Shah, T. et al (2007) 'Groundwater: A Global Assessment of Scale and Significance', in International Water Management Institute (ed) *Water for Food, Water for Life: A Comprehensive Assessment of Water Management,* Earthscan, London.

108 Shiklomanov, I. (1998) *Assessment of Water Resources and Water Availability in the World,* Report for the Comprehensive Assessment of the Freshwater Resources of the World, State Hydrological Institute, St Petersburg, Russia, cited in Gleick, P. (2000–2001) *The World's Water 2000–2001,* Island Press, Washington, DC, p52.

109 Leggitt, J. (2008) *When the Rivers Run Dry: What Happens When Our Water Runs Out?,* Eden Project Books, UK; Peter Gleick and the Pacific Institute have published freely online an historical chronology of all the wars and conflicts over water starting from 3000 BC, available at www.worldwater.org/conflictchronology.pdf, accessed 14 October 2008.

110 Bates, B. C., Kundzewicz, Z. W., Wu, S. and Palutikof, J. P. (eds) (2008) *Climate Change and Water,* Technical Paper of the Intergovernmental Panel on Climate Change, IPCC Secretariat, Geneva.

111 Shiva, V. (2002) *Water Wars,* South End Press, Cambridge, MA.

112 Klare, M. (2001) *Resource Wars: The New Landscape of Global Conflict,* Henry Holt Books, New York.

113 Dupont, A. and Pearman, G. (2006) *Heating up the Planet: Climate Change and Security,* Lowy Institute for Sustainable Policy, Sydney, Australia.

114 Myers, N. (1993) 'Environmental refugees in a globally warmed world', *BioScience,* vol 43, no 11, p758.

115 Sachs, J. (2005) *The End of Poverty: How Can We Make it Happen in our Lifetime,* Penguin Group, New York, pp44–45.

116 WCED (1987) *Our Common Future,* Oxford University Press, Oxford, p10.

6

Responding to the Complexity of Climate Change

The Overarching Moral, Economic, Scientific and Technological Challenge of Our Age

Will we stand by while drought and famine, storms and floods overtake our planet? Or will we look back at today and say that this was the moment when we took a stand? That this was the moment when we began to turn things around? The climate changes we are experiencing are already causing us harm. But in the end, it will not be us who deal with its most devastating effects. It will be our children and our grandchildren. Never has the failure to take on a single challenge so detrimentally affected nearly every aspect of our well being as a nation. And never have the possible solutions, had the potential to do so much good for so many generations to come. This is our generation's chance. It's a chance that will not last much longer, but if we work together and seize this moment, we can change the course of this nation (and world) forever.

Senator Barack Obama, 3 April 2006, Chicago, US[1]

In his closing words to the Australia 2020 Summit in April 2008, the recently elected Prime Minister of Australia, Kevin Rudd, stated that 'Climate change is the overarching moral, economic, scientific and technological challenge of our age'.[2] This understanding is now being voiced by many of the world's political leaders, such as former US Vice President, Al Gore, in calling the situation nothing less than a 'planetary emergency'.[3] The world's scientific community is also making its voice heard, with the 2007 report from the Intergovernmental Panel on Climate Change (IPCC) finding that CO_2 equivalent levels were at 455ppm which is widely considered to be approaching the range where dangerous impacts could result.[4] Dr Rajendra Pachauri, the chairman of the IPCC, states that 2015 will be 'the last year in which the world could afford a net rise in greenhouse gas emissions, after which "very sharp reductions" are required'.[5] UN Secretary-General Ban Ki-moon, when launching the Fourth Assessment Report of the IPCC,[6] said that 'slowing and even reversing the effects of climate change is the defining challenge of our age'.[7]

When considering the latest climate change science, and in light of the lack of progress at Copenhagen, it would be easy to despair. However, the stark reality of this situation is balanced by a growing realization that humanity has the capability to mitigate and adapt to climate change rapidly, and deliver strong economic growth as a result; the focus of the following chapters. The IPCC's Working Group on Climate Change Mitigation for the Fourth Assessment Report showed that the world has the capability to achieve rapid reductions in greenhouse gas emissions by 2020 and even 50–80 per cent cuts by 2050,[8] a position further supported by the 2009 update of the seminal book *Factor Four*, entitled *Factor Five: Transforming the Global Economy through 80% Improvements in Resource Productivity*.[9] The IPCC also showed that the economic costs of meeting this target globally were minimal – a reduction of less than 0.12 per cent GDP per annum between now and 2050,[10] hardly noticeable compared with the potentially devastating economic impacts of not acting. Discussing this with the authors, world-renowned sustainable development expert, Ernst von Weizsäcker reflected that, 'Communism collapsed because it wouldn't let prices tell the economic truth, Capitalism could collapse because we won't let prices tell the ecological truth.'

Leading us away from despair is the partial reassurance that there are now a vast array of opportunities to harness the market and deliver significant change, such that 'Creating the low-carbon economy will lead to the greatest economic boom in the U.S. since it mobilized for World War II', according to former US President Bill Clinton in late 2007.[11] Further, there are many significant co-benefits of reducing greenhouse gas emissions that can lead to considerable cost savings. As *The Stern Review* stated, '... co-benefits can significantly reduce the overall cost to the economy of reducing greenhouse gas emissions. There may be tensions between climate change mitigation and other objectives, which need to be handled carefully, but as long as policies are well designed, the co-benefits will be more significant than the conflicts.'[12] Stern supports this position, finding that:

> *Analyses carried out under the Clean Air for Europe programme suggest cost savings as high as 40% of GHG mitigation costs are possible from the co-ordination of climate and air pollution policies. Mitigation through land-use reform has implications for social welfare (including enhanced food security and improved*

clean-water access), better environmental services (such as higher water quality and better soil retention), and greater economic welfare through the impact on output prices and production.[13]

The European Environment Agency also showed that the additional benefits of acting to reduce global warming had the potential to deliver co-benefits related to mitigating air pollution in the order of €10 billion (US$13 billion) per year in Europe, and additional avoided health costs of €16–46 billion per year (US$20–58 billion).[14] In short, as Al Gore outlined in his 'A Generational Challenge to Repower America' address in 2008: 'When you connect the dots, it turns out that the real solutions to the climate crisis are the very same measures needed to renew our economy and escape the trap of ever-rising energy prices.'[15]

Despite growing evidence of both the challenges and opportunities over the last 30 years, there is still widespread hesitancy among some governments and business leaders resulting in a lack of action on a broad scale, and in some cases leading to efforts to block such progress. Much of this results from a lack of understanding, education and competency in the proven economic policies, scientific knowledge, business operations, and technological and design solutions now available – coupled with suitable economic structures for managing risk and rewarding action. Rather than seeking a 'silver bullet' solution – the one answer to save the world – it is becoming clear that what we need is more like what *Factor Four* and *Natural Capitalism* co-author Hunter Lovins calls a 'silver buckshot' approach: an integrated solutions-based portfolio of options, all travelling in the same direction and fixed on the same target and providing a range of complex and integrated challenges to be addressed within both the international and national context.

The OECD has argued that mitigating climate change is the most important of all environmental challenges because if humanity does not succeed then climate change will undermine and exacerbate all other environmental and social problems.[16] These environmental issues include greater intensity of weather-related natural disasters, a decline in water availability and shifting rainfall patterns, the loss of biodiversity (both on land and in the ocean due to ocean acidification), rising sea temperatures bleaching coral reefs, and sea-level rise. Such impacts will particularly affect the developing world. As Stern points out:

> *Climate change poses a real threat to the developing world. Unchecked it will become a major obstacle to continued poverty reduction. Developing countries are especially vulnerable to climate change because of their geographic exposure, low incomes, and greater reliance on climate sensitive sectors such as agriculture. For low-income countries, major natural disasters today can cost an average of 5% of GDP ... Millions of people will potentially be at risk of climate-driven heat stress, flooding, malnutrition, water related disease and vector borne diseases.*[17]

In light of the potential for massive development in China, Brazil, India and other rapidly emerging economies over the coming decades, the world is realizing that the current form of development that is 'fossil fuel based, automobile-centred, and thrives on a throwaway economy',[18] as Lester Brown puts it, is not going to deliver solutions that will allow for this growth to be sustained environmentally forever. It is now widely accepted that raising living standards globally using such traditional development models will lead to significant increases in demand for resources, increases in the generation of waste and emissions, and increased risk of conflict over resource shortages.[19] As discussed in previous chapters, there is compelling evidence that it is possible to significantly reduce poverty in our lifetime, and that such efforts are critical to enabling global population growth to stabilize this century. Earlier chapters have shown that the environmental, social and economic benefits of reducing global poverty and stabilizing global population levels this century are significant. However, should we be successful in achieving a substantial reduction in global poverty, serious consideration needs to be given to the potential this creates for an additional 2–3 billion people aspiring to consume to increasing levels of affluence, and contributing to increasing levels of greenhouse gas emissions and other environmental pressures. Already, ecological footprint studies show that humanity as a whole is using 40 per cent more resources than ecosystems of the earth can regenerate. Thus, if all developing nations achieved the current Western consumer lifestyle with current modes of development, this would rapidly push environmental pressures past ecological thresholds. Hence, while the levels of poverty reduction achieved in the last decade in Asian countries such as India and China are significant, there are also rising levels of demand for resources and environmental pressures right across the economy.

As Lester Brown explains:

> *If, for example, each person in China consumes paper at the current American rate, then in 2030 China's 1.46 billion people will need twice as much paper as is produced worldwide today. If we assume that in 2030 there are three cars for every four people in China, as there now are in the United States, China will have 1.1 billion cars. The world currently has 860 million cars. To provide the needed roads, highways, and parking lots, China would have to pave an area comparable to what it now plants in rice. By 2030 China would need 98 million barrels of oil a day. The world is currently producing 85 million barrels a day and experts from the International Energy Agency have warned in 2007 that we may never produce much more than that.[20]*

Facing Unprecedented Challenges and Opportunities

Appreciating the wide array of 21st-century challenges, climate change is clearly an overarching and immediate threat to be addressed. From the proceeding chapters it is clear that a significant effort to decouple economic growth from greenhouse gas emissions will be required in the coming decades on a global scale, and also in a manner that supports the reduction of poverty. This will be one of the most complex and wide-reaching endeavours ever to face the human race,[21] for a number of reasons:

Unprecedented speed

The speed of change needed across the world's economies to avoid dangerous climate change will require a massive effort. When considering the now common calls from climate scientists and policy analysts that the countries of the world must make significant reductions to emission levels in the coming decade, it is sobering to realize that according to the IPCC, carbon dioxide annual emissions grew by about 80 per cent between 1970 and 2004, and that the models predict an increase of global greenhouse gas emissions by 25 to 90 per cent (CO_2e) between 2000 and 2030.[22] This is complicated by the fact that, according to UNEP, 'One of the reasons for the limited impact of policies is the long lifespan (40–50 years and longer) of energy infrastructure. This means that technology and investment decisions from decades ago have created a path dependency for today's production and consumption patterns.'[23] Hence, efforts need to be further accelerated to compensate for such infrastructure legacies.

Unprecedented scale

At present, fossil fuels provide at least 80 per cent of global energy require-ments and are the basis of most of the industrial infrastructure and built environment the world has developed in the last 300 years.[24] In addition, greenhouse gas emissions arise from virtually all sectors of the economy in many different ways. Unlike other significant environmental issues – such as acid rain from sulphur dioxide pollution, which is relatively easy to respond to with a technical change in coal-fired power stations, or the reduction of the emissions of particular gases under the Montreal Protocol that were relatively easily replaceable – there is no one technical fix that can solve the climate change challenge. This is further complicated by the fact that, according to the New Economics Foundation, 'Implementation of environmental policies requiring substantial societal or cultural changes, such as a culture of environ-mental protection, or structural realignment, will meet with fierce resistance from sectors affected and from some parts of the public. Therefore, govern-ments tend to buy time or defer decisions when such 'hard' structural changes in overall policies are required – often until it is too late.'[25]

Unprecedented uncertainty

As the economic viability of a number of sectors of the economy – such as metal processing, cement and chemicals production, air transport and power stations – is currently tied to low energy costs, the future impacts from assigning a cost to greenhouse gas emissions through ecological tax reform or emissions trading schemes, present significant uncertainty. The fear of short-term losses has led to powerful vested interests forming blocking coalitions to prevent action on climate change since the early 1990s.[26] The *New York Times* editorialized in May 2007 that such a message 'is a hugely important message to policy makers everywhere ... Many of them have been paralysed by fears ... that a full-scale attack on climate change could cripple the economy.'[27] However such uncertainty is being responded to by a number of works including the 2009 book *Factor Five*, where the authors of this volume worked with Ernst von Weizsäcker to chronicle the vast array of cost-effective energy productivity improvements that could be achieved in such sectors by taking a whole system approach, making it possible even for heavy industries and fossil fuel companies to significantly reduce their energy usage and greenhouse gas emissions.[28]

Unprecedented need for education

As many countries have been blessed with access to cheap energy for so long, there has historically been relatively little attention given to reducing energy demand or generating renewable energy, accompanied by a lack of knowledge and skills in these areas. Abundant supplies of cheap energy have meant that when decision-makers have been faced with growth in energy demand they have usually just built more of the same form of supply infrastructure. Governments, keen to attract large industry, have often offered energy subsidies that have further made the price of energy artificially cheap. Hence many governments and companies now find themselves unprepared to focus on cost effectively reducing energy demand or generating onsite renewable energy. In Australia, recent surveys commissioned by the National Framework for Energy Efficiency (undertaken by Desha and Hargroves as discussed in Chapter 3), PriceWaterhouseCoopers,[29] Proudfoot Consulting,[30] Australia Industry Group[31] and the Australian Research Institute in Education for Sustainability[32] show that business leaders and key stakeholders like engineers and built environment professionals lack adequate education and training to ensure that Australia achieves cost-effective emissions reductions. These studies, which include discussions regarding similar global education challenges, highlight the unprecedented and urgent need for such capacity building.

Unprecedented need for collaboration

When facing the issues of climate change it is easy to become hypnotized by the complexity, and in order to meet this complexity with creativity and ingenuity the professions need to work together to inform each others' efforts. For instance, consider the nexus between economics and engineering. The study of economics, if well informed by science, can provide valuable guidance as to the potential impact on an economy from a range of strategies for emissions reduction. Also, a study of science, engineering and design, informed by economics, can provide valuable guidance as to the potential for our industrial economies to achieve such reductions in light of best practices and balanced by the potential impacts on the environment. On its own, a study of economics needs to be informed by what is physically possible. Likewise a study of science and engineering on its own cannot provide all the answers without being informed by economics as to the impacts on the economy from a range of potential engineering and design options. The merger of these professions is in its very early stages, and governments struggling to come to grips with the reality of the climate change issue and how it will affect their economies need to seek advice from both these and a range of other professions to balance assumptions and recommendations (further discussed in Chapter 7). As Stern points out, 'The scientific and economic framework provides a structure for the discussions necessary to get to grips with the global challenge and guidance in setting rational and consistent national and international policies.'[33]

Unprecedented need for cooperation

Responding to climate change requires unprecedented global cooperation and agreement. Ultimately a whole of global economy approach is needed, otherwise positive achievements in parts of the world may be offset by emissions growth in other parts. As *The Stern Review* points out, 'Because climate change is a global problem, the response to it must be international. It must be based on a shared vision of long-term goals and agreement on frameworks that will accelerate action over the next decade, and it must build on mutually reinforcing approaches at a national, regional and international level.'[34] Developing countries are understandably concerned about the fairness of any international agreements, and the levels of reductions required by each country need to be carefully considered as part of an overall global strategy, potentially on a per capita basis or a GDP-adjusted per capita basis.

Unprecedented interconnectivity

It may prove to be the case that the inherent complexities of responding to the climate crisis will also provide opportunities to assist other efforts. As negative impacts can be compounded in unpredictable ways through the planet's interconnected ecosystems, efforts to decouple greenhouse gas emissions can also be aligned with and positively reinforce efforts to decouple economic growth from a wide range of environmental pressures.

In Chapters 8–11 this concept is investigated for issues related to the loss of biodiversity and natural resources, water pollution and availability, waste production and air pollution. For instance:

- Countries that seek to contribute to their emissions reduction targets by investing in halting deforestation, improving soils to store carbon and assisting a shift to more appropriate forms of agriculture and forestry, particularly in developing countries, not only reduce emissions, but can also achieve improvements in the viability of forestry and agriculture, reduced risk from landslides, reduced loss of topsoil and reduced pressures on biodiversity (discussed in Chapter 8). This is especially viable, as reducing deforestation is a very cost-effective way to reduce greenhouse gas emissions globally, while investing in developing countries. As *The Stern Review* found, 'A study commissioned for the Review looking at 8 countries responsible for 70% of emissions from deforestation found that ... emission savings from avoided deforestation could yield reductions in CO_2 emissions for under $5/t$CO_2$, and possibly for as little as $1/t$CO_2$.'[35]

- Many nations of the world will face severe water shortages this century due to changes in rainfall, melting of glacial reserves and increasing temperatures from climate change, together with over-extraction and inefficient use. Yet many are now finding that action to reduce water consumption can yield multiple benefits such as reducing energy demand and greenhouse gas emissions at a national and state level, by reducing the need for storage, purification and distribution of potable water, and at the household level through reductions in hot water requirements, a significant energy consumer. The potential to save energy this way is significant as shown by the fact that the Californian Energy Commission, in their 2005 report *California's Water–Energy Relationship*,[35A] showed that water-related energy use makes up 19 per cent of all energy used in California, as discussed in Chapter 9.

- Another area of potential for reducing greenhouse gas emissions is through reducing waste production, such as reducing both the production of methane and the wastage of raw materials in municipal waste landfills. Efforts to reduce municipal waste, such as capturing the organic content for use in agriculture, recycling metals and plastics or shifting to biodegradable or minimal packaging, will not only reduce emissions but also reduce pressure on inorganic fertilizers and raw materials. This will lead to multiple benefits, as the mining and processing of non-renewable minerals and petrochemical resources is highly energy intensive compared to metal and plastics recycling (discussed in Chapter 10)

- Actions to reduce greenhouse gas emissions related to transport systems, urban planning, building regulations and energy generation will also have multiple benefits related to reductions in air pollution, such as reducing motor vehicle emissions.[36] Such benefits mostly relate to reducing damage to infrastructure and agriculture from acid rain from coal-fired power stations, and reduced impacts on human health, considering that there are approximately 800,000 deaths annually from ambient urban air pollution.[37] A study conducted by a leading Indian environmental NGO, the Centre for Science and Environment, revealed that about 10,000 people die prematurely in Delhi due to air pollution each year,[38] which is equivalent to an average of one death every 52 minutes (discussed in Chapter 11). Air pollution is a significant cost to economies, considering that:

- In 1995, the UK government calculated total costs of damage from acid rain to be over £18 billion mainly from building damage.[39]
- A European study found that tropospheric ozone causes measurable, regional-scale reductions on crop yields for 23 species of arable crops, costing Europe US$5.72–12 billion a year in lost production.[40]
- Particulate pollution under 10 microns (PM10) is predicted by the OECD to cause premature deaths and years of life lost of 3.1 million and 25.4 million respectively, by 2030.[41]
- A poll of tour guides found that one in ten tourists suffered pollution-linked health problems while visiting Hong Kong.[42] In Kathmandu, 17 per cent of tourists interviewed indicated that they would avoid visiting Nepal again because of poor air quality.[43]

Given these unprecedented challenges, and potential opportunities, in order to have a realistic chance of decoupling economic growth from greenhouse gas emissions and other environmental pressures on a global scale, business and governments around the world need to show considerable leadership. We next present an overview of evidence to date of such leadership from the business community and among national governments, particularly those with the ten largest economies, to demonstrate that in recent years significant progress has been made, providing a strong platform of experience to drive efforts in reducing greenhouse gas emissions while maintaining strong economic growth.

Signs of Change in the International Business Community

> *The global climate crisis will fundamentally reshape organisa-tions and management. It will bring in new career paths ... and change the structure of organisations and the way they are run. It's early days, and no one in the world knows its final impact, but there are already signs of the ground shifting. It will force businesses and managers to live with uncertainty, a world shaped by forces still emerging.*
>
> The Age, 20 August 2008[44]

Just over a decade ago many corporations were either supporting or participat-ing in active lobbying against action on climate change. Since then, there has been a sea-change in attitudes in the business community. This transformation is occurring because of the increased certainty of the science of climate change, and a greater understanding of the risks and opportunities it presents for businesses and society, particularly after the publication of *The Stern Review* in 2006. These factors, combined with rapidly growing markets for clean-tech and renewable energy, have contributed to many leading businesses now seeing climate change as a major business opportunity to improve their competitive advantage and reduce future risks. Companies are also increasingly facing new climate change-related regulations, whether at the state or national level, with which they need to comply. Hence, increasingly, chief executive officers and investors are realizing that the next major risk to the bottom line will be their reliance on generating greenhouse gases. As a result, investors are beginning to put pressure on companies to disclose climate-related risks and communicate their climate strategies. For example, during the US 2008 proxy season, investors filed a record 54 climate-related shareholder resolutions, twice as many as the previous season, most of which were seeking greater analysis and disclosure of business impacts related to climate change.[45] Furthermore, in 2008, organized by the Carbon Disclosure Project, an invitation to disclose greenhouse gas emissions performance and related strategies was sent to 3000 companies under the signature of 385 institutional investors with combined assets of US$57 trillion, resulting in 1550 responses.[46]

According to the FTSE Group, the UK equivalent of the US Dow Jones, there is growing awareness that 'the impact of climate change is likely to have an increasing influence on the economic value of companies, both directly, and through new regulatory frameworks. Investors, governments and society in general expect companies to identify and reduce their climate change risks and impacts, and also to identify and develop related business opportunities.'[47] In this age of rising climate change issues, companies do not want to be targeted by NGOs or the media as being slow to act on climate change, especially as according to a 2004 survey by the World Economic Forum, responding leaders felt that corporate reputation was a more important measure of success than stock market performance, profitability and return on investment.[48] Understanding these trends, a number of companies internationally have taken leadership in developing and implementing cost-effective strategies to respond to climate change, with many finding that taking such action has turned out to be far more profitable than they first thought, through a combination of energy efficiency, renewable energy and carbon offsets. For example, since 2003, investigations by the Climate Group, as part of the Carbon Down, Profits Up programme,[49] have shown that six early-moving major firms – Dupont, IBM, British Telecom, Alcan, NorskeCanada and Bayer – collectively saved over US$4 billion while reducing their carbon emissions by more than 60 per cent. Further investigations by the group showed that up to 2006, 43 large companies had significantly reduced their greenhouse gas emissions and saved a total of US$15 billion.[50] Businesses are also using their marketing and salesmanship to promote genuinely greener, more energy-efficient products to consumers. Sir Terry Leahy, Chief Executive of Tesco, stated that 'The key to success is to turn green consumption into a mass movement. By harnessing the buying power of millions of consumers we can drive change throughout the economy.'[51]

Other businesses are harnessing research and development opportunities to create new 'green' revenue streams. For example, in May 2005, General Electric, one of the oldest and largest corporations on the planet, announced

Ecomagination, a major new business driver that was expected to more than double revenues from cleaner technologies to US$25 billion by 2010 (from US$6.2 billion in 2004).[52] In May 2006, the company had already reported revenues of US$10.1 billion[53] from its energy-efficient and environmentally advanced products and services, and by 2008 this figure had grown to US$17 billion. As of May 2009, the portfolio contains over 80 products, with the company aiming to invest US$1.5 billion in researching cleaner technologies by 2010, having already invested over US$1.4 billion in 2008.[54] GE Chief Executive Jeffrey Immelt believes that, 'at some point in time, customers are going to say, "I don't want anything but an environmentally friendly product." It won't be acceptable to have something that is cheap but dirty.'[55] To this end, GE developed plans that aimed to reduce emissions by 30 per cent by 2008 (which they surpassed in 2008), and to improve the energy efficiency of their operations by 30 per cent by 2012.[56]

Global corporations are also beginning to address the implications and impacts of their products and services. For example, Wal-Mart announced in 2006 a US$500 million climate change commitment, including initiatives to increase truck fleet fuel efficiency by 25 per cent in three years and double it in ten years.[57] By 2008 they met their target of their whole fleet being 25 per cent more efficient, with the US component of the fleet now 38 per cent more efficient than it was in 2005.[58] As Wal-Mart Chief Executive Lee Scott observed, 'It will save money for our customers, make us a more efficient business, and help position us to compete effectively in a carbon-constrained world.'[59] The company also realized that changing the incandescent bulbs in its ceiling fan displays throughout its 3230 stores (40 bulbs per store) could save it US$6 million a year.[60] Wal-Mart's Chief Merchandising Officer John Fleming at a press conference at Merrill Lynch & Co.'s headquarters in New York said, 'We don't believe a person should have to choose between an environmentally friendly product and one they can afford to buy ... We want our merchandise to be both affordable and sustainable.'[61] Wal-Mart is aiming to open a proto-type store which is 25–30 per cent more efficient than the standard.[62] In addition, Wal-Mart has developed a strategy to influence its 60,000 suppliers to produce lower carbon products.[63] Work is under way to develop a Sustainability Index, based on a 15-question survey which all of Wal-Mart's suppliers will have to complete, and from life-cycle analyses undertaken by a consortium of universities in collaboration with manufacturers, retailers, NGOs and government organizations. It is hoped that this will enable customers to make more informed choices when shopping, and will create more incentive for the manufacture of sustainable products.[64]

It will of course be easier for some sectors of the economy to decouple greenhouse gas emissions than others, but the opportunity to dramatically improve energy productivity exists in every sector. Companies such as General Electric and Wal-Mart are among the first to make significant commitments to emissions reductions, partly because the energy-saving initiatives related to buildings, appliances and transportation are well supported and proven.

However, in other sectors, particularly heavy industry, the precedent for such initiatives is only now emerging. Encouragingly, a range of options exist even for the heavy industries to significantly reduce energy consumption[65] and emissions of greenhouse gases,[66] including:

- Up to 50 per cent reductions in the energy intensity of zinc, tin, copper and lead smelting by using advanced furnace technology and co-generation.[67]
- Up to 50 per cent reductions in the energy intensity of crushing and rock grinding in the mining sector.[68]
- Up to 80 per cent reductions in the energy intensity of the steel industry by using innovative processes such as electric arc furnaces with high levels of recycled steel, and near net shape casting technologies.[69]
- Between 30 and 80 per cent reductions in the energy intensity of the cement industry, by improving the current process to create Portland cement (30 per cent),[70] or by using innovations in geopolymer cement to replace Portland cement (80 per cent),[71] which can be used for most major purposes for which Portland cement is currently used.[72]
- Significant reductions in paper and pulp mills through investing in energy efficiency, co-generation and utilizing biomass as a source of energy. Paper and pulp mills can now even be retrofitted to become renewable electricity power generators through the use of black liquor gasification combined cycle technologies.[73]

Investigating such options, the Australian National Framework for Energy Efficiency[74] found that 30 per cent more efficiency gains could be made with a four-year or less payback period, and up to 70 per cent with an eight-year or less payback period across industry in Australia. Given these and many other such opportunities, many governments around the world are entering into voluntary agreements with industry to meet specific energy-use or energy-efficiency targets.[75] A number of industrial sector agreements and target programmes around the world have led to significant energy efficiency improvements, including:

- Canada: Industry Programme for Energy Conservation;[76]
- Denmark: Agreements on Industrial Energy Efficiency;[77]
- Germany: Declaration of German Industry on Global Warming Prevention;[78]
- Japan: Keidanren Voluntary Action Plan on the Environment;[79]
- Australia: Energy Efficiency Opportunities Program[80] (*with the Victorian government the only state to place mandatory requirements on businesses above a certain size to identify and implement energy efficiency opportunities of three years or less.*)

In the UK, such voluntary agreements have been taken a step further with energy-intensive companies being able to apply to sign a Climate Change

Agreement (CCA)[81] whereby the company agrees to commit to achieving a certain carbon reduction target or improving their energy efficiency, and in return receives exemption from 80 per cent of the carbon tax.[82] Overall, the signatories to the CCA programme exceeded their targets by the equivalent of 1 million tonnes of carbon (MtC) per year up to the first target period (2002), by 1.4 MtC a year up to the second target period (2004),[83] and by around 1.9 MtC[84] a year up to the third target period (2006). Through this process these businesses in the UK are saving over US$650 million from reducing greenhouse gas emissions.[85] Such progress in the UK business sector also strengthened bipartisan support for the 2008 energy bill, allowing the UK government to pass laws that make it the first country in the world to introduce legally binding legislation to cut greenhouse gas emissions by 80 per cent by 2050. The Netherlands government has also run since 1989 a major national programme to encourage energy efficiency in industry with negotiated formal binding agreements. The first Dutch long-term agreement scheme with industry had quantitative targets, to increase energy efficiency by 20 per cent by the year 2000 (compared to 1989), and for the whole of Dutch industry this target has been achieved.[86]

The UK and Netherlands experience has helped to inspire the Chinese government to adopt a similar programme with the 1000 largest heavy industry companies in China, with an estimated combined energy consumption of

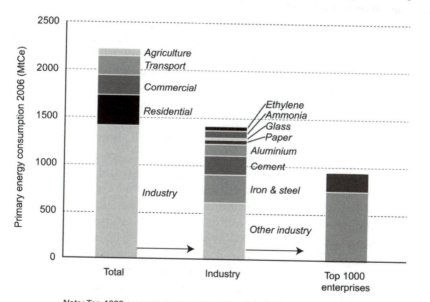

Note: Top-1000 program energy consumption is typically reported in final energy units (bottom segment). The shaded area at the top provides the MtCe equivalent of electricity generation, transmission, and distribution losses.

Figure 6.1 *Energy consumption of China, China's industrial sector and the top 1000 energy-consuming enterprises, 2005*

Source: LBNL (2009)[87]

around 33 per cent of national energy consumption,[88] as shown in Figure 6.1. After visiting the UK and Netherlands programmes in 2003, the Chinese government has worked with industry since 2006 to create China's Top 1000 Energy-Consuming Enterprises Program.[89] The goal of the programme is to contribute up to 25 per cent of the savings required to achieve the overall Chinese government target of a 20 per cent reduction in energy use per unit of GDP by 2010.[90] Such a target is unprecedented, with no other country having such strong mandatory energy efficiency targets for its heavy industries. Subsequently, the Chinese steel industry (responsible for over half of global production) experienced a decrease in overall energy consumption of 8.8 per cent between 2005 and 2006.[91] Such reductions by heavy industry are contributing to the nation's overall reductions in energy intensity of 3.7 per cent in 2007 and 4.6 per cent in 2008.[92] An initial review in 2008 by the Lawrence Berkeley National Laboratory showed that the programme is proceeding well and could even achieve 50 per cent more savings than planned in 2010.[93] Further investigations showed that in the first quarter of 2009 the programme was contributing significantly to assisting China achieve an overall 20 per cent cut in energy intensity by 2010.[94]

There are also significant potential reduction opportunities for light industry and the service sector – media, finance and banking, professional services, education, health and tourism – a sector that in OECD countries generates the majority of GDP and is responsible for as much as 70–80 per cent of employment.[95] However, in these sectors, energy costs are a small percentage of total costs, leading in the past to a minimal focus on reducing consumption.[96] As Amory and Hunter Lovins wrote in 1997, 'the average business spends (just) 1–2 per cent of their total costs on energy'.[97] Thus significant opportunities exist now in the service sector to firstly capitalize on the 'low hanging fruit', or easily realized reductions in energy usage, of up to 30–50 per cent of demand, and then to invest in energy from low-carbon sources, to become 'climate neutral' in regard to energy use. For example, in the UK, leading companies in the services sector such as Barclays Bank, Marks & Spencer, BSI, HSBC, Simmons & Simmons, Bradford and Bingley, Radio Taxis and BSkyB are a part of a growing wave of top British companies that claim to have achieved the net climate neutral status.[98] Throughout Europe many companies are committing to, and becoming, net climate neutral, such as Dutch multinational banking and insurance company ING which is reported to have been climate neutral since 2007. The UNEP Climate Neutral Network lists many other European companies that have committed to becoming climate neutral.[99] For instance, 20 Swedish companies have become net climate neutral and joined the UN Global Compact Caring for Climate Programme,[100] and in Australia numerous companies have now committed to becoming climate neutral from sectors that represent 70 per cent of the Australian economy and contribute significantly to Australia's GDP and employment.[101] News Corporation, for example, the global media empire headed by Rupert Murdoch, has committed to become climate neutral by 2010.[102] Furthermore, a number of other large companies –

PriceWaterhouseCoopers,[103] KPMG,[104] Energetics,[105] Bunnings Warehouse,[106] Fuji Xerox Australia, Westpac, National Australia Bank, ANZ, Insurance Australia Group and Swiss Re – have also committed to becoming climate neutral.[107]

In the US, there are now numerous government and NGO energy efficiency programmes working collectively with thousands of companies who are meeting their greenhouse gas reductions targets ahead of schedule and making money. For example, nearly 100 case studies charted by the Center for Energy & Climate Solutions for the Cool Companies Project demonstrate how businesses are earning the equivalent of 40–50 per cent returns on energy-saving investments.[108] Savings bring not only lower costs, but also measurable, documented productivity gains through improved product quality, working conditions and employee morale. The US Pew Center for Global Climate Change partner companies are also finding similar success,[109] as are the US EPA's Climate Leaders.[110] Leading US companies that are committed to (or already have) become climate neutral include Dell (computer manufacturer),[111] Google (internet search engine), Microsoft (computer software), The Cliff House (restaurant), Shaklee Corporation (pharmaceuticals, health goods), the Saunders Hotel Group (hotels and accommodation), Interface (carpet), Organic Bouquet (flowers), TripleE Better World Travel, (travel service provider), FedEx (hybrid delivery truck service), and PG&E (Californian energy supply company), to name a few.[112] Other major US Fortune 500 companies like PepsiCo and Whole Foods Supermarkets are now purchasing 100 per cent of their energy from low-carbon renewable sources, as are other US companies such as Mohawk Fine Papers, Inc. (Printing), the Dannon Company, Inc. (food and beverage), and the WhiteWave Foods Company (food and beverage).[113]

Considering such advances around the world, Hunter Lovins wrote in her contribution to the *Plan for Presidential Action for the First 100 Days in Office for the Next President of the United States*, (by the Presidential Climate Action Project), 'regardless of how severe the impact of climate change proves to be, and regardless of how drastically and how soon GHG come to be regulated at the federal level, these companies will be in a leadership position because by taking early action to deal responsibly with it, they cut their costs and got ahead of their competitors'.[114] Understanding this, companies such as DuPont, GE, Alcoa, Caterpillar, PG&E, Lehman Brothers and others, acting as members of the US Climate Action Partnership, or USCAP,[115] called for national legislation on carbon emissions in 2007, stating, 'In our view, the climate change challenge will create more economic opportunities than risks for the U.S. economy.'[116] Such calls for leadership were clearly answered then by President Elect Obama with the release of the Obama/Biden Energy Plan in 2008, which, among other targets, called for 80 per cent reductions in emissions over 1990 levels by 2050.[117] Clearly, with such strong signs of change in the international business community, the time to act is now. Indeed, as both Amory Lovins and Hunter Lovins have long been advocating, businesses who do not have ambitious strategies to respond to climate change will face significant future risks, including losing business opportunities, export opportunities, reputation and the goodwill of both the local and global community.

The international business community is increasingly calling on governments to take action through a number of significant communications, including the 2007 Bali Communiqué,[118] the 2008 Poznam Communiqué[119] and the 2009 Copenhagen Call,[120] issued collectively by the chief executives of over 150 major global businesses. The first of these, issued in November 2007 in the lead-up to UN climate change negotiations in Bali, called for a comprehensive and legally binding UN framework to tackle climate change to underpin rapid reductions of greenhouse gas emissions in line with scientifically based targets, and was supported by corporations including ANB AMRO, Philips, Sun Microsystems, Volkswagen, Johnson & Johnson, Tesco, Coco-Cola, Unilever and Vodaphone. The process, led by the Prince of Wales' UK and EU Corporate Leaders Groups on Climate Change, resulted in a business communiqué to government that was based on an appreciation of the science rather than what is considered politically palatable or 'reasonable'.

The Bali Communiqué states that:[121]

> *The scientific evidence is now overwhelming. Climate change presents very serious global social, environmental and economic risks and it demands an urgent global response. As business leaders, it is our belief that the benefits of strong, early action on climate change outweigh the costs of not acting:*
> * *The economic and geopolitical costs of unabated climate change could be very severe and globally disruptive. All countries and economies will be affected, but it will be the poorest countries that will suffer earliest and the most,*
> * *The costs of action to reduce greenhouse gas emissions in order to avoid the worst impacts of climate change are manageable, especially if guided by a common international vision,*
> * *Each year we delay action to control global emissions increases the risk of unavoidable consequences that will likely necessitate even steeper reductions in the future, causing potentially greater economic, environmental and social disruption, and*
> * *The shift to a low-carbon economy will create significant business opportunities. New markets for low carbon technologies and products, worth billions of dollars, will be created if the world acts on the scale required.*

This message, again clearly put forward in the Poznam Communiqué in 2008, and the Copenhagen Call in 2009, is forming a clear and consistent call for action to national governments, one that is being strengthened by the success of businesses around the world as outlined above.

Signs of Change within Regulations and Policies

In the lead-up to the Copenhagen Summit, in July 2009, the leaders of the G-8 countries US, Japan, China, Germany, France, UK, Russia and Canada agreed to a non-binding target of 80 per cent reductions in greenhouse gas emissions by 2050, with the intention of enabling the world as a whole to achieve a 50 per cent reduction by 2050.[122] Such targets, although non-binding, sent a strong signal that world leaders recognized the need to undertake purposeful policy and regulatory changes to achieve significant levels of decoupling. Whilst overall the Copenhagen Summit did not fulfil expectations during the lead-up and in the months afterwards, many nations made new commitments to stronger reduction targets with some bringing in new policies. For instance, the Brazilian government has committed to 36–38 per cent cuts in greenhouse gas emissions by 2020 below business as usual. This and other important developments, largely missed by the media post-Copenhagen, are well summarized in Deutsche Bank's 2010 report *The Green Economy: The Race is On.*[122A] This report shows that there were 154 new policies for help to drive action on climate change in nations around the world between September 2009 and March 2010. This is a significant increase on comparative periods, indicating that policy momentum is gathering rather than diminishing on climate change at the local and national level in many countries post-Copenhagen, contrary to the popular media perception.

We now provide a summary of leading policy changes by nations around the world on a range of topics, and then overview related efforts by the ten largest economies on the planet (Table 6.1). The world economy for the last 200 years has achieved remarkable economic growth partly because of access to cheap fossil fuels. It will take time to transition to a low-carbon economy, and there are significant barriers to change, not just from vested interests, but from a wide range of market, informational and institutional failures, together with the inherent complexity of the issues. Thus, in addition to policies to create a financial value for carbon emissions, such as emission trading schemes or carbon taxes implemented now in over 30 nations and 10 US states, effective decoupling of economic growth from greenhouse gas emissions is most likely to be achieved if countries also implement a range of related complementary policy measures and programmes.[123] Business, as explained above, is increasingly looking for clear and consistent leadership from government on climate change policy. The following pages briefly highlight how leading governments around the world are targeting mitigation opportunities with ambitious goals and policies. We then overview efforts in these areas by the 10 largest economies in he world, namely the US, Japan, China, Germany, France, the UK, India, Italy, the Russian Federation and Brazil.

The following examples of policy reform provide real-world examples from which others can learn and, we hope, inform the development of a suite of policy options suitable to each nation.

Climate neutral nations and cities

Nine nations – Norway, Portugal, Iceland, Pakistan, Costa Rica, the Maldives, Monaco, Ethiopia and Niue – have now committed to becoming very low carbon and even net climate neutral by 2050, if not before, and have joined the UNEP Climate Neutral Global Network.[124] Fifteen cities – Arendal, Norway; Rizhao, China; Vancouver, Canada; Växjö, Sweden; Aguascalientes, Mexico; Brisbane, Australia; Cape Town, South Africa; Cascais, Portugal; Copenhagen, Denmark; Curitiba, Brazil; Daejeon, South Korea; Niteroi, Brazil; Slough, England; Sydney, Australia; and Waitakere, New Zealand, have also signed up to the UNEP network. Hundreds of businesses and civil society organizations, who have committed to becoming climate neutral, have also joined. The network, a web-based project, is seeking to federate the small but growing wave of nations, local authorities, companies and civil society organizations who are pledging to significantly reduce emissions over time to develop zero-emission economies, communities and businesses.

2020 Greenhouse gas reductions regional targets (summarized in Table 6.1)

Leading the way is Costa Rica, which has committed to becoming net climate neutral by 2021. Following them is Norway, which has committed to 40 per cent greenhouse gas reductions by 2020 as part of their goal to become climate neutral by 2030. The EU has committed to a minimum 20 per cent reduction in greenhouse gas emissions (from 1990 levels) by 2020 and is pushing in international meetings for a global agreement of 30 per cent reductions by 2020. If the world will agree to the 30 per cent target by 2020 then the EU will adopt this stronger target.[125] Many other countries around the world have committed to strong 2020 greenhouse gas reduction targets, including Canada (17 per cent on 2005 levels), Japan (25 per cent from 1990 levels), South Korea (30 per cent below business as usual (BAU)), Russia (25 per cent from 1990 levels), Brazil (36.1 per cent to 38.9 per cent below BAU), India (20–25 per cent reduction in energy intensity on 2005 levels), Indonesia (26 per cent relative to BAU and by up to 41 per cent with international support), South Africa (34 per cent below BAU), Mexico (30 per cent below BAU levels), Thailand (22.5 per cent reduction in energy emissions), Israel (20 per cent below BAU), and Singapore (16 per cent below BAU levels).

China has committed to a 40–45 per cent reduction in carbon dioxide emissions per unit of GDP by 2020 compared to 2005 levels. The 11th Chinese Five-Year Plan calls for 20 per cent reductions in energy usage per unit of GDP from 2005 to 2010,[126] with early evidence showing that China is on target to achieve this.[127]

Energy efficiency targets

The EU currently has a non-binding target of 20 per cent energy efficiency improvement by 2020.[128] As noted above, in the UK the biggest 10,000 energy-using companies have to, by law, sign up to and achieve energy efficiency targets to receive an 80 per cent exception from the UK carbon tax.[129] Most of these companies have exceeded their energy efficiency targets ahead of time and overall saved £650 million (approximately US$1020 million) in the process. According to the British Prime Minister Gordon Brown, this will 'have committed our continent to a low carbon trajectory, demonstrating how Europe can provide the platform for Britain to achieve its aims nationally and internationally'.[130]

Of the rapidly growing transition economies in the world, China has the most impressive record for setting and achieving ambitious energy performance targets. In 1980, Chinese President Deng Xiaoping adopted the goal to quadruple GDP while only doubling energy consumption over the 20-year period between 1980 and 2000.[131] Investigations by the Lawrence Berkeley National Laboratory show that during this time China achieved greater than a sixfold increase in GDP, with a corresponding increase in energy use of a little over double.[132] This remarkable achievement not only affected Chinese industry and business, but affected the entire global economy, as estimates by the Lawrence Berkeley National Laboratory show that if this level of reduction in energy intensity had not been achieved, China would today be consuming two to three times more energy, making it by far the largest energy consumer in the world.[133] Again in 2000, Chinese officials committed China to a fourfold increase in GDP by 2020 with only a doubling in energy usage. To ensure this is achieved the Chinese government has committed to the ambitious energy efficiency goal of achieving a 20 per cent reduction in energy intensity by 2010. This ambitious goal is underpinned by numerous new policy initiatives and programmes, as outlined in Table 6.1.

Energy standards for buildings

Numerous efforts in the US, Europe, Australia, China and Japan are all working to improve building standards.[134] The UK Government's Code for Sustainable Homes legislates binding regulations for energy reduction with staggered targets – 25 per cent more efficient by 2010, 44 per cent by 2013, and 100 per cent or zero emissions by 2016. Now passed into law, the code sets minimum standards for both energy and water efficiency. In addition, the UK government has agreed that any home achieving a Level 6 sustainability rating will be exempt from stamp duty.[135] In France, the government has committed to ensuring that all new buildings should 'produce more energy than they consume' by 2020.[136] In Freiburg, Germany, a progressive energy-efficient housing standard has resulted in reductions of up to 80 per cent in energy use for space heating, by requiring energy consumption for heating purposes in households to be limited to $65kWh/m^2$ per annum for all construction under the Council's jurisdiction since 1992 (including construction on land bought from the Council and in projects funded by the Council). This is approximately a 70 per cent improvement on typical older European homes of $220kWh/m^2$ per annum.[137]

In 2008, the California Public Utilities Commission adopted the California Long-Term Energy Efficiency Strategic Plan, which includes the following commitments:

- All new residential construction will be zero net energy by 2020.
- All new commercial construction will be zero net energy by 2030.
- The heating, ventilation and air-conditioning industry will be re-shaped to deliver maximum performance systems.
- All eligible low-income customers will have an opportunity to participate in the Low Income Energy Efficiency Program and will be provided all cost-effective energy efficiency measures in their residences by 2020.[138]

To encourage the transition to zero net energy buildings, the Californian government has also passed laws that create two voluntary building energy efficiency codes that achieve 15 and 25 per cent higher energy efficiency/renewable energy standards than the current mandatory energy efficiency Californian building code standard.[139] The Californian government has also passed regulation that allows local government in California to choose to make these voluntary standards mandatory for new buildings in their county. This important policy initiative allows industry to learn from the leaders and build momentum for higher standards. Rapidly growing economies, such as China and India are also setting stronger energy efficiency and renewable energy requirements in building codes. According to the IPCC 'On 1 January, 2006, China introduced a new building construction statute that includes clauses on a mandatory energy efficiency standard for buildings ... [and] requires construction contractors to use energy efficient building materials and to adopt energy-saving technology in heating, air conditioning, ventilation and lighting systems in civil buildings.'[140]

Energy-efficient products and services

In the EU, energy demand in households accounts for 25 per cent of the final energy needs, with electricity used for domestic appliances in households showing the sharpest increase. The EU is responding to this issue by requiring energy labelling of household appliances demanding minimum efficiency requirements.[141] In America since 1978, California's energy-efficient appliance standards, combined with their energy-efficient building standards, (mentioned above) have saved more than US$56 billion in electricity and natural gas costs. While the US has increased per capita electricity consumption by nearly 50 per cent over the past 30 years, California's per capita electricity use has remained relatively flat.[142] In Japan the government has set strict energy-saving targets, focusing on 18 types of consumer and business electronics. Home and office air-conditioners, for instance, had to be redesigned to use 63 per cent less power by 2008.[143]

Since the late 1990s, China has developed a comprehensive programme of energy efficiency standards and labelling for household appliances, working

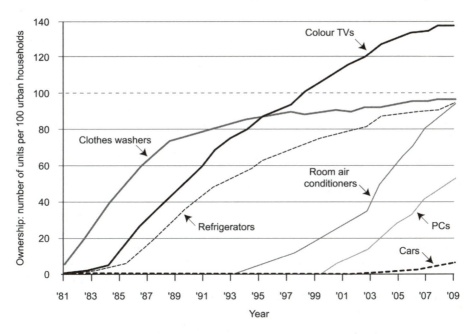

Figure 6.2 *Chinese urban appliance ownership*

Source: LBNL (2009)[144]

with Lawrence Berkeley National Laboratory's China Energy Group in an effort to respond to the rapid increase in the uptake of appliances by Chinese citizens[145] (see Figure 6.2). According to Lawrence Berkeley National Laboratory's, 'Standards enacted in China between 1999 (when the first new standard went into effect) and 2007 are expected to reduce growth of electricity consumption nationally by 110 TWh by 2020, saving consumers more than $100 billion cumulatively over this period.'[146] This work to improve Chinese appliance standards is very important because China is the largest global producer of major appliances and consumer electronics, providing over 50 per cent of the global supply for some products. By 2007, China was producing over 44 million refrigerators, 80 million air-conditioners and 85 million televisions annually. Hence, improving Chinese appliance standards has significant flow-on effects to reduce energy consumption and greenhouse gas emissions globally while increasing economic growth within China. An example of this is in the market of compact fluorescent lamps. China is already the world's largest manufacturer of this energy-efficient product, accounting for an estimated 80 per cent of global output, an industry with exports now worth around the US$2 billion mark.[147]

Disconnecting electricity utility profits from energy sales

A significant barrier to the uptake of energy efficiency has been the fact that, until recently, electricity and gas utilities increased their profits through generating greater sales.[148] Thus in the past there was little financial incentive for utilities to encourage their customers to take up energy efficiency opportunities and use less electricity and gas. The report *Aligning Utility Interests with Energy Efficiency Objectives: A Recent Review of Efforts at Decoupling and Performance Incentives*[149] shows that at least 25 states in the US have utility rate-payer-funded energy efficiency programmes in operation, all with very positive results. In short, all of these states have addressed traditional disincentives by introducing some type of cost recovery or savings sharing mechanism within these energy efficiency programmes for the electric utility.

Differential tariffs and smart meters

Several OECD countries have undertaken national roll-outs of smart meters to allow customers to monitor their energy consumption, and hence cost, in an effort to reduce consumption.[150] Such a mechanism is particularly successful when combined with differential tariffs to allow utilities to charge a greater cost during peak times. In Italy, the energy utility Enel Distribuzione SpA has installed more than 30 million electronic meters.[151] In 2004, Paolo Scaroni, Enel's Chief Executive, stated: 'Enel's 2 billion euro investment, including R&D costs and roll-out, will be paid back in 4 years in Italy alone.'[152] In 2003, Sweden announced that monthly readings would be required of all electricity meters by 2009. In September 2007, the Dutch government proposed that all 7 million households of the country should have a smart meter by 2013, as part of a national energy reduction plan.[153] Roll-outs are also under way in California and Pennsylvania in the US. According to John Hutton, the UK Secretary of State for Business, Enterprise and Regulatory Reform, smart energy meters should be brought in under an accelerated programme, as ten years is just simply, 'too long'.[154] In Australia, the Victoria government has committed to rolling out smart meters to 2.2 million homes and 300,000 businesses.[155]

Increasing the role of renewable energy

At least a third of the world's countries now have renewable energy targets,[156] with the level of renewable electricity generation capacity reaching an estimated 240 gigawatts (GW) worldwide in 2007; a 50 per cent rise over 2004, but still representing only 3.4 per cent of global power generation.[157] By setting bold targets for the amount of the country's electricity that will be sourced by renewable sources, national governments around the world are signalling to the market that innovation in renewable energy will be rewarded. Where countries and regions may not have bold targets, often states and cities are making strong commitments, thus signalling their support for greater national and global leadership on this issue. For instance, in November 2008, the Governor of California, Arnold Schwarzenegger, issued an executive order establishing the Renewable Portfolio Standard target for California that 'requires all retail sellers of electricity to serve 33% of their load with renewable energy by 2020. This builds on Million Solar Roofs Initiative which was adopted by the California Public Utilities Commission (CPUC) in 2005, and expanded by legislation Governor Schwarzenegger signed in 2006'.[158]

Increasing the use of feed-in tariffs (FITs)

FITs place a legal obligation on utilities to purchase electricity from renewable energy installations, whereby the tariff rate is guaranteed (in the best examples for a long period of up to 20 years), and is determined for each technology to ensure profitable operation of the installation. In 2008 it was established that as many as 36 countries (including 12 developing nations) and 10 states/provinces had brought in feed-in tariffs to encourage and support the renewable energy sector.[159] For instance, in the EU, FITs are widely used, with Germany, Denmark and Spain considered model countries achieving significant results. For Germany, where FITs have been in place and supported politically since 1990, its law has made it a world leader in renewable energy, generating billions of euros a year in exports, creating in the region of a quarter of a million jobs, saving nearly 100 million tonnes of carbon dioxide annually in recent years, and setting records for installed capacity across many technologies – all at the cost of around US$1.80 per household per month.[160] California has committed to and will soon be the largest US state to have implemented a FIT.[161] Among developing countries, India was the first to establish a FIT, followed by Sri Lanka and Thailand (for small power producers only), Brazil, Indonesia and Nicaragua. In the first half of 2005, feed-in policies were enacted in China, Ireland, Turkey and the US state of Washington. China's feed-in policy was part of a renewable energy promotion law enacted in February 2005.[162]

Reducing private vehicle transport greenhouse gas emissions

Much can be done to reduce the emissions from vehicles, as detailed in *Factor Five*.[163] New Zealand has committed to halving per capita transport emissions by 2040 by introducing electric cars and a requirement to use biofuels.[164] As of 2006, vehicles with low emissions already accounted for almost 11 million cars (21 per cent) on Japan's roads.[165] In Sweden, between 2007–2009, private car buyers have received a subsidy of SEK10,000 (aroundUS$1300) for zero- or low-emission vehicles, with the initiative becoming regarded as a success. While SEK250 million around US$32 million) was set aside for the scheme over three years, sales of 'eco-cars' are soaring with 45,000 vehicles sold in the nine months the scheme was operative in 2007 (44 per cent private sales).[166]

Improving freight and rail transport

Much can also be done to reduce the emissions from freight and rail transport through vehicle design, and improvements in operations, mode selection and logistics, as detailed in *Factor Five*.[167] In 2007 France committed to invest heavily in rail infrastructure to take freight transport off the roads and onto rail as part of France's 'Green Revolution'.[168] This is part of a more general trend in Europe that is seeking to reduce congestion on roads and reduce greenhouse gas emissions by making it more cost effective to transport freight by rail and sea. The EU Commission is promoting this transition.[169] China has committed to undertaking the world's most significant railway expansion since the US built its transcontinental line in the 1860s. Beijing plans to spend US$248 billion between now and 2020 on approximately 120,000 kilometres of new track, for freight and high-speed passenger transportation.[170]

Reducing traffic congestion and encouraging modal shifts

Over 15 cities in OECD countries have successfully implemented a congestion tax. London still stands out as an example, using revenue from its congestion tax to spend over €300 million (US$440 million) in improving and building safe bike paths and cycle lanes.[171] Hybrid cars have been made exempt from the congestion tax. Another interesting and cost-effective strategy to reduce congestion is to enable staff of government and business to work 10-hour days four days a week, instead of 8-hour days five days a week. The Utah government has instituted a four-day week affecting 17,000 government workers and saving the government around US$4 million a year through reduced electricity usage.[172] Marion County, Florida recently switched to a four-day working week for county workers and expects to save US$250,000 in the first year alone.[173] Employers are considering this to help staff cope with high oil prices and boost morale through maximizing their time with family.

Reducing growth in air transport greenhouse gas emissions

Unlike many other industries, although there are some promising options, there are few available technological or design options for reducing aviation's contribution to climate change significantly. Therefore, mandatory measures need to be introduced globally which apply fairly to all airlines, such as ensuring that all domestic aircraft emissions are included in emissions trading schemes, thus applying an international aviation emission charge to complement national and regional emissions trading schemes, with the funds raised to be invested in high-speed rail transport and telecommunications infrastructure to encourage the substitution of air travel with less emission-intensive alternatives.[174] The EU has also imposed tougher pollution limits on airlines from 2012,[175] stating that all airlines operating in or out of the EU will have to limit carbon dioxide emissions to 97 per cent of 2005 levels. From 2013, that figure will be reduced to 95 per cent.[176]

Reducing oil dependence

A number of countries have committed to significantly reducing their nation's oil dependency. Sweden, which was badly hit by the oil price rises in the 1970s, has committed to getting off oil by 2020. The country relies on fossil fuels mainly for transport, with only 32 per cent of the energy coming from oil in 2003, down from 77 per cent in 1970. Almost all of the country's heating was converted in the past decade to schemes that distribute steam or hot water generated by geothermal energy or waste heat. Iceland hopes by 2050 to power all its cars and boats with hydrogen made from electricity drawn from renewable resources. Brazil intends to power 80 per cent of its transport fleet with ethanol derived mainly from sugar cane by 2012.[177] Japan, the world's second largest economy with no domestic sources of fossil fuel has kept its oil consumption level since 1975, while world consumption has risen steadily, by dramatically diversifying its power sources over the years, becoming far less dependent on oil and cultivating a culture of conservation.[178] These plans are a part of broader sustainability plans like Hawaii's 2050 sustainability project, which has created a citizen-driven blueprint for the state's next half-century. The Hawaii 2050 strategy documents outline how the state can handle a tourist economy, a swelling population, friction between cultures, and a changing climate and environment.[179]

Further to these examples of policy reform, Table 6.1 presents a snapshot of specific government commitments and initiatives from the ten largest economies in the world to reduce energy consumption and increase levels of renewable energy generation. Such leadership illustrates the wealth of experience countries can now learn from to underpin efforts to achieve ambitious short- and long-term targets in these areas. These examples show that there is no longer any serious political risk in adopting such ambitious targets, and perhaps that the real risk is in not acting.

To conclude, climate change is now becoming a central part of government policy-making around the world. The ultimate goal of many of these targets and supporting policies is to cost effectively achieve significant reductions in greenhouse gas emissions in the order of 20–40 per cent by 2020 and 60–80 per cent by 2050.[180] Such examples of significant commitments by some of the worlds largest economies provide clear direction for other economies, in both developed and developing counties, to accelerate their progress towards significant greenhouse gas emissions reductions. The main barrier traditionally to national governments making such commitments has been their fear that it would harm economic growth and jobs, and we now consider this in the next chapter.

Table 6.1 *Energy consumption reduction and renewable energy targets set by the ten largest economies (ordered from largest to smallest)*

Country	Energy reduction and renewable energy targets
United States	• President Obama in 2009 committed to taking a global leadership role on climate change, announcing the formation of the Major Economies Forum on Energy and Climate. • In 2009, the Obama administration also announced that fuel consumption standards for US vehicles would be raised to 35.5 miles per gallon (15.44 kilometres per litre) by 2016 from the current 25 miles per gallon, which is four years earlier than previous US law. • In 2009 the American Clean Energy and Security Act of 2009, an energy bill that would establish a cap-and-trade scheme for greenhouse gases was approved by the House of Representatives by a vote of 219 to 212. While by the end of 2009 the bill had not yet been approved by the Senate it lists the goals of the US administration. If passed by the Senate, this bill commits the US to: – a 17% emissions reduction from 2005 levels by 2020 and about 80% by 2050; – a renewable electricity standard which requires each electricity provider supplying over 4 million MWh, to produce 20% of its electricity from renewable sources by 2020; – a new set of energy efficiency standards for lighting products, commercial furnaces and other appliances, requiring buildings to have 30% energy efficiency improvement by 2010 and 50% by 2016. • US State governments and city mayors have made strong commitments, including: – California has an executive order to reduce CO_2 emissions by 80% on 1990 levels by 2050. California has committed by law to sourcing 33% of all energy from renewables by 2020 achieving 20% by 2010. For instance, California aims to have a million solar roofs by 2017.[181] The new Solar Initiative calls for 3GW of solar photovoltaics by 2017 for homes, schools, businesses and farms. California leads the US and the world in many aspects of climate change policy and mitigation targets. These are outlined in detail by the annual California Energy Commission's Integrated Energy Policy reports.[182] States in the northeast and mid-Atlantic have set up the Regional Greenhouse Gas Initiative to cut emissions to 2005 levels between 2009 and 2015, and by a further 10% between 2015 and 2018. – As of October 2007 almost 750 American mayors had pledged their cities to meet the goals set forth in the Kyoto Protocol or reduce their emissions of greenhouse gases by at least 7% by 2012. Some have already met even more aggressive targets, ranging from a goal of 20% reduction by Portland to a goal of 42% reduction over the same timeframe by Sebastopol, California.[183]
Japan	• Japan's Kyoto Protocol commitment is to reduce greenhouse gas emissions by 6% on 1990 levels by the period 2008–2012. • As part of the Copenhagen Accord process, Japan has committed to achieve a 25% reduction in GHG emissions from 1990 levels by 2020. • The 2008 Action Plan for Achieving a Low-Carbon Society sets a long-term target of reducing Japan's current level of greenhouse gas emissions by 60–80% by 2050.[184] In October 2008, Japan introduced on a trial basis an Integrated Domestic Market for Emissions Trading, consisting of a Trial Emissions Trading Scheme, and options for procuring additional tradable credits.[185] • In 2009 the incoming prime minister of Japan, Yukio Hatoyama, announced a commitment of 25% reductions in greenhouse gas emissions over 1990 levels by 2020.[186]

Country	Energy reduction and renewable energy targets
	• The Japanese National Energy Strategy aims for: – 30% improvement of energy efficiency by 2030; – overall oil dependence reduced to lower than 40% by 2030 with an 80% target specifically for the transport sector. • Tokyo aims to reach a 20% share of renewables in primary energy consumption by 2020. Japan implemented a nationwide feed-in tariff system in late 2009.[187]
China	As part of the Copenhagen Accord process, the Chinese government formally committed to a 40–45% reduction in carbon dioxide emissions per unit of GDP by 2020 compared to 2005 levels. China has also committed to ambitious short-term energy efficiency targets, such as reducing energy intensity 20% by 2010 from 2005 levels.[188] The Chinese government has brought in a comprehensive range of policies[189] to enable such targets to be achieved, including: • Requiring the top 1000 largest businesses to achieve ambitious energy efficiency improvements per annum between 2005 and 2010.[190] • Implementing fuel consumption standards for passenger cars that are significantly higher than the US. • Implementing comprehensive energy efficiency standards for appliances.[191] • Implementing the National Energy Efficient Design Standard for Public/Commercial Buildings. • China's Renewable Energy Law aims to achieve: – 16% of primary energy from renewables by 2020;[192] – an increase in biofuel production to 15 billion litres by 2020;[193] – solar hot water coverage of 300 million square metres by 2020.[194] • Technology targets to be achieved by 2020 include generating 300GW of hydroelectric power, 30GW of wind power, 30GW of biomass power, 1.8GW of solar photovoltaics, and smaller amounts of solar thermal power and geothermal.[195] • By 2010, the emissions of nitrous oxide from industrial processes will remain stable at 2005 levels[196] (with a global warming potential of around 290 times CO_2). • Power producers with capacity greater than 5GW must increase power capacity from non-hydro renewables to 3% by 2010 and 8% by 2020.[197]
Germany	• As a member of EU15, Germany aims to fulfil the Kyoto Protocol commitment to reduce greenhouse gas emissions by 8% on 1990 levels by the period 2008–2012. • As a member of the G-8, Germany committed to 80% cuts by 2050 in July 2009. • As a member state of the EU in 2007 Germany committed to 20% reduction in greenhouse gas emissions by 2020 (increasing to a 30% reduction if international agreement is reached) and halving of 1990 levels by 2050.[198] • Energy productivity is to double from 1990 levels by 2020.[199] • Offered to set a target of 40% reduction below 1990 levels by 2020 if EU accepts a 30% greenhouse gas emissions reduction target. • National objective to supply 20% of electricity from renewable sources by 2020.[200]
France	• Aims to fulfil the Kyoto Protocol commitment to reduce greenhouse gas emissions by 8% on 1990 levels by the period 2008–2012, as member of EU15. • As a member of the G-8, France committed in principle to 80% cuts by 2050 in July 2009. • Member state of the EU's commitment for 20% reduction in greenhouse gas emissions by 2020 (increasing to a 30% reduction if international agreement is reached) and halving of 1990 levels by 2050.[201]

Table 6.1 *continued*

Country	Energy reduction and renewable energy targets

	• Policy targets for 7% of energy used to be provided by renewable sources by 2010, and 10% by 2015.[202] Tax credits, subsidies and grants are used to meet these targets, and fines or tax penalties are enforced to penalize non-compliance.[203]
	• The National Energy Efficiency Action Plan sets targets and actions to reduce greenhouse gas emissions by 25% from 1990 levels by 2020, and further targets to achieve this include:
	  – minimum of 9% energy savings over the period 2008–2016;
	  – decreasing energy intensity by 2% per year by 2015 and by 2.5% per year by 2030;
	  – reducing energy consumption in the construction industry by more than a third by 2020;
	  – lowering greenhouse gas emissions by 20% in the transport industry by 2020.[204]

United Kingdom	• Aims to fulfil the Kyoto Protocol commitment to reduce greenhouse gas emissions by 8% on 1990 levels by the period 2008–2012 as a member of the EU15. • As a member of the G-8, the UK committed in principle to 80 per cent cuts by 2050 in July 2009. • Member state of the EU's commitment for 20% reduction in greenhouse gas emissions by 2020 (increasing to a 30% reduction if international agreement is reached) and halving of 1990 levels by 2050.[205] • National objectives to reduce CO_2 emissions by 20% on 1990 levels by 2010 and by 80% on 2000 levels by 2050.[206] • London policy targets aim to reduce CO_2 emissions by 20% by 2010, relative to 1990 levels, and by 60% by 2050.[207]
India	• As part of the Copenhagen Accord process, the Indian government has formally committed to 20–25% reduction in emissions intensity of GDP by 2020 in comparison to the 2005 level. • The National Action Plan on Climate Change released in June 2008 sets targets to establish an effective, cooperative and equitable global approach based on the principle of common but differentiated responsibilities and relative capabilities enshrined in the UN Framework Convention on Climate Change (UNFCCC).[208] • In November, 2009 India announced an industry energy efficiency programme. A new law will outline average current energy usage for companies spanning major sectors, including cement, steel and power. • Industries will be required to meet energy efficiency standards and those who fail to do so will be able to purchase energy efficiency certificates from successful industries. • Under the National Action Plan, the National Solar Mission aims to develop a solar energy industry in India that can compete with the fossil fuel industries.[209] India is implementing a solar feed-in tariff in 2010. • The 11th Five-Year Plan contains mandatory and voluntary measures to increase efficiency in power generation and distribution, increase the use of renewable energy and encourage mass transit programmes. • Long-term targets by the year 2032 include renewable energy accounting for 15% of power; 20GW of solar capacity by 2022; 10% of oil consumption substituted by biofuels, synthetic fuels and hydrogen; and 100% use of solar hot water in all possible applications.[210] • Short-term targets by 2012 include full use of co-generation in the sugar and other biomass-based industries.[211]

Country	Energy reduction and renewable energy targets
	• Introduced mandatory labels for refrigerators, transformers, air-conditioners and tube lights in January 2010.
Italy	• Aims to fulfil the Kyoto Protocol commitment to reduce greenhouse gas emissions by 8% on 1990 levels by the period 2008–2012 as a member of the EU15.
	• As a member of the G-8, Italy committed in principle to 80% cuts by 2050 in July 2009.
	• Member state of the EU's commitment for 20% reduction in greenhouse gas emissions by 2020 (increasing to a 30% reduction if international agreement is reached) and halving of 1990 levels by 2050.[212]
	• Feed-in tariff targets 3000MW of solar photovoltaics by 2016, which equates to almost 1 million homes if used for residential installations.[213]
	• National objective and commitment to EU targets to increase share of electricity from renewable resources to 25% by 2010.[214]
	• Mandates for 1% blending for both ethanol and biodiesel.[215]
Russian Federation	• Aims to fulfil the Kyoto Protocol commitment to meeting the same 1990 greenhouse gas emissions levels by the period 2008–2012 as a member of the EU15.
	• As part of the Copenhagen Accord process, the Russian government has formally committed to a target of 22–25% reduction in emissions below 1990 levels by 2020.
	• As member of the G-8, Russia committed in principle to 60–80 per cent cuts by 2050 in July 2009.
Brazil	• As part of the Copenhagen Accord process, the Brazilian government has committed to 36.1–38.9 per cent cuts in greenhouse gas emissions by 2020 relative to business as usual by 2020.
	• Brazil's Energy Matrix Program sets mandatory requirements for: – at least 5% addition of biodiesel to fossil diesel by 2013;[216] – 10% of annual electricity consumption provided by alternative sources by 2020.[217]
	• Brazil's National Climate Change Plan aims to reduce annual deforestation rates by 40% from average 1996–2005 levels during 2006–2009, with a total decrease of over 70% by 2014–2017.[218]
	• The Amazon Protected Area programme aims to consolidate 600,000km² in new and existing protected areas by 2012. The Coalition of Developing Nations provides funds from the International Carbon Trading Scheme to assist this programme.[219]

Source: Based on *The Stern Review* (2006)[220] and updated by The Natural Edge Project, with references added.

Notes

1 The Australian 2020 Summit was a 'by invitation' event and involved 1000 representatives from across the Australian community and Cheryl Desha was invited to represent the work of The Natural Edge Project.

2 For further information on Prime Minister Kevin Rudd's views on climate change see www.pm.gov.au/topics/climate.cfm, accessed 11 August 2008.

3 Barringer, F. and Revkin, A. C. (2007) 'Gore warns Congress of 'planetary emergency', *New York Times*, 22 March.

4   IPCC (2007) *Climate Change 2007: Synthesis Report*, Contribution of Working
     Groups I, II and III to the Fourth Assessment Report of the Intergovernmental
     Panel on Climate Change, Cambridge University Press, Cambridge.

5   Milmo, C. (2007) 'Too late to avoid global warming', *Independent* (UK), 19
     September.

6   IPCC (2007) *Climate Change 2007: Synthesis Report*, Contribution of Working
     Groups I, II and III to the Fourth Assessment Report of the Intergovernmental
     Panel on Climate Change, Cambridge University Press, Cambridge.

7   UN (2007) 'Ban Ki-moon urges climate change breakthrough in Bali after dire
     report released', *UN News Centre*, 17 November.

8   IPCC (2007) *Climate Change 2007: Synthesis Report*, Contribution of Working
     Groups I, II and III to the Fourth Assessment Report of the Intergovernmental
     Panel on Climate Change, Cambridge University Press, Cambridge, p104.

9   von Weizsäcker, E., Hargroves, K., Smith, M., Desha, C. and Stasinopoulos, P.
     (2009) *Factor Five: Transforming the Global Economy through 80%
     Improvements in Resource Productivity*, Earthscan, London.

10   IPCC (2007) *Climate Change 2007: Synthesis Report*, Contribution of Working
     Groups I, II and III to the Fourth Assessment Report of the Intergovernmental
     Panel on Climate Change, Cambridge University Press, Cambridge, p104.

11   Reuters (2007) 'Bill Clinton: "Green" economy offers great rewards', *Reuters*,
     2 November.

12   Stern, N. (2006) *The Stern Review: The Economics of Climate Change*,
     Cambridge University Press, Cambridge, p302.

13   Stern, N. (2006) *The Stern Review: The Economics of Climate Change*,
     Cambridge University Press, Cambridge, p278.

14   EEA (2006) *Air Quality and Ancillary Benefits of Climate Change*, Technical
     Report no 4, European Environment Agency, Copenhagen.

15   Gore, A. (2008) 'Al Gore: A generational challenge to repower America',
     Transcript, 17 July, www.wecansolveit.org/pages/al_gore_a_generational_
     challenge_to_repower_america/, accessed 12 July 2009.

16   Mellgren, D. (2008) 'OECD issues warning on climate change action or else half
     the world will suffer', *The Associated Press*.

17   Stern, N. (2006) *The Stern Review: The Economics of Climate Change*,
     Cambridge University Press, Cambridge, pp104–105.

18   Brown, L. (2008) *Plan B 3.0: Mobilizing to Save Civilization*, W. W. Norton &
     Company, New York, p14.

19   Klare, M. (2001) *Resource Wars – The New Landscape of Global Conflict*,
     Metropolitan Books, New York.

20   Brown, L. (2008) *Plan B 3.0: Mobilizing to Save Civilization*, W. W. Norton &
     Company, New York, p13.

21   Stern, N. (2006) *The Stern Review: The Economics of Climate Change*,
     Cambridge University Press, Cambridge, see 'Summary of conclusions'.

22   IPCC (2007) *Climate Change 2007: Mitigation of Climate Change*, Contribution
     of Working Group III to the Fourth Assessment Report of the Intergovernmental
     Panel on Climate Change, Cambridge University Press, Cambridge, see 'Summary
     for policymakers'.

23   UNEP (2007) *Global Environment Outlook: Environment for Development
     (GEO-4) Report*, UNEP, p332.

24   Schneider, S. and Azar, C. (2002) 'Are the costs of stabilising the atmosphere
     prohibitive?', *Ecological Economics*, vol 42, pp73–80.

25 NEF (2006) *The UK Interdependence Report: How the World Sustains the Nation's Lifestyles and the Price it Pays,* New Economics Foundation, London, cited in UNEP (2007) *Global Environment Outlook: Environment for Development (GEO-4) Report,* UNEP, p467.

26 Obama, B. (2006) 'Oil & alternative fuels – Energy independence and the safety of our planet', 3 April 2006.

27 Editorial (2007) 'The warming challenge', *New York Times,* 5 May, cited in Lovins, H. 'The economic case for climate action', in PCAP (2008) *Plan for Presidential Action for the First 100 Days in Office for the Next President of the United States,* Presidential Climate Action Project, US.

28 von Weizsäcker, E., Hargroves, K., Smith, M., Desha, C. and Stasinopoulos, P. (2009) *Factor Five: Transforming the Global Economy through 80% Improvements in Resource Productivity,* Earthscan, London.

29 PWC (2008) *Carbon Countdown: A Survey of Executive Opinion on Climate Change in the Countdown to a Carbon Economy,* PriceWaterHouseCoopers, Australia.

30 Proudfoot Consulting (2007) *Meeting the Corporate Energy Challenge: Are Companies Walking the Talk on Energy Efficiency?,* Proudfoot Consulting, Australia.

31 Australia Industry Group (2007) *Environmental Sustainability and Industry, Road to a Sustainable Future,* AIG, Australia.

32 Lyth, A., Nichols, S. and Tilbury, D. (2007) *Shifting Towards Sustainability: Education for Climate Change Adaptation in the Built Environment Sector,* a report prepared by the Australian Research Institute in Education for Sustainability.

33 Stern, N. (2006) *The Stern Review: The Economics of Climate Change,* Cambridge University Press, Cambridge, p319.

34 Stern, N. (2006) *The Stern Review: The Economics of Climate Change,* Cambridge University Press, Cambridge, see 'Summary of conclusions'.

35 Stern, N. (2006) *The Stern Review: The Economics of Climate Change,* Cambridge University Press, Cambridge, pp244–247.

35A Californian Energy Commission (2005) California's Water–Energy Relationship, Californian Energy Commission, www.energy.ca.gov/2005publications/CEC-700-2005-011/CEC-700-2005-011-SF.PDF.

36 Mellgren, D. (2008) 'OECD issues warning on climate change action or else half the world will suffer', *The Associated Press.*

37 Campbell-Lendrum, D. and Corvalán, C. (2007) 'Climate change and developing-country cities: Implications for environmental health and equity', *Journal of Urban Health,* vol 84, no 1, pp109–117.

38 CSE (1999) 'Sick of air pollution', Press Release, Centre for Science and Environment, 5 June, Delhi, India.

39 Farmer, A. (1997) *Managing Environmental Pollution,* Routledge Publishing, New York.

40 Holland, M., Kinghorn, S., Emberson, L., Cinderby, S., Ashmore, M., Mills, G. and Harmens, H. (2006) *Development of a Framework for Probabilistic Assessment of the Economic Losses Caused by Ozone Damage to Crops in Europe,* Centre for Ecology and Hydrology, Natural Environment Research Council, Bangor, Wales.

41 UNEP (2007) *Global Environment Outlook: Environment for Development (GEO-4) Report,* UNEP.

42 Agence France-Presse (2006) *Hong Kong Pollution Leaves Tourists Choking,* Agence France-Presse.

43 Clean Air Initiative for Asian Cities Centre (2007) *2007 Annual Report: Clean Air Initiative for Asian Cities Centre,* Clean Air Initiative for Asian Cities Centre, Manila, the Philippines.

44 Gettler, L. (2008) 'Company structures and career paths shift with global warming', *The Age,* 20 August.

45 Rauber, C. (2008) 'Investors file flurry of global-warming resolutions', *San Francisco Business Times,* 6 March.

46 Carbon Disclosure Project (undated) Homepage, www.cdproject.net/, accessed 22 August 2009.

47 FTSE4Good Index Series (2006) *Market Consultation on the FTSE4Good Climate Change Criteria,* FTSE Group, cited in Lovins, H. (2007) 'The economic case for climate action', in PCAP (2008) *Plan for Presidential Action for the First 100 Days in Office for the Next President of the United States,* Presidential Climate Action Project.

48 Sosnowchik, K. (2004) 'Between blue and yellow: What's in a name?', *Green@work,* May/June.

49 The Climate Group (2004) *Carbon Down, Profits Up,* the Climate Group, London; the Climate Group (2005) *Carbon Down, Profits Up,* the Climate Group.

50 The Climate Group (2004) *Carbon Down, Profits Up,* the Climate Group.

51 Lean, G. (2007) 'Green giants join forces to fight carbon emissions', *Independent* (UK), 25 March.

52 Environmental Leader (2008) 'GE reports on progress of Ecomagination, sets new goals', *EL Daily,* 29 May.

53 The Climate Group (2007) *Carbon Down, Profits Up* (third edition), the Climate Group.

54 General Electric Company (2009) 'Ecomagination: Our commitments', http://ge.ecomagination.com/our-commitments/index.html, accessed 12 September 2009.

55 Environmental Leader (2008) 'GE reports on progress of Ecomagination, sets new goals', *EL Daily,* 29 May.

56 General Electric Company (2009) 'Ecomagination: Our Commitments', http://ge.ecomagination.com/our-commitments/index.html, accessed 12 September 2009.

57 Roner, L. (2005) 'Wal-Mart – An environmental epiphany?' *Climate Change Corp.Com,* 7 December.

58 Alliance to Save Energy (undated) 'Wal-Mart is serious about sustainability', http://ase.org/content/article/detail/5740, accessed 25 August 2009.

59 Lash, J. and Wellington, F. (2007) 'Competitive advantage on a warming planet', *Harvard Business Review,* March.

60 Fishman, C. (2006) 'How many lightbulbs does it take to change the world? One. And you're looking at it', *Fast Company Magazine,* no 108, p74.

61 Gogoi, P. and Herbst, M. (2007) 'Wal-Mart: Measuring just how green; the retailing giant launched a potentially groundbreaking initiative to measure suppliers' energy use – how hard will it push for change?', *Business Week Online,* 26 September.

62 Alliance to Save Energy (undated) 'Wal-Mart is serious about sustainability', http://ase.org/content/article/detail/5740, accessed 25 August 2009.

63 The Climate Group (2007) *Carbon Down, Profits Up* (third edition), the Climate Group.

64 Wal-Mart (2009) 'Sustainability Index', http://walmartstores.com/Sustainability/9292.aspx, accessed 12 September 2009.

65 von Weizsäcker, E., Hargroves, K., Smith, M., Desha, C. and Stasinopoulos, P. (2009) *Factor Five: Transforming the Global Economy through 80% Improvements in Resource Productivity,* Earthscan, London.

66 Smith, M., Hargroves, K., Stasinopoulos, P., Stephens, R., Desha, C. and Hargroves, S. (2007) *Energy Transformed: Sustainable Energy Solutions for Climate Change Mitigation*, The Natural Edge Project, Australia.

67 Ausmelt Technologies (undated) Homepage, www.ausmelt.com.au/home.htm, accessed 12 July 2009.

68 Pokrajic, Z. and Morrison, R (2009) 'A simulation methodology for the design of eco-efficient comminution circuits', Proceedings of the XXIV International Mineral Processing Congress, Beijing.

69 Weizsäcker, E., Hargroves, K., Smith, M., Desha, C. and Stasinopoulos, P. (2009) *Factor Five: Transforming the Global Economy through 80% Improvements in Resource Productivity,* Earthscan, London.

70 Humphreys, K. and Mahasenan, M. (2002) *Towards a Sustainable Cement Industry,* World Business Council for Sustainable Development, Geneva, see 'Substudy 8: Climate change'; Kim, Y. and Worrell, E. (2002) 'CO_2 emission trends in the cement industry: An international comparison', *Mitigation and Adaptation Strategies for Global Change*, vol 7, no 2, pp115–133.

71 Smith, M., Hargroves, K., Desha, C. and Stasinopoulos, P. (2009) 'Factor 5 in eco-cements', ECOS, CSIRO, no 149.

72 CSIRO (undated) 'Geopolymers: Building blocks of the future', www.csiro.au/science/ps19e.html, accessed 4 September 2008.

73 Worrell, E. and Galitsky, C. (2004) *Emerging Energy-Efficient Technologies in Industry: Case Studies of Selected Technologies*, Ernest Orlando Lawrence Berkeley National Laboratory, Environmental Energy Technologies Division, US.

74 Energy Efficiency and Greenhouse Working Group (2003) *Towards a National Framework for Energy Efficiency – Issues and Challenges Discussion Paper*, Energy Efficiency and Greenhouse Working Group, Australia.

75 Price, L. et al (2003) *Voluntary Agreements for Increasing Energy-Efficiency in Industry: Case Study of a Pilot Project with the Steel Industry in Shandong Province, China*, Lawrence Berkeley National Laboratory, US.

76 McKenzie, R., (1994) 'Canada's National Partnership Strategy for Industrial Energy Efficiency', International Energy Agency Conference Proceedings – Industrial Energy Efficiency: Policies and Programs, Washington, DC, 26–27 May.

77 Togeby, M., Johannsen, K., Ingrslev, C., Thingvad, K. and Madsen, J. (1999) 'Evaluations of the Danish Agreement System', Proceedings of the 1999 American Council for an Energy-Efficient Economy Summer Study on Energy Efficiency in Industry, Washington, DC.

78 Ramesohl, S. and Kristof, K. (1999) 'What is the role of energy-related voluntary approaches in the Post-Kyoto climate policy? A process oriented analysis of the "Declaration of German Industry on Global Warming Prevention"', in Energy Efficiency and CO_2 Reduction: The Dimensions of Social Change: 1999 European Council for an Energy-Efficient Economy Summer Study, 31 May–4 June, Mandelieu, France.

79 Worrell, E. and Price, L. (2001) *Barriers and Opportunities: A Review of Selected Successful Energy-Efficiency Programs*, Lawrence Berkeley National Laboratory, US.

80 Department of Resources, Energy and Tourism (formerly the Department of Industry, Tourism and Resources) (undated) Homepage, www.energyefficiencyopportunities.gov.au/, accessed 10 April 2008.

81 House of Commons Environment, Food and Rural Affairs Committee (2004–2005) *Climate Change: Looking Forward,* Ninth Report of Session, House of Commons Environment, Food and Rural Affairs Committee, UK

82 Kirby, A. (undated) 'UK industry succeeding: UK beats greenhouse gas targets', *BBC News Online,* 7 April 2003.

83 UK Government (2006) *Explanatory Memorandum to the Climate Change Agreement,* Office of Public Sector Information (OPSI), UK.

84 DEFRA (2007) *Climate Change Agreements: Results of the Third Target Period Assessment,* Department for Environment, Food and Rural Affairs, London.

85 Kirby, A. (undated) 'UK industry succeeding: UK beats greenhouse gas targets', *BBC News Online,* 7 April 2003.

86 *Novem* (2002) 'Voluntary agreements on energy efficiency in industry in the Netherlands: The second generation', *Novem,* August.

87 Lawrence Berkeley National Laboratory (2009)*China Energy Group: Sustainable Development Through Energy Efficiency,* Lawrence Berkeley National Laboratory, Berkeley, CA.

88 Wang, X. (2006) 'Top-1000 Enterprises Energy Efficiency Program: Policy design and implementation', Supporting documentation for the Energy Foundation's Forum on Implementing China's 2010 20-Percent Energy Efficiency Target, 9–10 November 2006.

89 Price, L. and Wang, X. et al (2008) *China's Top-1000 Energy-Consuming Enterprises Program: Reducing Energy Consumption of the 1000 Largest Industrial Enterprises in China,* Lawrence Berkeley National Laboratory, Berkeley, CA.

90 Lawrence Berkeley National Laboratory (2009) *China Energy Group: Sustainable Development through Energy Efficiency,* Lawrence Berkeley National Laboratory, Berkeley, CA.

91 Gao, Y. (2007) 'Energy consumption of China's steel industry down 8.8%', *China Daily,* 18 February.

92 Zhou, N., Levine, M. and Price, L. (2009) 'Overview of current energy efficiency policies in China', submitted to *Energy Policy* (in press).

93 Price, L. and Wang, X. et al (2008) *China's Top-1000 Energy-Consuming Enterprises Program: Reducing Energy Consumption of the 1000 Largest Industrial Enterprises in China,* Lawrence Berkeley National Laboratory, Berkeley, CA.

94 Levine, M., Zhou, N. and Price, L. (2009) *The Greening of the Middle Kingdom: The Story of Energy Efficiency in China,* Lawrence Berkeley National Laboratory, Berkeley, CA.

95 Ahmad, N., Lequiller, F., Marianna, P., Pilat, D., Schreyer, P. and Wölfl, A. (2003) *Statistics Brief: Comparing Growth in GDP and Labour Productivity: Measurement Issues,* OECD.

96 Lovins, A. and Lovins, H. (1997) *Climate: Making Money, Making Sense,* Rocky Mountain Institute, Colorado.

97 Lovins, A. and Lovins, H. (1997) *Climate: Making Money, Making Sense,* Rocky Mountain Institute, Colorado.

98 Business for Social Responsibility (2008) *Who's Going 'Carbon Neutral'? A Compilation by Business for Social Responsibility,* Business for Social Responsibility, San Francisco, CA.

99 UNEP Climate Neutral Network (undated) Homepage, www.grida.no/, accessed 7 March 2008.

100 UN Global Compact (2009) *Twenty Climate-Neutral Frontrunners Join Caring for Climate,* United Nations Global Compact, New York.

101 Grady, K. (2003) 'Climate change and the Australian economy', Conference Presentation, Business Council of Australia.

102 News Corporation (2007) 'News Corporation launches global energy initiative: Commits to become carbon neutral by 2010 and engage audiences around the world on issue', Press Release, 5 May.

103 Gettler, L. (2006) 'PwC plans to become carbon neutral', *The Age*, 16 December.

104 KPMG (2008) *KPMG's Journey to Climate Neutrality*, KPMG, Australia.

105 Australian Greenhouse Office (undated) 'Greenhouse friendly', www.climatechange.gov.au/greenhousefriendly/products/index.html#energetics, accessed 4 November 2008.

106 Bunnings (undated) 'Bunnings and sustainability', www.bunnings.com.au/contact-us_bunnings-sustainability.aspx, accessed 12 July 2009.

107 WWF (2007) 'WWF welcomes ANZ commitment to become climate neutral by end of 2009', Media Release, 3 May.

108 Center for Energy & Climate Solutions (undated) 'Energy and climate', www.energyandclimate.org/, accessed 4 December 2008; Cool-Companies.com (undated) 'Hype about hydrogen', www.cool-companies.org, accessed 4 December 2008; Capital E (undated) Homepage, www.cap-e.com, accessed 4 December 2008.

109 Pew Center for Global Climate Centre (undated) 'Global warming: Emission reduction targets of companies', www.pewclimate.org/companies_leading_the_way_belc/targets/, accessed 4 December 2008.

110 Climate Leaders is an EPA industry–government partnership that works with companies to develop comprehensive climate change strategies, see www.epa.gov/stateply/, accessed 12 July 2009.

111 Gross, G. (2007) 'Dell to go "carbon neutral" by late 2008', *Washington Post*, 26 September.

112 Business for Social Responsibility (2008) *Who's Going 'Carbon Neutral'? A Compilation by Business for Social Responsibility*, Business for Social Responsibility.

113 US EPA (2009) 'US EPA 2009 Green Power Partnership: Top 50 company list', www.epa.gov/grnpower/toplists/top50.htm, accessed 12 September 2009.

114 Lovins, H. (2007) 'The economic case for climate action', in PCAP (2008) *Plan for Presidential Action for the First 100 Days in Office for the Next President of the United States*, Presidential Climate Action Project, US.

115 As of May 2007, USCAP members included: Alcan Inc.; Alcoa; American International Group, Inc. (AIG); Boston Scientific Corporation; BP America Inc.; Caterpillar Inc.; ConocoPhillips; Deere & Company; the Dow Chemical Company; Duke Energy; DuPont; Environmental Defense; FPL Group, Inc.; General Electric; General Motors Corp.; Johnson & Johnson; Marsh, Inc.; National Wildlife Federation; Natural Resources Defense Council; the Nature Conservancy; PepsiCo; Pew Center for Global Climate Change; PG&E Corporation; PNM Resources; Shell; Siemens Corporation; and World Resources Institute.

116 USCAP (2007) *A Call for Action – Consensus Principles and Recommendations from the U.S. Climate Action Partnership: A Business and NGO Partnership*, USCAP.

117 Obama and Biden (2008) 'Barack Obama and Joe Biden: New energy for America', www.barackobama.com/pdf/factsheet_energy_speech_080308.pdf, accessed 12 July 2009.

118 Prince of Wales Corporate Leaders Group on Climate Change (2007) 'The Bali Communiqué', www.balicommunique.com/communique.html, accessed 13 February 2008.

119 Prince of Wales Corporate Leaders Group on Climate Change (2008) 'The Poznam Communiqué', www.copenhagencommunique.com/the-communique/previous-communiques, accessed 19 August 2009.

120 Prince of Wales Corporate Leaders Group on Climate Change (2008) 'The Copenhagen Call', www.copenhagencommunique.com, accessed 19 August 2009.

121 Prince of Wales Corporate Leaders Group on Climate Change (2007) 'The Bali Communiqué', www.princeofwales.gov.uk/content/documents/Bali%20Communique.pdf, accessed 7 June 2010.

122 CBC News (2009) 'Recession slows climate change progress: Obama', *CBC News*, 9 July.

122A Deutsche Bank Climate Change Advisors (2010) *Global Climate Change Policy Tracker – The Green Economy, The Race is* On, Deutsche Bank Group, www.dbcca.com/dbcca/EN/investment-research/investment_research_2296.jsp

123 Centre for International Economics (2008) 'Discussion paper for the 9th National Business Leaders Forum for Sustainable Development', reports commissioned by the Property Council and the Australian Sustainable Built Environment Council.

124 UNEP (undated) 'Climate Neutral Network', www.climateneutral.unep.org, accessed 7 March 2008.

125 *Environment News Service* (2007) 'Europe to cut greenhouse gases 20 percent by 2020', *Environment News Service*, 8 March.

126 Levine, M., Zhou, N. and Price, L. (2009) *The Greening of the Middle Kingdom: The Story of Energy Efficiency in China*, Lawrence Berkeley National Laboratory, Berkeley, CA.

127 Levine, M., Zhou, N. and Price, L. (2009) *The Greening of the Middle Kingdom: The Story of Energy Efficiency in China*, Lawrence Berkeley National Laboratory, Berkeley, CA.

128 EurActiv (2008) 'Commission: Binding energy efficiency targets not excluded', Euractiv.com, 25 February.

129 House of Commons Environment, Food and Rural Affairs Committee (2004–2005) *Climate Change: Looking Forward*, Ninth Report of Session, House of Commons Environment, Food and Rural Affairs Committee; Kirby, A. (2003) 'UK industry succeeding: UK beats greenhouse gas targets', *BBC News Online*, 7 April; UK government (2006) *Explanatory Memorandum to the Climate Change Agreements (Eligible Facilities) (Amendment) Regulations*, UK government.

130 Number10.gov.uk (2007) 'Prime Minister calls for global action on climate change', Number10.gov.uk, 19 November 2007.

131 Levine, M., Zhou, N. and Price, L. (2009) *The Greening of the Middle Kingdom: The Story of Energy Efficiency in China*, Lawrence Berkeley National Laboratory, Berkeley, CA.

132 Lawrence Berkeley National Laboratory (2009) *China Energy Group: Sustainable Development through Energy Efficiency*, Lawrence Berkeley National Laboratory, Berkeley, CA.

133 Levine, M., Zhou, N. and Price, L. (2009) *The Greening of the Middle Kingdom: The Story of Energy Efficiency in China*, Lawrence Berkeley National Laboratory, Berkeley, CA.

134 The Insulation Council of Australia and New Zealand (2006) 'ICANZ applauds ACT 5-Star decision', Press Release, 20 February.

135 BBC (2006) 'Zero carbon homes plan unveiled', *BBC News*, 13 December.
136 Deutsche Well (2007) *Sarkozy Promises Green Revolution for France*, Deutsche Well, Germany.
137 Clinton Climate Initiative (2008) 'C40 Cities: Buildings, Freiburg, Germany', Clinton Climate Initiative.
138 The Climate Group (2007) 'Top Actions by States and Regions – California', www.theclimategroup.org/what_we_do/states_and_regions/california, accessed 12 July 2009.
139 California Energy Commission (2007) *Integrated Energy Policy Report*, California Energy Commission, CA.
140 IPCC (2007) *Climate Change 2007: Mitigation of Climate Change*, Contribution of Working Group III to the Fourth Assessment Report of the Intergovernmental Panel on Climate Change, Cambridge University Press, Cambridge, see 'Policies, instruments and co-operative arrangements'.
141 European Commission (undated) 'Energy efficiency', http://ec.europa.eu/energy/efficiency/index_en.htm, accessed 12 July 2009.
142 The Climate Group (2007) 'Top actions by states and regions – California', www.theclimategroup.org/what_we_do/states_and_regions/california, accessed 12 July 2009.
143 Faiola, A. (2006) 'Turn off the heat – how Japan made energy saving an art form', *Guardian* (UK), 17 February.
144 Lawrence Berkeley National Laboratory (2009) *China Energy Group: Sustainable Development Through Energy Efficiency*, Lawrence Berkeley National Laboratory, Berkeley, CA.
145 Lawrence Berkeley National Laboratory (2009) *China Energy Group: Sustainable Development through Energy Efficiency*, Lawrence Berkeley National Laboratory, Berkeley, CA.
146 Lawrence Berkeley National Laboratory (2009) *China Energy Group: Sustainable Development Through Energy Efficiency*, Lawrence Berkeley National Laboratory, Berkeley, CA.
147 China Sourcing Reports (2006) *Compact Fluorescent Lamps*, China Sourcing Reports, Global Sources, Singapore
148 Smith, M., Hargroves, K., Stasinopoulos, P., Stephens, R., Desha, C. and Hargroves, S. (2007) *Energy Transformed: Sustainable Energy Solutions for Climate Change Mitigation*, Griffith University, ANU and The Natural Edge Project, Australia, see Lecture 4.4.
149 Kushler, M. (2006) *Aligning Utility Interests with Energy Efficiency Objectives: A Recent Review of Efforts at Decoupling and Performance Incentives*, American Council for an Energy-Efficient Economy, p5; Smith, M. and Hargroves, K. (2007) 'Smart approaches to electricity use', *CSIRO ECOS Magazine*, no 135, p12.
150 Smith, M. and Hargroves, K. (2007) 'Smart approaches to electricity use', *CSIRO ECOS Magazine*, no 135, p12.
151 Enel SpA (2008) 'ENEL Energia offers fixed price for electricity and gas', Press Release, 30 January.
152 Enel SpA (2004) 'IBM and ENEL will team to offer automated metering solution world wide', Press Release, 18 March.
153 Parliamentary Office of Science and Technology (2008) 'Smart metering of electricity and gas', *Postnote*, no 301.
154 Davies, J. (2007) 'Smart meters win minister's backing: John Hutton says 10 years is too long to wait for smart energy meters to be rolled out', *Computing*, 12 November.

155 Department of Primary Industries (2009) 'Smart meters: Advanced metering infrastructure for Victoria', www.dpi.vic.gov.au/dpi/dpinenergy.nsf/LinkView/ 4EC2E4EA42B821FCCA2572B10079A930A8BAF6E4E66C900FCA2572B2000 4C403, accessed 19 August 2009.

156 REN21 (2007) *Renewables Global Status Report*, REN21 Renewable Energy Policy Network for the 21st Century, Paris.

157 Renewable Energy Network for the 21st Century and Worldwatch Institute (2007) cited in Editorial (2008) 'Renewable energy surges forward', *The Japan Times Online*, 16 March.

158 The Climate Group (2007) 'Top Actions by States and Regions – California', www.theclimategroup.org/what_we_do/states_and_regions/california, accessed 12 July 2009.

159 REN21 (2007) *Renewables Global Status Report*, REN21, Paris Renewable Energy Policy Network for the 21st Century, Paris.

160 Mendonca, M. (2007) 'Energy, ethics and feed-in tariffs', *Renewable Energy World.Com*, 30 April.

161 California Energy Commission (2007) *Integrated Energy Policy Report*, California Energy Commission.

162 REN21 (2008) *Global Status Report: Policy Landscape / Power Generation Promotion Policies*, Renewable Energy Policy Network for the 21st Century, Paris.

163 von Weizsäcker, E., Hargroves, K., Smith, M., Desha, C. and Stasinopoulos, P. (2009) *Factor Five: Transforming the Global Economy through 80% Improvements in Resource Productivity*, Earthscan, London.

164 UNEP (undated) 'Climate Neutral Network', www.climateneutral.unep.org/ cnn_contentdetail.aspx?m=175&amid=666, accessed 7 March 2008.

165 Faiola, A. (2006) 'Japanese putting all their energy into saving fuel', *Washington Post Foreign Service,* 16 February 2006.

166 Vidal, J. (2006) 'Sweden plans to be the world's first oil-free economy', *Guardian* (UK), 2 February; Simpson, P. V. (2008) 'Eco-car subsidy could break budget', *The Local*, 1 March.

167 von Weizsäcker, E., Hargroves, K., Smith, M., Desha, C. and Stasinopoulos, P. (2009) *Factor Five: Transforming the Global Economy through 80% Improvements in Resource Productivity*, Earthscan, London.

168 Chrisafis, A. (2007) 'Sarkozy puts France on green track', *Guardian* (UK), 26 October.

169 EU Commission (2007) *EU Seeks To Shift Freight to Rail and Shipping*, EU Commission.

170 *Business Week* (2008) 'China's Great Railway Expansion', *Business Week*, 23 October.

171 Taylor, M. (2008) 'City's two-wheel transformation', *Guardian* (UK), 9 February.

172 *Associated Press* (2008) 'Utah is going to a 4-day workweek. In an effort to save energy, state employees will get Friday off', *Associated Press*, 3 July.

173 *Earth First* (2008) 'Some rural students get 4-day school week due to high fuel costs', *Earth First,* 25 July.

174 von Weizsäcker, E., Hargroves, K., Smith, M., Desha, C. and Stasinopoulos, P. (2009) *Factor Five: Transforming the Global Economy through 80% Improvements in Resource Productivity*, Earthscan, London.

175 IPCC (1999) *Special Report – Aviation and the Global Atmosphere, Summary for Policymakers*, Intergovernmental Panel on Climate Change, Cambridge University Press, Cambridge.

176 *EU Business News* (2008) 'European Union forces CO_2 caps on airlines', *EU Business News*, 25 October.

177 Vidal, J. (2006) 'Sweden plans to be the world's first oil-free economy', *Guardian* (UK), 2 February.

178 Faiola, A. (2006) 'Turn off the heat – how Japan made energy saving an art form', *Guardian*, UK, 17 February.

179 Hawaii 2050 Sustainability Task Force (2008) 'Hawaii 2050 Sustainability Plan sets direction for state's future', *PR Newswire*.

180 Smith, M., Hargroves, K., Stasinopoulos, P., and Desha, C.(2008) 'Analysis of the costs of inaction versus the costs of action on climate change for Australia', Submission to the Garnaut Review, The Natural Edge Project and Griffith University Business School, www.naturaledgeproject.net/Documents/TNEPSubmission.pdf, accessed 12 July 2009.

181 REN21 (2006) *Renewables Global Status Report 2006 Update,* Renewable Energy Policy Network for the 21st Century, Paris.

182 California Energy Commission (2007) *Integrated Energy Policy Report*, California Energy Commission.

183 Wilson, S. (2007) 'US Grassroots Tackle Climate Change', *BBC News*, 11 July.

184 Mori, Y., Kikuyama, Y. and Day, J. (2009) 'Japan implements integrated market for emissions trading linked to Kyoto mechanisms on trial basis', Martindale-Hubbell, Tokyo.

185 Young, T. (2008) '500 businesses join Japan's emissions trading scheme', *BusinessGreen.com*, 17 December.

186 McCurry, J. (2009) 'Japan's new prime minister promises ambitious greenhouse gas cuts: Yukio Hatoyama seeks to reduce CO_2 emissions by 25% below 1990 levels by 2020', *Guardian* (UK), 7 September.

187 REN21 (2006) *Renewables Global Status Report 2006 Update,* Renewable Energy Policy Network for the 21st Century, Paris.

188 Levine, M., Zhou, N. and Price, L. (2009) *The Greening of the Middle Kingdom: The Story of Energy Efficiency in China*, Lawrence Berkeley National Laboratory, Berkeley, CA.

189 Levine, M., Zhou, N. and Price, L. (2009) *The Greening of the Middle Kingdom: The Story of Energy Efficiency in China*, Lawrence Berkeley National Laboratory, Berkeley, CA.

190 Price, L. and Wang, X. et al (2008) *China's Top 1000 Energy-Consuming Enterprises Program: Reducing Energy Consumption of the 1000 Largest Industrial Enterprises in China*, Lawrence Berkeley National Laboratory, Berkeley, CA.

191 Levine, M., Zhou, N. and Price, L. (2009) *The Greening of the Middle Kingdom: The Story of Energy Efficiency in China*, Lawrence Berkeley National Laboratory, Berkeley, CA.

192 NDRC (2007) *National Climate Change Program*, National Development and Reform Commission, China.

193 REN21 (2006) *Renewables Global Status Report 2006 Update,* Renewable Energy Policy Network for the 21st Century, Paris.

194 Liu, Y. (2005) 'Shanghai embarks on 100,000 solar roofs initiative', *China Watch*, 10 November, Worldwatch Institute, Washington, DC.

195 NDRC (2007) *National Climate Change Program*, National Development and Reform Commission, China.

196 NDRC (2007) *National Climate Change Program*, National Development and Reform Commission, China.

197 REN21 (2006) *Renewables Global Status Report 2006 Update*, Renewable Energy Policy Network for the 21st Century, Paris.

198 European Commission (2007) *Combating Climate Change: The EU Leads the Way* (2008 edition), European Union.

199 German Federal Ministry of Economic Affairs and Technology (2007) *National Energy Efficiency Action Plan (EEAP) of the Federal Republic of Germany*, European Commission.

200 German Federal Ministry of Economic Affairs and Technology (2007) *National Energy Efficiency Action Plan (EEAP) of the Federal Republic of Germany*, European Commission.

201 European Commission (2007) *Combating Climate Change: The EU Leads the Way*, European Union.

202 REN21 (2006) *Renewables Global Status Report 2006 Update*, Renewable Energy Policy Network for the 21st Century, Paris.

203 EU (2007) *France – Renewable Energy Fact Sheet*, European Union.

204 French Republic (2008) *Energy Efficiency Action Plan for France*, European Commission.

205 European Commission (2007) *Combating Climate Change: The EU Leads the Way*, European Union.

206 DEFRA (2006) *Climate Change: The UK Programme 2006*, UK Department of State for the Environment, Food and Rural Affairs, London.

207 REN21 (2006) *Renewables Global Status Report 2006 Update*, Renewable Energy Policy Network for the 21st Century, Paris.

208 Sabha, L. (2008) 'Impact of climate change and National Action Plan on Climate Change', Press Release, Ministry of Environment and Forests.

209 Government of India (2008) *National Action Plan on Climate Change*, Government of India.

210 REN21 (2006) *Renewables Global Status Report 2006 Update*, Renewable Energy Policy Network for the 21st Century, Paris.

211 REN21 (2006) *Renewables Global Status Report 2006 Update*, Renewable Energy Policy Network for the 21st Century, Paris.

212 European Commission (2007) *Combating Climate Change: The EU Leads the Way*, European Union.

213 REN21 (2006) *Renewables Global Status Report 2006 Update*, Renewable Energy Policy Network for the 21st Century, Paris.

214 European Union (2007) *Italy – Renewable Energy Fact Sheet*, European Union.

215 European Union (2007) *Italy – Renewable Energy Fact Sheet*, European Union.

216 Nass, L. L., Pereira, P. A. and Ellis, D. (2007) 'Biofuels in Brazil: An overview', *Crop Science*, vol 47, pp2228–2237.

217 Dutra, R. M. and Szkloa, A. S. (2008) 'Incentive policies for promoting wind power production in Brazil: Scenarios for the Alternative Energy Sources Incentive Program (PROINFA) under the new Brazilian electric power sector regulation', *Renewable Energy*, vol 33, no 1, pp65–76.

218 WWF (2008) 'Brazil falls short with forest emission reduction ambitions', WWF, 3 December.

219 Laurance, W. F. (2007) 'A new initiative to use carbon trading for tropical forest conservation', *Biotropica*, vol 39, no 1, pp20–24.

220 Stern, N. (2006) *The Stern Review: The Economics of Climate Change*, Cambridge University Press, Cambridge, Table 21.1.

7

Decoupling Economic Growth from Greenhouse Gas Emissions

Appreciating the Cost of Inaction on Climate Change

Efforts to date by the nations of the world to reduce environmental pressures, such as greenhouse gas emissions, have largely been motivated by a wide range of factors in addition to improving environmental conditions. These include: improving resource productivity, reducing negative impacts on public health, reducing dependence on fossil fuels, and improving industry competitiveness, particularly in capturing growing global markets in 'clean', 'green' products and services. However, as this book, and the many resources that have informed it, are showing, one of the leading drivers for change in the coming decades will be the costs to economies around the world of not acting to reduce a range of environmental pressures. In the case of greenhouse gas emissions, valuing the costs of inaction for nations and the global economy is a very complex task, and few studies proclaim to have quantified it. The 2006 review of the economics of climate change by UK economist Sir Nicholas Stern, *The Stern Review*,[1] is one of the few studies that have made a solid attempt at this, resulting in significant international attention. This area was further investigated in 2008 by a study from the OECD, *The Costs of Inaction on Key Environmental Challenges*.[2]

Costs from inaction to reduce greenhouse gas emissions will come from a wide range of causes, including (to name only a few):

• damage to infrastructure and the built environment from an increase in intensity of natural disasters, including fires, storms, hailstorms, ocean surges, flooding and cyclones;

- health-related costs due to more frequent heat waves and cold snaps, along with the spread of vector-borne diseases, such as Dengue fever and Ross River virus;
- reduced agricultural production from increased temperatures affecting crops, along with significant changes and variations in rainfall patterns;
- reduced revenue from nature-based tourism, such as tourism dependent on healthy coral reefs, and snow conditions in alpine regions;
- costs related to coastal protection, accommodation and retreat from rising sea levels and enhanced storm surges;
- reductions to the carrying capacity of grazing land for livestock due to higher temperatures and lower availability of water;
- increases in peak electricity demand due to the use of air-conditioners in response to rising temperatures, along with more frequent heat waves;
- increased losses from forest fires due to reduced water availability and higher average temperatures;
- increased risk of conflict over resources such as oil, water and timber, and declining food production.

In 2006, *The Stern Review*, after analysing a broad range of such costs of inaction, concluded that each year on average, 'the costs of action to the global economy would be roughly 1% of GDP, while the costs of inaction could be from 5–20% of GDP' depending on whether positive feedbacks are unleashed or not, as explained in Chapter 1.[3]

> *If we don't act the overall costs and risks of climate change will be equivalent to losing at least 5% of global GDP each year, now and forever. If a wider range of risks and impacts is taken into account, the estimates of damage could rise to 20% of GDP or more … The investment that takes place in the next 10–20 years will have a profound effect on the climate in the second half of this century … and could create risks of major disruption to economic and social activity, on a scale similar to those associated with the great wars and the economic depression of the first half of the 20th century. And it will be difficult or impossible to reverse these changes.*
>
> Sir Nicholas Stern, *The Stern Review*, 2006[4]

This work was one of the first to place an economic value on the option of not acting to reduce greenhouse gases, and on its publication it captured the attention of economists, policy-makers and business leaders around the world. The power of the findings is that they marked the moment when the cost of not acting went from a discussion of the probabilities of potential negative impacts from sea-level rises and temperature rises to a more tangible discussion for governments and policy-makers – namely a high likelihood of a significant negative impact on GDP. The challenge for government, however, is that these reductions in GDP will hit hardest in the future, while political attention and business strategy is firmly focused on performance in the very short term. Hence, as well as implementing the portfolio of climate change mitigation policies discussed here in the second half of this chapter, governments need to also address those factors currently leading to a short-term focus by business. These factors include the current structure of executive bonus packages which currently reward short-term quarterly profit results rather than profit results over the longer term. These factors also include the fact that superfund investors, which are investing citizens' superannuation to get the best return over a 20- to 30-year period to help with retirement, are currently required by fiduciary duty law to maximize quarterly returns rather than being encouraged to invest for the long term. How to address these barriers to longer-term investment and innovation, we covered in detail in Chapter 9 of our first book *The Natural Advantage of Nations, Business Opportunities, Innovation and Governance in the 21st Century*. Hence we will not cover it again here in detail; but it is important to note that this is a major issue upon which governments need to act to help enable large investment funds, CEOs and boards to make the longer-term investments needed to help business to reduce their greenhouse gas emissions without fear of their quarterly stock price being negatively affected. Such changes to corporate law and fiduciary duty are in the long-term interests of all, including business.

A large part of the challenge to understand the economic reality of the situation, as discussed earlier in this publication, is that many of these negative environmental impacts are externalized from the market, meaning they are not usually given an economic value, and hence as far as many past modelling exercises were concerned they were hidden or do not exist. Economists have explained for decades that our high pollution levels[5] and current unsustainable development paths arise largely from the fact that the environmental and social costs of development are not reflected in the costs of products and services to the market. For instance, as Stern points out, 'Those who create greenhouse gas emissions as they generate electricity, power their factories, flare off gases, cut down forests, fly in planes, heat their homes or drive their cars, do not have to pay for the costs of the climate change that results from their contribution to the accumulation of those gases in the atmosphere.'[6] So, with the costs of greenhouse gas emissions and pollution externalized from the prices of goods and services in the market, it is very difficult to accurately estimate the costs on the economy and thus estimate the economic cost benefits of taking action to reduce them. Furthermore, accurately assessing these costs is complicated by government interventions, such as perverse subsidies, which can lead to an even further reduction in the price of a range of emissions-intensive goods and services that result in their increased uptake, and lead to the increase in the environmental pressures associated with them.

In order to attract corporate investment to create jobs and help make domestic industries more internationally competitive, governments often provide subsidizes to businesses, such as the agricultural sector in response to international competition, and to fossil fuel-based industries in response to high costs for infrastructure development and maintenance. The intended result is to create jobs, encourage new industries, maintain existing industries in the face of international competition, and ensure essential services such as electricity and water are made more affordable, particularly to low-income citizens. However, such subsidies, which lower the costs of products and services, such as electricity and water, lead to inefficient or wasteful use whilst also discouraging investments in energy and water efficiency, further compounding the environmental pressure, and hence the costs of inaction. There are many examples of environmental pressures increasing in regions around the world, whereby the situation is being made worse through perverse subsidies:

- increasing algal blooms and higher nitrogen levels in groundwater and waterways, because of excessive use of subsidized fertilizers;
- overuse and wastage of water, because of the subsidies for the use of water;
- wastage of electricity, with appliances, equipment and lights being left on when not needed because of the subsidies for electricity;
- continued reliance on fossil fuel-based energy, encouraged by subsidies which also distort the market and make it harder for renewable options to compete.

UNEP and the Worldwatch Institute have identified at least US$650 billion worth of perverse subsidies globally, per annum, that are either directly or indirectly contributing to the degradation of the environment.[7] The reality is that a proportion of the costs that result from the increased environmental pressures from subsidized activities, such as those above, are borne directly by governments – and therefore citizens – through health care costs and public taxes. The remaining burden is borne by individuals through health-related impacts, and by the environment itself as the increased levels of toxins and pollution lead to the degradation of ecosystems.

When considering intervention into the market by providing subsidies, governments need to understand the broader implications in the short and long term, and undertake comprehensive cost–benefit analyses that use modern valuation methods to include historically externalized environmental and social costs. It is important to note that, in broad terms, this approach is not new. The famous British economist, Arthur Cecil Pigou, was one of the first economists to suggest the need to acknowledge the existence of externalities and the need to find ways to quantify their costs in his 1920 classic, *The Economics of Welfare.*[8] He described, for instance, how the smoke pouring from factories in Manchester, England, although being a sign of a growing industrial estate, had many indirect costs to the economy. Such costs, including extra laundry, repair of corroded buildings and the need for additional artificial lighting due to this smoke, were assessed in 1920 at £290,000 annually. Through this basic estimation of costs, not including health-related costs,

Pigou showed that for every £100 steel makers earned, they were doing £200 worth of damage. In effect, pollution victims (taxpayers) were subsidizing pollution causers, and as a result making the whole society dirtier and unhealthier. In this case the fact that the factories did not have to pay the direct costs (the £200) of the impacts caused by the smoke meant that little was done to reduce emissions. Shutting down the factories was, of course, not an option, but allowing unrestricted emissions turned out to be economically detrimental when the wider impacts were considered. Perhaps the government could have assigned a cost, or tax, on the level of smoke to encourage factories to reduce emissions. If set at an appropriate level this may have led to better economy-wide outcomes, especially if in doing so the factories also made a series of savings such as directly reducing costs for cleaning the stacks and indirectly improved productivity through a healthier workplace. A well-designed government response may have also seen some of the savings on the £200 returned to the factories to invest in further initiatives and research, and to offset the cost of changes to reduce emissions.

Many economic experts have argued for the externalized costs of greenhouse gas emissions to be internalized through putting a price on greenhouse gas emission pollution. This would result in higher prices for electricity and reductions in government subsidies for the industry for this very reason, as the increased price would encourage efficiency and reduced consumption, and promote exploration for alternatives to fossil fuel-based electricity, leading to reduced negative impacts. Economists argue that price particularly matters in the case of reducing greenhouse gas emissions to provide an incentive to replace inefficient appliances, cars, technologies with more efficient models and to enable new low-carbon alternative energy industries to compete with established fossil fuel industries.

Some go further like Ernst von Weizsäcker, who argued in *Factor Five*, 'Ultimately, resource consumption should be so expensive that total resource consumption rests in a perfect balance with sustainable supplies of renewable (or recycled) resources, and the resulting ability of the biosphere to assimilate the associated pollution and by-products.'[9] However, this is not the case in our current society, where the major reason why environmental degradation occurs is because the current balance reached in many economies around the world makes it cheaper to degrade nature than to care for it.[10]

Traditionally, certain interests in society have strongly opposed such efforts. Such interests have argued that taking action on climate change, through implementing a carbon price signal, would significantly harm the economy and lead to job losses. This argument has been used time and again to hinder and even halt progress at major international meetings on climate change. Many experts now argue, however, that purposeful climate change policy and effective implementation can achieve higher economic growth than business as usual, not less. We explain next why such varying assessments on the cost of action on climate change exist and examine the evidence to see who is right on this important question.

Estimating the Cost of Action on Climate Change

George Monbiot, in his book, *Heat*, summed up the debate about the global costs of action on stabilizing greenhouse gas emissions as follows:[11] 'I have not come across such wildly varying claims in any other field. Bjorn Lomborg's extraordinarily accurate figure – US\$37,632 billion – occupies one extreme; at the other end are people who claim that cutting carbon emissions will actually make us money, as the requirement to invest in new technologies will stimulate economic growth and energy efficiency will lead to financial efficiency.'

The reason that these estimates of the cost of action vary so much is that action is required across the entire economy, to differing levels, and over medium to long timeframes. In order to model this intricacy, a number of assumptions need to be made, and it is in these assumptions that much of the variability is created. In efforts to economically model the potential future costs of action on climate change, assumptions must be made about variables, such as: the potential economic benefits of various options in both the short and long term; how the cost of alternatives may vary in the future; and the rate that new technologies and practices will be taken up in the marketplace.

Tackling this issue, *The Stern Review*, having analysed the costs of action and inaction on climate change-related activities, concluded that the costs of action to the global economy would be roughly 1 per cent of GDP, while the costs of inaction could range from 5 to 20 per cent of GDP.[12] *The Stern Review* explains that the range of costs of inaction depends on assumptions about the level of direct and indirect impacts on environmental and human health, the effects of positive feedbacks being triggered, and the disproportionate burden on the poor and vulnerable. According to Stern, most economic modelling of the costs of stabilizing greenhouse gas levels finds that it would cost the economy anywhere between –1.0 per cent and 3.5 per cent of GDP by 2050.[13] *The Stern Review* explains in detail how this is due to the choice of assumptions made by economists upon which they build their economic models. In other words, depending on the assumptions modellers make about how rapid and how costly different strategies and actions will be, economic modelling has shown a range of outcomes leading to either slightly higher or slightly lower economic growth. Thus the interrogation by decision-makers of cost estimates in this area based on the validity of particular assumptions is vitally important to ensure that policies and strategies encourage investment which can lead to large greenhouse gas reductions, while contributing to economic and jobs growth.

When developing a set of assumptions to underpin economic modelling of the costs of action on climate change, economists need to be informed by knowledge and understanding in a range of areas related to research and development, education and capacity building, construction and implementation, operation and maintenance, financing, etc. In order to improve the estimates of the cost of action from economic models, economists need to work with a range of other professionals to inform efforts. In particular, economic modelling must be well informed by science and engineering if it is to make assumptions about the potential for engineered systems to simultaneously contribute to both economic growth and the reduction of environmental pressures – like the potential for renewable energy to replace fossil-based energy for example. This is because economic modelling needs to be informed by what is physically possible, and likewise, as previously pointed out, science and engineering on their own cannot provide all the answers without being informed by economics as to the impacts on the economy from a range of potential engineering and design options.

Next we explore a set of assumptions made in economic models of the costs of action to reduce greenhouse gas emissions, and in each case provide a summary of the latest advances and understanding from the engineering profession to inform assumptions made by economic models. Furthermore, this chapter seeks to provide decision-makers with a concise list of core considerations that need to be scrutinized to interpret the outcomes of economic modelling. The purpose of this chapter, and the leading work it presents, is to assist in achieving greater accuracy in estimations of the costs, and benefits, of action to reduce greenhouse gas emissions in an attempt to accelerate such efforts. The structure for the chapter is based on the seminal 1997 work of Repetto and Austin, which identified seven underlying assumptions that were found to explain 80 per cent of the differences in the results of various economic climate models at the time.[14] Repetto and Austin found that, for a 60 per cent carbon reduction by 2020, these seven assumptions can predetermine whether the model shows a 7 per cent decrease in GDP (shown as the worst case in Figure 7.1), or a 5 per cent per annum increase in GDP (shown as the best case), a swing of 12 per cent. Furthermore, and most importantly, as the results show, if the models are able to assume closer to the best case for each of the assumptions, the models show that the greater the target, say 60 per cent CO_2 abatement, the greater the positive impact on the economy.

To demonstrate the robustness of their approach, Repetto and Austin in 1997 also applied their analysis to a target that had received a great deal of modelling by 1997 – that of reducing US carbon emissions to 1990 levels by 2010 and stabilization of emissions thereafter. For the US, it has been calculated that this would require a 26 per cent reduction below projected business-as-usual emissions by 2020. This target had been analysed extensively in preparation for the COP-3 meeting in Kyoto in December 1997. Repetto and Austin found again that under favourable assumptions there was a positive increase in GDP per annum (2.4 per cent higher) and under unfavourable assumptions, there was a slight negative effect on GDP (2.4 per cent lower) by 2020. Repetto and Austin show that in this case the four assumptions that have the biggest impact were around:

1   the potential level of energy efficiency improvement;
2   the level of global cooperation;
3   whether carbon-tax or emissions-trading-permit revenues are recycled to reduce other taxes;
4   assumptions about the costs of inaction.[15]

This is a significant result as it indicates that if strategies can lead to outcomes close to the best case scenario in each of the four areas, this can actually lead to increasing economic growth, and furthermore the more aggressive the target the greater the economic growth can be. The results of course also indicate that if efforts to reduce greenhouse gas emissions are not close to the best case scenario, for instance through poor strategy and implementation, or the impact of conflict and corruption, then the greater the target for reduction the greater the negative impact on the economy. However, in the absence of such disruptive influences, and assuming that most nations can achieve close to the best case scenario, and even if the strategies lead to a net decrease in GDP (as the most pessimistic economic models predict), this will only slightly delay both people's wealth and the size of the economy reaching higher levels over the coming century.[15A] In 2002, Professor Stephen Schneider and Professor Christian Azar published findings in the paper 'Are the costs of stabilising the atmosphere prohibitive?',[16] which pointed out that the estimates by some economists of significant costs of purposeful action incorrectly assume that the cost will be borne in the short term. The research found, rather, that if countries, business and citizens focus on investing over time, first in the most cost-effective methods of mitigation, such as energy efficiency, and then more systemic options, the costs can be spread out over at least a number of decades, and economic growth will continue to be strong. Schneider and Azar showed that those arguing the case that nations cannot afford to take action on climate change because it will cost too much are ill informed because they have not accounted for the predicted growth of the global economy of 2–3 per cent a year throughout the 21st century. This means that by 2100 the global economy will have grown in size an order of eight to ten times what it was in 2000. As Schneider and Azar explain:

> *Top–down (economic) models typically suggest that the cost of a 50% reduction of global CO_2 emissions from baseline by 2050 would cost some 1–4% of global GDP, and a 75–90% reduction by 2100 would cost some 3–6%. But since these studies also assume that global income grows by 2–3% per year, this abatement cost would be overtaken after a few years of income growth. Thus, the cost of 'climate insurance' amounts to 'only' a couple of years delay in achieving very impressive growth in per capita income levels. To be ten times richer (than in 2000) in 2100 AD versus 2102 AD would hardly be noticed and would likely be politically acceptable as an insurance.*

Therefore, as the direct costs of inaction stand to increase in the future, significant efforts need to be focused on achieving the best case scenarios to provide the best long-term economic growth strategies for the world's economies.

The seven underlying assumptions identified by Repetto and Austin as

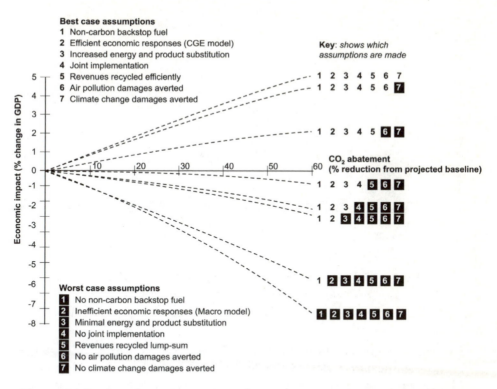

Figure 7.1 *Predicted impacts on GDP for various CO_2 abatement targets in 2020 – the effects of changing underlying assumptions one by one*

Source: Repetto and Austin (1997)[17]

significantly affecting the outcomes of economic modelling are summarized as follows.

1 Assumptions about the availability of non-carbon backstop fuels

Does the economic model assume non-fossil energy alternatives will become available in the future at a competitive price? Repetto and Austin found that some economic models completely excluded renewable technologies and thus massively overestimated the costs of action to reduce emissions. Even though renewable energy currently provides a small percentage of the current world energy demand of 138PWh (or 138 trillion KWh), estimates of the technical potential for harnessing renewable energy are in the range 152–1205PWh annually (see Figure 7.2 for a breakdown). Hence if the majority of the world's energy services were delivered using electricity, rather than oil, petroleum and natural gas, even the lowest estimate of 152PWh would be greater than the current global energy demand. Furthermore, if energy efficiency and demand management opportunities are harnessed to their full potential, as outlined in

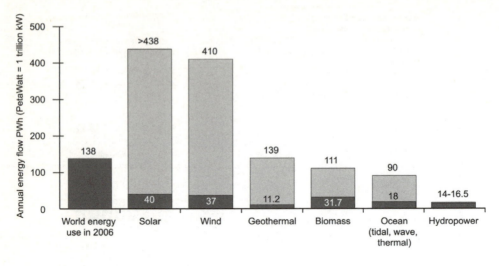

Figure 7.2 *Estimated technical potential of renewable resources relative to world energy consumption*

Source: Based on data for world energy use,[18] solar,[19] wind,[20] geothermal,[21] biomass,[22] ocean[23] and hydro[24]

Factor Five, world energy demand could be reduced in the order of 40–80 per cent,[25] significantly reducing the demand to be met by renewable sources. Many studies have been released that show staggering potential for expansion of the renewable energy sector, such as that by the Renewable Energy Policy Network for the 21st Century (REN21), suggesting that 'By 2050 renewable energy could contribute from up to 50% (in China, for example) to more than 90% (Australia) of national electricity demand, and in the range of 40% (Germany) to 80% (Indonesia) of national heating supply.' REN21's research shows that 'Targets for renewable energy now exist in at least 58 countries worldwide, including 13 developing countries, all EU countries, and in many states/provinces in the US and Canada.'[26]

Repetto and Austin found that other economic models recognized non-fossil energy sources but assumed 'that their availability is limited so that their prices will rise when used in greater volumes'.[27] However, in practice this is not the case, as recent innovations are enabling rapid improvements and cost reductions in the renewable energy sector. There have been cost reductions in several important areas of low-carbon technology over the last two decades. Also economies of scale and increased skill development tend to help bring down the manufacturing costs of different low-carbon technologies.

2 Assumptions about the efficiency of economic responses

Does the model assume that firms and consumers will reallocate their expenditures efficiently as energy prices increase? This assumption involves the reallocation of resources to reduce energy demand as the price of energy is increased, and the availability of opportunities to do so. There is a common assumption that most of the cost-effective improvements in energy efficiency and demand management have already been realized, but this assumption is flawed as there are in fact significant opportunities across the global economy, now detailed by a range of technical investigations and analysis showing that 30–90 per cent energy reduction opportunities commonly exist throughout most sectors of the economy.[28] For instance, the 2009 book *Factor Five*,[29] showed that in the order of 80 per cent improvements in energy productivity could be achieved across each of the major energy-intensive sectors (see Table 2.1 on page 36) through a whole systems approach, including: residential[30] and commercial[31] buildings; heavy industry such as steel[32] and cement;[33] light industry such as data centres[34] and pulp and paper;[35] agriculture;[36] the food and hospitality sector, including supermarkets[37] and restaurants;[38] and the transportation sector, including vehicle design,[39] discouraging car use,[40] increased public transport,[41] and modal shifts for freight carriage.[42] As Repetto and Austin explain, 'Most models assume a steady annual percentage improvement in energy efficiency, constant across all industries and over time.'[43] Hence these models inevitably underestimate the potential for energy savings, leading to an overestimate of the cost of action to reduce greenhouse gas emissions.[44] As well as being the quickest, easiest and most cost-effective way for business, government and households to reduce greenhouse emissions, reducing energy demand can also lead to significant infrastructure cost reductions. For instance, reductions to the level of electricity demand, particularly during peak periods, could effectively delay or even avoid the need to build new power stations, and reduce maintenance requirements on the electricity grid. This is particularly important as in practice, in order to deliver 1kW to the end-user the power station may actually need to generate in the order of 6–10kW to overcome the losses throughout the distribution system.[45] So, governments across the world are now investigating ways to improve existing regulatory frameworks to reward electricity utilities for helping their customers to use electricity more efficiently and effectively.[46]

A particular area to be considered under this assumption is transportation. Economic models and strategies for economic development often assume that building roads and highways for cities will lead to higher economic growth than encouraging and supporting the use of sustainable transport modes such as railways, buses, cycling and walking. However, a 1999 report to the World Bank[47] prepared by Australian transport experts Professor Peter Newman and Professor Jeff Kenworthy found that governments and cities that emphasize public transport, cycling and walking, can actually deliver stronger economic growth than a focus on providing roads for private vehicles and freight.[48] A number of economic benefits can result from a transition to low-carbon and sustainable transportation, including reducing transportation costs to business (particularly through better freight vehicle design and modal shifting[49] along with increasing video conferencing[50]), reducing congestion costs (currently costing nations billions of dollars and set to rise significantly by 2020[51]), reducing health costs and absenteeism, and improving productivity (with the risk of obesity and diabetes halving,[52] and absenteeism reducing by up to 80 per cent[53] in staff that cycle to work), and direct financial benefits to households (including avoiding a second car[54]).

3 Assumptions about energy and product substitution

To what extent does the model assume substitution among energy sources, energy technologies, products and production methods?

Substitution of Energy Source: A number of studies and investigations have been undertaken since the early 1980s that provide a wealth of information to support the proposal that renewable energy generation can not only contribute to peak demand periods throughout the day but can also make a meaningful contribution to base load power.[55] The main misunderstanding is that renewable forms of energy generation are at the whim of weather conditions. However, a range of options exist that are not dependent on weather conditions, such as co-generation, geothermal, biomass, tidal and types of hydro.[56] And even weather-dependent options such as solar, wind or tidal generators can be connected to a grid to allow them to be located across a state or region, taking advantage of differing wind, wave or tidal regimes.[57] After an extensive study of weather patterns for the UK, doctoral candidate Graham Sinden from Oxford University found that, 'between 1970 and 2003, there was not an hour, let alone a day or a week, with no wind across the UK.'[58]

To enable the integration of small-scale renewable energy plants into the grid a number of changes need to be made to develop what is now being referred to as a 'smart grid', and the overall balance of various levels of power generation will be affected, including the optimal mix of conventional base, intermediate and peak load power stations.[59] However, to maintain the reliability of the generating system at the same level, some additional peak load plant may be needed, along with allocation of back-up options for base and intermediate supply, estimated to be for instance between one-fifth and one-third of the wind capacity.[60] Furthermore, because the back-up is a peak load gas turbine plant, it does not have to be run continuously and can quickly be shut off while the turbines are generating adequate electricity. The need for back-up supply can be further reduced through the use of a range of emerging options for storage such as holding heat in water, rocks or thermo-chemical systems like ammonia.[61] Additionally, by taking a small-scale distributed approach to energy generation a range of benefits can be achieved, with Rocky Mountain Institute demonstrating that there are over 200 benefits compared to centralized plants that are rarely factored into economic models.[62] Such benefits include: shorter lead times for construction; reduced demand overshoot through shorter projected demand periods[63] (particularly as the various government initiatives outlined in Chapter 6 are set to at least slow the growth in demand for energy, having already flattened in California,[64] Sweden[65] and the Netherlands[66]); shorter lead times leading to shorter returns on investment;[67] and a decreased burden on utility cash flow.[68]

Substitution of Products: As described in the previous chapter, over time citizens, businesses and governments replace appliances, cars, equipment and infrastructure with new models. Purposeful and effective government policies can ensure that when this occurs, the new models purchased are far more energy efficient, and have produced far fewer greenhouse gas emissions in the manufacture, than the models they are replacing. This enables the economy over time to become far more energy efficient for minimal cost and can be applied across the economy, from electrical equipment to buildings.

Substitution of Production Methods: In the book *Factor Five*, we showed that there is significant potential to reduce carbon dioxide emissions through making changes to production methods such as changing from Portland cement to geopolymer cements or from oxygen blast furnaces to electric arc furnaces for steel making. Furthermore, targeting the reduction in non-CO_2 greenhouse gases through design or substitution, can be a cost-effective way to reduce overall emissions, with recent modelling by Massachusetts Institute of Technology (MIT) suggesting that strategies to reduce non-CO_2 emissions can reduce the costs of climate change abatement by up to two-thirds.[69] As Repetto and Austin explain, 'Economic models differ in the degree to which they represent these substitution possibilities. Highly aggregated models cannot incorporate the possibility of substituting one product for another.'[70] Thus economic models that fail to adequately model substitution effects, a very important strategy, will overestimate the costs of reducing greenhouse gas emissions.

4 Assumptions about involvement in joint implementation

Does the model assume that nations will take advantage of joint implementation? These approaches allow, for instance, a major multinational company to achieve a targeted emissions reduction by energy-saving measures at any of its facilities around the world, or at partner facilities, hence providing greater flexibility. Since CO_2 has the same effect on climate wherever it is released, companies should be incentivized to find the lowest-cost abatement possibilities wherever they occur. As part of the Kyoto Protocol, the Clean Development Mechanism (CDM) is an opportunity for corporations to create tradable carbon credits through investment in greenhouse gas reduction projects in the developing world. As Environment Business Australia explains:

> *Australia's efficiency in mining (both resource extraction and metals processing) and power generation is high. Now that Australia has ratified Kyoto, this efficiency would become a strong positive. Australia is highly regarded in these areas and the skills of heavy industry are exportable to developing countries who need to either build or modernize entire industry sectors. For example transforming Chinese power stations into efficient*

and less emissions-intensive sources of energy would provide a winning combination. Australia would be well-placed to embark on CDM projects of this nature.[71]

This can then provide a cost-effective way to help developing countries rapidly achieve a peaking in their greenhouse gas emissions, particularly through efforts to stop deforestation, the cheapest form of greenhouse gas abatement after energy efficiency.[72]

5 Assumptions about revenue recycling

Does the model assume that revenues raised from energy taxes or auctioned-off permits will be used to reduce taxes on labour and capital? Economic models usually assume that new revenue gained by carbon taxes or emission-trading permits will be distributed evenly across government spending. However, as Repetto and Austin show in detail in their report, if 'revenues are used to reduce existing taxes that penalize work, savings, and investment this would lower the net cost of reducing emissions and even have a net economic benefit. Some economic models even suggest that the substitution of a carbon tax for other taxes could provide net economic benefits, irrespective of the environmental gains.'[73] As we showed in Chapter 3, in 1994, modelling commissioned by the UK government showed that where revenues from pollution taxes were used to reduce employers' non-wage labour costs such as social security payments, superfund payments and payroll tax, this would help create 2.2 million jobs.[74] There is strong evidence that, as long as carbon tax revenue is recycled effectively, a carbon tax would have a strong employment dividend and could be used to assist the economy to become far more energy efficient.[75] One of the early examples of revenue recycling was the UK Climate Change Levy, which applied only to business energy use and was introduced in 2001. Under the levy most of the revenues gained from the slight increase to energy costs to business were returned to business by way of a 0.3 percentage point cut in employers' national insurance contributions for each employee. In a study of the performance of the programme, Cambridge Econometrics found in 2005 that it brought business investment forward on energy efficiency, and estimated that it will reduce overall unit costs for business by 0.13 per cent by 2010.[76] As part of the levy programme, the government also introduced other measures to help business raise energy efficiency levels, including climate change agreements as mentioned in Chapter 6; enhanced capital allowances for energy-saving technologies; and funding for the UK Carbon Trust which has provided education and training in energy efficiency and low-carbon sustainable energy to UK businesses.[77]

6 Assumptions about air pollution damages

Does the model assume that reductions in fossil fuel consumption will decrease air pollution damages? Action on climate change will also reduce other significant environmental pressures such as air pollution, as further presented in Chapter 11. Costs related to air pollution have been estimated to range from 2 to 4 per cent of GDP,[78] with the World Bank estimating in 2007 that Chinese air pollution health costs were in the order of 3.8 per cent of GDP.[79] Studies in Europe and the US estimate that the non-climate benefits of reducing greenhouse gas emissions, many associated with air pollution, would probably be as large, or larger, than the benefits of avoiding climate change.[80] These studies, quoted in the 1996 IPCC assessment, reported that the estimated economic savings from reduced air pollution damages may be sufficiently large to offset from 30 to 100 per cent of greenhouse gas reduction costs.[81] So there are clear opportunities for simultaneously improving health and cutting greenhouse gas emissions, as shown in Chapter 11, most obviously through policies related to transport systems, urban planning, building regulations and energy generation.[82] The *OECD Environmental Outlook to 2030* points out that other sources of air pollution will also be reduced by strong action on climate change, stating that 'Ambitious climate change policies would also lead to reductions in sulphur oxides of 20–30% and in nitrogen oxides of 30–40% by 2030.'[83] Despite these studies, some economic models of the costs of action to reduce greenhouse gas emissions have not taken the co-benefit of reduced air pollution into account. It is very important to note that most economic models assessing the costs of action versus inaction on climate change have ignored other significant co-benefits, such as:

- Investing in forests and habitat restoration to increase carbon storage provides significant economic co-benefits through maintaining vital ecosystem services and underpinning related business activities such as eco-tourism (see Chapter 8).
- Reducing the consumption of fresh water can also reduce consumption of energy, such as through the use of water-efficient shower-heads that reduce residential water demand (saving the utility energy) and reduce the volume of water to be heated (saving the resident energy). Investing in such energy/water nexus opportunities can be highly cost effective with rapid returns on investment; however, to date such opportunities have been largely ignored in economic modelling (see Chapter 9).
- Reducing greenhouse gas emissions through greater material productivity strategies such as recycling and remanufacturing can significantly reduce both energy and water consumption. Further reducing waste from a range of processes can lead to reduced toxins in the environment and potential impacts on human health (see Chapters 10 and 11).

7 Assumptions about climate change damages

Does the model assume that reductions in fossil fuel consumption will avert environmental damages associated with climate change? As Repetto and Austin explain: 'Most models used to simulate the economic impacts of carbon taxes and emission trading schemes have been adaptations of existing models designed for energy planning or for general macroeconomic forecasting, and were not able to incorporate the benefits of preventing climate change, or equivalently, the costs of doing nothing.'[84] There are a range of potential damages related to climate change that will result in significant costs to economies, including increasingly frequent and more intense natural disasters, reduced agricultural production, reduced revenue from nature-based tourism, relocation or protection from rising sea levels and storm surges, reductions to the carrying capacity of grazing land for livestock, increases in peak electricity use, increased losses from forest fires, increased risk of conflict over resources and increased health-related costs.[85] For instance, the 2008 Australian government's modelling of climate change included just one of the four main areas of potential damage and future costs and found that achieving a 25 per cent cut in greenhouse gas emissions by 2020 would result in a reduction of economic growth output of just over 0.1 per cent per annum until 2050 whereupon action on climate change starts to boost economic growth. So, if the modelling had included more of the foreseeable damage-related costs it is likely that the overall economic outcome would have been a net boost to economic growth from the early days of action.[86]

Economic modelling therefore is most useful to policy- and decision-makers when it is clear about the assumptions that it makes, and when it provides a range of estimates of potential costs and benefits to the economy, based on such assumptions. Decision-makers and policy-makers can then use this understanding about the effects of assumptions on the economic models to better design policy – in particular to improve performance in the areas that were assumed to have a low positive impact but have been identified as having potential for improvement – and to focus efforts on the most cost-effective ways to reduce greenhouse gas emissions with the fastest rates of return on investment.

Support for Ambitious Commitments to Emissions Reductions Targets

The clear message from analyses like that of Repetto and Austin is that, done effectively, ambitious greenhouse gas emission reduction targets can deliver a range of direct and co-benefits, while reducing risk of future costs. A combination of energy efficiency, demand management, sustainable transport and renewable energy opportunities can be harnessed to achieve cost-effective emissions reductions as shown in *Factor Five*. Furthermore, such ambitious targets can delay and even avoid the need for costly energy supply infrastructure. As far back as 1987, *Our Common Future*[87] showed that large greenhouse gas emissions reductions could be cost effectively and rapidly achieved through a range of energy efficiency and demand management approaches, In the 1991 book *Beyond Interdependence*, the author of the introduction to the book, Jim MacNeill built on *Our Common Future* with his colleagues and brought together further evidence to support ambitious commitments to emissions reduction targets, stating that 'an increasing number of studies show that industrialised nations can make substantial reductions in greenhouse gas emissions through energy efficiency and other measures that, at best, return a profit, and at worst, break even'.[88]

MacNeill and colleagues argued that the opportunities to improve energy efficiency in particular make it possible to achieve short-term targets very cost effectively. For example, they quoted from a Canadian study which showed that 20 per cent cuts could be achieved by 2005 with energy efficiency providing 75 per cent of the reductions. The remainder of the target could be achieved through substituting competitive non-fossil fuel sources of energy. This study showed that an investment of C\$74 billion would yield a net benefit of C\$150 billion on the basis of energy savings alone.[89] The team cited work by Tim Jackson of Lancaster University in the UK, stating in 1991 that he had 'calculated that a combination of energy efficiency measures and high efficiency gas-fired electricity generation could reduce CO_2 emissions from the UK stationary sector (i.e. utilities and buildings) by 46.5 per cent over current levels'.[90] Further studies presented included a study by Swedish state power company Vattenfall and the University of Lund which showed that CO_2 emissions in Sweden from the heat and power sectors could be reduced by a third between 1987 and 2010, mainly though energy efficiency improvements and a shift to biomass-based power generation. MacNeill and colleagues then outlined a range of studies showing that the structural adjustment costs to shift national economies to 50 per cent reductions in greenhouse gas emissions or more over the longer term were affordable.

One of the first such studies discussed was the 1989 study by McKinsey & Company, commissioned by the Netherlands Ministry of Housing, Physical Planning, and Environment:

> *McKinsey & Company [were commissioned] to analyse the potential for reducing two greenhouse gases, CO_2 and CFCs, in three regions, OECD, Eastern Europe and the rest of the world. These measures apply to approximately two-thirds of all greenhouse gas emissions and they cover a sufficiently broad range of actions to provide a fair assessment of policy opportunities ... The most important conclusion of the study, was that from a purely technical point of view it appears possible to reduce greenhouse gas emissions by almost 50 per cent by the year 2005 relative to then-prevailing levels, and at the same time to continue economic growth at a realistic pace in each of the three target areas.*[91]

As a result of the investigation McKinsey concluded that many measures to mitigate greenhouse gas emissions would be quite profitable and would 'more than offset the initial investment and incremental operational costs [through] a variety of energy efficiency measures in for example, transportation, space heating, and industrial process heat and significant net afforestation. Implementation of these measures might eventually result in a 30–40 per cent reduction in greenhouse gas emissions over time.'[92] By the mid-1990s, these economic and technical results were further backed up by new and important technical studies by the IPCC and other experts,[93] and books like *Factor Four* in 1997.[94] These studies showed that significant reductions in greenhouse gas emissions would be cost effectively achievable over the longer term. The growing consensus was also shown in 1997, when a group of 2500 economists, including six Nobel laureates, led by Kenneth Arrow and Robert Solow, issued the following declaration at a January 1997 meeting of the American Economics Association:

> *The balance of evidence suggests discernible human influence on global climate. As economists, we believe that global climate change carries with it significant environmental, economic, social and geopolitical risks and that preventative steps are justified. Economic studies have found that there are many potential policies to reduce greenhouse gas emissions for which the total benefits outweigh the total costs. For the United States in particular, sound economic analysis shows that there are policy options that would slow climate change without harming American living standards, and these measures may in fact improve U.S. productivity in the longer run.*[95]

Since 2000, numerous comprehensive studies and investigations have been published which provide business and governments around the world with detailed guidance on how to achieve large reductions of greenhouse gas emissions reductions using existing technologies. The following list of studies, published in the last ten years, demonstrates that the most effective strategies use a portfolio of options, including energy efficiency, demand management, renewable energy, fuel switching, transport planning, and emissions trading and ecological taxation opportunities. The following list of detailed studies shows that it is possible to achieve ambitious greenhouse gas reduction targets, with existing technologies, in the order of at least 20–40 per cent by 2020, and 60–100 per cent by 2050, whilst maintaining strong economic and jobs growth. A sample are listed here:

- Interlaboratory Working Group (2000) *Scenarios for a Clean Energy Future*, Oak Ridge National Laboratory, Berkeley, CA, Lawrence Berkeley National Laboratory, CA and National Renewable Energy Laboratory, CO.
- Jochem, E., Favrat, D., Hungerbahler, K., Rudolf von Rohr, Ph., Spreng, D., Wokaun, A. and Zimmermann, M. (2002) 'Steps towards a 2000 watt society – A White Paper on R&D of energy-efficient technologies', Fraunhofer Institute for Systems and Innovation Research.

- Torrie, R., Parfett, R. and Steenhof, P. (2002) 'Kyoto and beyond: The low emission path to innovation and efficiency', Report for David Suzuki Foundation and Canadian Climate Action Network, Canada.
- Lovins, A., Datta, K., Feiler, T., Rábago, K., Swisher, J., Lehmann, A. and Wicker, K. (2002) *Small Is Profitable: The Hidden Economic Benefits of Making Electrical Resources the Right Size*, Rocky Mountain Institute, CO.
- Turton, H., Ma, J., Saddler, H. and Hamilton, C. (2002) *Long-Term Greenhouse Gas Scenarios: A Pilot Study of How Australia Can Achieve Deep Cuts in Emissions*, Australia Institute Paper no 48, the Australia Institute.
- Mintzer, I., Leonard, J. A. and Schwartz, P. (2003) *US Energy Scenarios for the 21st Century*, Pew Center on Global Climate Change, US.
- Department of Trade and Industry (2003) *Our Energy Future – Creating a Low Carbon Economy*, Energy White Paper, UK Department of Trade and Industry, Version 11.
- Bailie, A., Bernow, S., Castelli, B., O'Connor, P. and Romm, J. (2003) *The Path to Carbon Dioxide-Free Power: Switching to Clean Energy in the Utility Sector*, a study by Tellus Institute and Center for Energy and Climate Solutions for the World Wildlife Fund, US.
- Jochem, E. (eds) (2004) *Steps towards a Sustainable Development: A White Book of R&D for Energy Efficient Technologies*, Fraunhofer Institute for Systems and Innovation Research.
- Saddler, H., Diesendorf, M. and Denniss, R. (2004) *A Clean Energy Future for Australia: Energy Strategies*, WWF, Canberra.
- Lovins, A. B., Datta, E. K., Bustnes, O. E., Koomey, J. G. and Glasgow, N. J. (2004) *Winning the Oil Endgame: Innovation for Profits, Jobs and Security*, Rocky Mountain Institute, CO.
- Belhaj, M. and Norrman, J. (2004) 'Low carbon economy', discussion paper for the European Regional Network on Sustainable Development workshop, IVL Swedish Environmental Research Institute Ltd.
- National Institute for Environmental Studies (2005) *Japan: Low Carbon Society Scenarios toward 2050*, National Institute for Environmental Studies, Japan.
- Stern, N. (2006) *The Stern Review: The Economics of Climate Change*, Cambridge University Press, Cambridge.
- Makhijani, A. (2007) *Carbon-Free and Nuclear-Free: A Roadmap for U.S. Energy Policy*, Nuclear Policy Research Institute and the Institute for Energy and Environmental Research.
- Smith, M. and Hargroves, K. (2007) 'Analysis of the costs of inaction versus the costs of action on climate change for Australia', a submission by Griffith University, ANU and The Natural Edge Project to the Garnaut Review, Australia.
- Diesendorf, M. (2007) *Paths to a Low Carbon Future: Reducing Australia's Greenhouse Gas Emissions by 30 per cent by 2020*, Sustainability Centre, Australia.

- Hatfield Dodds, S., Jackson, E. K., Adams, P. D. and Gerardi, W. (2007) *Leader, Follower or Free Rider? The Economic Impacts of Different Australian Emission Targets by 2050*, Climate Institute, Sydney.
- Helweg-Larsen, T. and Bull, J. (2007) *Zero Carbon Britain*, Centre for Alternative Technology Publications.
- IPCC (2007) *Climate Change 2007: Mitigation of Climate Change*, Contribution of Working Group III to the Fourth Assessment Report of the Intergovernmental Panel on Climate Change, Cambridge University Press, Cambridge.
- National Institute for Environmental Studies (2007) *Japan Scenarios towards a Low Carbon Society – Feasibility Study for 70% CO_2 Emission Reduction by 2050 Below 1990 Level*, National Institute for Environmental Studies, Japan.
- Smith, M., Hargroves, K., Stasinopoulos, P., Stephens, R., Desha, C. and Hargroves, S. (2007) *Energy Transformed: Sustainable Energy Solutions for Climate Change Mitigation*, Griffith University, ANU, The Natural Edge Project, and CSIRO, Australia.
- Department of Trade and Industry (2007) *Meeting the Energy Challenge: A White Paper on Energy*, Department of Trade and Industry, UK.
- Institute of Public Policy Research, WWF and RSPB (2007) *80 Per Cent Challenge: Delivering a Low Carbon Britain*, Institute of Public Policy Research, WWF and Royal Society for the Protection of Birds, UK.
- McKinsey & Company (2007) *Curbing Global Energy Demand Growth: The Energy Productivity Opportunity*, McKinsey & Company.
- Gorner, S., Lewis, A., Downey, L., Slezak, J., Michael, J. and Wonhas, A. (2008) *An Australian Cost Curve For Greenhouse Gas Reduction*, McKinsey Consulting, Australia/New Zealand.
- Pembina Institute and David Suzuki Foundation (2008) *Deep Reductions, Strong Growth: An Economic Analysis Showing that Canada Can Prosper Economically while Doing its Share to Prevent Dangerous Climate Change*, Pembina Institute and David Suzuki Foundation.
- von Weizsäcker, E., Hargroves, K., Smith, M., Desha, C. and Stasinopoulos, P. (2009) *Factor Five: Transforming the Global Economy through 80% Improvements in Resource Productivity*, Earthscan, London.
- ClimateWorks Australia (2010) *Low Carbon Growth Plan for Australia*, Climate Works Australia.

To make it easy to access this wealth of knowledge, most of these studies are freely available online. This knowledge, combined with a growing level of experience in implementing solutions successfully in economies around the world, provides a realistic foundation for hope that our global community has a realistic chance of stabilizing greenhouse gas emissions in the coming century.

However, given the urgency and the scale of the response needed, the reality may be that what is needed is in fact a bipartisan national/international approach, implemented with 'war-time' urgency. Such a bipartisan effort would call for significant cooperation across governments and within national economies, reminiscent of the achievements of the co-operation between the Allies during World War II, which in the period 1939–1945, for instance, led to huge jobs growth with unemployment falling in the US from 14.6 per cent to 1.9 per cent, and GDP grew 55 per cent in six years. In 1942 US annual economic growth was 12 per cent – that is 12 times more than in the 2007–2008 financial year.[96] Wages grew 65 per cent over the course of the war to far outstrip inflation, and company profits boomed, all at a time when personal consumption was dampened by the sale of war bonds, some basic goods and foods were rationed, and at the height of the mobilization 42 per cent of the economy was directed towards the war effort:[97]

> *… the United States must build planes and tanks and guns and ships to the utmost limit of our national capacity. We have the ability and capacity to produce arms not only for our own forces, but also for the armies, navies, and air forces fighting on our side. Let no man say it cannot be done. It must be done – and we have undertaken to do it. I have just sent a letter of directive to the appropriate departments and agencies of our Government, ordering that immediate steps be taken: First, to increase our production rate of airplanes so rapidly that in this year, 1942, we shall produce 60,000 planes, 45,000 tanks, 20,000 anti-aircraft guns and 6,000,000 deadweight tons of merchant ships as compared with a 1941 completed production of 1,100,000.*
> President Franklin D. Roosevelt, 6 January 1942[98]

By the end of the Second World War, the US had far exceeded these ambitious targets – by, for example, producing a staggering 229,600 aircraft between 1942 and 1944.[99] Effectively the orders of the president and the imperative of the war galvanized a nation to take immediate action to refocus its industrial system towards a new goal – as, for instance, corset makers began producing grenade belts and webbing, and even merry-go-round makers produced gun mounts, and astonishingly, as Brown points out, 'from early 1942 through the end of 1944, nearly three years, there were essentially no cars produced in the United States'.[100] Although there is a great deal to learn from the period of industrial development, the challenge faced by climate change and environmental systems decline is that it is gradual and its early impacts are easily ignored, unlike the events of Sunday morning, 7 December 1941, which led to President Roosevelt stating that the rapid creation of 'a multitude of implements of war will give the Japanese and the Nazis a little idea of just what they accomplished in the attack at Pearl Harbor'.[101] However, as there has not yet been a unifying and immediately compelling force to rapidly respond to reducing environmental pressures, perhaps lessons can be learned from the rapid peacetime industrialization of many Asian economies, and in particular the 'Asian Tigers' of South Korea, Singapore, Taiwan and Hong Kong.

The rapid transformation of these countries' economic production demonstrates what can be achieved when a nation's government, private sector, and research and education institutions work together towards a clear vision to rapidly position themselves for new and emerging markets. In each of the 'Asian Tigers' the rapid industrialization was underpinned by high personal savings rates, the encouragement of investment, and the prioritization of skills and capacity building. In his work *The Rise of the Korean Economy*,[102] Byung-Nak Song lists 'the most important components of the Korean model and necessary base for countries attempting to grow at high rates over a sustained period of time. These include a long-term national vision, communitarian capitalism, competent leaders, an ability to manage change and innovate, and cultural congruency.'[103] Clearly each of these characteristics in some form will be needed to also enable a rapid shift to sustainable development. However, unlike the progress of the Asian Tigers, which led in most cases to increasing levels of pressure on the environment, the creativity and ingenuity of a nation's governments, private sector, civil society, and research and education sector, needs to be focused on a clear vision to decouple economic growth significantly from environmental pressures.

The examples of the 'Allies in World War II' and the 'Tiger economies' also highlight the key role played by government in enabling rapid economy-wide transformations to occur, in both war and peace time. These two historical examples illustrate the key role of government in planning and coordination, investing in and directing research and development, providing incentives to drive new investment, and supporting research and capacity building, to enable such a rapid transformation. In more recent times the potential for governments to take a leadership role in driving economic development that both reduces environmental pressures and enhances economic growth was clearly shown in the response to the 2008 global economic crisis. As can be seen in Figure 7.3, countries such as South Korea and China invested significant proportions of their total fiscal stimulus into what is referred to as a 'green stimulus'. An outstanding example is that of South Korea, spending by far the highest percentage (81 per cent) of its stimulus package – some US$30 billion (or 2.3 per cent of its annual GDP) – on green investment in order to create green jobs.

South Korea's stimulus package is a valuable example of leadership, and includes payments for:

- Housing: US$6 billion for:
  - the construction of 1 million green homes;
  - energy efficiency upgrades for 1 million homes;
  - energy conservation improvements in villages and schools;
  - the installation of LED lighting in public facilities.
- Cars: US$1.8 billion towards the development of fuel-efficient vehicles, such as electric and hybrid cars, by automakers Hyundai and Kia.
- Trains and bikes: US$7 billion for:

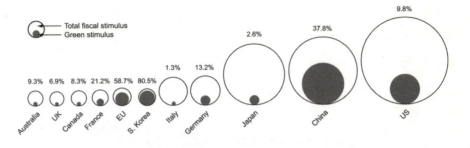

Figure 7.3 *Eco-friendly components of fiscal stimuli 2008–2009*

Source: Based on data from HSBC[104]

- – the expansion of electrified tracks;
- – the construction of new high-speed rail links;
- – the construction of more than 4000km of bicycle paths.
- Water: US$11.1 billion for river restoration and water resource management.
- Forestry: US$1.7 billion for:
  - – forestry management, including tree planting to increase carbon sink capacity;
  - – the construction of new facilities that use wood as biomass energy.
- Recycling: US$670 million for resource recycling, including the construction of electricity plants that run on the methane emissions generated from incinerating rubbish.

The South Korean government believes that such investments will drive economic growth and help position South Korean companies at the forefront of the next wave of innovation – the green economy.

Hence, it is clear that government, working with business, universities and the community, can rapidly transform the focus of its entire economy, and that a key part of any decoupling agenda will be the rapid innovation and development of low-carbon technologies and practices across all sectors of the economy. Many are now also realizing that this will require the development of a range of complementary options through a portfolio approach, and will need full commitment from governments, the private sector and civil society if it is to yield meaningful results.

A Framework for Decoupling Greenhouse Gas Emissions – Stabilization Trajectories

Innovation is, by its nature, unpredictable. Some technologies will succeed and others will fail. The uncertainty and risks inherent in developing low-emission technologies are ideally suited to a portfolio approach ... While markets will tend to deliver the

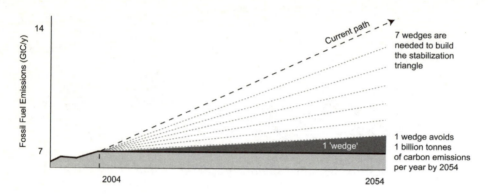

Figure 7.4 *A stabilization triangle for reducing carbon emissions from fossil fuels*

Source: Pacala and Socolow (2004)[105]

least-cost short-term option, it is possible they may ignore technologies that could ultimately deliver huge cost savings in the long term.

Sir Nicholas Stern, *The Stern Review*, 2006[106]

Understanding the need for a portfolio approach, in 2004 economists Pacala and Socolow of Princeton's Carbon Mitigation Initiative proposed a 'stabilization triangle' in *Science*.[107] The paper identified 15 existing technologies that could each prevent 1 billion tonnes (1Gt) of global carbon emissions each year, shown in Table 7.1.

Of these, the authors showed that just seven of the available 'wedges' would stabilize carbon emissions from fossil fuel use by 2054 relative to 2004 levels, effectively stopping the growth of, or peaking, these emissions, as seen in Figure 7.4. Once the levels of carbon emissions from fossil fuels have peaked, then they need to be further reduced to fall within the ability of the global biosphere to assimilate such emissions – estimated to require a further four wedges. Further action is also required to reduce the remaining gases including CO_2 from deforestation and peat thaw, along with a range of non-CO_2 gases from industry and manufacturing, which as Chapter 1 outlined, when converted to an equivalent volume of CO_2 represent 27 per cent of total greenhouse gas emissions. This work by Pacala and Socolow presents a solid case to show that there exists a range of realistic technological options for achieving significant reductions in greenhouse gas emissions. Furthermore, the authors readily acknowledge that their list of 15 'wedges' excludes many other potentially significant areas of greenhouse gas reductions. As Pacala reflects, 'For efficiency improvements we had only three examples and there were many more we could have added in. It is amazing how much of a wedge you get just out of replacing the remaining incandescent light bulbs with compact fluorescents. Also the number of options for biological sequestration is really large.'[108]

Table 7.1 *15 existing technologies that in 2004 were estimated to prevent 1 billion tonnes a year worth of carbon emissions by 2054*

Existing technology	Action required (in relation to 2004 figures)
Car efficiency	• Doubling fuel efficiency of 2 billion cars from 30 to 60 miles per gallon (12.75 to 25.5 kilometres per litre)
Reducing car dependency	• Decreasing the number of car miles travelled by half
Green buildings	• Using best efficiency practices in all residential and commercial buildings
Decarbonizing energy supply	• Replacing 1400 coal electric plants with natural gas-powered facilities
	• Capturing and storing emissions from 800 coal electric plants
	• Producing hydrogen from coal at six times the 2004 rate and storing the captured CO_2
	• Capturing carbon from 180 coal-to-synfuels plants and storing the CO_2
	• Adding double the current global nuclear capacity to replace coal-based electricity
	• Increasing wind electricity capacity by 50 times the 2004 level, for a total of 2 million large windmills worldwide
	• Producing current coal-based electricity with twice today's efficiency
	• Installing 700 times the current capacity of solar electricity
	• Using 40,000 square kilometres of solar panels (or 4 million windmills) to produce hydrogen for fuel cell cars
Reducing CO_2 emissions through agriculture	• Increasing ethanol production 50 times by creating biomass plantations with area equal to one-sixth of world cropland
Conserving forests	• Eliminating tropical deforestation and creating new plantations on non-forested land to quintuple current plantation area
Conserving soils	• Adopting conservation tillage in all agricultural soils worldwide

Source: Pacala and Socolow (2004)[109]

Pacala and Socolow provided a strong counter to the argument that major new technologies need to be developed before significant mitigation of emissions can begin. Most of the 'wedges' are based on existing technologies and build on areas of the economy that have reached entry-level maturity in the market. Their work is complemented by the large range of studies listed earlier which also demonstrate that large reductions can be achieved with existing knowledge and technologies. The fact that so many existing low-carbon technologies are ready highlights to what extent there has been significant failure to get the right policies and incentives to ensure rapid uptake of such technologies and greenhouse gas reduction strategies. This means that much of the policy and industrial strategy used to achieve development in the past will need to be critically reassessed if it is to continue to deliver strong progress well into the future. Effectively the challenge now is not 'what' to do or 'how' to do it, but rather 'where' it can be done and by 'when' within the context of each nation's economy. Designing a strategy to transition a national economy in such a way as to maximize the overall economic growth and stability while delivering large sustained emissions reductions is going to be the challenge of the 21st century, and will be a key component of any national strategy for sustainable development.

The complexity of the decoupling challenge arises from understanding that even if every nation, company and community on the planet agreed to become climate neutral it could not happen overnight. According to UNEP's fourth *Global Environmental Outlook*, 'Due to inertia in economic, social, cultural and institutional systems, transitions to more sustainable modes of production and consumption are slow and cumbersome. Typically, it takes 30–50 years or more before such changes are fully implemented, although the first improvements can be seen at a much earlier stage.'[110] It does not make financial sense to simply discard large amounts of existing industries and replace them with new ones overnight. Nor does it make sense to do nothing until such infrastructure is ready to be replaced. Adjunct Professor Alan Pears from RMIT University, Australia reflected to the authors, suggestions for several alternatives:

> *Technological innovation, behaviour change and redirection of discretionary expenditure can all accelerate the rate of change and enhance the economics of early closure or modification of high emission facilities. For example, we know that efficient, well-managed existing office buildings use two-thirds less energy than the worst buildings: improved management and carefully selected upgrades can bring the poor performers up to much more efficient levels. Similarly, detailed analysis of industrial processes often identifies key elements of systems that are driving inefficiency, and modification can significantly improve performance. Behaviour change also offers potentially large savings: throughout business and industry, a lot of equipment is simply left running when not needed. And skilled operators who are given effective feedback can drive processes much more efficiently than others.[111]*

In *Factor Five*, we have outlined how to do this for most of the major greenhouse gas-emitting sectors of the economy. *Factor Five* shows that rapid change is possible and the knowledge and proven models of success already exist for most major sectors of the economy. What is needed now is a major effort in retraining parts of the workforce, though updating vocational and higher education takes time, as well as rebuilding protocols, design standards, health and safety standards, checks and balances, building financing structures, effective metering and monitoring, creating accreditation and performance assessment, and influencing or building new supply chains, manufacturing plants, transport and freight options.

A sophisticated strategy to reduce greenhouse gas emissions needs to focus on the most cost-effective short-term opportunities from efficiency improvements, fuel switching, avoided deforestation and personal behaviour changes, whilst investing in R&D to further reduce the costs of biofuels, wind, solar and hydrogen options, as shown in Figure 7.5, taken from *The Stern Review*. An

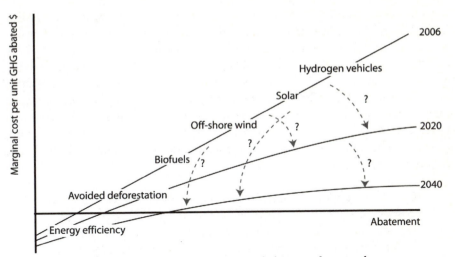

Figure 7.5 *Relative marginal costs of climate change abatement per unit greenhouse gas*

Source: Stern (2006)

effective strategy will deliver both the short-term emissions reductions cost effectively, but will also create conditions required to underpin ongoing sustained levels of reduction by lowering the cost of future options.

> *Historical experience shows that technological development does not stand still in the energy, or other sectors. There have been major advances in the efficiency of fossil-fuel use; similar progress can also be expected for low-carbon technologies as the state of knowledge progresses ... The cost of technologies tends to fall over time, because of learning and economies of scale ... Using a portfolio of technologies is cheaper because individual technologies are prone to increasing marginal costs of abatement, making it cheaper to switch to an alternative technology or measure to secure further savings. There is also a lot of uncertainty about which technologies will turn out to be cheapest so it is best to keep a range of technology options open. It is impossible to predict accurately which technologies will experience breakthroughs that cause costs to fall and which will not.*
> Sir Nicholas Stern, *The Stern Review*, 2006[112]

As well as investing in R&D of low-carbon technology, nations need to take stock of their infrastructure, and plan and implement changes needed to support low-carbon forms of buildings, energy and transportation. Such infrastructure transformation needs to be transitioned according to its lifespan as part of standard creation, maintenance and upgrading of such systems, all being complex processes.

Understanding this, economists Repetto and Austin cite economic studies for the US and Canadian economies in the late 1990s which showed that the key is to adopt policies which 'encourage early development of energy-efficient and low-carbon technologies and discourage long-lived investments in carbon-intensive energy facilities'.[113] Further work by Adjunct Professor Alan Pears, shown in Figure 7.6, highlights the reality that, for long-lasting assets, if economy-wide emissions reductions are to be achieved, the strategy will need to include actions to improve existing plants, to affect the process of expansions and refurbishments, and to influence the design of new projects. Pears explains:

> *[Greenhouse Gas] Emission reduction sounds like a daunting prospect, and many people imagine that we will have to freeze in the dark, shut down industry, and face misery. But remember, we don't have to slash greenhouse gas emissions in a couple of years – we are expected to phase in savings over decades. This allows us to take advantage of the fact that most energy producing or using equipment, from fridges and computers to cars and power stations, has to be replaced every 5 to 30 years. So we can minimize costs by making sure that, when old equipment is replaced, low greenhouse-impact alternatives are installed. For example, by 2020, most of Australia's coal-fired power stations will be more than 30 years old – and they will have to be re-built or replaced: renewable energy, cogeneration and high efficiency energy supply technologies (such as fuel cells) could replace them.*
>
> Professor Alan Pears, RMIT, 2006[114]

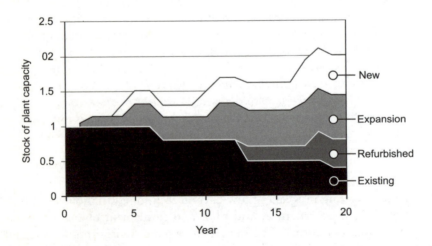

Figure 7.6 *Simplified schematic of large industrial plant assets over time*

Source: Courtesy of Alan Pears[115]

For equipment with a more rapid turnover, the performance of existing equipment may not be so important. However, it is surprising how long many old items of equipment actually remain in use (often while their efficiency deteriorates), so there is a case for strategies that encourage their retirement – as long as new alternatives are close to long-term optimum efficiency. As Stern points out:

> *Costs would start to rise very rapidly if emissions had to be reduced sharply before the existing capital stock in emissions-producing industries would otherwise be replaced and at a speed that made structural adjustments in economies very abrupt and hence expensive. Abrupt changes to economies can themselves trigger wider impacts, such as social instability, that are not covered in economic models of the costs of mitigation ... Technological change eventually has to get annual emissions down to their long-run sustainable levels without having to accelerate sharply the retirement of the existing capital stock, if costs are to be contained.*[116]

Given the complexity of broad-scale changes to industrial economies, there is a need for a greater level of urgency and sophistication around the realities of developing cost-effective strategies and policies. *The Stern Review* explored 'stabilization trajectories' in detail, highlighting two distinct phases:

- global emissions need to stop growing, that is, emissions levels need to peak;
- there needs to be a sustained reduction of annual greenhouse gas emissions across the entire global economy of anywhere between 3 to 5 per cent per annum depending on the timing of the peak and the requirement for emissions reductions.

A range of potential trajectories were suggested, which would achieve different final stabilization concentrations, as shown in Figure 7.7.

Before considering these findings further we pause to clarify some assumptions about the levels of greenhouse gas emissions, how they are arrived at, and the units used to represent them. The y axis of Figure 7.7 shows 'Global emissions' in units of $GtCO_2e$, meaning 'billion (giga) tonnes of carbon dioxide equivalent'. The 2005 amount for the 'business-as-usual' trajectory of around $46GtCO_2e$ is arrived at by adding the IPCC[117] estimates of around $26GtCO_2$ from fossil fuel-related emissions only (equivalent to 7.2GtC which is used as the current level in Figure 7.4), around $8GtCO_2$ from peat and permafrost releases combined with deforestation-related emissions, and around $12GtCO_2e$ from emissions of non-CO_2 greenhouse gases. This last category is an important one and is calculated as the equivalent volume of CO_2 based on each of the non-CO_2 gas's global warming potentials (GWPs). For example the volume of

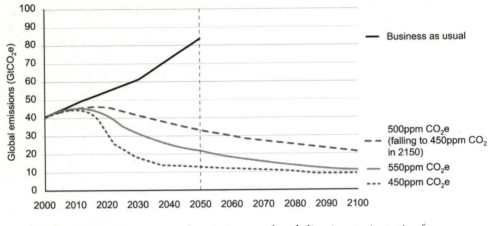

Figure 7.7 *Business-as-usual emissions and stabilization trajectories for 450–550ppm CO_2e*

Source: Based on data from Stern (2006)

methane (CH_4) is multiplied by 21, as it is 21 times more effective at warming the atmosphere than CO_2. The volume of sulphur hexafluoride (SF_6) is multiplied by 16,300 times, meaning that its relatively limited emissions actually carry a much larger global warming potential. Hence this is why the curves in Figure 7.7 begin at around $40GtCO_2e$ for the year 2000. When considering how low the emissions need to be in 2050, the best case scenario of around $8-10GtCO_2e$ is reached by assuming, first, that by 2050 the high GWP non-CO_2 gases will be mostly removed from industrial activity, as there is no way to absorb them from the atmosphere. Second, it is assumed that the current level of removal from the atmosphere of CO_2 and CH_4 of around $11.7GtCO_2$ per year will be reduced to around $9GtCO_2$ by 2050.

With these assumptions in mind, each of the trajectories in Figure 7.7 peak between 2012 and 2018, with the IPCC calling for the peak by 2015.[118] However given the amplifying affect of the various feedback loops such as permafrost or sea-ice melt, even a peak in 2015 may not secure such a limit in temperature increase. As the Australian Garnaut Climate Change Review concluded:[119]

> *A target concentration of around 450ppm CO_2e has been widely discussed in the literature, and was the basis of the 25–40% emissions reduction proposal for developed countries discussed at the Conference of Parties in Bali. Achieving stabilization at 450ppm CO_2e target would require ... global emissions peaking around 2010. A less ambitious target, leaving much higher risks of dangerous climate change, is to restrict greenhouse gas concentrations to 550ppm CO_2e ... [this would require] global emissions ... peaking by 2030. These stabilization paths are only illustrative, as there are multiple paths to any specific concentra-*

Table 7.2 *Illustrative emissions paths to stabilization*

Stabilization level (CO$_2$e)	Date of peak global emissions	Global emissions reduction rate (% per year)
450ppm	2010	7.0
500ppm (falling to 450ppm in 2150)	2010	3.0
	2020	4.0–6.0
	2030	5.0–5.5
550ppm	2015	1.0
	2020	1.5–2.5
	2030	2.4–4.0
	2040	3.0–4.5

Source: Stern (2006)

tion target. However, they make the point that only urgent, large, and effective global policy change leaves any hope of holding atmospheric concentrations at the 450ppm or even the 550ppm levels.

Modelling undertaken for *The Stern Review* indicates that for example a 450ppm trajectory with a peak in emissions by 2010 would need to be followed by a sustained reduction of 7.0 per cent per year, while the 550pm trajectory with a peak in 2030 would need to be followed by a sustained reduction of 2.5–3.0 per cent, as shown in Table 7.2. Stern pointed out that:

Paths (with a late peak) requiring very rapid emissions cuts are unlikely to be economically viable ... [however] early abatement paths (with an early peak) offer the option to switch to a lower emissions path if at a later date the world decides this is desirable. This might occur for example, if natural carbon absorption weakened considerably or the damages associated with a stabilisation goal were found to be greater than originally thought. Similarly, aiming for a lower stabilisation trajectory may be a sensible hedging strategy, as it is easier to adjust upwards to a higher trajectory than downwards to a lower one.[120]

As can be seem from Table 7.2 the date of the peaking in global emissions has a significant impact on the level of sustained annual reductions, or tailing, then required to achieve the desired global stabilization goal. *The Stern Review* states that: 'The longer action is delayed, the harder it will become. Delaying the peak in global emissions from 2020 to 2030 would almost double the rate of [annual] reduction needed to stabilise at 550ppm CO$_2$e. A further ten-year delay could make stabilisation at 550ppm CO$_2$e impractical, unless early actions were taken to dramatically slow the growth in emissions prior to the peak.'[121] Since *The Stern Review* was published in 2006, global CO$_2$e emissions are tracking higher than predicted and several significant non-linear positive feedbacks have been unleashed, as discussed in Chapter 1, placing further urgency on the issue.

Key to managing an ambitious approach to emissions reduction is to achieve a balance in the timing of the emissions peak and the corresponding requirement for a tailing. According to Stern, 'Pathways involving a late peak in emissions may effectively rule out lower stabilisation trajectories and give less margin for error, making the world more vulnerable to unforeseen changes in the Earth's system.'[122]

The challenge is the range of combinations of 'peaks' and corresponding 'tails' (i.e. trajectories), that may deliver a given stabilization level, especially when considering that each trajectory may have a different impact on the economy. A late peak will allow short-term reduction levels to be relaxed but will then require a greater level of annual sustained reduction to meet the overall target. An early peak will require a rapid short-term reduction level, but these efforts will be rewarded by a lower level of required sustained annual reductions, providing greater flexibility. As Figure 7.8 shows, there are a range of 'peaks' and corresponding 'tails' that may deliver any given stabilization level. Both sets of trajectories in Figure 7.8 are the result of modelling a stabilization level of 550ppm; however, each will have a different impact on the economy. A late peak, shown by the '2030 high peak' curve, will allow a slow short-term reduction level but will require a 4.0 per cent annual sustained reduction, whereas an early peak, shown by the '2020 low peak' curve, will require a rapid short-term reduction level but will afford a level of sustained reduction at 1.5 per cent per annum.

It is vital, then, that the nations of the world and business focus on working together to peak global emissions as soon as possible. *The Stern*

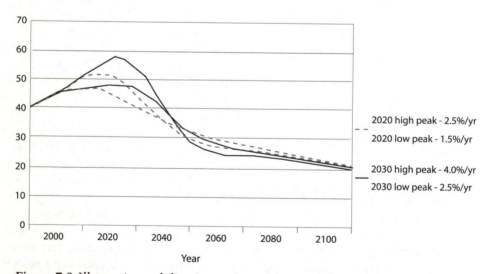

Figure 7.8 *Illustrative stabilization trajectories to stabilize at 550ppm* CO_2e

Source: Stern, N. (2006)

Review points out that, 'Given that it is likely to be difficult to reduce emissions faster than around 3% per year, this emphasises the importance of urgent action now to slow the growth of global emissions, and therefore lower the peak'.[123]

Understanding this imperative to move early, as we showed in Chapter 6, businesses across the globe have already begun to build strategies and make commitments to sustained reductions. For example the inaugural members of the Chicago Climate Exchange in 2005 (including DuPont, ST Microelectronics, Baxter Health Care, the City of Chicago, Natural Capitalism Inc. and 12 other businesses) contracted to reduce their emissions by 1 per cent a year. In 2008 the Exchange had over 330 members – companies, cities, states, counties, universities, NGOs and others with new members being required to reduce their emissions by 2 per cent a year.[124] Salt Lake City's Mayor Rocky Anderson stated in a letter to the Seattle Mayor: 'In Salt Lake City we have been working diligently since 2002 to meet the greenhouse gas emissions reduction goal set forth in the Kyoto Protocol. If every local and state government entity, every business, and every individual takes available, effective measures to significantly reduce greenhouse gas emissions, we can reverse the trend toward global warming. If we do not, the consequences will be devastating.' Salt Lake City set a goal to reduce emissions by 3 per cent per year for a ten-year period, with its long-term goal to reduce emissions 70 per cent by 2040. By 2007 the city had already achieved a 31 per cent reduction in CO_2 emissions in its municipal operations over the 2001 baseline, surpassing its goal to meet the Kyoto Protocol standard by 148 per cent, and seven years early.[125]

A benefit of using stabilization trajectories as the basis for policy development is that it allows nations to capitalize on already abundant opportunities for short-term reductions to achieve the peak, while also building the experience and economies of scale to seriously tackle the issue of tailing through sustained reductions. The beauty of the sustained reductions model is that it allows an economy to stage out the activities it undertakes to allow for certain industries, or even nations, to be given more time, or 'head room', to respond, while the industries or nations that can make short- and medium-term gains contribute to achieving the average overall reduction. As Stern points out, 'It will be cheaper, per tonne of GHG, to cut emissions from some sectors rather than others because there will be a larger selection of better-developed technologies in some ... However, this does not mean that the sectors with a lack of technology options do nothing in the meantime. Indeed, innovation policies will be crucial in bringing forward clean technologies so that they are ready for introduction in the long term.'[126] Hence strategies and policies to achieve stabilization trajectories will no doubt dominate national economic development strategies in the coming decades.

Another level of complexity is evident when considering each country's role in relation to global stabilization goals. First, efforts across the economy of each country need to be combined, and then the efforts of each country need to be

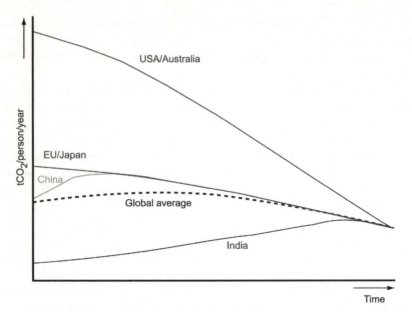

Figure 7.9 *A stylized illustrative scenario showing contraction and convergence for different countries, with 'head room' for the rapidly developing economies*

Source: Garnaut Climate Change Review (2008)

aggregated to achieve the global stabilization curve. The Australian Garnaut Climate Change Review outlined the need to develop country-specific trajectory curves based on per capita emissions to be aggregated to achieve the overall global stabilization trajectory, as shown in Figure 7.9.[127] As the report pointed out: 'Broad international agreement will require acceptance of global limits on emissions, sharing of rights to emissions across countries within these limits, and international collaboration to help achieve the national restrictions.'[128] Furthermore, such per capita allowances may be weighted against the economic activity of a particular country to further allow a meaningful allocation.

It is widely agreed that expecting the rapidly developing countries such as China and India to stop completely consuming fossil fuels is unreasonable considering that developed countries have capitalized on fossil fuels for decades to underpin their development. The strength of the stylized scenario presented in Figure 7.9, is that it provides flexibility for both China and India to address emissions within rapidly emerging economies. Furthermore China,[129] Brazil and India[130] are all now making increasingly significant commitments to improving energy performance. For instance, a major 2009 analysis entitled *2050 China Energy and CO$_2$ Emissions Report*[131] by China's National Development and Reform Commission and the Development Research Center of the State Council shows that energy growth in China will significantly slow by 2020 and energy growth and carbon emissions will peak around 2030 if the government continues to be serious about 'strengthened measures' to improve energy efficiency and accelerates uptake of renewable energy options. This is a very important and encouraging study. The fact that by 2020 China's energy growth will have significantly slowed gives the world as a whole a chance to peak global emissions by 2020 if all nations implement the full array of potential solutions as outlined in books such as *Factor Five*. Further encouraging signs are emerging from other leading emerging economies like Brazil, which has committed to achieving close to 40 per cent greenhouse gas reductions by 2020 from business-as-usual levels. To conclude, as a national strategy will seek to balance improvements in various parts of the economy over time to meet its annual reduction goals, an international strategy would need to balance improvements in various countries over time to allow for the most cost-effective overall transition. Such a global programme would understand that the conditions in various countries will favour the realization of specific opportunities for reductions in emissions, such as reducing defor-estation, changing to particular agriculture types and techniques, particular transportation options (due to density or social structures), or types of renew-able energy generation, and that these efforts need to be appropriately combined to achieve the overall goals. Furthermore, the interplay between the timing of infrastructure cycles, as mentioned above, between countries will affect the ability for various countries to implement changes, and such timelines again need to be considered as part of a global programme. Hence not only will the development of national strategies to stabilize greenhouse gas emissions to preferred levels present an enormous challenge, the need to then combine efforts internationally to achieve the overall stabilization presents an unprecedented – yet possible – global challenge.

Notes

1   Stern, N. (2006) *The Stern Review: The Economics of Climate Change*, Cambridge University Press, Cambridge, Chapters 3–6.

2   OECD (2008) *The Costs of Inaction on Key Environmental Challenges*, OECD, Paris.

3   Stern, N. (2006) *The Stern Review: The Economics of Climate Change*, Cambridge University Press, Cambridge, p10.

4   Stern, N. (2006) *The Stern Review: The Economics of Climate Change*, Cambridge University Press, Cambridge, p10.

5   Aylward, B., Bishop, J. and Barbier, E. B. (1991) *Guidelines for Applying Environmental Economics in Developing Countries*, International Institute for Environment and Development (IIED), Gatekeeper Series no LEEC 91–02, London; Conway, A. G. (1991) 'A role for economic instruments in reconciling agricultural and environmental policy in accordance with the polluter pays princi-ple', *European Review of Agricultural Economics*, vol 18, no 3–4, pp467–484.

6   Stern, N. (2006) *The Stern Review: The Economics of Climate Change*, Cambridge University Press, Cambridge, see 'Introduction'.

7   Roodman, D. (1999) *The Natural Wealth of Nations: Harnessing the Market and the Environment*, Worldwatch Environment Alert Series, W. W. Norton and

Earthscan, London. This publication provides a detailed discussion of government subsidies and the environment.

8   Pigou, A. (1932) *The Economics of Welfare*, fourth edition, Macmillan, London.

9   von Weizsäcker, E., Hargroves, K., Smith, M., Desha, C. and Stasinopoulos, P. (2009) *Factor Five: Transforming the Global Economy through 80% Improvements in Resource Productivity*, Earthscan, London.

10 Daily, G. C. and Ellison, K. (2002) *The New Economy of Nature: The Quest to Make Conservation Profitable*, Island Press, Washington, DC.

11 Monbiot, G. (2006) *Heat. How to Stop the Planet Burning*, Penguin Books, p51.

12 Stern, N. (2006) *The Stern Review: The Economics of Climate Change*, Cambridge University Press, Cambridge, 'Executive summary', p10.

13 Stern, N. (2006) *The Stern Review: The Economics of Climate Change*, Cambridge University Press, Cambridge, p10.

14 Repetto, R. and Austin, D. (1997) *The Costs of Climate Protection: A Guide for the Perplexed*, World Resources Institute, Washington, DC.

15 Repetto, R. and Austin, D. (1997) *The Costs of Climate Protection: A Guide for the Perplexed*, World Resources Institute, Washington, DC.

15A OECD (2008) *OECD Environmental Outlook to 2030*, OECD, Paris.

16 Schneider, S. and Azar, C. (2002) 'Are the costs of stabilising the atmosphere prohibitive?', *Ecological Economics*, vol 42, issues 1–2, pp73–80.

17 Repetto, R. and Austin, D. (1997) *The Costs of Climate Protection: A Guide for the Perplexed*, World Resources Institute, Washington, DC.

18 EIA (2006) *International Energy Annual 2006*, World Energy Consumption, Energy Information Administration.

19 Gross, R., Leach, M. and Bauen, A. (2003) 'Progress in renewable energy', *Environment International*, vol 29, pp105–122 (estimating 40PWh/y); Fridleifsson, I. (2003) 'Status of geothermal energy amongst the world's energy sources', *Geothermics*, vol 32, pp379–388 (estimating 438PWh/y).

20 Hoogwijk, M., de Vries, B. and Turkenburg, W. (2004) 'Assessment of the global and regional geographical, technical and economic potential of onshore wind energy', *Energy Economics*, vol 26, pp889–919 (37PWh/y); Gross, R., Leach, M. and Bauen, A. (2003) 'Progress in renewable energy', *Environment International*, vol 29, pp105–122 (40PWh/y); de Vries, B., van Vuurenb, D. and Hoogwijk, M. (2007) 'Renewable energy sources: Their global potential for the first half of the 21st century at a global level: An integrated approach', *Energy Policy*, vol 35, pp2590–2610 (61PWh/y); Hoogwijk, M., de Vries, B. and Turkenburg, W. (2004) 'Assessment of the global and regional geographical, technical and economic potential of onshore wind energy', *Energy Economics*, vol 26, pp889–919 (96PWh/y); Fridleifsson, I. (2003) 'Status of geothermal energy amongst the world's energy sources', *Geothermics*, vol 32, pp379–388) (178PWh/y); Sovacool, B. and Watts, C. (2009) 'Going completely renewable: Is it possible (let alone desirable?)', *The Electricity Journal*, vol 22, no 4, pp 95–111 (410PWh/y); Jacobson, M. (2009) 'Review of solutions to global warming, air pollution, and energy security', *Energy & Environmental Science*, vol 2, pp148–173 (410PWh/y).

21 IGA (2001) *Information Report in Support of Submission: 'Contribution of Geothermal Energy to Sustainable Development'*, International Geothermal Association (11.2PWh/y); Stefansson, V. (2000) 'Competitive status of geothermal energy', *Proceedings of World Geothermal Congress*, International Geothermal Association, Japan (22.4PWh/y); Gross, R., Leach, M. and Bauen, A. (2003) 'Progress in renewable energy', *Environment International*, vol 29, pp105–122 (40PWh/y); Bertani, R. (2003) 'What is geothermal potential?', *Newsletter of the*

International Geothermal Association, no 53, July–September, p2 (41.7PWh/y); and WEA (2000) *World Energy Assessment – Energy and the challenge of sustainability*, UNDESA, UNDP, WEA, WEC, p517 (139PWh/y).

22   Yamamoto, H., Fujino, J. and Yamaji, K. (2001) 'Evaluation of bioenergy potential with a multi-regional global-land-use-and-energy model', *Biomass and Bioenergy*, vol 21, no 3, pp185–203 (31.7PWh/y); IEA Bioenergy (2007) 'Potential contribution of bioenergy to the world's future energy demand', Media Release, IEA Bioenergy (55.6PWh/y); de Vries, B., van Vuurenb, D. and Hoogwijk, M. (2007) 'Renewable energy sources: Their global potential for the first half of the 21st century at a global level: An integrated approach', *Energy Policy*, vol 35, pp2590–2610 (59PWh/y); Fischer, G. and Schrattenholzer, L. (2000) 'Global bioenergy potentials through 2050', *Biomass & Bioenergy*, vol 20, pp151–159 (62.5PWh/y); Fridleifsson, I. (2003) 'Status of geothermal energy amongst the world's energy sources', *Geothermics*, vol 32, pp379–388 (76.7PWh/y); and Rockefeller Foundation (2008) 'A sustainable biofuels consensus', www.uneptie.org/energy/bioenergy/documents/pdf/SBC_April08.pdf, accessed 12 July 2009 (111PWh/y).

23   IEA (2007) *Energy Technologies at the Cutting Edge*, International Energy Technology Collaboration, International Energy Agency.

24   Fridleifsson, I. (2003) 'Status of geothermal energy amongst the world's energy sources', *Geothermics*, vol 32, pp379–388 (13.9PWh/y); Sovacool, B. and Watts, C. (2009) 'Going completely renewable: Is it possible (let alone desirable?)', *The Electricity Journal*, vol 22, no 4, pp 95–111 (14.4PWh/y); IHA (2000) *Hydropower and the World's Energy Future: The Role of Hydropower in Bringing Clean, Renewable, Energy to the World*, International Hydropower Association (14.4PWh/y); Boyle, G. (2004) *Renewable Energy*, Oxford University Press, Oxford (15PWh/y); Bartle, A. (2002) 'Hydropower potential and development activities', *Energy Policy*, vol 30, no 14, pp1231–1239 (15PWh/y); Jacobson, M. (2009) 'Review of solutions to global warming, air pollution, and energy security', *Energy & Environmental Science*, vol 2, pp148–173 (16.5PWh/y).

25   von Weizsäcker, E., Hargroves, K., Smith, M., Desha, C. and Stasinopoulos, P. (2009) *Factor Five: Transforming the Global Economy through 80% Improvements in Resource Productivity*, Earthscan, London.

26   REN21 (2007) *Renewables Global Status Report*, Renewable Energy Policy Network for the 21st Century, Paris.

27   Dean, A. and Hoeller, P. (1992) 'Costs of reducing CO_2 emissions: Evidence from six global models', *OECD Economic Studies*, vol 19 (Winter), pp15–47, cited in Repetto, R. and Austin, D. (1997) *The Costs of Climate Protection: A Guide for the Perplexed*, World Resources Institute, Washington, DC.

28   Schmidheiny, S. (1992) *Changing Course: A Global Business Perspective on Development and the Environment*, MIT Press, Boston, MA; Halliday, C. O., Hart, S. and Ahuja, G. (1996) 'Does it pay to be green? An empirical examination of the relationship between emission reduction and firm performance', *Business Strategy and the Environment*, vol 5, pp30–37; von Weizsäcker, E., Lovins, A. and Lovins, L. H. (1997) *Factor Four: Doubling Wealth, Halving Resource Use*, Earthscan, London; Lovins, A. and Lovins, L. H. (1997) *Climate: Making Sense and Making Money*, Rocky Mountain Institute, CO; Hawken, P., Lovins, A. B. and Lovins, L. H. (1999) *Natural Capitalism: Creating the Next Industrial Revolution*, Earthscan, London; Schaltegger, S. and Synnestvedt, T. (2002) 'The link between "green" and economic success: Environmental management as the

crucial trigger between environmental and economic performance', *Journal of Environmental Management*, vol 65, pp339–346; Schmidheiny, S. and Watts, P. (2002) *Walking the Talk, The Business Case for Sustainable Development*, World Business Council for Sustainable Development, Greenleaf Publishing, Sheffield, UK; McDonough, M. and Braungart, M. (2002) *Cradle to Cradle – Remaking The Way We Make Things*, North Point Press, NY; Innovest Strategic Value Advisors (2004) *Corporate Environmental Governance: A Study into the Influence of Environmental Governance and Financial Performance*, Innovest Strategic Value Advisors; Jochem, E. (ed) (2004) *Steps Towards a Sustainable Development: A White Book of R&D for Energy Efficient Technologies*, Fraunhofer Institute for Systems and Innovation Research; Hargroves, K. and Smith, M. H. (eds) (2005) *The Natural Advantage of Nations: Business Opportunities, Innovation and Governance in the 21st Century*, Earthscan, London.

29 von Weizsäcker, E., Hargroves, K., Smith, M., Desha, C. and Stasinopoulos, P. (2009) *Factor Five: Transforming the Global Economy through 80% Improvements in Resource Productivity*, Earthscan, London.

30 Clinton Climate Initiative (2008) 'C40 Cities: Buildings, Freiburg, Germany', Clinton Climate Initiative, US.

31 US EPA (2004) 'Boston's Saunders Hotel Group awarded for energy efficiency and good environmental practices', Press Release, 18 November, US EPA.

32 Worrel, E., Price, L. and Galitsky, C. (2004) *Emerging Energy-Efficient Technologies in Industry: Case Studies of Selected Technologies*, Ernest Orlando Lawrence Berkeley National Laboratory, Berkeley, CA.

33 Smith, M., Hargroves, K., Desha, C., and Stasinopoulos, P. (2009) 'Factor 5 in eco-cements', CSIRO *ECOS* Magazine, no 149.

34 Google (2009) 'Efficient Computing – Introduction', Google.com, www.google.com/corporate/green/datacenters/, accessed 3 April 2010.

35 Catalyst Paper Corporation (undated) 'Environmental manufacturing principles', www.catalystpaper.com/socialresponsibility/socialresponsibility_environment_ma nufacturingprinciples.xml, accessed 23 March 2009.

36 UK Carbon Trust (2006) *Agriculture and Horticulture: Introducing Energy Saving Opportunities for Farmers and Growers*, UK Carbon Trust, Oxford, UK.

37 Tesco (2008) *Sustainability Report: More Than the Weekly Shop: Corporate Responsibility Review*, Tesco Inc.; Whole Foods Market (2008) *Whole Foods Market 2008 Annual Report,* Whole Foods Market, Texas.

38 Bordeaux Quay (undated) 'Eco pages: Saving energy', www.bordeaux-quay.co.uk/ ecopages/eco_saving_energy.php, accessed 25 February 2009: Whole Foods Market (2008) *Whole Foods Market 2008 Annual Report,* Whole Foods Market, Texas; Carvalho, M. D. (2007) 'The Acorn House bears fruit', www.communityenergy.info/index_nu.php?page=20, accessed 3 April 2010.

39 Lovins, A. B. (2007) 'Reinventing the wheels: The automotive efficiency revolution', *Economic Perspectives*, vol 1, no 2.

40 Diaz, O. E. (2001) 'Car free Bogotá: The response to the transportation challenge', *The New Colonist*, www.newcolonist.com/bogota.html, accessed 3 April 2010.

41 Northern Territory Government (2007) *NT Greenhouse Gas Emissions – Transport*, Northern Territory Government.

42 Freight on Rail (2009) 'Useful facts and figures', www.freightonrail.org.uk/ FactsFigures.htm, accessed 9 April 2009; Frey, C. and Kuo, P. (2007) 'Assessment of potential reduction in greenhouse gas (GHG) emissions in freight

transportation', *Proceedings, International Emission Inventory Conference*, US Environmental Protection Agency, Raleigh, NC, 15–17 May.

43 Manne A. S. and Richels, R. G. (1990) 'The costs of reducing U.S. CO_2 emission: Further sensitivity analyses,' *The Energy Journal*, vol 11, no 4, pp69–78, cited in Repetto, R. and Austin, D. (1997) *The Costs of Climate Protection: A Guide for the Perplexed*, World Resources Institute, Washington, DC.

44 De Canio, S. (1993) 'Barriers within firms to energy efficiency investments', *Energy Policy*, vol 21, no 9, pp901–914.

45 Lovins, A. B. (2005) 'More profit with less carbon', *Scientific American*, September.

46 Kushler, M. (2006) *Aligning Utility Interests with Energy Efficiency Objectives: A Recent Review of Efforts at Decoupling and Performance Incentives*, American Council for an Energy Efficient Economy, Washington, DC, p5.

47 Kenworthy, J., Laube, F., Newman, P. and Barter, P. (1997) *Indicators of Transport Efficiency in 37 Cities*, Report to World Bank, ISTP, Murdoch University, Western Australia.

48 Newman, P. (1998) 'Transport', interview transcript from Radio National Earthbeat, 12 September.

49 Chrisafis, A. (2007) 'Sarkozy puts France on green track', *Guardian* (UK), 26 October.

50 Porteous, J. (2009) 'Videoconferencing to cut public sector airfares and emissions', *CSIRO ECOS Magazine*, April–May.

51 BTE (2007) *Estimating Urban Traffic and Congestion Cost Trends for Australian Cities*, Working Paper no 71, Bureau of Transport and Regional Economics, Department of Transport and Regional Services, Canberra.

52 WHO (2000) *Transport, Environment and Health*, WHO Regional Office for Europe, Copenhagen.

53 Shayler, M. et al (1993) *Bikes Not Fumes: The Emission and Health Benefits of a Modal Shift from Motor Vehicles to Cycling*, Cyclist's Touring Club, Surrey.

54 NRMA (2003) 'True running costs of cars revealed by NRMA Consulting', NRMA, 11 July 2003, www.mynrma.com.au/cps/rde/xchg/mynrma/hs.xsl/releases2003_4.htm, accessed 3 April 2010.

55 Diesendorf, M. (2007) *Greenhouse Solutions with Sustainable Energy*, UNSW Press, Sydney.

56 Dickson, M. H. and Fanelli, M. (2004) *What is Geothermal Energy?*, Istituto di Geoscienze e Georisorse, CNR, Pisa.

57 Outhred, H. (2003) *National Wind Power Study*, A report prepared for the Australian Greenhouse Office, Version 8. This study explores readily accepted wind energy penetration levels in Australia's electricity networks; Focken, U., Lange, M., Monnich, K. and Waldl, H. (2002) 'Short-term prediction of the aggregated power output of wind farms – statistical analysis of the reduction of the prediction error by spatial smoothing effects', *Journal of Wind Engineering and Industrial Aerodynamics*, vol 90, pp231–246.

58 Sinden, G. (2005) *Wind Power and the UK Resource*, Environmental Change Institute, Oxford University, Oxford.

59 Martin, B. and Diesendorf, M. (1982) 'Optimal thermal mix in electricity grids containing wind power', *Electrical Power & Energy Systems*, no 4, pp155–161.

60 Dale, L., Milborrow, D., Slark, R. and Strbac, G. (2004) 'Total cost estimates for large-scale wind scenarios in UK', *Energy Policy*, no 32, pp1949–1956.

61 Lovegrove, K. et al (2007) *Closed Loop Thermo-chemical Energy Storage System Using Ammonia*, ANU Solar Thermal Energy Research, Canberra.

62   Lovins, A. B. et al (2002) *Small is Profitable: The Hidden Economic Benefits of Making Electrical Resources the Right Size*, Rocky Mountain Institute, CO, p173.
63   Swisher, J. (2005) *Cleaner Energy, Greener Profits: Fuel Cells as Cost-Effective Distributed Energy Resources*, Rocky Mountain Institute, CO.
64   Shirley, W. (2006) *Decoupling Utility Profits From Sales*, Prepared for Arizona Decoupling Stakeholder Meeting, Regulatory Assistance Project (RAP), US.
65   Miljo, S. (2005) *Swedish Report on Demonstrable Progress*, Ministry of Sustainable Development, Sweden.
66   Netherlands Environmental Assessment Agency and National Institute for Public Health and the Environment (2004) *Environmental Balance 2004 – Summary*, Netherlands Environmental Assessment Agency and National Institute for Public Health and the Environment.
67   Hoff, T. E. and Herig, C. (1997) 'Managing risk using renewable energy technologies', in Awerbuch, S. and Preston, A. (eds) *The Virtual Utility: Accounting, Technology and Competitive Aspects of the Emerging Industry*, Kluwer Academic, Boston, MA, p22, Figure 7.
68   Kahn, E. (1978) *Reliability Planning in Distributed Electric Energy Systems*, Lawrence Berkeley National Laboratory, Berkeley, CA, p333; Lovins, A. B. (1981) 'Electric utility investments: Excelsior or confetti?', *Journal of Business Administration*, vol 12, no 2, pp91–114; Lovins, A. B. (1982) 'How to keep electric utilities solvent', *Energy Journal*, cited in Lovins, A. B. et al (2002) *Small is Profitable: The Hidden Economic Benefits of Making Electrical Resources the Right Size*, Rocky Mountain Institute, CO.
69   Reilly, J., Jacoby, H. and Prinn, R. (2008) *Multi-Gas Contributors to Global Climate Change: Climate Impacts and Mitigation Costs of Non-CO$_2$ Gases*, MIT Press, Boston, MA.
70   Repetto, R. and Austin, D. (1997) *The Costs of Climate Protection: A Guide for the Perplexed*, World Resources Institute, Washington, DC.
71   Environment Business Australia (2002) *The Business Case for Ratifying Kyoto*, Environment Business Australia.
72   Stern, N. (2006) *The Stern Review: The Economics of Climate Change*, Cambridge University Press, Cambridge.
73   Repetto, R. and Austin, D. (1997) *The Costs of Climate Protection: A Guide for the Perplexed*, World Resources Institute, Washington, DC.
74   DRI et al (1994) *Potential Benefits of Integration of Environmental and Economic Policies*, Graham and Trotman and Office for Publications of the European Communities, Brussels.
75   Proops, J., Faber, M. and Wagenhals, G. (1993) *Reducing CO$_2$ Emissions: A Comparative Input-Output Study for Germany and the UK*, Springer Verlag, Berlin.
76   UK Treasury (2006) *The Climate Change Levy Package*, UK Treasury.
77   UK Treasury (2006) *The Climate Change Levy Package*, UK Treasury.
78   OECD (2008) *OECD Environmental Outlook to 2030*, OECD, Paris.
79   World Bank (2007) *Cost of Pollution in China: Economic Estimates of Physical Damages*, World Bank, Washington, DC.
80   Ekins, P. (1995) 'Rethinking the costs related to global warming: A survey of the issues', *Environmental and Resource Economics*, vol 6, no 3, pp231–277; Jorgenson, D., Goettle, R., Gaynor, D., Wilcoxen, P. and Slesnick, D. (1995) *Social Cost Energy Pricing, Tax Recycling and Economic Change*, Final Report submitted to the US EPA, EPA contract no 68-W2-0018, August, cited in Repetto, R. and Austin, D. (1997) *The Costs of Climate Protection: A Guide for the*

Perplexed, World Resources Institute, Washington, DC.

81 IPCC (1996) *Climate Change 1995: The Economic and Social Dimensions of Climate Change*, Contribution of Working Group III to the Second Assessment Report of the Intergovernmental Panel on Climate Change, Cambridge University Press, Cambridge.

82 Mellgren, D. (2008) 'OECD: World must act on climate change', *The Economic Times*, 5 March, http://economictimes.indiatimes.com/news/international-business/OECD-World-must-act-on-climate-change/articleshow/2840577.cms, accessed 3 April 2010.

83 OECD (2008) *OECD Environmental Outlook to 2030*, OECD, Paris.

84 Repetto, R. and Austin, D. (1997) *The Costs of Climate Protection: A Guide for the Perplexed*, World Resources Institute, Washington, DC.

85 Smith, M., Hargroves, K., Stasinopoulos, P., and Desha, C. (2008) 'Analysis of the costs of inaction versus the costs of action on climate change for Australia', Submission to the Garnaut Review, The Natural Edge Project and Griffith University Business School, Australia.

86 Pears, A. (2008) 'The national picture: The Pears Report', *Renew Magazine – Technology for A Sustainable Future*.

87 WCED (1987) *Our Common Future*, Oxford University Press, Oxford.

88 MacNeill, J., Winsemius, P. and Yakushiji, T. (1991) *Beyond Interdependence: The Meshing of the World's Economy and the Earth's Ecology*, Oxford University Press, Oxford, citing Goldenberg, J., Johannson, T., Reddy, A. and Williams, E. (1985) *Energy for Development*, World Resources Institute, Washington, DC.

89 The DPA Group Inc. (1989) *Study on the Reduction of Energy-Related Greenhouse Gas Emissions*, commissioned by the Ontario Ministry of Energy (with support from all the federal and provincial energy departments of Canada), cited in MacNeill, J., Winsemius, P. and Yakushiji, T. (1991) *Beyond Interdependence: The Meshing of the World's Economy and the Earth's Ecology*, Oxford University Press, Oxford.

90 Jackson, T. (1991) 'The least cost greenhouse planning: Supply curves for global warming abatement', *Energy Policy*, vol 19, cited in MacNeill, J., Winsemius, P. and Yakushiji, T. (1991) *Beyond Interdependence: The Meshing of the World's Economy and the Earth's Ecology*, Oxford University Press, Oxford.

91 MacNeill, J., Winsemius, P. and Yakushiji, T. (1991) *Beyond Interdependence: The Meshing of the World's Economy and the Earth's Ecology*, Oxford University Press, Oxford.

92 MacNeill, J., Winsemius, P. and Yakushiji, T. (1991) *Beyond Interdependence: The Meshing of the World's Economy and the Earth's Ecology*, Oxford University Press, Oxford.

93 Such as: Ishitani, H. and Johansson, T. B. et al (1996) *Climate Change 1995: Impacts, Adaptation and Mitigation Options*, Contribution of Working Group II to the Second Assessment Report of the Intergovernmental Panel on Climate Change, Cambridge University Press, Cambridge, see Chapter 19; Nakicenovic, N. et al (1995) *Global Energy Perspectives to 2050 and Beyond*, World Energy Council and International Institute for Applied Systems Analysis, London; Lazarus, M. (1993) *Towards a Fossil Free Energy Future – the Next Energy Transition*, Stockholm Environment Institute, Boston Center, Boston, MA and Greenpeace International, Amsterdam.

94 von Weizsäcker, E., Lovins, A. B. and Lovins, L. H. (1995) *Factor Four: Doubling Wealth, Halving Resource Use*, Earthscan, London.

95 Arrow, K., Jorgenson, D., Nordhaus, W., Krugman, P. and Solow, R. (undated) 'Economists' letter on global warming', cited in United Eco-Action, http://uneco.org/Global_Warming.html#Economists' Letter on Global Warming, accessed 12 August 2008.

96 Walton, F. (1956) *Miracle of World War II: How American Industry Made Victory Possible*, Macmillan, New York, cited in Brown, L. (2008) *Plan B 3.0: Mobilizing to Save Civilization*, W. W. Norton & Company, New York.

97 Harrison, M. (2000) *The Economics of World War II: Six Great Powers in International Comparison*, Cambridge University Press, Cambridge.

98 Roosevelt, F. (1942) '9th State of the Union Address', www.ibiblio.org/pha/policy/1942/420106a.html, accessed 25 August 2009.

99 Goodwin, D. (1994) *Franklin and Eleanor Roosevelt: The Home Front in World War Two*, Simon and Schuster, New York.

100 Vatter, H. (1985) *The US Economy in World War II*, Columbia University Press, New York, cited in Brown, L. (2008) *Plan B 3.0: Mobilizing to Save Civilization*, W. W. Norton & Company, New York.

101 Roosevelt, F. (1942) '9th State of the Union Address', www.ibiblio.org/pha/policy/1942/420106a.html, accessed 25 August 2009.

102 Song, B. (1997) *The Rise of the Korean Economy*, Oxford University Press, Oxford.

103 Song, B. (1997) *The Rise of the Korean Economy*, Oxford University Press, Oxford.

104 Robins, N., Clover, R. and Singh, C. (2009) *A Climate for Recovery – The Colour of Stimulus Goes Green*, HSBC Global Research, London.

105 Pacala, S. and Socolow, R. (2004) 'Stabilization wedges: Solving the climate problem for the next 50 years with current technologies', *Science*, vol 305, p968.

106 Stern, N. (2006) *The Stern Review: The Economics of Climate Change*, Cambridge University Press, Cambridge, p407.

107 Pacala, S. and Socolow, R. (2004) 'Stabilization wedges: Solving the climate problem for the next 50 years with current technologies', *Science*, vol 305, p968.

108 The Climate Group (2004) 'Stephen Pacala: Profile', www.theclimategroup.org/our-news/interviews/2004/10/15/stephen-pacala/, accessed 3 April 2010.

109 Pacala, S. and Socolow, R. (2004) 'Stabilization wedges: Solving the climate problem for the next 50 years with current technologies', *Science*, vol 305, p968.

110 UNEP (2007) *Global Environment Outlook: Environment for Development (GEO-4) Report*, UNEP, p44.

111 Personal Communication, 11 September 2009.

112 Stern, N. (2006) *The Stern Review: The Economics of Climate Change*, Cambridge University Press, Cambridge.

113 Jaccard, M. and Montgomery, W. D. (1996) 'Costs of reducing greenhouse gas emissions in the USA and Canada', *Energy Policy*, vol 24, no 10/11, pp889–898, cited in Repetto, R. and Austin, D. (1997) *The Costs of Climate Protection: A Guide for the Perplexed*, World Resources Institute, Washington, DC.

114 Cited in Smith, M. and Hargroves, K. (2006) 'The first cuts must be the deepest', *CSIRO ECOS Magazine*, no 128, December–January.

115 Pears, A. (2004) 'Misconceptions about Energy Efficiency – Its Real Potential: Some Perspectives and Experiences', Background paper for International Energy Agency Energy Efficiency Workshop, Paris April.

116 Stern, N. (2006) *The Stern Review: The Economics of Climate Change*, Cambridge University Press, Cambridge.

117 IPCC (2007) *Climate Change 2007: Mitigation of Climate Change,* Contribution of Working Group III to the Fourth Assessment Report of the Intergovernmental Panel on Climate Change, Cambridge University Press, Cambridge, Figure SPM 1.
118 IPCC (2007) *Climate Change 2007: Synthesis Report,* Contribution of Working Groups I, II and III to the Fourth Assessment Report of the Intergovernmental Panel on Climate Change, Cambridge University Press, Cambridge, p104.
119 Garnaut Climate Change Review (2008) *Garnaut Climate Change Review Final Report,* Garnaut Climate Change Review, Australia.
120 Stern, N. (2006) *The Stern Review: The Economics of Climate Change,* Cambridge University Press, Cambridge.
121 Stern, N. (2006) *The Stern Review: The Economics of Climate Change,* Cambridge University Press, Cambridge.
122 Stern, N. (2006) *The Stern Review: The Economics of Climate Change,* Cambridge University Press, Cambridge.
123 Stern, N. (2006) *The Stern Review: The Economics of Climate Change,* Cambridge University Press, Cambridge.
124 Lovins, H. (2007) 'The economic case for climate action' in PCAP (2008) *Plan for Presidential Action for the First 100 Days in Office for the Next President of the United States,* Presidential Climate Action Project.
125 Salt Lake City Green (undated) 'Climate Action Plan', www.slcgreen.com/CAP/default.htm, accessed 4 June 2008, cited in Lovins, H. (2007) 'The economic case for climate action', in PCAP (2008) *Plan for Presidential Action for the First 100 Days in Office for the Next President of the United States,* Presidential Climate Action Project.
126 Stern, N. (2006) *The Stern Review: The Economics of Climate Change,* Cambridge University Press, Cambridge.
127 Garnaut Climate Change Review (2008) *Garnaut Climate Change Review Final Report,* Garnaut Climate Change Review, Australia.
128 Garnaut Climate Change Review (2008) *Garnaut Climate Change Review Final Report,* Garnaut Climate Change Review, Australia, p27
129 *Energy Bulletin* (undated) 'China Outlines 10 programs for energy efficiency', www.energybulletin.net/3566.html, accessed 13 February 2008.
130 India Bureau of Energy Efficiency (undated) Homepage, www.bee-india.nic.in/, accessed 13 February 2008.
131 Hepeng J. (2009) 'Chinese emissions could peak in 20 years', *New Scientist,* 20 August.

8

Decoupling Economic Growth from Loss of Biodiversity and Ecosystem Resilience

The development of this chapter has been advised by Mr Conor Kretch, the Executive Director of the COHAB Initiative (Co-Operation On Health and Biodiversity).[1]

The Complex Challenge of Reducing Loss of Biodiversity and Ecosystem Resilience

Ecosystems vary greatly in size and composition, ranging from a small community of microbes in a drop of water, to the entire Amazon rain forest. The very existence of people, and that of the millions of species with which the planet is shared, is dependent on the health of our ecosystems.

UNEP, GEO-4, 2007[2]

Now that over half the world's population lives in cities, it is easy to forget that the economy, indeed our existence, is wholly dependent on the earth's biodiversity, the health of ecosystems and the services they freely provide. A lack of attention in this area has resulted in unsustainable trends, with UNEP finding that 'current biodiversity changes are the fastest in human history. Species are becoming extinct a hundred times faster than the rate shown in the fossil record.'[3] This century will see unprecedented biodiversity loss unless policies and actions significantly change, with the UN, finding that:

> *Since 2000, 6 million hectares of primary forest have been lost annually ... In the Caribbean, average hard coral cover declined from 50% to 10% in the last three decades ... 35% of mangroves have been lost in the last two decades. While protected areas cover some 13% of the world's land area, these are unevenly distributed. Only some half a percent of marine areas are covered. And not all of these areas are effectively managed. The average abundance of species is declining – 40% loss between 1970 and 2000. Species present in rivers, lakes and marshlands have declined by 50% ... Habitats, such as forests and river systems are becoming fragmented ... The intensification of fishing has led to a decline of large fish. In the North Atlantic, their numbers have declined by 66% in the last 50 years'.[4]*

Such rates of species loss is set to accelerate due to unmitigated climate change, as shown in a study published in *Nature* in 2004 predicting that by 2050 as a result of climate change 'between 15 and 37 per cent of the species on the earth might be committed to extinction'.[5]

There are a range of reasons why we need to significantly reduce the rate and scale of loss of both biodiversity and resilience of the planet's ecosystems. Clearly the loss of biodiversity is irreversible, because once species are lost they cannot be replaced. Furthermore, the extinction of a particular species can have devastating effects on the ecosystem function and services as a whole. As discussed by authors such as Diamond, in the book *Collapse*, the loss of biodiversity and habitat is a factor in soil degradation and deterioration of water quality which can have direct impacts on the economic growth of cities and nations, as experienced by many past civilizations.[6]

The threat of environmentally induced economic decline poses a real risk to the nations of the world in the coming decades. As explained in earlier chapters, this is due to the negative effects of unmitigated climate change combined with the other environmental pressures such as biodiversity loss and degradation of natural resources. Along with a lack of activity and investment to reduce greenhouse gas emissions, not acting to reduce the loss of habitat and biodiversity will also lead to a measurable adverse impact on GDP. Just as *The Stern Review* found that the costs of action were much less compared to inaction on climate change, economists have found that the costs of action on habitat/biodiversity protection and restoration to be much less than the costs of inaction. A landmark EU UNEP study on The Economics of Ecosystems and Biodiversity, commissioned by the G8+5 Environment Ministers, concluded that, by 2050, cumulative economic costs from the loss of ecosystems services and biodiversity, under 'business as usual', would be equivalent to around 7 per cent of GDP per annum – equivalent to around US$2–4.5 trillion each year.[6A] By comparison, the costs of action are very small. As Lester Brown showed in *Plan B 3.0: Mobilizing to Save Civilization*, an annual budget to restore global habitat/ecosystem services and protect biodiversity would cost around an additional US$110–130 billion per annum, or approximately 0.2 per cent of current global GDP. This difference in costs exists because it is much cheaper to avoid further degradation and restore habitat today than to wait and try to pay for the full costs of ecological rehabilitation after ecological systems completely collapse. Once ecosystems collapse, there is no guarantee that efforts to restore them will be successful, as ecosystem collapse is often irreversible. These important economic cost–benefit studies build on from the most comprehensive global investigation ever into the state of the world's natural systems published in 2000, the Millennium Ecosystem Assessment, initiated by the then secretary-general of the United Nations, Kofi Annan. The Millennium Ecosystem Assessment set out to investigate the consequences for human well-being from the impact of various environmental pressures, and to establish the scientific basis to inform action to enhance the conservation and sustainable use of ecosystems. The main findings of the assessment relevant to this discussion are summarized as follows:

> *Over the past 50 years, humans have changed ecosystems more rapidly and extensively than in any comparable period of time in human history, largely to meet rapidly growing demands for food, fresh water, timber, fibre and fuel. This has resulted in a substantial and largely irreversible loss in the diversity of life on Earth ... with some 10 to 30 per cent of the mammal, bird and amphibian species currently threatened with extinction.*
>
> *The changes that have been made to ecosystems have contributed to substantial net gains in human well-being and economic development, but these gains have been achieved at growing costs in the form of the degradation of many ecosystem services, increased risks of nonlinear changes, and the exacerbation of poverty for some groups of people. These problems, unless addressed, will substantially diminish the benefits that future generations obtain from ecosystems. The degradation of ecosystem services could grow significantly worse during the first half of this century and is a barrier to achieving significant development goals such as the United Nations Millennium Development Goals.*
>
> *The challenge of reversing the degradation of ecosystems while meeting increasing demands for services can be partially met under some scenarios considered by the Assessment, but will involve significant changes in policies, institutions and practices that are not currently under way. Many options exist to conserve or enhance specific ecosystem services in ways that reduce negative trade-offs or that provide positive synergies with other ecosystem services.*[7]

The main message of the Millennium Ecosystem Assessment was that human actions are putting such a strain on the environment that the ability of the planet's natural systems to sustain future generations can no longer be taken for granted. According to the Assessment, the main factors contributing to biodiversity loss and declining ecosystem services are: land use changes (usually associated directly or indirectly with increasing populations, like conversion to agriculture); unsustainable use and exploitation of natural resources (especially fisheries and forestry); invasive alien species; pollution (e.g. nutrient loading of rivers and groundwater and bio-accumulative pesticides) and climate change.[8] Furthermore, as the OECD explains:

> *While these are the immediate sources of the loss of biodiversity, the underlying problem is that biodiversity is usually not fully accounted for by consumers in the market place[9] – there is often no distinction between biodiversity-friendly goods and those that damage biodiversity. Without government intervention, the market place has difficulty making that distinction. That so few policies have been enacted to mitigate biodiversity loss is an indicator of the strength of the underlying market failure, especially since there is considerable evidence for direct and indirect values of biodiversity that are not reflected in the market.[10]*

The Assessment also showed that ecosystem services are vital to preventing disease and sustaining good health.[11] It is known that the natural ecological cycles of many infectious disease organisms – viruses, bacteria, fungi and parasites – can be distorted by ecosystem change, including the loss of biodiversity, and the introduction of invasive species, potentially leading to the emergence of diseases in species not previously affected. Such complex relationships between hosts, carriers and ecosystems cannot yet be fully understood or replicated artificially, and relying on technology to combat disease through medicine, or on changing human behaviour to reduce transmission risks, would entail significant risks and costs.

The concept that services provided by ecosystems, such as clean air, soil formation and fertility, and the water cycle, could be threatened on a large enough scale by human activity to actually threaten their ongoing viability can be difficult to comprehend, as the enormity of the global biosphere makes it easy to think that these 'services' will be always abundant. However, the reality is that the scale of human development over the last 300 years has grown to the point that it now threatens these critical services in locations all around the world. Clean air is threatened by acid rain, dust storms and the increasing levels of greenhouse gas pollution. Soil formation is threatened by a range of modern farming practices including the overuse of chemical fertilizers and pesticides rather than organic material, tillage practices that destroy soil structure and do not allow for land to regenerate, and the clearing of vast areas of forest, leaving land susceptible to erosion and landslides. The availability of freshwater too is threatened by over-extraction from underground stores, industrial pollution pumped into waterways, and growing agricultural consumption based on inefficient practices.[12]

The assessment also pointed out that 'at the same time … with appropriate actions it is possible to reverse the degradation of many ecosystem services over the next 50 years, but the changes in policy and practice required are substantial and not currently underway'.[13] In an attempt to align efforts and increase cooperation between nations the UN initiated a Convention on Biological Diversity (CBD) which was signed by 168 countries by 1993. However, as at the end of 2009, the 190 countries that have signed are still not enough to allow global ratification.

Economic Risks and Benefits Associated with Biodiversity and Natural Systems

Nature provides numerous crucial services to the economy, including: the purification of soil, water and air; the storage and cycling of fresh water; pollination of crops; disposal of organic wastes; control of pest and disease by insects, birds and other organisms; and the prevention of soil erosion and sediment loss – to name a few. Each of these, regardless of whether they currently have a financial value, will begin to have financial implications, as the service is affected by environmental pressures. The challenge is that most of these services cannot be substituted with technology or human-made processes on a meaningful scale, and hence need to be protected.[14] For example, in May 2007 *ScienceDaily* reported a 'pollination crisis' with a 'decline in bee diversity and abundance linked to habitat loss and disease in Europe together with a 50% drop in the number of managed honeybee colonies throughout North America'. This presented a significant risk as more than 80 per cent of crops in Europe are pollinated by insects. As the services provided by bees could not be replicated, 'Each year, Irish growers import hundreds of commercial bumblebee colonies from mainland Europe to improve fruit quality and yield.'[15]

The longer nations delay action the higher the risk to business, and the higher the costs to governments, and therefore citizens, will be. In their publication, *Business and Ecosystems: Ecosystem Challenges and Business Implications*, the World Resources Institute, World Business Council for Sustainable Development, Earthwatch Institute and IUCN have identified the following major risk areas related to biodiversity and natural systems decline:[16]

- Operational risks: including higher costs due to resource scarcity (water, fuel and wood products), direct loss of assets to flooding or storm surges, or loss of hydroelectric generation capacity due to siltation.
- Regulatory and legal risks: including new user fees and increased government regulation. Where ecosystem change is brought about by corporate

activities, additional risks include environmental liabilities and fines, rejection of development applications, and lawsuits by local communities affected by the loss of biodiversity and natural systems decline.

- Reputational risks: including pressures from NGOs or regulators for not adopting green procurement principles, or investing in activities that degrade ecosystems.
- Market and product risks: including the enforcement of green procurement policies, or loss of customers who favour environmentally certified products.
- Financing risks: as financial institutions adopt more rigorous lending requirements, such as the Equator Principles, businesses face more difficulty in accessing finance or credit for operations that may result in or be at high risk from ecosystem change.

Furthermore, as explained in Chapter 1, natural systems have thresholds, which if passed, can lead to a rapid loss of species and resilience. Once such ecological thresholds are crossed, often habitats and ecosystems cannot be restored easily or cheaply.[17] The Millennium Ecosystem Assessment documented several cases of natural systems being pushed beyond their thresholds, including algal blooms from overuse of nitrogen fertilizers, fishery collapses from overfishing, bleaching of coral reefs from temperature increases, and desertification from deforestation and agricultural practices.[18] The OECD shares these concerns, stating that, 'While some environmental impacts are potentially "reversible", there are many areas in which this is not the case. In the presence of such nonlinear effects, the costs of preventing environmental degradation in the first place (mitigation) will be less than the costs of addressing the impacts of the environmental problem once it has occurred (restoration).'[19] As discussed earlier, this has been demonstrated by the 2009 EU UNEP interim report for the G8+5 on *The Economics of Ecosystems and Biodiversity*.

Conversely, there are significant job creation and economic benefits from restoring, maintaining and protecting biodiversity and ecosystems. Investing in the ecological infrastructure of nations creates jobs. For instance, in Bolivia, protected area tourism generates over 20,000 jobs, indirectly supporting over 100,000 people; in Wales, just three of its National Parks support directly and indirectly nearly 12,000 jobs. Conserving 20–30 per cent of global fisheries oceans through a network of Marine Protected Areas could create 1 million jobs, and help to sustain a marine fish catch worth US$70–80 billion per year. The economic benefits from protecting biodiversity and maintaining and restoring habitat are likely to be in the hundreds of billions to trillions of dollars per annum, including:[20]

- Eco-tourism: the benefit of what is known as 'charismatic mega fauna' and 'biodiverse ecosystems', such as the Great Barrier Reef, to the tourism industry is difficult to calculate but clearly runs to the hundreds of billions of dollars internationally, with eco-tourism being one of the largest contributors to the GDP of Costa Rica and Bhutan. Beginning in the

1990s, the eco-tourism market has been growing 20–34 per cent per year, three times faster than the industry as a whole.[21] The International Eco-tourism Society estimates the global eco-tourism market alone will be worth US$473 billion by 2015, much of which relies on such biodiverse ecosystems.[22]

- Pharmaceuticals: the pharmaceutical market is worth around US$640 billion per annum, and of all drugs sold, 25–50 per cent are derived from or partly inspired by natural sources. Indeed, finding just a small number of additional blockbuster drugs from the remaining biodiversity would justify significant conservation for bio-prospecting.[23] The 2009 EU UNEP report on *The Economics of Ecosystems and Biodiversity* found that herbal and alternative health product markets also depend significantly on the world's biodiversity, with the market estimated at US$22 billion per annum. Similarly, the biotechnology sector derives many products from natural sources. It has a market of around US$70 billion.

- Watershed management: the ability of marshes and wetlands to play an integral part in filtering wastewater is often overlooked. However, the services provided by ecosystems through watersheds globally runs into the tens of billions, as in the now famous case of New York City saving hundreds of millions of dollars by maintaining its natural watershed rather than building a water purification plant.[24]

- Pollination in agriculture: the production of over 75 per cent of global crops depends on pollination. A 2005 study calculated the economic value from pollination services at €153 billion (US$201 billion) or 9.5 per cent of the economic value of world agricultural food production.[25]

- Cooling cities: many of the world's cities are planting trees. At a city level, Tokyo, for example, has been planting trees and shrubs on the rooftops of buildings to help offset the urban heat island effect and cool the city.[26] Also, a US study of the economic and social values of planting trees on the streets and in the parks of five western US cities, including Cheyenne, Wyoming, and Berkeley, California, found that the community benefits were greater than two dollars for every dollar spent. Mature trees in cities can reduce air temperatures by 2–5°C, and in cities which have extremely cold winters, trees can help reduce wind speed dramatically and thus reduce heating bills.[27]

- Resilience to natural disasters: the resilience of ecosystems is a critical determinant as to the levels of damage and costs to human life, costs to the economy and costs to the environment from natural disasters.[28] For instance, in Asia, the 2004 tsunami would have been less disastrous if the mangroves, serving as a natural barrier, had not been removed for tourism and shrimp farming; and in the northern Pakistan earthquake of 2005, local people claim that intact forest cover prevented landslides which caused extensive damage elsewhere. The World Bank has estimated that, for the poorest countries, the cost of natural disasters represents more than 13 per cent of GDP.[29]

Reduced resilience of ecosystems can also exacerbate the risks and impacts related to conflict. A workshop on disaster prevention, relief and recovery, held as part of the Second International Conference on Health and Biodiversity (Galway, Ireland) in February 2008 reported that competition over access to ecosystem goods and services can contribute to, and become a cause of conflict – the consequences of which can negatively impact on ecosystems in both the short and long term. The workshop report advised that greater recognition needs to be given to the potential positive role that conservation and ecosystem management can play in conflict prevention and resolution and peace building.[30] Projects based on the conservation and sustainable use of biodiversity in parts of Cambodia in the aftermath of the Khmer Rouge regime have demonstrated the significant value of biodiversity for post-conflict community rebuilding, economic redevelopment and public health protection.[31] Biodiversity-related projects also have an important role in supporting good community relations and social cohesion.[32] Another inspiring example comes from Africa and was developed by Kenyan Nobel laureate Wangari Maathai, who organized women in Kenya and several nearby countries to plant 30 million trees, and thus the worldwide Billion Tree Campaign was launched in 2007, administered by UNEP.[33] The campaign reported, as of October 2007, that it had received pledges to plant a total of 1.2 billion trees by year end, with 431 million already planted. Among the leaders are Mexico, which pledged to plant 250 million trees, and Ethiopia, which promised to plant 60 million trees to commemorate its millennium celebration. Senegal signed up for 20 million trees. Indonesia pledged to plant 80 million trees. The Ministry of Environment and Forestry of Turkey has confirmed that 150 million trees had been planted as part of the Billion Tree Campaign.

Globally there has been growth in protected areas in the last three to four decades, and by 2003, 12 per cent of the world's land area was devoted to protected areas.[34] A leader in protected areas is Costa Rica, which has over 25 per cent of the country's territory in protected areas. And this percentage is growing through private and public sectors to further enhance eco-tourism and also to plant millions of trees to help achieve Costa Rica's target of net climate neutrality by 2021 respectively. This proactive stance on forest protection in Costa Rica is important because Costa Rica has roughly 4 per cent of the world's species within its borders.

However, as outlined by the Millennium Ecosystem Assessment, countries such as Costa Rica are the exception to the rule. For most countries, the substantial changes in policy and practice, required to halt the loss of biodiversity and the degradation of essential ecosystems, are not currently under way to a meaningful extent. Whilst most governments have signed the UN Convention on Biological Diversity, most are only now starting to understand that the situation is critical and that much greater commitments and action must be taken now on a meaningful scale to underpin our present and future economic growth and prosperity. For instance, conservation efforts need to be expanded beyond biodiversity hotspots or particular populations, to the creation of wildlife corridors, with programmes to work with farmers and land managers to build biodiversity and vegetation back into the landscapes in ways that enable species to move north and south to adapt to climate change across the continents. Such efforts also need to be strategically aligned with programmes related to reforestation, revegetation, reversing soil erosion, soil carbon sequestration and the protection of biodiversity, where appropriate.

The following pages bring together and overview some of the most cost-effective strategies to support decoupling the loss of biodiversity and the resilience of ecosystems from economic growth. The following pages add further weight to the emerging consensus from publications such as the 2009 EU UNEP interim report on *The Economics of Ecosystems and Biodiversity* and *Plan B 3.0: Mobilizing to Save Civilization*[35] by Lester Brown, which demonstrate the economic benefits of acting to reduce environmental pressure and investing to restore the planet's ecological infrastructure.

Responding to the Challenge of Deforestation

Deforestation leads to greater rainfall run-off and associated flooding and soil erosion. The primary economic impact of deforestation that is set to increase with further inaction, is the reduction of the natural system's resilience to shocks, such as flash floods or cyclones. Which can lead to such events causing significantly more damage.[36] Worldwide, areas with a high level of erosion risk from water are projected to increase from 20 million km^2 in 2000 to nearly 30 million in 2030, across all regions of the world. Similar risks also exist for estuarine forests, or mangroves, as the Food and Agriculture Organization of the UN (FAO) points out, 'the destruction of huge areas of coastal mangroves around the Irrawaddy River delta in Myanmar in the last few decades amplified the flooding and worsened devastation'.[37] According to the Worldwatch Institute, in China's Yangtze basin in the same year, heavy rainfall, compounded by upstream deforestation (with over 85 per cent of forest cover lost), triggered flooding across the extremely densely settled floodplain, that killed 3700 people, dislocated 223 million and inundated 60 million acres of cropland. This US$30 billion disaster forced a logging moratorium and a US$12 billion crash programme of reforestation.[38] Another example is Bangladesh, which suffered its most extensive flood of the century in the summer of 1998. Two-thirds of this low-lying nation at the mouth of the Ganges and Brahmaputra rivers was inundated and 30 million people were left temporarily homeless. Some 10,000 miles of roads were heavily damaged, and the rice harvest was reduced by 2 million tonnes. Damage estimates exceeded US$3.4 billion, as logging up river in the Himalayas of north India and Nepal exacerbated the disaster, as did the fact that the region's rivers and floodplains had been filled with silt and constricted by development.[39]

In addition to reforestation, investing in other forms of natural capital provides protection and resilience from natural disasters. In Viet Nam, tropical cyclones have caused a considerable loss of livelihood resources, particularly in coastal communities. Mangrove ecosystem rehabilitation along much of Viet Nam's coastline is an example of a cost-effective approach to improving coastal defences while restoring biodiversity and ecosystems, as well as generating local livelihoods. Since 1994, the Viet Nam National Chapter of the Red Cross has worked with local communities to plant and protect mangrove forests in northern Viet Nam. Nearly 120 km² of mangroves have been planted, with substantial resulting benefits; as although planting and protecting the mangroves cost approximately US$1.1 million, it saved US$7.3 million per year in dyke maintenance. During the devastating typhoon Wukong in 2000, project areas remained unharmed, while neighbouring provinces suffered huge losses in lives, property and livelihoods. The Viet Nam Red Cross has estimated that some 7750 families have benefited from mangrove rehabilitation. Family members can now earn additional income from selling crabs, shrimp and molluscs, while also increasing the protein in their diets.[40]

Other countries are beginning to recognize the economic, social and environmental costs associated with deforestation. China, New Zealand, the Philippines, Sri Lanka, Thailand and Viet Nam have all implemented total or partial bans on deforestation.[41] Most brought in these bans after similar experiences to those mentioned above. But simply stopping logging is often not enough to ensure that natural systems will regenerate, as restoration of forests will also be required. South Korea offers one of the best examples of reforestation to the rest of the world. When the Korean War ended, half a century ago, the almost completely mountainous country was largely deforested. Since around 1960 the South Korean government has invested in a major national reforestation effort, utilizing village cooperatives involving hundreds of thousands of people digging trenches and creating terraces to support trees on barren mountain slopes. Se-Kyung Chong, researcher at the Korea Forest Research Institute, writes:

> The result was a seemingly miraculous rebirth of forests from barren land. Today forests cover 65 per cent of the country, an area of roughly 6 million hectares. While driving across South Korea in November 2000, it was gratifying for me to see the luxuriant stands of trees on mountains that a generation ago were bare ... We can reforest the Earth![42]

South Korea is also showing that there is a vast unrealized potential in all countries to lessen the demands that are shrinking the earth's forest cover, having one of the highest paper recycling rates in the world at 77 per cent. South Korea also made a concerted effort to shift from using wooden chopsticks to plastic and metal alternatives, and the government has banned the use of disposable chopsticks in many restaurants.[43] Following this leading effort, Bian Jiang, the Secretary-General of the China Cuisine Association has called on restaurant operators across China to phase out one-use cutlery, stating that 'the country produces and discards more than 45 billion pairs of wooden chopsticks every year, at a cost to the environment of about 25 million trees'.[44]

As part of its investigation into the economics of climate change, the UK *Stern Review* recommended not just slowing down but stopping completely further deforestation as a cost-effective way to mitigate climate change. According to the FAO, deforestation, particularly the burning of forests is 'responsible for between 25 and 30 per cent of the greenhouse gases released into the atmosphere each year – 1.6 billion tonnes'.[45] *The Stern Review* puts the opportunity cost of stopping deforestation in eight countries responsible for 70 per cent of emissions at US$5–10 billion per annum and the cost of ongoing management of the forests at US$12–93 million per annum.[46] But *The Stern Review* did not investigate the cost benefits of coupling halting deforestation efforts with investments in restoration and reforestation. There is significant potential in currently semi-degraded land to sequester carbon further and help to restore the landscape and reduce soil erosion and thus further reduce costs to society from environmental degradation. Lester Brown writes about an important study by Swedish energy firm, Vattenfall,[47] which has examined the large-scale potential for foresting wasteland to sequester carbon dioxide. This study shows that there are 1.86 billion hectares of degraded land in the world that were once forestland, cropland or grassland. This study finds that half of this land, approximately 930 million hectares, is suitable for reclamation at an affordable price. As Brown reports, 'Vattenfall estimates that the maximum technical potential of these 930 million hectares is to absorb roughly 21.6 billion tons of CO_2 per year ... [and that] there is potential for government working with the private sector to leverage private investment to solve this problem and thus reduce the amount of tax payer funding required to address climate change.'[48]

Responding to the Challenge of the Loss of Topsoil and Desertification

According to the Asia-Pacific Forestry Commission, approximately a third of all cropland is currently losing topsoil faster than new soil is forming, reducing the land's inherent productivity.[49] For example, Ethiopia, a country that struggles to provide enough food for its citizens, is losing close to 2 billion tonnes of topsoil a year, washed away by rain from its highly erodible soils on steeply sloping land.[50] The accelerating soil erosion over the last century can be seen in the enormous dust bowls that are forming in various locations around the world as vegetation is destroyed and wind erosion soars out of control. Among the regions that stand out are northwest China and the Sahelian region of Africa. Each of these is associated with a familiar pattern of overgrazing, deforestation and agricultural expansion onto marginal land, followed by retrenchment as the soil begins to erode and disappear.[51]

Conserving the Earth's topsoil must involve at least the following two steps. The first step is to retire the highly erodible land that cannot sustain further farming and return the natural vegetation cover. 10 per cent of the earth's land surface is fertile enough for crops, and of this percentage, one-tenth is estimated to account for at least half of all excess erosion. In the US, this first step has involved retiring 14 million hectares of land at a cost of US$125 per hectare, totalling US$2 billion over a ten-year period.[52] The second step involves using conservation practices on the remaining land to restore eroded and degraded land. This initiative includes providing an economic incentive to encourage farmers to adopt conservation practices such as contour farming, strip cropping and, increasingly, minimum-till or no-till farming. It has been estimated that this costs roughly US$1 billion per year in the US.[53]

Lester Brown discusses the global cost implications for retiring land and adopting conservation practices:[54]

> *In expanding these estimates to cover the world, it is assumed that roughly 10 per cent of the world's cropland is highly erodible and should be planted to grass or trees before the topsoil is lost and it becomes barren land. In both the United States and China, the two leading food-producing countries, which account for a third of the world grain harvest, the official goal is to retire one tenth of all cropland. In Europe, it likely would be much less than 10 per cent, but in Africa and the Andean countries it could be substantially higher than that. For the world as a whole, converting 10 per cent of cropland that is highly erodible to grass or trees seems a reason-able goal. Since this costs roughly $2 billion in the United States, which represents one eighth of the world cropland area, the total for the world would be roughly $16 billion annually.[55] Assuming that the need for erosion control practices for the rest of the world is similar to that in the United States, we again multiply the U.S. expenditure by eight to get a total of $8 billion for the world as a whole. The two components together – $16 billion for retiring highly erodible land and $8 billion for adopting conservation practices – give an annual total for the world of $24 billion [which is less than the estimated US market for ice cream and frozen desserts in 2012 of US$427.6 billion[56]].*

As stated above, 10 per cent of the earth's land surface is fertile enough for crops, but 40 per cent is suitable for rangeland, categorized as land that is too steep, dry or simply not fertile enough for crop farming. Rangeland supports more than 50 per cent of the world's 3.3 billion cattle, sheep and goats.[57] An estimated 200 million people worldwide depend on rangelands to graze their cattle, sheep and goats in countries in Africa, the Middle East, Central Asia, Mongolia and northwest China. Most rangelands are commonly accessible and suffer from overgrazing due to the lack of controls on access and use.[58] In China, responsibility for farming has shifted from state-organized production teams to farm families. This has led to a rapid increase in numbers of sheep and goats being farmed. As Lester Brown writes: 'While the United States has only 9 million sheep and goats, China has 366 million. Concentrated in China's western and northern provinces, sheep and goats are destroying the land's protective vegetation. The wind then does the rest, removing the soil and converting productive rangeland into desert.'[59]

In Africa and parts of Asia the spread of desertification is a serious threat to hundreds of millions of people. In the north of Africa the Sahara is advancing.[60] Nigeria is losing 351,000 hectares of rangeland and cropland to desertification each year. China's desertification is also a serious problem. A leading Chinese scholar on the issue, Wang Tao, when speaking on the exponentially rising levels of desertification in his country, explains that, 'From 1950 to 1975 an average of 1,560 square kilometres of land turned to desert each year. Between 1975 and 1987, this climbed to 2,100 square kilometres a year. From then until the century's end, it jumped to 3,600 square kilometres of land going to desert annually.'[61] Large-scale efforts aimed at holding off desertification are under way in China and Africa. For example the Great Green Wall in the north of China is projected to plant a 4480km (2800 mile) corridor of trees to combat shifting sands from the Gobi Desert,[62] along with the Saharan Green Wall of Africa, a partnership between the EU and African nations to expand the planted forest network by 5 million hectares to keep back the Sahara.[63]

The UN Plan of Action to Combat Desertification focuses on the world's dryland regions, containing nearly 90 per cent of all rangeland, and estimates that restoration of rangelands would cost approximately US$183 billion over 20 years.[64] The key restoration measures include: improved economic incentives to stop overstocking; revegetation with appropriate rest periods; and the identification of periods when grazing would be banned, and thus sustainable rangeland management techniques required.[65] This is a costly undertaking, but Brown argues that every dollar invested in rangeland restoration yields a return of $2.5 in income from the increased productivity of the rangeland ecosystem.[66] The alternative to action would cause a loss not only of land productivity but of livelihood. Though not quantified here, restoring this vulnerable land will also have carbon sequestration benefits.[67] For example, one activity that involves a good use of restoring vulnerable land is the planting in Africa and Asia of *Jatropha curcas*, a 4 foot (1.2 metre) perennial shrub that produces seeds which can be used to produce biodiesel; this covers wasteland and sequesters carbon.[68] BP and D1 Oils have announced that they are to form a 50:50 joint venture, to be called D1-BP Fuel Crops Limited, to accelerate the planting of *Jatropha curcas*. The joint venture has been established in order to make more sustainable biodiesel feedstock available on a larger scale. Under the terms of the agreement, BP and D1 Oils intend to invest around US$160 million over the next five years.

Responding to the Challenge of the Depletion of Global Fisheries

Fisheries are collapsing throughout the world. Atlantic stocks of the heavily fished bluefin tuna – a large specimen of which, headed for Tokyo's sushi restaurants, can bring in US$100,000 – have fallen by a staggering 94 per cent. The harvest of the Caspian Sea sturgeon, source of the world's most prized caviar, fell from a record 27,700 tonnes in 1977 to just 461 tonnes in 2000.[69] A 2003 landmark study by a Canadian–German research team published in *Nature* concluded that '90 per cent of the large fish in the oceans had disappeared over the last 50 years'.[70] It will take years for such long-lived species to recover, even if fishing were to stop altogether. One focus for the restoration of oceanic fisheries is the establishment of a worldwide network of marine reserves, which would cover roughly 30 per cent of the ocean's surface, and cost an estimated US$13 billion per year.[71]

Fisheries management is limited by imperfect information and imperfect control, making it impossible to precisely gauge the size of the stock, its growth rate and its relationship with other stocks. In addition to imperfect information, regulation is imperfect, especially for the high seas fisheries which are not controlled by any one government. There are now many examples of stocks being fished to commercial extinction. In 2007, the FAO reported that the proportion of overexploited and depleted stocks rose from 10 per cent in 1974 to 25 per cent in 2005.[72] Unsustainable fishing practices in many parts of the world mean that there is limited potential for further expansion of the sector in the short or medium term. The fisheries sector is one where environmental pressures can lead to 'irreversible' collapse of the system. Thus the long-term costs of unsustainable fishing practices are significantly greater than costs of action to ensure that the economic, social and environmental benefits of fishing can be continued. The OECD has listed some of the different types of costs arising from unsustainable fisheries management:

> *These include direct economic consequences, such as lost receipts for fishers and vessel owners from falling catches. There are also indirect consequences, such as lost earnings for workers and foregone profits of fish-processing and related industries. Then there is the additional loss of 'use values', including those costs which can be difficult to value due to their non-market characteristics, such as reduced recreational opportunities. And finally, there are costs associated with damage to marine ecosystems.*[73]

Therefore, the costs of unsustainable fisheries management can be considerable. The OECD[74] highlights this through reference to a number of studies, including one study of 15 'overfished' fish stocks in US waters by Sumaila and Suatoni.[75] In this study the direct income from commercial fishery yields and recreational fishing was calculated for two specific scenarios. The first scenario assumed continued excessive fishing and income was based on the most recent catch levels, referred to as the 'recent catch' scenario. The second scenario assumed the stock was able to rebuild through management by Regional Fishery Management Councils and estimated that income, referred to as the 'rebuilding' scenario. For each of the 15 fish stocks the study estimated the two incomes, assuming that for each specific fish stock the duration of the calculation would be the time required to bring the stock up to a manageable level under the second scenario, referred to as the 'target rebuilding year'. The study estimated that continuing the existing excessive fishing management regime under the recent catch scenario would lead to a loss of US$373 million (reducing from US$566.7 million down to US$193.7).[76]

In addition to lost income from reduced population levels of fish, there are other costs from continuing unsustainable commercial and recreational fishing practice. When a fishery collapses often others also bear some of the direct costs, including taxpayers. For example, in response to the collapse of the cod stock in Canada in the early 1980s substantial public funds were spent on income support (including fishers' unemployment benefits) and government assistance programmes (expenditures towards restructuring, sectoral adjustment and regional economic development). An estimated CA$3.5 billion was spent on these structural adjustment programmes.[77] However, prior to the collapse a range of effective structural adjustments could have ensured the sustainability of the industry and avoided the collapse of the fisheries and the economic impacts that resulted. For example, investing in efforts to improve fisheries management practices such as structural adjustment in order to reduce the number of fishing permits and fishing companies able to fish the resource.

Unfortunately, it is now too late for such efforts in the Atlantic cod fisheries, but many other fisheries around the planet are now facing similar challenges, and without progressive efforts stand to experience the same fate:

> *Just as cod was once perceived as Canada's 'Newfoundland currency', tuna is largely considered the 'chicken of the sea' – cheap and plentiful. Where the landed value of cod in Atlantic Canada was at its peak of $1.4 billion in 1968, it dropped to just $10 million by 2004. Trends for some tuna species are cause for concern. In 2001, for example, landed value of yellowfin tuna in the Western Central Pacific Ocean was US$1.9 billion, but three years later it had dropped by more than 40 per cent to US$1.1 billion.*[78]

If nations do not heed the warnings from the UN, UNEP and the OECD concerning currently unsustainable fishery practices the costs in the short to medium term will be significant. The fisheries sector employs about 40 million fishers and fish farmers across the world, most living in developing countries,[79] who depend on healthy fisheries.[80] Fishery resources also contribute to the livelihoods of coastal or island communities. In many of these countries, fish is an essential part of the diet, providing 22 per cent and 19 per cent of animal proteins consumed in Asia and Africa respectively.[81] Fish is also recommended as part of a healthy diet due to the presence of omega-3 fatty acids, such as eicosa-pentaenoic acid (EPA) and docosa-hexaenoic acid (DHA), which have significant health benefits. In 2004, the US Food and Drug Administration gave 'qualified health claim' status to EPA and DHA, stating that 'supportive but not conclusive research shows that consumption of EPA and DHA may reduce the risk of coronary heart disease'.[82] People with certain circulatory problems, such as varicose veins, benefit from fish oil as it stimulates blood circulation and increases the breakdown of fibrin, a compound involved in clot and scar formation, and additionally has been shown to reduce blood pressure.[83] There is also strong scientific evidence that these fatty acids significantly reduce blood triglyceride levels,[84] and regular intake reduces the risk of secondary and primary heart attack.[85]

For all of these reasons, economic, public health and the quality of natural systems, it is important that fishery resources be managed sustainably. However, such management will always be faced with the challenge of uncertainties from imperfect information and imperfect control. Such uncertainties need to be managed if fisheries are to be kept below thresholds that lead to a given stock being fished into commercial extinction, as this will result in the permanent loss of all of the benefits indicated earlier.

Responding to the Challenge of the Growth of Invasive Species and the Loss of Wildlife

Another direct cost from failure to act on reducing environmental pressures is the issue of invasive species. According to Environment Canada, invasive species are defined as 'plants, animals, and micro-organisms that have been relocated to environments outside of their natural past or present distribution. They are harmful species whose introduction or spread threatens the environment, the economy or society.'[86] Plant species that are introduced to an area, say by tourism, can interfere with agricultural crops and reduce yields, degrade water catchments and impact on water supply and freshwater ecosystems, and as a result increase control costs. Animal species, especially insects, when introduced to new areas of crops, livestock and vegetation can have devastating effects on plant life, agricultural yield and ecosystem health, leading to increasing pest control costs. The introduction of micro-organisms, say from the discharge of a ship's ballast water, introduces harmful organisms to the receiving natural system, including diseases, bacteria and viruses, thereby, for instance, degrading commercially important fisheries.

Biologist Edward Wilson has claimed that the introduction of alien species is second only to habitat loss as the leading cause of extinctions worldwide. Major economies around the world are paying significant costs related to invasive species, including:

- The cost of invasive species to the US economy is estimated to exceed US$138 billion per year over the next 50 years, with an estimated 50,000 species having been introduced into the US.[87]
- The economic cost of invasive species to the Canadian economy, from only 16 invasive species, is estimated to be CA$13–35 billion, with damage to the agricultural and forestry industries resulting in an estimated CA$7.5 billion of lost revenue annually.[88]
- Rapid economic growth and giant infrastructure projects have allowed invasive species to spread throughout China and inflict more than US$14.5 billion of damage to the nation's economy annually, according to a study published in *BioScience*.[89]

While it should be acknowledged that there is considerable uncertainty in estimating the total economic costs of invasions, these estimates of the economic impacts indicate the seriousness of the problem. Most countries are now affected in some way by invasive species that add significant costs to the economy. Chief Scientist for the World Conservation Union in 2000, Jeffrey McNeely, recounts such issues as part of research undertaken by the Global Invasive Species Programme (created in 1997 to provide information to implement the Convention on Biological Diversity), saying:

> *Every nation on earth is already grappling with complex and costly invasive species problems, such as zebra mussels affecting fisheries, mollusc diversity, and electric power generation in Canada and the USA, water hyacinth choking African waterways, rats extirpating native biota on oceanic islands, and deadly new diseases attacking both temperate and tropical countries … the Varroa Mite, a serious pest in honeybee hives, has recently invaded New Zealand and is expected to have an economic cost of NZ$400–900 million [US$184–414 million], forcing beekeepers to alter the way they manage hives. Beekeepers argue that had border rules been complied with or had surveillance systems detected it earlier, then the problem could have been avoided. It appears that it now is too late to eradicate the mite, requiring a mitigation plan that is expected to cost NZ$1.3 million [US$600,000] in its first stage.[90]*

According to the UN Millennium Ecosystem Assessment a number of direct risks to the economy from continued loss of biodiversity will increase over the coming decade. The UNEP fourth *Global Environment Outlook* stated 'Current biodiversity changes are the fastest in human history. Species are becoming extinct a hundred times faster than the rate shown in the fossil record.'[91] The latest findings of IUCN – the International Union for Conservation of Nature – on the percentage of birds, mammals and fish that are vulnerable or in immediate danger of extinction is as follows: 12 per cent of the world's nearly 10,000 bird species; 20 per cent of the world's 5416 mammal species; and 39 per cent of the fish species analysed.[92] The World Parks Congress estimates that US$25 billion in additional annual support is required to establish and maintain an effective global system of protected areas.[93] Additional areas needed, including those encompassing the biologically diverse hotspots not yet included in designated parks, would cost between US$500 million and US$5 billion a year over five years, yielding a total of US$30 billion per annum.[94]

To conclude, biodiversity, ecosystems and ecosystem services underpin economic activity and quality of life around the world, however they are given little consideration in economic decision-making. The costs of inaction in this area long term will be in the same order of magnitude as the costs of inaction that are now being estimated for climate change, as pointed out in the 2009 EU UNEP interim report on *The Economics of Ecosystems and Biodiversity*. There are a range of areas where action can be taken to reduce such future risks and costs combining to an additional annual investment in the order of US$110–130 billion per annum. This figure includes efforts to stop further deforestation (US$5–10 billion), additional tree planting to sequester carbon ($20 billion), stopping land degradation and protecting topsoil (US$24 billion), restoring rangelands (US$9 billion), protecting and restoring fisheries (US$13 billion), and protecting biological diversity (US$31 billion).

Another area of additional investment needed is more funding to stop illegal trade in endangered species, the black market for which is worth around US$10 billion per annum and involves the trade of approximately 350 million plant and animal species. Some 150 nations are working together to try to address this through the UN Convention on International Trade in Endangered Species of Wild Fauna and Flora (CITES). Complementing such efforts, a number of NGOs and governments have launched successful campaigns to discourage the purchase of souvenirs or clothing made from endangered wildlife. Improved law enforcement and serious penalties for poaching can also influence the wildlife trade – for instance, panda smugglers in China can be sentenced to life in prison. Furthermore, researchers are investigating alternatives to wildlife products used for traditional medicines, clothing and ceremonies, some that have been used for many generations in certain cultures. There also is the need to ensure adequate wildlife corridors to allow species to continue to migrate, especially with predicted impacts of climate change.

Finally, it is important to note that the UN Millennium Ecosystem Assessment in 2005 showed that relative decoupling of economic growth from the loss of ecosystem resilience and the use of ecosystem services has already been achieved, stating that 'Growth in the use of ecosystem services over the past five decades was generally much less than growth in GDP.' So a commitment of just 0.2 per cent of additional GDP expenditure by the nations of the world, for the initiatives outlined by this chapter and the supporting documents, would significantly assist efforts to achieve absolute decoupling and to create systems that allow ecosystem restoration to be correlated with economic growth.

Notes

1 The authors are grateful to the World Resources Institute for permission to reproduce sections of the Millennium Ecosystem Assessment synthesis reports,
Ecosystem Services: A Guide for Decision Makers, and the methodology in this
chapter. This chapter is to be cited as Smith, M., Hargroves, K. and Kretch, C.
(2009) 'Decoupling economic growth from loss of biodiversity and Ecosystem
Resilience', in Smith, M., Hargroves, K. and Desha, C. (2010) *Cents and
Sustainability: Securing Our Common Future by Decoupling Economic Growth
from Environmental Pressures*, Earthscan, London.

2 UNEP (2007) *Global Environment Outlook: Environment for Development
(GEO-4) Report*, UNEP.

3 UNEP (2007) *Global Environment Outlook: Environment for Development
(GEO-4) Report*, UNEP.

4 CBD (2006) *Global Biodiversity Outlook 2*, Secretariat of the Convention on
Biological Diversity, Montreal.

5 Thomas, C. et al (2004) 'Feeling the heat: Climate change and biodiversity loss',
Nature, 8 January, vol 427, no 6970, pp87–180, cited in Kunzig, R. (2008) 'Is
focusing on "hot spots" the key to preserving biodiversity? Preserving biodiversity
in rich habitats is good. But global warming and other new threats may call for a
new strategy', *Scientific American*, October 2008 special edition.

6 Diamond, J. (2006) *Collapse: How Societies Choose to Fail or Succeed*, Viking
Press, New York.

6A TEEB (2009) *The Economics of Ecosystems and Biodiversity for National and
International Policy Makers, The Economics of Ecosystems and Biodiversity,
UNEP and EU*, Welzel+Hardt, Wesseling, Germany.

7 Millennium Ecosystem Assessment (2005) *Ecosystems and Human Well-Being:
Synthesis Report*, World Resources Institute, Island Press, Washington, DC.

8 Lovejoy, T. (2009) 'Climate change's pressures on biodiversity', in Worldwatch
Institute (2009) *State of the World 2009: Into a Warming World*, Worldwatch
Institute, Washington, DC.

9 OECD (2004) *Handbook of Market Creation for Biodiversity: Issues in
Implementation*, OECD, Paris.

10 OECD (2008) *OECD Environmental Outlook to 2030*, OECD, Paris.

11 Millennium Ecosystem Assessment (2005) *Ecosystems and Human Well-Being:
Synthesis Report*, World Resources Institute, Island Press, Washington, DC.

12 For further details about such threats and impacts refer to Brown, L. (2008) *Plan
B 3.0: Mobilizing to Save Civilization*, W. W. Norton & Company, New York;
UNEP (2007) *Global Environment Outlook: Environment for Development
(GEO-4) Report*, UNEP.

13 Millennium Ecosystem Assessment (2005) *Ecosystems and Human Well-Being:
Synthesis Report*, World Resources Institute, Island Press, Washington, DC.

14 For an excellent general discussion of biodiversity and its value, see Millennium
Ecosystem Assessment (2005) *Ecosystems and Human Well-Being: Synthesis
Report*, World Resources Institute, Island Press, Washington, DC, see
'Biodiversity synthesis report'.

15 Science News (2007) 'Declining bee numbers raise concerns over plant
pollination', *ScienceDaily*, 11 May.

16 Athanas, A., Bishop, J., Cassaram, A., Donaubauer, P., Perceval, C., Rafiq, M.,
Ranganathan, J. and Risgaard, P. (2006) *Business and Ecosystems: Ecosystem
Challenges and Business Implications*, WRI, WBCSD, Earthwatch Institute, IUCN.

17 OECD (2008) *OECD Environmental Outlook to 2030*, OECD, Paris.

18 Millennium Ecosystem Assessment (2005) *Ecosystems and Human Well-Being: Synthesis Report*, World Resources Institute, Island Press, Washington, DC.

19 OECD (2008) *OECD Environmental Outlook to 2030*, OECD, Paris.

20 Millennium Ecosystem Assessment (2005) *Ecosystems and Human Well-Being: Synthesis Report*, World Resources Institute, Island Press, Washington, DC.

21 Mastny, L. (2001) *Treading Lightly: New Paths for International Tourism*, Worldwatch Paper 159, Worldwatch Institute, Washington, DC, p15.

22 The International Eco-tourism Society (TIES) (2006) *TIES Global Ecotourism Fact Sheet*, TIES, Washington, DC.

23 OECD (2002) *Handbook of Biodiversity Valuation: A Guide for Policymakers*, OECD, Paris.

24 Heal, G. (2000) *Nature and the Marketplace: Capturing the Value of Ecosystem Services*, Island Press, Washington, DC.

25 Gallai, N., Salles, J.-M., Settele, J. and Vaissière, B. (2009) 'Economic valuation of the vulnerability of world agriculture confronted with pollinator decline', *Ecological Economics*, vol 68, no 3, pp810–821.

26 Chang-Ran Kim (2002) 'Tokyo turns to rooftop gardens to beat the heat', *Reuters*, 7 August; Casey Trees (undated) Homepage, www.caseytrees.org, accessed 12 October 2007.

27 Wolf, K. (1998) 'Urban forest values: Economic benefits of trees in cities', fact sheet, Center for Urban Horticulture, Seattle, WA; McPherson, G. et al (2005) 'Municipal forest benefits and costs in five US cities', *Journal of Forestry*, December 2005, pp411–416, cited in Brown, L. (2008) *Plan B 3.0: Mobilizing to Save Civilization*, W. W. Norton & Company, New York.

28 Masundire, H., Rizvi, A. and Rietbergen, S. (2006) *Ecosystems, Livelihoods and Disasters: An Integrated Approach to Disaster Risk Management*, IUCN.

29 World Bank (2006) *Hazards of Nature, Risks to Development*, World Bank, Washington, DC.

30 COHAB Initiative Secretariat (2008) *Summary Report*, from the Second International Conference on Health and Biodiversity, Galway, Ireland, February.

31 COHAB Initiative Secretariat (2008) *Summary Report*, from the Second International Conference on Health and Biodiversity, Galway, Ireland, February.

32 See, for example, Chivan, E. S. and Bernstein, A. (2008) *Sustaining Life: How Human Health Depends on Biodiversity*, Oxford University Press; also see the website of the COHAB Initiative www.cohabnet.org, accessed 12 July 2009.

33 UNEP (undated) 'Billion Tree Campaign', www.unep.org/billiontreecampaign/, accessed 25 March 2008.

34 Chape, S. et al (2003) *United Nations List of Protected Areas*, IUCN, Gland, Switzerland and Cambridge, UK and UNEP-WCMC, Cambridge.

35 Brown, L. (2008) *Plan B 3.0: Mobilizing to Save Civilization*, W. W. Norton & Company, New York.

36 Masundire, H., Rizvi, A. and Rietbergen, S. (2006) *Ecosystems, Livelihoods and Disasters: An Integrated Approach to Disaster Risk Management*, IUCN, see Media Release, www.iucn.org/en/news/archive/2006/08/30_pr_disaster.htm, accessed 23 March 2008.

37 FAO (2008) 'Intact mangroves could have reduced Nargis damage – Destruction of mangroves has exposed coastal communities to cyclone', FAO Newsroom, 15 May.

38   Bright, C. (2000) *State of the World Report, Anticipating Environmental Surprise*, Worldwatch Institute, Washington, DC, Chapter 2, pp22–38.
39   Bright, C. (2000) *State of the World Report, Anticipating Environmental Surprise*, Worldwatch Institute, Washington, DC, Chapter 2, pp22–38.
40   IIED (2003) *The Millennium Development Goals and Conservation; Managing Nature's Wealth for Society's Health*, International Institute for Environment and Development, London, Chapter 3: 'Climate change – Biodiversity and livelihood impacts'.
41   Durst, P. et al (2001) *Forests Out of Bounds: Impacts and Effectiveness of Logging Bans in Natural Forests in Asia-Pacific*, FAO, Asia-Pacific Forestry Commission, Bangkok.
42   Chong, S. K. (2005) 'Anmyeon-do Recreation Forest: A millennium of management', in Durst, P. et al (2005*) In Search of Excellence: Exemplary Forest Management in Asia and the Pacific*, Asia-Pacific Forestry Commission, FAO Regional Office for Asia and the Pacific, Bangkok, pp251–259.
43   Coonan, C. (2008) 'A green tax triumph – China introduces tax on disposable chopsticks', *Independent* (UK).
44   Juan, S. (2007) 'Call to abandon wooden chopsticks', *China Daily*, 8 October.
45   FAO (2006) 'Deforestation causes global warming: Key role for developing countries in fighting greenhouse gas emissions', FAO Newsroom, 4 September.
46   Stern, N. et al (2006) *The Stern Review: The Economics of Climate Change*, Cambridge University Press, Cambridge.
47   Vattenfall (2007) *Global Mapping of Greenhouse Gas Abatement Opportunities up to 2030: Forestry Sector Deep-Dive*, Vattenfall, Stockholm.
48   Brown, L. (2008) *Plan B 3.0: Mobilizing to Save Civilization*, W. W. Norton & Company, New York.
49   Durst, P. B. et al (2001) *Forests Out of Bounds: Impacts and Effectiveness of Logging Bans in Natural Forests in Asia-Pacific*, FAO, Asia-Pacific Forestry Commission, Bangkok.
50   UNEP (2002) *Africa Environment Outlook: Past, Present, and Future Perspectives*, UNEP, Nairobi.
51   Youlin, Y., Squires, V. and Qi, L. (eds) (2002) *Global Alarm: Dust and Sandstorms from the World's Drylands*, Secretariat of the UN Convention to Combat Desertification, Bangkok, pp15–28.
52   Wolf, E. C. (1988) 'Reclaiming the future', in Brown, L. et al (1988) *State of the World 1988*, W. W. Norton & Company, New York, p174, using data from FAO, 'Fuelwood supplies in the developing countries', Forestry Paper 42.
53   Wolf, E. C. (1988) 'Reclaiming the future', in Brown, L. et al (1988) *State of the World 1988*, W. W. Norton & Company, New York, p174, using data from FAO, 'Fuelwood supplies in the developing countries', Forestry Paper 42.
54   Brown, L. (2008) *Plan B 3.0: Mobilizing to Save Civilization*, W. W. Norton & Company, New York.
55   Brown, L. (2008) *Plan B 3.0: Mobilizing to Save Civilization*, W. W. Norton & Company, New York.
56   *Foodweek* (2008) 'US ice cream market continues to grow', *Foodweek Online*, 14 January 2008, www.foodweek.com.au/main-features-page.aspx?ID=1273, accessed 3 April 2010.
57   Land area estimate from Wood, S., Sebastian, K. and Scherr, S. J. (2003) *Pilot Analysis of Global Ecosystems: Agro-ecosystems*, International Food Policy Research Institute and WRI, Washington, DC, p3; livestock counts from FAO (1995) *The State of Food and Agriculture*, FAO, Rome, p175.

58   Number of pastoralists from FAO (2003) *The State of Food Insecurity in the World,* FAO, Rome, p15.

59   Brown, L. (2008) *Plan B 3.0: Mobilizing to Save Civilization*, W. W. Norton & Company, New York.

60   UN Population Division (2007) *World Population Prospects: The 2006 Revision Population Database*, UN Population Division.

61   Tao, W. et al (2004) 'A study on spatial-temporal changes of sandy desertified land during last 5 decades in north China', *Acta Geographica Sinica*, vol 59, pp203–212; Tao, W. (2004) Cold and Arid Regions Environmental and Engineering Research Institute (CAREERI), Chinese Academy of Sciences, e-mail to author, 4 April; Tao, W. (2002) 'The process and its control of sandy desertification in northern China', CAREERI, Chinese Academy of Sciences, seminar on desertification, held in Lanzhou, China, May.

62   BBC (2001) 'China's Great Green Wall', *BBC News*, 3 March.

63   *Biopact* (2007) 'EU and Africa to build a Green Wall across the Sahara', *Biopact*, 9 December.

64   Brown, L. (2008) *Plan B 3.0: Mobilizing to Save Civilization*, W. W. Norton & Company, New York.

65   UN (undated) Convention to Combat Desertification, www.unccd.int/main.php, accessed 26 March 2008.

66   Brown, L. (2008) *Plan B 3.0: Mobilizing to Save Civilization*, W. W. Norton & Company, New York.

67   Dregne, H. E. and Chou, N. T. (1992) 'Global desertification dimensions and costs', in UNEP (1992) *Degradation and Restoration of Arid Lands*, UNEP.

68   Jatropha World (undated) Homepage, www.jatrophaworld.org/, accessed 26 March 2008.

69   Leahy, S. (2007) 'Atlantic bluefin going way of northern cod', *Interpress Service News Agency*, 24 August; Williams, T. (1994) 'The last bluefin hunt', in Harms, V. et al (1994) *The National Audubon Society Almanac of the Environment*, Grosset/Putnam, New York, p185; Roberts, C. (2007) *The Unnatural History of the Sea*, Island Press, Washington, DC, p280; Volkov, K. (2001) 'The caviar game rules', *Reuters* (IUCN Environmental Media Award winner); 2007 quota from UNEP (2007) '2006 ban on caviar lifted', Press Release, 2 January.

70   Myers, R. and Worm, B. (2003) 'Rapid worldwide depletion of predatory fish communities', *Nature*, vol 432, pp280–283.

71   Balmford, A. et al (2004) 'The worldwide costs of marine rotected areas', *Proceedings of the National Academy of Sciences*, vol 101, no 26, pp9694–9697.

72   FAO (2007) *The State of World Fisheries and Aquaculture 2006*, FAO, Rome.

73   OECD (2008) *OECD Environmental Outlook to 2030*, OECD, Paris.

74   OECD (2008) *OECD Environmental Outlook to 2030*, OECD, Paris.

75   Sumaila, U. R. and Suatoni, L. (2006) *Economic Benefits of Rebuilding US Ocean Fish Populations*, Fisheries Centre Working Paper no 2006-04, University of British Columbia, Vancouver.

76   Sumaila, U. R. and Suatoni, L. (2006) *Economic Benefits of Rebuilding US Ocean Fish Populations*, Fisheries Centre Working Paper no 2006-04, University of British Columbia, Vancouver, Table 1.

77   OECD (2006) *Subsidy Reform and Sustainable Development: Economic, Environmental and Social Aspects*, OECD, Paris.

78   *Business Wire* (2008) 'Learning from cod collapse to save tuna', *Business Wire*, 18 February.

79   FAO (1999) *The State of World Fisheries and Aquaculture 1998*, FAO, Rome.
80   FAO (2005) *Increasing the Contribution of Small-Scale Fisheries to Poverty Alleviation and Food Security*, FAO Technical Guidelines for Responsible Fisheries, no 10, FAO, Rome.
81   FAO (2005) *Increasing the Contribution of Small-Scale Fisheries to Poverty Alleviation and Food Security*, FAO Technical Guidelines for Responsible Fisheries, no 10, FAO, Rome.
82   US Food and Drug Administration (2004) 'FDA announces qualified health claims for omega-3 fatty acids', Press release, US Food and Drug Administration.
83   Morris, M. C., Sacks, F. and Rosner, B. (1993) 'Does fish oil lower blood pressure? A meta-analysis of controlled trials', *Circulation*, vol 88, no 2, pp523–533.
84   Harris, W. S. (1997) 'n-3 fatty acids and serum lipoproteins: Human studies', *American Journal of Clinical Nutrition*, vol 65 (5 Supplement), pp1645S–1654S; Sanders, T. A. B., Oakley, F. R., Miller, G. J., Mitropoulos, K. A., Crook, D. and Oliver, M. F. (1997) 'Influence of n-6 versus n-3 polyunsaturated fatty acids in diets low in saturated fatty acids on plasma lipoproteins and hemostatic factors', *Arteriosclerosis, Thrombosis, and Vascular Biology*, vol 17, no 12, pp3449–3460; Roche, H. M. and Gibney, M. J. (1996) 'Postprandial triacylglyc-erolaemia: The effect of low-fat dietary treatment with and without fish oil supplementation', *European Journal of Clinical Nutrition*, vol 50, no 9, pp617–624.
85   Bucher, H. C., Hengstler, P., Schindler, C. and Meier, G. (2002) 'n-3 polyunsaturated fatty acids in coronary heart disease: A meta-analysis of random-ized controlled trials', *The American Journal of Medicine*, vol 112, no 4, pp298–304; Burr, M. L., Sweetham, P. M. and Fehily, A. M. (1994) 'Diet and reinfarction', *European Heart Journal,* vol 15, no 8, pp1152–1153; Willett, W. C., Stampfer, M. J., Manson, J. E., Colditz, G. A., Speizer, F. E., Rosner, B. A., Sampson, L. A. and Hennekens, C. H. (1993) 'Intake of trans fatty acids and risk of coronary heart disease among women', *The Lancet*, vol 341, no 8845, pp581–585.
86   Environment Canada (undated) 'Questions and answers: What are invasive alien species?', www.ec.gc.ca/eee-ias/default.asp?lang=En&n=02101A38-1#ws2A6F42D7, accessed 7 July 2009.
87   Pimentel, D., Lach, L., Zuniga, R. and Morrison, D. (1999) *Environmental and Economic Costs Associated with Non-Indigenous Species in the United States*, College of Agriculture and Life Sciences, Cornell University, US.
88   Environment Canada (undated) 'Questions and answers: To what extent do invasive alien species impact our economy?', www.ec.gc.ca/eee-ias/default.asp?lang=En&n=02101A38-1#ws2A6F42D7, accessed 7 July 2009.
89   Mack, R. et al (2008) 'China's booming economy is sparking and accelerating biological invasions', *BioScience*, vol 58, pp317–324.
90   McNeely, J. (2000) *Global Strategy for Addressing the Problem of Invasive Alien Species – A Result of the Global Invasive Species Programme (GISP)*, IUCN–World Conservation Union, Switzerland, p7.
91   UNEP (2007) *Global Environment Outlook: Environment for Development (GEO-4) Report,* UNEP, see Media Release, www.unep.org/geo/geo4/media/media_briefs/Media_Briefs_GEO-4%20Global.pdf, accessed 23 March 2008.
92   Species Survival Commission (2007) *IUCN Red List of Threatened Species*, www.iucnredlist.org, accessed 12 September 2008.

93 World Parks Congress (2003) 'Message of the 5th IUCN World parks congress to the convention on biological diversity', www.internationalwildlifelaw.org/WPCCBD.pdf, accessed 26 March 2008.

94 Myers, N., Mittermeier, R. A., Mittermeier, C. G., da Fonseca G. A. B. and Kent, J. (2000) 'Biodiversity hotspots for conservation priorities', *Nature,* vol 403, pp853–858.

9

Decoupling Economic Growth from Freshwater Extraction

The Complex Challenge of Freshwater Extraction and Use

We have in the past been concerned about the impacts of economic growth upon the environment. We are now forced to concern ourselves with the impacts of ecological stress – degradation of soils, water regimes, atmosphere, and forests – upon our economic prospects.

Our Common Future, 1987, p5

Fresh water is essential for life on our planet and is a critical component of most forms of economic development – ranging from primary sector activities to industrial production, energy generation and service sector development. The critical nature of water to human survival and economic activity explains why, historically, civilizations, cities and towns have grown and prospered next to, or with access to, plentiful sources of fresh water. However, history has shown that the manner in which water is used can be a significant factor in the long-term success or failure of a society, with the legacy of the world's first recorded civilization, Sumeria, being that of an environmental disaster.[1] The demise of Sumaria was largely due to irrigation practices that caused the increased salinity of agricultural land – with a Sumerian clay tablet recording that 'the earth turned white'. Despite the growing levels of soil salinity, the Sumer rulers had based their wealth and power on having a food surplus, and thus they required the farmers to continue irrigating and farming the salty land, inevitably leading to food shortages. Without enough food to feed and pay for large armies, their civilization was vulnerable and finally fell in 2370 BC to the Akkadian Empire from the north.

Just as the survival of past ancient civilizations has been threatened by poor water management, so is the long-term survival and sustainability of many rural and urban settlements in many parts of the world. In the 21st century, climate change threatens to significantly reduce water availability and lead to greater frequency of droughts in many countries and regions of the world. Studies by the International Water Management Institute have estimated that by the year 2025, one-third of the world's population will face absolute water scarcity.[2] According to the OECD this number could rise to two-thirds by around 2050 unless serious efforts are made to decouple economic growth from freshwater extraction.[3]

Climate change is set to exacerbate freshwater shortages significantly. It is already changing the water cycle and affecting water availability. Rising temperatures are boosting evaporation rates, altering rainfall patterns and melting glaciers that feed rivers during the dry season. In fact, the effects of climate change on these parts of the water cycle are so significant that the IPCC in 2008 released a new technical report on *Climate Change and Water* which concluded that:[4]

- *Globally, the area of land classified as very dry has more than doubled since the 1970s. There have been significant decreases in water storage in mountain glaciers and northern hemisphere snow cover. Shifts in the amplitude and timing of run-off in glacier- and snowmelt-fed rivers, and in ice-related phenomena in rivers and lakes, have been observed.*
- *By the middle of the 21st century, many semi-arid and arid areas (e.g. the Mediterranean Basin, western US, southern Africa, northeastern Brazil and Murray Darling Basin, Australia) are particularly exposed to the impacts of climate change and are projected to suffer a decrease of water resources due to climate change.*
- *Globally, the negative impacts of future climate change on freshwater systems are expected to outweigh the benefits. By the 2050s, the area of land subject to increasing water stress due to climate change is projected to be more than double that with decreasing water stress.*
- *Water supplies stored in glaciers and snow cover are projected to decline in the course of the century, thus reducing water availability during warm and dry seasons in regions supplied by melt water from major mountain ranges, where more than one-sixth of the world's population currently lives.*

Furthermore, climate change that leads to increasing average global temperatures will also directly reduce agricultural yields in many countries and areas, including southern Europe, the US and Australia.[5] For instance, an Australian study found that over the next 100 years, unmitigated climate change is forecast to devastate the Murray Darling Basin, which is the major food bowl for Australia. In one unmitigated scenario put forward by the Garnaut Climate Change Review, irrigation will continue in the Basin in the immediate term, but by 2030, economic production will fall by 12 per cent. By 2050 this loss will increase to 49 per cent and, by 2100, 92 per cent will be lost due to climate change.[6] The reality is that drought conditions have prevailed in many parts of rural Australia since 2000 and most of the 50,000 farmers in the Murray Darling Basin are already operating on less than 20 per cent of their normal water allocations.[7] Such impacts from climate change will add significant pressure to the economies of the world and this, combined with the fact that in many parts of the world – such as West Asia, the Indo-Gangetic Plain in South Asia, the North China Plain and the High Plains in North America – freshwater extraction rates are exceeding the natural water replenishment rates, means that decoupling water extraction from economic growth will prove to be a crucial component of economic development this century.

To date, in order to achieve the steady increases in food production required by the growing world population, countries have not only relied on irrigation from rivers but also from groundwater supplies. However, almost all of the world's wells now have falling water levels and declining yield, and many have run dry. Today in the US, groundwater provides drinking water for over half the population. The same applies in much of Europe, India, China and many other countries.[8] Together with the massive volumes of water used for agriculture, this means that many countries are in a classic overshoot-and-decline mode, with the potential risk only becoming clear when wells run dry. Developing nation economies are particularly sensitive to the surface-water impacts of climate change and subsequent overuse of groundwater because their economies and society are heavily dependent on the agriculture sector, which contributes 20–60 per cent of their nations' GDP. For example, the groundwater overdraft rate exceeds 25 per cent in China and 56 per cent in parts of northwest India.[9]

The issue of water availability and climate change will not just impact upon farmers and agriculture. Supplying fresh water is now a critical issue for many cities. Traditionally, many cities have relied largely on a network of dams to collect and store fresh water to meet urban demand. In the 21st century, when climate change is forecast to reduce and alter rainfall patterns in many parts of the world, this highly centralized approach cannot guarantee adequate future water supplies for rising populations as it is heavily reliant on rainfall falling in small geographical areas where there are dammed water catchments. This is a major challenge facing water supply authorities and utilities in the 21st century. Even without factoring in the risks from long-term climate change, some water supply authorities are struggling to keep pace with demand. According to a 2003 report by the US government's General Accounting Office, *Freshwater Supply: States' Views of How Federal Agencies Could Help Them Meet the Challenges of Expected Shortages*,[9A] current trends in rising water demand mean that at least 36 US states are anticipating local, regional, or state-wide water shortages by 2013 under 'normal conditions', with 46 US states anticipating water shortages under 'drought conditions' by 2013. Longer term, this report noted that 'Water supply conditions in all regions of the United States are likely to be affected by climate change in the future, either through increased demand for water associated with higher temperatures or changes in supply because of changes in precipitation and runoff patterns.' Already, some cities in the US are having to rely on piping water from other regions to meet their needs. In the US, cities such as San Diego, Los Angeles, Las Vegas, Denver and El Paso, are increasingly meeting their needs by taking a percentage of the irrigation water previously allocated for farming.[10] Hence, with rural and city implications in mind, this chapter focuses on how to decouple economic growth from freshwater extraction, both for agriculture and city supplies.

Economic Benefits Associated with Reducing Freshwater Consumption

Investments in water efficiency, demand management, rainwater and storm water harvesting and reuse to decouple freshwater extraction from economic growth have strong economic multipliers because they lead to multiple cost benefits, as well as creating local jobs and boosting the local economy. An economic impact study of the Malaysian Muda irrigation project reported that not only was water use reduced, but substantial indirect economic benefits were found in a range of other associated sectors of the regional economy. The study found that for every dollar of direct benefits, another 83 cents were generated in the form of downstream or indirect effects.[11] A study of a number of water-efficient irrigation investment projects in India found economic multipliers of as much as three times.[12] Such initiatives that deliver associated multiplier effects are a key part of the decoupling process. For example, water efficiency savings in business, industry and residential supply can also result in reduced wastewater treatment costs and energy savings from reduced water distribution and from reducing the amount of water needing to be heated. The amount of energy needed for pumping water for agriculture, and to distribute and heat water for use in businesses, commercial buildings and homes, is significant. The Californian Energy Commission 2005 report, *California's Water–Energy Relationship*,[12A] showed that water-related electricity use makes up 19 per cent of all energy used in California. Thus once the return on investment from water efficiency initiatives are achieved, usually within one to four years, business, industry and households do not just have lower annual water and water treatment costs but also lower energy costs too. If they then choose to invest this money in additional cost-effective water and energy saving opportunities, still more funds can be generated over time, further stimulating economic activity. Water efficiency and recycling investments have a high economic multiplier because they reduce demand for water resources and can thus delay, and even in some cases prevent, the need to build new water supply infrastructure such as dams, desalination plants and water treatment plants. Dr Peter Gleick, director of the Pacific Institute, showed in 2003, in his *Science* journal paper 'Global freshwater resources: Soft-path solutions for the 21st century',[12B] that the annual cost of ensuring all globally have access to clean water through investing in more large-scale centralized dams and treatment plants would cost around US$180 billion per annum to at least 2025. However, this figure can be reduced to an annual cost of US$10–25 billion, if the emphasis is on investing in water efficiency, demand management, rain and stormwater harvesting and water recycling at appropriate scale.

As Wolff and Gleick explain, 'water efficiency reduces the size, duration and frequency of peak water system loads. Peak loads determine the size of capital facilities required, hence capital costs. Lower peak loads mean that existing capital facilities can serve more customers, avoiding or reducing the expense of these facilities. Lowering peak water demand and usage also reduces peak energy usage by water utilities to pump, treat and handle water, providing further cost savings.'[13]

Research led by Professor White at the Institute for Sustainable Futures (Australia), indicates that for cities and towns facing the need to build more water supply infrastructure, investing in water efficiency can result in water savings of greater than 30 per cent, and can yield net present value economic benefits in excess of AU$100 million for some capital cities.[14] Research by the Pacific Institute has come to a similar conclusion for California, finding that despite progress already made in water efficiency, a further one-third of California's current urban water use can be saved through conservation and efficiency in the residential, commercial, institutional and industrial sectors.[15] Its report also showed that once the potential energy efficiency saving co-benefits were taken into account from water efficiency initiatives, virtually all water efficiency investments were financially worthwhile. In particular, the report found that at least 85 per cent of the savings can be achieved at costs below what it would cost to tap into new sources of supply and without the negative social, environmental and economic impacts that any new major dam project would bring. In a separate 2005 report that investigated the wider Californian economy including agriculture, the Pacific Institute found that water efficiency measures could reduce overall water usage to 20 per cent below 2000 levels by 2030, even with a growing population and a strong economy.[16]

With this type of research under way, water efficiency programmes are becoming better understood and this experience is leading to the development of robust and cost-effective long-term strategies. As more programmes come to fruition, short-term economic benefits are also being identified, by studies such as the 2009 US study by the Alliance for Water Efficiency, which showed that for the US economy:[17]

Table 9.1 *Example of the true cost of ambient water
and hot water (US$/kL)*

Purchase cost	1.13[†]
Wastewater treatment costs[*]	0.75
Wastewater pumping costs	0.05
Wastewater discharge costs (volume charge)	0.40
True cost for ambient water	2.33
Heating to 80°C[**]	2.80
True cost of hot water	5.13

Note: * Based on assumption of typical treatment costs of an anaerobic digester
** Costs for heating to 80°C using steam produced by a gas boiler
† Based on Brisbane Water supply costs
Source: UNEP Working Group for Cleaner Production in Food (2004)[18]

- *The economic output benefits of investments in water efficiency range between US$2.5 and 2.8 million per million dollars of direct investment.*
- *GDP benefits range between US$1.3 and 1.5 million per million dollars of direct investment.*
- *Employment potential ranges between 15 and 22 jobs per million dollars of direct investment.*
- *Direct investment in the order of US$10 billion in water/energy efficiency could save between 20 and 40 trillion litres of water, with resulting energy reductions as well.*

For businesses, water efficiency saves money directly through reduced water costs, and indirectly by reducing wastewater treatment requirements (including energy requirements and the cost of chemicals) and trade waste disposal. These hidden costs of water usage are rarely properly evaluated and so potential cost savings from water-efficiency improvements tend to be underestimated. For example, in the food processing industry, some of the hidden components include the purchase price, treatment of incoming water, heating or cooling, treatment of wastewater, disposal of wastewater, pumping, maintenance (e.g. pumps and corrosion of pipe-work and equipment) and capital depreciation.[19] Table 9.1 provides an example of evaluating the full costs of water at ambient temperature, and of hot water, to businesses in the food processing industry. The results show that while the nominal purchase cost of the water is US$1.13, the true cost is actually US$2.33 for water at ambient temperature, and US$5.13 for water heated to 80°C.

Despite such a strong economic and financial case, little effort has been made by most businesses, farmers and most cities on the whole to improve the efficiency of water use, leading to high levels of wastage, even though significant opportunities have been shown to still exist to increase productivity, as shown in *Factor Five*.[20] This is particularly true in the agricultural sector where the true cost of water has been heavily subsidized, with farmers in many parts of the world paying very little to nothing at all for water, as shown in Figure

9.1. Thus OECD households or industries are potentially paying as much as 100 times more for water compared to the prices paid by farmers.[21] However, even with this comparative cost discrepancy, water usage by industry and urban businesses is still very cheap, where water costs typically, in OECD countries, represent less than 2 per cent of the total operating costs of most businesses and households. Hence, as for energy, the lack of a strong price signal for industry and residential consumers has resulted in most water efficiency opportunities in many countries being largely ignored.

A range of studies now show that increasing water prices can induce conservation. For instance, in Bogor, Indonesia, an increase in the water tariff from US$0.15 to US$0.42 per cubic metre resulted in a 30 per cent decrease in household demand for water. In Goa, India, increased water tariffs induced a 50 per cent reduction in water use over a five-year period by a fertilizer factory, and in Sao Paulo, three industries reduced water consumption by 40–60 per cent in response to the establishment of effluent charges.[22] The structures of water-pricing tariffs for households and commercial buildings vary considerably among OECD countries, but there is a trend away from fixed charges (e.g. based on dwelling size or number of occupants) and toward two-part tariffs which include both a small fixed component (to reflect fixed costs such as connection or metering costs) and a volumetric component to reflect the levels of water consumed. By charging consumers based on the actual volume of water used, volumetric pricing systems provide incentives for efficient water use. Some countries have also been experimenting with 'peak pricing' arrangements, especially seasonal pricing, in order to better manage demand.[23]

Another reason why large water efficiency opportunities exist globally is that urban water utilities have not had incentives to encourage their customers

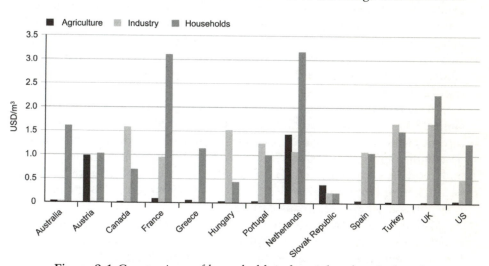

Figure 9.1 *Comparison of household, industrial and agricultural water prices for a selection of OECD countries*

Source: Adapted from OECD (2001)[24]

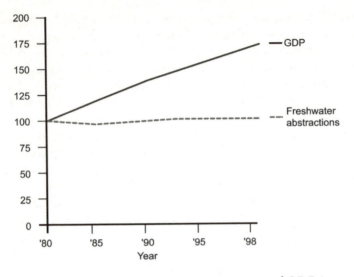

Figure 9.2 *Freshwater extraction per unit of GDP in OECD countries, 1980–1998*

Note: Not including Australia, Belgium, France, Greece, Ireland, Italy, Luxembourg, Mexico, Netherlands, New Zealand, Norway, Portugal and the UK.
Source: OECD (2002)[25]

to use water more efficiently. Rather, they have simply been required to ensure supply and to keep selling more water to customers, much like energy utilities. Governments and the water supply industry have also historically addressed increasing demand for water by building more dams or more desalination plants, rather than encouraging greater water efficiency.[26] However, a range of market-based strategies, policies and demand management programmes can be used to encourage consumers to value water efficiency, rain and stormwater harvesting and water recycling, reducing overall freshwater demand on the limited resource, and reducing and delaying the need to invest in new dams and storage and treatment works.

To support this there have been numerous technical innovations that now enable 50–90 per cent water efficiency savings, most of which have a short return-on-investment period, as shown in Tables 9.2 and 9.3.[27] However, despite the significant potential for decoupling through water efficiency, reuse and recycling opportunities, most countries have only achieved relative decoupling of economic growth from freshwater extraction (see Figure 9.2), with only a few examples of absolute decoupling.

With this theory and reality in mind, we now explore a portfolio of options that can assist nations to achieve absolute decoupling of economic growth from freshwater extraction across the major areas of global freshwater usage in agriculture, industry, cities and buildings. According to the UN, the major global uses of freshwater include agriculture (69 per cent, mostly for irrigation), followed by urban, which includes industry (23 per cent) and buildings

(8 per cent, for drinking water and sanitation).[28] Hence we focus first on agriculture (grazing and cropping), followed by cities (industry and buildings).

Decoupling Economic Growth from Freshwater Extraction for Grazing

Decoupling economic growth from freshwater extraction on farms can be achieved through a combination of technology, policy and management actions. In *The Natural Advantage of Nations* we discussed the necessary policy and water-trading market mechanisms needed to underpin efforts to decouple economic growth from freshwater extraction in the agricultural sector, featuring pioneering work in this field by Dr Mike Young and Dr Jim McColl.[29] Here we focus on farming practices, and considering that of the total land used by agriculture, most is for livestock grazing (69 per cent, 3488Mha) followed by cropland (28 per cent, 1405Mha),[30] we will first look at ways to reduce freshwater extraction and irrigation by maintaining healthy pastures, followed by the potential to reduce freshwater extraction for crops.

Grazing pastures have tended to lose productivity over time, leading farmers to invest in more irrigated water, chemicals, fertilizers and the machinery to undertake traditional pasture improvement techniques to maintain pasture productivity. In the late 1980s, Allan Savory published *Holistic Management*[31] which explored a new way to restore pasture health and productivity while reducing artificial inputs and required irrigation levels. Savory helped to change the understanding of the underlying causes of grazing land productivity loss, and his methods have now been applied to 30 million hectares of grazing land globally with remarkable and economically attractive

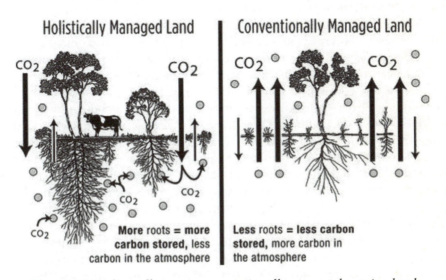

Figure 9.3 *Holistically versus conventionally managed grazing land*

Source: Holistic Resource Management[32]

results. Furthermore, as the IPCC has concluded that the majority of the mitigation potential for the agriculture sector arises from soil carbon storage,[33] Savory's methods have shown that there is significant potential to enable greater levels of carbon to be stored in the plants and soil, as shown in Figure 9.3 and explained in the following paragraphs.

Up until the end of the 20th century, 'set stocking', also known as continuous grazing, was the standard agricultural practice, involving livestock browsing on one piece of land for an extended period of time. 'Conservative' stocking rates allowed the livestock to graze selectively, preferring some species while leaving others untouched.[34] With this practice, the extent of defoliation is largely determined by which species the livestock find most palatable.[35] Over many months in the same paddock, continuous grazing tends to reduce the amount of vegetation and the height of the preferred species as there is minimal time for regrowth and recovery. As the grasses and plants lose their height they also have less surface area to undertake photosynthesis and subsequently less capacity to grow large root systems or rapidly regrow. Set stocking also reduces the resilience of grasses and plants that are not grazed which can become 'rank' or 'tired'.[36] Furthermore, in set stocking livestock tend to form sprawling 'camps' where they rest and these areas can become bare due to frequent trampling, leading to soil erosion and land degradation issues. And once land degradation occurs on one part of the landscape over time it tends to spread.[37] In contrast, historically, as the plants and the animals were evolving together, herds of closely packed livestock roamed the landscape, regularly moving to new areas to miminize risk of attack from predators. Savory realized that the problem was one of concentration, where domesticated grazers – with stockpeople guarding them and killing their predators – have no reason to clump together. Their impact on the land is therefore scattered and erratic.

Acknowledging these differences, Savory proposes a new grazing method called 'holistic resource management', which promotes 'time control grazing', 'a grazing management method where stock are moved through a number of paddocks at high stock density ... Stock moves are based on growth rate of pasture and its consequent physiological requirement for rest'.[38] Under this method large groups of stock graze for up to 14 days in a comparatively small paddock, before the paddock is then left to rest and recover for 30–100 days.[39] The short-duration and high-density grazing forces livestock to eat whatever grasses and vegetation are available, and not just those species it prefers. The short duration that the stock spend in each paddock prevents them from forming habitual camps, and with the regular movement of the dense herd, plants and grasses are 'mulched' (pushed back into the soil) through hoof action. Livestock manure is also more evenly spread out across the landscape reducing the potential for local over-fertilizing, and the need to add artificial fertilizers in other areas. Savory also recommends a return to natural native grasses and perennial plants as these tend to have greater resilience as they have co-evolved to thrive with only natural levels of rainfall. The combination of these changes leads to more soil biota activity, improved soil structure and hydraulic properties, and increased and more active root systems of plants, enabling soils to become more porous and stable. This also leads to higher infiltration of water into the soils and reduced surface water run-off and evaporation. Organic matter in the topsoil helps it hold a greater amount of water, which can lessen the need for irrigation dramatically. This means plants and grasses are able to grow longer in dry periods because more of the natural rainfall is stored in the soil. Furthermore, more active and extensive root systems, higher soil organic matter, and greater soil biota activity all means that grazing pastures have the capacity to store significantly more carbon than they currently do using the set stocking method.

Decoupling Economic Growth from Freshwater Extraction for Cropping

In *Factor Five*[40] our team worked with Professor von Weizsäcker to compile world-leading examples of water productivity improvements in agriculture. The research showed that through a whole system approach, using a combination of the following five strategies, up to 80 per cent reductions in freshwater extraction can be achieved:

1   appropriate selection and rotation of crop species;
2   sub-surface drip irrigation and irrigation scheduling;
3   advanced deficit irrigation strategies;
4   rainwater harvesting;
5   reusing urban stormwater and recycled water for peri-urban agriculture.

Here we summarize each strategy, updating the work in *Factor Five*, and incorporating leading findings from research undertaken by the Pacific Institute, based on interviews with Dr Peter Gleick.[41]

1 Appropriate selection and rotation of crop species

Selecting crops that are well suited to the intended biophysical and climatic conditions can deliver in the order of 50 per cent water savings. Furthermore, due to the foreseeable impacts of altered climatic conditions, not only is it important to choose appropriate crops, the variety of the crop, referred to as the varietal, is also important, with some offering lower water requirements, heat shock resistance, drought tolerance, higher protein levels, and resistance to new pests and diseases. For instance, researchers have developed drought-tolerant 'Tuxpeño' corn that can increase harvests by 40 per cent under drought conditions.[42] Additionally, researchers have been able to modify wheat varieties through intensive plant breeding to increase production even in hot climates and provide strong built-in resistance to major diseases.[43] Once appropriate crop species and varietals have been selected, water productivity can be further increased using crop rotation. Investigations of innovative crop rotation by leading farmers by the Australian National University (ANU) have verified that rotating rice and wheat crops can lead to significantly less water consumption overall. The trial grew wheat as a winter crop in rotation with a summer 'temperate Japonica' rice crop, and found that through precise and efficient use of flood irrigation for the rice crop the soil moisture levels were maintained during winter to allow a wheat crop to use little or no further irrigation, meaning that on average both crops can be harvested over the year for around the same level of irrigation as the most water-efficient wheat crop.[44]

2 Sub-surface drip irrigation and irrigation scheduling

Significant potential exists to reduce water consumption in agriculture as, in many countries, over 90 per cent of irrigated land surface receives water by flooding or through open channels. Water efficiency savings through sub-surface drip irrigation can be as high as 50–80 per cent, and can be made more affordable for use in the developing world.[45] However, currently only a few countries, namely Cyprus, Israel and Jordan, are fully utilizing the potential of drip irrigation, with the method used on only 1–3 per cent of irrigated land in India and China, and on roughly 4 per cent of agricultural land in the US.[46] Furthermore, by combining drip irrigation with appropriate watering schedules, informed by water sensors, water usage has been shown to reduce by 17 per cent, and crop yields to increase by as much as 8 per cent.[47]

3 Advanced deficit irrigation strategies

A growing body of international work shows that water consumption can be significantly reduced in orchards and vineyards using advanced 'deficit irrigation'. This method sees the application of water at below the full requirement for the particular crop, causing it to be more efficient with its water and reducing evapo-transpiration.[48] For instance, in Turkey, deficit irrigation strategies were shown to increase the yield of a winter wheat crop by 65 per cent.[49] Similar positive results have been described for cotton.[50] As documented in *Factor Five*:

> *One exciting area of research and development in this field has been that of the partial dry zone irrigation technique that is allowing farmers to achieve still more significant reductions in water application. It is called 'partial root-zone drying' because at any one time only half the root-zone is in a drying state. Using two rows of drip-line irrigation, instead of the usual one, one part of the root system side of the plant is kept wet while the other side is dried. The grower irrigates through one line at a time, two or three times a week for a couple of weeks (whatever local conditions dictate), then the same on the other line – that pattern continues throughout the season. The drying roots send a hormonal message to the rest of the plant that it is deprived of*

water, so the leaf stomata close, preventing excess moisture loss and reducing excessive shoot growth. In other words the plant is 'tricked' into believing it's stressed and the end result is a plant which uses the water it has, far more efficiently than it otherwise would use. This allows up to 50 per cent reductions in the total amount of water needed to irrigate many crops on top of traditional drip irrigation.[51]

4 Rainwater harvesting

A wide variety of small-scale innovations are available which can catch and store rainfall for agriculture as well as aquifer and groundwater replenishment – collectively referred to as 'rainwater harvesting' technology.[52] In addition to storage containers (rainwater tanks and bladders), rainwater harvesting can include micro-dams, and channels and stream diversions that direct rainfall and river flow out over flood plains to rehydrate them, boosting productivity. Rainwater harvesting techniques are particularly important in those parts of the tropics where there is a long dry period after the wet season or in dry temperate climates where rainfall is infrequent and light. A grazing and fruit farm in the coastal tropics of Australia demonstrates this well. Owner Adrian Pozzebon had a choice in the mid-1990s to either address the water shortage or close the farm, reflecting:

> *This farm, being in the dry tropics, received rain for only a few months a year, from December through to February, which quickly flowed through the streams and rivers out to sea. So for the rest of the year the property relied on extracting bore water in large volumes, at about 75,000 gallons [284,000 litres] an hour. Over time the quality of the bore water decreased and the salinity levels in it increased significantly. We had no choice. We had to change practices or we would have had to close the farm. We figured that the key was learning how to restore the natural hydrology and slow down the flow of water through the landscape. We invested in natural structures across our creeks so that when the rains came these structures spread the water out over the floodplain effectively.*[53]

The results of this rainwater harvesting have been remarkable and were quickly achieved, including a near complete halt to the use of bore water pumping, significantly reducing salinity and improving productive land capacity. According to Pozzebon, 'The results have been so impressive that there are now at least six other farms that I am aware of trying aspects of this strategy in the dry tropics of Far North Queensland.'[54]

5 Reusing urban stormwater and recycled water for peri-urban agriculture

The FAO estimates that across 50 countries, 20 million hectares are already directly or indirectly irrigated with wastewater[55] – close to 10 per cent of the total irrigated area of the world.[56] 70 per cent of Israeli municipal wastewater is treated and reused, mainly for agricultural irrigation of non-food crops. Yet in virtually all other cities, most of the water which falls on that city is running out to sea as stormwater. Recycling stormwater and treated water from sewerage and reusing it for non-potable water applications therefore offers a significant way to assist peri-urban agriculture or replenish and store water in underground aquifers under or near cities in preparation for future droughts due to climate change.

Decoupling Urban Economic Growth from Freshwater Use in Industry

Globally, industry is the second largest user of fresh water in the world after agriculture. The potential to achieve significant reductions in net water usage and freshwater usage in a number of sectors and industries is significant because many industrial processes do not need fresh potable water. Many companies are finding that water efficiency and onsite water recycling measures are an effective way to reduce operating costs. Similarly, companies and organizations in the services sectors (for example in tourism, research, education and health) are finding that they too can achieve large water savings cost effectively. The examples shown in Table 9.2 demonstrate that across most sectors 60–95 per cent reductions in freshwater use can be achieved (further details are available in the online resource, *Water Transformed: Sustainable Water Solutions for Climate Change Adaptation*).[57]

Decoupling Economic Growth from Freshwater Use in Cities

Significant potential exists to reduce water consumption in cites through a range of mechanisms as shown in Table 9.3 (see also *Factor Five*). A number of cities have achieved significant per capita freshwater use reductions through implementing a suite of progressive water conservation programmes as part of a broad demand management programme. These cities include Jerusalem, Israel; Mexico City, Mexico; Los Angeles, California; Seattle, Washington State; Beijing, China; Singapore; Boston, Massachusetts; Waterloo, Canada; Bogor, Indonesia; and Melbourne, Sydney, and Brisbane, Australia. Sydney has been able to reduce its 2010 per capita water usage levels to 1970 levels largely through its water efficiency and demand management programmes. This is also true of Seattle, which started implementing demand management programmes in the 1990s, and by 2007 had reduced per capita water usage by 35 per cent. There is also significant potential to reduce the need for freshwater and

Table 9.2 *Best practice case studies demonstrating the potential for decoupling*

Sectors	Best of sector case studies
Steel manufacture	In the steel sector, water is used primarily for cooling and environmental treatment in the steelmaking process. There are two main methods for making steel: oxygen blast furnace (OBF) and electric arc furnace (EAF). Compared to OBF methods, EAF methods use 85% less water, and 70% less energy per tonne of steel.[58] BlueScope Steel's Port Kembla Steelworks in Australia has shown that a fivefold improvement in water efficiency can also be achieved in OBF steel making, reducing water use from 55 to 9 million litres per day.[59]
Aluminium manufacture	In the aluminium sector, water is largely used for cooling and environmental treatment in the aluminium smelting process. Alcoa, in their European Mill Products business, which includes casthouse and rolling mills, has achieved a 95% reduction in water consumption through installing a closed-loop system that recirculates process water, and has committed to 70% reductions in potable water use throughout all global operations.
Paper manufacture	Visy, through its Australian paper and pulp mill in Tumut, New South Wales has achieved an 80% reduction in the average water consumed by pulp and paper mills compared to elsewhere in the world. In accordance with its site-based ISO14001 certified environmental management system, no water is discharged off the site, and treated wastewater is used for the irrigation of pastures.[60]
Information and communication technology manufacture	With manufacturing plants all over the world, and many in very dry places, Intel has invested US$100 million on water efficiency measures, saving more than enough water to supply 180,000 homes for a year. Intel's 1000 acre (405 hectare) operation in Arizona includes processing equipment that uses 75% less water than the industry average (from 25 to 8 million litres per day). Additionally, Intel constructed a system that treats wastewater and then injects it into the local aquifer, treating and injecting more than 3.5 billion gallons (13.2 billion litres) of drinking-quality water into the aquifer since its inception in 2000.[61]
Chemical manufacture	Since 2002, Qenos, a leading chemicals and plastics company, has reduced its annual freshwater consumption by over 30%, saving 1.2 billion litres of water per year.[62]
Food processing	Oberti Olives olive processing plant in Madera, California processes in the order of 128 tonnes of olives per day, involving washing, curing, storing and packaging. Through installing a best practice membrane filtration system to enable water reuse, the company has reduced its freshwater use by 91%, equating to more than 3.5 million litres per day.[63]
Beverage industry	Breweries, on average, use about 6–8 litres of water per litre of product. Fosters Brewery at Yalata, Queensland has achieved a 75% improvement in water efficiency since 1993,[64] using only around 2 litres of water per litre of product.[65] Pacific Coca-Cola has also reduced its can line's need for rinse-water by 79%, using air instead of water to clean the insides of cans.[66]
Tourism and hospitality	The Hyatt Regency Sanctuary Cove resort, Queensland, Australia has reduced water use by more than 65%, from 140 million litres in 1996 to 54 million litres in 2000, saving AU$85,372 per year.[67]
Medical and health	Saint Petersburg hospital in Florida, US has saved 50% of its water,[68] while St Andrew's War Memorial Hospital in Brisbane, Australia has reduced its water use by 68%, from 105 to 33 million litres per year, in just four years.[69]
University campuses	The Queensland University of Technology in Brisbane, Australia reduced water consumption by 50% between 2004 and 2007, equating to 200 million litres per year, and has since reduced its consumption by a further 5–10% across its campuses.[70] The University of Queensland, Brisbane, Australia has reduced water usage by 48% since 2003.[71] The University of California's Santa Barbara campus reduced water usage by nearly 50% between 1987 and 1994, saving US$3.7 million, excluding energy and maintenance savings.[72]

Source: Compiled by The Natural Edge Project, based on Smith et al (2010),[73] with references added.

groundwater extraction through rainwater and stormwater harvesting, especially those cities situated on or near the coast. Currently, in most coastal cities, significant amounts of water is either used once, or falls on roads and roofs as rain, and then flows directly out to sea. However, as an example of what is possible, in two very different parts of the world, Singapore (population 3.5 million)[74] and Orange County[75] in southern California (2.3 million) have both made commitments to maximize the use of available fresh water through aggressive water-recycling schemes. Singapore and Orange County have also developed schemes that will use a dual membrane process to recycle domestic wastewater (sewage) to levels that approach the quality of distilled water. The basic cost to treat and recycle water using the dual membrane process is about 55 cents a kilolitre on top of the cost of treatment to secondary effluent standards. To compare, seawater desalination techniques cost about US$1.40 a kilolitre. While Singapore built four plants that recycle 20 per cent of water that is currently discharged into the ocean, Orange County commissioned one large recycling plant to treat the municipal wastewater before its use in recharging natural groundwater supplies. The recycled water mixes with existing groundwater supplies for six months to a year before it is pumped to the surface, treated and delivered through the water distribution system. Another area of significant opportunity for cities is from addressing water leakages. Most urban areas throughout the world are losing 30–50 per cent of their water supply through leakage. For instance, Mexico City found that its water system was losing 1.9 billion m^3 of water every year due to leakage. Jerusalem reduced its annual consumption of water by 14 per cent from 1989 to 1991 just by instituting a leak detection and repair system.[76]

Addressing leaks in buildings, residential and commercial, is important because the building sector is the third highest user of fresh water globally after agriculture and industry. Leakage of water in commercial buildings can be as much as 30 per cent of the overall building's consumption,[77] with roughly a third of this water wasted in leaking pipes, another third used in amenities (toilets, showers, etc.) and the final third in cooling towers. In the last 10–20 years a wide range of enabling technologies have been invented which, used together, can enable residential and commercial buildings to reduce their water use significantly. For example, technologies now exist to enable 80 per cent or better efficiency improvements in amenities and cooling towers. Through utilizing such technologies Melbourne University's new Faculty of Economics and Commerce building has achieved 90 per cent reductions in mains-supplied freshwater usage. The building achieves this through utilizing all the water-efficient amenities, reducing cooling demand by utilizing natural ventilation, using chilled beam cooling technology, and by the installation of highly efficient dry hybrid water coolers,[78] combined with rainwater harvesting and greywater reuse. Enabling technologies now also exist to help different commercial buildings – commercial laundromats, restaurants, hospitals – to achieve large cost-effective freshwater savings.

Residential buildings can also reduce their freshwater usage significantly through the use of efficient showerheads and water-efficient appliances, toilets and taps. Combining these can improve the water efficiency for an average home by over 60 per cent.[79] Rainwater tanks and greywater recycling systems can further significantly reduce demand for potable water, as can designing gardens to be drought tolerant.[80] For example, the Currumbin Ecovillage, in Australia, has shown that through using these strategies it is also possible to achieve self-sufficiency in water supply for a residential estate.[81] As Table 9.3 shows, many of these water-efficient technologies also achieve significant

Table 9.3 *Enabling technologies in water efficiency and potential for decoupling*

Sector	Enabling technologies
Buildings	• Various low-flow showerhead designs exist to reduce water consumption by 50–75%,[82] resulting in sizable reductions in water consumption along with the requirement for water heating. • Low-flow aerators reduce tap water flow by 30–50% and can also reduce the energy costs of heating water by up to 50%. • Water-efficient appliances such as front-loading domestic washing machines are 40–75% more efficient than top loading options. • Toilets using 6/3 litre dual flush systems are capable of reducing water usage by 67% compared with conventional models.[83]
Commercial buildings	• Waterless urinals use liquid-repellent coatings and a lighter-than-urine biodegradable liquid to trap odours, and can save between 150,000 and 230,000 litres per year.[84] • Ultra-efficient water urinals can flush with as little as a half a litre. • Hybrid dry air/water cooling systems for large buildings have been optimized to reduce typical consumption of water by as much as 75%.[85]
Commercial laundromats	• Highly efficient washers can reduce water consumption by 35–50% and achieve energy savings of up to 50%, with highly efficient washers requiring 50% less detergent.
Restaurants	• Boiler-less compartment food steamers have been developed that use 90% less water. • Water-efficient commercial dishwashers can save 25% of water usage. Payback periods for installing small efficient commercial dishwashers range between one and four years. • Pre-rinse spray valves account for 14% of water consumption in commercial kitchens. Replacing a traditional pre-rinse spray valve can save 25–80% of this water.
Medical and health	• Steam sterilizers are utilized widely in hospitals, pharmaceutical manufacturing, and research institutions to disinfect surgical instruments in hospitals, research and development laboratories and in the manufacture of products where sterilization is essential. Among many strategies, most sterilizers can be retrofitted with heat exchangers to cool condensate without the need to dilute the hot condensate water with tap water thus enabling the water to be reused. • Traditional X-Ray film processing generally uses a constant flow of potable water to cool the machine and develop the film, and 98% saving of water use can be achieved by recycling this water for use in the equipment.

Source: NDRC (2009)[86] unless otherwise noted

energy savings as well. For further detail on how these enabling technologies can be used to improve the water efficiency of commercial buildings see the online textbook , *Water Transformed: Sustainable Water Solutions for Climate Change Adaptation.*[87]

There is significant potential to decouple economic growth from fresh water extraction by outlining how to reduce freshwater usage in the major areas of agriculture, industry and buildings (residential and commercial) (for a further detailed explanation on how to achieve decoupling economic growth from freshwater extraction, see the online textbook *Water Transformed: Sustainable Water Solutions for Climate Change Adaptation*).[88]

Notes

1   Brown, L. (2008) *Plan B 3.0: Mobilizing to Save Civilization*, W. W. Norton & Company, New York.
2   Seckler, D., Amarasinghe, U., Molden, D., de Silva, R. and Barker, R. (1998) *World Water Demand and Supply, 1990 to 2025: Scenarios and Issues*, Research Report 19, International Water Management Institute (IWMI), Colombo, Sri Lanka; Seckler, D., Baker, R. and Amarasinghe, U. A. (1999) 'Water scarcity in the twenty-first century', *International Journal of Water Resources Development* (Special Double Issue: Research from IWMI), vol 15, no 1/2, pp29–42.
3   OECD (2002) *Sustainable Development Strategies: A Resource Book*, OECD, Paris.
4   Bates, B. C., Kundzewicz, Z. W., Wu, S. and Palutikof, J. P. (eds) (2008) *Climate Change and Water*, Technical Paper of the Intergovernmental Panel on Climate Change, IPCC Secretariat, Geneva.
5   Stern, N. (2006) *The Stern Review: The Economics of Climate Change*, Cambridge University Press, Cambridge, p104.
6   Garnaut, R. (2008) *The Garnaut Climate Change Review Final Report*, Cambridge University Press, Cambridge.
7   Craik, W. and Cleaver, J. (2008) *Modern Agriculture Under Stress – Lessons from the Murray-Darling*, The Murray-Darling Basin Commission, MDBC Publication Number: 46/08, Australia; Cooley, H., Christian-Smith, J. and Gleick, P. (2009) *Sustaining Californian Agriculture in an Uncertain Future*, Pacific Institute, CA.
8   Brown, L. (2008) *Plan B 3.0: Mobilizing to Save Civilization*, W. W. Norton & Company, New York.
9   Briscoe, J. (2008) *India's Water Economy: Bracing for a Turbulent Future*, World Bank, Washington, DC.
9A United States General Accounting Office (2003) *Freshwater Supply: States' Views of How Federal Agencies Could Help Them Meet the Challenges of Expected Shortages*, United States General Accounting Office, www.gao.gov/new.items/d03514.pdf.
10 Brown, L. (2008) *Plan B 3.0: Mobilizing to Save Civilization*, W. W. Norton & Company, New York.
11 Bell, C., Hazell, P. and Slade, R. (1982) *Project Evaluation in Regional Perspective: A Study of an Irrigation Project in Northwest Malaysia*, World Bank and Johns Hopkins University Press, Baltimore and London, p326.
12 Bhattarai, M., Barker, R. and Narayanamoorthy, A. (2003) 'Who benefits from irrigation investments in India? Implication of irrigation multiplier estimates for

cost recovery and irrigation financing', A workshop paper presented at the ICID regional meeting in Taipei, Taiwan, 10–12 November, vol 1, pp285–296.

12A Californian Energy Commission (2005) *California's Water–Energy Relationship*, Californian Energy Commission, www.energy.ca.gov/2005publications/ CEC-700-2005-011/CEC-700-2005-011-SF.PDF.

12B Gleick, P. (2003) 'Global freshwater resources: Soft-path solutions for the 21st century', *Science*, vol 302, no 5650, pp1524–1528.

13 Wolff, G. and Gleick, P. (2002) *The Soft Path for Water*, World Water Atlas, Island Press, Washington, DC.

14 White, S. (2009) Personal communication with Professor Stuart White, University of Technology Sydney, Institute for Sustainable Futures, 14 April.

15 Gleick, P. et al (2003) *Waste Not, Want Not: The Potential for Urban Water Conservation in California*, Pacific Institute, CA.

16 Gleick, P., Cooley, H. and Groves, D. (2009) *California Water 2030: An Efficient Future*, Pacific Institute, CA.

17 Mithcell, D., Beecher, J., Chesnutt, T. and Pekelney, D. (2008) *Transforming Water: Water Efficiency as Stimulus and Long-Term Investment*, Alliance of Water Efficiency, Chicago, IL.

18 Pagan, R., Prasad, P., Price, N. and Kemp, E. (2004) *Food Processing Eco-Efficiency Manual*, UNEP Working Group for Cleaner Production in Food, Australia Industry Group.

19 Pagan, R., Prasad, P., Price, N. and Kemp, E. (2004) *Food Processing Eco-Efficiency Manual*, UNEP Working Group for Cleaner Production in Food, Australia Industry Group.

20 von Weizsäcker, E., Hargroves, K., Smith, M., Desha, C. and Stasinopoulos, P. (2009) *Factor Five: Transforming the Global Economy through 80% Improvements in Resource Productivity*, Earthscan, London.

21 OECD (2004) *OECD Environmental Strategy: 2004 Review of Progress*, OECD, Paris

22 OECD (2004) *OECD Environmental Strategy: 2004 Review of Progress*, OECD, Paris.

23 OECD (2004) *OECD Environmental Strategy: 2004 Review of Progress*, OECD, Paris.

24 Adapted from OECD (2001) *Environmental Indicators for Agriculture, Volume 3: Methods and Results*, OECD, Paris, cited in OECD (2004) *OECD Environmental Strategy: 2004 Review of Progress*, OECD, Paris.

25 OECD Secretariat (2002) *Indicators to Measure Decoupling of Environmental Pressure and Economic Growth*, OECD, Paris.

26 Troy, P. (ed) (2008) *Troubled Waters: Confronting the Water Crisis in Australia's Cities*, ANU E-Book Publication.

27 Cohen, R., Ortez, C. and Pinkstaff, C. (2009) *Making Every Drop Work: Increasing Water Efficiency in California's Commercial, Industrial, and Institutional (CII) Sector*, Natural Resources Defense Council, New York.

28 FAO and IFAD (2006) 'Water for food, agriculture and sustainable livelihoods', in United Nations (2006) *The Second UN World Water Development Report*, UN World Water Assessment Programme.

29 Hargroves, K. and Smith, M. (eds) (2005) *The Natural Advantage of Nations: Business Opportunities, Innovation and Governance in the 21st Century*, Earthscan, London.

30 Bates, B. C., Kundzewicz, Z. W., Wu, S. and Palutikof, J. P. (eds) (2008) *Climate Change and Water*, Technical Paper of the Intergovernmental Panel on Climate

Change, IPCC Secretariat, Geneva.

31 Savory, A. and Butterfield, J. (1988) *Holistic Management: A New Framework for Decision Making* (second edition), Island Press, Washington, DC.

32 FAO and IFAD (2006) 'Water for food, agriculture and sustainable livelihoods', in UN (2006) *The Second UN World Water Development Report,* United Nations World Water Assessment Programme.

33 Holistic Resource Management (2009) 'A solution to climate change is right under our feet: Putting carbon in the soil and keeping it there', www.holisticmanagement.org/n9/about/carbon.php, accessed 29 July 2009.

34 Allan, C. (1994) 'Grazing management – the animal factor', *Proceedings 9th Annual Conference of Grassland Society NSW*, 13–14 July, pp77–82.

35 Allan, C. (1994) 'Grazing management – the animal factor', *Proceedings 9th Annual Conference of Grassland Society NSW*, 13–14 July, pp77–82.

36 Ticehurst, J. (1996) 'Over grazed but under stocked: A comparison of grazing systems in the Southern Tablelands, New South Wales, Australia', Honours thesis, ANU.

37 Ticehurst, J. (1996) 'Over grazed but under stocked: A comparison of grazing systems in the Southern Tablelands, New South Wales, Australia', Honours thesis, ANU.

38 Cook, G. (1994*)* 'A simple explanation of time control grazing', *Proceedings of the 9th Annual Conference of the Grassland Society, NSW Department of Agriculture*, 13–14 July, pp113–114.

39 Hacker, R. (1993) 'A brief evaluation of time control grazing', *Proceedings of the 8th Annual Conference of the Grassland Society NSW Department of Agriculture*, pp82–89.

40 von Weizsäcker, E., Hargroves, K., Smith, M., Desha, C. and Stasinopoulos, P. (2009) *Factor Five: Transforming the Global Economy through 80% Improvements in Resource Productivity,* Earthscan, London, see Chapter 4.

41 Gleick, P., Cooley, H. and Groves, D. (2009) *California Water 2030: An Efficient Future*, Pacific Institute, CA; Cooley, H. et al (2008) *More with Less: Agricultural Water Conservation and Efficiency in California – A Special Focus on the Delta*, Pacific Institute, CA; Cooley, H. Christian-Smith, J. and Gleick, P. (2009) *Sustaining Californian Agriculture in an Uncertain Future*, Pacific Institute, CA.

42 Khan, S., Hanjraa, M. and Mua, J. (2008) 'Water management and crop production for food security in China: A review', *Agricultural Water Management*, vol 96, no 3, pp349–360.

43 World Water Forum (2000) 'Scientists and farmers create improved crops for a water-scarce world', Press Release, World Water Forum, 21 March.

44 Dumaresq, D. (2009) Personal Communication with Dr David Dumaresq, Australian National University, 24 March.

45 Shah, T. and Keller, J. (2002) 'Micro-irrigation and the poor: Livelihood potential of low-cost drip and sprinkler irrigation in India and Nepal', in Sally, H. and Abernethy, C. (eds) *Private Irrigation in Sub-Saharan Africa*, FAO/IWMI, International Water Management Institute, Colombo, pp165–183; Sijali, I. V. and Okuma, R. A. (2002) 'New irrigation technologies', in Blank, H. G., Mutero, C. M. and Murray-Rust, H. (eds) *The Changing Face of Irrigation in Kenya: Opportunities for Anticipating Change in Eastern and Southern Africa*, IWMI, Colombo.

46 Brown, L. (2008) *Plan B 3.0: Mobilizing to Save Civilization*, W. W. Norton & Company, New York.

47 Cooley, H. et al (2008) *More with Less: Agricultural Water Conservation and Efficiency in California – A Special Focus on the Delta*, Pacific Institute, CA.

48 Chaves, M., Santos, T., Souza, R., Ortuno, M., Rodrigues, M., Lopes, C., Maroco, J. and Pereira, J. (2007) 'Deficit irrigation in grapevine improves water use efficiency while controlling vigour and production quality', *Annals of Applied Biology*, vol 150, pp237–252; Fereres, E. and Soriano, M. A. (2006) 'Deficit irrigation for reducing agricultural water use', *Journal of Experimental Botany*, vol 58, no 2, pp147–159.

49 Ilbeyi, A., Ustun, H., Oweis, T., Pala, M. and Benli, B. (2006) 'Wheat water productivity and yield in a cool highland environment: Effect of early sowing with supplemental irrigation', *Agricultural Water Management*, vol 82, pp399–410.

50 Ilbeyi, A., Ustun, H., Oweis, T., Pala, M. and Benli, B. (2006) 'Wheat water productivity and yield in a cool highland environment: Effect of early sowing with supplemental irrigation', *Agricultural Water Management*, vol 82, pp399–410; Raes, D., Geerts, S. and Vandersypen, K. (2008) 'More food, less water', in Raymaekers, B. (ed) *Lectures for the XXIst Century*, Leuven University Press, Leuven, Belgium, pp81–101; Geerts, S. et al (2008) 'Introducing deficit irrigation to stablize yields of quinoa (*Chenopodium quinoa Willd*)', *European Journal of Agronomy*, vol 28, pp427–436; Spreer, W., Ongprasert, S., Hegele, M., Wünnsche, J. and Müller, J. (2009) 'Yield and fruit development in mango (*Mangifera indica L. cv. Chok Anan*) under different irrigation regimes', *Agricultural Water Management*, vol 96, pp574–584.

51 von Weizsäcker, E., Hargroves, K., Smith, M., Desha, C. and Stasinopoulos, P. (2009) *Factor Five: Transforming the Global Economy through 80% Improvements in Resource Productivity*, Earthscan, London.

52 Practical Action (undated) 'Rainwater harvesting technical factsheets', http://practicalaction.org/?id=rainwater_harvesting, accessed 21 February 2009.

53 Smith, M. and Hargroves, K. (2007) 'Water: Vital for our future', in Khoo, V. (2007) *Australian Innovation: Towards A Sustainable Future*, CL Creations, NSW Australia.

54 Smith, M. and Hargroves, K. (2007) 'Water: Vital for Our Future', in Khoo, V. (2007) *Australian Innovation: Towards A Sustainable Future*, CL Creations, NSW Australia.

55 UN World Water Development Report (2003) *Water for People, Water for Life*, UNESCO, Paris.

56 Ensink, J., Mahmood, T., van de Hoek, W., Raschid-Sally, L. and Amerasinghe, F. (2004) 'A nation-wide assessment of wastewater use in Pakistan: An obscure activity or a vitally important one?' *Water Policy*, vol 6, pp1–10.

57 Smith, M., Hargroves, K., Stasinopoulos, P. and Desha, C. (2010) *Water Transformed: Sustainable Water Solutions for Climate Change Adaptation*, Griffith University, Australian National University, The Natural Edge Project, Australia, www.naturaledgeproject.net/Sustainable_Water_Solutions_Portfolio.aspx.

58 von Weizsäcker, E., Lovins, A. and Lovins, H. (1997) *Factor Four: Doubling Wealth, Halving Resource Use*, Earthscan, London

59 Hird, W. (2005) 'Recycled water – case study: BlueScope Steel, Port Kembla Steelworks', Presented at the International Conference on Integrated Concepts on Water Recycling, Wollongong, NSW, Australia, 14–17 February.

60 AusCID (2003) *Sustainability Framework for the Future of Australia's Infrastructure Handbook*, Australian Council for Infrastructure and Development (Contributions by Toyne, P., Tate, A., Hargroves, K. and Smith, M.).

61 Cohen, R., Ortez, C. and Pinkstaff, C. (2009) *Making Every Drop Work: Increasing Water Efficiency in California's Commercial, Industrial, and Institutional (CII) Sector*, Natural Resources Defense Council, New York, United States.

62 City West Water (undated) 'Water use efficiency project: Ongoing efforts at Quenos', www.citywestwater.com.au/business/docs/Qenos-Case_Study.pdf, accessed 1 August 2009.

63 Pacific Institute (1999) *Sustainable Use of Water California Success Stories*, the Pacific Institute, CA.

64 Fosters Group (2007) 'Yatala Brewery: Water usage facts', Fosters Group.

65 Davis, C. (2007) 'Crystal balling water for industry', *Waste Management and Environment (WME)*, Industrial Water Supplement, November.

66 Hawken, P., Lovins, A. B. and Lovins, L. H. (1999) *Natural Capitalism*, Earthscan, London, 'Chapter 11: Aqueous solutions', p225.

67 SaveWater (undated) 'Case studies', www.savewater.com.au/how-to-save-water/in-business/hospitality/case-studies, accessed 2 August 2008.

68 South Florida Water Management District (undated) 'Hospital case study: A St Petersburg hospital saves 50% of its water use!', www.swfwmd.state.fl.us/conservation/waterwork/casestudy-hospital.html, accessed 7 August 2009.

69 St Andrews War Memorial Hospital (2008) 'St Andrew's Hospital beats all expectations in reducing water usage', www.uchealth.com.au/sawmh/index.php?option=com_content&task=view&id=53, accessed 21 June 2009.

70 Queensland University of Technology, Brisbane (QUT) (2009) 'Sustainability@QUT', www.fmd.qut.edu.au/pdfs/Sustainability_Feb_2009_FINAL.pdf, accessed 13 August 2009.

71 University of Queensland, Queensland (2009) 'UQ Saves More Water', www.uq.edu.au/news/index.html?article=18669, accessed 13 August 2009.

72 Pacific Institute (1999) *Sustainable Use of Water: California Success Stories*, Pacific Institute, CA.

73 Smith, M., Hargroves, K., Stasinopoulos, P. and Desha, C. (2010) *Water Transformed: Sustainable Water Solutions for Climate Change Adaptation*, Griffith University, Australian National University, The Natural Edge Project, Australia. www.naturaledgeproject.net/Sustainable_Water_Solutions_Portfolio.aspx.

74 Lee, P. O. (2005) *Water Management Issues in Singapore*, Institute of Southeast Asian Studies, Singapore.

75 Groundwater Replenishment System (undated) 'Orange County Groundwater Replenishment Scheme', www.gwrsystem.com, accessed 2 August 2009.

76 UNESCO (undated) 'Eliminating unhealthy water/providing clean water for all', www.unesco.org/education/tlsf/TLSF/theme_a/mod02/www.worldgame.org/wwwproject/what04.shtml, accessed 12 July 2009.

77 Department of Environment, Water, Heritage and the Arts (DEWHA) (2007) *Water Efficiency Guide: Office and Public Buildings*, DEWHA, Australia.

78 Muller Industries (2009) '5 stars for Melbourne University', *Muller Industries News*, April.

79 Stasinopoulos, P., Smith, M., Hargroves, K. and Desha, C. (2008) *Whole System Design: An Integrated Approach to Sustainable Engineering*, Earthscan, London, and The Natural Edge Project, Australia.

80 Troy, P. (2008) *Troubled Waters: Confronting the Water Crisis in Australia's Cities*, ANU Epress.

81 Corrumbin Ecovillage (undated) 'Sustainability objectives',

http://theecovillage.com.au/site/index.php/C4/, accessed 18 April 2009.

82 von Weizsäcker, E., Lovins, A. B. and Lovins, L. H. (1997) *Factor Four: Doubling Wealth, Halving Resource Use*, Earthscan, London.

83 Caroma (undated) 'Caroma dual flush system', www.caromauk.com/innovate/idea_1.htm, accessed 12 July 2009.

84 Hawken, P., Lovins, A. B. and Lovins, L. H. (1999) *Natural Capitalism*, Earthscan, London, p221.

85 von Weizsäcker, E., Hargroves, K., Smith, M., Desha, C. and Stasinopoulos, P. (2009) *Factor Five: Transforming the Global Economy through 80% Improvements in Resource Productivity*, Earthscan, London.

86 Cohen, R., Ortez, C. and Pinkstaff, C. (2009) *Making Every Drop Work: Increasing Water Efficiency in California's Commercial, Industrial, and Institutional (CII) Sector*, Natural Resources Defense Council, New York, United States.

87 Smith, M., Hargroves, K., Stasinopoulos, P. and Desha, C. (2010) *Water Transformed: Sustainable Water Solutions for Climate Change Adaptation*, Griffith University, Australian National University, The Natural Edge Project, Australia. http://www.naturaledgeproject.net/Sustainable_Water_Solutions_Portfolio.aspx.

88 Smith, M., Hargroves, K., Stasinopoulos, P. and Desha, C. (2010) *Water Transformed: Sustainable Water Solutions for Climate Change Adaptation*, Griffith University, Australian National University, The Natural Edge Project, Australia, www.naturaledgeproject.net/Sustainable_Water_Solutions_Portfolio.aspx.

10

Decoupling Economic Growth from Waste Production

The development of this chapter has been undertaken by Peter Stasinopoulos, Michael Smith and Karlson Hargroves.

The Complex Challenge of Addressing Waste Production

Since 1980, annual global resource extraction (by mass) has increased by 36 per cent and is expected to grow to 80 billion tonnes in 2020.[1] Alongside such growth in material flows, most cities of the world are seeing significant increases in municipal waste production. For instance, in China's urban areas, municipal waste production is projected to increase by more than three times between 2000 and 2030.[2] Much of this waste is widely regarded by the community as undesirable as it has the potential to create a range of health and environmental pollution problems, as identified in *Our Common Future*: 'Another poorly used resource is solid wastes, the disposal of which has become a major problem in many cities, with much of it dumped and uncollected. Promoting the reclamation, reuse, or recycling of materials can reduce the problem of solid waste, stimulate employment, and result in savings of raw materials.'[3] The reality is that land-filling municipal waste uses space which is becoming increasingly scarce and valuable in and around cities, particularly in rapidly growing economies like India and China. Most importantly from an economic point of view, land-filling assumes that the cost of disposal is small and the value gained from recycling the waste negligible, which is often no longer the case considering the value of recycled materials such as plastics, glass, rubber, metals and organic compost.

Land-filling also has the potential to devalue property, contaminate land and pollute surface and groundwater, threatening human health, ecosystem health, biodiversity and potable water supplies. In addition, greenhouse gas emissions are created from the energy used to transport waste and from decomposing organic materials in the fill. Given that even small amounts of hazardous waste can cause widespread and long-term contamination of soil and water, there is significant value in nations pursuing sound waste management practices. Furthermore, given the finite nature of non-renewable resources such as minerals and metals, there is value in recycling and recovering materials and resources from the municipal waste stream, simultaneously reducing the amount of waste going to landfill while also reducing the demand for virgin materials to be extracted from the biosphere. As demonstrated by the growing recycling industry (including steel, glass, rubber and cardboard packaging industries), recycling of these materials can be profitable while also directly reducing energy demand and greenhouse gas emissions.

The good news is that average levels of waste production, and land-filled volumes, appear to be growing less than GDP among OECD countries, indicating a relative decoupling trend at least has been achieved,[4] as shown in Figure 10.1. In most OECD countries, citizens have embraced domestic recycling, which has led to a significant increase in materials available to be recycled. Technical innovations now enable most major waste streams to be recycled, from plastics through to metals, paper, glass and even e-waste. Moreover, technologies and processes now exist to automatically separate many of the major waste streams into component materials. By 2005, for the OECD, the amount of municipal waste disposed of in landfills had fallen to 49 per cent from 64 per cent in the mid-1990s; 30 per cent was being recycled, a 12 per cent improvement on the mid-1990s; and 21 per cent was being incinerated or otherwise treated, compared with 18 per cent in the mid-1990s.[5] In 1980 the US recycled only 9.6 per cent of its municipal rubbish, compared with 32 per cent in 2008.[6] A similar trend can be seen in Europe, where some countries, such as Austria and the Netherlands, now recycle 60 per cent or more of their municipal waste. The UK's recycling rate, at 27 per cent, is low, but it is increasing rapidly, having nearly doubled between 2006 and 2008.[7]

However, given the rapid growth being experienced in waste production, there is still immense potential to improve recycling levels of most major waste streams in most OECD countries.[8] For example, the EU's Landfill Directive (1999) requires member states to reduce the amount of biodegradable waste disposed to landfills to 75 per cent of 1995 levels by 2010, then to 50 per cent by 2013 and 35 per cent by 2020.[9] However, while countries such as the Netherlands and Denmark already meet the 2020 target, the European Commission reported in 2005[10] that most EU countries were not on track, and in 2007 took legal action against Italy for failing to comply with its directives.[11] In the US, at least five states have reported fewer than ten years of remaining capacity for land-filling, leading to increased shipment of solid

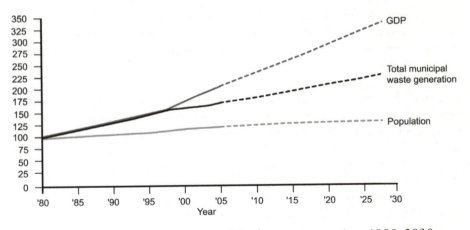

Figure 10.1 *OECD country municipal waste generation, 1980–2030*

Source: OECD (2008), p238

waste between states and regions.[12] In 2003, 39 million tonnes of waste (around 16 per cent of all waste generated) was shipped around the country with New York as the largest exporter and Pennsylvania the largest importer, impacting on increased greenhouse gas emissions associated with transportation, in addition to increased risks of spills and other potentially hazardous incidents.[13]

The experience of the last two decades has shown that, while traditional approaches like recycling have slowed the rate of waste to landfill and subsequently the rate of growth of environmental pressures concerning waste, overall levels of waste generation are still growing. Furthermore, attempting to curb the still expanding stream of waste being produced is a complex challenge, which includes addressing such factors as:

- The high variability in approaches to reuse and recycling, as well as waste collection, treatment and disposal in various countries and regions. In transitioning economies for example, as little as 50 per cent of municipal waste is collected and/or treated appropriately.[14]
- The globalization of trade, which makes trans-boundary movement of some types of waste attractive and cost effective for disposal in countries prepared to accept waste for a fee, especially for the more complicated products that are hazardous or difficult to recycle, such as electric and electronic appliances.
- The insidious nature of illegal trans-boundary waste movement, which makes hazardous waste in particular difficult to track. For example, between 2004 and 2006, 5 per cent of inspected trans-boundary waste transportation within and from the EU was illegal.[15] While some illegal shipments from EU countries stay within Western Europe, many go to developing regions, such as Africa and Asia, causing problems there.

- The difficulty in finding information about reuse and recycling opportunities, given that existing data networks are often insufficient to give a real-time and coherent view of how different materials are flowing through the economy.[16]

Hence without a substantial change in thinking about resources and waste, such complexities will see the global levels of waste generation continue to rise significantly over the next decade. Indeed, the OECD has concluded that:

> *With continuous growth in the global demand for materials and the amounts of waste generated and disposed of, conventional waste policies alone may not be enough to improve material efficiency and offset the waste-related environmental impacts of materials production and use. New integrated approaches – with stronger emphasis on material efficiency, redesign and reuse of products, and waste prevention – could be used to counterbalance the environmental impacts of waste throughout the entire life-cycle of materials.*[17]

A number of countries are already adopting such policies and strategies, including the EU thematic strategies on 'Sustainable Use of Natural Resources'[17A] and on 'Waste Prevention and Recycling',[17B] Japan's 'Sound Material-Cycle Society',[18] China's 'Circular Economy',[19] and the US's Resource Conservation and Recovery Act.[20] These strategies are using a portfolio of options building on from the previous 'reduce, reuse, recycle' hierarchy to form strategies to 'refuse, reduce, reuse, remanufacture, repair, refurbish, recondition and recycle', such as:

- **Rethinking design (refuse and reduce)**: encouraging early stage holistic design options to reduce waste production. By refusing to accept waste as a necessary by-product, this can open up a number of design options to eliminate waste from a range of systems, by encouraging greater emphasis on the entire life cycle. 'Lean thinking' is a concept focused around this notion, made popular through the Japanese manufacturing industry, comprising a set of tools that can assist in identifying and eliminating waste or 'muda' (in addition to improving flow and avoiding overburdening the system) during product manufacture.[21] In 2001 Japan enacted a Fundamental Law for Establishing a Sound Material-Cycle Society which provided a framework for policies to comprehensively and systematically transform to a 'sound material-cycle society'.[22] As of 2008, policies are in place to govern source reduction, reuse and recycling of products such as containers and packaging, electric household appliances, construction materials, food waste and end-of-life vehicles, as well as in a number of specific manufacturing industries,[23] in addition to promoting green purchasing by government agencies and independent administrative institutions.[24]

- **Reuse**: encouraging consumers to purchase used goods and components. Reusing products and components, primarily at the organization and community level, extends the useful lives of products, and hence the service they can deliver before needing to invest in recycling or disposal. Such policies within organizations can be very low cost, and even basic initiatives can accumulate to significantly reduce waste and offset other purchasing decisions. For example in the tourism industry, a major Holiday Inn hotel in the centre business district of Melbourne, Australia, has implemented an environmental policy and programme that aims to reduce resource consumption, including a set of relatively simple policies for reusing a variety of products. Through the programme, the hotel targeted a 44 per cent reduction in waste but instead achieved a 77 per cent reduction in three months.[25] Standard practice is now that plastic chemical containers and food packaging are cleaned and reused, printing is done on both sides of the paper, scrap paper is used as note pads, cardboard boxes are used as recycle bins, and old linen, towels and half-used toiletries are donated to charities for the homeless.

- **Remanufacture**: changing business and public attitudes towards purchasing remanufactured goods (also referred to as repaired, refurbished or reconditioned). Providing economic and other incentives such as extended warrantees through business and government collaborations promotes the purchasing of remanufactured goods (goods that have been made with refurbished components).[26] For example, remanufactured goods already make up a US$50 billion market in the US, including automobile components, photocopiers, toner cartridges, furniture, ready-to-use cameras and personal computers, yet studies show that this market could be significantly increased.[27] Markets for second-hand cars, clothes and jewellery are also already extensive.[28]

- **Recycling**: building plants with the latest sorting and processing technologies. Establishing government and industry collaborations that address major barriers to building additional recycling industries is necessary in order to lift overall recycling rates. There are increasing precedents to ensure that recycling infrastructure is located in the most economically and environmentally efficient locations, usually those that accommodate easy access to local reliable feedstock supplies and recycled materials markets. For example, recycling infrastructure can benefit from incorporating drop-off centres for the local community, from being located in an industrial park, or from being located near other processing facilities and waste management facilities that can pre-treat or post-treat the materials.

- **Recycling**: creating markets for recycled content. Establishing government and industry collaborations that build markets for products with recycled content. For example, recycling rates can be lifted through 'buy recycled' alliances for organizations such as business, government, schools and education sector networks. Such alliances involve policies that stipulate the purchase of recycled-content office products such as notepads, sticky labels, facial and toilet tissue, copy paper, hand towels, pencils, calendars, presentation folders, refillable whiteboard markers, envelopes, print cartridges, timber equipment and furniture.[29]

With such components of resource policies and strategies in mind, we now consider a number of strong economic drivers for government and business to focus on decoupling waste production from economic growth. We then look at each of the options described above in more detail, with regard to opportunities to achieve absolute decoupling of waste to landfill through rethinking design, reuse, remanufacturing and recycling.

Economic Drivers for Decoupling Waste Production from Economic Growth

As the finite nature of raw materials such as oil, rubber and precious metals begins to affect the pricing of inputs in manufacturing processes, there are a number of emerging economic drivers for factoring out waste from manufacturing and production processes. These previously disregarded 'externalities' include the production costs, the cost and potential liability in managing hazardous and toxic waste, and the costs of acquiring, managing and maintaining disposal sites. Decoupling of waste production from economic growth occurs as these costs are successively identified and removed alongside improved organizational performance, further fuelled by the strengthening performance of the recycling industry. At a basic level, waste can be thought of as an 'unsaleable product' as it costs the organization to produce it without capturing any further benefit. Such costs may include for example: the acquisition of too much 'raw' component material (such as paper, plastics, chemicals, fabrics, wood and metal) which is later discarded as off-cuts or leftovers; transportation of these excess inputs and their packaging to the point of use/processing/product manufacture; costs related to the overconsumption of energy and water for given processes or services; and costs of processing, collecting and disposing of the waste. There are therefore financial incentives driving the identification of such issues and the designing of waste out of the system. The result can include significantly lower operating costs, including the potential for using this 'waste' onsite. It may even uncover revenue-making opportunities in on-selling to others or converting the waste into other saleable products. As Amory Lovins from the Rocky Mountain Institute reflects:[30]

> *It is extremely profitable to wring out waste, even today when nature is valued at approximately zero, because there is so much waste – quite an astonishing amount after several centuries of market capitalism. In the American economy, the material that we extract from the planet, that we mobilize for economic purposes, and process and move around and ultimately dispose of, totals about 20 times the body weight of a person per day. So*

*worldwide this resource flow is in the order of a half-trillion tons
per year. And what happens to it? Well, only about 1% of it ends
up in durable goods; the system is about 99% waste. That's a
business opportunity.*

Another driver for reducing waste is the need to reduce hazardous and toxic
waste generation, to avoid negative public and environmental health impacts
and associated potential liability and remediation costs. For example, under
the Massachusetts Toxics Use Reduction Act (1989), manufacturers have
voluntarily and cost effectively reduced their total use of toxic chemicals by 40
per cent, their by-product releases by 70 per cent, and their site releases to air,
water and soil by 91 per cent.[31] In addition to waste being a lost resource and a
potential liability, waste disposal imposes a significant cost on government, in
the acquisition, management and long-term maintenance of disposal sites.
There are also public costs associated with increased air pollution from incineration, loss of public land, risks from the spread of disease, and hazardous
waste leaching from landfills into groundwater supplies or being released into
the air. In the economic literature, when such 'externality' costs related to
landfill are taken into account, recycling has been found to almost always be
economically efficient.[32] This is increasingly being acknowledged by governments through a variety of types of recycling programmes,[33] green (plant)
waste composting and organic waste processing using methods such as vermi-
culture. For example, a study conducted by the Technical University of
Denmark found that in 83 per cent of cases, recycling is the most efficient
method to dispose of household waste.[34] Furthermore, a study of municipal
waste and landfill in Israel found that for 51 per cent of the municipalities, it
would be (economically) efficient to adopt recycling, even without accounting
for externality costs.

As recycling rates improve, the emergence of recycling industries is also
driving demand for further increasing recycling rates, and subsequently making
growing contributions to national economies. For example, recycling employs
over 1.5 million employees in more than 50 countries, with an annual turnover
exceeding US$160 billion, and is estimated to process over 600 million tonnes
of commodities annually.[35] US EPA studies show that the reuse and recycling
industry consists of approximately 56,000 establishments that employ over 1.1
million people, generate an annual payroll of nearly US$37 billion, and gross
over US$236 billion in annual revenues.[36] The recycling industry is also
contributing to reducing greenhouse gas emissions per unit of product in the
manufacturing industry. Not only does the use of recycled materials lead to
reductions in the consumption of raw materials, there are also significant
reductions in the energy required to produce inputs from recycled materials
compared to raw resources, as the recovered materials have already been
extracted and processed. For example, aluminium can be produced from
recyclate using 95 per cent less energy,[37] while the recycling of other materials
also achieves considerable energy savings, including copper (70–85 per

cent),[37A] lead (60–80 per cent),[37B] zinc (60–75 per cent)[37C] magnesium, (95 per cent),[37D] paper (64 per cent),[37E] plastics (70–80 per cent)[37F] and glass (60–70 per cent).[38] Indeed, such advanced resource efficiency strategies in product manufacture can enable a much greater decoupling of economic growth from waste production by not only reducing the costs of material inputs, but also enabling a market of secondary materials that are, in many cases, cheaper than the equivalent primary materials.

Decoupling Economic Growth from Waste Production – By Rethinking Design

Since *Our Common Future* was published, there have been numerous innovations in product, process and policy design that can reduce the amount of waste being generated and ensure that most products can be readily reused, remanufactured or recycled. Good design approaches can also ensure that if waste is to be generated, it can later become a useful material resource. As Hawken et al wrote in *Natural Capitalism* more than a decade ago, 'by the time the design for most human artefacts is completed but before they have actually been built, about 80–90 per cent of their life-cycle economic and ecological costs have already been made inevitable'.[39] These facts have led many in the design professions to call for more attention to be paid to the design decisions made in the earlier phases of projects, where changes cost the least and which can lead to better considered decisions, lower life-cycle costs, and fewer late changes. This focus on the early stages of design is known as 'front-end design'.[40] Spending more time and money at the front-end of any project design, whether it be in the built environment, chemical, pharmaceutical or other product development, has been shown to be a cost-effective way to achieve large resource efficiency improvements which reduce the amount of resources needed and waste produced.[41]

Alongside the front-end design approach, product stewardship seeks to clearly establish the implications of product design with respect to waste production and to ensure that products do not end up as waste but can be remanufactured or recycled into new products. Product stewardship essentially requires key participants throughout the product chain – from manufacturer to consumer – to share responsibility for the products they produce, handle, purchase and use. This includes improving the efficiency of resource use in products, increasing resource recovery, minimizing the generation of waste (including hazardous substances), improving the management of post-consumer waste by ensuring recyclability, and reducing the risks to human health from poor management of products.

In some cases, businesses may incur extra costs in investing in research and development, and in retooling factories to achieve better product design, which could be a potential disadvantage in terms of cost competitiveness with other companies. However, to encourage all companies to embrace product steward-ship approaches, governments can provide a level playing field by regulating non-participants and giving industry certainty that there will be no significant short-term loss of competitive advantage from 'doing the right thing'. This 'co-regulatory approach' to product stewardship involves a combination of industry self-regulation and government regulation to ensure that non-participants do not gain a competitive advantage. The strongest form of product stewardship regulation is 'extended producer responsibility' (EPR) regulation, which can be implemented using one or a combination of two models:

- an individual producer responsibility (IPR) model, which requires producers to take responsibility for their own products only; and/or
- a collective producer responsibility (CPR) model, which requires producers to take responsibility for all products of the same type as their own.

There is good reason to recommend that IPR provides better incentives for producers to invest in product design over CPR. Although IPR faces challenges such as the potential requirement for additional administration work, duplicated infrastructure, increased transport and a supplementary system to handle orphaned products (where accessing the producer is not possible). IPR policies provide producers with full control over their products and thus the opportunity to coordinate product design features with end-of-life processing features.[42] In contrast, CPR policies may actually provide disincentives for producers to invest in product design, since any enhancement to their products will subsidize the cost for competitors that process the products at end-of-life.[43]

EPR regulation was first introduced in Germany in 1991 (the 'German Packaging Ordinance') to extend producers' responsibility for their products and packaging, beyond production and delivery through to the entire life cycle, especially take-back and end-of-life management. The initial motivation was to require producers to take back and process their packaging – typically requiring up-front investment costs – and to thus provide an economic incentive for producers to invest in packaging that would generate less waste and fewer toxins, contain recycled materials, and which would be more durable, reusable and recyclable.[44]

To date, most EPR policies aim to shift the responsibility of product and packaging disposal away from municipalities and towards producers and their supply chains. For example, since 1991, Germany's packaging ordinance has enabled consumers to leave packaging with producers, distributors and retailers while enabling producers to incorporate the costs for end-of-life processing into their products' sale price. As of June 2001, the packaging ordinance required that at least 65 per cent of packaging be recovered and that at least 45 per cent be recycled. The German government also aims to use the ordinance to increase the share of beverages in reusable and ecologically safe drink packaging to 80 per cent.

The first ever EPR policy for electrical and electronic equipment was implemented by the Taiwanese government in 1998, requiring producers to take back and recycle products such as televisions, refrigerators, washing machines, air-conditioners and computers, regardless of where they were sold.[45] In 2001, Japan enforced its Home Recycling Appliance Law (also enacted in June 1998),[46] which required consumers to pay a combined fee for retailers to take back discarded air-conditioners, televisions, refrigerators and washing machines and for producers to recycle them. Japan's law also required that at least 50–60 per cent of these end-of-life appliances would be recycled by producers and that all CFC gases would be recovered from air-conditioners and refrigerators.

Policies that place the responsibility for end-of-life products on producers are a necessary initial step to address the waste management challenges that virtually all nations face.[47] However, in this form, the effectiveness of many of these EPR policies towards decoupling economic growth from waste generation is compromised by two main factors. First, a cheaper market has emerged for developed countries to export end-of-life products, such as cars,[48] home appliances[49] and electronic equipment,[50] as 'second-hand' or 'for recycling', even though many of these products are simply illegally dumped. Cars and home appliances are also being abandoned or dumped domestically rather than being sent for processing. Second, these policies increase recycling rates but, depending on their specific policy instruments, may not have an effect on preventing waste in the first place, through product design.[51] Further, putting end-of-life responsibility back onto the producers incentivizes them to design less waste into their product's life cycle but it is not a guarantee. In response to the second complication, some EPR policies are now also explicitly requiring that producers and their supply chains consider the life cycle environmental impacts of their products at the design stage. For example, the German packaging ordinance has been amended to include specific requirements for minimizing packaging volume and weight, and minimizing selected heavy metals.[52]

The most comprehensive EPR policies have been implemented by the EU and apply to all of the member states, requiring action from both governments and private enterprise. Examples are noted here:

- **End-of-Life Vehicles Directive.**[53] Since 2002 this directive has required producers and governments to cooperate in reducing waste from road vehicles.[54] Producers have been encouraged to limit the use of hazardous substances in vehicles, design vehicles for disassembly, reuse and recycling, and incorporate recycled content into vehicles. Producers have also been required to use coding standards that identify components and materials that are suitable for reuse and recycling, and provide disassembly information for new vehicles and components. Governments have been required to establish and operate systems to reuse and recycle vehicles at no cost to vehicle owners. As of 2006, the directive has required that governments recover at least 75–85 per cent of end-of-life vehicles by weight, and reuse and recycle 70–80 per cent by weight, depending on the production date.

- **Waste from Electrical and Electronic Equipment Directive.**[55] Since 2004 this directive has required producers of a wide range of electrical and electronic equipment to address issues related to both design and end-of-life management in order to reduce waste. Producers have been encouraged to design equipment with less waste, and that are easily disassembled, reused and recycled. Producers have also been required to take back and recycle equipment at no cost to consumers. As of 2006, the directive has required that producers take back at least an average of 4kg end-of-life equipment per capita annually, recover at least 70–80 per cent by weight, and reuse or recycle at least 50–80 per cent by weight, depending on the equipment type.
- **Restriction of Hazardous Substances Directive.**[56] Since 2006 this directive has required producers to eliminate lead, mercury, cadmium, hexavalent chromium, polybrominated biphenyls (PBB) and polybrominated diphenyl ethers (PBDE) from their products. However, there are currently exceptions for using limited quantities of these substances in some products, including lead in glass, steel alloys, aluminium alloys, copper alloys and solder; mercury in fluorescent lamps; cadmium in plating; and hexavalent chromium in some types of refrigerators.

These three EU EPR policies have also triggered a response internationally, most rapidly from those Asian industries and governments that were at risk of losing a significant export market into the EU due to non-compliant products, with the percentage of Restriction of Hazardous Substances-compliant producers rising from 51 per cent to over 93 per cent in the nine months prior to the directive coming into force.[57] Governments, especially in Asian countries, are now developing a range of supporting policies that help to provide a level playing field. One such policy is South Korea's Resource Recycling of Electrical and Electronic Equipment and Vehicles Act,[58] which, since 2008, has required producers, retailers and processors to cooperate in reducing waste from electronic and electrical equipment and road vehicles. In each case, producers have been required to limit the use of hazardous substances, to provide materials and recycling information, and have been encouraged to design for reuse and recycling. Retailers have also been required to take back products and packaging at no cost to consumers, and producers have been required to reuse and recycle their end-of-life products, including end-of-life vehicles.[59] In China, the Administrative Measure on the Control of Pollution Caused by Electronic Information Products[60] has, since 2007, required producers to eliminate the same hazardous substances as the EU's Restriction of Hazardous Substances Directive from their products, in addition to incorporating degradable and recyclable materials. Further Waste from Electrical and Electronic Equipment-type policies are being developed by China,[61] Thailand[62] and Taiwan,[63] while Restriction of Hazardous Substances-type policies are being developed by Argentina, Australia, Japan, the US[64] and Taiwan.[65]

Decoupling Economic Growth from Waste Production – By Reuse and Remanufacturing

Product reuse and remanufacturing includes: reusing products in their current state; repairing faulty products or reconditioning worn products before reuse; and remanufacturing products for use by first disassembling and then rebuilding 'new' products with the original component materials. Where products have a finite lifespan or 'end-of-life' in meeting a particular need, reusing or remanufacturing whole products or their individual components can be a cost-effective or even profitable strategy to curb waste generation. By extending product life, and enabling products to provide more services (increasing service intensity) before they are then remanufactured or recycled, these processes provide significant opportunities to decouple economic growth from waste generation.[66] Product life-cycle expert Walter Stahel has shown, many decades ago, that such approaches can also save significant amounts of energy whilst creating more jobs. In his 1981 report *Jobs for Tomorrow: The Potential for Substituting Manpower for Energy* he showed that:

> *Roughly three quarters of all industrial energy consumption is associated with the extraction or production of basic materials, while only about one quarter is used in the transformation of materials into finished goods such as machines or buildings. The converse is true of labour, about three times as much being used in the conversion of materials to finished products as is required in the production of materials.*[66A]

Table 10.1 provides a number of examples from industry, retail and within the community which highlight the potential for product reuse and remanufacture to assist in decoupling economic growth from waste generation.

However, while reuse can reduce materials and energy consumption through avoiding the manufacturing of new products from scratch, the costs of labour need to be factored into the business case, particularly with regard to product collection and transportation to the point of processing. Within the spectrum of end-of-life products that are currently available for reuse, the majority are suited to repair, reconditioning and remanufacturing, which could be facilitated for example through a product 'take-back' requirement as part of an EPR policy. Table 10.2 highlights a number of take-back models, including mandatory take-back, which can provide producers with incentives to reuse end-of-life products while also addressing the labour cost of collection.

The technical costs involved in reintroducing a product to the market typically correlate with how far upstream the supply chain the product is sent.[67] For example, products that are directly reused often go back to retailers,[68] as is the case for second-hand clothes and jewellery. Meanwhile, products that are reconditioned or remanufactured often go back to producers[69] for specialized activities such as disassembly, sorting, cleaning, testing, component

Table 10.1 *Examples of product reuse and remanufacturing opportunities*

Direct reuse

Packaging: A study for the American Reusable Pallet and Container Coalition compared reusable plastic containers to single-use display-ready paper corrugated trays for ten different types of fresh produce, finding that the reusable plastic containers require 39% less total energy, produce 95% less total solid waste and generate 29% less total greenhouse gas emissions.[70]

Construction materials: EcoFlex have developed building blocks based on reused tyres, using them as containers that are then filled with crushed recycled concrete, gravel, sand or soil. Displacing higher-cost structural materials such as masonry blocks, quarry rock and concrete, EcoFlex units can reduce the cost of constructing retaining walls by more than 25%, concrete slabs and hardstands by 15%, rural roads and erosion control systems by 28%, and waterway protection systems by 40%.[71]

Reconditioning

Carpet: Milliken Carpet reconditioned about 61,000m^2 (almost 500 tonnes) of carpet in the office of GTE Telops[72] at a cost of US\$18–24/m^2, almost doubling its useful life. In contrast, replacing the carpet would have cost about US\$30–42/m^2 plus installation for new carpet, and about US\$12,300 to dispose of the old carpet, plus removal and transportation.

Remanufacturing

Heavy machinery: Caterpillar,[73] a manufacturer of earth-moving and construction equipment, offers customers a significant discount if they return their used products. It then produces remanu-factured products for less than 70% of the cost of manufacturing new products, giving its equipment three to four lives through a combination of careful design and increasing the quality of parts, considerably reducing the waste stream to landfill. Remanufactured products include engines, fuel pumps, injectors, oil coolers, cylinder packs and hydraulic assemblies, each of which is disassembled by hand with every component down to the last screw being recovered and cleaned.

Home electronics: Sony Computer Entertainment Europe,[74] has a service exchange system to handle warranty returns in Europe, Australia and New Zealand, where the faulty consoles are picked up from the customer and immediately replaced by a remanufactured console. Faulty consoles are sent to centralized repair centres in the region of sale, with 85% returned to full working order, 9% receiving more complex repairs and 6% used for spare components. In addition to reducing the waste stream, the system reduces customers' waiting time from several weeks to 24–48 hours and also reduces the company's costs for warranty repairs.

Photocopiers: A study of Fuji Xerox's photocopiers showed that remanufacturing can reduce the life-cycle resource consumption and waste by up to 60% when the photocopiers are designed for disassembly and remanufacturing.[75]

Sharing

Cars: A study of a Dutch car-sharing programme with 337 customers showed that, compared to a purchase system, the number of cars in use and the required parking space was 44% lower, the cars were 24% more fuel efficient and the average car mileage was 33% lower.[76]

Laundry: A review of professional and industrial laundry service performance showed that, compared to household washing and drying, these services can consume up to 80% less water, 85% less detergent and 77% less energy, and emit 33% less carbon dioxide. The resource efficiency improvements arise as a result of better cost control of input resources, economies of scale, better equipment, and more skilled and knowledgeable operators.[77]

Power drills: A study comparing the material intensity of customer-owned electric drills for 150 households with that of two shared professional electric drills for the same households showed that the material intensity per hole drilled was tenfold higher for the two shared drills due to the shared use and higher quality of the drills.[78]

Books: A study of Finland's public libraries showed that the shared use of books reduces paper consumption by 32,000 tonnes and carbon dioxide emissions by 13,800 tonnes annually, assuming every book is loaned 60 times each year.[79]

Source: Compiled by The Natural Edge Project with references as cited

Table 10.2 *Take-back models and examples for end-of-life products*

Model	Description	Example
Donation	Users give items for recycling at end of life	Bottle banks
Coercion	Legal penalties and charges force users to sort and submit items for recycling	Microchipped wheelie bins
Deposit	Items remain the property of the producer. A deposit is charged that is forfeited if the item is lost	Returnable packaging
Buy-back	Producer pays for items at end-of-life	Car batteries, trade-in discounts on white goods, cell phones
Mandatory take-back	The law requires the producer to take back items at end-of-life and carry the cost of disposal in an acceptable way	Extended producer responsibility policies
Dustman	Third party is paid to dispose of items, perhaps recovering value by recycling	Tyres, scrap cars, skip hire, domestic refuse
Steptoe	Third party recycler buys items and recovers value by recycling	Waste paper, toner cartridges, rags – and bones
Lease	Goods are leased or hired to user. Ownership is retained by producer	Photocopiers, electric vehicle batteries, construction plant
Service	User purchases a service not an item. Ownership of the 'tools' is retained by producer	Public transport

Source: Lee (2008)[80]

matching and reassembly, then resale – as is the case with some computers and office equipment. The potential for product reuse also varies considerably, depending on factors such as the quality and quantity of product available, the geographical and national context (including serviceability and demand) and the type of reuse, including challenges such as safety, reliability, amenity and durability of the reused or remanufactured product. However, the likelihood of significant waste reduction, economic viability and technological viability is potentially far greater for products that are intentionally designed for reuse and remanufacturing.

Decoupling Economic Growth from Waste Production – By Recycling

In cases where reusing or remanufacturing end-of-life products is not viable, recycling the component materials in products may still be cost effective or even profitable. Product recycling involves converting post-consumer waste to production-ready raw materials, which then form the input materials for other new products. Since the publication of *Our Common Future*, changes to waste recycling rates have varied between countries for each type of waste. Recycling rates in both OECD[81] and non-OECD[82] countries have generally increased, with the markets for many recyclable materials growing due to both policy incentives and favourable commercial conditions.[83] This is especially the case in China, which in 2006 was by far the world's leading waste paper importer and recycler, in order to meet rapidly growing demand for paper and paper products.[84] Recycling may be a labour- and energy-intensive option when compared to reuse, but can be a very energy-effective option when compared to virgin production. The technical cost of recycling is generally higher compared with reused products, as recycled products are returned further upstream in the supply chain to the producer or materials supplier.[85] However, despite the higher relative technical cost, producers generally favour recycling, especially when required to take back products under an EPR. This is because recycling enables producers to terminate liability for the product and its service, whereas reuse would require producers to ensure adequate product and service quality for an extended life.[86]

There is significant scope to increase the recycling rates of virtually all types of materials currently ending up in landfill. Here we consider a number of classes of materials and the potential for decoupling waste generation from economic growth:

- **Metals:** virtually all metals can be recycled into high-quality metal, where recycled metals require 60–95 per cent less energy to produce than virgin metals.[87] Recycling rates are growing due to surging metal commodity prices,[88] which are making recycling very cost effective compared to producing virgin metals even without subsidy or regulation. However, there is still further scope to increase metal recycling rates. For example, in 2007, global crude steel production reached over 1.3 billion tonnes while approximately 480 million tonnes of scrap was recycled.[89]
- **Plastic:** compared to plastics made from virgin materials, recycled plastics require 80–90 per cent less energy to produce.[90] While technologies exist to recycle virtually all types of plastics, the supporting infrastructure exists mainly for polyethylene terephthalate (PET) and high-density polyethylene (HDPE) – those used to make bottles – and sometimes for polyvinyl chloride (PVC) and low-density polyethylene (LDPE). The remaining types of plastics, including polypropylene (PP) and polystyrene (PS), are often collected but then land-filled or incinerated (sometimes with energy recovery).[91] In many developed countries, the recycling rate is highest for plastic bottles and packaging, at about 30 per cent, while the overall recycling rate is less than 20 per cent.[92]
- **Paper:** Compared to paper made from virgin materials, recycled paper requires 64 per cent less energy to produce and creates 35 per cent less water pollution and 74 per cent less air pollution.[93] Most waste paper and cardboard – including used office paper, envelopes, cardboard boxes, newspapers, magazines and telephone books – can be recycled.[94] There is demand for paper of various grades.[95] High-grade paper can be recycled into paper products such as office paper, envelopes, toilet paper and tissues, whereas lower-grade paper can often only be recycled into cardboard and insulation. Paper fibre can be recycled four to six times,

depending on its grade, so paper waste cannot be completely eliminated but it can be significantly reduced, especially by combining pre-recycled paper with paper products made from wood pulp.[96] Some paper products are generally not available for recycling, such as material from libraries, archives, wall papers and sanitary paper. These products make up 15–20 per cent of total paper and cardboard consumption, so the maximum achievable recycling rate is about 80–85 per cent.[97]

- **Organic materials:** waste organic materials, most of which are from farming processes, are a major component of landfill. A range of options exist for recycling organic material directly into new value-adding processes, such as composting for soil improvement, a food source for animal raising and a fuel to provide energy.[98] Recycling organic materials back into farming processes can reduce costs and improve yields by restoring microbial activity and soil fertility, thereby reducing the need for chemical fertilizer, the cost of which is increasing; and by restoring minerals, trace elements and other nutrients that cannot be made by plants but are essential for the health of humans and livestock. Organic materials that cannot be cost effectively returned to farming processes can be sold on the domestic horticultural market, used as fuel or converted into fuel. Removing organic waste from landfill has the added benefit of making all other products available for reuse in a relatively clean state. Even at the level of municipal waste streams, which has a smaller organic waste component than farming waste, separating organic materials from the waste stream for composting or anaerobic digestion is more cost effective than land-filling or incineration.[99]

- **Construction and demolition materials:** building deconstruction can make both preassembled building components (such as windows, cabinets, carpets and finish flooring) and basic building components (such as bricks, timber beams, plastic pipes and glass) available for reuse. Virtually all other materials that are not reusable can be recycled.[100] There is extensive scope to increase construction and demolition material recycling rates. In the US, about 20 per cent of these materials are recycled[101] while the rest go to landfill, where they make up 40 per cent of all solid waste, as in many countries.[102] There are numerous opportunities to use reused and recycled construction and demolition materials in new constructions.[103] The cost of the deconstruction process can be offset through: the avoidance of disposal costs, which are increasing in many countries; the avoidance of purchasing new materials for new constructions; and selling reused and recycled materials in the sufficiently available markets.[104] The deconstruction process can also create jobs.[105]

- **Electrical and electronic equipment:**[106] electrical and electronic equipment can contain recoverable levels of several valuable and precious materials. Recycling can play a key role in helping maintain a secure supply of many metals by providing an additional, affordable source.[107] These products are also a relatively rich source of plastics and silicon, the recovery of which can help meet the demand in the expanding solar cell market.[108] There is extensive scope to increase recycling rates in many countries. For example, in Australia, from an end-of-life computer, only about 20 per cent of the plastics, 5 per cent of the lead and virtually no other substances are recycled.[109]

- **Tyres:** tyres are 100 per cent recyclable.[110] A range of options exist for converting tyres into shred, chips, granulate and powder, which can then be used as raw materials for new products and processes.[111] These raw materials are valuable because they maintain many of the chemical and physical properties of the tyres.[112] Tyres can also be decomposed into component materials or used to create energy via a range of processes.[113] Even simply incinerating waste tyres can be cost effective, since tyres contain at least the same amount of energy as coal.[114] There is extensive scope to increase tyre recycling rates in many countries. Globally, an estimated 1.2 billion used tyres are discarded annually and billions already stockpiled. By far, the current leading contributor is the US, which discards about 270 million tyres annually.[115] There are also ample markets for recycled tyre materials in industries such as construction, manufacturing and environmental restoration.[116] Since the rubber in tyres is mostly petroleum-based synthetic rubber,[117] the cost effectiveness of tyre recycling will probably increase with the price of oil, which has been increasing quite rapidly since late 2003 and even more rapidly since early 2007.[118]

The target recycling rates of waste materials currently required by some government policies are ambitious but there is a growing range of options that demonstrate that achieving these targets can be cost effective (see Table 10.3). The technical costs of waste recycling are increasingly being demonstrated as at least cost neutral in developed and transitioning countries. Depending on the combination of technology and policy, this can also be affordable in developing countries. With innovations in materials and recycling emerging rapidly, and with the growing markets for recycled materials and products, the cost effectiveness of recycling all types of waste materials and products will probably increase.

Table 10.3 *Examples of product reuse resulting in reduced resource consumption and waste*

Metals

Steel cans: Steel cans – mainly used for packaging food, aerosols, paints, chemicals and bottle caps – are the most recycled form of packaging and are 100 per cent recyclable. Steel can recycling has been increasing and reached 67% in 2006, globally. Leaders include Belgium, Germany, Japan, the Netherlands, Austria, Switzerland, Ireland and China, all of whom recycle more than three-quarters of their waste steel cans.[119] The US and China recycle the greatest mass of steel cans – more than 1 million tonnes each.[120] Steel's magnetism makes it relatively easy to extract from mixed waste and thus can offset the relatively high costs of manual separation.

Plastics

Pyrolysis: The pyrolysis process is a special case of the thermolysis process that converts waste plastics to liquid diesel.[121] The process involves heating the plastics to 385–425°C in the absence of oxygen, then catalytically converting and condensing the resulting vapours to produce diesel. A typical commercial thermolysis plant can convert 7–10 tonnes of plastics into about 7000–10,000 litres of diesel per day. The process can handle a variety of plastics, including dirty, mixed plastics such as those in landfill.[122] Of the total process output, 90% is typically hydrocarbon distillate, 5–7% is char and 2–5% is non-condensable gases, which are cleaned in a scrubber and then mixed with the burner's fuel.[123] Pyrolysis diesel generally performs similarly to conventional diesel and also has a few advantages. Tests have shown that, compared to conventional diesel, it has a similar octane number[124] (35–50 compared with 35–45), has far lower sulphur content (1–50 ppm compared with 500–2000), and burns hotter and cleaner due to its higher light hydrocarbon fraction and negligible sulphur content.[125] A thermolysis plant's burner is usually fuelled by natural gas, but can also be fuelled by the diesel it makes. The burner requires about 24–28 litres of diesel per hour – a fraction of the plant's output. Producing pyrolysis diesel costs about 30–40 cents per litre and is usually excise-free.

Alternate feedstock: Australian researcher Professor Veena Sahajwalla has developed a method for using waste plastic to replace coal as a source of carbon in the steel-making process. Plastic can replace up to 30% of the coal and also acts as a fuel so power requirements are reduced. Some 40% of the world's steel is produced in electric arc furnaces operating at 1600°C, which is hot enough to eliminate pollutants such as dioxins.[126]

Paper

Network: Office Chonai-kai (Office Community Network) was established by Tokyo Electric Power Company to collect, sort and recycle waste paper.[127] The network links several offices in Tokyo's business districts and enables cost-effective collection for offices that otherwise would be limited by the costs of a dedicated collection vehicle or by the lack of a local collection point. The network has grown from servicing about 30 offices in 1991 to more than 1000 offices, 900 member companies and 40 paper collection companies in 2001. Office Chonai-kai's economic viability is ensured by reducing client costs while paying for collection and operations through the 'three economics'; where member companies pay 17.6 yen/kg to recycle paper rather than 28.5 yen/kg to dispose of it, as well as collection costs, and 5.8 yen/kg to maintain the Office Chonai-kai secretariat. The initiative was also instrumental in the business community's acceptance of office copy paper with a whiteness rating of 70 (using less bleach and other chemicals, and incorporating recycled newspaper) rather than 80 (made from virgin pulp or bleached recycled paper), which is now stipulated as a standard in Japan's Green Purchasing Law, formulated in 2000. As Whiteness 70 paper is cheaper to produce, its acceptance presents a large and cost-effective market for recycled paper in Japan.

Organic materials

Animal raising: In outer-urban Manila, Philippines, domestic pig rearing is a traditional source of income. Commercial pig feed is relatively costly so pig raisers often use their own organic food waste as a supplement or replacement. Pig raisers can also purchase additional food waste at about half the cost of the commercial feed through a collection and distribution network, which collects organic waste from city restaurants and distributes it among the pig raisers. In addition to reducing waste to landfill and supporting local business, using this food waste as pig feed has more than doubled profits, even after accounting for the additional costs, such as transportation.[128]

Fuel and new materials: Waste-to-energy facilities convert waste into energy and useful materials.[129] Waste, particularly organic waste, is combusted to recover the energy for use in electricity production and to shrink its volume by 70–95%. The remaining materials, a combination of ash and metals, are separated and can be sold to secondary markets. The recovery of ferrous metals (steel and iron) is common, while the recovery of non-ferrous metals is increasing. The ash residue has physical properties similar to concrete, so it can be used as road aggregate and asphalt mixture, or in the construction of cement blocks, as well as a landfill roadbed material and landfill cover.

Waste-to-energy facilities employ extensive pollution control technologies, including selective non-catalytic reduction to reduce nitrogen oxides, scrubbers to reduce acidic gases, carbon injection to reduce mercury and trace organics, and bag houses to reduce soot, smoke and metals. In the US, facilities employing these pollution control technologies reduced emissions of several hazardous substances by 94–99% between 1990 and 2005.[130] Waste-to-energy facilities also destroy bacteria and pollutants, prevent methane generation and reduce the demand for landfill space. A study of various waste management strategies in the US context suggests that waste-to-energy may be the most favourable strategy with respect to net carbon emissions, acidification and smog, but may be more costly to implement.[131] However, in countries with higher landfill fees, such as EU countries and Japan, the waste-to-energy strategy would be more cost competitive or even most favourable. Indeed, waste-to-energy facilities already process a large portion of waste in these countries.[132]

Construction and demolition materials

Insulation: Bonded Logic Inc. has developed UltraTouch natural cotton fibre insulation, a building insulation material made from 85% post-industrial recycled denim. UltraTouch has low toxicity, fire retardance, mould and mildew resistance, and pest resistance, and produces an acoustic rating about 30% higher than traditional insulations. UltraTouch is produced in a zero material waste process that uses less energy than producing fibreglass insulation and diverts about 200 tonnes of landfill waste per month.[133]

Solid surfaces: Syndesis Inc. have developed Syndecrete, a solid-surfacing material that is an alternative to materials such as wood, stone and petroleum-based solid and laminating materials. Syndecrete contains up to 40% recycled materials such as plastic regrinds, glass chips, wood chips and brass shavings. Syndecrete is less dense than concrete but has twice the compressive strength.[134]

Deconstruction: Alex Fraser Group[135] was established in 1879 as a metals dealer. In the 1950s, the Group moved into demolitions, where it dismantled thousands of large industrial and manufacturing complexes such as gasworks, factories and power stations. In the 1980s, the Group expanded into salvaging, reusing and recycling construction and demolition materials (such as concrete, bricks, masonry and rubble) into useful products (such as specification road bases and construction materials). The Group is now Australia's leading recycler in the industry and leading supplier of sustainable civil construction materials, with the capacity to produce 3 million tonnes of material per year, now recycling up to 98% of every demolition project.

Tyres

Decomposition: The Molectra® process, invented in Australia by John Dobozy, recovers all component materials of tyres without waste, residue or emissions, which eliminates costs associated with pollution and waste disposal. The process integrates mechanical, chemical and microwave treatments to cleanly and efficiently break tyres down into base materials – oil, carbon, rubber granules, steel and plastic fibres – which are valuable commodities.[136]

Source: Compiled by The Natural Edge Project, sources as cited

Notes

1 OECD (2008) *OECD Environmental Outlook to 2030*, OECD, Paris, p240.
2 Hoornweg, D., Lam, P. and Chaudhry, M. (2005) *Waste Management in China: Issues and Recommendations*, Urban Development Working Papers, no 9, World Bank, Washington, DC, p6.
3 Khouri-Dagher, N. (1985) *Waste Recycling: Towards Greater Urban Self-Reliance*, prepared for the World Commission on Environment and Development (WCED), cited in WCED (1987) *Our Common Future*, Oxford University Press, Oxford, 'Chapter 9: The urban challenge'.
4 OECD (2008) *OECD Environmental Outlook to 2030*, OECD, Paris.
5 OECD (2008) *OECD Environmental Data Compendium*, OECD, Paris.
6 Economist.com (2007) 'The truth about recycling', *The Economist*, print edition, 7 June, www.economist.com/science-technology/technology-quarterly/displaystory.cfm?story_id=9249262 .
7 OECD (2008) *OECD Environmental Outlook to 2030*, OECD, Paris.
8 Kallman, M. (2008) 'Talking trash: The world's waste management problem', Earth Trends Environmental Information, World Resources Institute, 18 June.
9 The European Commission (1999) Council Directive 99/31/EC.
10 European Commission (2005) *National Strategies for the Reduction of Biodegradable Waste going to Landfills*, Report from the Commission to the Council and the European Parliament pursuant to Article 5(1) of Directive 1999/31/EC on the landfill of waste, 30 March.
11 Fisher, I. (2007) 'European Commission sues to force Italy to take out the garbage', *The New York Times*, 7 May.
12 American Society of Civil Engineers (2005) 'Solid waste C+', Infrastructure Report Card, ASCE.
13 Kallman, M. (2008) 'Talking trash: The world's waste management problem', Earth Trends Environmental Information, World Resources Institute, 18 June.
14 OECD (2008) *OECD Environmental Outlook to 2030*, OECD, Paris, pp246, 249.
15 IMPEL (2006) *IMPEL-TFS Seaport Project II: International Co-operation in Enforcement Hitting Illegal Waste Shipments*, Project Report, IMPEL (Implementation and Enforcement of Environmental Law).
16 OECD (2007) *Measuring Material Flows and Resource Productivity: The OECD Guide*, OECD, Paris.
17 OECD (2008) *OECD Environmental Outlook to 2030*, OECD, Paris, p237.
17A Europa (undated) 'Sustainable use of natural resources', http://ec.europa.eu/environment/natres/, accessed 18 October 2008.
17B Europa (undated) 'Waste', http://ec.europa.eu/environment/waste/, accessed 18 October 2008.
18 Environment Agency, Japan (2000) *The Challenge to Establish the Recycling-Based Society: The Basic Law for Establishing the Recycling-Based Society Enacted*, government of Japan, Tokyo; Ministry of the Environment, Japan (2000) *The Basic Act for Establishing a Sound Material-Cycle Society*, government of Japan, Tokyo.
19 Sanders, S. and Dempsey L. L. P. (2008) *Circular Economy of the People's Republic of China*, English translation.
20 US EPA (2003) *Beyond RCRA: Prospects for Waste and Materials Management in the Year 2020*, US EPA, Washington, DC.
21 Holweg, M. (2007) 'The genealogy of lean production', *Journal of Operations Management*, vol 25, no 2, pp420–437.

22   Ministry of the Environment, Japan (2000) *The Basic Act for Establishing a Sound Material-Cycle Society*, government of Japan, Tokyo.

23   Ministry of the Environment, Japan (undated) 'Laws: Waste and recycling', www.env.go.jp/en/laws/recycle/, accessed 15 August 2008.

24   Ministry of the Environment, Japan (2008) 'Basic policy on promoting green purchasing', www.env.go.jp/en/laws/policy/green/, accessed 15 August 2008.

25   Hubbard, F. (2007) Personal communication with Frank Hubbard, Director, Sustainability, InterContinental Hotels Group Australia/New Zealand/South Pacific, 15 August.

26   Knight, M. (2004) *The Remanufacturing Equation: Remanufacturing is a $50-billion Market, and Assemblers Own the Skills and Knowledge to Compete*, Circuits Assembly.

27   King, A. M., Burgess, S. C., Ijomah, W. and McMahon, C. A. (2006) 'Reducing waste: Repair, recondition, remanufacture or recycle?', *Sustainable Development*, vol 14, no 4, pp257–267.

28   King, A. M., Burgess, S. C., Ijomah, W. and McMahon, C. A. (2006) 'Reducing waste: Repair, recondition, remanufacture or recycle?', *Sustainable Development*, vol 14, no 4, pp257–267.

29   Eco Buy (undated) 'Now open for business to business', www.brwmg.vic.gov.au/news/documents/ECO-BuyBusinessWasteWise.ppt, accessed 10 October 2009.

30   Lovins, A. (undated) 'Amory Lovins' natural capitalism lecture', *ABC: The Slab*, Australia, www.abc.net.au/science/slab/natcap/default.htm, accessed 25 September 2008.

31   Toxic Use Reduction Institute (undated) 'TURAdata', www.turi.org/turadata, accessed 12 July 2009.

32   Lavee, D. (2007) 'Is municipal solid waste recycling economically efficient?', *Environmental Management*, vol 40, no 6, pp926–943.

33   Lavee, D. (2007) 'Is municipal solid waste recycling economically efficient?', *Environmental Management*, vol 40, no 6, pp926–943; Brisson, I. E. (1997) *Assessing the Waste Hierarchy: A Social Cost Benefit Analysis of Municipal Solid Waste Management in the European Union*, AKF Publishing, Copenhagen.

34   *The Economist* (2007) 'The truth about recycling', *The Economist*, 7 June, www.economist.com/science-technology/technology-quarterly/displaystory.cfm?story_id=9249262.

35   Oliver, R. (2008) 'About recycling', CNN Asia, http://edition.cnn.com/2008/WORLD/asiapcf/02/03/eco.about.recycling/, accessed 15 October 2009; Bureau of International Recycling (undated) 'Welcome to BIR', www.bir.org/welcome/welcome.asp, accessed 15 October 2009.

36   R. W. Beck Inc. (2001) *US Recycling Economic Information Study: Executive Summary*, a study prepared for the National Recycling Coalition, National Recycling Coalition, Inc.

37   British Metals Recycling Association (undated) 'What is metals recycling?', www.recyclemetals.org/whatis.php, accessed 23 August 2008; Bureau of International Recycling (undated) 'About recycling', www.bir.org/aboutrecycling/index.asp, accessed 23 August 2008; Eurometrec (undated) 'Position papers', www.eurometrec.org/, accessed 23 August 2008.

37A British Metals Recycling Association (undated) 'What is metals recycling?', www.recyclemetals.org/whatis.php, accessed 23 August 2008; Eurometrec (undated) 'Position papers', www.eurometrec.org/, accessed 23 August 2008.

37B British Metals Recycling Association (undated) 'What is metals recycling?', www.recyclemetals.org/whatis.php, accessed 23 August 2008; Bureau of International Recycling (undated) 'About recycling', www.bir.org/aboutrecycling/index.asp, accessed 23 August 2008; Eurometrec (undated) 'Position papers', www.eurometrec.org/, accessed 23 August 2008.

37C British Metals Recycling Association (undated) 'What is metals recycling?', www.recyclemetals.org/whatis.php, accessed 23 August 2008; Eurometrec (undated) 'Position papers', www.eurometrec.org/, accessed 23 August 2008.

37D Ditze, A. and Scharf, C. (2008) 'Recycling of magnesium', Papierflieger Verlag, Clausthal-Zellerfeld, Germany, p7.

37E Bureau of International Recycling (undated) 'About recycling', www.bir.org/aboutrecycling/index.asp, accessed 23 August 2008.

37F Bureau of International Recycling (undated) 'About recycling', www.bir.org/aboutrecycling/index.asp, accessed 23 August 2008; Recoup (2004) 'Recycling plastic bottles: The energy equation' (factsheet), www.recoup.org/shop/product_documents/33.pdf, accessed 12 July 2009.

38 Ohio government (undated) *Recycling in Ohio. Glass Recycling.* Ohio government's Division of Recycling and Litter Prevention.

39 Hawken, P., Lovins A. and Lovins, L. H. (1999) *Natural Capitalism: Creating the Next Industrial Revolution*, Earthscan, London.

40 OECD (2008) *OECD Environmental Outlook to 2030*, OECD, Paris, pp246, 249.

41 Stasinopoulos, P., Smith, M., Hargroves, K. and Desha, C. (2008) *Whole System Design – An Integrated Approach to Sustainable Engineering*, Earthscan, London and The Natural Edge Project, Australia.

42 van Rossem, C., Tojo, N. and Lindhqvist, T. (2006) *Extended Producer Responsibility: An Examination of its Impact on Innovation and Greening Products*, report commissioned by Greenpeace International, Friends of the Earth and the European Environmental Bureau, p8.

43 Tojo, N. (2004) 'Extended producer responsibility as a driver for design change: Utopia or reality?', Doctoral dissertation, Lund University, Lund, Sweden, pp266, 268, 269.

44 Federal Ministry for the Environment, Nature Conservation and Nuclear Safety (2005) 'Ordinance on the Avoidance and Recovery of Packaging Wastes of 21 August 1998, as last amended by Article 1 Third Amending Ordinance of 24 May', German government, Berlin.

45 Chen, J. L. (2001) 'Some observations on recycling of electrical home appliances activities in Taiwan', *Proceedings EcoDesign 2001: Second International Symposium on Environmentally Conscious Design and Inverse Manufacturing*, Tokyo, pp935–938.

46 Ministry of the Environment, Japan (undated) 'Law for the Recycling of Specified Kinds of Home Appliances (outline)', government of Japan, Tokyo.

47 Some developing countries, while not producers of a great deal of manufactured products, may be burdened with vast volumes of waste from developed countries.

48 Fergusson, M. (2007) *End of Life Vehicles (ELV) Directive: An Assessment of the Current State of Implementation by Member States*, European Parliament, p57.

49 Tasaki, T., Terazono, A. and Moriguchi, Y. (2005) 'Effective assessment of Japanese recycling law for electrical home appliances: Four years after the full enforcement of the law', *Proceedings of the 2005 IEEE International Symposium on Electronics and the Environment*, 16–19 May, pp243–248.

50 Puckett, J., Byster, L., Westervelt, S., Gutierrez, R., Davis, S., Hussain, A. and Dutta, M. (2002) *Exporting Harm: The High-tech Trashing of Asia*, Basel Action Network; Puckett, J., Westervelt, S., Gutierrez, R. and Takamiya, Y. (2005) *The Digital Dump: Exporting Re-use and Abuse to Africa*, Basel Action Network.

51 Walls, M. (2006) *EPR Policies and Product Design: Economic Theory and Selected Case Studies*, OECD, Paris, pp16–18, 35.

52 Federal Ministry for the Environment, Nature Conservation and Nuclear Safety (2005) 'Ordinance on the Avoidance and Recovery of Packaging Wastes of 21 August 1998, as last amended by Article 1 Third Amending Ordinance of 24 May', German government, Berlin, p 37.

53 EU (2000) 'Directive 2000/53/EC of the European Parliament and of the Council of 18 September 2000 on end-of life vehicles', *Official Journal of the European Union,* vol 43, L 269, 21 October 2000, p34, www.ecodesign-company.com/documents/ELV-directive.pdf.

54 'Vehicle' refers to any motor vehicle intended for use on the road, with or without bodywork, having at least four wheels and a maximum design speed exceeding 25km/h, and its trailers, with the exception of vehicles that run on rails and of agricultural tractors and machinery.

55 EU (2003) 'Directive 2002/96/EC of the European Parliament and of the Council of 27 January 2003 on waste electrical and electronic equipment (WEEE)', *Official Journal of the European Union*, vol 46, L 37, 13 February 2003, pp24–38.

56 EU (2003) 'Directive 2002/95/EC of the European Parliament and of the Council of 27 January 2003 on the restriction of the use of certain hazardous substances in electrical and electronic equipment (RoHS)', *Official Journal of the European Union*, vol 46, L 37, 13 February 2003, pp19–23.

57 Global Sources (2005) *RoHS Compliance Readiness Survey: Mainland China, Taiwan, Hong Kong and South Korea*, Global Sources, Singapore, p3.

58 Yun, J. And Park, I. (2007) *Act for Resource Recycling of Electrical and Electronic Equipment and Vehicles: English Translation*, Eco-Frontier, Seoul.

59 End-of-life vehicle processors perform operations such as dismantling, reusing, recycling and shredding.

60 Ministry of Commerce (2006) *Administrative Measure on the Control of Pollution Caused by Electronic Information Products*, People's Republic of China, Beijing.

61 Ferris, T. and Zhang, H. (2005) 'Global regulatory policy development and implementation: Focus on China', Presentation, IEEE International Symposium on Electronics in the Environment, New Orleans, 17 May.

62 Manomaivibool, P., Lindhqvist, T. and Tojo, N. (2007) *Extended Producer Responsibility in a Non-OECD Context: The Management of Waste Electrical and Electronic Equipment in India*, Report commissioned by Greenpeace International, Lund University, Lund, Sweden, p1.

63 Raymond Communications cited in Franklin, R. (2006) 'China RoHS and China WEEE', RoHSWell.com, www.rohswell.com/News/Genl006.php, accessed 3 April 2010.

64 Bradley, T. (2006) *Compliance: Beyond RoHS*, Electronics, Design, Strategy, News (EDN), Massachusetts, US.

65 Raymond Communications cited in Franklin, R. (2006) 'China RoHS and China WEEE', RoHSWell.com, www.rohswell.com/News/Genl006.php, accessed 3 April 2010.

66 See Stahel, W. R. (1994) 'The utilization-focused service economy: Resource efficiency and product life extension', in Allenby, B. R. and Richards, D. J. (eds) *The Greening of Industrial Ecosystems*, National Academy Press, Washington, DC, p179.

66A Stahel, W. (1976/1981) *Jobs for Tomorrow: The Potential for Substituting Manpower for Energy*, Report to the Commission of the European Communities (now European Commission), Brussels/Vantage Press, New York, http://www.product-life.org/en/about.

67 Stahel W. R. (1994) 'The utilization-focused service economy: Resource efficiency and product life extension', in Allenby, B. R. and Richards, D. J. (eds) *The Greening of Industrial Ecosystems*, National Academy Press, Washington, DC, p181.

68 King, A. M., Burgess, S. C., Ijomah, W. and McMahon, C. A. (2006) 'Reducing waste: Repair, recondition, remanufacture or recycle?', *Sustainable Development*, vol 14, no 4, pp257–267.

69 King, A. M., Burgess, S. C., Ijomah, W. and McMahon, C. A. (2006) 'Reducing waste: Repair, recondition, remanufacture or recycle?', *Sustainable Development*, vol 14, no 4, pp257–267.

70 Franklin Associates (2004) *Life Cycle Inventory of Reusable Plastic Containers and Display-Ready Corrugated Containers Used for Fresh Produce Applications*, Executive Summary, Reusable Pallet and Container Coalition, Washington, DC; Singh, S. P., Chonhenchob, V. and Singh, J. (2006) 'Life cycle inventory and analysis of re-usable plastic containers and display-ready corrugated containers used for packaging fresh fruits and vegetables', *Packaging Technology and Science*, vol 19, no 5, pp279–293.

71 EcoFlex (undated) Homepage, www.ecoflex.com.au, accessed 30 May 2008.

72 Waste Reduction Resource Centre (undated) 'Case study No. 9638 – GTE TELOPS', http://wrrc.p2pays.org/indsectinfo.asp?INDSECT=35, accessed 22 August 2008.

73 Scott, J. T. (2008) 'Case study 3: Caterpillar', in Management Education Services, *Managing the New Frontiers*, Management Education Services, Panama City, FL.

74 Parker, D. and Butler, P. (2007) 'An introduction to remanufacturing', www.remanufacturing.org.uk/pdf/story/1p76.pdf, accessed 14 October 2009.

75 Kerr, W. and Ryan, C. (2001) 'Eco-efficiency gains from remanufacturing: A case study of photocopier remanufacturing at Fuji-Xerox in Australia', *Journal of Cleaner Production*, vol 9, no 1, pp75–81.

76 Heiskanen, E. and Jalas, M. (2003) 'Can services lead to radical eco-efficiency improvements – A review of the debate and evidence', *Corporate Social Responsibility and Environmental Management*, no 10, pp186–198.

77 Heiskanen, E. and Jalas, M. (2003) 'Can services lead to radical eco-efficiency improvements – A review of the debate and evidence', *Corporate Social Responsibility and Environmental Management*, no 10, pp186–198.

78 BMBF (1998) cited in Heiskanen, E. and Jalas, M. (2003) 'Can services lead to radical eco-efficiency improvements – A review of the debate and evidence', *Corporate Social Responsibility and Environmental Management*, no 10, pp186–198.

79 Mäki (1999) cited in Heiskanen, E. and Jalas, M. (2003) 'Can services lead to radical eco-efficiency improvements – A review of the debate and evidence', *Corporate Social Responsibility and Environmental Management*, no 10, pp186–198.

80 Lee, C. (2008) 'Closed loops to reduce waste and increase profits', Presentation, Futurengineering, Cambridge, England, p11.

81 OECD (2007) *OECD Environmental Data Compendium: Waste*, OECD, Paris, pp25–26; OECD (undated) 'Stan database for structural analysis', http://stats.oecd.org/wbos/Index.aspx?DatasetCode=STAN08BIS&lang=en, accessed 16 October 2008.

82 van Beukering, P. (2001) 'Recycling, international trade and the environment: An empirical analysis', Presentation at the Science & Culture of Industrial Ecology: ISIE 2001 Meeting, 12–14 November, Leiden, Netherlands, p3.

83 Johnston, N. (2005) *Improving Recycling Markets*, OECD, Paris, p9.

84 Magnaghi, G. (2006) *The Evolution of the Recovered Paper Market: Comparing 2006 with 2005*, Bureau of International Recycling.

85 King, A. M., Burgess, S. C., Ijomah, W. and McMahon, C. A. (2006) 'Reducing waste: Repair, recondition, remanufacture or recycle?', *Sustainable Development*, vol 14, no 4, pp257–267.

86 Stahel, W. R. (1994) 'The utilization-focused service economy: Resource efficiency and product life extension', in Allenby, B. R. and Richards, D. J. (eds) *The Greening of Industrial Ecosystems*, National Academy Press, Washington, DC, pp181, 183–186.

87 British Metals Recycling Association (BMRA) (undated) 'What is metals recycling?', www.recyclemetals.org/whatis.php, accessed 23 August 2008; Bureau of International Recycling (undated) 'About recycling', www.bir.org/aboutrecycling/index.asp, accessed 23 August 2008; Eurometrec (undated) 'Position papers', www.eurometrec.org/, accessed 23 August 2008.

88 *Oxford Economics* (2007) 'High commodity prices are here to stay', *Oxford Economics*, Autumn, Oxford, UK; Global Info Mine (undated) 'Commodity mine', www.infomine.com/commodities/, accessed 22 August 2008.

89 International Iron and Steel Institute (2008) *World Steel in Figures*, IISI, Brussels, pp6, 23.

90 Bureau of International Recycling (undated) 'About recycling', www.bir.org/aboutrecycling/index.asp, accessed 23 August 2008; Eurometrec (undated) 'Position papers', www.eurometrec.org/, accessed 23 August 2008.

91 Eureka! Recycling (undated) 'Recycling plastic: Complications & limitations', www.eurekarecycling.org/PDFS/Recycling_Plastic_Complications.pdf, accessed 23 August 2008.

92 Container Recycling Institute (undated) 'Graphs: Plastic bottle statistics', www.container-recycling.org/plasrate/graphs.htm, accessed 23 August 2008; Sustainability Matters (2008) 'Record plastics recycling could fill the MCG five times', www.sustainabilitymatters.net.au/news/2062-Record-plastics-recycling-could-fill-the-MCG-five-times, accessed 23 August 2008.

93 Bureau of International Recycling (undated) 'About recycling', www.bir.org/aboutrecycling/index.asp, accessed 23 August 2008; Eurometrec (undated) 'Position papers', www.eurometrec.org/, accessed 23 August 2008.

94 Australian Plantation Products and Paper Industry Council (A3P) (undated) 'Paper recycling', www.a3p.asn.au/keyissues/recycling.html, accessed 23 August 2008.

95 The State of Queensland (Environmental Protection Agency) (undated) 'Reduce, reuse, recycle', www.epa.qld.gov.au/environmental_management/waste/waste_minimisation/reduce_reuse_recycle/, accessed 23 August 2008.

96 Bureau of International Recycling (undated) '10 questions on paper recovery and recycling', www.bir.org/aboutrecycling/10questions/tenquestions.asp, accessed 23 August 2008; Confederation of European Paper Industries (undated) 'Recycling facts', www.cepi.org/Objects/1/files/Recycling%20Factsheet.pdf, accessed 23 August 2008.

97 Bureau of International Recycling (undated) '10 questions on paper recovery and recycling', www.bir.org/aboutrecycling/10questions/tenquestions.asp, accessed 23 August 2008; Eurometrec (undated) 'Position papers', www.eurometrec.org/, accessed 23 August 2008; Confederation of European Paper Industries (undated) 'Recycling facts', www.cepi.org/Objects/1/files/Recycling%20Factsheet.pdf, accessed 23 August 2008.

98 Dai Rees and Practical Action (2005) 'Recycling and reuse of resources – Organic waste', http://practicalaction.org/practicalanswers/product_info.php?cPath=71& products_id=181, accessed 13 August 2008.

99 Hogg, D., Favoino, E., Nielsen, N., Thompson, J., Wood, K., Penschke, A., Economides, D. and Papageorgiou, S. (2002) *Economic Analysis of Options for Managing Biodegradable Municipal Waste*, Final Report to the European Commission.

100 Conchran, K. and Villamizar, N. (2007) 'Recycling construction materials: An important part of the construction process', *Construction Business Owner*, June; Reardon, C. and Fewster, E. (2008) 'Waste minimisation', in Australian government, *Your Home Technical Manual*, fourth edition, Commonwealth of Australia.

101 US EPA (1998) cited in Napier, T. (2008) *Construction Waste Management*, Whole Building Design Guide, National Institute of Building Sciences, US.

102 US EPA (1998) cited in Napier, T. (2008) *Construction Waste Management*, Whole Building Design Guide, National Institute of Building Sciences, US; OECD (2003) *Environmentally Sustainable Buildings: Challenges and Policies*, OECD, Paris; Reardon, C. and Fewster, E. (2008) 'Waste minimisation', in Australian government, *Your Home Technical Manual*, fourth edition, Commonwealth of Australia.

103 Conchran, K. and Villamizar, N. (2007) 'Recycling construction materials: An important part of the construction process', *Construction Business Owner*, June.

104 Conchran, K. and Villamizar, N. (2007) Recycling construction materials: An important part of the construction process', *Construction Business Owner*, June; Neun, D. and Grothe, M. (2001) *A Report on the Feasibility of Deconstruction: An Investigation of Deconstruction Activity in Four Cities*, prepared by National Association of Home Builder Research Center for US Department of Housing and Urban Development, Washington, DC; US EPA (undated) 'Construction and demolition materials', www.epa.gov/epawaste/nonhaz/industrial/cd/index.htm, accessed 12 October 2008.

105 Neun, D. and Grothe, M. (2001) *A Report on the Feasibility of Deconstruction: An Investigation of Deconstruction Activity in Four Cities*, prepared by National Association of Home Builder Research Center for US Department of Housing and Urban Development, Washington, DC; US EPA (undated) 'Construction and demolition materials', www.epa.gov/epawaste/nonhaz/industrial/cd/index.htm, accessed 12 October 2008.

106 Hargroves, K., Stasinopoulos, P., Desha, C. and Smith, M. (2007) 'Engineering Sustainable Solutions Program: Industry Practice Portfolio – E-Waste Education Courses', The Natural Edge Project, Australia.

107 Ruediger Kuehr cited in UN University (2007) UN, *Industry, Others Partner to Create World Standards for E-Scrap Recycling, Harvesting Components*, UN University, Tokyo.

108 Skinner, L. (2005) 'Solar silicon market a seller's paradise', *Renewable Energy World*, 14 February; van Sark, W. G., Brandsen, G. W., Fleuster, M. and Hekkert, M. P. (2007) 'Analysis of the silicon market: Will thin films profit?', *Energy Policy*, vol 35, no 6, pp3121–3125.

109 Environment Victoria (2005) *Environmental Report Card on Computers 2005: Computer Waste in Australia and the Case for Producer Responsibility*, Environment Victoria, Carlton, Australia, pp8–9.

110 European Tyre Recycling Association (2004) 'Introduction to tyre recycling: 2004', www.etra-eu.org/ac121.htm, accessed 13 October 2008.

111 European Tyre Recycling Association (2004) 'Introduction to tyre recycling: 2004', www.etra-eu.org/ac121.htm, accessed 13 October 2008; Waste Online (undated) 'End of life vehicle and tyre recycling information sheet', www.wasteonline.org.uk/resources/InformationSheets/vehicle.htm, accessed 13 October 2008.

112 European Tyre Recycling Association (2004) 'Introduction to tyre recycling: 2004', www.etra-eu.org/ac121.htm, accessed 13 October 2008.

113 Waste Online (undated) 'End of life vehicle and tyre recycling information sheet', www.wasteonline.org.uk/resources/InformationSheets/vehicle.htm, accessed 13 October 2008.

114 Bureau of International Recycling (undated) 'Tyres', www.bir.org/aboutrecycling/tyres.asp, accessed 12 October 2008; Waste Online (undated) 'End of life vehicle and tyre recycling information sheet', www.wasteonline.org.uk/resources/InformationSheets/vehicle.htm, accessed 13 October 2008.

115 Amirkhanian, S. N. (2001) 'Utilization of crumb rubber in asphaltic concrete mixtures – South Carolina's experience', in Dhir, R. K., Limbachiya, M. C. and Paine, K. A., 'Recycling and Reuse of Used Tyres', Proceedings of the International Symposium Organised by the Concrete Technology Unit, University of Dundee, UK, 19–20 March, pp163–174; Paul, J. (1998) cited in Morin, J. E. and Farris, R. J. (2001) *ANTEC 2001: Plastics, the Lone Star: Conference Proceedings*, Society of Plastics Engineers, Dallas, US, 6–10 May 2001.

116 European Tyre Recycling Association (2004) 'Introduction to tyre recycling: 2004', www.etra-eu.org/ac121.htm, accessed 13 October 2008.

117 European Tyre Recycling Association (2004) 'Introduction to tyre recycling: 2004', www.etra-eu.org/ac121.htm, accessed 13 October 2008.

118 Index Mundi (undated) 'Crude oil (petroleum) monthly price', http://indexmundi.com/commodities/?commodity=crude-oil&months=300, accessed 5 September 2008.

119 Association of European Producers of Steel for Packaging (2007) 'Two thirds of Europe's steel packaging gets recycled: A significant contribution to reducing energy consumption and carbon footprint', APEAL Press Release, Brussels; International Iron and Steel Institute (2008) 'Steel packaging: A recycling success story', Media Release, IISI, Brussels.

120 International Iron and Steel Institute (2008) 'Steel packaging: A recycling success story', Media Release, IISI, Brussels.

121 Sheirs, J. (2006) 'Overview of commercial pyrolysis processes for waste plastics', in Sheirs, J. and Kaminsky, W. (eds) *Feedstock Recycling and Pyrolysis of Waste Plastics*, John Wiley and Sons; Zadgaonkar, A. (2006) 'Process and equipment for conversions of waste plastics into fuels', in Sheirs, J. and Kaminsky, W. (eds) *Feedstock Recycling and Pyrolysis of Waste Plastics*, John Wiley and Sons.

122 Cynar PLC (undated) 'Operating features of ThermoFuel', www.cynarplc.com/thermo-fuel-features.asp, accessed 14 October 2008; EnvoSmart Technologies (2006) 'EnvoFuel – frequently asked questions', http://envosmart.com/2006/uploadedfiles/envofuel_faq.pdf, accessed 16 October 2008; Ozmo Energy (undated) 'Plastic waste recycling', www.ozmoenergy.com/recycling/, accessed 16 October 2008.

123 Cynar PLC (undated) 'Operating features of ThermoFuel', www.cynarplc.com/thermo-fuel-features.asp, accessed 14 October 2008.

124 Cetane number (or cetane index) is a measure of the ease with which the fuel is ignited in an engine and is important with respect to low-temperature startability, warm-up, and smooth, even combustion. Cetane number is analogous to the octane rating for petrol.

125 Cynar PLC (undated) 'Operating features of ThermoFuel', www.cynarplc.com/thermo-fuel-features.asp, accessed 14 October 2008; EnvoSmart Technologies (2006) 'EnvoFuel – frequently asked questions', http://envosmart.com/2006/uploadedfiles/envofuel_faq.pdf, accessed 16 October 2008; Ozmo Energy (undated) 'Plastic waste recycling', www.ozmoenergy.com/recycling/, accessed 16 October 2008.

126 Australian Museum (undated) 'University of New South Wales Eureka Prize for Scientific Research', www.physics.usyd.edu.au/~gekko/press/eureka_05/eureka_05.htm, accessed 16 October 2008; Catalyst (2008) 'Meet Professor Veena Sahajwalla', *Australian Broadcasting Corporation Catalyst Stories*, 6 March.

127 Japan for Sustainability (2002) 'Office Chonai-kai: A paper recycling success story', www.japanfs.org/en/public/ngo01.html, accessed 12 August 2008; Office Chonai-kai (undated) 'About us', www.o-cho.org/eigo/f_about.html, accessed 12 August 2008; Office Chonai-kai (2001) 'Whiteness 70 is just right', Sample Chapter, Office Chonai-kai, www.o-cho.org/eigo/f_book.html, accessed 12 July 2009.

128 Dai Rees and Practical Action (2005) *Recycling and Reuse of Resources – Organic Waste*, Practical Action, UK.

129 Energy Recovery Council (undated) Homepage, http://wte.org/, accessed 5 September 2008; Stehlik, P. (2002) 'Some aspects contributing to improved process and equipment design in the field of waste-to-energy and environmental protection', in Afgan, N. H. and de Carvalho, M. C. R. (eds) *New and Renewable Technologies for Sustainable Development*, Kluwer Academic, Norwell, MA, pp443–458.

130 Stevenson, W. (2002) *Emissions from Large MWC Units at MACT Compliance, Memorandum to Docket A-90-45*, US EPA, North Carolina, US.

131 Thorneloe, S. A., Weitz, K. and Jambeck, J. (2007) 'Application of the U.S. decision support tool for materials and waste management', *Waste Management*, vol 27, no 8, pp106–1020.

132 Metro Vancouver (undated) 'Examples of waste-to-energy facilities in Europe and Japan', www.metrovancouver.org/services/solidwaste/zerowaste/PDF%20documents/Waste-to-EnergyFacilities.pdf, accessed 5 September 2008; Stengler, E. (2005) 'The European position', *Waste Management World*, November/December.

133 Brownell, B. (2004) *Transmaterial*, Transstudio, p55; Bonded Logic Inc. (undated) Homepage, www.bondedlogic.com/, accessed 20 September 2008.

134 Brownell, B. (2005) *Transmaterial*, Princeton Architectural Press; Syndesis (undated) 'Syndecrete', www.syndesisinc.com/index-syndecrete.html, accessed 30 June 2008.

135 Alex Fraser Group (undated) Homepage, www.alexfraser.com.au, accessed 4 October 2008.

136 Molectra® Technologies (undated) 'The Molectra® Technology', www.molectra.com.au/technology.aspx, accessed 28 August 2008.

11

Decoupling Economic Growth from Air Pollution

The Complex Challenge of Air Pollution

It is no wonder that we have managed fundamentally to alter the chemical composition of the atmosphere. For we have treated it as an unlimited resource, available to all in unlimited quantities, at no charge.

Dr Richard L. Sandor, creator of the
Chicago Climate Exchange, 1998[1]

In addition to greenhouse gas emissions, biodiversity loss, freshwater extraction and waste production, air pollution, particularly from fossil fuel combustion, is an environmental pressure that needs to be decoupled from economic growth, in large part because it causes significant adverse health effects. The WHO estimates that more than 400,000 people die prematurely each year from causes directly attributable to outdoor air pollution,[2] and a further 1.6 million deaths are caused by indoor air pollution.[3]

More than 2 billion people across the world have no access to electricity and thus depend on crop waste or coal, dung or wood to meet their energy needs. The cooking and heating with such solid fuels on open fires or stoves without chimneys or adequate ventilation leads to significant indoor air pollution. This indoor smoke contains a range of harmful pollutants including small soot or dust particles that are able to penetrate deep into the lungs. In many developing countries, indoor smoke is responsible for an estimated 3.7 per cent of the overall disease burden.[4] Particulate pollution under 10 micrometres, or microns (PM_{10}) for instance, is predicted to cause 3.1 million premature deaths and 25.4 million years of life lost by 2030.[5] PM_{10} levels, as prescribed by the WHO guidelines, are exceeded in many countries, especially in Mexico, Greece and Turkey.[6]

The OECD projects health impacts of air pollution, based on current trends, to increase worldwide, with the number of premature deaths linked to inhaling particulate matter more than doubling by 2030. Air pollution is of course a particular problem for large cities, as a 1999 study conducted by a leading Indian environmental NGO revealed – about 10,000 people die prematurely in Delhi due to air pollution each year,[7] which is equivalent to an average of one death every 52 minutes. Furthermore, a study by the World Bank in 2000 found that for 18 cities in Central and Eastern Europe, 18,000 premature deaths a year could be prevented, and US$1.2 billion a year in working time lost to illness could be regained by achieving EU air pollution standards for dust and soot.[8]

Air pollution also causes a number of direct financial impacts and can be a significant cost to economies:

- In 1995, the UK government calculated that the total costs of damage from acid rain, caused mainly by sulphur emissions from coal-fired power stations, were over £18 billion (US$28.8 billion) – mostly related to the damage of buildings.[9] Not only do acid rain and persistent organic pollutants attack infrastructure, through corroding steel and cement, they also contribute to the contamination of water, and the loss of resilience of ecosystems, nature's ability to accommodate shocks such as natural disasters.
- Tropospheric ground-level ozone, formed through the interaction of ultraviolet light with hydrocarbons and nitrogen oxides formed mainly from fossil fuel combustion, causes health-related issues,[10] along with damage to agriculture and rubber products. Ozone is vitally important to protect the earth from ultraviolet rays in the stratosphere, but when created at sea level it causes a range of problems. A European study found that tropospheric ozone causes measurable, regional-scale reductions in crop yields for 23 species of arable crops, costing Europe US$5.72–12 billion per year in lost production.[11] In addition, ozone's oxidizing effect causes rubber to decompose and disintegrate, with damage to rubber goods from ozone exposure in the UK estimated to cost the economy £85 million per year (US$135 million per year).[12]
- Poor indoor air quality from lack of ventilation, the presence of off-gases from paints and various materials, and indoor sources of air pollution, costs OECD economies through ill health, absenteeism and lost productivity. For instance, poor indoor air quality in Australia's homes, offices, factories and buildings has been estimated to cost the country as much as AU$12 billion (US$10.5 billion) a year due to ill health and lost production, and in the US the cost is US$170 billion.[13]
- Air pollution can also harm the lucrative tourism sector, as sulphur and nitrogen oxides result in corrosion of buildings and heritage structures,

such as the Taj Mahal in India and the Colosseum in Rome. A survey of 150 tour guides in Hong Kong found that half of the tourist visitors had complained about the air pollution. The poll of tour guides also found that one in ten tourists suffered pollution-linked health problems while visiting Hong Kong.[14] In Kathmandu, 17 per cent of tourists interviewed indicated that they would avoid visiting Nepal again because of poor air quality.[15]

A range of studies from across the world, summarized in the *OECD Environmental Outlook to 2030*,[16] have reported economic losses of 2–4 per cent of GDP in cities and countries because of air pollution, with most of the economic costs coming from increased health costs. For example, in 1995 India's economic growth rate was 4 per cent, economic losses due to health costs of air pollution were estimated to be 4.5 per cent of India's gross domestic product – which meant that the entire economic growth for that year was invested in addressing health costs resulting from air pollution.[17] In China also, the World Bank estimated in 2007 that Chinese air pollution health costs were at about 3.8 per cent of GDP.[18] However, addressing such costs is problematic as the causes can require action not just within the cities but on a regional scale. For instance, a large share of air pollution in Beijing and Hong Kong comes from sources, mostly industry, outside the cities. This is one of the main reasons why it was such a challenge for Beijing to reduce its air pollution for the 2008 Olympics. The Chinese government spent US$20 billion greening the city to reduce air pollution by investing in rail, retrofitting factories with cleaner technology, building urban parks, taking half of the city's vehicles off the roads in the lead-up to and during the Olympics, stopping most construction and shutting down dozens of factories. Despite this, the level of particulate pollution in Beijing was significantly worse than Athens, Atlanta and Sydney, the host cities of the three previous Olympics. Researchers found that, 'Particulate air pollution did drop by about one-third during the two-week Olympic period. But coarser particulate matter, PM_{10}, exceeded levels the WHO considers safe about 81 per cent of the time, while the smaller particulate pollution $PM_{2.5}$, which can cause more serious health consequences, exceeded WHO guidelines 100 per cent of the time'.[19] Many cities around the world are affected by regional effects such as the Southeast Asian haze which is caused by massive forest burning. In 1997 and 2006, smoke from slash-and-burn land clearing caused an environmental disaster that is estimated to have cost the Asia Pacific region over US$4 billion.[20] Other forms of air pollution that influence whole regions include problems of acidification from industrial sulphur and nitrous oxide emissions. Acidification has been reduced in Europe and North America, but is now a growing problem in parts of Asia, where acidic deposition has increased.[21]

Addressing air pollution is therefore a complex challenge and requires a multi-faceted approach that tackles urban, industrial and regional sources of various particulates and pollution. As *Our Common Future* stated in 1987:

> *Atmospheric pollution, once perceived only as a local urban-industrial problem involving people's health, is now also seen as a much more complex issue encompassing buildings, ecosystems, and maybe even public health over vast regions. During transport to the atmosphere, emission of sulphur and nitrogen oxides and volatile organic compounds are transformed into sulphuric acid and nitric acids, ammonium salts and ozone. They fall to the ground, sometimes many hundreds or thousands of kilometres from their origins, as dry particles, or in rain, snow, frost, fog and dew.[22]*

Considerable progress has been made since *Our Common Future* was published in preventing and controlling air pollution in many parts of the world, partly due to strong government policy measures and multilateral agreements which have driven market uptake of technological innovations in this area. At the national level, many countries have clean air legislation that sets emission and ambient air quality standards to protect public health and the environment. This has led to significant success stories, such as the considerable and rapid reduction of carbon monoxide pollution from automobiles.[23] At the regional level, there are a number of agreements, including the Convention on Long Range Trans-boundary Air Pollution,[24] the Canada-US Air Quality Agreement,[25] European Union agreements,[26] the ASEAN Haze Agreement,[27] the Malé Declaration on the Control and Prevention of Air Pollution in South Asia[28] and the Air Pollution Information Network for Africa, a regional science-policy network. Internationally, the Stockholm Convention on Persistent Organic Pollutants[29] regulates the use and emission of certain persistent organic pollutants (POPs), the Helsinki Protocol focuses on the reduction of sulphur emissions and their trans-boundary movements (as outlined in Chapter 2) and the Montreal Protocol regulates the emissions of ozone depleting chemicals.

Six common pollutants are the leading cause of harm to human health and the environment – namely sulphur dioxide (SO_2), nitrous oxide (N_2O), tropospheric ozone (O_3), lead (Pb), carbon monoxide (CO) and particulate matter (PM) – and are often used as the main indicators of air quality by regulatory agencies.[30] In this chapter we consider how to decouple economic growth from the production and emissions of these major air pollutants, with the exception of carbon monoxide, which has been well covered by a major US National Research Council Review.[31] Recommended targets for air pollution levels in this chapter are based on the recommendations from the WHO,[32] such as the specific interim targets and air quality levels for particulate matter (PM_{10} and $PM_{2.5}$), as shown in Table 11.1.

In this chapter we will show that, as with other major environmental pressures, the costs of action on air pollution are affordable and significantly less than the costs of inaction. We will also examine a range of innovations in policy and enabling technologies that have helped to reduce the overall costs of

Table 11.1 *WHO interim targets and air quality guidelines (AQG) for particulate matter – annual mean concentrations (micrograms per cubic metre, µg/m³)*

Target	PM_{10}	$PM_{2.5}$	Basis for the selected target level
Interim Target 1	70µg/m³	35µg/m³	These levels are associated with about a 15% higher longer-term mortality risk relative to the AQG level
Interim Target 2	50µg/m³	25µg/m³	In addition to other health benefits, these levels lower the risk of premature mortality by an average of 6% relative to the Interim Target 1 level (IT-1)
Interim Target 3	30µg/m³	15µg/m³	In addition to other health benefits, these levels reduce the mortality risk by an average of 6% relative to the IT-2 level
Air Quality Guideline (AQG)	20µg/m³	10µg/m³	These are the lowest levels at which total cardiopulmonary and lung cancer mortality have been shown to increase with more than 95% confidence in response to long-term exposure to $PM_{2.5}$

Source: WHO (2005)[33]

action on reducing air pollution. We begin with a discussion of ways to decouple sulphur dioxide, as it was the cause of the first major recorded air pollution health disaster, the 1952 London smog, and is also a significant factor in the acidification of thousands of lakes in the northern hemisphere. Then we investigate ways to decouple nitrous oxides, a precursor to the formation of tropospheric ozone, a major component of photochemical smog, with the first city to experience photochemical smog on a massive scale being Los Angeles. We then investigate the decoupling of lead, particularly from leaded petrol and, finally, we consider airborne particulates, which are a serious threat to human health.

Economic Benefits Associated with Reducing Air Pollution

In most cases where air pollution has been reduced, the economic benefits have been found to far outweigh the costs of taking action.[34] Significant advances have been achieved over the last few decades both in the scientific understanding of air pollution and in the technological innovations to reduce it. Through these advances, air quality has been improved dramatically in many cities, especially in the OECD, at much less cost than first anticipated. The US EPA, for instance, conducted an extensive study which found that the total benefits of the Clean Air Act programmes 1970–1990 saved the US economy US$22 trillion.[35] In other words, if US air pollution trends in 1970 had continued to 1990, then the measurable economic, social, health and environmental costs to the US economy would have been an extra US$22 trillion. By comparison, the actual cost of achieving the pollution reductions observed over the 20-year period was US$523 billion, a relatively small expense compared to the estimated costs of the impacts avoided. While there are successes in both developed and developing countries, major challenges remain, particularly in rapidly developing cities in Asia and South and Central America. Currently, only a few major cities in Asia have pollution levels below WHO guideline limits.[36] There is a significant risk of air pollution worsening in the future if strong action is not taken, due to the expected exponential increases in energy use, vehicle ownership and industrial growth. In Beijing, for instance, approximately 1300 new vehicles are registered each day, while in Bangalore, India, the daily figure is more than 900.[37]

Before investigating the specific forms of air pollution, and building on from the last four chapters, we first highlight the fact that measures to reduce air pollution will also contribute to reducing greenhouse gas emissions, as outlined in Table 11.2. This is due to the fact that each of the forms of air pollution considered in this chapter results mainly from either the burning of fossil fuels[38] or from emissions from industrial processes, which are also the main contributors to carbon dioxide (CO_2) and other greenhouse gas emissions. This 'co-benefits' approach is supported by the Intergovernmental Panel on Climate Change (IPCC), which stated in its Fourth Assessment Report (2007) that 'Integrating air pollution abatement and climate change mitigation policies offers potentially large cost reductions compared to treating those policies in isolation.'[39] Accounting for the co-benefits of reduced air pollution and reduced greenhouse gas emissions can have significant impacts on the cost effectiveness of climate and air pollution policy. As the OECD states:

> The co-benefit relationship suggests that co-ordination of policy efforts in these areas could deliver important cost savings. For example, van Harmelen et al[40] found that to comply with agreed or future policies to reduce regional air pollution in Europe, mitigation costs are implied, but these are reduced by 50–70% for SO_2 and around 50% for NO_x when combined with greenhouse gas related policies. Similarly, in the shorter-term, van Vuuren et al[41] found that, for the Kyoto Protocol, about half the costs of climate policy might be recovered from reduced air pollution control costs.[42]

Clearly, aligning investments to decouple economic growth from both greenhouse gas emissions and air pollution simultaneously will increase the economic efficiency of such investments.

Table 11.2 *Actions to reduce urban air pollution which also reduce greenhouse gas emissions*

City	Initiative
Curitiba, Brazil	The now famous case of Curitiba successfully uses a bus rapid transit system with dedicated bus lanes to provide cost-effective transport options that are comparable with private car use, thus reducing fossil fuel consumption and air pollution. Some 70% of commuters use transit, despite per capita income well above the national average. Curitiba has now achieved one of the lowest ambient air pollution levels in the country,[43] and this success has inspired many other cities to also invest in effective rapid bus transit, such as the TransMilenio in Bogotá, Colombia, the Orange Line of Los Angeles, California, the Transmetro system in Guatemala City, and the Metrobús of Mexico City.[44]
Bogotá, Colombia	In 1998 Bogotá mayor, Enrique Penalosa, began an urban renewal campaign inspired by the success of Curitiba. Modelled on Curitiba's bus system, a new TransMilenio bus rapid transit system was built which now carries over 1.4 million passengers per day. Furthermore, a doubling of parking costs was imposed, along with a 20% increase in fuel taxes. The proceeds directly funded the upgrades to the public transport system. Curitiba and Bogotá are showing that sustainable transport – cycling, walking and buses – can comfortably manage over 50% of commutes, with reduced air pollution and greenhouse gas emissions, as well as improved health and economic outcomes. In Bogotá, 85 per cent of residents now live within 500 metres of a bus service.[45]
Guayaquil, Ecuador	In Guayaquil, Ecuador, in 2006, Mayor Nebot opened the first 15km (9.3 miles) of the Metrovia bus rapid transit system to provide a cleaner, higher-quality service and reduce trip times in key travel corridors. Now, in 2008, the bus system has been expanded to 45km (28 miles) and serves over 200,000 daily passengers. Also since 2006, the city has run 'car-free Sundays', closing streets to traffic to encourage thousands of residents to participate in city life by walking and riding bicycles.
Mexico City, Mexico	In 2007, the mayor of Mexico City launched a new 'Plan Verde' ('Green Plan') committed to expanding Metrobus (the city's bus rapid transit system), and increasing pedestrian and bicycle paths. The plan also included other measures to reduce air pollution, such as an expansion of the 'Hoy no circula' (or 'Today don't drive') programme, where drivers are prohibited from using their vehicles one weekday per week based on their licence plate numbers – from 2008, 'Hoy no circula' included Saturday as well as weekdays.[46]
Stockholm, Sweden	Stockholm introduced a congestion pricing scheme on a trial basis in 2005. It extended its public transport system to support the increased patronage, assessed the effectiveness of the trials using several different perspectives and held a referendum to determine whether to introduce it permanently.[47] The public transport network was enhanced with 197 new buses and 16 new bus lines. Extra 'park and ride' facilities were built with 1800 new parks, and existing parking lots were made more attractive.[48] The trial resulted in an overall 22% reduction in congestion,[49] and on approach roads into the city queuing times in the morning fell by as much as a third, and were halved for outbound traffic in the evening.[50] Road use in the inner city, as measured by kilometres travelled, also fell by 14%,[51] and there was an average 10% reduction in air pollutants.[52] In the subsequent referendum, the public, which had initially had reservations about the scheme, voted for its continuation.[53] A cost–benefit analysis was undertaken as part of the trial period to assess its viability, and showed significant net benefits of SEK1048 million per year (over US$150 million).[54]
Vancouver, Canada	'EcoDensity', Vancouver's sustainability initiative, has led to investment in measures to encourage and facilitate walking and cycling to significant effect, leading to changes in planning policies to facilitate the uptake of cooperative car programmes. As a result, trips made by walking have increased by 44% and walking now accounts for 27% of all trips into the city centre.[55] The new 'Evergreen Line' uses advanced light rapid transit technology to offer a rapid transit service around Vancouver's northeast sections. It offers high frequency (3.0 minutes between trains), high speed (maximum speed of 80km/hour) and a high peak hour capacity of 10,400 persons.[56]

Source: The Natural Edge Project (2008) compiled by Smith, Hargroves and Reeve.

Decoupling Economic Growth from Sulphur Dioxide Emissions

Sulphur emissions result from various sources but mainly from the burning of fossil fuels. One of the first cities to suffer on a large scale from sulphur pollution was London. By the 1600s, coal became widely used for domestic heating in London, in addition to expanded industrial use as the city grew. As the UN Environment Programme states, 'Indications are that smoke concentrations were so heavy in the 1700s in London that some buildings had to be repainted every three years to hide the effects of smoke particle deposition.'[57] Particulate sulphates, derived from coal combustion in the atmosphere, provide hygroscopic sites for fog droplet nucleation, making it easier for fogs to form. The government at the time was able, from the turn of the last century, to reduce sulphur emissions largely by shifting a percentage of domestic heating from coal to electricity. However, despite the fact that sulphur pollution and the number of fog days was in decline, stagnant weather conditions in 1952 helped create one of the worst air pollution disasters in Britain's history. Early in December 1952, a cold fog descended upon London, and because of the cold, Londoners began to burn more coal than usual. The resulting air pollution was trapped by an inversion layer formed by the dense mass of cold air. Concentrations of air pollutants built up dramatically. The problem was made worse by the fact that low-quality, high-sulphur coal was still being used for home heating in London in order to permit export of higher-quality coal. Sooty smoke produced peak daily concentrations of black smoke of $5000\mu g/m^3$ (compared with the WHO 24-hour maximum limit of $100–150\mu g/m^3$),[58] and daily average SO_2 levels of $3000–4000\mu g/m^3$ (compared with the WHO 24-hour maximum limit of $100–150\mu g/m^3$).[59] This formed a solute sulphuric acid with water in the atmosphere and the acidity of the rain reached dangerous levels. The smog lasted for five days, eventually extending over a 50km radius. Approximately 4000 deaths occurred as a result of inhaling the pollution, particularly affecting the elderly and the sick and those with chest problems.[60] This ushered in the first national Clean Air Act for the UK, variations of which were copied by OECD countries in the second half of the 20th century.

As *Our Common Future* outlined, significant further impetus for decoupling economic growth from sulphur emissions came soon after this incident:

> *Damage first became evident in Scandinavia in the 1960s. Several thousand lakes in Europe, particularly in southern Scandinavia, and several hundreds in North America have registered a steady increase in acidity levels to the point where their natural fish populations have declined or died out. The same acids enter the soil and groundwater, increasing corrosion of drinking water piping into Scandinavia ... Some of the greatest observed damage has been reported in Central Europe which is currently receiving*

more than one gram of sulphur on every square meter of ground each year, at least five times greater than national background levels. By 1985, the Federal Republic of Germany reported leaf damage in its forest plot samples nationwide amounting to 50 per cent. Many reports show soils in parts of Europe becoming acidic throughout the tree rooting layers.[61]

Our Common Future sounded a stern warning that 'Europe may be experiencing an immense change to irreversible acidification, the remedial costs of which could be beyond economic reach'.[62] A range of studies subsequently showed that the costs of damage from sulphur pollution were significant. In 1995, the UK government calculated total costs of damage from sulphur to be over £18 billion (US$28 billion), while the costs of action were no more than £1–3 billion (US$1.5–4.6 billion).[63] Table 11.3 shows that most studies published give a range of estimates of the costs and damages caused by sulphur pollution, due mainly to the fact that health costs are hard to estimate accurately. Most early studies have focused on the health costs and the costs of damaging and eroding buildings and infrastructure. The more recent studies have also taken into account the cost impacts on crops, forests and ecosystems. This explains why the more recent studies predict a higher, but probably more accurate, estimate of the costs of inaction on sulphur emissions.

Table 11.3 *Estimates of damage costs from sulphur emissions (per tonne emitted)*

Study	Country	Damage cost US$ / tonne emitted	Comment
Hohmeyer[64] (1988)	West Germany	1589–8533	Lower estimate – plant life 61%, human health 16% Higher estimate – plant life 76%, human health 17%
Pearce[65] (1992)	UK	4661	Building costs 74%
ECOTEC[66] (1992)	UK	861–5191	Health costs 21–87%
	Germany	3959–4,368	Health costs 77–85%
Alfsen et al[67] (1992)	Norway	500–8960	Health costs 80–90%
ExternE[68] (1998)	Austria	18,000	Study addressed costs of
	Belgium	22,776–24,282	impacts on health, crops,
	Denmark	5980–8432	building materials, forests and
	Finland	2054–2972	ecosystems
	France	15,000–30,000	
	Germany	3600–27,376	
	Greece	3956–15,664	
	Iceland	5600–10,600	
	Italy	11,400–24,000	
	The Netherlands	12,410–15,162	
	Portugal	9920–10,848	
	Spain	8438–19,166	
	Sweden	4714–5620	
	United Kingdom	12,054–20,050	

Source: Ekins (2002)[69]

In the second half of the 20th century, significant reductions in sulphur pollution were achieved in OECD countries. Clean air legislation ensured that the use of coal for domestic heating and cooking was phased out, and replaced by the use of electricity and natural gas. Switching to electricity in homes and industry rather than burning coal directly meant that local pollution was negligible, but it did cause regional pollution problems. For example, in the 1970s and 1980s, only 10 per cent of the sulphur pollution in Switzerland was produced in Switzerland. Italy was responsible for more than 20 per cent of Switzerland's sulphur pollution, with France and Germany each generating some 15 per cent of the sulphur pollution that lands in Switzerland. Norway is also a major recipient of trans-boundary sulphur pollution – almost half its sulphur pollution originates in the UK, Germany, the Russian Federation or Poland.[70] These levels of trans-boundary sulphur pollution have been monitored in Europe since 1977.[71] Because of this, and the fact that other sources of air pollution similarly have a regional basis, many nations signed up to the Convention on Long Range Trans-boundary Air Pollution in 1979.[72] The Convention came into force in 1983 and catalysed stronger policies and greater exchange of information, research and cooperation between monitoring efforts to combat the discharge of air pollutants, including sulphur.[73] Known as the 'Helsinki Protocol', the agreement established a standard target of 30 per cent reduction in national emissions of signatory countries from 1980 levels. This has been subsequently updated twice and the UNECE Second Sulphur Protocol in 1994 committed nations to targets of reductions of 62 per cent by the year 2000, 70 per cent by 2005 and 80 per cent by 2010.[74] These global agreements helped to stimulate and provide incentives to innovation and reduce business competitiveness issues.

According to the OECD:

> *Emissions of sulphur dioxide from all sources were absolutely decoupled from economic growth for all three OECD regions during 1980–98: emissions decreased by over 50%, while GDP grew by almost 61%. Of the three OECD regions, decoupling was most pronounced in Europe, where emissions fell by 70% and GDP grew by 44%. In OECD Pacific emissions fell by 17% and GDP increased by 81%. In OECD North America, the corresponding figures were 27% and 72% respectively ... Emissions reductions have been due mainly to a switch from high sulphur solid and liquid fuels to natural gas in the energy industries, industry and domestic sectors, the construction of new power plants, and the use of low-sulphur coal and flue gas desulphurisation.*[75]

Some nations did not sign up to the Second Sulphur Protocol, fearing that the costs of achieving the 80 per cent reduction goal would be too great. However, since 1980, two parallel, but equally important, developments have helped to reduce the mitigation costs of sulphur pollution. First, structural changes and

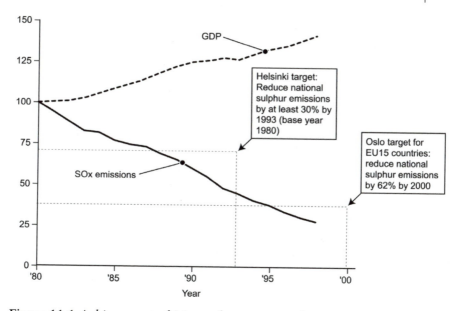

Figure 11.1 *Achievement of 16 members party to the UNECE Convention on Long Range Trans-boundary Air Pollution (CLRTAP)*

Note: Parties include Austria, Belgium, Canada, Czech Republic, Denmark, Finland, France, Germany, Hungary, Italy, Luxembourg, Netherlands, Norway, Slovak Republic, Sweden and Switzerland.
Source: OECD (2002)[76]

energy management – energy-saving and energy-efficiency measures like the use of wind and solar energy and the switch to natural gas and low-sulphur fuels – have significantly reduced sulphur emissions.[77] Second, the use of primary measures – advanced combustion and combustion modifications – or secondary measures – like flue gas desulphurization, denitrification (selective catalytic reduction), precipitators (e.g. electrostatic precipitators), bag-houses and catalytic/thermal oxidation – have also reduced sulphur emissions.[78] These innovations (see Table 11.4) changed the costs of meeting the requirements of the Second Sulphur Protocol. In practice, the single most successful measure for the reduction of sulphur oxides has been the introduction and implementation of flue gas desulphurization on medium-size and large combustion installations in power plants and district heating.[79]

Today the UK government celebrates its achievement, along with Europe, of reducing sulphur emissions by over 70 per cent, as seen in Figure 11.2. As UK Economist Paul Ekins writes:

> *[the result of this achievement] was that the environmentally sustainable goal of 90 per cent reductions is attainable with essentially no negative impacts on economic growth at all. In this case, economic growth and environmental sustainability have proved to be remarkably compatible.*[80]

Table 11.4 *Enabling technologies that have reduced sulphur pollution*

Pressurized fluidized bed boilers	Pressurized fluidized bed boilers involve air under pressure being injected into a fine mixture of coal, lime and sand, until the whole mass behaves like a boiling fluid. The process achieves highly efficient combustion and reduces sulphur emissions by up to 90%. This process also reduces NO_x and greenhouse gas emissions because combustion temperatures are lower.
Flue gas desulphurization	Flue gas desulphurization involves scrubbers that remove sulphur from emissions after combustion, either by passing them through a powdered lime filter (dry scrubbers) or an alkaline liquid (wet scrubbers). Many systems achieve reductions of 80–95%, and can easily be fitted to existing stations. Flue gas desulphurization is one of the main sulphur reduction methods adopted in the US, Japan and Europe.
Integrated gasification combined cycle	Integrated gasification combined cycle utilizes low-quality solid and liquid fuels and is able to meet the most stringent emission requirements. The system uses a combined cycle format with a gas turbine driven by the combusted syn-gas from the gasifier, while the exhaust gases are heat exchanged with water/steam to generate superheated steam to drive a steam turbine. The process produces no sulphur or nitrous oxide emissions and is much more efficient than traditional coal-fired systems.

Source: Compiled by the Authors led by Michael Smith.

Industry has rapidly taken up these technological innovations to meet and exceed sulphur reduction targets at a fraction of the original projected cost. In the US, for instance, using a market emissions trading scheme enabled the reduction of sulphur emissions more quickly and cheaply than anticipated. In 1992 economists predicted that sulphur reductions would cost US$500–750 per tonne and industry predictions were in the range US$1000–1500 per tonne. The sulphur market opened in 1992 at approximately US$250 a tonne, decreasing to US$130 per tonne in 1995 and US$66 per tonne in 1996. US sulphur emissions fell during this period from 1992 to1996 by 37 per cent while the US economy continued to grow.[81] According to *The Economist* in 1997: 'There is a precedent in America, where a law allowing power companies to trade their right to emit sulphur dioxide has proved highly successful. The government determines what the allowable emissions from each power plant are. Those plants that can clean up cheaply, and thus emit less than allowed, are then free to sell their unused rights to those for whom pollution control would be costly. Overall, this has cut sulphur emissions faster and more cheaply than anyone predicted'.[82] According to Dr Richard Sandor, the then Chairman and Chief Executive Officer of Environmental Financial Products, and the driving force behind the US sulphur and carbon markets, 'This major success interests both the environmental and business communities because it reflects the win-win possibility of emissions trading. Turning this possibility into a probability includes such conditions as strictly limiting and precisely measuring pollution levels, and enabling industry to comply with the law using flexible and creative instruments'.[83]

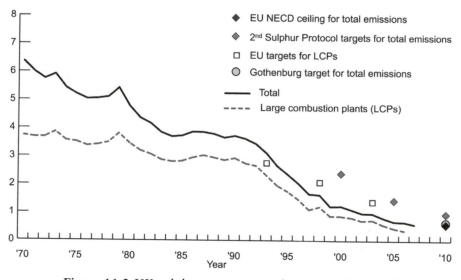

Figure 11.2 *UK sulphur emissions and targets: 1970–2010*

Note: NECD = National Emissions Ceilings Directive
Source: AEA Energy & Environment, DEFRA (2009)[84]

Decoupling Economic Growth from Nitrous Oxide, Tropospheric Ozone and Photochemical Smog

Air pollutants are described as either primary or secondary. Usually, primary pollutants are substances directly emitted from a process, such as sulphur dioxide released from coal-fired power stations. Secondary pollutants are not emitted directly, but form when primary pollutants react with other molecules in the atmosphere. Photochemical smog is largely the result of the formation of secondary pollutants. In the case of Los Angeles, in the early 1950s Professor Haagen-Smit of the California Institute of Technology proved that city smog was caused by photochemical atmospheric chemical reactions occurring when light shines on a mixture of nitrogen oxides, carbon monoxide and volatile organic compounds in the air. These reactions lead to tropospheric ozone formation, as well as to the formation of a large variety of air pollutant chemicals including aldehydes (which cause eye irritation), peroxyacyl nitrates and fine particles. Following this discovery Professor Haagen-Smit faced significant opposition from the automobile lobby, and his conclusions were challenged. However, by the mid-1950s there was general agreement as to the cause of the smog,[85] and a network of air-monitoring stations was established in Los Angeles. These monitoring stations found that for instance, in the late 1950s, peak ozone concentrations were above the air quality standard for more than 300 days per year.

Along with automobiles, the other major source of air pollutants in California was found to be the oil-powered electric power plants and in 1957

Professor Haagen-Smit researched how to reduce air pollution from this sector.[86] Through these investigations he pioneered technologies and design strategies to bring about major reductions in hydrocarbon and nitrogen oxide emissions. Using these findings, the Californian government brought into force strict emission standards through the mid-1960s. As a result there was a large and steady decline in hydrocarbon emissions. According to UNEP, 'By 1990, the number of days per year with peak 1-hr average ozone concentration greater than the Federal air quality standard of 0.12ppm had declined to roughly 160 per year. That downward trend has continued such that by 2006 far less than 100 days per year exceed 0.12ppm ozone, and days with ozone concentrations above 0.2ppm are rare indeed.'[87] Stronger standards for nitrous oxide pollution from cars resulted in research which led to the invention of the catalytic converter, a device now widely used to reduce air pollution from internal combustion engines. However, despite the significant reductions in levels from the 1950s and 1960s, more still needs to be done to reduce emissions.

Reducing tropospheric ozone and photochemical smog levels has other significant benefits. Evidence of the harmful effects to vegetation and agricultural crops caused by tropospheric ozone has accumulated over recent decades.[88] For instance, it is estimated that in 1989 annual US crop losses caused by tropospheric ozone were in the order of US$3 billion.[89] And a further study by MIT in 2007 found that if stronger global action is not taken to reduce tropospheric ozone the levels will grow 50 per cent by 2100, resulting in crop production falling by an estimated additional 10–12 per cent.[90]

Decoupling Economic Growth from Lead Pollution

Leaded petrol was originally hailed as one of the greatest inventions of the 1920s, as it was an inexpensive way to increase its octane rating and reduce abnormal combustion to improve engine operation. However in the 1970s, studies were undertaken in the US which demonstrated the dangerous effects of lead on human health, and it was found that lead dust from sources such as petrol and paint could be ingested, damaging the nervous system, kidney functioning and harming intellectual development, with children found to be particularly vulnerable.[91] At the same time, new vehicle technologies – such as the catalytic converter – were being developed to reduce vehicular emissions, and internal combustion engines using catalytic convertors required the use of unleaded petrol, with even small amounts of lead ruining converter performance.

With the realization of the impact of lead on human health, governments around the world – starting with the US – required oil companies to reduce the amount of lead in petrol and to introduce unleaded petrol to the market. Other OECD countries rapidly followed suit, and major emerging economies have also made the switch over the last decade. China began the switch to unleaded petrol in cities in 1997 and is now lead free. India began its lead phase-out in Delhi in 1998 and is now also completely lead free. In 2002, only one African country,

Sudan, had banned lead in petrol.[92] As recently as 2005, 81 countries had still not banned leaded petrol.[93] However, by 2006 almost all African nations had made a significant commitment to ban leaded petrol,[94] due mostly to the work of the Partnership for Clean Fuels and Vehicles launched at the 2002 World Summit on Sustainable Development in Johannesburg, South Africa.[95]

Economists have calculated that making gasoline unleaded rarely costs more than 2 cents a litre and countries can save five to ten times as much as that through health and economic cost savings.[96] The World Bank points out that when the US converted to unleaded gasoline, it saved more than US$10 for every US$1 invested due to reduced health costs, savings on engine maintenance and improved fuel efficiency.[97] Leaded gasoline, because it contains lead salts and halogen acids, causes greater corrosion of automobile exhaust systems and requires more frequent oil and spark plug changes. Now that lead is banned across almost all of Africa, UNEP and the Partnership for Clean Fuels and Vehicles have launched a new campaign to get lead banned worldwide. As of 2009, there are still at least 15 countries using leaded petrol, with more than 270 million people still being exposed daily to unsafe levels of lead from leaded petrol.[98] With significant precedents available, it is time that these countries follow suit to protect the health and well-being of current and future generations.

Decoupling Economic Growth from Particulate Pollution ($PM_{2.5}$–PM_{10})

The most important air pollutant from a disease perspective is fine particulate matter. The WHO believes that reducing levels of one particular type of pollutant, PM_{10}, (particular matter smaller than 10 micrometres, or 'microns'), could reduce deaths in polluted cities by as much as 15 per cent every year[99] – with 500,000 attributed deaths recorded in Asia and the Pacific in the year 2000 alone.[100] Particulate matter includes a wide range of pollutants ranging from airborne smoke to soot, dust and liquid droplets from fuel combustion. Combustion of fossil fuels is the principal source of fine particle emissions, including the burning of coal, oil, diesel fuel, gasoline and wood in transportation, power generation and space heating. Older coal-fired power plants, industrial boilers, diesel- and gasoline-powered vehicles, and wood stoves are major sources of such pollution. High-temperature industrial processes such as metal smelting and steel production are also significant sources. The health impacts of particles depend considerably on their physical and chemical characteristics. Particle size is important, as this influences how easily and deeply the particles are able to penetrate the lungs. Particles larger than 10 microns in diameter generally do not penetrate into the lungs, and have a short residence time in the atmosphere, but PM_{10} will enter the nasal cavity and $PM_{2.5}$ can enter the bronchia and lungs. These smaller particles have been proven, through epidemiological research, to be linked to adverse effects on health, and even at levels well below the current standards of many nations, the smaller particles have proved to adversely affect the health of those exposed. In fact, scientists have not been able to identify a threshold below which health effects do not occur.

Even without a threshold, the WHO's air quality standards recommend that the concentration of suspended particulates should be less than 90µg/m³. In many cities, however, this number is several times higher, with cities such as Beijing experiencing levels of $PM_{2.5}$ and PM_{10} that are often three times higher than the WHO recommendation. When exposed to such particles, people with heart or lung diseases, and the elderly, are at a higher risk, with health effects resulting from exposures lasting as little as 24 hours or less. Long-term exposures of a year or more have been linked to the development of lung diseases, such as chronic bronchitis. Those exposed to the particles who already have lung disease may not be able to breathe as deeply or vigorously as normal, and may have respiratory symptoms including coughing, phlegm, chest discomfort, wheezing and shortness of breath. Even those without such a pre-existing condition may experience these symptoms as well as an increase in susceptibility to respiratory infections, although they are unlikely to experience more serious effects.

Since particulate air pollution is produced from numerous sources, it needs to be addressed through an integrated approach which reduces particulate pollution through a range of strategies, including:

- emission control devices for motor vehicles;
- cleaner-burning gasoline and diesel fuels (along with alternate fuels and power sources);
- dust control for roads, construction and landfills;
- landscaping, barriers and fencing to reduce windblown dust;
- programmes to reduce emission from wood stoves and fireplaces;
- controls for industrial facilities.

In developing countries, the two main sources of PM_{10} and $PM_{2.5}$ pollution come from the prevalence of two- and three-wheeled motorized vehicles and dependence on biomass and coal for cooking. Two billion people worldwide burn wood, dung and crop residues indoors for home cooking and heating. According to the WHO, this results in the premature deaths of an estimated 1.6 million people each year from breathing elevated levels of indoor smoke – resulting in indoor air pollution being the fourth leading cause of death in poor developing countries.[101] The WHO has estimated that indoor smoke from solid fuel causes about one-third of lower respiratory infections, about one-fifth of chronic obstructive pulmonary disease and approximately 1 per cent of cancers of the trachea, bronchus and lung. The Partnership for Clean Indoor Air, which involves over 160 partners worldwide, is assisting efforts to address this problem by funding projects in Asia, Africa and Latin America to identify and demonstrate effective approaches for increasing the use of clean, reliable, affordable, efficient and safe home cooking and heating practices that reduce people's exposure to indoor air pollution. The Partnership for Clean Indoor Air, for instance, is promoting the design of more efficient wood-burning cooking stoves.[102] These more energy-efficient stoves and solar cookers dramatically reduce indoor air pollution. As Lester Brown explains:

> One of aid's more promising projects is the distribution of 780,000 highly efficient wood cook-stoves in Kenya that not only use far less wood than a traditional stove but also pollute less. Kenya is also the site of a solar cooker project sponsored by Solar Cookers International. These inexpensive cookers, made from cardboard and aluminium foil and costing $10 each, cook slowly, much like a crockpot. Requiring less than two hours of sunshine to cook a complete meal, they can greatly reduce firewood use at little cost. They can also be used to pasteurize water, thus saving lives.[103]

The 2009 WHO analysis of the health benefits of interventions to reduce indoor air pollution from solid fuel use concluded that 'from a public health point of view, there should be a continued emphasis on the promotion of improved stoves, as well as other locally appropriate means to reduce exposures within solid fuel-using households'.[104] Progress is also being made to find alternatives to the two- and three-wheel motorized vehicles currently used throughout Asia. Motorcycles and 'baby taxis' constitute the majority of vehicles in many Asian and developing countries, many of which employ two-stroke engines which emit 50 times the amount of air pollution compared to modern automobiles. Envirofit,[105] an independent, non-profit company established at Colorado State University in 2003, is now working to distribute affordable retrofit kits that will both reduce air pollutant emissions in particulates, CO and hydrocarbons by over 70 per cent while also improving the fuel efficiency of two-stroke engines by 30–50 per cent. Originally developed for snowmobiles, the direct injection technology of the kits has now been adapted so that the retrofit system eliminates the carburettor, and fuel is instead introduced directly into the engine cylinder, thus conserving more unburnt fuel. Envirofit's retrofit engine kit costs about US$300, which may sound a lot for people in a developing economy, but governments are sponsoring micro-financers to lend taxi drivers the money for their installation. At the moment, taxi drivers make US$3–5 a day, but after their motorcycles are fitted with the kit, they can expect their income to increase by US$1–2 a day due to the engines' improved fuel efficiency. This provides the taxi driver with a 30 per cent pay rise which enables drivers to pay back their loans within a year. Clearly, these types of programmes and incentives, effectively implemented, can play a significant role in reducing air pollution and associated health implications, in small-vehicle dominated cities.

In the following chapter, we consider a unique case of the use of public interest litigation to reducing air pollution in one of the worlds most congested cities, Delhi in India.

Notes

1   Sandor, R. (1998) 'Trading gases', *Our Planet*, vol 9, no 6,.
2   WHO (2005) *Air Quality Guidelines for Particulate Matter, Ozone, Nitrogen Dioxide and Sulfur Dioxide: Global update 2005, Summary of Risk Assessment*, WHO.
3   UNEP (2007) *Global Environment Outlook: Environment for Development (GEO-4) Report*, UNEP.
4   WHO (2005) 'Factsheet No 292: Indoor air pollution and health', WHO, June.
5   UNEP (2007) *Global Environment Outlook: Environment for Development (GEO-4) Report*, UNEP.
6   World Bank (2006) *World Development Indicators*, World Bank, Washington, DC.
7   CSE (1999) 'Sick of air pollution', Press Release, Centre for Science and Environment, 5 June.
8   Sheram, K. and Soubbotina, T. P. (2000) *Beyond Economic Growth – Meeting the Challenges of Global Development*, World Bank, Washington, DC.
9   Farmer, A. (1997) *Managing Environmental Pollution*, Routledge, New York.
10 Levy, J., Schwartz, J. and Hammitt, J. K. (2007) 'Mortality risks from ozone exposure', *Risk in Perspective*, Harvard Centre for Risk Analysis, Boston, vol 15, no 2, pp1–5.
11 Holland, M., Kinghorn, S., Emberson, L., Cinderby, S., Ashmore, M., Mills, G. and Harmens, H. (2006) *Development of a Framework for Probabilistic Assessment of the Economic Losses Caused by Ozone Damage to Crops in Europe*, Centre for Ecology and Hydrology, Natural Environment Research Council, Bangor, Wales.
12 Watkiss, P. (2004) *Damage Costs for Air Pollution*, DEFRA, London.
13 Brown, S. (1998) 'Beating the $12 billion cost of polluted air', CSIRO Press Release.
14 Agence France-Presse (2006) *Hong Kong Pollution Leaves Tourists Choking*, Agence France-Presse, Hong Kong.
15 Clean Air Initiative for Asian Cities Centre (2007) *2007 Annual Report: Clean Air Initiative for Asian Cities Centre*, Clean Air Initiative for Asian Cities Centre.
16 OECD (2008) *OECD Environmental Outlook to 2030*, OECD, Paris.
17 CSE (1996) 'Press Release', Centre for Science and Environment, 29 September.
18 World Bank (2007) *Cost of Pollution in China: Economic Estimates of Physical Damages*, World Bank, Washington, DC.
19 Wang, W., Primbs, T., Tao., S., Zhu, T. and Simonich, M. (2009) 'Atmospheric particulate matter pollution during the 2008 Beijing Olympics', *Environmental Science and Technology*, 19 June.
20 ASEAN (2003) *ASEAN Haze Agreement*, The Association of South East Asian Nations, Jakarta.
21 UNEP (2007) *Global Environment Outlook: Environment for Development (GEO-4) Report*, UNEP.
22 World Commission on Environment and Development (1987) *Our Common Future*, Oxford University Press, Oxford, p179.
23 Committee on Carbon Monoxide Episodes in Meteorological and Topographical Problem Areas (2003) *Managing Carbon Monoxide Pollution in Meteorological and Topographical Problem Areas*, National Research Council, National Academies Press, Washington, DC.

24 UNECE (1979–2005) *The Convention on Long Range Trans-boundary Air Pollution*, United Nations Economic Commission for Europe, Geneva.

25 Environment Canada (2006) *Canada-U.S. Air Quality Agreement*, Environment Canada, Gatineau, QC.

26 EU (1996) 'Council Directive 96/62/EC of 27 September 1996 on ambient air quality assessment and management', *Official Journal of the European Union*, vol 296, pp55–63, Environment Council, European Commission, Brussels; EU (1999) 'Council Directive 1999/30/EC of 22 April 1999 relating to limit values for sulphur dioxide, nitrogen dioxide and oxides of nitrogen, particulate matter and lead in ambient air', *Official Journal of the European Union*, vol 163, pp41–60, Environment Council, European Commission, Brussels; EU (2002) 'Council Directive 2002/3/EC of the European parliament and of the council of 12 February 2002 relating to ozone in ambient air', *Official Journal of the European Union*, vol 67, pp14–30, Environment Council, European Commission, Brussels.

27 ASEAN (2003) *ASEAN Haze Agreement*, The Association of South East Asian Nations, Jakarta.

28 UNEP/RRC-AP (2006) *Malé Declaration on the Control and Prevention of Air Pollution in South Asia and its Likely Trans-boundary Effects*, UNEP Regional Resource Centre for Asia and the Pacific, Bangkok.

29 Stockholm Convention (2000) *Stockholm Convention on Persistent Organic Pollutants*, Stockholm Convention.

30 UNEP (2007) *Global Environment Outlook: Environment for Development (GEO-4) Report*, UNEP.

31 Committee on Carbon Monoxide Episodes in Meteorological and Topographical Problem Areas (2003) *Managing Carbon Monoxide Pollution in Meteorological and Topographical Problem Areas*, National Research Council, National Academies Press, US.

32 WHO (2005) *Air Quality Guidelines for Particulate Matter, Ozone, Nitrogen Dioxide and Sulfur Dioxide: Global Update 2005, Summary of Risk Assessment*, WHO.

33 WHO (2005) *Air Quality Guidelines for Particulate Matter, Ozone, Nitrogen Dioxide and Sulfur Dioxide: Global Update 2005, Summary of Risk Assessment*, WHO.

34 UNEP (2007) *Global Environment Outlook: Environment for Development (GEO-4) Report*, UNEP.

35 US EPA (1999) *The Benefits and Costs of the Clean Air Act 1990 to 2010*, US Environmental Protection Agency, Washington, DC.

36 Clean Air Initiative for Asian Cities Centre (2007) *2007 Annual Report: Clean Air Initiative for Asian Cities Centre*, Clean Air Initiative for Asian Cities Centre.

37 Clean Air Initiative for Asian Cities Centre (2007) *2007 Annual Report: Clean Air Initiative for Asian Cities Centre*, Clean Air Initiative for Asian Cities Centre.

38 UNEP (2007) *Global Environment Outlook: Environment for Development (GEO-4) Report*, UNEP; Sharma, A. and Roychowdhury, A. (1996) 'Slow murder, the deadly story of vehicular pollution in India', *State of the Environment*, Series 3, Centre for Science and Environment, New Delhi.

39 IPCC (2007) *Climate Change 2007: Mitigation of Climate Change*, Contribution of Working Group III to the Fourth Assessment Report of the Intergovernmental Panel on Climate Change, Cambridge University Press, Cambridge, see 'Summary for policymakers'.

40   Van Harmelen, T. et al. (2002) 'Long-term reductions in costs of controlling regional air pollution in Europe due to climate policy', *Environmental Science & Policy*, vol 5, no 4, pp349–365.

41   Van Vuuren, D. P. and den Elzen, M. J. E. et al (2006) 'Exploring the ancillary benefits of the Kyoto Protocol for air pollution in europe', *Energy Policy*, no 34, pp444–460.

42   OECD (2008) *OECD Environmental Outlook to 2030*, OECD, Paris.

43   Hawken, P., Lovins A. and Lovins, L. H. (1999) *Natural Capitalism: Creating the Next Industrial Revolution*, Earthscan, London.

44   Pilloton, E. (2007) 'Transportation Tuesday: Curitiba public transit', *InHabitat*, 11 December.

45   Runyan, C. (2008) 'Bogotá designs transportation for people, not cars', *World Resources Institute (WRI) Features*, vol 1, no 1.

46   Kete, N., Hildalgo, S. and Ward, C. (2008) 'How we move: Sustainable transport around the world', World Resources Institute.

47   Stockholmförsøket (2006) 'About the Stockholm trials', www.stockholmsforsoket.se/templates/page.aspx?id=2431, accessed 4 July 2008.

48   Stockholmförsøket (2006) 'About the Stockholm trials', www.stockholmsforsoket.se/templates/page.aspx?id=2431, accessed 4 July 2008.

49   Stockholm STAD (2006) 'Evaluation of the effects of the Stockholm trial on road traffic', Stockholm STAD, Sweden, p9.

50   Stockholm STAD (2006) 'Evaluation of the effects of the Stockholm trial on road traffic', Stockholm STAD, Sweden, p23.

51   Stockholm STAD (2006) 'Evaluation of the effects of the Stockholm trial on road traffic', Stockholm STAD, Sweden, p41.

52   Transportation Alternatives (2008) 'Congestion pricing, international examples', www.transalt.org/campaigns/congestion/international, accessed 4 July 2008.

53   Stockholmförsøket (2006) 'Referendum on the implementation of congestion charges in the city of Stockholm', www.stockholmsforsoket.se/templates/page.aspx?id=10215, accessed 4 July 2008.

54   Transek (2006) *Cost-Benefit Analysis of the Stockholm Trial*, Transek AB, Sweden, p11.

55   COV (2007) *Transportation Plan Update – A Decade of Progress*, City of Vancouver, Canada.

56   ERTP (2008) *Evergreen Line Transit Project: Business Case – Executive Summary*, Translink, British Columbia, p3.

57   UNEP Assessment Report (2005) *The Asian Brown Cloud: Climate and Other Environmental Impacts*, Centre for Clouds, Chemistry and Climate, UNEP, see 'Part I: The South Asian haze: Air pollution, ozone and aerosols'.

58   WHO (2005) *Air Quality Guidelines for Particulate Matter, Ozone, Nitrogen Dioxide and Sulfur Dioxide: Global update 2005, Summary of Risk Assessment*, WHO.

59   WHO (2005) *Air Quality Guidelines for Particulate Matter, Ozone, Nitrogen Dioxide and Sulfur Dioxide: Global update 2005, Summary of Risk Assessment*, WHO.

60   Wise, W. (2001) *Killer Smog: The World's Worst Air Pollution Disaster*, IUniverse Inc.

61   WCED (1987) *Our Common Future*, Oxford University Press, Oxford.

62   WCED (1987) *Our Common Future*, Oxford University Press, Oxford.

63   Farmer, A. (1997) *Managing Environmental Pollution*, Routledge Publishing, London.

64 Hohmeyer, O. (1988) *Social Costs of Energy Consumption*, Springer Verlag, Berlin.

65 Pearce, D. (1992) *The Secondary Benefits of Greenhouse Gas Control*, CSERGE Working Paper 92-12, University College, London.

66 ECOTEC (1992) 'A cost-benefit analysis of reduced air deposition: UK natural and semi-natural ecosystems – An assessment framework for evaluating the benefits of reduced acid deposition', Working Paper 1 for the Department of the Environment, April, ECOTEC Research and Consulting Ltd, Birmingham, cited in Ekins, P. (2002) *Economic Growth and Environmental Sustainability: The Prospects for Green Growth*, Routledge Publishing, London.

67 Alfsen, K., Brendemoen, A. and Glomsrod, S. (1992) 'Benefits of climate policies: some tentative calculations', Discussion Paper no 69, March, Central Bureau of Statistics: B 8131, Dep:0033, Oslo 1, cited in Ekins, P. (2002) *Economic Growth and Environmental Sustainability: The Prospects for Green Growth*, Routledge Publishing, London.

68 ExternE (1998) 'An assessment of impacts from air pollution', ExternE – EC Study on the Externalities of Energy, no 6 (March) pp9–11, cited in Ekins, P. (2002) *Economic Growth and Environmental Sustainability: The Prospects for Green Growth*, Routledge Publishing, London.

69 Ekins, P. (2002) *Economic Growth and Environmental Sustainability: The Prospects for Green Growth*, Routledge Publishing, London.

70 UNECE (2002) *25 Years of Successful International Cooperation to Protect our Environment*, United Nations Economic Commission for Europe, Geneva.

71 UNECE (2002) *25 Years of Successful International Cooperation to Protect our Environment*, United Nations Economic Commission for Europe, Geneva.

72 UNECE (1979–2005) *The Convention on Long Range Trans-boundary Air Pollution*, United Nations Economic Commission for Europe, Geneva.

73 UNECE (1979) *Protocol to the 1979 Convention on Long Range Trans-boundary Air Pollution on Further Reduction of Sulphur Emissions*, United Nations Economic Commission for Europe, Geneva.

74 UNECE (1994) *The 1994 Oslo Protocol on Further Reduction of Sulphur Emissions*, United Nations Economic Commission for Europe, Geneva.

75 OECD (2002) *Indicators to Measure Decoupling of Environmental Pressure and Economic Growth*, OECD, Paris.

76 OECD (2002) *Indicators to Measure Decoupling of Environmental Pressure and Economic Growth*, OECD, Paris.

77 Sliggers, J. and Kakebeeke, W. (2004) *Clearing The Air: 25 years of the Convention on Long Range Trans-boundary Air Pollution*, United Nations Economic Commission for Europe, Geneva.

78 Sliggers, J. and Kakebeeke, W. (2004) *Clearing The Air: 25 years of the Convention on Long Range Trans-boundary Air Pollution*, United Nations Economic Commission for Europe, Geneva.

79 Sliggers, J. and Kakebeeke, W. (2004) *Clearing The Air: 25 years of the Convention on Long Range Trans-boundary Air Pollution*, United Nations Economic Commission for Europe, Geneva.

80 Ekins, P. (2002) *Economic Growth and Environmental Sustainability: The Prospects for Green Growth*, Routledge Publishing, London.

81 Hawken, P., Lovins, A. and Lovins, L. H. (1999) *Natural Capitalism: Creating the Next Industrial Revolution*, Earthscan, London.

82 *The Economist* (1997) 'Money to burn?' *The Economist* (print edition), 4 December, vol 344, no 8033, p86.

83 Sandor, R. (1998) 'Trading gases', *Our Planet*, vol 9, no 6.

84 AEA Energy & Environment (2009) 'Air quality: Emissions of sulphur dioxide 1970–2007, United Kingdom', e-*Digest Statistics*, UK Department of Environment, Food and Rural Affairs.

85 Haagen-Smit, A. and Fox, M. (2009) 'Ozone formation in photochemical oxidation of organic substances', *Industrial and Engineering Chemistry*, vol 48, p1484.

86 Bonner, J. (1989) *Arie J. Haagen-Smit (1900–1977): A Biographical Memoir*, US National Academy of Sciences.

87 UNEP (2009) *The Asian Brown Cloud: Climate and Other Environmental Impacts,* Centre for Clouds, Chemistry and Climate, UNEP, see 'Part I: The South Asian haze: Air pollution, ozone and aerosols'.

88 US EPA (1997) *The Benefits and Costs of the Clean Air Act, 1970 to 1990*, report prepared for US Congress, US Environmental Protection Agency, Washington, DC.

89 Adams, R. M., Glyer, J. D., Johnson, S. L. and McCarl, B. A. (1989) 'A reassessment of the economic effects of ozone on United States agriculture', *Journal of Air Pollution Control Association*, vol 39, no 7, pp960–968; Adams, R. M., Hamilton, S. A. and McCarl, B. A. (1985) 'An assessment of the economic effects of ozone on US agriculture', *Journal of Air Pollution Control Association*, vol 35, pp938–943.

90 Stauffer, N. (2007) 'Human-generated ozone will damage crops, according to MIT study: Could reduce production by more than 10 percent by 2100', *MIT News*, MIT Energy Initiative.

91 Agency for Toxic Substances and Disease Registry (undated) 'Case studies in environmental medicine: Lead toxicity cover page', www.atsdr.cdc.gov/csem/lead/pbcover_page2.html, accessed 15 August 2008.

92 Lean, G. (2006) 'UN hails green triumph as leaded petrol is banned throughout Africa', *Independent* (UK), 1 January.

93 Lead Group Inc. (2005) '81 Countries possibly still to ban leaded petrol as at 20th Oct 2005', www.lead.org.au/fs/fst27superseded.html, accessed 12 July 2009.

94 Lean, G. (2006) 'UN hails green triumph as leaded petrol is banned throughout Africa', *Independent* (UK), 1 January.

95 UNEP (undated) 'Partnership for Clean Fuels and Vehicles Programme', www.unep.org/PCFV/, accessed 11 August 2008.

96 World Bank (2002) *Toward an Unleaded Environment: World Bank Support to Transition Economies*, World Bank, Washington, DC.

97 World Bank (2002) *Toward an Unleaded Environment: World Bank Support to Transition Economies*, World Bank, Washington, DC.

98 World Bank (2002) *Toward an Unleaded Environment: World Bank Support to Transition Economies*, World Bank, Washington, DC.

99 WHO (2006) 'World Health Organization challenges world to improve air quality: Stricter air pollution standards could reduce deaths in polluted cities by 15%', WHO News Releases.

100 Cohen, A. J., Anderson, H. R., Ostro, B., Pandey, K., Krzyzanowski, M., Künzli, N., Gutschmidt, K., Pope, C. A., Romieu, I., Samet, J. M. and Smith, K. R. (2004) 'Mortality impacts of urban air pollution', in WHO, *Comparative Quantification of Health Risks: Global and Regional Burden of Disease Attributable to Selected Major Risk Factors*, vol 2, World Health Organization, Geneva, Chapter 17.

101 WHO (2002) *World Health Report: Reducing Risks, Promoting Healthy Life*, World Health Organization, Geneva.

102 Bryden, M. et al (2005) *Design Principles for Wood Burning Cook Stoves*, Partnership for Clean Indoor Air, Aprovecho Research Center, US EPA, Shell Foundation.

103 Brown, L. (2008) *Plan B 3.0: Mobilizing to Save Civilization*, W. W. Norton & Company, New York.

104 Mehta, S. and Shahpar, C. (2009) *The Health Benefits of Interventions to Reduce Indoor Air Pollution from Solid Fuel Use: A Cost-Effectiveness Analysis*, WHO-CHOICE, Evidence and Information for Policy, World Health Organization.

105 Envirofit (2007) 'Engine retrofit kit helps Filipinos breathe easier', *CSIRO ECOS Magazine*, October–November, p139.

12

Reducing Air Pollution through Public Interest Litigation: The Delhi Pollution Case

On invitation from and working closely with the authors, this chapter was developed by Dhruv Sanghavi, a young attorney from India.[1]

The Role of the Super-Administrator

If mere enactment of laws relating to the protection of environment was to ensure a clean and pollution free environment, then India would, perhaps, be the least polluted country in the world. But it is not so. There are stated to be over 200 Central and State statutes which have at least some concern with environmental protection, either directly or indirectly. The plethora of such enactments has, unfortunately not resulted in preventing environmental degradation which, on the contrary, has increased over the years.[2]

The above lamentation of the Supreme Court of India reflects the state of environmental affairs in India, where despite numerous legislative mechanisms to combat environmental issues, very little seems to have been achieved. A major cause for this lack of action may have resulted from the fact that the government agencies wield vast powers to regulate various polluters but are reluctant to use their power to discipline violators.[3] How then can a society seek to combat the growing number of environmental issues that are threatening to have significant impacts on both quality of life and on the quality of the environment and ecosystems within it, given such examples of reluctant administrations? The answer to this important question may in fact lie with the judiciary that has the power to take it upon itself to play the proactive role of a super-administrator.

The Constitution of India, like many other constitutions in the civilized world, provides fundamental rights for every person within India. Every person, under the constitution, has the liberty to approach a constitutional court for protection against violation of these rights. In light of the serious nature of the decline of environmental systems and the impacts on the quality of life for the people of India, the concept of 'right to life' may actually be reasonably interpreted as a right to live with dignity, as distinct from a mere 'animal existence',[4] which would then include the right to a healthy environment that is free from hazardous substances and toxic pollutants.[5] Based on this interpretation, the Supreme Court of India has handed out severe penalties for violators of this right.

In this chapter, we examine the mechanisms that the Indian judiciary has adopted to tackle environmental issues, looking at both their successes and failures. As the main case point, we study the Delhi Pollution Case,[6] which resulted in the rapid transition of fuel used by public transport vehicles (including taxis) from diesel to compressed natural gas (CNG) between 28 July 1998 and 1 December 2002,[7] and which led to Delhi, the third most polluted[8] city in the world at the time,[9] to be awarded the Clean Cities International Award by the Clean Cities Program of the US Department of Energy in 2003.[10]

Environmental Jurisprudence in India

The Indian Constitution is among the few in the world that contains specific provisions on environmental protection.[11] Since the right to life has become the basis for environmental litigation in India, the Indian Constitution is the primary reference for all other environmental regulations in the country.[12] The Indian Constitution guarantees the right to life,[13] and provides directive principles of state policy to protect and improve the health of its citizens,[14] and to protect and improve the environment.[15] The Constitution also imposes a similar fundamental duty upon the citizens.[16] Although the directive principles and fundamental duties are not judicially enforceable by themselves, many become enforceable through the expanding interpretation of the right to life. In the Sariska Case,[17] the Supreme Court of India viewed its role thus:

> *A great American judge emphasizing the imperative issue of environment said that he placed the Government above big business, individual liberty above Government, and environment above all ... The issues of environment must and shall receive the highest attention from this Court.*

Encouraged further by an atmosphere of freedom in the aftermath of the 1975–1977 Proclamation of Emergency, by the Indira Gandhi Government,[18] which had caused widespread denial of civil and political rights, the Supreme Court of India entered one of its most creative periods.[19] The 'right to life' was interpreted as not just a right to mere existence, and further that pollution of the environment would amount to its violation. Furthermore, it was pointed out that the right to live with human dignity becomes illusory in the absence of a humane and healthy environment.[20] This position was notably supported in 1987 by the Andhra Pradesh High Court in the case of T. Damodar Rao v. The Special Officer, Municipal Corporation of Hyderabad[21] where the court observed:

> There can be no reason why practice of violent extinguishment of life alone should be regarded as violative of Article 21 of the Constitution. The slow poisoning by the polluted atmosphere caused by environmental pollution and spoliation should be regarded as amounting to violation of Article 21 of the Constitution.

Most constitutional courts of the country have now held that environmental degradation violates the fundamental right to life – thus giving power to the otherwise judicially unenforceable directive principles of state policy and fundamental duties.

Until the 1970s, little attention was focused on environmental law; and environmental issues wherever possible were dealt with in ordinary criminal courts,[22] or by using principles of Tort law like nuisance, negligence and absolute liability. Two early post-independence laws[23] touched on water pollution,[24] with the earliest laws aimed at controlling air pollution being related to smoke nuisance in 1905 and 1912.[25] The legislation was, at best, scattered and limited in its scope. During the 1970s, pursuant to the 1972 UN Conference on the Human Environment, the Constitution of India was amended[26] to include provisions that explicitly provided for the protection and improvement of the environment. This marked the beginning of modern environmental jurisprudence in India, with the Wild Life (Protection) Act in 1972, the Water (Prevention and Control of Pollution) Act in 1974, the Forest (Conservation) Act in 1980, the Air (Prevention and Control of Pollution) Act in 1982 and the Environment (Protection) Act in 1986 (to name a few such laws) enacted in order to meet the provisions of these obligations.

The Parliament enacted the nationwide Air Act in 1974 to implement the decisions taken at the 1972 UN Conference on the Human Environment. The Act aims at providing for the prevention, control and abatement of air pollution. The 1974 Water Act provides for State Pollution Control Boards to carry out the objects of prevention and control of water pollution with a view to maintaining or restoring the 'wholesomeness' of water. To enable an integrated approach to environmental problems, the Air Act expanded the authority of the central and state boards established under the Water Act, to include air pollution control.[27] States not having water pollution boards were required to set up air pollution boards.[28] The general functions of the Central Pollution Control Board under the Air Act are to improve the quality of air and to prevent, control and abate air pollution in the country. The Act particularly provides for the Central Board to: advise the central government on any matter concerning air pollution; plan and cause to be executed nationwide programmes for the prevention and control or abatement of air pollution; coordinate the activities of and provide technical guidance to state boards; carry out research and investigations relating to the problems of air pollution; and lay down standards for the quality of air. The Air Act specifically provides for the state boards to lay down standards for atmospheric emissions from industrial plants and automobiles. It further provides for state government to give necessary instructions to authorities with a view to ensuring compliance with emissions standards for automobiles.

The 1986 Environment (Protection) Act (EPA) was enacted to support the improvement of the environment and the prevention of hazards to human beings, other living creatures, plants and property. Although there were existing laws dealing directly or indirectly with a number of environmental matters, it was found necessary to have general legislation for environmental protection that would also supplement and reinforce both the Air and Water Acts. While the existing laws focused on specific categories of hazardous substances, some major environmental hazards were not covered. The objective behind the enactment of the EPA was based on the need for a general legislation, citing the multiplicity of regulatory agencies and the pursuant need for an authority which can assume the lead role for studying, planning and implementing long-term requirements for environmental safety. The EPA was also enacted to give direction to and coordinate a system of speedy and adequate responses to emergency situations threatening the environment. The EPA is effectively an 'enabling' law which articulates the essential legislative policy on environmental protection and delegates wide powers to the executive to enable bureaucrats to frame necessary rules and regulations.[29] The Act empowers the central government to 'take all such measures as it deems necessary or expedient for the purpose of protecting and improving the quality of the environment and preventing and abating environmental pollution'.[30] It specifically provides for the planning and control of a nationwide programme for the prevention, control and abatement of environmental pollution; laying down standards for the quality of the environment in its various aspects; and laying down standards for emissions or discharge of environmental pollutants from various sources.[31]

While the above legislation provides a bureaucratic framework for environmental protection the functioning of the Pollution Control Boards has always left much to be desired. The board members, even today, are appointed rather arbitrarily without much attention to qualifications and credentials. The bureaucratic framework was mostly ineffective until 1987 when the Air Act was amended. With this amendment, the state boards gained the power to cut off electricity and water supply to industries and even cause closure of industries.[32] However, despite their apparent power, the boards have not yet fulfilled their potential as enforcement agencies. They have no authority to impose fines, cannot threaten imprisonment for non-compliance, and are reliant on the courts to enforce their orders.[33] Their power to shut down polluting factories is often compromised by their reluctance to bring about unemployment and economic dislocation.[34] These boards have been a complete failure in so far as abatement of vehicular pollution is concerned, laying down ambient air quality standards without setting any mechanism to achieve the same. Funding for the boards is also a serious problem. Although the Water Cess Act of 1977 attempted to raise funds for the boards while regulating water consumption, the money generated by the cess (charge) provides very modest revenue for the operating budgets of the state boards. As one example, the state of Karnataka Board had a 1993 budget of Rs41.416 million to pay for the monitoring of over 138,000 industrial units in the state.[35] This amounts to about Rs300 (approximately US$6) per industrial unit. As a result, the Karnataka Board was only able to monitor 8966 of the state's industrial units, a meagre 6.5 per cent. Furthermore, the Karnataka Board has lacked the resources to effectively prosecute and shut down offending industries. From the inception of the Water and Air Acts, in 1974 and 1981 respectively, until 1994, it had launched only 87 prosecutions under the Water Act and 37 prosecutions under the Air Act, resulting in the closing of only 22 industrial units. Despite whatever limited successes the Pollution Control Boards may have had, declining air and water quality continue to cause a serious challenge to India.[36]

Public Interest Litigation in India

As in many countries in the world, India's Constitution provides for a person to approach the Supreme Court[37] or a High Court[38] to remedy a breach of any fundamental right guaranteed by it. However, there are instances wherein the infringement is not exclusive to a person, but a segment of society as a whole, such as environmental damage and pollution from industry. Thus, the question arises of how an individual personally can seek to remedy such infringement through litigation. This is resolved by the concept of public interest litigation wherein litigation is aimed, not at personal enforcement of rights but rights of the public at large. In the 1960s and 1970s, the concept of litigation in India was still in its rudimentary form and was seen as being mainly used as a private pursuit for the vindication of private vested interests. Litigation in those days consisted mainly of some action initiated and continued by certain individuals, usually addressing their own grievances or problems. Even this was restricted by the limited resources available to those individuals. There was very little organized effort to take up wider issues that affected classes of consumers or the general public at large.

Another major obstacle in the way of litigation relating to public issues was the narrow and rigid construction of the doctrine of *locus standi*. *Locus standi* refers to the standing enjoyed by a litigant, as one's standing is required for the court to hear one's case. The classical concept of *locus standi* requires a person's individual or personal rights to be infringed before he or she can be heard. The construction of such a doctrine would require litigants, in cases addressing issues that derogate rights of society at large, to establish that they have suffered a special injury over and above the injury suffered by the public at large. This narrow construction of standing left, more or less, no scope for action against issues relating to the protection of rights of the poor, illiterate and prisoners, as well as exploitation of labour practices, the protection of heritage monuments like the Taj Mahal, and public health issues like pollution from industries, automobiles, quarrying and mining. The rule of *locus standi* has more recently been relaxed by the courts for such purposes with a view to enable a citizen of India to approach the courts to vindicate legal injury or legal wrong caused to a section of the people by way of violation of any statutory or constitutional rights.[39]

In the 1980s, the Supreme Court lowered the standing barriers by widening the concept of 'the person aggrieved', and pioneered the concept of public interest litigation (PIL) in India. Now a public-spirited individual or group could move a Constitutional Court under either Article 32 or Article 226 of the Constitution without the traditional doctrine of *locus standi* and the practical difficulties of litigation, such as the high costs of such action – and with this the judiciary had taken a leap in the field of protection of fundamental and other rights of the people of India. Petitions in public interest could now be received in the form of a letter addressed to the court if so directed by the judge nominated for this purpose.[40] This innovative strategy has been evolved by the Supreme Court for the purpose of providing easy access to justice to the weaker sections of Indian society and it is a powerful tool in the hands of public-spirited individuals and social action groups for combating exploitation and injustice, and securing for the underprivileged segments of society their social and economic entitlements. It is a highly effective weapon in the armoury of law for bringing social justice to the common man.[41]

Justice Krishna Iyer[42] made a forceful plea that the 'law should not be closed shop ... [or else] ... the system will crumble under its own insensitivity'. Thereafter in S. P. Gupta (commonly known as the first Judges' case)[43] and in Bandhua Mukti Morcha,[44] Justice Bhagwati evolved the concept of 'public inquiry' and allowed a public-spirited citizen to approach the court for redress of public injury relating to environment, human rights, administration of justice, arbitrary action of the executive and investigation of cases involving persons occupying high public offices, etc. The Supreme Court demonstrated in the case of Sheela Barse v. Union of India[45] that it was of the view that 'in public interest litigation both the party structure and the matters in controversy are sprawling and amorphous, to be defined, redefined and adjusted and readjusted, ad hoc, according to the exigencies of the emerging situations'.[46] Through the mechanism of public interest litigation the courts have succeeded in extending the principles of precaution and 'polluter pays' to various environmental litigations that could not have been possible through regular adversarial litigation. The mechanism has facilitated the court to better exercise its constitutional discretionary power to make the law of the land[47] in its absence in the form of legislation.

Most environmental litigation in India has been in the form of public interest litigation cases and is based upon the fundamental 'right to life' as protected by the constitution. The judiciary has interpreted the right to life as being a right to dignity, which includes the right to a clean and wholesome environment. The courts have relocated[48] or shut down polluting industries[49] and brick kilns;[50] caused municipal authorities to act to de-silt rivers, clean up sewage systems,[51] lay down and implement noise-abatement measures,[52] etc., in furtherance of this right to life. It is through this mechanism of public interest litigation, that the Supreme Court addressed the once chronic problem of vehicular pollution in Delhi.

M. C. Mehta v. Union of India
(Vehicular Pollution Case)

Air pollution in Delhi

The Supreme Court's involvement in the Vehicular Pollution Case originated over concerns that the city's polluted air was slowly poisoning its citizens.[53] A study conducted by a leading Delhi-based environmental NGO, the Centre for Science and Environment, revealed that about 10,000 people die prematurely in the city due to air pollution, mainly from industry, refineries and vehicles, each year[54] – equivalent to an average of one death every 52 minutes. While in 1995 India's economic growth rate was 4 per cent, economic losses due to the health costs of pollution were estimated to be 4.5 per cent of India's gross domestic product – which meant that the entire economic growth for the year was invested in addressing health costs resulting from pollution.[55] When investigating the main cause of the pollution leading to the health-related costs it was found that most of the air pollution in Delhi stemmed from vehicles.[56] Though industries, thermal power plants and domestic activity also contribute to air pollution in cities, the transport sector is the largest emitter of carbon monoxide (CO), nitrogen oxides (NO_x) and hydrocarbons (HC) into the air. Petrol-run vehicles contribute most of the CO, HC and lead (Pb), while diesel vehicles are the chief source of particulate matter and sulphur dioxide (SO_2), with 90 per cent of the particulate pollution in Delhi caused by automobiles, particularly the diesel ones.[57] While noting the alarming difference in the levels of particulate levels in California and Delhi in a public lecture in city, Dr Shankar Prasad, the Community Health Adviser on the California Air Resources Board, pointed out that:

> *If small particulate pollution level in California ever reached the same levels as in Delhi today, Californian environmental authorities would have declared an emergency, shutting all emission sources in the city and taking vehicles off the road.*[58]

Presently, vehicles emit 1300 tonnes of pollutants into Delhi's air every day – which is more than the sum of vehicular pollutants in Mumbai, Calcutta and Bangalore.[59] The biggest tragedy is that the health impact of vehicular pollution is intangible, so one tends to ignore it.[60] With low levels of awareness among the general public and very low government investment in research and development, the automobile industry has little incentive to introduce cleaner technology into the Indian market.

Mahesh Chandra Mehta[61] was a regular litigation lawyer in Delhi until 1984 when he was first exposed to environmental issues while in the process of filing a case which sought to remedy the problem of acid rain defacing the Taj Mahal.[62] This led him to make an in-depth inquiry into the pollution problem that might have caused the acid rain. Mehta visited various industries to discover that the highly obsolete technologies employed by them were causing high levels of sulphur dioxide pollution and contributing to the acid rain problem at the Taj Mahal. Mehta reflected to the authors that he was surprised to find that automobile manufacturing plants employed the same technology as in the late 1940s due to the fact that up to the early 1990s there was a limited number of companies operating in the closed economy and they were not incentivized or required to invest in research and development and nor did the government. This alarmed Mehta who, based on his investigations, saw the impending catastrophe facing the city of Delhi and went on to file the Vehicular Pollution Case[63] in 1985 that sought to address the rising problem of pollution in the city of Delhi, most of which is attributable to vehicular emissions.[64]

The case, filed in 1985, involved numerous parties, including automobile manufacturers, petroleum companies, governments of Delhi and India, and public transport operators. As required in the interests of justice, each of these parties was fairly heard before the court passed any substantial orders. On 14 November 1990, five years after the filing of the case, the court acknowledged that heavy vehicles like buses and trucks in the city were the main contributors to the air pollution problem in Delhi. The Union Ministry of Environment and Forests, for the first time on public record through an affidavit, acknowledged that pollution in Delhi was mainly due to the rise in the number of vehicles. The court directed the Delhi administration to suspend the registration of vehicles that were in infringement of the relevant emissions control law. It also directed the Ministry of Environment and Forests to conduct experiments with catalytic converters to confirm their effectiveness, which led to the court ordering all new vehicles to be fitted with catalytic converters at the latest by 1 July 1990 to abate the threat of air pollution.[65] This marked the beginning of the court's proactive involvement in abating the problem of air pollution in Delhi.[66]

In early 1991, the Association of Automobile Manufacturers intervened as party to the litigation, to present its arguments in the case.[67] Since the submissions made by the association were very technical, the Ministry of Environment and Forests agreed to the setting up of a high-level review committee chaired by retired Justice K. N. Saikia[68] to undertake a range of investigations, including:

- assessing the technologies available in the world for vehicular pollution control;
- assessing the current status of technology available in India for controlling vehicular pollution;
- assessing low-cost alternatives for operating vehicles at reduced pollution levels in the metropolitan cities of India;
- examining the feasibility of measures to reduce/eliminate pollution from motor vehicles, both on short-term and long-term bases and make appropriate recommendations in this regard;
- making specific recommendations on administrative/legal regulations required for implementing its recommendations.[69]

Based on recommendations made by the Justice Saikia Committee in 1991,[70] the court, for the first time, considered the possibility of compressed natural gas (CNG) as a transportation fuel and ordered the Delhi Transport Corporation (DTC) to introduce a pilot fleet of CNG-run buses. However, as Mehta explained to the authors during the development of this chapter, this original intent was affected by strong pressure from the industry: 'The court had initially decided to introduce a pilot fleet of one hundred CNG-run buses, midway the order being dictated, scientists brought in by the Association of Indian Automobile Manufacturers raised a hue and cry in court restricting the fleet to a meagre five buses.'[71] During the course of the litigation, however, the court's focus shifted from one scheme to another and the issue of CNG faded into the background, only to be reconsidered in late 1996, when the Supreme Court pressed the central government to set an example for others by converting all its vehicles to CNG.[72] In the meanwhile, in early 1992, the court's attention shifted to focusing on bringing down emissions from all public buses,[73] and throughout 1994, the court exerted pressure on the government to ensure that all new vehicles in the four largest cities of India – Delhi, Mumbai, Calcutta and Chennai – would be fitted with catalytic converters and use lead-free petrol by April 1995.[74] Also, the court had time and again sought technical solutions to reduce harmful emissions from two- and three-wheelers[75] and diesel trucks and buses.[76] On 7 January 1998, the Attorney General presented the draft of an order proposed to be made by the Ministry of Environment and Forests, central government to constitute an authority under the 1986 Environment (Protection) Act, to be called the Environment Pollution (Prevention and Control) Authority,[77] under the chairmanship of Mr Bhurelal. The court welcomed this proposal and referred this authority for the technical solutions mentioned above.[78] The Bhurelal Committee was constituted on 29 January 1998.[79]

The case took its most significant turn through the court's order of 28 July 1998, expressing distress at the apathy of the state, lax implementation of its orders and delaying tactics employed by vested interests. The Supreme Court, for the first time, based on recommendations made by the Bhurelal Committee, *mandated that all public transport vehicles in Delhi should be converted to a single fuel mode of CNG in a phased, time-bound manner.*[80] The court, for the first time, applied significant pressure on the hitherto non-complying administration and warned that failure to implement these deadlines would invite contempt of court proceedings.

The court stated:

> *Realising the urgency and importance of protection and improvement of the environment, this Court has given directions from time to time and impressed upon the authorities to take urgent steps to tackle the acute problem of vehicular pollution in Delhi. Assurances have been held out to the Court through various affidavits filed by competent officers that effective steps shall be taken in a phased manner within a specified time-span. In spite of the matter having engaged the attention of this Court for a long time and lengthy debates on each hearing, precious little appears to have been done by the State Administration to check and control the vehicular pollution ... In the white paper published by the Government of India, a deadline of 1-4-1998 had been proposed for implementation of major actions. No concrete steps have however, been taken to date in spite of the assurances.*[81]

The court was of the opinion that in order to arrest the growing menace of air pollution certain steps were required to be taken immediately and directed to restrict the plying of commercial vehicles, including taxis, which were more than 15 years old, by 2 October 1998. The court also directed that goods vehicles, which caused much congestion and air pollution, be restricted from plying during daytime within city limits by 15 August 1998. In the meanwhile, emphasizing the direct relationship between the quality of fuel and the level of air pollution, the court also took steps in mandating the quality of traditional transportation fuel. In this regard, the Bhurelal Committee recommended that the sulphur content in diesel be restricted to a maximum of 0.05 per cent and benzene content in petrol be restricted to 1 per cent. The Ministry of Petroleum and Natural Gas undertook to comply with the committee's recommendations by 1 April 2000 and 1 October 2000 respectively.[82] In 1999 and 2000, the court mandated the introduction of Euro emission norms for private vehicles, first for Euro I[83] standards then Euro II.[84]

By 26 March 2001, the court had received many applications seeking extensions of the deadline to convert the entire city bus fleet to the single fuel mode of CNG beyond the 31 March 2001 deadline, in spite of the court making it abundantly clear on each date of hearing that the question of allowing buses other than those running on CNG after 31 March 2001 would never arise. In the applications filed for extension of time, difficulties being faced by the transporters included:

- non-availability of CNG conversion kits;
- conversion of CNG at reasonable prices;
- the lack of stabilization of CNG technology in respect to public transport.

These contentions were, however, not acceptable to the court as the applicants were seen to be 'sleeping over' for almost the entire time provided for implementation and no difficulties had been pointed out earlier.

The court, making it amply clear that the administration and private transporters had 'failed to show sufficient earnestness' in implementing its orders, noted:

> *With a view to check rapid deterioration of air quality in Delhi, which was becoming a health hazard besides being an environmental enemy, certain directions have been issued by this Court from time to time ... Unfortunately, neither the governmental authorities nor the private bus operators acted seriously or diligently in taking steps for the purposes of complying with the aforesaid directions and this was in spite of the fact that we had issued strong caution to all concerned in our order dated 28-7-1998 that failure to comply with the aforesaid directions could render the concerned punishable for committing contempt of court ... The extensions have now been sought finding that the deadline is fast approaching ... Orders of this court cannot be treated lightly. They are to be complied with in letter and in spirit.*[85]

While denying a blanket extension of the deadline for conversion, as that 'would amount to putting premium on the lapses and inaction of the administration and private transport operators', the court did make certain relaxations, outlined in Table 12.1. With a view to mitigate the sufferings of the commuting public in general and school children in particular it extended the deadline to 30 September 2001. The court also directed that no commercial vehicle which did not conform to its order dated 28 July 1998 would be registered in Delhi after 1 April 2001.

However, this deadline was also not met and the administration, for similar reasons, applied to the court for a further extension. On 28 September 2001, the court, in order to protect public interest, made an interim extension of the deadline to 18 October 2001, when the matter was to be taken up for further consideration. The relaxation was, however, made subject to the following conditions:[86]

- The Union of India and the government of Delhi would take all appropriate steps to ensure that diesel is not adulterated, by checking the quality of diesel not only at petrol pumps, but also in the vehicles that use diesel, by ensuring that the sulphur content did not exceed 0.05%.

Table 12.1 *Relaxations made by the Supreme Court through its order dated 26 March 2001 in response to the ramifications of the implementation of its order dated 28 July 1998*

Sr. no.	Relaxation	Extension of deadline
1	The schools that had as of 31 March 2001 placed firm orders for replacement or conversion of school buses owned by them to CNG mode, but who have not so far obtained such buses running in CNG mode were permitted to run their existing buses, equal to the number of buses for which conversion orders have been placed, was in hand, provided such buses were not more than eight years old, up to 30 September, 2001.	30.09.2001
2	1880 existing DTC buses, including existing CNG buses which were not more than eight years old, since DTC had placed orders for 1880 CNG buses. This was subject to the condition that out of those 1880 buses, a full complement of buses for schools, namely 860 buses plus the requisite spare buses shall be deployed for school duty and the existing buses will be replaced as and when the new CNG buses are delivered.	30.09.2001
3	The owners of 3100 contract-carriage buses, which also plied as school buses, were allowed to ply their existing buses, equal to the number of existing buses for which they had already taken steps for conversion to CNG, provided such buses were not more than eight years old.	30.09.2001
4	Any other bus operators, that would by 31 March 2001, place firm orders for CNG buses or for conversion to CNG mode, were permitted to operate an equal number of their existing buses, which were not more than eight years old.	30.09.2001
5	All operators of all-India tourist buses were permitted to ply their existing buses, provided they were not more than eight years old.	30.09.2001

Source: M. C. Mehta v. Union of India (2001)[87]

- Strict action would be taken against defaulters, including cancellation of their licences/permits.

On 18 October 2001 the deadline was once again extended to 31 January 2002.[88] In spite of accommodations made by the court, the Delhi administration once again filed an intervention application seeking extension of time to run diesel buses, only to be dismissed with costs. The court noted:

> *It is made clear, and it is obvious in our constitutional set-up, that orders and directions of this Court cannot be nullified or modified or in any way altered by any administrative decision of the Central or State Governments. The administrative decision to continue to ply diesel buses is, therefore, clearly in violation of this Court's orders.*[89]

Combating resistance to the court orders

The case was unexpected by the automobile and petroleum industries which were hitherto unchallenged due to non-implementation of the law and insulation from international competition. Right from its inception the case had been riddled with obstruction from parties with vested interests. A combination of bureaucratic inertia, concerns over cost, the seeming magnitude of the new infrastructure requirements and the likely disruptions to the municipal transport system on which the bulk of the population depends may have been the basis for much of the resistance to change and might have accounted for the sometimes fierce opposition to CNG buses.[90] However, the obvious impacts from vehicular pollution on the health of people in Delhi continued to be a driving inspiration pushing the case forward.

In early 2001, the Union of India had hurriedly set up the R. A. Mashelkar Committee to produce a report with regard to vehicular pollution, after 31 January 2001, when an order[91] was passed condemning the apathy on the part of the government in carrying out the court orders. The composition of the Mashelkar Committee was such that none of its members were doctors or experts in public health. In its report, the said committee recommended that emission norms should be laid down, and choice of fuel should be left to the users. The committee seemed to have overlooked the fact that such norms had been in place for over two decades and yet Delhi was the third most polluted city in the world.[92] The court noted, as it dismissed the report, that 'it was naïve of the Mashelkar Committee to expect that merely laying down fresh emission norms will be effective or sufficient to check or control vehicular pollution'.[93]

It is perceived that delaying tactics were employed by the administration, expecting the court to give in to the pressure of non-implementation. Various contentions were later raised before the court at an extremely delayed stage of the case to 'deliberately frustrate the orders'[94] of the Supreme Court in carrying out the conversion smoothly, leading to the court stating:

> *This Court has been extending the time with regard to conversion of commercial vehicles. Time was first extended to 30-9-2001, and then to 31-1-2002. It is during the period of January 2001 to February 2002, that action has been taken by the Union of India, which leaves us with no doubt that its intention, clearly, is to frustrate the orders passed by this Court with regard to conversion of commercial vehicles to CNG. The manner in which it has been sought to achieve this object is to try and discredit CNG as the proper fuel and, secondly, to represent to the Court that CNG is in short supply and, thirdly, delay the setting up of adequate dispensing stations.*

Each of the above contentions was then categorically dealt with, before being rejected by the court.

1 Questions as to the scarcity of supply of CNG

The plea of the government that CNG was in short supply was seen as being entirely untenable and a deliberate attempt to 'frustrate' the conversion. Particulars filed by the court showed that no CNG had been imported as of the date of the order and that indigenous supply was 'far in excess of what is supplied to the transport sector'. The court held that even if CNG, an essential commodity, was in short supply, 'priority must be that of public health, as opposed to the health of the balance sheets of private companies'. The court further noted that, 'if crude oil could be imported and supplied to refineries for manufacture of petrol and diesel, there was no reason why CNG cannot be imported, if need be, so as it ensures less pollution'.[95] The court went on to order the Union of India to give priority to the transport sector including private vehicles all over India with regard to the allocation of CNG such that only if after Delhi and other cities with polluted air were adequately supplied, could it be allocated to, 'industries, preference being shown to public sector undertakings and power projects'.[96]

2 Concerns that CNG was not the proper alternative fuel

It was contended before the court that low-sulphur diesel should be regarded as a clean fuel and buses be permitted to run on this rather than being forced to convert to CNG.[97] It was pointed out that 'ultra-low-sulphur diesel' with sulphur content of not more than 0.001 per cent was available in some other countries. While the court directed the Bhurelal Committee to look into and examine the suggestion, it also noted that 'diesel, especially of the type available in India could not be regarded as a clean fuel'.[98] During the course of arguments, it was contended by the Union of India that diesel and CNG are 'not materially different' in the matter of air pollution and instead of a 100 per cent switch-over to CNG, a mix of CNG and diesel buses of equal proportion would result in a difference of pollution levels of only about 2 per cent.[99] The court, relying upon extensive statistical evidence, rejected this contention as 'patently untenable'. The court cited data from the Automotive Research Association of India to show that the pollution potential of emissions from CNG was far less than even Euro IV standards. It stated that in terms of particulate emissions, 'CNG vehicles were 15 times better than Euro II diesel vehicles and only Euro IV diesel vehicles were comparable to CNG vehicles'.[100]

These comparisons, the court noted, could be made in the case of 500ppm sulphur (low-sulphur) diesel being used and underscored concerns relating to rampant adulteration of fuel in Delhi. It had directed the Bhurelal Committee[101] to submit a report in this regard, which reflected that fuels contained contaminants to the extent of up to 20 per cent in samples taken from fuel stations.[102] The court stated, 'Merely lowering sulphur and benzene content in diesel and petrol respectively would have little effect unless and until

Table12.2 *Comparison of CNG-certified test data from Automotive Research Association of India (ARAI) with emission norms for buses as cited by the Supreme Court of India in its order dated 5 April 2002*

Sr. no.	Particulars	Sulphur level in diesel	Hydrocarbons	Carbon monoxide	Nitrogen oxide	Particulate matter
1	1992 Standards	–	3.5	14.4	18	No standard
2	1996 Standards	–	2.4	11.2	14.4	No standard
3	Bharat Stage I, April 2000	–	1.23	4.9	9	0.40
4	Bharat Stage II (Euro-II Standards), October 2001	500ppm (0.05%)	1.1	4.0	7	0.15
5	Euro III Standards	350ppm (0.035%)	0.66	2.1	5	0.10
6	Euro IV Standards	50–10ppm (0.005–0.001%)	0.46	1.5	3.5	0.02
7	Ashok Leyland CNG Bus	Nil	0.04*	2.92	2.91	0.01**
8	TELCO CNG Bus	Nil	0.25*	1.68	3.42	0.03

Note: * Non-methane hydrocarbons are a small fraction of total hydrocarbons in CNG vehicles.
** Certificate from ARAI says particulates negligible.
Source: Order in M. C. Mehta v. Union of India (2002)[103]

the oil companies guarantee that the fuel which was sold from the dispensing stations is pure and unadulterated ... It is not surprising that there is stiff resistance to the implementation of the orders of this Court for switchover to gas which cannot be adulterated and will undoubtedly cause financial loss...'[104]

3 Concerns that perhaps there was little precedent internationally

During the course of the case, it was repeatedly argued before the court, on behalf of the Union of India, that no other city in the world had introduced CNG buses at the scale directed by the Supreme Court. Both the state government and the Union of India had urged that the CNG technology was still 'evolving and experimental'.[105] While the court acknowledged that it was true that most of the cities in the industrialized world do not have large numbers of CNG buses, it also noted growing numbers of CNG buses being introduced around the world to meet the 'stringent norms in the future'. It noted that in the US, CNG buses accounted for 18 per cent of the then current bus orders and 28 per cent of the potential orders. Beijing also had resorted to an alternative fuel strategy whereby 18,000 buses would be fuelled by CNG, LPG and electricity, to 'clean up the air because of the approaching Olympic Games in 2008', and the Ministry of Environment in South Korea aimed at introducing 20,000 natural gas buses into its fleet. The court used the above facts to assert its stand that alternative fuels like CNG, LPG and electricity were a preferred technology, 'which critically polluted cities like Delhi needed as a leapfrogging technological option'.[106]

4 Concerns of the possibility of a pipeline breakdown interrupting supply

The Union of India had argued that a breakdown in the pipeline would lead to disruption in supply of fuel to the city and could paralyse the transport system, should it be solely dependent on CNG. The court, however, rejected this contention, on the basis of the 'available information that suggested that the possibility of the pipeline breaking down was remote'. Furthermore, the court noted that 'the pipeline itself stored up to three months of gas supply needed for Delhi'.[107]

Having reasonably rejected each contention raised against the conversion to CNG, the Supreme Court went on to mandate the supply and conversion and laid down a detailed plan to convert the entire fleet of public transport buses within the following 'seven to eight months'.[108] The court levied a heavy fine at the rate of Rs500 (approximately US$10) per bus per day, increasing to Rs1000 (approximately US$20) per bus per day after 30 days of operation of buses with effect from the following day of the order.[109] Despite the resistance from enforcement agencies and countless attempts to subvert its orders, the court maintained its independence from private interests in seeking to champion the public good. By relying on the most up-to-date research provided to it by unbiased sources, the court was able to counter the arguments of its opposition, while it continued to push for more environmentally friendly transport options.[110] As Figure 12.1 shows, the majority of the buses in Delhi were converted to the single fuel mode of CNG by the end of the year 2003.

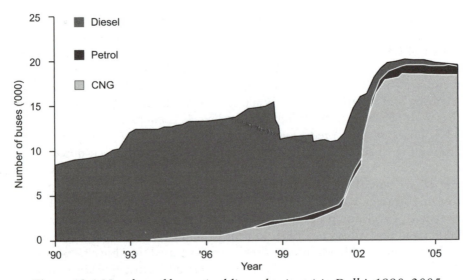

Figure 12.1 *Number of buses (public and private) in Delhi, 1990–2005*

Source: Narain and Krupnick (2007)[111]

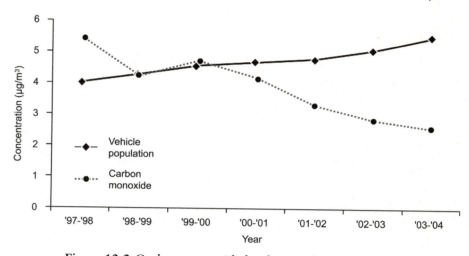

Figure 12.2 *Carbon monoxide levels in ambient air of Delhi*

Source: National Air Quality Monitoring Program (2004)[112]

Environmental impact of the court orders

A number of recent studies have attempted to measure the success of the various interventions in improving Delhi's air quality. The Central Pollution Control Board monitors various criteria pollutants such as sulphur dioxide, nitrogen dioxide, PM_{10} and suspended particulate matter at 10 sites located at Nizamuddin, Ashok Vihar, Janakpuri, Siri Fort, Netaji Nagar, Town Hall, Shahzadabagh, Shahdara, Najafgarh road and Bahadur Shah Zafar road in Delhi. Out of these ten sites, the first six are categorized as residential and the next three are industrial, while the remaining one represents the busiest traffic intersection site. The Central Pollution Control Board findings for carbon monoxide and sulphur dioxide, shown in Figures 12.2 and 12.3, demonstrate clearly the impact of the CNG conversions post-2002.

However, other air pollutants have not shown such improvements, as Kathuria reported in the 2004 paper 'Impact of CNG on vehicular pollution in Delhi: A note':[113]

> *Daily ambient air quality data from June 1999 to September 2003 from the busiest crossing in Delhi do not indicate an all-round improvement in ambient quality. The NO_x has risen after the conversion whereas suspended particulate matter and PM_{10} have shown only marginal fall; CO has shown a significant decline.*

Such findings need to be considered in the context of Delhi's population growth, with the population rising from 9.42 million in 1991 to 13.78 million by 2001. This population growth has driven the growth in vehicle use, as can

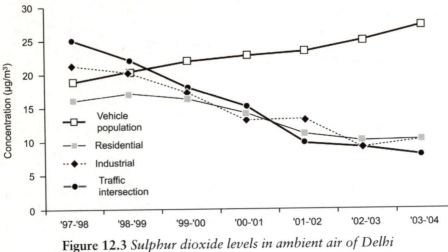

Figure 12.3 *Sulphur dioxide levels in ambient air of Delhi*

Source: National Air Quality Program (2004)[114]

be seen in Figure 12.4; with only a small percentage of new vehicles in Delhi run on CNG and the majority being petroleum fuelled.

As previously pointed out, in 2003 Delhi received the Clean Cities International Award given by the US Department of Energy's Clean Cities Program.[115] However, it is still far from being a clean city with respect to air quality and there are still further challenges ahead. The growth in the number of vehicles on the road is likely to continue with the introduction of very cheap automobiles.[116]

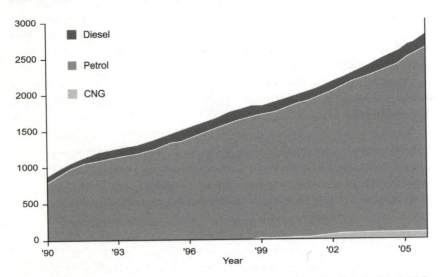

Figure 12.4 *Number of vehicles on the Road in Delhi, 1990–2005*

Source: Narain and Krupnick (2007)[117]

Critical Analysis of Judicial Activism on Environmental Issues

While the impact of the Vehicular Pollution Case is for all to see, it is important to examine whether the mechanism adopted by the Indian judiciary is a sustainable approach. Is it proper for the judiciary to play the activist role of a super-administrator, thus making law, which is otherwise the prerogative of the elected legislature? What could be the drawbacks in adopting such a drastic mechanism? The final part of this chapter critically analyses the activist role adopted by the judiciary as discussed above.

Division of power and the constitutional role of the judiciary

It is for the elected legislature to enact law, the judiciary to interpret the law and the executive to enforce the law and run a country. The Indian Constitution, unlike the US Constitution, does not provide for the concept 'substantive due process', which 'involves a judge's notion of reasonableness [over] that of a duly elected legislature'.[118] Also, unlike its US counterpart, the Indian judiciary elects itself and the electorate has no role to play in the process. Succinctly articulated by Abraham Lincoln, 'democracy is the government of the people, by the people, for the people', and it is for the people to enact the laws they want to be governed by. Quite reasonably, and in consonance with the very basic tenets of democracy, it is for an elected legislature to enact positive law and not the judiciary, except under extraordinary circumstances that justify the discretionary power granted by Article 142. The drafting committee while debating the draft Constitution of India decided that 'due process of law' should be substituted by the more specific 'procedure established by law', in the language of Article 21, similar to Article 31 of the Japanese Constitution of 1946.[119] What the framers of the Constitution consciously avoided, judicial activism has brought in by the back door.[120] It is not for the judiciary to play the role of a super-administrator; it is rather a humble interpreter of law and not an emperor who adjudicates on a whim.[121] The power granted by Article 142 is an extraordinary discretionary power vested in the Supreme Court of India and it must be very careful while treading the activist path. Any unrestrained trespass into the territory of the legislature might confirm Lord Acton's declaration: 'all power tends to corrupt and absolute power corrupts absolutely'.[122]

Precedents and questions of stability and sustainability

The concept of legal precedent occupies a very important place in jurisprudence in any country. As Professor Roscoe Pound has stated 'Law must be stable, yet it cannot stand still.'[123] Similarly, Justice Aharon Barak says, 'Stability without change is degeneration. Change without stability is anarchy.'[124] Thus while laws and their interpretations must evolve along with time, drastic changes in either are to be considered with the utmost caution.

The Constitution of India provides that the decisions of the Supreme Court are fully binding as precedents for all courts in India,[125] thus stating the law of the land. Each judgement and order of the Supreme Court, and stability in the same are, thus, of utmost national importance, lest the law should change as per the whim of the judge. However, as presented above, the Supreme Court was of the view that, 'in public interest litigation both the party structure and the matters in controversy are sprawling and amorphous, to be defined, redefined and adjusted and readjusted, ad hoc, according to the exigencies of the emerging situations'.[126]

With due respect, this sort of result-oriented jurisprudence requires embarrassing legal gymnastics from judges, disregarding the consequent instability of the law of the land. If the apex judicial body of the land itself 'shows scant respect for precedents, it may well encourage the High Courts and the subordinate courts to follow suit, leading to judicial indiscipline and anarchy'.[127]

Every 'activist decision' of the Supreme Court sets a precedent which binds the High Courts of the country to act similarly in similar instances. This might throw open the floodgates, unintentionally, encouraging illegitimate litigation in the guise of being in the public interest. For example, while the fuel mode on which public transport vehicles should run is essentially a matter of state policy – the prerogative of the executive – the Vehicular Pollution Case sets a very strong and binding precedent whereby all constitutional courts of the country will be bound to look into policy matters, transgressing their constitutional jurisdiction. Parties with *mala fide*, or bad faith, vested interests might challenge policies of the state in the 'public interest' merely because the policy might be to the detriment to their private business.[128] While judicial activism through the mechanism of public interest litigation was introduced with a noble motive, the constitutional courts have become an open market, where those without standing try to manipulate the mechanism to achieve private ends.[129] There have been numerous frivolous cases filed at the Supreme Court masquerading as public interest litigations, which in the words of Justice Pasayat can be termed as 'private interest litigations' or 'publicity interest itigation' or even '*paisa* (money) interest litigation', but not 'public interest litigation'.[130]

Suddenly closing the floodgates seems impossible because precedents in favour of such litigation are very strongly in place and a sudden departure may lead to the loss of prestige, which the judiciary can ill afford. While the courts have laid down stringent tests for petitions in public interest before they are entertained, it still bleeds the judiciary of precious resources. The Indian judiciary currently faces a vast backlog of cases, and the Supreme Court of India itself hears about 60,000 cases in a year, which comprise civil and criminal appeals besides constitutional matters. Given the vast number of frivolous cases of public interest litigation filed every year, the noble intentions of meeting the ends of 'complete justice', with which the concept was ushered in and the bar of *locus standi* lowered, are hardly served. The US Chief Justice John Roberts, writing about the US Supreme Court, which only hears a small fraction of the cases the Supreme Court of India hears, had this to say about the problem, 'so long as the Court views itself as being ultimately responsible for governing all aspects of our society, it will, understandably, be overworked'.[131]

Strengthening bureaucracies

'(Judicial) activism … is excessivism when a court undertakes responsibilities normally discharged by other co-ordinate organs of the government.'[132] A court in its activist stance may be able to mandate functions of these organs on a case-by-case basis, which cannot cover every environmental issue faced by society. A situation of rampant environmental degradation clearly indicates a weak bureaucracy. It is these bureaucracies that need to be strengthened, lest the effects of judicial activism should remain skin deep – addressing case-specific, ad hoc issues. In a scathing comment, noted environmental lawyer Shyam Divan called the Supreme Court's activism a mistake of judgement, arguing that 'judicial activism has restricted the growth of a responsible and independent bureaucracy'.[133]

As seen in the Vehicular Pollution Case, the court mandated the entire conversion to the single fuel mode of CNG to its very intricate detail. However, one of the most severe criticisms of this judgement is that it essentially deals with the conversion in New Delhi, with a few directions regarding other cities. While the Supreme Court of India chose to play the role of a super-administrator, it might have rather lost an opportunity to mandate the functioning of all Pollution Control Boards, state and central, in exercise of its discretionary powers, thus covering the entire nation simultaneously.

A Caution on the Use of a Constitutional Court in matters of Public Interest

The mechanism of public interest litigation is a radical approach to safeguarding the citizen's right to a clean and healthy environment, and the Delhi Vehicular Pollution Case is a fine example of how, over a short period of time, living conditions can be drastically improved. However, it is not free from its faults and every judiciary must beware of its treacherous pitfalls before treading this path to 'complete justice'. Judges are, after all, men and women, learned but not infallible in their judgements. Given that the court possesses little, if any, expertise in matters of science and environment, it has to rely on 'expert opinion', which in itself is not homogeneous across various think-tanks; giving an impression that with every judgement regarding environmental policy, courts may be unduly influenced by expert opinion leading to inadequate consideration of opposing views, which may in fact create significant risk of consequences in the future. It was Mahatma Gandhi who advocated that the means used for achieving a particular result must also be as acceptable as the result itself. Writing in *Young India*, 17 July 1924, he said: 'They say, "means are after all means". I would say, "means are after all everything". As the means so the end ... There is no wall of separation between the means and the end. Indeed, the Creator has given us control (and that too, very limited) over means, none over the end. Realisation of the goal is in exact proportion to that of the means. This is a proposition that admits of no exception.' Involving a constitutional court in matters of public interest should be a sparingly used mechanism, which should not be adopted hastily, but rather as a 'last resort' after all other means have failed, rather than adopted as means to short-circuit through other legitimate forums.

In the Vehicular Pollution Case, the Supreme Court of India engaged in the case as a forum of the first and last resort, causing it to examine each fact, contention and argument, and refer to the various committees, reports and expert opinion for the first time. While situations like those that prevailed in Delhi demand instant action to safeguard the constitutional rights of the people, it must be noted that it took the Court nearly two decades to satisfactorily assess and rule on the issue of air pollution in Delhi. The authors submit that air pollution may have been resolved expeditiously had the Supreme Court been engaged as a forum of the last resort. However, the direct threat to human health, the lack of progress to date and the level of vested interests may have in fact warranted an out-of-the-ordinary response.

Alexander Hamilton described the judiciary as the weakest branch of government, because it lacks control over the purse or the sword.[134] Former US President Andrew Jackson once reportedly observed, '[US Supreme Court Justice] John Marshall has made his decision. Now let him enforce it',[135] while President Roosevelt threatened to 'pack' the Supreme Court with judges who would not show restraint and accept the legislative wisdom.[136] If the other branches of government withdraw their support and if people refuse to obey orders of the judiciary, the courts would be severely weakened. Civil society groups and those who may now look to the judiciary for further environmental activism need to recognize what is at stake; they cannot afford to win one case at the cost of a discredited and diminished judiciary.[137]

Notes

1   Dhruv Sanghavi is primarily an international tax and funds lawyer. His practice areas include international taxation, international tax litigation, globalization, structuring of inbound/outbound investments, structuring of offshore funds, mergers and acquisitions, etc. He received a Bachelors degree in Commerce and Economics in 2004 and the LLB degree in early 2008 from the University of Mumbai. Sanghavi has also been, and continues to be, involved with numerous environmental interest movements in India.

2   Indian Council for Enviro-Legal Action v. Union of India (1996) Vol. 5 Supreme Court Cases (SCC), p303.

3   Divan, S. and Rosencranz, A. (2001) *Environmental Law and Policy in India – Cases, Materials and Statutes*, Oxford University Press, New Delhi.

4   This concept has been argued for in a number of cases of Indian law, including: Maneka Gandhi v. Union of India (1978) 1 SCC 248; Charles Shobraj v. Supdt,

Central Jail (1978) 4 SCC 104; Francis Coralie Mullin v. Administrator, Union Territory of Delhi (1981) 1 SCC 608; Sunil Batra v. Delhi Admn (1978) 4 SCC 494; M. Nagraj v. Union of India (2006) 8 SCC 212.

5   Charan Lal Sahu v. Union of India (1990) 1 SCC 613.

6   M. C. Mehta v. Union of India, Civil Writ Petition No. 13029 of 1985.

7   Narain, U. and Krupnick, A. (2007) *The Impact of Delhi's CNG Program on Air Quality*, Resources for the Future, RFF Discussion Paper no 07-06.

8   'The United States Environmental Protection Agency (USEPA) has mandated that the annual average levels of $PM_{2.5}$ particles in the air should not exceed 15 mg/cum. The Indian annual national average standard for PM_{10} is 60 mg/cum, but most cities, including Delhi register PM_{10} levels above 150–200 mg/cum on an annual basis.' M. C. Mehta v. Union of India (2002) 4 SCC 356.

9   M. C. Mehta v. Union of India (2002) 4 SCC 356, at 364.

10   For more information on the Clean Cities Program refer to: www1.eere.energy.gov/cleancities/participating_countries.html, accessed 12 July 2008.

11   Divan, S. and Rosencranz, A. (2001) *Environmental Law and Policy in India – Cases, Materials and Statutes*, Oxford University Press, New Delhi.

12   Rosencranz, A. and Jackson, M. (2003) 'The Delhi Pollution Case and the limits of judicial power', *Columbia Journal Environmental Law*, Spring.

13   The Constitution of India, Article 21: 'No person shall be deprived of his life or personal liberty except according to the procedure established by law.'

14   The Constitution of India, Article 39(e): 'The State shall, in particular, direct its policy towards securing – (e) that the health of and strength of workers, men and women, and the tender age of children are not abused …'; Article 47: 'The State shall regard the raising of the level of nutrition and the standard of living of its people and the improvement of public health as among its primary duties …'.

15   The Constitution of India, Article 48A: 'The State shall endeavour to protect and improve the environment and to safeguard the forests and wild life of the country.'

16   The Constitution of India, Article 51A (g): 'It shall be the duty of every citizen of India – (g) to protect and improve the natural environment including forests, lakes, rivers and wild life, and to have compassion for all living creatures.'

17   Tarun Bharat Sangh, Alwar v. Union of India, Civil Writ Petition No. 509 of 1991, 14 May 1992.

18   Issued on the grounds of 'internal disturbance' threatening the security of India, the proclamation was revoked in March 1977 after the Indira Gandhi government was swept out of power in a national election.

19   Divan, S. and Rosencranz, A. (2001) *Environmental Law and Policy in India – Cases, Materials and Statutes*, Oxford University Press, New Delhi.

20   State of M. P. v. Kedia Leather & Liquor Ltd (2003) 7 SCC 389.

21   All India Reporter (AIR) 1987 Andhra Pradesh High Court (AP) 171.

22   The Indian Penal Code, 1860 imposes a fine on a person who, 'voluntarily fouls the water of any public spring or reservoir'.

23   Section 12(1) of the Factories Act, 1948: 'Effective arrangements shall be made in every factory for the treatment of wastes and effluents due to the manufacturing process carried out therein, so as to render them innocuous, and for their disposal.' River Boards established under the River Boards Act of 1956 for the regulation and development of inter-state rivers and river valleys were empowered to prevent water pollution.

24   Divan, S. and Rosencranz, A. (2001) *Environmental Law and Policy in India – Cases, Materials and Statutes*, Oxford University Press, New Delhi.

25 Bengal Smoke Nuisance Act of 1905 and the Bombay Smoke Nuisance Act of 1912.

26 The Constitution (Forty-Second Amendment) Act, 1976.

27 Air Act, Section 4.

28 Air Act, Section 5.

29 Divan, S. and Rosencranz, A. (2001) *Environmental Law and Policy in India – Cases, Materials and Statutes*, Oxford University Press, New Delhi.

30 Environment (Protection) Act, Section 3(1).

31 Environment (Protection) Act, Section 2(ii).

32 Environment (Protection) Act, Section 31-A.

33 Kuik, O. J. et al (1997) *Pollution Control in the South and North*, Sage Publications, California, US, p75.

34 Pravinbhai J. Patel v. State of Gujarat, (2) Guj. L. Rep. 1210 (1995).

35 Kuik, O. J. et al (1997) *Pollution Control in the South and North*, Sage Publications, California, US, p75.

36 Rosencranz, A. and Jackson, M. (2003) 'The Delhi Pollution Case and the limits of judicial power', *Columbia Journal Environmental Law*, Spring.

37 The Constitution of India, Article 32.

38 The Constitution of India, Article 226. The jurisdiction of the High Courts under this Article is wider than that of the Supreme Court under Article 32. While the breach of a fundamental right is a pre-condition to move the Supreme Court under Article 32, the writ jurisdiction of the High Courts can be invoked for 'any other purpose' as well.

39 Indian Banks' Assn v. Devkala Consultancy Service (2004) 11 SCC 1.

40 State of West Bengal v. Sampat Lal (1985) 1 SCC 317; Indian Banks' Assn v. Devkala Consultancy Services (2004) 11 SCC 1.

41 State of H. P. v. Parent of a Student of a Medical College (1985) 3 SCC 169.

42 Fertilizer Corporation Kamgar Union, Sindri and Others v. Union of India (UOI) and Others (1981) 1 SCC 568.

43 S. P. Gupta v. Union of India and Another (1981) Supp SCC 87: AIR 1982 Supreme Court (SC) 149.

44 Bandhua Mukti Morcha v. Union of India and Others (1991) 4 SCC 174.

45 Sheela Barse v. Union of India and Others (1988) 4 SCC 226: AIR 1988 SC 2211.

46 Rao, M. (2004) *Public Interest Litigation, Legal Aid and Lok Adalats*, Eastern Book Company, Delhi, India.

47 The Constitution of India, Article 142(1): 'The Supreme Court in the exercise of its jurisdiction may pass such decree or make such order as is necessary for doing complete justice in any cause or matter pending before it, and any decree so passed or order so made shall be enforceable throughout the territory of India in such manner as may be prescribed or under any law made by Parliament and, until provision in that behalf is so made, in such manner as the President may by order prescribe.'

48 M. C. Mehta v. Union of India (1998) 9 SCC 448.

49 M. C. Mehta v. Union of India (Kanpur Tanneries Case) 1992 Supp 2 SCC 637; Vellore Citizens' Forum v. Union of India AIR 1996 SC 2175.

50 M. C. Mehta v. Union of India (1998) 9 SCC 149.

51 Ratlam Municipality v. Vardichand AIR 1980 SC 1622.

52 Church of God (Full Gospel) in India v. K. K. R. Majestic Colony Welfare Association and Others (2000) 7 SCC 282.

53 Rosencranz, A. and Jackson, M. (2003) 'The Delhi Pollution Case and the limits of judicial power', *Columbia Journal Environmental Law*, Spring.

54 CSE (1999) 'Sick of air pollution', Press Release, Centre for Science and Environment, 5 June, http://old.cseindia.org/AboutUs/press_releases/au4_060599.htm, accessed 3 June 2010.
55 CSE (1996) 'Press Release', Centre for Science and Environment, 29 September, http://old.cseindia.org/AboutUs/press_releases/au4_0929.htm, accessed 3 June 2010.
56 Sharma, A. and Roychowdhury, A. (1996) *Slow Murder: The Deadly Story of Vehicular Pollution in India*, Centre for Science and Environment, Delhi, India.
57 M. C. Mehta v. Union of India (1999) 6 SCC 9.
58 CSE (1999) 'Press Release', Centre for Science and Environment, 9 September, http://old.cseindia.org/AboutUs/press_releases/au4_090999.htm, accessed 3 June 2010.
59 Sharma, A. and Roychowdhury, A. (1996) *Slow Murder: The Deadly Story of Vehicular Pollution in India*, Centre for Science and Environment.
60 CSE (1996) 'Press Release', Centre for Science and Environment, 3 November, http://old.cseindia.org/AboutUs/press_releases/au4_1103.htm, accessed 3 June 2010.
61 M. C. Mehta is the most active environmental lawyer practicing at the Supreme Court of India. He has filed and argued numerous environmental public interest litigations which include the Vehicular Pollution Case, the Taj Trapezium Case, the Ganga Pollution Case and Oleum Gas Leak Case, to name but a few.
62 M. C. Mehta v. Union of India, Civil Writ Petition No. 13381 of 1984.
63 M. C. Mehta v. Union of India, Civil Writ Petition No. 13029 of 1985.
64 M. C. Mehta v. Union of India, AIR 1991 SC 1132; Mehta, M. C. (2007) Personal Communication, 5 July 2007.
65 M. C. Mehta v. Union of India, AIR 1991 SC 1132.
66 The orders have now been enforced in many other cities in India.
67 Order in M. C. Mehta v. Union of India, Civil Writ Petition No. 13029 of 1985 dated 16 January 16 1995.
68 Justice K. N. Saikia served as a Judge of the Supreme Court of India from 14 December 1988 to 28 February 1991.
69 M. C. Mehta v. Union of India (1991) 2 SCC 353.
70 Orders in M. C. Mehta v. Union of India, Civil Writ Petition dated 3 October 1991 and 25 October 1991.
71 Mehta, M. C. (2007) Personal Communication, 5 July.
72 M. C. Mehta v. Union of India, 1997 (4) SCALE 7 (SP).
73 Order in M. C. Mehta v. Union of India, Civil Writ Petition No. 13029 of 1985 dated 8 January 1992.
74 M. C. Mehta v. Union of India, 1997 (4) SCALE 4 (SP); 1997 (4) SCALE 5 (SP); 1997 (4) SCALE 6 (SP).
75 M. C. Mehta v. Union of India, 1997 (4) SCALE 9 (SP); 1997 (4) SCALE 10 (SP); 1997 (4) SCALE 11 (SP).
76 M. C. Mehta v. Union of India, 1997 (3) SCALE 24 (SP).
77 EPPCA, more popularly known as the Bhurelal Committee.
78 M. C. Mehta v. Union of India (1998) 2 SCC 435.
79 This five-member committee was originally composed of a representative from the Central Pollution Control Board, the Automobile Manufacturers Association of India, the Centre for Science and Environment (an environmental NGO), the Transport Department and the Central Vigilance Commission. Because the committee was designed to express the interests and expertise of the major affected parties, the Supreme Court has consistently looked to the committee as

its fact-finding commission and has relied almost exclusively on its findings when making its decisions in the Delhi Pollution Case.

80   Refer to Table 12.1.
81   M. C. Mehta v. Union of India (1998) 6 SCC 63.
82   Order dated 5 May 2000 (2001) 3 SCC 767, at 768.
83   Equivalent of India-2000 norms as notified by the Government of India on 28 August 1997.
84   M. C. Mehta v. Union of India 1997 (1999) 6 SCC 14.
85   M. C. Mehta v. Union of India (2001) 3 SCC 756.
86   M. C. Mehta v. Union of India (2003) 10 SCC 567.
87   M. C. Mehta v. Union of India (2001) 3 SCC 756.
88   M. C. Mehta v. Union of India (2003) 10 SCC 566.
89   M. C. Mehta v. Union of India (2002) 4 SCC 356.
90   Divan, S. and Rosencranz, A. (2001) *Environmental Law and Policy in India – Cases, Materials and Statutes*, Oxford University Press, New Delhi.
91   M. C. Mehta v. Union of India, (2002) 4 SCC 376.
92   Order in M. C. Mehta v. Union of India, Civil Writ Petition No. 13029 of 1985, dated 5 April 2002.
93   Order in M. C. Mehta v. Union of India, Civil Writ Petition No. 13029 of 1985, dated 5 April 2002.
94   Order in M. C. Mehta v. Union of India, Civil Writ Petition No. 13029 of 1985, dated 5 April 2002.
95   Order in M. C. Mehta v. Union of India, Civil Writ Petition No. 13029 of 1985, dated 5 April 2002.
96   Order in M. C. Mehta v. Union of India, Civil Writ Petition No. 13029 of 1985, dated 5 April 2002.
97   M. C. Mehta v. Union of India (2001) 3 SCC 756.
98   M. C. Mehta v. Union of India (2001) 3 SCC 756.
99   Order in M. C. Mehta v. Union of India, Civil Writ Petition No. 13029 of 1985, dated 5 April 2002.
100 Order in M. C. Mehta v. Union of India, Civil Writ Petition No. 13029 of 1985, dated 5 April 2002.
101 M. C. Mehta v. Union of India (2003) 10 SCC 564.
102 Order in M. C. Mehta v. Union of India, Civil Writ Petition No. 13029 of 1985, dated 5 April 2002.
103 Order in M. C. Mehta v. Union of India, Civil Writ Petition No. 13029 of 1985, dated 5 April 2002.
104 Order in M. C. Mehta v. Union of India, Civil Writ Petition No. 13029 of 1985, dated 5 April 2002.
105 Order in M. C. Mehta v. Union of India, Civil Writ Petition No. 13029 of 1985, dated 5 April 2002.
106 Order in M. C. Mehta v. Union of India, Civil Writ Petition No. 13029 of 1985, dated 5 April 2002.
107 Order in M. C. Mehta v. Union of India, Civil Writ Petition No. 13029 of 1985, dated 5 April 2002.
108 Order in M. C. Mehta v. Union of India, Civil Writ Petition No. 13029 of 1985, dated 5 April 2002.
109 Order in M. C. Mehta v. Union of India, Civil Writ Petition No. 13029 of 1985, dated 5 April 2002.
110 Rosencranz, A. and Jackson, M. (2003) 'The Delhi Pollution Case and the limits of judicial power', *Columbia Journal Environmental Law*, Spring.

111 Narain, U. and Krupnick, A. (2007) 'The impact of Delhi's CNG program on air quality', Resources for the Future, a Discussion Paper RFF DP 07-06.

112 National Air Quality Monitoring Program (undated) 'Highlight: Air quality assessment', www.cpcb.nic.in/oldwebsite/Highlights/Highlights04/ch-2.html, accessed 12 July 2008.

113 Kathuria, V. (2004) 'Impact of CNG on vehicular pollution in Delhi: A note', *Transportation Research*, Part D 9, pp409–417.

114 National Air Quality Monitoring Program (undated) 'Highlight: Air quality assessment', www.cpcb.nic.in/oldwebsite/Highlights/Highlights04/ch-2.html, accessed 12 July 2008.

115 National Cooperative Highway Research Program (NCHRP) (1997) 'Relationships among implemented transportation control measures, emissions, and measured pollutant levels', *NCHRP Research Results Digest #217*, Transportation Research Board, Washington, DC.

116 'The world's cheapest car', *Time Magazine*, 10 January 2008.

117 Narain, U. and Krupnick, A. (2007) 'The Impact of Delhi's CNG Program on Air Quality', Resources for the Future, a Discussion Paper RFF DP 07-06.

118 Justice B. N. Srikrishna, 'Skinning a cat' 2005 (8) SCC (J) 3.

119 H. M. Seervai (2005) *Constitutional Law of India*, Vol. 1, fourth edition, Universal Law Publishing Co Ltd, p971.

120 Justice B. N. Srikrishna, 'Skinning a cat' 2005 (8) SCC (J) 3.

121 Editorial, 'The interpreters: Judiciary should not stray from the rule book', *Times of India*, 17 September 2005.

122 Lord Acton, in a letter to Bishop Mandell Creighton, 1887.

123 Pound, R. (1923) *Interpretations of Legal History*, p1.

124 Barak, A. (2002) 'A judge on judging: The role of a supreme court in a democracy, *Harvard Law Review*, vol 16, pp28–53.

125 The Constitution of India, Article 141: 'The law declared by the Supreme Court shall be binding on all courts within the territory of India.'

126 Sheela Barse v. Union of India (1988) 4 SCC 226: AIR 1988 SC 2211.

127 Justice B. N. Srikrishna, 'Skinning a cat', 2005 (8) SCC (J) 3.

128 An analogy may be drawn to the 'infamous Dred Scott v. Sandford [see www.ebc-india.com/lawyer/articles/#Note17] where the US Supreme Court virtually supported slavery by denying the power of the Federal Government to abolish this practice. The preposterous reasoning put forward by the Judges, ignoring clear provisions of law, was that black people were not citizens and could not, therefore, claim constitutional protections. Moreover, since slaves were chattels of the slave-owners, freeing them from slavery meant forfeiture of the slave-owner's property without compensation – something, which in the thinking of those activist Judges was unfair and unreasonable.' Excerpted from 'Skinning a Cat' by Justice B. N. Srikrishna, 2005 (8) SCC (J) 3.

129 Dhruv Sanghavi: Interview with Justice Srikrishna, Retired Judge, Supreme Court of India, 21 July 2007.

130 Chief Justice R. C. Lahoti's speech on law day (2005) 5 SCC 1.

131 Judge John Roberts, as quoted in Gibbs, N. (2005) '5 things to know about John Roberts', *Time Magazine*, 28 August 2005.

132 Sathe, S. P. (2001) 'Judicial activism: The Indian experience', *Journal of Law and Policy*, vol 6, no 29.

133 Divan, S. (2002) 'A mistake of judgment', *Down to Earth*, 30 April.

134 Sathe, S. P. (2001) 'Judicial activism: The Indian experience', *Journal of Law and Policy*, vol 6, no 29.

135 Bailey, T. and Kennedy, D. (2002) *The American Pageant: A History of the Republic* (12th edition), Wadsworth Publishing, Kentucky, US, p267.

136 Bork, R. H. (1990) *The Tempting of America: The Political Seduction of the Law,* Touchstone Books, Florida, US.

137 Rosencranz, A. and Jackson, M. (2003) 'The Delhi Pollution Case and the limits of judicial power', *Columbia Journal Environmental Law*, Spring.

Index

earthscan

publishing for a sustainable future

Factor Five

Transforming the Global Economy through 80% Improvements in Resource Productivity

*Ernst von Weizsäcker, Karlson 'Charlie' Hargroves,
Michael H. Smith, Cheryl Desha and Peter Stasinopoulos*

'Building on our 1997 collaboration in *Factor Four* this exciting synthesis combines a powerful efficiency toolkit with farsighted policy insights - vital to ensure that efficiency's gains are not offset but reinforced to create a richer, fairer, safer, and cooler world.' *Amory B. Lovins, Chairman and Chief Scientist, Rocky Mountain Institute*

'The exciting thing about *Factor Five* is the combination of boldness and realism.' *Lester Brown, President, Earth Policy Institute*

'The scientific assessment of climate change requires urgent action in mitigating greenhouse gas emissions... particularly in industries like cement and steel. These sectors could reduce emissions by 80% on an economically viable basis. *Factor Five* provides several such win-win strategies.' *Dr R K Pachauri, Chair of the Intergovernmental Panel on Climate Change*

The 21st century will see monumental change. Either the human race will use its knowledge and skills and change the way it interacts with the environment, or the environment will change the way it interacts with its inhabitants.

In this update to the 1997 International Best Seller, *Factor Four*, Ernst von Weizsäcker again leads a team to present a compelling case for sector wide advances that can deliver significant resource productivity improvements. The purpose of this book is to inspire hope and to then inform meaningful action in the coming decades to respond to the greatest challenge our species has ever faced – that of living in harmony with our planet and its other inhabitants.

Spanning dozens of countries including China and India and examining innumerable cases of innovation in design, technology and policy, the authors leave no engineering and economic stone unturned in their quest for excellence. The book tackles sustainable development and climate change by providing in depth Factor 5 resource productivity studies of the following sectors: Buildings, Industry, Agriculture, Food and Hospitality, and Transportation.

Hardback • £24.99 • 448 pages • ISBN 9781844075911 • 2009

www.earthscan.co.uk